TO TRY MEN'S SOULS

TO
TRY
MEN'S
SOULS

Loyalty Tests in American History

BY HAROLD M. HYMAN

UNIVERSITY OF CALIFORNIA PRESS

Berkeley and Los Angeles

1959

UNIVERSITY OF CALIFORNIA PRESS
Berkeley and Los Angeles, California

CAMBRIDGE UNIVERSITY PRESS
London, England

© 1959 by The Regents of the University of California

Library of Congress Catalog Card No. 59-8761

DESIGNED BY KENNETH KRAL

Printed in the United States of America

To the Memory of a Beloved Friend

WILLIAM J. HANDELSMAN

PREFACE

"There seems no reason," Herman Melville noted soon after Lee surrendered, "why patriotism and narrowness should go together, or why intellectual impartiality should be confused with political trimming, or why serviceable truth should be kept cloistered because not partisan." Melville felt that post–Civil War problems required for solution little "but common sense, and Christian charity." Then he added: "Little but these? They are much." [1]

Common sense and Christian charity have been largely absent from the history of loyalty tests in the United States. Few persons know that there *is* such a history and that it offers, in the Beardian phrase, insight from hindsight. But this may be too optimistic. In times of crisis, it is a rare event to find individuals seeking solutions for the problems of their time from the lessons of the past. Even Woodrow Wilson, trained in the art of history, remarked in 1918 that "nobody ever before fought a war like this," and concluded that the stories of earlier conflicts offered few guides to America's World War I needs. [2]

Optimistic or no, I have tried in this book to draw together the history of loyalty tests throughout the long span of American development for what purposes it may serve. It seemed to me that the best way to do this was to re-create as much of the story as possible as it occurred on the stage of history, concentrating on the loyalty-testing aspect of each incident, rather than from the vantage point of the backward look. To be sure this approach involved certain limitations. It imposed, for example, an episodic scheme, for the history of loyalty tests is spasmodic rather than continuous. Loyalty tests are crisis products. They emerge from the felt needs of authorities during wars, rebellions, and periods of fear of subversion.

Another limitation derives from the nature of the greatly varied sources used for this book. They offered no simple picture to draw, no convenient hero to extol or villain to condemn. There is, surely, no easy conservative-against-liberal line. Champions of loyalty tests in America's colonial and national history included James I, Sam Adams, George Mason, George III, Washington, Jefferson, Hamilton, Lincoln, Jefferson Davis, Wilson, Martin Dies, Franklin Roosevelt, Truman, and Eisenhower. Nor is there a clear answer to the question concerning the utility of tests of loyalty, for there is in this history rarely an opportunity to know from the records for what use the test of the moment was designed. One can say that most loyalty tests of the past were both failures and successes for certain purposes.

The records did permit me to estimate why loyalty tests came into existence at certain times, what forms they took, how authority administered them, and with what gains to the cause the tests were supposed to support. Most of this book deals with loyalty tests in the form of oaths of loyalty. Our first settlers brought the patterns of medieval statecraft with them to the New World and oaths played primary parts in the histories of the emerging nationalisms of that time. As Reformation pressures forced ecclesiastic institutions into subserviency to secular states, religious oaths began to test political orthodoxy as well as churchly conformity. Men in power and men seeking power and salvation used loyalty oaths to help create what Thorstein Veblen once called "a sense of partisan solidarity." [3] Our ancestors found that loyalty oaths possessed the virtue of convenience. Few devices of government can offer more benefit than to force potential enemies to expose themselves by refusing to swear. It is this aspect of loyalty oaths—self-identification by the person being tested —which makes them loyalty tests. It matters little what such oaths were termed. Oaths of office, of allegiance, of religious conformity are loyalty tests when they are used to create internal security and to reveal potential enemies to a cause. Only in the twentieth century has the popularity of the oath form of test lessened at all, giving way to or being supplemented in very recent years by indices of allegiance which seem, at least, more sophisticated and modern.[4]

To be sure the utility of and necessity for loyalty tests have rarely been questioned, even among the victims of a government's policies, during the existence of the emergency that inspired the test of the moment. Criticisms emerge after the passions of emergencies fade. Thus West Virginians, whose state was born in a spasm of divided loyalty attended by a congeries of competing loyalty tests, wrote into their 1872 constitution their belated antipathy toward "political tests, requiring persons . . . to purge themselves by their own oaths . . . [which] are repugnant to the principles of free government and are cruel and oppressive." [5] But later generations of West Virginians in 1917 and in 1950 followed other Americans in most states in requiring loyalty-oath tests of their fellow citizens.

In 1918, Secretary of War Newton D. Baker replied to a suggestion for a national test oath with this comment: "It may be that the formulation and repetition of some particular pledge will be of fundamental help, but I am not quite sure." [6] I hope that this book may serve to remove some of the uncertainty.

There are many individuals and institutions whose aid and facilities were generously offered to make this research possible. Financial support was obtained from the Fund for the Republic of the Ford Foundation, and from the Social Science Research Council, the latter with a grant for research on the history of American military policy. The most devoted and able research assistance was that of Miss Vera Waltman, of Washington, D.C., which she sustained even in the heat of summer. Mr. and Mrs. Earl Glauert graciously helped examine the large collections in the libraries of the University of North Carolina and Duke University. Professor and Mrs. Harold Shapiro, of the Arizona State College, Tempe, submitted to readings of substantial portions of the manuscript, and were always ready with critical comments. My colleagues at the University of California, Los Angeles, deserve my thanks for their unfailing encouragement, and Mrs. Grace H. Stimson, of the staff of the University of California Press, gave patient, useful editorial advice.

I want also to express my thanks to Mr. John Lord O'Brian of Washington, D.C., who freely offered his recollections of Wilson's wartime administration. Mr. Bruce Bielaski, of New York City was equally generous in his memories of his Department of Justice career in that period. Mr. Francis Biddle, of Washington, provided significant comments on later problems in internal security, as did Professor Robert Cushman, who was also kind enough to read portions of this manuscript dealing with the early years of World War II.

Librarians and archivists across the country performed their miracles in finding materials, always graciously and patiently. I hope that the staffs of these institutions realize the extent of my obligation. I want especially to mention in gratitude the personnel in the Library of Congress Manuscripts Division, and in the Justice Department and Army Records sections of the National Archives. Those in charge of the Southern Historical Collection at the University of North Carolina, and at Duke University Library, combed those manuscripts collections for my use. The finest kind of assistance was similarly offered at the New York Public Library, the New-York Historical Society, the Maryland Historical Society, the State Historical Society of Wisconsin, the Virginia State Library, and the Huntington Library.

Three ladies of my family, Ferne, Lee, and Ann, assisted in ways peculiar to their several talents. They must share with me at least some responsibility for any inadequacies of this book.

H. M. H.

CONTENTS

ILLUSTRATIONS

CHAPTER I

Old Loyalties in the New World

There was a tale told in England three hundred years ago of a stolid farmer who disgustedly watched his field trampled by rebel and royal forces readying for battle near Marston Moor. Challenged to declare for king or Parliament, he replied, "What, be they two at it again?" [1] From the turbulent reign of Henry VIII until long after James II had fled his former kingdom, successive generations and factions of Englishmen were "at it."

During those centuries England shared in the concatenation of change and strain which all Europe was experiencing. Explorations reaped vast rewards from Asian, African, and American commerce, twisting Europe's economy far from accustomed medieval paths, pitting Continental powers against each other in contests for colonies half a world away. Lutheran Protestantism and its disputatious offspring rent asunder the European fabric of Roman Catholic unity. The tragic century of warfare which followed in the name of the Prince of Peace kept all Europe in continuing tension, and made questions of national defense and internal security paramount considerations for all rulers.

In this world at war, every king knew himself to be dependent for survival upon the unalloyed fidelity of his subjects. Each ruler chose the only true path toward divine salvation which he permitted his people, and equated right religious observance with good citizenship. Thus, treason and heresy mixed in the lexicon of statecraft; piety and patriotism were on the agenda of all royal courts. So it was in England.

With Henry VIII's break from Roman ecclesiastical domination, England commenced a long adventure in religious experimentation and political growth. The theological predilections of successive monarchs combined with the pressures of international crises to keep Englishmen on an erratic pendulum of dogmatic change. Henry substituted his considerable self for the Pope in the English religious edifice, but maintained the Catholic faith against Protestant novelties. Edward VI and Somerset permitted some doctrines of the new heresy to penetrate England's churches. Mary Tudor's devoted attempts to restore her realm to Roman regularity failed, and in the process she broke her heart and bloodied her land. Then, during Elizabeth I's long half-century of power, England found a religious equilibrium which most Englishmen accepted. Anglican theological latitudinarianism, structured in a state-church under royal control, buttressed by the patriotism that helped repel the Spanish Armada, and enforced by the apparatus of the state as a condition of good citizenship, seemed to solve the problem of religious disputation. But, on the Catholic right as on the Protestant left, determined champions of the old Romanism and of the new Calvinism refused to risk the safety of their immortal souls for the earthly rewards of conformity. Such stubborn subjects also risked the immediate punishments for disobedience.

Slowly, pragmatically, imperfectly, the Tudor monarchs created an internal security system to deal with deviationists. They faced few restrictions at a time when Magna Charta was neither prop to Parliament nor bar to king. England's monarchs, fearing invasion from without and plagued with treason, intrigues, and dissent within, demanded loyalty.

Henry VIII contributed a series of loyalty tests to measure the worthwhileness of individual Englishmen. These tests of political respectability and religious conformity were loyalty oaths which stated that the subscriber affirmed Henry's legitimate kingship, the equal legitimacy of each of Henry's successive consorts and offspring, and the rectitude of the popeless Catholic church Henry had created. By 1539, for example, Englishmen of many classes had publicly to state that "having now the veil of darkness of the . . . Bishop of Rome clearly taken away from my eyes, [I] do utterly testify . . . that . . . [no] foreign potentate hath . . . any jurisdiction . . . within this realm." [2]

Nonjurors, by the simple act of refusing to swear loyalty, were self-confessedly guilty of disloyalty; nonconformists in religion were automatically suspect enough to warrant application of the royal oath test. Both unhappy kinds of Englishmen, if persistent in their folly, faced Henry's powerful loyalty enforcement administration, which made Erasmus describe England as a land where "a scorpion lay sleeping under every stone." [3] Nonjurors and dissenters became the subjects for

2

the king's bills of attainder and property confiscation decrees. Many went to prison and into exile. Some met death.

Mary Tudor and Elizabeth I refined Henry's loyalty tests (modifying the religious clauses to suit their opposite purposes) and created a more sophisticated enforcement apparatus. By the end of Elizabeth's reign, England was honeycombed with a network of justices of the peace, pursuivants, civil courts, militia units, ecclesiastical investigating commissions, spies, informers, *agents provocateurs,* and port officers, all empowered to administer the current loyalty tests to all Englishmen.

Elizabeth, unlike her royal predecessor and successors, never deluded herself concerning the real purpose of her loyalty program. "I will not open windows into men's souls," she said, and cared little what men really believed so long as they observed the ritual of the Anglican creed and performed for England as events demanded. This most pragmatic of queens deserved the perceptive tribute of a pamphleteer who, writing in 1600, analyzed Elizabeth's achievements in loyalty-testing:

The main point is the weakening of the domestic enemies, for . . . the land is divided into four sorts of persons, viz. 1. religious protestants, 2. political protestants, 3. religious papists, 4. political papists, the first whereof only were found to be sure to the state, the other three dangerous. . . . [The Queen has] for the diminishing and weakening of the three latter made laws that every man . . . in Parliament or any state or possession in the land shall take his corporal oath for the maintenance of the religion now established.

It was so efficient; the royal oath requirement made conscientious members of the three "dangerous" classes expose themselves by non-juring, so that "the number of these sorts is much diminished and daily doth decrease." Nor did Elizabeth neglect the danger of subversion from immigrants, or permit disaffected subjects to spread their heresies to other parts of her realm. As the same chronicler recorded, "There is no person neither stranger nor subject that may depart out of the realme without license [and loyalty oath] . . . nor enter without being examined by Commissioners for that purpose in every Port towne." [4]

As the aging Elizabeth surveyed her long reign, she knew that England was stronger than when she had become queen, and that her willingness to accept security as the goal of her "loyalty" program had contributed significantly toward realizing that increased strength. A royal successor as competent as she might have been able to perpetuate her achievement. James I was not the man for the job.

James felt himself more God's partner than servant. This proud, literate, stubborn prince, who mixed political philosophy with governing, believed that "there is not a thing so necessary to be known by the people . . . next to the knowledge of their God, as the right knowledge of allegiance." He was master of England and head of the Anglican Church. All Englishmen, he inflexibly determined, would obey him.[5] For the first two years of his reign, James contented himself with the loyalty-testing program Elizabeth had left him, merely substituting his name for hers in the oaths of allegiance and of religious supremacy. Then, in 1605, the abortive Gunpowder Plot implicated all Catholics in treason and murder.

James wrote a new loyalty-oath law designed to make a "difference between the civilly obedient Papists and the perverse disciples of the [Gun] Powder Treason." The new oath formula required Englishmen to swear loyalty to James, including his secular and religious prerogatives, even in the face of papal excommunication of the king. James succeeded in his purpose of confusing English Catholics concerning the extent of papal power. Exulting in an opportunity for a polemical fight, he plunged into an inky scholastic contest with literary enemies of his loyalty invention. He also enforced its provisions with great severity.[6]

The impact of James's determined Anglicanism fell upon certain Protestants as well as Catholics. Calvinist theology had penetrated deeply into England by this time, and many Anglicans accepted the Genevan's views. English Calvinists hoped to cleanse Anglicanism of its remnants of Roman ritual. As "good " Anglicans, they had no trouble swearing loyalty to James as head of that church. But they were deeply troubled that this prince, whose Scottish upbringing had failed to steer him toward Calvinism, should uphold Anglican tenets over those of Calvin. "I shall make them conform themselves, or I will harry them out of the land," James replied to dissenters' demands for a Calvinist interpretation of Anglican theology and ecclesiastical structure. James did his best to make good his threat.

Despite these continuing tensions, England was ready early in James's reign to expand from the Old World into the New, and to plant its first permanent colonies on the shores of America.[7] As Englishmen made their ways to Virginia, New England, and Maryland, they bore with them the problems of the homeland they had left. Loyalty tests were an invisible cargo which traveled to the English colonies in America.

In the century from Henry VIII to James I, Englishmen dreamed and died to plant their nation's flag and make their personal fortunes in the seductive reaches of America. James dreamed with them, and gladly gave his royal assent to exploitative commercial schemes. One such joint-stock venture, the Virginia Company, received his charter in 1606. James came personally to the company's meetings in London, where he made each of the ambitious promoters swear to "bear to the uttermost true faith and allegiance to the King's majesty . . . and . . . [to] assist and defend all authorities granted under his Majesty's hand and annex't unto the Crown . . . against all forrain enemies . . . whatsoever." [8]

Through the succession of charter changes that followed upon the first precarious years of the Jamestown settlement, one constant note is the king's and company's nominal agreement (they agreed on little else) that only loyal men should go to Virginia. How else could profits remain in loyal pockets, the encroaching French and Spanish be kept out, and the true (Anglican) Word of God be spread among the savages? So the first charter of Virginia required every company officer and colonist to swear to the lengthy oath of allegiance and supremacy of which James was so proud. In this way, hopefully, nonjuring Catholics would be self-excluded. A few Catholics did go to Virginia, however; James's deliberately ambiguous oath formula concerning papal authority seduced some Catholics into taking his oath. Catholic participation in settling Virginia was one result of his casuistry which James had not foreseen! [9]

Profitless initial exploitation of Virginia impelled James to issue a new charter in 1609. It repeated his earlier order that none should go there "but such, as first shall have taken the Oath of Supremacy," for James confessed himself "loath, that any person should be permitted to pass [to Virginia] that we suspected to affect the superstitions of the Church of Rome." Rather than add to the duties of his already overburdened oath-enforcing administration, James authorized Virginia Company officials to screen all prospective colonists, and "to tender and exhibit the said oath to all such persons who shall, at any time, be sent and employed in the said voyage." [10]

In nominal obedience to royal dictates, the company's directors enjoined the colony's military commanders that "no man [in Virginia] shall willingly absent himself, when he is summoned to take the Oath of Supremacy, upon pain of death." Any soldier in the colony who refused the oath was to be "committed to the galleys." And, in the perpetual optimism of the promoter, considering the existing paucity of settlers and settlements, the company ordained that "all Governors of Town or Towns, Fort or Forts, shall be ready (when so be it they shall be summoned thereto) to take their Oaths of Allegiance unto his Majesty." In reality, however, the struggling colony could ill afford to compound its perpetually undermanned state by denying admission or existence to anyone who came to Virginia in those grim first years of settlement. Survival and profits consistently took precedence over loyalty tests in Virginia.[11]

In 1619 the company's directors, safely based in London, sought a new way to spur their despairing colonists to provide profits for the investors. They permitted local self-government in Virginia, subject always to company control and royal intervention. A measure of political democracy—timid, experimental, novel—came to America.

Late in April of that year, Sir George Yeardley reached Jamestown bearing his commission as governor of the colony and news of the company's decision concerning local suffrage. At the end of June the first Virginia Assembly met in the wooden church building, in as impressive a ceremony as the weak colony could stage. Governor Yeardley entered first, splendidly dressed, as was his bodyguard. Sword-begirt councilors followed him, and behind them, two by two, the newly elected burgesses arranged themselves facing Yeardley and his appointed council. An Anglican minister prayed for divine aid. Then the burgesses and councilors, "before they were freely admitted . . . were called to order by name and so every man (none staggering at it) took the oath of Supremacy, and then entered the Assembly." [12]

The new local assembly reënacted existing colonial provisions against recusancy, and approved the London directors' decision that all immigrants embarking from England for Virginia had first to take the king's oath. As a double check, all future colonists had to produce a certificate from an English magistrate testifying that they had duly taken that loyalty test. The magistrates, as a further administrative control, were to forward their registers of oath takers to the company's directors at frequent intervals. Colonization and loyalty-testing were becoming complicated.

They became still more complicated when Virginia affairs entered into the developing dispute between the Anglican monarch and Puritan members of Parliament in England. Religion, constitutional privileges, and politics were stern enough imperatives to involve even far-off Virginia. James's predilections tended toward centralization of royal authority, the colony showed no profits, and the company's directors were troublesome Puritans. In part using Virginia's alleged (and actual) remissness in enforcing his loyalty-oath requirement as an excuse, James, early in 1623, appointed a special commission to investigate the company's affairs and to determine "whether all that have gone to the plantations have taken the Oath of Supremacy." The rigged commission reported negatively, and the loyalty test became one of the formal charges against the company which led James, in 1624, to void its charter and name Virginia as a royal province directly under his control.[13]

Virginians found little change in their lives. As a profession of obedience to royal command, the Virginia Assembly, which continued to meet despite the lack of kingly authority to do so, ordered that its militia commander at Point Comfort should board all incoming vessels and receive from their captains a true list of all passengers, and that "the said commander of the fort . . . administer unto them the oaths of allegiance and supremacy." [14]

When James was succeeded in 1625 by his son, Charles I, Virginians joined Englishmen everywhere in celebrating the occasion by renewing their oaths of allegiance with appropriate name changes. Charles soon indicated that he would continue his father's loyalty-testing program with increased intensity and scope. Royal orders required that every prospective emigrant for Virginia take the oaths of allegiance and supremacy, or produce oath certificates from justices of the peace or Anglican ministers. Port officers registered each oath taker's name on lists which went regularly to the Privy Council. Nonjurors were, at best, denied a place on shipboard; at worst they were imprisoned, often while their families were forced to leave England for Virginia. In consistent inconsistency, port officers in some areas, and at some times, swore minors, women, and children as young as three years, while a change of official, place, or time exempted such from the need to swear. The Privy Council fumed, but could do little to regularize procedures.

In any event, these loyalty-testing procedures were always more effective on paper than in reality, whether promulgated by the king or by Virginia assemblymen. Lax port officers permitted many nonjurors to go their ways unchallenged by oath tests, an inattention often sweetened with bribes and favors. Class consciousness impelled some port officials to gloss over all rules requiring dealings with any but "persons of quality"; common clay thus often went unsworn. Involuntary transportation to Virginia's perils was a favored penalty which some English magistrates levied upon hapless "sturdy beggars" who infested the kingdom's prisons, and oath administrators often felt that such folk did England better service abroad than at home, sworn or not. Ship captains, anxious for the money and land bounties awaiting the bringer of settlers, arranged for smuggling unswearable passengers or for forging oath certificates. King and Privy Council might, as they did in 1637, protest the "disorderly passing and departing out of the Kingdom into America," but reforms were always spasmodic.[15]

Those who survived the nightmare of transatlantic travel faced the same loyalty barrier when they reached Virginia. In compliance with royal orders and the colonial assembly's regulation, the fort at Point Comfort became the first view of Virginia most immigrants enjoyed. Its commander received from every ship's captain a list of passengers, whom he assembled while still aboard, and from whom—men, women, and children—he required oaths of allegiance. Nonjurors could not land, but must retrace the weary miles to England, there to await arraignment before a royal court. But in Virginia as in England, the letter of the law was often less than a total barrier to bribery, evasion, or mere sloppy administration.[16]

Royal Governor Sir Francis Wyatt ordered, in 1626, a general tightening of the Point Comfort loyalty-testing system, and imposed a tax of six shillings on each oath-taking immigrant to cover the expenses of notarizing and registering the necessary documents. Since most immigrants were poor folk who had had to sell their services for years ahead in order to secure passage from England, the tax fell on those who assumed the immigrants' labor contracts. Virginia's planters and merchants were eager for laborers. But they were far less anxious to part with hard money, which, as one group of Virginians declared, "is not . . . to be had but with exceeding difficulty and inconvenience." The problem temporarily passed as less diligent royal governors succeeded Wyatt, and evasions of the regulation again became easy. But by 1638 oath enforcement was again rigorous. A deputation of Virginia planters appealed to incumbent Governor Sir John Harvey (a stormy petrel in the royal service) for a relaxation of the oath tax. It injured trade and discouraged immigration, according to the Virginians. And the Virginia oath system was unnecessary, the planters claimed, since English regulations were supposed to ensure that all emigrants from the mother country were already sworn. Should Virginians beggar themselves because English officials were lax? Should loyal immigrants be prevented from entering Virginia because no one could afford to buy them the luxury of a needless second swearing of a loyalty oath?

This was one of Harvey's sweeter moments. He forwarded the complaints to the Privy Council, which, while considering the issue, temporarily suspended the oath tax, requiring the posting of a bond equal to the tax in the interim. Then a third party entered the picture.

8

Captain Richard Morison was then commander of the Virginia fort at Point Comfort. Most of his income derived from a share in the six-shilling tax he collected for administering the oaths to immigrants. He pleaded with the Privy Council for "all perquisites received by his predecessor," noted that his royal commission granted him the tax-collecting privilege, and pictured all sorts of dire, if unstated, perils to the Empire if Virginia's immigrants entered unsworn and he remained unpaid. Morison pleaded with the Privy Council to ignore the "clamors of the traders" and keep the tax, and let him keep his income.

A year and a half later (hardly laggard by seventeenth-century standards) the Privy Council's decision reached Virginia. Morison won; the Council decided that

The keeping of a register by the petitioner [Morison] of all passengers into that colony and the administering of the oaths of allegiance and supremacy to them is very necessary and of great importance for his Majesty's service and the benefit of the plantation in general, and that the imposition of payment of 6 s. per poll is but a thing of small value and was agreed to . . . by the General Assembly of the whole colony and by several acts of the courts there, and [the Privy Council] are therefore of opinion that the same is fit to be continued.

Continued pressure by Virginians finally achieved a more palatable solution—payment of the oath tax in tobacco, the value of which Virginians could manipulate in their favor, instead of in scarce sterling. The ritual swearing continued as before.[17]

Governor Harvey figured less pleasantly in another episode involving the oath requirement. In earlier years he had been a royal commissioner whose adverse report had resulted in Virginia's subjection to direct royal control; his governorship of that colony in 1630 was in part a kingly reward for such services. However faithful a servant of the king, Harvey had never learned to moderate his temper. Certainly any governor of Virginia needed saintly qualities to get along with the quarrelsome colonists. In any event, everyone was nervous; the colony was poor, the Indians were worrisome, the colonial assembly was unsure of its status under royal authority—it required little to set off an explosion.

Harvey behaved boorishly. He arrested Virginians on flimsy charges, knocked teeth from the mouth of an impertinent assemblyman with his stick, extracted money with great energy, replaced councilors with his favorites, silenced a minister whose interpretations of Holy Writ displeased him; the list of other grievances is long. Harvey found the Virginia Assembly demanding an increasing voice in public affairs. In short, he was in a position similar to that which his beloved monarch, Charles I, was facing in England in regard to Parliament.

Shrewdly, protesting Virginians asserted that Harvey was "soft" toward Catholics. In 1629 Virginia had prevented Catholic Lord Baltimore from settling in that colony because he would not take the oath of supremacy. Pridefully if inexactly, the colonists boasted that "no papists have been suffered to settle . . . among us." But the Virginians could not know that Harvey had secret royal instructions to coöperate with the Catholic colony of Maryland, now nibbling at lands which Virginians claimed as their own. In 1634, Harvey, by royal orders, welcomed one of the Baltimore clan to Jamestown. The next year the Virginia situation blew wide open.

Harvey set off the fuse when he decided to arrest several Virginia assemblymen for treason, because they had circulated written criticisms of his administration. Instead, they arrested Harvey, accused *him* of treason, and shipped him to England in chains, along with charges to the Privy Council that Harvey "denieth to administer the oath of allegiance to those that went . . . [to Virginia] to plant, as obliged by his instructions, and that he is in favor of the popish religion." Royal intervention exonerated Harvey and returned him to the Virginia governorship. There, he contented himself with seizing the property of those who had unseated him and sending them to English jails. Virginians, like all Englishmen, were learning that loyalty tests were tricky political weapons.[18]

Virginia's internal situation was forcibly, if temporarily, stabilized, and the colony's authorities continued to enforce the royal loyalty tests. Maryland's unwelcome presence at their doorstep inspired Virginians to prevent Catholic influence from infiltrating into official positions. A 1641 Virginia act "Concerning Popish Recusants" required all colonial officials to swear to the oaths James had established and Charles had continued. If any Virginian "by any sinister or secret means" secured appointment to a post, and then refused the oath, he stood self-condemned of popish recusancy by his nonjuring, lost his position, and incurred a fine of a thousand pounds of tobacco. Two years later, royal Governor Berkeley guided the acquiescent Virginia Assembly into ruling that he had the power to eject nonconformists and nonjurors from the colony "with all convenience." But all loyalty-testing directives seemed fated for poor enforcement, and required constant nagging from "higher-up" to recall officialdom to its duty. A bloody Indian attack on Virginia's spreading outposts in 1644 evoked this reminder from the Assembly:

. . . whereas by the late bloody Massacre divers businesses have wanted their present dispatch and especially the administration of the Oath of Allegiance, a matter of noe mean consequence in these dangerous times. It is therefore ordered that the Commanders of each County forthwith do see to the due execution thereof.[19]

Of course, not even the most diligent servant of the king really wanted everyone to swear the royal oaths. There was, for instance, Thomas Cheyney, whom a Virginia sheriff jailed for speaking disrespectfully of royalty. At his trial, Cheyney refused the proffered oaths of allegiance and supremacy, and the judge ordered him to receive "thirty stripes on his bare back, well laid on till the blood come." But Cheyney was lucky; "the Court, finding by . . . [his] discourse that he is disturbed in the brain, talking wildly and distractedly . . . , order a suspension of his punishment." [20] In those critical times few Englishmen were able to claim lunacy when confronted by their nation's or their colony's loyalty tests.

Virginia, the first of the English-speaking New World colonies, did not long remain the sole American outpost of the British Empire. Other Englishmen were making their way to nearby Maryland and to New England's shores. In either area, whether as members of the initial commercial organization of the Anglican Virginia colony or under its later royal control, as participants in the search for an independent theocracy which the Calvinist Puritans pursued in New England, or as adventurers in the Catholic proprietary colony of Maryland, new Americans carried their heritage of England's loyalty problems with them.

New England, north of Virignia's extensive boundaries, proved to be the next point of attention for Englishmen interested in exploiting and settling in America. In 1620, King James granted a charter to the Council for New England, which, like the Virginia Company, hoped to make profits from its ventures. James enjoined the directors of the council "to minister and give the Oaths of Allegiance and Supremacy . . . to all . . . persons, which . . . go or pass to the said colony in New England." [21] But James's loyalty program impelled a nonprofit-seeking group to be first in New England, in defiance of the royal grant and royal loyalty regulations.

In the English Midlands village of Scrooby there lived, early in the seventeenth century, a group of Protestant dissenters who called themselves Separatists, for, finding no hope of salvation in "the profane mixture" of orthodox Anglicanism or Catholicism, they wished to separate from both. Such convictions made them recusants and nonjurors. Hounded by pursuivants and oath administrators, jailed, mobbed, and vilified by lawful and extralegal mobs, a remnant of the Scrooby Separatists evaded the oath test all emigrants were supposed to take, and escaped to Holland. Despite the hurt they had suffered, these simple, poor people still loved England. After a decade of hospitable Dutch exile, the Separatists, in obedience to their interpretation of Calvin's creed, decided to establish themselves in the wilderness of America and thus, in isolation, to keep God's Word inviolate under English authority.[22]

Lengthy, tortuous negotiations with England resulted in a promise from James I that he "would connive at them, and not molest them, provided they carried themselves peaceably." Royal approval achieved an agreement that the Separatists return to England and make preparation to settle themselves in part of the Virginia Company's lands, with exemption from royal oath tests and from overt conformity to the Anglican ritual. When, finally, they sailed from England, one of their number, the diarist William Bradford, recorded that "they knew they were pilgrims." The story of the first American religious refuge was begun.

On the wintry November day in 1620 when the *Mayflower* dropped anchor in American waters, her passengers found themselves far from the Virginia lands to which their arrangement with the Virginia Company in London entitled them to go. No man knew who had the right to claim jurisdiction over land or government. The Pilgrim elders decided to build where they were, despite the absence of authority.

But non-Pilgrim "strangers" (Anglicans in the main) would be with them on shore. How could the two groups coexist in this inhospitable land, unless some prearranged authority provided security? And how, if their years of suffering were to be worthwhile, could the Pilgrims realize their dream of a perfect church-state, a Zion in this new Canaan, unless they succeeded in building that life where the *Mayflower* had brought them?

The Pilgrims pondered the matter, and achieved an answer in a combination loyalty test, church covenant, and fundamental constitution, which we know as the "Mayflower Compact":

In the Name of God, Amen. We whose names are underwritten, the loyal subjects of our dread sovereign, Lord King James, . . . Having undertaken, for the Glory of God and advancement of the Christian faith and honor of our King and Country, a voyage to plant the first colony in the northern parts of Virginia, do by these presents solemnly and mutually in the presence of God and one another, covenant and combine ourselves into a civil body politic, for our better ordering and preservation of the ends aforesaid; and by virtue hereof to enact, constitute and frame such just and equal laws, ordinances, constitutions, and offices, from time to time, as shall be thought most meet and convenient for the general good of the colony, unto which we promise all due submission and obedience.[23]

Those who signed paid the formal price of initial admission into the Plymouth colony and to participation in local government. That this was not too high a price history has recorded in the relatively amicable relations that Pilgrims and "strangers" enjoyed in Plymouth. Of course, the loyalty shoe had changed feet. The Pilgrim brand of Calvinism was orthodoxy, the sole source of law and enforceable by law. Anglicans were the dissenters in Plymouth. But the colony was too poor, its people were too few in number, and the threats to its existence were too great for the Pilgrims of Plymouth to expend much energy on internal squabbles. That kind of activity occurred with greater frequency in the colony that the Puritans, theological cousins to the Pilgrims, soon established nearby.

In the decade after the Pilgrims reached New England, a new monarch, Charles I (1625–1649), succeeded his father on the throne. Charles soon proved himself even more determined than James had been to wipe religious dissent from England. The new king's coercive apparatus, directed by such able loyalty enforcers as Bishop Laud and Thomas Wentworth, worked overtime.

Charles's particular ire was directed at a group of Calvinist dissenters who called themselves "God's People." During the swings of the religious pendulum, these nonconformists decided that the Anglican Church was a desirable framework for worship, *if,* and it was a large qualification, they might cleanse it of Catholic remnants with a harsh Calvinist brush. Hence the popular name of Puritans, which was no compliment in their time, soon clung to them.

The king's police clung to them, too, for Puritans were prominent leaders in the struggle Parliament was then launching against arbitrary royal action. As the last years of the 1620's passed, increasing royal persecutions against Puritans caused one of their leaders, John Winthrop, to predict that "God will bring some heavy affliction upon this land, . . . but if the Lord seeth it will be good for us, He will provide a shelter and a hiding-place for us . . . as a Zoar for Lot." [24]

Unlike the Pilgrims, the Puritans as a group were politically important and economically well fixed. One party of Puritans decided to emulate their Pilgrim fellow Calvinists and emigrate to America. *They,* however, would go as honorable adventurers. As Anglicans, even dissident Anglicans, the Puritans were ready and willing to swear the king's oaths. Neither nonjurors nor recusants, they were yet the severest critics of the incumbent regime. Two decades later, their doctrinal brethren, still easily able to swear the king's oath of allegiance, cut off the royal head.

The Puritans, shrewd businessmen and lawyers among them, combed the promotional literature that various joint-stock companies were spreading to encourage emigration to America. They finally decided to go to Massachusetts Bay, and arranged that the charter they signed should go with them to the New World (a most unusual procedure, permitting the Puritans to evade the charter restrictions requiring all laws in the future colony to conform to England's, and to escape the normal requirement that the "forms of . . . oaths [must be] warrantable by the laws and statutes of . . . England"). From its inception, the Puritan enterprise in New England was a heady mixture of piety and profit, and it produced a colonial hybrid.[25]

King Charles approved the charter, and welcomed the chance to rid England of some of this troublesome neo-Anglican sect who took oaths of allegiance freely enough, yet rarely ceased prattling of the need for Calvinistic reforms in his church and for restrictions upon his power. In March, 1630, the Puritan company embarked, honorable participants in a commercial venture, discreet comrades in a search for a religious Utopia, bound in a spirit that a future governor of the colony they were to establish set to rhyme:

> Let Men of God in Courts and Churches watch
> O'er such as do a Toleration hatch,
> Lest that ill Egg bring forth a Cockatrice,
> To poison all with Heresie and Vice.
> If Men be left, and otherwise Combine,
> My Epitaph's, I DY'D NO LIBERTINE.[26]

Even before they left England, the Puritan leaders agreed that settlers who proved "not conformable to their government were not to remain within the limits of the grant." To be "conformable" in Massachusetts, the Puritans soon made it clear, meant participation in their church and obedience to their state. A small group of Puritan leaders—

14

ministers and magistrates—established rigid controls over both church and state in the little colony. In 1634 they paid England's monarchs the accolade of emulation by establishing a loyalty test for all residents, Puritan and non-Puritan, to swear (which, of course, violated the charter requirement that any oaths the colony used had to conform to England's). But the Puritans had the charter with them, so, for the moment, who in England could see the discrepancy? The oath read:

I (A.B.) being by God's providence, an Inhabitant, and Freeman, within the Jurisdiction of this Commonwealth, do freely acknowledge myself to be subject to the Government thereof: And therefore do here swear by the great and dreadful Name of the Everliving God, that I will be true and faithfull to the same, and will accordingly yield assistance and support thereunto, with my person and estate, as in equity I am bound; and will also truly endeavour to maintain and preserve all the liberties and privileges thereof, submitting myself to the wholesome Laws and Orders made and established by the same. And, further, that I will not plot or practice any evil against it, or consent to any that shall do so; but will timely discover and reveal the same to lawfull authority now here established, for the speedy preventing thereof. . . . So help me God in the Lord Jesus Christ.[27]

Puritan leaders, as internal troubles mounted, increasingly valued the utility of this oath. When, in 1639, the first printing press in the English-speaking colonies began operation in Boston, the first item struck off was the loyalty oath, followed by an almanac and the famed *Bay Psalm Book*. Loyalty, efficiency, and piety were the trade-marks of Puritan New England.

From the first, prominent Puritans defended their oath test against the many opponents to their rule and against critics of the oath law. John Cotton, for instance, in a passage that James I might have penned, defended the use of coercive tests to achieve political and religious conformity:

But (say you) it doth make men hypocrites, to compel men to conform the outward man for fear of punishment. If it did so, yet better to be hypocrites than profane persons. Hypocrites give God part of His due, the outward man, but the profane person giveth God neither the outward nor inward man.[28]

There *were* enemies to the Puritan control of Massachusetts for the Calvinist oligarchy to combat. In the supercharged theological atmosphere of the Bay colony, nonconforming interpretations of Holy Writ were deemed disloyal. Roger Williams, as a case in point, denied the right of the Puritan lawmakers to offer a sacred oath to men who might be unregenerate. Williams saw such oaths as blasphemy rather than piety. His protests aroused the colony's casuists, and so much sound and fury rose that the lawmakers revoked the oath law. But they reënacted it only two years later, when Williams was gone from the colony, a banished, vanquished enemy to Massachusetts' law and order.

Other critics of Massachusetts' oath policy, unlike Williams, took the colony to task at a farther, safer distance from her magistrates, and criticized Massachusetts' test oath mainly on the basis that it was not the oath that royal regulations required. Thomas Lechford, for instance, the first trained lawyer to practice in New England, waited until he returned to England to expose Puritan practices he had found distasteful. In his *Plain Dealing* (1642), Lechford described how the Puritan authorities had ruled that

Every free-man, when he is admitted, takes a strict oath, to be true to the [Massachusetts] society, or jurisdiction: In which oath, I do not remember that ordinary saving, which is and ought to be in all oaths to other lords, [that is,] saving the faith and truth which I bear to our sovereign Lord the king, though I hope it may be implied.[29]

Samuel Maverick and Robert Child braved the wrath of the ruling Puritan group when they sought to mesh New England more closely with the growing Presbyterian movement which in the mid-1640's was enveloping the mother country. Maverick, a discreet sort, kept quiet so long as he was under Puritan control; Child rashly broke into print in Boston. In a *Remonstrance to the Governor and General Court of Massachusetts Bay* (1646), Child pointed to the Puritan oath as a contradiction to the limitations of the Puritans' charter, from which, Child insisted,

. . . proceeds fears and jealousies of . . . undue oaths, being subject to exposition, according to the will of him or them that gives them, and not according to the true and unbowed rule of law, which is the true interpreter of all oaths to all men, whether judge or judged.

For his temerity, the Massachusetts authorities fined Child, destroyed his books and papers, and warned him to drop his literary pursuits. But protests such as Child's reached England, and Massachusetts felt impelled to match the propaganda of its detractors. John Winthrop and some Puritan confreres assembled a document which compared, most favorably for Massachusetts, the Magna Charta and English common law with some discreetly chosen sections of the colony's regulations. The Puritan apologists denied that the Massachusetts loyalty test conflicted in any way with English oath laws, and asserted that in any event no one in Massachusetts had to take the former. They did not say that nonjurors were disfranchised and banished from the colony, and that banishment could easily mean death. Nor did the Puritan writers see anything amiss in their bland assumption that they possessed precisely the same power to create oaths as did England's Parliament. In complete duplicity and contradiction to fact, they claimed that

> . . . our polity and fundamentals are framed according to the laws of England and according to the charter, so that the petitioners (if they had not cast off all modesty) must needs be ashamed of this complaint. . . . They should have done well to have told us what oaths and covenants they mean [in their complaint], for . . . deceit lies hid in generalities. We know of no oaths we impose on any, other than such as are allowed by our charter, and were in practice by the company in London (as occasion required) before we came to these parts.[30]

Child, emboldened by reports of English support in his dispute, wrote to Presbyterian members of Parliament. But Puritan censors apprehended his letters, and Child found it healthier to take himself to England. There he joined with his brother John, and with William Vassal, another refugee from Boston, in writing *New England's Jonas Cast Up in London* (1647), which severely criticized the Massachusetts authorities for administering oaths which "cannot be warranted by the letters patents, and seem not to concur with the [royal] oath of allegiance . . . enforced upon all." [31]

Such reports reinforced the king's ministers in their dislike of the course of colonial events. Plymouth had no legal right to govern herself; Massachusetts was violating the charter its leaders had cunningly removed abroad, increasing its population at an alarming rate through a continued Puritan exodus from England, and expanding its boundaries. Such influential courtiers as Sir Ferdinando Gorges, to whom James and Charles had given grants of land which Massachusetts was infringing, pressed claims for redress before the royal court. The perpetually bankrupt monarch was especially receptive to arguments that the emigrating dissenters were removing vast quantities of wealth from England. "Suffering such swarms to go out of England," warned one anti-Puritan councilor, "will overthrow trade."

Early in 1634 Charles decided to end the emigration evil. Royal orders enjoined every port officer to prevent anyone from leaving who refused the oath, or who, oath or not, could not prove that he had paid his taxes and owed no debts. In a single month, as a result of Charles's attempt to sift emigration, eleven ships, fully loaded, were returned to English docksides to await the royal pleasure. Port officials removed all nonjurors and all sworn passengers and crew whom the officials thought *might* be perjurers. For three years Charles did his best to prevent the spread of subversion to the colonies by keeping nonjurors in England. But strict enforcement was beyond the capabilities of his administrative staff. Too few officials, of whom many sympathized with their victims' religious views, and too many more pressing problems confronting the king worked in New England's favor. In addition to these limits upon his power to check emigration from England, Charles was really facing a problem of reverse migration of Puritans back to England from America, who hoped to help their faith in the growing internal strife in the mother country.[32]

If Charles could do little to check the growth of the increasingly unpopular Puritan colony, the possibility of royal revocation of the colony's charter was a more immediate road to control. Sir Ferdinando Gorges, whose claims to New England areas the Puritans disputed; Thomas Morton, whose trading post at Merrymount had burned from Puritan torches; and other enemies of the Puritan colony gathered to press this approach to the Privy Council. In 1637 English authorities ordered the recall and cancellation of the colony's charter, and commissioned Gorges as governor of New England.

It was crisis in Boston. The Puritans warned a royal investigating committee not to remove the charter, or "the common people here will conceive that his Majesty hath cast them off and thereby they are freed from their allegiance." And the Puritans were ready to support their words by defying the British Empire, if necessary. Bostonians manned cannon, ready to meet a British "invasion," and ordered that all residents reswear the colonial oaths of allegiance in order to guarantee internal security.

God, as the Puritans saw it, was on their side. Gorges' ship sank at the start of its voyage from England. The Bay colony maintained its independent course. Correspondence about the colonial test oath and the disputed charter continued between Boston and Whitehall, while Puritan agents in England spoke shrewdly worded disclaimers of disobedience to the irate monarch. But Massachusetts did not obey Charles's orders to produce its charter for inspection, or repeal its loyalty oaths in deference to the royal oath tests. Indeed, when the Puritan colony helped to organize the New England Confederation as a regional alliance against Indian marauders, Winthrop satisfiedly recorded that the delegates "omitted the oath to bear true faith and allegiance to our sovereign Lord King Charles, seeing that he had

violated the privileges of Parliament and had lost much of his kingdom and many of his subjects." [33]

There was even sweeter revenge coming for Massachusetts. Events in
England were ever her ally, preventing successive rulers from devoting
full or consistent attention to colonial affairs. By the mid-1640's, the
religious tensions, constitutional disagreements, and crises of allegiance
which had driven the Pilgrims and the Puritans to New England, were
too explosive to be contained. Civil war erupted in England, resulting
in the execution of a king and the transmutation of a monarchy into a
religious commonwealth. Few of the participants in these great events
had time to consider far-off New England.

Maryland soon followed Virginia, Plymouth, and Massachusetts Bay
as the fourth in the constellation of English-speaking colonies in America. Its inception, location, and history were tightly bound up in a
complex loyalty-testing tale.

George Calvert had been a secretary of state for James I, but he had
to resign his office in 1625 when, because of his Catholic leanings, he
refused to swear the required oaths of allegiance and supremacy. But
Calvert retained royal favor, became Lord Baltimore, and received a
personal grant to part of Newfoundland, where he found the climate
frigid and the income inconsiderable. In 1629 Calvert decided to visit
Virginia. The colony's councilors, knowing he must refuse, insisted he
take the royal test oaths. Exultant Virginians gloated as the rebuffed
Catholic noble sailed away from Jamestown for England. There Calvert petitioned Charles I for a royal grant to land and proprietary governing powers in part of the Virginia patent he had found so attractive.
England would benefit, Calvert argued, if some of her loyal Catholic
subjects could emigrate to America, there to build a buffer against
foreign colonial expansion, and to check the spread of radical Protestantism as well. Catholic exertions in America would gain the king
more than confiscations of Catholics' estates in England. True, emigrants must, by royal orders, swear the test oaths. But what royalty had
proposed, it could dispose; were not, Calvert asked, the test oaths in
force "for reason of State; for the safety of the king and kingdom more
than religion?" [34] Calvert could have hit upon no shrewder arguments
to convince a monarch who was finding dissenting Protestants rather
than Catholics his most troublesome subjects.

Virginia had agents on hand to combat Calvert's claims. One of
these agents, William Claiborne, held land in the area Calvert wanted,
and had been one of the Jamestown councilors who required Calvert to

swear allegiance there. When Calvert won a vast royal grant of land out of the original Virginia patent, with almost unrestricted powers of government (the new colony's laws were to conform to England's, and no religious establishment was specified), it boded ill for harmonious relations with Virginia.[35] Triumphant Calvert initiated the many preparations needed to launch his proprietary colony in America. His death bequeathed his title, rights, religion, and dreams to his son, Cecilius.

While Cecilius Calvert slowly recruited his company, his enemies whispered that he intended to flood America with Catholic soldiers and nuns to serve Spanish interests. Ironically, Calvert's real trouble was recruiting enough Catholics, of whom few with any funds volunteered. Finally, in October, 1630, the *Ark* and the *Dove* weighed anchor, only to be turned back to London. An informant had reported to the Star Chamber that the ships had departed with their passengers "abusing the king's officers and refusing to take the oath of allegiance." Calvert hurried to the Privy Council, which sent one of its best pursuivants to the ships. He reported that

According to your Lordship's order . . . I offered the oath of allegiance to all and every [one of] the persons aboard, to the number of 128, who took the same, and inquiring of the master of the ship whether any more persons were to go on the said voyage, he answered that some few others were shipped who had forsaken the ship and given over the voyage, by reason of the stay of the ships.

The deceit of some of the Catholic passengers, who took the oaths with personal reservations, soon compounded with treason. Once more at sea, the two vessels stopped by the Isle of Wight and secretly embarked sixty-five additional passengers, including two Catholic priests who had arranged this discreet rendezvous rather than swear the test oath. Their complements full, the ships proceeded to America.[36] Cecilius appointed his brother, George Calvert, as resident lieutenant governor, and warned the entire company to preserve good order and unity among themselves, and to "suffer no scandal or offence to be given to any of the Protestants." Therefore, all Catholic services were to be held as quietly as possible, and no Catholic was to argue about, or boast of, his faith to others on board. The Catholic passengers disobeyed this order immediately by conducting services almost in sight of England.

Calvert had enjoined the expedition to steer clear of the unfriendly Anglican stronghold at Point Comfort. This order, too, was disobeyed. The ships stopped at Jamestown, and benefited from the toadying character of incumbent Governor Harvey, who knew that Charles I was increasingly friendly to Catholics. From Jamestown the vessels beat their way northward. In March, 1634, they dropped anchor at St. Mary's, the passengers finally obeying one of their proprietor's orders. George Calvert assembled them ashore, and administered

. . . an oath of allegiance to his Majesty unto all and everyone upon the place, after having first publicly in the presence of the people taken it themselves; letting them know that his Lordship gave particular directions to have it one of the first things to be done, to testify to the world that none should enjoy the benefits of his Majesty's gracious grant . . . but such as would give a public assurance of their fidelity and allegiance. . . .

How diligently the Calverts sought to contradict the disloyalty allegations their enemies were casting about in England, by requiring public loyalty oaths in Maryland! But the very loyalty oaths their colonists swore contradicted the Calverts, *if* loyalty oaths were a valid guide to loyalty. The oaths George Calvert administered on the first day of landing were not those ordained by English law, but were Calvert-tailored, carefully omitting all mention of the Anglican king's religious supremacy. And, simultaneously with the oath ceremony, the Catholic priests at hand erected a crude cross and held public Mass, thus defying the third of the proprietor's injunctions.[37]

Once settled into the hard life in the wilderness, Maryland's colonists found themselves engaged in bitter boundary disputes with their Virginia neighbors. Blood spilled, and after years of tortuous negotiations the Privy Council finally awarded the contested territory to the Calverts, by no means sweetening relations between the two colonies. Calvert governors permitted a representative assembly to meet in Maryland, but rigged it with a system of proxy votes. Through devoted (and well-paid) supporters of proprietary rights, the Calverts finally defeated Jesuit aspirations to control the colony, in part by welcoming as many Protestants into Maryland as possible. By 1638 Calvert felt his rule solid enough to permit the assembly to initiate laws, with a veto power remaining in the proprietor's hands.

Under Calvert guidance, the Maryland Assembly created an oath test for all residents, especially recipients of land grants, to take. Its lengthy provisions required pledges of fidelity to the Calvert family and appointees, promises to prevent and expose any conspiracies against the proprietor's command, and assertions of eternal allegiance. It did *not* impose loyalty to king or country, give precedence to any church, or deal at all with the vexed question of abjuration of papal power. Rather, the Maryland oath of fidelity specifically stated that it was "not

[in] any wise understood to infringe or prejudice Liberty of Conscience, in point of Religion." All adult inhabitants had to take the oath. Nonjuring imposed loss of office and land rights until a second refusal, when the nonjuror forfeited all property and suffered perpetual banishment. Women, as weaker creatures (and nonproperty-owners) merely faced imprisonment "until such time as they will take the same oath."

As a matter of fact, the Calverts at first enforced only one part of the test law. Primarily interested in money, the proprietors wasted no time in deriving revenues from the only immediate resource the colony offered—land. Nonjurors were pretty much left alone so long as they were peaceable, and did not seek a land patent from the proprietors. Men who applied for land, paid their money, and swore the oath, got the land. If they refused the oath, the Calverts did not want them as landholders, with consequent suffrage, office-holding, and militia privileges.[38]

By 1640, four American colonies had adopted differing loyalty-testing laws and policies. Virginia, initially a commercial venture, now a royal colony, vigorously used the statutory form which successive monarchs and Parliaments had created. Plymouth, self-governing because unauthorizedly in being, made the Mayflower Compact an initial base for residence and franchise, plus the essential requirement of church membership on which all other rights hinged. Its bigger Puritan neighbor at Massachusetts Bay, like Virginia a commercial enterprise in origin, closely followed the Pilgrim pattern of effective self-government; the Puritans of Boston created a snug identity of Calvinist church and state, buttressing both by a strict oath of allegiance to the colony and to the pious purposes of its magistracy. And Maryland, a propietary colony under the sole rule of a single individual, also wrote a special loyalty test into law.

Obviously, the royal oath requirement had failed to standardize the kind of English colonies or colonists that planted the royal ensign in America. Royal, self-governing, and proprietary colonies formed part of the rich diversity that created an enduring heritage of differentiation in American local government, but such diversity was not what English administrators desired from their oath regulations.

And in another, more immediate sense, 1640 signaled the failure of the royal oath. Civil war came to England, and affected every colony. The echoes of that conflict soon tested the efficacy of the colonial loyalty tests, whether proprietary, royal, or self-governing in origin, whether Anglican, Catholic, or Calvinist in inspiration.

CHAPTER II

Torchbearers of Colonial Loyalty-Testing

Crisis crossed the Atlantic when news of England's two political up-heavals of the seventeenth century reached North America. Colonists added local issues and tensions to the causes of political rupture which sufficed for Englishmen. Emulating royal and rebel practices at home, England's colonists in America used loyalty tests as weapons of ideology, political partisanship, and peculation. In America as in England there were men like Cromwell's lieutenant John Lilburne, who condemned such prostitution of patriotic purpose. Lilburne, who in writing *Rash Oaths Unwarrantable* in 1647 was obviously a good bit ahead of his time, stated that

Oaths . . . now are nothing but cloaks of knavery, and breeders of strife and mischief. Therefore for shame lay them all down and press them no more upon any man whatsoever, for he that conscientiously makes nothing of an oath, will make as little of breaking his oath, whensoever it shall make for his profit, ease, or preferment, whereas to him that conscientiously scruples an oath, his bare word . . . is the sincerest tie in the world.[1]

Lilburne's advice found few takers. Roundhead and Royalist seeded England and the Empire with a rich crop of tests of fidelity. Samuel Pepys, that attentive diarist, might privately bemoan that "we have more cause to be sorry for the many oaths that we have already taken and broken," but made no public protest. Those who did suffered.[2]

England's first civil war was Catholic Lord Baltimore's supreme test of political tightrope-walking. In 1643 he returned to England to watch the ominous growth of Calvinist power there. In his absence a Virginia expedition under William Claiborne invaded Maryland and forcefully retook Claiborne's former property. Almost simultaneously, a profane, violent, demagogic supporter of England's parliamentary cause, Richard Ingle, incited insurrection against Calvert rule. Calvert's deputy indicted Ingle for high treason, since the latter had cursed Charles I in no uncertain terms. Ingle temporarily fled Maryland.

Calvert's subsequent return to Maryland, after he had proved to suspicious English Parliamentarians that he was no friend to royalism or oppressor of Protestantism, was marred by a second "visit" from Ingle, who occupied St. Mary's, forced Calvert to flee to Virginia, and began a loyalty-testing spree among Marylanders. Ingle's loyalty-testing program was based on two oaths: one, Parliament's current "Solemn League and Covenant," and the second, an oath of his own devise which demanded submission to himself as Parliament's legal representative in Maryland, which he was not.

More interested in spoils than in statecraft, Ingle worded his test oath so that all "good" Catholics must reject it. Delighted at their nonjuring, Ingle banished the most prominent, whipped and jailed lesser fry, and confiscated their properties, with special attention to Jesuits. But his very excesses alienated even Protestant Marylanders. In 1646 Calvert retook the colony, and found it in an uproar. His and Ingle's adherents were bent on mutual extermination.

Calvert, perpetually bedeviled by his own delicate tenure as a Catholic proprietor in an empire now dominated by Calvinist rebels, decided upon clemency for Ingle's defeated followers. He proclaimed an oath of amnesty and allegiance for them to take after surrendering their arms. All landholders, no matter how firm their past resistance to Ingle, had to swear this oath as a bonus of allegiance to the proprietor which Calvert prescribed "shall not be understood . . . only for the present, but shall firmly . . . bind in futurity." Nonjurors would be social lepers, excluded from legal rights and denied neighborly assistance by all (a serious matter on the frontier). But Ingle was only the beginning of Calvert's troubles. As John Bozman, the early historian of the colony, suggests, "from the imposition of the [Calvert] oath of fidelity . . . flowed all the bloodshed which eventually ensued." [3]

Trying to please all theological and political sides, Calvert welcomed Protestant dissenters from royalist Virginia, appointed a Protestant, William Stone, to govern Maryland, and returned to England to guard his interests before an unfriendly Parliament. While the Catholic noble toadied to Presbyterian burghers, Parliament sent commissioners to Maryland to impose new loyalty tests on the colony. But Calvert took advantage of Cromwell's assumption of dictatorial rights to assert that the parliamentary envoys were shorn of authority. He ordered

Governor Stone to reassert full proprietary rights in Maryland and reissue the Calvert oath of fidelity, along with an act decreeing religious toleration to take the sting from his oath order (resulting in the famed Toleration Act of 1649). Calvert's assembly, although it enacted his oath law and toleration measure, warned him that "an occasion is given to much perjury, when swearing becomes common"; too-numerous oaths "little prevail on men of little conscience." Such ethical niceties failed to appreciate Calvert's heroic agility in the shifting sands of religious dispute surrounding him in England and Maryland.[4]

A loud protest against the oath test soon echoed across Maryland, surprising Calvert by its vehemence and source. Puritan settlers, many of whom Calvert had succored from royalist Virginia vengeance, castigated the proprietor's oath because it forced them to agree to religious toleration, which, one Puritan Marylander complained, "we conceive not agreeable to the terms on which we came hither, nor to the liberty of our consciences as Christians and free subjects of the Commonwealth of England." According to these Protestant complainants, Calvert was unjust to require them to swear to defend "to the last drop of blood" colonial officers who were in turn sworn to support a Catholic lord and to tolerate the hated Catholic faith. Action followed words, but what all the words had to do with loyalty is open to question. Maryland's Puritans were protesting against the grim tenacity of Catholic rule in the colony in the face of growing Protestant numbers, against their deep-seated hatred of all Catholic existence, and against their equally firm antipathy to the reimposition of rents and fees due the Calverts which the new oath order seemed to make perpetual.

The old Calvert nemesis, William Claiborne, was on the Maryland scene as one of the temporarily unemployed parliamentary commissioners. Using the oath issue as a pretext, Claiborne deposed Governor Stone and required all Marylanders now to swear allegiance to the Commonwealth, abjuring their "perpetual" oaths to the Calverts. Claiborne revoked the Toleration Act, disfranchised all Catholics and nonjurors, and his Puritan assembly in Maryland proved itself as ruthless an exterminator of dissent as its big brother in England.

Calvert, defending his authority before Cromwell's Parliament, faced angry agents of the insurgent Maryland Puritans, who denounced his oath for being "without any relation to, or mention of, the supreme authority of England." [5] In Calvert's behalf, one of his supporters in England, John Langford, penned an emotional, effective *Refutation* of the insurgents' claims. Langford noted that Calvert had appointed a Protestant as governor of Maryland, and that he had briefed prospective Protestant immigrants into Maryland that the proprietor's oath was a condition of landholding. None had then objected that the oath infringed religious conscience. No, Langford asserted, the Protestant troublemakers had "no regret to the oath till they were as much refreshed with their entertainment [in Maryland] . . . as the snake in the fable was in the countryman's breast." Protestants "of much better quality" than the complainants swore the Calvert oath, recognizing it as a just test of their fidelity to the Baltimore family's rights to suzerainty over the colony.[6] A similar defense of Calvert's rights and oaths found expression in John Hammond's *Leah and Rachel*. According to Hammond, Maryland Protestants were after more earthly gains than loyalty to England or religious uniformity in their objections to the Calvert oath:

. . . it was that sweet, that rich, that large country [Maryland] they aimed at; and finding themselves in a capacity not only to capitulate, but to oversway those that had so received and relieved them, began to pick quarrels first with the Papists, next with the oath, and lastly declared their averseness with all conformity, wholly aiming . . . to deprive the Lord Proprietor of all his interest in that country and make it their own.[7]

While ink spilled in London, blood spilled in Maryland, where the claimants for domination met in martial enmity, each seeking to pave the way to victory by sending oath commissioners about the colony demanding loyalty oaths of all settlers. Governor Stone's arms were weaker. When the smoke of battle cleared, Stone had lost and Claiborne's victorious party celebrated by disfranchising, imprisoning, and attainting Stone's supporters and all who had sworn Calvert's oaths in the most recent spate of loyalty-testing. It seemed that Calvert's cause was lost in Maryland.[8]

Patiently, incredibly patiently, Calvert continued to press his cause before Cromwell. In 1657, England's dictator, who was mellower toward "loyal Catholics" than he had been a decade earlier, ordered Maryland returned to Calvert control, and Calvert to amnesty his former enemies in the colony, reinstitute the Toleration Act, and alter the disputed Calvert oath to include a statement of primary allegiance to the existing republic in England. All Marylanders over sixteen years of age had to swear, or lose landholding rights, and face possible banishment from the turbulent colony. But those in Maryland who wished to (meaning the most devoted supporters of Calvert's rights, and the many feeders at his generous trough of office and preferment) could elect to swear by the original loyalty test of Calvert supremacy in preference to the new formula.[9]

Early in 1658 Calvert returned to Maryland with Cromwell's restoration order. The Claiborne "government" bent with the changing wind and dissolved itself out of existence; its once belligerent members swore to Calvert rule with meek obedience. Calvert's agents saw to it that all residents pledged their fidelity by either of the two available tests of loyalty. But many Maryland consciences remained uneasy, and thwarted ambitions yearned for revenge when opportunity again opened. Maryland was one place where no oath seemed a powerful enough cement to bind together the disparate elements of its population.

Calvert was himself largely responsible for the refusal of old wounds to heal. In 1661, when news of the restoration of Charles II reached Maryland, Calvert reimposed his original loyalty test as the sole legitimate passport to respectability in his colony, and added to its already stringent terms a statement of the subscriber's agreement that any criticism of Baltimore policies was automatically an act of treason. For the moment, Maryland's cowed Puritans accepted what they could not prevent, took the "new" oath, and waited.[10]

When Charles Calvert, third Lord Baltimore, sailed from Maryland in 1676 for a visit "home" to England, he left an apparently serene colony. Only a year earlier, when Calvert assumed the proprietary title, he had heard renewed the oaths of fidelity which had become a family fixture in Maryland. But troubles erupted soon after his departure. From neighboring Virginia came news of wild unrest and rebellion. Calvert officials determined to prevent the conflagration from spreading to Maryland, jumped to the conclusion that several local mass meetings were hatching plots against Calvert rule (the meetings were actually seeking to prepare defenses against a rumored French and Indian invasion), and condemned the assemblies as rebellious acts. Affairs in Maryland grew causelessly critical. Then came news of the suppression of revolt in Virginia. But the reasons that had impelled Marylanders to protest at all—high rents and taxes, Calvert nepotism, unjust representation, inadequate protection against Indians, and the proprietor's vexed oath of fidelity—made the unrest continue.

An anonymous, Protestant-penned *Complaint from Heaven with a Hue and Cry and a Petition out of . . . Maryland* (1676) soon appeared in England. It detailed Calvert offenses, and found as the "greatest consequence" Calvert's assumption "that he is an absolute prince in Maryland, . . . as our gratious sovereign in England." As proof, the pamphleteer submitted for examination the Calvert oath.

27

That oath had once lost Maryland to the Calvert clan; it now was losing the colony for England, for Calvert's servitors in imposing the proprietor's loyalty test showed that the king's power did not penetrate the colony. "Loyal" Marylanders, the writer urged, were caught in a trap. If they swore Calvert's oath, they denied their king. If they refused the oath, they suffered contumely and banishment: "And for this they begin to hang and fine people . . . under the cloak of fidelity." This rugged choice was obnoxious to all ethical men: "Some have taken it [the Calvert oath] by persuasion, some by compulsion out of fear and threatenings, others and the most part will not take it, and they are threatened with banishment and no protection of the law, to be prosecuted as mutinous and rebels."

In place of the oath to the "Young Pope," Maryland's Protestants wanted Charles II (how ironical that this pro-Catholic king should receive this plea!) to take over Maryland as his grandfather had assumed royal control over Virginia, and to impose the "King's . . . only due Oath of Allegiance and Supremacy." The Calvert oath had reduced Maryland to a country "divided in factions and affections," where "the papists and other turncoats sworn for the proprietary vapor and domineer," and those who preferred the royal oath were "crowded out." [11]

Hardly surprisingly, Charles II failed to heed the Protestant plea. Calvert's officials sternly repressed incipient unrest in Maryland with all the current tools of authority: test oaths, prisons, gallows, banishments, and confiscations. But Calvert disliked the reports of repression which reached England. He pressured Protestant officeholders to attest to a distorted description of serenity in Maryland which he circulated about England, envisaging a loyal population, sworn to fidelity, justly ruled, disturbed only by a few radical malcontents. Unfortunately for this traditionally agile Calvert footwork, events moved too fast for distorted propaganda to counter.

Charles Calvert had an unfortunate affinity for going to England at the wrong time. In 1685 he left Maryland for another visit, leaving a committee in the colony to rule in his name. He observed the threatening course of events in England as James II drifted toward disaster. In 1688 the Privy Council ordered Calvert to proclaim the birth of James's son in Maryland. Then a seemingly irrelevant issue unnecessarily exacerbated tempers.

Calvert had named William Joseph to act as governor. A tactless, insensitive soul, Joseph addressed a meeting of the colony's assembly with a lengthy tribute to the divine-right theory of government, then demanded that each representative swear anew the proprietor's oath. Some assemblymen decided to test Joseph's mettle, and asserted that they had once sworn that oath as members of a previous assembly, and need not again. Joseph insisted. "Refusing allegiance implies rebellion," he ranted, and threatened the nonjurors with prison, fines, and exile, for he now had cause, he warned them, "to suspect your loyalty." The cowed representatives compromised and swore the oath individually, thus salving their collective dignity. But this needless ruckus added fuel to the fire of colonial indignation.[12]

Then news of the English Revolution of 1688–89 reached Maryland. Which king had their proprietor chosen; had he picked the winning Protestant side? Calvert's elasticity produced a quick submission to William and Mary, but his orders to Maryland to proclaim the new monarchs were delayed, and his colonists knew only that weeks passed with no word from him on this burning issue. To militant Maryland Protestants, now organized in a "Protestant Association," Calvert's silence meant that he had decided to support the exiled Stuart king. Suspense and indecision, and the tensions of impending Indian warfare, mingled with formless fears of Catholic persecution. For once Governor Joseph was silent, fearing to make a move that future authority might condemn. Silence now was no substitute for leadership. In mid-1689, John Coode and the Protestant Association took to arms, proclaimed William and Mary as rulers, and, in good seventeenth-century form, issued an apologia for their act.

Coode's condemnation of the Calvert rule centered on the test-oath issue. Calvert's failure to proclaim William and Mary as the rightful rulers of England proved, Coode asserted, that the Calvert loyalty-testing program had always been a discreet mask for Catholic expansion. Therefore the Calverts had always been disloyal (to the brand-new monarchs!) and deserved punishment rather than revenues from Maryland. Naturally, Governor Joseph condemned Coode as a rebel. Once more two governments claimed undivided allegiance in Maryland. Each asserted itself as the only proper recipient of loyalty; each imposed old and new loyalty tests with fine abandon. Caught in the middle, as undecided as were many Englishmen in this conflict of loyalties, some Marylanders sought to steer a middle way, but few could safely do so. When, in August, 1689, Coode's faction controlled almost all Maryland, he made it an act of treason to assert that Calvert had ever rightfully been the proprietor of Maryland. The penalty for treason was death.

Confusion reigned in Maryland. Political murders became common; offices remained vacant for want of men willing to take a partisan plunge by swearing loyalty to one side or the other. From adherents of both camps, tearful petitions describing the gory turn of events in Maryland made their slow way to England.[13] News of crisis in his colony surprised Calvert, who had supposed everything serene there. Despite his protests, the Privy Council decided to consider the disposition of Maryland. Anxious months passed as the royal ministers sought a legitimate way to deprive Calvert of all his rights in the colony. The best they could do was to justify King William's arbitrary assumption of governmental powers in Maryland; the Calvert clan retained its land and revenue rights. "Trimming" had paid off again for the Calverts.

Maryland's rebel Protestant government, under Coode's minatory association, was barely maintaining power when the first royal governor, Lionel Copley, arrived in the colony. In April, 1692, Copley administered the royal oaths of allegiance to all Marylanders. The Calvert family and the Calvert oath of fidelity had finally lost their hold on the colony.[14] With Protestant supremacy established, merely two decades more were required to transmute Maryland into as anti-Catholic a colony as any Anglican or Calvinist could desire; by 1717, Maryland had disfranchised Catholics unless they swore loyalty by the royal formula, and had commissioned special port officers to "impose an additional duty of 20 shillings on each Papist immigrant, status to be determined by offering each immigrant the Oaths of Allegiance and Abjuration, and the Maryland Test Oath Act." In final salute to the lesson in loyalty-testing they had learned when Catholics ruled Maryland, the Protestant legislators ordained that "any one refusing is by refusing deemed a Papist." [15] Maryland had gone full circle.

Far less elastic in matters of conscience than pragmatic Lord Baltimore, Sir William Berkeley, royal governor of Virginia, cast his own and his colony's lot with the Stuart monarchs during England's first civil war. With saucy impudence, Berkeley rejected the authority of Cromwell's Commonwealth and continued enforcing the royal oaths of allegiance and supremacy.

Warships achieved what Cromwell's proclamations concerning loyalty could not, and parliamentary commissioners succeeded in carrying out their instructions to

. . . cause all the several acts against Kingship and the House of Lords to be published . . . [in Virginia]; to administer an oath to all the inhabitants; . . . to be true and faithful to the Commonwealth as it is now established without a King or House of Lords, also to give liberty to those who have taken the [parliamentary test oath called the] Engagement.[16]

Neither side had resources to carry on war. Virginia's leaders, over Berkeley's protests, achieved a compromise with the commissioners. Nonjurors had a year of grace to leave the colony (a proviso that was never enforced), but only those sworn to the new oath could vote or hold office. During most of Cromwell's rule, Virginia was substantially self-governing for the first time in its history. A few nonjurors presented problems to the colony's policy makers; if Berkeley remained quiet, other devoted Royalists made much of the sudden shift of loyalties. One magistrate, for instance, rejected this "strong horrid imposition by oath." To this purist, "the whole oath seemed so detestable and sacreligious . . . that I did not only refuse it, but utterly detest the thought of it." Damning the parliamentary oath as a "heretical imposition" contrary to his "tender conscience," this brave man had courage to face the Cromwellian commissioners and tell them that he "would suffer the execution of death before my own door rather than derogate from those Kingly principles which I have ever been naturally endowed with." But his example found few emulators, and Virginia, so far as loyalty tests were concerned, found little difficulty during the years of the first English civil war.[17]

With Charles II's restoration in 1660, Virginia recalled Berkeley as governor. Again a royal colony, Virginia imposed severe punishments upon republicans; the royal tests of allegiance and supremacy reappeared as prerequisites for office and suffrage. In the swift turnover, some officials, a few ministers, and a scattering of citizens could not shift quickly enough, refused the oaths, and faced the penalties. Berkeley turned his fierce attention upon the "turbulent" Quakers, whose meetings he felt were seditious and whose refusal to swear loyalty was self-convicting treason. Shrewdly, he let it be known that Quaker women were proselytizing among Negro slaves, which deprived the Friends of popular support. Berkeley's sheriffs raided Quaker meetings and dragged men and women worshipers to prison for their nonjuring.

Berkeley was no man to treat the royal test oaths with levity, or permit anyone else to do so. Events were to prove, however, that not even the presence of this devoted servant of the king in the governor's office, nor a colonial assembly committed to the most stringent application of loyalty tests, could save Virginia from a terrible crisis of allegiance.[18]

Virginia's loyalty problem of the mid-1670's originated in the dissatisfaction of western Virginians with the low prices tobacco was bringing, the high taxes they were paying, and the poor protection against Indian raiders those taxes were providing. Men of the west believed that Berkeley's favorites were protecting the Indians in order to benefit from the fur trade. Nepotism was certainly rife; the Virginia burgesses who had taken office in 1661 were still in session a decade and a half later. Events indicated that Berkeley would not protect western Virginians against Indians, could not raise the price of tobacco, and chose not to lower taxes. In part, these accusations were true. Berkeley's hand-picked council divided the spoils of office among each other with a rare disregard for the colony's welfare, and left unanswered numerous petitions for redress from western counties. Even by seventeenth-century standards, this system of organized corruption was expensive and inefficient. To frontiersmen, the worst manifestations of Berkeley's rule evidenced themselves in the Indian menace; Berkeley's minions controlled the lucrative fur trade with the native tribes. The conclusion seemed obvious: Berkeley protected red subjects more than white. A brief flaring of angry refusals to pay taxes in the western counties in 1673 achieved nothing. But the anger remained.

Berkeley unwittingly fanned the flame of western anger when he refused to approve a petition from the frontier counties for an expedition against marauding Indians. Disgruntled Virginians assembled in April, 1676, at Jordan's Point, in Charles City County. Out of this meeting the west found a voice and a leader. Nathaniel Bacon, a man in his mid-thirties, with the impressive marks of English university education still with him, had arrived in Virginia only two years earlier. His social connections secured him a place in Berkeley's select coterie, but Bacon made the mistake of reaching out too far and too soon, by demanding a share in the fur-trade monopoly. Berkeley ousted him from the council.

Bacon retired to western Virginia to make an honest living, but soon felt the financial squeeze common to most tobacco growers. He gathered round him a group of equally thwarted advocates of a get-rich-quick program. There was John Cheesman whose Quaker wife had suffered under Berkeley's ungentle ministrations, and for whose offenses Cheesman had lost his attractive official post. William Drummond had lost heavily in a land-title dispute with Berkeley, and never forgave the forceful governor. And there were others like these who wanted position, power, and status, as well as revenge and wealth.[19]

At this meeting Bacon castigated Berkeley's policies, catalogued western grievances, and asked the undivided backing of the western counties. Such was the birth of Bacon's Rebellion, and none can say how premeditated was its conception or how spontaneous its generation. Whatever its parentage, whether in sincere social protest or sinister conspiracy, it grew with the forced feed of frustration until it disrupted Virginia and unsettled her neighbors.

The Jordan's Point meeting authorized Bacon to act as its representative, and in that capacity he applied to Berkeley for an Indian-hunting commission. Berkeley's reply was an order for Bacon's supporters to disperse. Under Bacon's skillful manipulation, his followers defied the governor. Berkeley, furious at this disobedience, assembled his pliant council, and heard these gratifying words:

We cannot out of duty to God, his most sacred Majesty, and this country, but declare . . . that . . . Mr. Bacon's proceedings are . . . rash, illegal, unwarrantable, and most rebellious, and consequently destructive to all government and laws, he having not only endeavoured to seduce and draw his most sacred Majesty's subjects from their duty and allegiance, but by diverse scandalous papers by him sent about the country, endeavouring to traduce his Majesty's government here.

The flow of prose boiled down to the council's declaration that Bacon was a traitor and his followers were rebels. In his proclamation, Berkeley likened Bacon's rationale of Indian incursions to an Englishman's using the excuse of a threatened foreign invasion of the homeland as justification for treason against the king. What a king (and, obviously, a king's viceroy) decided was right; resistance was impious, seditious, and vile. Deviation from this rigid standard was rebellion, and Bacon had persisted in rebellious error after due warning from Jamestown.[20]

It was late for words. Under the stigma of outlawry, Bacon and his men declared their preference to be called traitors rather than be killed by Indians. Some of them attributed Berkeley's patriotism to economic motives: "Rebel forfeitures would be loyal inheritances," they grumbled. But Berkeley's stern proclamations were having their effect. Bacon watched his supporters melt away. He had to act or lose leadership—and perhaps much else. So he assembled his remaining men and marched into the wilderness after Indians. His vigorous campaign won the plaudits of western Virginia, utterly countering the force of Berkeley's successive proclamations.

That wily governor was no fool. He realized that the time was at hand for concessions, and issued a call for new elections to replace the despised burgesses who had been in office for fifteen years. But his hope of capturing western support by liberality met the solid obstacle of

Bacon's score of dead Indians. Western Virginia elected the declared rebel and several of his officers to seats in the House of Burgesses. Bacon the traitor was now Bacon the legislator.

But, Bacon wondered, was it safe to go to Jamestown? When he finally went, he traveled prepared. Forty armed men formed an impressive bodyguard as his sloop made its slow way down the winding course of the James River. Then, with Jamestown in sight, came the roar of cannon and musketry directed against them; Berkeley would have no truck with traitors. After a secret nocturnal excursion into Jamestown, where he conspired with Marylanders and North Carolinians to export his brand of rebellion to Virginia's neighbors, Bacon returned to his sloop. There followed a hectic day of flight in the tangled inlets of the James. Then Berkeley captured Bacon. The two faced each other. "Mr. Bacon, have you forgotten to be a gentleman?" demanded Berkeley. Bacon, suddenly hopeful, promised future good behavior, and a public recantation of past error. For the moment he was a chastened reformer, a defeated rebel.

A few days later, before the convened assembly, Bacon bent his knee and begged for pardon. He confessed that he had been guilty of "diverse late unlawful, mutinous, and rebellious practices," and swore the royal oath of allegiance which he had, in Berkeley's opinion, so consistently violated. Again an honorable citizen and assemblyman, Bacon, the recent rebel, enjoyed reappointment as an executive councilman (perhaps the better for Berkeley to keep watch on him).

News of Bacon's pardon and promotion spread rapidly through Virginia. As Bacon wrote to his worrying wife, it was amusing to see

. . . fortune sport herself with poor mortals, sometimes mount[ing] them up in the air (as boys do tennis balls) that they may come with the greater violence down, and then strike them against the earth that they may with the greater speed mount up in the air.[21]

The question with Nathaniel Bacon seemed ever centered on discerning whether he was on his way up or down. His momentary rise to Berkeley's favor proved a prelude to disaster. Bacon's ambition remained as overweening as ever. He was a ready auditor to rumors that Berkeley was using him as a puppet; the governor failed to initiate promised reforms or grant Bacon the long-desired commission to fight Indians. When pressed, Berkeley suggested that Bacon forget the whole thing. Bacon departed Jamestown for his western home where meditation upon his situation resulted in his decision again to pit himself against the governor's forces. Soon the beat of muster drums sounded in the western foothills, and Bacon was leading five hundred men on Jamestown. There this overwhelming force surrounded Berkeley in the state house, and forced him to surrender, but could not at first pry loose the commission upon which Bacon's claim to legitimacy rested. Threats to murder the vanquished governor, the council, and the assembly finally evoked the commission for Bacon to raise arms and men, enslave Indians, and carry on governmental functions in the troubled frontier areas. Then the Bacon-dominated assembly generated a stream of statutes in support of their chieftain and region: an act of oblivion and pardon "for the late distractions that have arisen"; a cancellation of confiscation and imprisonment penalties against these victorious insurgents (social revolutionaries? democratic visionaries?); a denial of multiple offices and a termination of the hated Indian fur-trade monopoly.

With his reforms accomplished, and the governor's commission lending him the guise of constitutional leader, Bacon mustered his men and recruited across Virginia. At the falls of the James River he called a halt, and with impressive ceremonies administered the royal oaths of allegiance and supremacy to his troops. But he was not satisfied; many men were enlisted in his corps whose loyalty to himself Bacon distrusted, and most of his little army had either been in opposition to him until this time or at least had failed to support him overtly. Distrustful, unsure of his own authority, anxious to prepare for eventualities, Bacon came up with what seemed to him the original idea of requiring each man to swear a special loyalty oath to himself:

They should not conceal any plot or conspiracy of hurt against his person, but immediately reveal the same to him or to such others by whom he might come to the knowledge of it.

That if any harm or damage was intended towards any of his men, whether by surprise or otherwise, or any conference used, or council kept about the same, to discover it.

That no correspondence should be had with the heathen, and . . . That no news or information should be sent out lest himself or army by such intelligence should be endangered either in repute or otherwise.[22]

With this loyalty test as his symbol of security, Bacon introduced an internal police system among his troops. No Berkeley spy, no would-be Bacon, would find an easy way to take his place, *if* the oath test had effect. Unfortunately, the doughty governor busied himself with sending spies into Bacon's corps who found no trouble at all in swearing Bacon's oath. Berkeley meanwhile also mustered troops in the most

Royalist county of eastern Virginia, serving to confirm the impression, spread by Bacon's agents, that the governor was more interested in fighting Bacon than in suppressing Indians. It made Berkeley bitter to realize that Bacon was still the "darling of the people."

When Bacon heard of Berkeley's martial activities, he angrily turned his army eastward once more. Berkeley abandoned dignity and colony, and took ship to Accomac, on the Eastern Shore, temporarily out of Bacon's reach. Nathaniel Bacon, whose family had written him off as a spoiled failure in England, was now, two short years after arriving in Virginia, master of the colony. His troops toured Virginia, separating loyal sheep from Berkeley's goats, administering Bacon's oath with great energy, under authority of the commission Berkeley had granted him to fight Indians. As one observer later recalled:

Mr. Bacon . . . sent out Parties of Horse Patrolling through every county, carrying away prisoners all whom he distrusted might any more molest his Indian Prosecution, yet giving liberty to such as pledged him their Oaths to return home and live quiet; the copies or contents of which Oaths . . . were very strict, though little observed.

If he was now king in Virginia in all but name, Bacon worried about how the King of England would react to reports of events in his disturbed colony. He knew that few of his followers, however ready to defy Berkeley, would support open defiance of royal authority, and that he received popular support because most Virginians were convinced that he had legal authority to fight Indians. To ensure the continued loyalty of his troops, and simultaneously to convince them of *his* loyalty to the Crown, Bacon had them reswear to the royal oath tests, and to a new oath Bacon wrote requiring them to approve the proposition that Bacon was serving the king by exiling the king's governor, rejecting the king's laws, and appropriating royal revenues. As a public relations man, Nathaniel Bacon lacked the light touch.[23]

Consider the meeting of influential planters Bacon assembled in August, 1676, at Middle Plantation. He demanded that these important men swear his oath, which by now addressed Bacon as "General by the consent of the people," and required subscribers to oppose even royal forces from England at Bacon's command, testify that all Berkeley's acts had been illicit and Bacon's actions legitimate, and maintain Bacon's secrets inviolate. The stubborn planters at first refused to sign, but after hours of wrangling, climaxed by Bacon's locking them in the building and implying he might burn it, they acquiesced. Many of those who signed later regretted their haste, for their signatures placed them on record as Bacon men. But for the moment Bacon was triumphant. He pronounced Berkeley a traitorous outlaw. The tables had turned completely.

To keep them that way, Bacon sent armed patrols to tour Virginia and require all officials—sheriffs, judges, militiamen, justices of the peace, Anglican ministers—to swear to both Bacon's oath and the royal tests of loyalty. Then, ever unsure of his own authority, Bacon required *all* Virginians to take these loyalty tests, and his commissioners applied themselves to the enlarged task with delighted energy. Most Virginians swore, either in sincere conviction, honest confusion, or concealed perjury. Bacon imprisoned nonjurors and applied their forfeited property to defraying the mounting expenses of his administration. He also executed one of Berkeley's spies among his men, unearthed (incredibly) by the agent's refusal to swear to the Baconian formulas of fidelity.

As the midsummer heat reached its peak, Bacon launched an amphibious expedition against Berkeley's peninsular stronghold, and personally led another force westward against the obstreperous Indians. While Bacon floundered in the woods, Berkeley captured the first expedition through the treachery of a Bacon man who had willingly sworn the latter's oaths in order to serve the royal governor. After hanging Bacon's lieutenants, Berkeley in turn took the offensive, and easily recaptured Jamestown. Within a week Bacon was again at that unhappy town's walls. His greatest asset proved to be the unwillingness of Virginians to die in this confused congeries of causes. Berkeley again had to retreat across the bay, and, by Bacon's orders, Jamestown was put to the torch. Still claiming legitimacy, Bacon issued proclamations blaming Berkeley for the pyromaniacal act and condemning the "late" governor as a proved traitor.

Now, in mid-September, Bacon began to enjoy the fruits of victory. His soldiery, lax in discipline, enriched themselves by appropriating the property of "disloyal" Virginians, caring little whether their victims had sworn loyalty to Bacon, Berkeley, or anyone else. Bacon was busy, too, maintaining formal control over governmental affairs. He was not a happy man in victory. Time was his enemy: time for Berkeley's reports to get to England; time for Virginians to reconsider their oaths to Bacon in favor of earlier oaths to king and Berkeley (this was happening); time for Berkeley to regroup his forces and stir up disaffection among Bacon's troops and among Virginians generally. The situation, with two governments each claiming sole allegiance, could not remain static.

Bacon decided upon a dual course of severity and moderation. He enforced a novel, strict discipline upon his troops, thus hoping to gain the gratitude of the oppressed Virginians. At the same time he set himself to ensuring the loyalty of the colonists. Armed with a new oath of loyalty to himself, Bacon went to the center of Royalist sentiment in Gloucester County, where his soldiers assembled the citizenry at the courthouse. He ordered them to swear to resist any of Berkeley's forces, to "fly together as in a common calamity, and . . . stand or fall in defense of . . . the country." [24] The Gloucestermen pleaded to be left neutral, unsworn, uncommitted. Bacon saw no neutrality possible, divided all Virginians into friends or foes, and established his oath as the symbol of foe or ally. A Gloucester minister who was encouraging others to refuse Bacon's oath went to jail. Bacon's lengthy oratory so affected his unhappy audience that "the people's minds became quickly flexible." He added to the confusion by asserting that each man could himself determine, *after swearing,* if the oath was repugnant to individual conviction. If so, then Bacon promised to release that person from its obligation. But neither Bacon nor Berkeley treated their respective tests of loyalty as lightly as this in practice.[25]

Then, in October, 1676, a greater enemy than Berkeley conquered Bacon. Ill with dysentery, Bacon "died much dissatisfied in mind, inquiring ever and anon after the arrival of the frigates and forces from England, and asking if the guards were strong about the house." His rebellion endured a little while. Bacon's mantle of leadership fell upon the willing shoulders of Joseph Ingram, whom Bacon had earlier named lieutenant governor. But Ingram could neither command the same love from his men as Bacon had evoked, nor as ably lead them in combat. By bribery, intimidation, and promises of pardon, Berkeley defeated Ingram's dwindling army. Bacon's empire began a rapid collapse. His lieutenants fled, most of them being recaptured by Berkeley or by coöperative governors of neighboring colonies. Drummond, in chains, heard Berkeley's unconvincing display of bluff heartiness end with a death sentence. Cheesman escaped the hangman by dying in prison. Lesser rebels received sentences of imprisonment, exile, and property confiscation. Most of the rank and file were freed after abjuring Bacon's oaths and reswearing the royal loyalty tests.

In Berkeley's victorious train had come Virginians who had suffered at Bacon's ungentle hands. Other Virginians, in an agony of repentance over the support and oaths they had given Bacon, flooded Berkeley with accusations against neighbors less agile at switching loyalties than themselves. Private feuds mixed inextricably with statecraft. Fearful colonists sought to prove that they had sworn Bacon's oaths under duress, with mental reservations, and with full intention of violating them at the earliest opportunity. The situation needed a Solomon. It had Berkeley, who, as one observer noted, "would have hanged half the Country, if . . . let . . . alone." [26]

Fortunately for Virginia, he was not long let alone. A royal commission arrived from England with pardons for all save Bacon. At first Berkeley ignored this limit upon his unbalanced search for vengeance. His bills of attainder embraced ever-larger numbers of those who had sworn Bacon's oaths, and confiscated their properties in favor of more persistent loyalists. Berkeley saw no variations possible in allegiance, no degrees of sincerity, no half tones of loyalty. Otto Thorpe, for instance, had sworn allegiance to Bacon to protect his wife from threatened harm. Thorpe later refused to aid the rebel chief, and had lost all his property as a consequence. Despite his helpless protestations, Thorpe went to jail when Berkeley returned to power, and his property faced another confiscation. Berkeley's victims rotted in Virginia's prisons while their appeals to England for redress made slow, costly rounds of ministerial offices.

Some undoubted Bacon supporters, after such rugged treatment, repented and received forgiveness, indicating that Berkeley preferred public conversion to unspectacular consistency in matters of loyalty. Arthur Long, former captain in Bacon's troop, achieved a full pardon when he appeared before the assembly and spoke this formula of recantation:

[I] most humbly upon my knees with a rope around my neck implore the pardon of God, my King, the Honorable Governor, Council, and Magistrates . . . and humbly crave the benefit of his Majesty's most gracious acts of mercy and pardon for my treason and rebellion.

Long abjured his former oaths to Bacon, informed on erstwhile comrades in Bacon's cause, reswore his fidelity to king and governor, and lived. To accommodate the hundreds like Long, Berkeley created a special loyalty test for the occasion:

I, AB, do willingly and heartily declare, that I know, and in my conscience believe . . . [myself] to be in open rebellion against the King's most sacred Majesty, and against the Right Honourable the Governor of Virginia, . . . which rebellion I do in my heart abhor and protest, and do therefore most willingly, freely and from my heart swear allegiance to the King's most excellent Majesty; and that I will with my life, and whole estate, serve and obey the . . . Governor, . . . and use my utmost endeavour to my life's end, to take, seize, kill, and destroy all such persons whatsoever, as either now are, or hereafter shall be in such rebellion as is recited. This oath I do most heartily, freely, and willingly take, in the presence of Almighty God. So help me God.[27]

And so the dismal Virginia loyalty-testing tale ended in wholesale proscriptions. Berkeley could not altogether turn back the clock to the placid pre-Baconian times. Royal orders maintained many of the reforms the rebels had initiated, and by Charles II's command Berkeley returned to England to justify his harsh repression, which earned from the monarch Berkeley had served so diligently the comment that more men had died as punishment for a petty rebellion in Virginia than had perished in England for executing the king's father. Perhaps this was a fitting epitaph for a tragic misadventure in confusion and conceit which, however disguised in words of loyalty, succeeded only in disrupting a colony and ruining the lives of hundreds of people. Bacon's Rebellion, its causes enmeshed in complexities of imperial economics, selfish statesmanship, and personal ambitions, could not solve its need for a clear definition of loyalty by any of the successive tests of allegiance which emanated from both sides in the conflict. Indeed, it solved nothing, and at a great cost.[28]

While England writhed in the torment of civil war, Massachusetts, freed from earlier threats of royal control, continued to crush nonconformity with a heavy hand. Bay residents who advocated supporting the king, or acknowledged Parliament or Cromwell as suzerain over the colony, met swift and displeased reaction from the Puritan magistrates. In 1652, for instance, the colony's General Court complained of dissident residents whose "offensive speeches" were cause "whereby their fidelity to this government may justly be suspected." To quiet such undesirables, the colonial legislature decreed that any magistrate could require Massachusetts' oath of fidelity of all known nonjurors, suspected backsliders from past oaths, and "strangers." Nonjuring incurred money fines and, if repeated, exile from the colony.[29]

Charles II's restoration faced Massachusetts with the immediate problem of recognizing the returned monarch. A year and a half after Charles returned to London, Massachusetts was one of two lonely nonproclaimers (the other was her Puritan offshoot and neighbor, New Haven). The worried Bostonians turned for advice to the primary source of earthly wisdom, the elders of their church. Those sages recommended that Massachusetts' "allegiance and subjection to the King's Majesty is to be acknowledged," but the form of that submission was to be that old irritant, the colony's own oath of fidelity. It seemed in England that Massachusetts was at best disrespectful, and at worst disloyal.[30]

The colony's tactlessness provided opportunity for her numerous enemies to attack her once more. One such enemy narrated to the Privy Council in 1661 how close the colony was to actual independency, and how suspicious was its refusal to use the royal tests of loyalty as English law and the colony's charter required. The colony's oath, the council heard, was illegal and subversive, and discriminated against Anglicans. Samuel Maverick reappeared in print with a popular description of New England as he had seen it in 1660. In this vindictive essay Maverick noted how, during the English civil war, the Puritans tore down the royal coat of arms and substituted the seal of the colony; he provided his readers with a text of Massachusetts' oaths so that

. . . it may be judged what esteem they have of the laws of England, swearing their subjects to submit to laws made only by themselves. And, indeed, to allege a statute law of England in one of their courts would be a ridiculous thing.[31]

Others added their voices to the clamor: Quakers told tales of sufferings; Sir Ferdinando Gorges petitioned for the return of his Maine lands which Massachusetts had seized; Anglican Royalists exposed the colony's harboring the attainted executioners of the king's father.

Lord Clarendon gave the colony's agents in London specific orders that the "rules and prescriptions of the . . . [Massachusetts] charter for administering and taking the [royal] oath of allegiance be henceforth duly observed." The order reached Boston, and nothing was done. Then, for two more years, war and diplomacy claimed the king's attention. In 1664 Charles appointed a special commission to report on New England conditions, and one commissioner was the Puritans' stubborn enemy, Samuel Maverick. Despite Clarendon's injunction to Maverick to be objective, that worthy commissioner rarely let his judgment get the better of his feelings. He took full advantage of the royal instruction to ascertain how well Massachusetts had complied with the king's orders concerning loyalty tests.[32]

Bostonians welcomed the commissioners with veiled hostility, first being sure to hide their precious charter, prepare the colony's cannon, and assemble the militia, while Massachusetts agents in England pleaded with the king to revoke the investigating committee's authority. On the Boston scene, Maverick roundly condemned a Puritan stratagem to disguise the colony's disputed oath test as part of a property qualification for suffrage and office-holding. Unabashed, Massachusetts at first stood stubbornly firm. Her leaders would not use the king's test oaths in the colony, ostensibly because the colony's oath declared enough loyalty to the king to satisfy the royal appetite, but actually, and obviously, because the royal loyalty formula gave precedence to the king over the colony. The commissioners, angered, repeated the admonition that Charles II had given them before they left England, that "our subjects in those parts do not submit to our government but look upon themselves as independent," and the injunction that the "rules . . . for the administration and taking of the [royal] Oath of Allegiance be henceforth strictly and duly observed." Frightened, the Massachusetts leaders belatedly promised to comply with the oath order. But they were too late. The royal commissioners were already en route to England with a report of the colony's determined refusal to obey.[33]

In their report of December, 1665, the commissioners, in part on the basis of the test-oath dispute, recommended to the king that he suspend the colony's vaunted charter and make Massachusetts a royal colony. Once more, however, events worked in Massachusetts' favor; external war and internal discord absorbed England's attention. Massachusetts used the emergency wisely. She sent troops to support England's armies and masts to aid her navy, and imposed unwontedly strict repressive policies within her borders to suppress enemies to her way of life. Chief sufferers in the name of emergency security were those Bay residents who had supplied the 1664 commission with evidence. By her leaders' cleverness, Massachusetts gained another slice of time as an independent colony, and signaled her victory by reimposing the original colonial oath of fidelity.[34]

In 1671 Massachusetts again came to the Privy Council's attention. Claimants for the Maine and New Hampshire lands that the Bay colony had seized charged that the latter, in direct violation of royal orders, was refusing to disgorge her two prizes and was vigorously enforcing her test oaths among the unhappy populations there. After inconclusive deliberations, the Privy Council decided to avoid the suggested use of direct military force to obtain obedience, and sent another royal commission, this time with secret orders to act as spies, to find witnesses to Massachusetts misrule, and to report back to the royal ministers. But another war with Holland interfered to prevent this commission from leaving England. Massachusetts was still benefiting from events far beyond her ability to control.[35]

Five years later, a revived English interest in enforcing imperial mercantilist legislation impelled an unprecedentedly searching inquiry into Massachusetts' relations with England and the Empire. By this time Massachusetts was a center of organized evasion of commerce controls, "by which," a royal administrator lamented, "the . . . King's revenue [is] inexpressibly impaired." To counteract the evil, King Charles appointed a Privy Council committee to oversee colonial affairs. These Lords of Trade and Plantations appointed a special agent, Edward Randolph, to spy out irregularities in the conduct of New England's colonies. For Massachusetts, Randolph was a bitter choice. He was related to the Mason family, on whose New Hampshire grant Boston had trod roughly. When Randolph arrived in Massachusetts, he was prepared for a cool reception, and reciprocated it enthusiastically.[36]

Shunned by the "respectable" residents, Randolph surrounded himself with the discontented and the disfranchised. From such sources he easily amassed enough information to report to his London superiors that many Bay residents, loyal to royal interests, were subject to "daily abuses and discouragements," which "makes them conceal themselves till it shall please his Majesty to resolve upon the reducing of this plantation to due obedience." Randolph soon seized upon his chief target. The Massachusetts oath of fidelity became the theme upon which he rang the changes of subjective partisanship in a mounting flood of derogatory reports to England.

One report offered privy councilors (for the first time) the complete texts of the Puritan loyalty tests, and Randolph criticized each deviation and omission from English forms. These oath tests were "the laws most derogatory and contradictory to those of England," he insisted in a personal appearance before the Lords of Trade. To prove his point, he again assembled the colony's enemies to offer testimony concerning how the loyalty tests suppressed legitimate dissent. The attorney general of England, impressed by this cacophony of criticism, easily concluded that in Massachusetts "no treason or rebellion exists for what pertains to the King," and that the absence of the royal oaths was a serious bar to royal rights. England's solicitor general decided that

The oaths of Allegiance and Supremacy are not required to be taken, in such manner as the laws of England direct. This, I humbly conceive, ought to be provided for, as necessary for obliging the subjects there to their obedience and loyalty to their sovereign.[37]

Then Massachusetts did Randolph and its other enemies a favor. Realizing the obvious, that Randolph's information came from informants within the colony, Puritan authorities began intensive loyalty investigations of their own to unearth the defectors in their midst, banishing nonjurors and punishing perjurers. And, despite repeated royal orders to obey imperial trade regulations, Massachusetts continued in its illicit commerce with foreign areas.

Randolph pressed his attack before the Lords of Trade, pointing out that violators of the Navigation Acts faced no penalties in Boston while nonjurors from the colony's unlawful oath test, especially Anglicans, faced "so severe and determinate penalties." He pleaded for royal forces to protect his informants, who were the few loyal Englishmen in the colony. Randolph derided Massachusetts' defense for its house-to-house loyalty probe, denying that anyone had tried to fire Boston as the colony's agents claimed, asking what connection loyalty tests had with incendiarism in any event, insisting that behind Massachusetts' nonsense about fearing fire was its subversion in requiring its own loyalty tests.

His attack threw the colony's agents into confusion. They stammered a foolish charge that Boston's enemies were the real authors of the vexed oaths, who had placed them in the Bay colony's statute books and enforced them for four decades just to get the colony into trouble in London. Retreating from this logical trap, the agents finally admitted Massachusetts' error, and offered to suggest to the colony's leaders the rectitude of the royal oath. They were forty years too late.

Randolph pressed his advantage. He proposed that all colonials who took the royal oath tests be admitted to free status and office-holding, that no nonjurors to England's oaths hold office in any colony, and that compulsory attendance at Calvinist services give way to equally required conformity to Anglican rituals. In short, Randolph proposed an end to the church-state theocracy of Massachusetts Bay. Largely through the device of criticizing the Puritan loyalty test, he pierced the heart of Puritan Massachusetts. The Lords of Trade agreed, recommending to the Privy Council and Charles II that the colony's "indecent forme" of loyalty test permanently die because

. . . by the unseasonable enjoining of this oath, it looks very suspicious that all things stand not so fair, in reference to many of his Majesty's good and loyal subjects there. . . . So that . . . their Lordships . . . advise that his Majesty do . . . signify his resentment at the enjoining of that oath, which, however intended, seems to be a snare in the way of many of his good subjects there. . . . That the said oath is derogatory to his honor, as well as defective in point of their own duty.

Soon, over Charles's signature and seal, Massachusetts' General Court read the dread order of their sovereign strictly requiring them to replace the colony's oath with the king's, and ordering them to cease harassing supporters of royal rule and oath.[38] Late in 1678 the General Court ordered that every adult male in the colony swear the royal oaths, making sure that Charles heard full accounts of their overt obedience to his orders.

Randolph, meanwhile, had amassed more secret information against the colony. Its obedience was a sham, he insisted. Whole villages remained unsworn and unpunished for their sinister nonjuring; Anglicans still did not hold office; recusants from Calvinist services still faced dire punishment. But Charles was then too busy with dissenters in England to worry much over distractions in New England. For the moment, the attack on Massachusetts' oath, charter, and way of life diminished. Randolph contented himself with a stream of needling reminders to king and Privy Council that their orders concerning the royal loyalty test were still largely unenforced in Massachusetts, the outlawed colonial oath was still very much in vogue, and Randolph's friends were still very much in trouble.

Then, in 1681, Randolph received greater opportunity to press his attack. In that year he returned to Boston as royal customs collector for New England, commissioned to enforce the trade regulations which Massachusetts residents hated quite as much as they disliked Randolph personally. One local muse expressed his feelings on hearing this news:

> Welcome, Sir, welcome from the eastern shore,
> With a commission stronger than before,
> To play the horse-leech; rob us of our fleeces,
> To rend our land, and tear it all to pieces. . . .
> Boston, make room, Randolph's returned, that hector,
> Confirm'd at home to be the sharp collector; . . .
> So Royal Charles is now about to prove
> Our Loyalty, Allegiance and our Love,
> In giving license to a publican
> To pinch the purse, . . . to hurt the man,
> Patience raised Job unto the heights of fame,
> Let our obedience do for us the same.

Unfortunately for Massachusetts, neither its leaders nor Randolph possessed Job's patience. Randolph found himself beset with uncooperative colonists, intimidated subordinates and witnesses, social ostracism, and a recrudescence of the colonial oath directed against his informants. Massachusetts' agents in England, meanwhile, assured the king that his oath order "is cheerfully obeyed and always shall be so."

Randolph, thwarted in Boston, returned to England to warn the Privy Council that the colony's agents were outright liars. His reports fitted in well with the predilections of the new monarch, James II, to centralize imperial administration and suppress dissent. In October, 1684, James proclaimed Massachusetts' charter suspended. A half century of independence was ended; Massachusetts was to be a royal colony under the command of Joseph Dudley (former Massachusetts agent, now a turncoat to his former oath and colony), with Randolph as one of his councilors, and with the king's specific "will and pleasure . . . that no person shall be admitted . . . or have a vote . . . until he hath taken the [royal] Oath of Allegiance." [39]

Deep despair came to Boston with the news of the charter's demise: "The symptoms of Death are on us," wailed Samuel Sewall. Randolph's sharp, distrustful eyes peered for evidences of nonconformity to the royal oath order. He pleaded with the Privy Council to restrict emigration to New England to those able to swear the statutory oath of allegiance "or we shall have multitudes of fanaticks flock over hither." His customs commissioners made it part of their antismuggling duties to check on immigrants' oath certificates; his agents delighted in enforcing the English oaths in religious services, for absence or deviationism from Anglican services was now a crime. And Randolph knew even greater joy when Sir Edmund Andros arrived from England, bearing James II's orders to centralize all New England and New York into a single "Dominion of New England."

But Randolph's dreams collapsed in December, 1688, when Boston heard of the Glorious Revolution in England and the exile of James II. Dudley and Randolph found themselves in the indignity of the "Common Gaol." As Increase Mather put it:

Mr. Dudley in a peculiar manner is the object of the people's displeasure. . . . They deeply resent his correspondence with that wicked man Mr. Randolph for the overturning of the [independent Massachusetts] government. . . . These have made him vile in the eyes of all.

Randolph, musing on the shift of fate, derided the New Englanders' protestations of loyalty to the new Protestant monarchs, William and Mary, as a mere Puritanical subterfuge to permit the happy colonists "to return to their former government; [and they] used this as a means." Perhaps. What is certain is that the Massachusetts loyalty test, which had endured for five decades, had at last died. Boston's joy at the 1688–89 revolution in England later tempered when William and

Mary maintained many of their predecessor's trends toward imperial centralization, and required the royal loyalty tests as one of the first acts of their reign. Never again was Massachusetts to know freedom from royal control or from English loyalty oaths.[40]

The stirring events in England, which so disturbed affairs in Maryland and Massachusetts, soon settled down to a familiar pattern of loyalty-testing and repression of religious or political dissenters. William and Mary's coöperative Parliaments created new omnibus loyalty tests for their common safety. As assurance of purity, the new tests required subscribers to assert their loyalty "in the plain and ordinary sense of the words . . . as they are commonly understood by protestants." The Catholic threat inspired a degree of toleration for recusant Protestants, who received royal dispensation to swear allegiance without promising conformity to the official creed of England.

New test oaths opened old, deep wounds in England's religious society. Anglican clergymen who had once sworn allegiance to the exiled James II found it beyond the elastic limits of their consciences to abjure those oaths, renounce that king, and assume new loyalty obligations to an obvious, though victorious, usurper. Faced with this bitter choice, hundreds of Anglican priests seceded from their church (and their salaries) to maintain their faith. They would not, despite obloquy and hardship, affirm their loyalty to William. As in all earlier crises of loyalty, some men and women died for their stubborn consistency.

Conversely, as in earlier times, most men rationalized the changes, altered their own viewpoints, and signed the necessary loyalty tests of the new realm. Eternal oaths of loyalty to James gave way to similar oaths to his revolutionary successor, then, more legitimately, to Queen Anne, and then to the Hanoverian monarchs. By this time, successive generations of Englishmen had seen so many alterations in their kings, religion, and loyalty-oath tests, that cynicism regarding all three became part of England's folklore in the eighteenth century. *Gulliver's Travels* mocked loyalty tests in prose, and children versified the theme in "The Vicar of Bray," whose slippery soul easily made all necessary changes in his successive sacred vows, and concluded that "Whatsoever King shall reign, I'll still be Vicar of Bray, Sir." Such satires intoned a dirge for all that the tens of thousands of oaths, and the uncountable hurts and tears of two hundred years, had failed to accomplish.[41]

News of England's second revolution in half a century traveled to America, where, as has already been shown concerning Massachusetts and Maryland, it provoked crises of conscience. In other colonies also, authorities had to decide whether to continue honoring James II, to whom they had already sworn "eternal" loyalty, or to take a great chance and declare for William, who might win or lose. The fall of Andros' New England Dominion and Calvert's proprietorship resulted from wrong or delayed choices. In Massachusetts as in Maryland, grievances of long standing inspired more or less popular movements to unseat legitimate colonial authorities. In both colonies, loyalty tests performed prominent parts in preparing people's minds for revolt.[42]

New York's was a different story, but no less turbulent. Its revolt beginning in 1689 was spontaneous in generation, unplanned, chaotic, based on formless fears of disloyalty rather than on concrete needs for loyalty. Beginning in discontent and ending in disorder, it fed on the fires of faction. However bedecked in the dressings of loyalty, Leisler's rebellion in New York meant tragedy for the participants and the colony. Serving little purpose, it gave the prize of death to the losers. The victor received nothing he had not owned before the race began to be the first to declare loyalty.

Jacob Leisler's story began when he arrived in New Amsterdam as a common soldier of the Dutch West India Company. He married a wealthy widow, which connected him with the elite of the colony, a connection that Van Cortlandts, Bayards, and Van Rensselaers acknowledged most unenthusiastically. In 1664 Leisler helped force Peter Stuyvesant to surrender to a British squadron. Now a citizen of New York, Leisler willingly swore the Duke of York's oath of fidelity, which became the standard royal oath when James II traded his ducal title for a royal one. Many English residents, however, were far from pleased with the new dispensation, sometimes registering violent resentment at the inequitable representation afforded them. All New Yorkers were unsettled by continuing border disputes, and the menace of Catholic France's Indian allies was a fearful thing on the overlong New York frontier. Commercial intrigues, territorial pretensions, religious bigotry, and personal ambitions mingled in an unhealthy stew.[43]

In 1684 Leisler became a militia captain of Suffolk County. As he rose in prominence, disturbing rumors of Charles II's secret pro-Catholicism and of James II's blatantly open Romanism beset the colony. Worried New Yorkers thought they saw a menacing increase in Catholic power along the Hudson as well. A former governor, Dongan, was a Romanist. At strategic Albany, bastion against French and Indian penetration and source of lucrative furs, a Catholic was militia commander. Sir Edmund Andros' centralizing experiment in the name of

James II included New York. Rumors spread that present Governor Nicholson, too, was a secret adherent of Rome. Increasing tension, fed on wild imaginings, afflicted the colony. Then crisis crossed the ocean in 1689, when the first confused reports of James II's forced abdication circulated through the unquiet city. Governor Nicholson needed a ready answer to the host of questions the rumors unloaded upon him. Should he, on the basis of mere hearsay, commit treason against James II by proclaiming some unknown person as monarch? He decided to wait for definite word from Governor Andros in Massachusetts or from England, meanwhile imposing a censorship to keep as many unwelcome rumors as possible out of New York. Unfortunately for Nicholson, jubilant Massachusetts Puritans put Andros in prison and flooded New York with accounts of events in England which Nicholson's agents were powerless to stop. In this uncertain situation, military power suddenly assumed a novel importance in New York. The prospects were hardly encouraging.

Fort James, principal defense of Manhattan Island, commanding the maritime approaches to the strategic Hudson, was crumbling into ruins, its cannon decrepit, its powder stores impure, and most of "the small number of soldiers in the fort . . . infirm and old." Nicholson, giving no official reason for his actions, enlarged his council and mustered several militia companies to reinforce the fort's garrison. This accident sent Jacob Leisler to Fort James; another chance decision by Nicholson placed Leisler's name on the roster of councilmen.[44]

Through the early summer of 1689 the governor's council argued, but accomplished little. Its decision to apply all customs receipts to repairing the fort met Leisler's refusal to pay customs on some wine he had ordered, on the ostensible ground that the customs collector was a Catholic. Only Leisler knew whether his stubborn stand was devotion to his own pocket, to Protestant purity, or to demagoguery. In any event, the population vibrated with rumors: Governor Nicholson was a Catholic (he was not); a Catholic altar was built into Fort James (again, no); former Governor Dongan was preparing a warship to plague the city (no, he wanted only to go as far away as possible). All waited, unsure of what was to come. Irate colonists in several counties deposed some local officers they felt untrustworthy, and news of an abortive plan Nicholson had hatched to free Andros from the Boston prison came home to torment the perplexed New York governor. If only he could know what events were occurring in England he would be able to commit his loyalty with some safety. To be first to get the news from England was a matter of prime importance. Since all incoming ships must stop at Fort James, the man who controlled the fort had by far the best chance to make the right choice. He might also control the city and the colony.[45]

Militiamen at Fort James vastly outnumbered the few regulars under Nicholson's appointee, Colonel Nicholas Bayard. On May 30, 1689, the militia officer of the day engaged Colonel Bayard in a heated argument over precedence which culminated in a personal appearance of the disputants before Governor Nicholson. Aggrieved at this petty interruption, Nicholson shouted that "if they should any more so trouble him he would set the town afire." An eavesdropping militiaman quickly spread garbled reports of the governor's incendiary intentions around the city. His story was a trigger that unleashed the energies of accumulated fears and discontents. New York City woke the next morning to the unnerving beat of militia drums, and the citizen-soldiers hurried to the fort. There, resolving to secure the place against all Catholic attempts at control, they seized Fort James in the name of the Protestant King of England. Militia officers forced the storeroom keys from a cowed governor, renamed the fort in honor of William of Orange, and summoned all absent comrades, including Jacob Leisler, to join them.

Captain Leisler was officer of the guard on June 3, 1689, when word arrived from Long Island that strange sails were heading toward New York City. Assembled, the militia prepared either for battle or for celebrating the long-awaited news from England. Their trepidation found expression in widespread refusal to obey Colonel Bayard's orders, for many felt him tarred with the Nicholson-Andros brush of tyranny and popery. Bayard, disgusted, left the fort. Into the place of command, at this critical juncture, stepped Jacob Leisler. His force of four hundred men gave him control over the city.[46] No ships appeared, but Leisler decided to retain command despite the absence of an emergency. He signaled his decision by requiring his troops to swear loyalty to himself as the legitimate trustee of William and Mary's sovereignty and property:

Whereas our intention tended only to the preservation of the protestant religion, and the fort of this city, . . . till safe arrival of the ships that we expect every day from his royal highness the prince of Orange with orders for the government of this country . . . then and without delay we shall execute the said orders punctually; declaring that we do intend to submit and obey not only the said orders, but also the bearer thereof.

With this declaration of loyalty and intent, Leisler defined his position. He considered himself the emergency on-the-spot representative

ganda that the Albany authorities were pro-Catholic supporters of the exiled James II.

Leisler's techniques were proving too effective for Albany's comfort. The city's officials decided to fight disloyalty allegations with loyalty tests, and required every soldier and civilian in the town to swear again the royal oaths, to prove that there were "few or none in our posts but do abhor and detest all popery . . . but will with all cheerfulness and readiness abide by the oath of allegiance to the . . . majesties." This loyalty probe unearthed one soldier who refused the oaths as a matter of conscience. He received a dishonorable discharge and disappeared into the forest.[50]

As an adjunct to loyalty-testing, Albany tried to set a backfire of disloyalty among Leisler's supporters by spreading messages from Colonel Bayard that Leisler had no legitimate authority, that those who were aiding him might later find royal condemnation as traitors, and that he, Bayard, was the sole bearer of a genuine commission to lead the New York militia. As if in defiant reply, Albany learned that an armed force from New York City was nearing the northern outpost. Early in November, 1689, Leisler's lieutenant, Jacob Milborne, appeared at Albany with fifty soldiers. He harangued the assembled residents, accusing Albany authorities of complicity in a Catholic, Stuart conspiracy. But Milborne's oratorical and martial ardor dissipated when Albany's Mohawk allies donned war paint. In sudden recollection of important affairs in New York City, Milborne departed. Close behind went Nicholas Bayard, hopeful for an opportunity to injure Leisler.

A month later Bayard's opportunity seemed at hand. A royal messenger from England arrived at Fort William with communications addressed to the colony's legitimate authorities. But who were they? Leisler and Bayard both sought the mantle of legality which delivery of this communication would give the recipient. Leisler won, and happily read what seemed to be a royal approval of all he had done. The letter was addressed to "Francis Nicholson, . . . and in his absence to such as for the time being take care of preserving the peace and administering the laws . . . in New York." Surely, Leisler exulted, this description fitted him. In celebration, he threw Bayard out of the fort, styled himself lieutenant governor, dissolved his puppet Committee of Safety, appointed a council composed of his most trusted subordinates, and appropriated Nicholson's former church pew. The fruits of power were his. He soon learned, however, that they required fiscal fertilizer to provide nourishment.

Leisler had thus far avoided the problem of securing revenues by stretching existing credit facilities to the limit. But in December, 1689, he imposed new taxes. Popular resistance immediately became evident. Posters announcing the new tax levy were torn down; merchants refused to pay; Leisler's collectors met physical abuse. In swift retribution, Leisler created a special, arbitrary tax court, and employed his idle troops in crushing resistance. He blamed the troubles on the seditious activities of his enemies, and inferred that the Pope and King James II were really at fault. Bayard went to prison as the leader of unrest; ministers and merchants learned that criticism of the "lieutenant governor" led to jail on disloyalty charges. Leisler made it painfully obvious to New York City that disloyalty meant questioning his authority. He fumed while an entire city, Albany, stubbornly refused to recognize him as constitutional viceroy of the colony.

Early in 1690 Leisler learned that a French and Indian raid had decimated Schenectady, frighteningly close to Albany. Leisler blamed the tragedy on Albany's delinquency in acknowledging his mastership; Albany blamed Leisler. Connecticut, which sought to arbitrate between the two, found more acrimony than agreement on defense measures issuing from a hurriedly assembled conference. But Albany was caught is a cross fire, and Leisler seemed a lesser evil than Indians. Albany reluctantly accepted Leisler's authority and his representative, Milborne, as the city's commander. In emulation of his chief, Milborne created a duplicate of Leisler's apparatus of repression in the northern city. Leisler was at the pinnacle of his power.[51]

To mark the event, Leisler initiated colony-wide elections for a new assembly. The assembly convened on schedule, with Leisler ignoring the fact that many of its members were determinedly unsworn to his or to the royal oaths. For Leisler now wanted money more than overt evidence of loyalty, money to finance an invasion of Canada. He imposed high taxes, confiscated ships, arms, and foodstuffs in disregard of protests, and ignored his agents' warnings that his program was feeding the fires of discontent. Leisler suffered a rude awakening when a group of conspirators almost succeeded in assassinating him. He imprisoned the would-be murderers and sent a baker's dozen of Bayard's friends, innocent of anything but their association with the unruly colonel, to keep them company in jail.

Leisler publicly professed to believe that Catholic, Stuart machinations were behind the plot. Again he ordered all inhabitants—men, women, and children—to assemble at Fort William and swear loyalty to England's monarchs and to himself as their viceroy. He felt that this multiple swearing would force the inhabitants to

. . . persist in their design to preserve the fort and the City and to surrender to his Majesty on order to the exclusion of the late King James, to that purpose we enjoin all the inhabitants of this city forthwith to appear in Fort William to declare their intention and give their sign of their fidelity with subscribing to this present with us declaring that the relinquent[s] to this our order shall be deemed and esteemed enemies to his Majesty and country and shall be treated accordingly.

Since even the most inveterate anti-Leislerians professed as much loyalty to William and Mary as did Leisler himself, the loyalty-testing went off without much incident. A few residents, correctly fearing that their appearance might be the first step to Leisler's prisons whether they swore or not, fled to safer areas. In any event, Leisler felt his base secure. He began his onslaught on Catholic Canada.

Perhaps, if Leisler's cherished scheme had been successful, official and popular plaudits might have greeted his vision. But the invasion failed. He found himself surrounded by recrimination, despite his over-worked repressive machinery which filled the jails of the province with critics of Leisler and his works. Indeed, the not unsympathetic governor of neighboring Connecticut warned the irate Leisler that "a prison is not a catholicon for all state ills, though much favored by you." Leisler, unwilling to listen, unable to halt for fear that his unstable system woud collapse under him, proclaimed a second invasion of Canada. It became the signal for a revolt against him.

Leisler acted swiftly in an arena he understood better than statecraft or strategy. New orders reimposing old loyalty tests issued from Leisler's headquarters; his forces systematically sought to crush resistance.[52] It was a time of intense confusion, which seemed inevitably heading toward a climactic intracolonial civil war. Then, in January, 1691, a ship sailed into New York Bay. From it stepped the man for whose delay the colony had paid a fearful price—Governor Nicholson's official replacement, or at least his herald, Major Richard Ingoldsby, had arrived.

Ingoldsby, flanked by a file of British soldiers he had brought with him, demanded control over Fort William, or, as he warned Leisler, "I must esteem you no friend to their Majesties." Here was Leisler's supreme test. He had ever claimed willingness to surrender all power to the proper representative of the Protestant monarchs. With the moment at hand Jacob Leisler found that he could not give up the sweet supremacy he had enjoyed. He ordered his men to obey no one but himself "until the arrival of his majesty's further orders." Still pretending to be acting as militant housekeeper for the distant rulers of England, Leisler prepared to battle Ingoldsby. Each side recruited among the general populace, each claiming to be acting in the spirit and the letter of true loyalty to the Crown. Weeks passed in tense stalemate. Bloodshed seemed imminent as skirmishes presaged bigger battles, when the tardy Governor Henry Sloughter appeared—and demanded Leisler's surrender. Leisler could do no more. There was no way for him to question Sloughter's legitimacy. Then, to his anger and surprise, Leisler found himself under arrest for "treacherously levying war against our sovereign." He and his officers went to the prisons where they had sent so many who had earlier questioned Leisler's power. Leisler's rebellion was ended.

Swiftly, Leisler's foes gathered. They demanded that Sloughter hasten a trial for the beaten man. That uneasy governor deprecated such haste, and angered Bayard and others by releasing some of Leisler's men upon their oaths of future loyalty. But for Leisler and Milborne, both of whom denied the jurisdiction of the court and the validity of the charges facing them, Sloughter could do nothing. The biased court found them guilty of treason, attainted them and their property, and ordered death as their penalty. On March 16, 1691, Jacob Leisler stepped to the scaffold, and spoke for the last time to the people he had so recently ruled. Although he confessed some errors, he maintained that all he had done had been in the spirit of loyalty to the Protestant rulers of England. He insisted that only his efforts had saved New York from becoming prey to Catholic conquests, and accused his detractors of being the real traitors. Then he died.

In his wake New York experienced years of bitter partisan strife as Leisler's enemies continued to proscribe all who had sworn Leisler's special oaths. Accusations and counteraccusations of disloyalty dotted the docket books of the courts until fresher winds from England arrived to clear away some of the acrimony. The Privy Council granted pardons to six Leislerian officers, who were immediately upon release from prison elected to the colonial assembly, where they proceeded to legislate against their past tormentors. Leisler's son obtained a parliamentary reversal of the attainder against his father on the grounds that he had been "barbarously murdered." Still later another Parliament pronounced that Leisler's assumption of control of Fort William in 1689 had been perhaps indiscreet, but hardly treason. But no one— king, Parliament, or historian—has really decided whether Jacob Leisler was a patriot, a traitor, or a greedy demagogue. Or perhaps someone has. In a Boston prison, Edward Randolph, who certainly knew enough about loyalty and disloyalty, heard about Leisler. Randolph felt this way about it: "Leisler and his partners made true the proverb, 'Set beggars on horseback and they will ride to the devil.' " [53] This may describe Jacob Leisler, but fails to justify the claims to loyalty, or accusations of disloyalty, which center on Leisler's name.

With much pain and suffering, Britain's Empire slowly settled into the paths of peace after the tumultuous events surrounding the Glorious Revolution in the mother country. The Catholic menace, now symbolized by France rather than by Spain, still seemed a real and present danger. In the mid-1690's, Englishmen the world over pledged loyalty to their Protestant sovereigns by swearing to an "association oath" which named William as rightful monarch and required the subscribers to "declare that we will be enemies to all persons that have been his enemies." [54] Seemingly, with almost all English colonials swearing royal loyalty oaths, the Empire should have been secure, and the problems concerning loyalty tests which had so long bedeviled imperial administration should have ended. The problems did not end. Men—ambitious, unscrupulous, patriotic—continued to twist words of loyalty to their own uses.

So far as administration was concerned, imperial officials after 1689 consistently required all colonial administrators to swear to the new loyalty tests which English monarchs from William of Orange to George III required. As new American colonies—Pennsylvania, Georgia, Canada, and East Florida—graced the imperial map, the loyalty tests spread to include their areas and peoples. Usually this was a peaceful process. Wise British officials in charge of recently conquered Canada permitted the Catholic population to modify the English oaths to square with their religious convictions. Less wise officials in Nova Scotia refused to modify the test-oath requirements; they expelled the "Acadians" from their homes in a horrid, unplanned exile which brought death from disease, starvation, and shipwreck to thousands of simple folk whose only offense was a refusal to abandon old oaths to France for new oaths to England. But these were aberrations which seemed inevitable after a war or in the midst of preparations for war.[55]

More normally, colonial loyalty-testing occurred regularly at news of a king's demise and his successor's ascent to the throne. Thus, a traveler recorded how in Williamsburg, Virginia, in 1702, news of William III's death "caused general grief and consternation." Assembled dignitaries and militia made solemn ceremony of proclaiming the sad news. Then, at noon, the solemn band suddenly struck up a lively tune, crepe was removed from flags and cannon, and the royal governor, his mourning clothes doffed for vivid official dress, proclaimed the new monarch, Anne. After an afternoon and night of feasting, drinking, and dancing, solemnity returned with the next dawn, when the militia again assembled and the colony's officials swore new loyalty oaths to their new queen.[56] And so it went as royal flesh met mortal end. Kings passed on, years passed by, and such spectacular ceremonies served to bind the distant parts of the Empire together. Loyalty tests, part of the trappings of peaceful succession, were a necessary cement to bind the sprawling settlements of England's offshoots into a semblance of unity.

But there were occasions when these ceremonies scarcely clothed baser motives, when England's loyalty tests became tools for personal aggrandizement rather than props to imperial unity. In view of what had gone before, it is hardly surprising that one such incident should occur in Massachusetts. There, Joseph Dudley was still royal governor in 1714, when Queen Anne died. With appropriate ceremony, Dudley acknowledged her passing and proclaimed George I as the new king. In accordance with imperial practice as established by Anne, Dudley maintained all the colony's officials, including himself, in office, until specific word should arrive from England. He and his council swore new loyalty oaths to the new king. For six months Dudley's numerous enemies in Boston waited, hoping that each incoming vessel might bring Dudley's replacement. Devious machinations resulted in the council's deposing Dudley and assuming executive control of the colony. There followed lengthy arguments concerning the legitimacy of the move and the mutual accusations of disloyalty. Fortunately, no blood spilled. Early in 1715 royal orders finally arrived; George I reappointed Dudley to the governorship, and the insubordinate council, tired of onerous executive duties, gladly relinquished the reins of power to the man they had deposed. Governor and council again swore loyalty to George I, and Samuel Sewall, one of the councilors, prayed as he swore (admitting to no hypocrisy!), "The Lord help us to be faithfull." [57]

Such ardent pledges of fidelity by royal formula did not prevent Massachusetts from briefly resurrecting her own loyalty test, long-condemned by royal orders. An Anglican divine in Boston, John Checkley, unsettled the Puritans by his preachments. In 1719 Checkley dared to criticize Calvinist doctrines. His impiety roused the ire of the Puritan leaders of the colony, who responded almost automatically to the stimulus of disaffection by legislating that any magistrate might tender the colony's (illegal) loyalty test to "any person whom they suspected to be disaffected to his Majesty or to his Government." Hardly was the ink dry on this unusual document when Checkley found two magistrates at his door asserting that he was suspected of disloyalty, and ordering him to swear the special oath of loyalty to the colony. Checkley, as an Englishman and an Anglican, had no objections to swearing loyalty to his king. But he heatedly objected to having his patriotism suspected, and to the illicit form of oath facing him. If he took the oath, he felt, he would be admitting the charges. So he refused, and escaped prison only by posting a heavy money bond and by promising to tone down his anti-Calvinist preachments (which was precisely what the Puritans wanted).

For four years Checkley resisted the oath test, even against the crushing weight of one of Cotton Mather's sermons. But the stubborn Anglican could not convince his friends and neighbors that by nonjuring he did not admit to the disloyalty which made the oath necessary. He finally capitulated in 1724, and took the oath. The Massachusetts General Court, satisfied, immediately repealed the oath law. All that Checkley lost was the right to preach what he felt to be true. Had he tried the same tricks forty or more years earlier, he would have met a harsher fate.[58]

In this instance Massachusetts succeeded with its slippery use of a loyalty test as a political weapon directed at a specific individual. There were other occasions, in other colonies, when colonial officials tried the same device with less fortune. Royal Governor Belcher of New Hampshire, for instance, claimed the right to refuse to offer the required loyalty oath to any elected assemblyman he did not like. Hampshiremen in the colonial legislature boycotted their duties, including appropriating Belcher's salary, until the cowed viceroy yielded and administered the oath to whomever the assembly was willing to accept in membership, which is an important privilege of American legislative bodies today. In another similar case, Governor Cornbury of New Jersey fell prey to his cliquish council's suggestion that he refuse to administer the required oaths to certain elected assemblymen the councilors disliked. It took time, but Cornbury's arbitrariness received Board of Trade censure.

Generally, throughout the American colonies, the royal oath tests remained a procedural form and received scant attention from their subscribers. It was the transcolonial prerequisite for suffrage, office-holding, and naturalization until it stood in the way of attracting par-

ticularly desirable immigrants, such as sailors or vintners, when pragmatic needs of empire took easy precedence over the theoretical benefits
of strictly administered loyalty oaths.[59]

As the decades of the eighteenth century passed, new generations of
American colonists grew to maturity in a land of developing importance in Britain's Empire. These colonists, like their forebears, swore
the royal loyalty tests and took their turns at the reins of local government. Benjamin Franklin as a postal official and George Washington
as a militia officer and a surveyor were but two colonists who swore
loyalty to George II. Thousands of other colonists soon thereafter
joined Franklin and Washington in rebellion against that king's successor. The investment of time and energy which successive English
kings had made in enforcing loyalty tests ultimately failed to hold the
Empire together.

CHAPTER III

Insurrection Becomes Independence

In 1763 the British Empire celebrated a global victory. A little more than a decade later, the most populous, politically advanced, and seemingly fully patriotic part of that Empire erupted in outright rebellion. Ever since the American Revolution, historians have argued the desirability and necessity for the separation from Britain. Few students of the period, however, have considered the "how" of the Revolution, or dealt with the political mechanisms which ultimately proved capable of transforming thirteen disparate, distant colonies into a relatively unified enemy to royal rule.

Loyalty tests played a primary role in structuring the Revolution. They helped spur the creation of an American patriotism and accelerated the development of a decade of discontent. Loyalty tests served to place Americans in increasingly extreme positions regarding allegiance to the English king, and, finally, made a declaration of independence inevitable.

When put into individual terms, this transcolonial process is reduced to human scale. The experience of a young Virginian named Samuel Shepard is instructive and introductory. "I am come home to a nest of rebels," lamented Shepard, whose legal training in London had kept him from his native Virginia through the early 1770's. Now returned, he joined with old friends in a few draughts, and incautiously supported Britain when one of the roisterers cursed the English king. Only later did Shepard recall "an eagerness in the assenting noises of the company which should have warned me of a trap." Shepard did not know until it was too late that his loyalty was being tested and that he had failed the test. A member of an illicit unit of local government of whose very existence Shepard knew nothing jailed him on "disloyalty" charges, and a sobered Shepard heard this rough advice:

You will learn not to think and talk aloud in this place, for we are going to have a hard time, and we can't have treasonable talk to weaken our cause. . . . You are most fortunate in not having old man Pat Henry at the tavern; he would have addressed the people and you would have fared badly.

Shepard made his peace and pledged his loyalty to the new powers that were in Virginia.[1] His bewilderment mirrored the reaction of an entire generation of British-Americans as the exultation of victory over France in 1763 became the bitterness of revolt against England in 1776.

Britain's need for increased revenue inspired her statesmen to impose imperial taxes, new commerce restrictions, and novel enforcements of existing regulations. Faced with unprecedented demands, colonists from Maine to Georgia organized unparalleled resistance. The Stamp and Townshend acts inspired colonists to boycott British goods, organize citizens' committees to see that merchants and consumers abided by the boycott, and arrange for "spontaneous" mobs to coerce stubborn individuals who refused to join in the boycott, or, worse, promised compliance and then violated their pledges. Boycott breakers found their names published in libelous broadsides and themselves or their property pelted with stones, dung, or sticky "overcoats" of tar and feathers. Twice these rough and ready tactics succeeded; twice pocket-conscious Parliaments repealed the obnoxious legislation. Colonists exulted in their possession of techniques and organizations adequate to cow the mightiest empire in the world.

Resistance against taxation was, however, far from conspiracy for treason. Most Americans, radical or conservative, believed in local rights and joined in the boycotts of the 1760's with, as Jeremy Belknap later described it, "the warmest expressions of duty and loyalty to the King . . . and [his] constitutional authority, together with a determined resolution not to submit to the dangerous innovations then making." [2] Conservatives found it far easier to rouse mobs than to call them to heel; learned that in helping to create anti-boycott committees they had innocently helped to sow seeds of sedition. And there were a few Americans who wanted to go further than boycotts and who now knew how to realize their dreams.

Increasing numbers of colonists slowly discerned the existence of a new allegiance, built with great labor upon the writings of Sam Adams and the words of Patrick Henry, spread with vast energy by covert committees of correspondence and Sons of Liberty, reinforced with stunning impact by news of the Boston Massacre, the plundering of the *Gaspée,* and the Boston Tea Party. Colonial conservatives, recoiling from lawlessness, pleaded with royal officers to invoke England's treason laws against turbulent committeemen.

But the king's administrators, weak in real power and fearing to bring matters to a head, temporized. As late as December, 1773, royal governor Thomas Hutchinson of Massachusetts merely recommended that Britain terminate the colony's turbulent town meetings which had created the first committees of correspondence. Hutchinson, along with his colleagues in the colonial bureaucracy and supporters among the conservative citizenry, failed to see that the intercolonial committee structure was transforming itself into effective units of local government, and amoeba-like, was extending tentacles of power into expanding arenas of social and political control.

Elastic, illicit, and irresponsible, these local committees came under the control of radical spokesmen, men like Sam Adams, Patrick Henry, Thomas Jefferson, and John Hancock, who wielded their flexible instruments of pressure with consummate skill.[3] Each successive crisis increased radical power and committee functions. When the Intolerable Acts of 1774 brought overt rebellion to the American colonies, these Whig committees possessed superb organization, with representation in almost every community. Royal authorities and their colonial Tory supporters were unprepared. And yet, as late as 1774, when Britain imposed military rule over unquiet Boston, almost all Americans were still prating words of loyalty to George III.

General Thomas Gage assumed the royal governorship of Massachusetts in April, 1774. His mission was to conciliate as well as to punish. Tories wailed as Gage delayed, and later, when he sought to crush subversion by force, his belated choice brought on open war. Gage's first orders suspended sessions of Massachusetts' colonial assembly. In illicit meetings, its personnel found inspiration, and sometimes participation, in the Whig program of organized economic resistance to British tax programs.

In June, 1774, the Massachusetts assembly created a new boycott agreement, the Solemn League and Covenant, which ardent Massachusetts committeemen transmuted into a loyalty test, holding that an individual's "refusal to come into agreement [to boycott British goods] must evidence a disposition inimical to . . . the common safety." To enforce the covenant, committeemen assumed vigilante powers under the very guns of Gage's garrison and in the halls of British justice where colonial jurymen refrained from issuing indictments against committeemen's excesses. The covenant test was, for the Whigs, a huge success, with "every adult of both sexes putting their names to it, saving a very few." For those like poor John Andrews, who refused to identify himself with either the numerous Whigs or the Tory minority of Boston, there was only the contumely of both, so that this would-be neutral had to burn horse manure for want of a nonpartisan firewood dealer to sell him more ordinary fuel. And for outright Tories who sold supplies to the British Army, accepted royal office as colonial councilmen, and—perhaps worst of all!—publicly protested against the actions of the Whig committees, there was the threat of far worse to come if British power exposed them to Whig vengeance.[4]

Gage finally decided to end the Whig nonsense once and for all. Late in June he ordered the arrest of all whose support of the covenant implied committee participation. But Gage met a blank wall of simulated ignorance. Stubborn (or intimidated) grand jurymen blighted each attempt at procedural prosecution in the courts. Gage fumed while subscriptions to the covenant mounted and Tories met increasingly harsh treatment at Whig hands. He complained to his superiors that "tho' I hear many things against this and that person, yet when I want to descend to particular points, and want people to stand forth in order to bring crimes home to individuals by clear and full evidence, I am at a loss."

Gage could punish no one for signing the covenant. British and Tory prestige plummeted to low levels and Tories added humiliation at British weakness to their hurts from Whig strength. Successively, Gage banned all public meetings and intercolonial support for blockaded Boston. He could enforce none of his prohibitions, but each abortive order added firmness to Whig concepts of loyalty to colonial rights.[5] To a very few radicals, Gage's prohibitions added justification for outright separation from Great Britain, but time had yet to pass and blood to spill before the extreme Whigs could realize such dreams.

By midsummer, 1774, Whig committees began expanding their organization into the rural counties of the back country. It was from one such western Massachusetts committee that a call came in August for an intercolonial congress to consider the further defense of colonial rights, still in the name of loyalty to the king. The First Continental Congress assembled the next month in Philadelphia. Its members were far from united in spirit, with conservatives joining in its meetings to keep radicals in check. Out of its hectic deliberations the Congress produced a uniform boycott regulation for all the colonies. This Continental Association, passed by an extralegal Congress, designed even with cautious conservative participation to defy the British Crown and ministry, soon developed into the colonists' first standard loyalty test.

Congress, however, possessed no power to enforce its Continental Association. In a reciprocal exchange of illicit grants of power, it called upon Whig committeemen in every colony to enforce the boycott program. Thus the intercolonial committee system received a veneer of legality and prestige from the Congress and in turn provided that assembly with an efficient executive arm. Congress ordered Whig committees to obtain subscriptions and obedience to the association from all colonists and

. . . attentively to observe the conduct of all persons, . . . and when it shall be made to appear, to the satisfaction of any such committee, that any person . . . has violated this association, that such committee so forthwith cause the truth of the case to be published . . . to the end, that all such foes to the rights of British-America may be publicly known, and universally condemned as the enemies of American liberty; and thenceforth we will break off all dealings with him or her.

The line of loyalty was clearer now than ever before. Support or defiance of the association boycott oath was the test of allegiance of the moment. With practiced efficiency and bland assurances of continued loyalty to the king, Whig committees enforced the provisions of the oath by social ostracism, economic pressure, and physical terrorism. But to enforce the association the Whig committees had to extend their influence and control into novel areas of colonial life and government. In the process they took a long step toward outright independence from the Crown.[6]

From England came orders to all royal governors to check the association and crush the Whig committees. It was too late. Lord Dunmore, royal governor of Virginia, disclosed how tardy that order was when he reported in December, 1774, that his power in Virginia was "entirely disregarded, if not overturned." In a tone of petulant helplessness, Dunmore complained that

The Associations . . . are now enforcing . . . with the greatest rigour. A Committee has been chosen in every County . . . to carry the Association . . . into execution, which Committee assumes an authority to inspect the books, invoices, and all other secrets of the trade and correspondence of the Merchants; to watch the conduct of every inhabitant, without distinction, and to send for such as come under their suspicion . . . to interrogate them respecting all matters, which, at their pleasure, they think fit objects of their inquiry; and to stigmatize . . . such as they find transgressing what they are now hardy enough to call the laws of the Congress, which stigmatizing is . . . inviting the vengeance of an outrageous and lawless mob to be exercised upon the unhappy victims.

With few exceptions, the picture Dunmore painted found reproduction in all the colonies. It was not a happy time to be a royal governor or a Tory; one unhappy loyalist described the latter appellation as a "name as dangerous to the person so aspersed, as mad dog to the canine species in England." Years later a prominent Tory, Daniel Leonard, remembered how British officialdom and their colonial supporters watched the Whig committees hatch "the eggs of sedition." He "saw the small seed when it was planted," and "watched . . . until it has become a great tree." [7] By early 1775, the Whig tree was too strong, and its roots were too intertwined with the basic economic and political society of the colonies, for British orders or Tory enmity to cut it down. And it was from enforcing the loyalty test of the association that the Whig colossus took its first firm growth, and nourished itself on the heady drink of power.

In defense of the association, New England ministers, Congregational in dogma and Whiggish in politics, apostrophized nonjurors as satanic dupes of British tyranny, to such effect that a bitter English official denounced them for inculcating "war, bloodshed, and massacres, as though all these were the express injunction of Jesus Christ." General Gage black-listed one such propagandizing minister as "the most dangerous character to the King's cause in the . . . colony." Shrewd South Carolina committeemen sent fundamentalist Protestant preachers on proselytizing tours into backwoods communities, armed with Biblical exhortations to sign the association. North Carolina Whigs staged parades in which effigies of local nonassociators, along with those of the Pope, Lord North, the Devil, and General Gage, were consumed in fires fed by confiscated properties of boycott-breaking merchants. New York committeemen, with John Jay and James Duane at their head, spread handbills scheduling mass swearing ceremonies and public hearings to decide penalties for nonjurors.[8]

Under such pressures, in the almost complete absence of effective royal or Tory countermeasures, signatures to the association mounted with astonishing rapidity. Some colonists signed, as did Joseph Galloway, in the hope that their participation in Whig affairs would keep the radical element in check. But many men who signed the association under duress must have felt as did this anonymous "Pausing American Loyalist":

To sign, or not to sign!—That is the question
Whether t'were better for an honest man to sign
And to be safe—or to resolve
Betide what will, against "associations"
And, by retreating, shun them. To fly—I reck
Not where—and, by that flight, t'escape
Feathers and tar, and thousand of other ills
That loyalty is heir to: 'tis a consummation
Devoutly to be wished. To fly—to want—
To Want?—perchance to starve! Ay, there's the rub!
For in that chance of want, what ills may come
To patriots rage, and when I have left my all,
Must give me pause! There's the respect
That makes us trim, and bow to men we hate.
For, who could bear th' indignities o' th' times,
Congress' decrees, and wild Convention plans,
The laws controll'd, and injuries unredressed,
The insolence of knaves, and thousand wrongs
Which patient . . . [loyal] men from vile rebels take,
When he, sans doubt, might certain safety find,
Only by flying? Who would bend to fools,
And truckle thus to mad, mob-chosen upstarts,
But that the dread of something after flight
(In that blest country, where, yet, no moneyless
Poor wight can live) puzzles the will,
And makes ten thousands rather sing—and eat,
Than fly—to starve on Loyalty!
Thus, dread of want makes cowards of us all;
And, thus, the native hue of Loyalty
Is sicklied o'er with a pale cast of trimming;
And enterprises of great pith and virtue,
But, unsupported, turn their streams away,
And never come to action.[9]

Physical force was every Whig committee's ultimate pressure upon reluctant citizens. Such unrestricted power often proved too much for novice committeemen to cope with. Irresponsibility led to brutal excess which local law officers, too frightened to act or themselves sympathetic to Whig acts, refused to punish. As one despondent Boston Tory expressed it, "We lead a devil of a life." Chief among the satanic aspects of loyalist life were the Whig committees.[10]

Some case histories exist of how Whig committees enforced loyalty to the association, and, by doing so, became centers of revolutionary sentiment and training grounds for revolutionary assumptions of governmental functions. Ten days after news of Boston's Tea Party reached Worcester, Massachusetts, for instance, local Whigs organized a committee called the American Political Society. It assumed police and judicial functions in administering the association, sent delegates to the provincial assembly, and, in short, became the town's local government. The Worcester group was theoretically subject to the discipline of the colony's Committee of Safety. Actually, however, Worcester's Whigs had a free hand in dealing with their Tories, and were their own court of last resort and highest appeal. By late 1775 the society had completed a loyalty census of all Worcester's inhabitants. Loyal men had signed the association; disloyal men (and women) had not. It was, for the moment, as simple as that.[11]

Whig committeemen in Virginia had similar ideas. In March, 1775, they questioned a resident on charges of prejudicing others against signing the association oath or obeying its injunctions. Refusing to recant, the nonjuror was "published as one of the enemies to America"; children stoned him, adults smeared his home with paint and filth, and he could neither buy nor sell from cowed tradesmen. Unable to secure police protection (the sheriff was also in charge of the Whig committee), the nonjuror, after suffering three months of such treatment, capitulated, signed the test, and was let alone—briefly.

Committeemen in Barnstable, Massachusetts, conducted an investigation into their town moderator's loyalty because he opposed the association, and revealed how expertly they had woven a web of surveillance about the town. Trusted neighbors of the suspect man had for a year kept careful notes on his words and deeds; these he had to explain away, in addition to swearing the association, in order to escape the consequences of his earlier errors. As one Connecticut merchant expressed it, the consequences of nonassociating were "a sort of political death or disfranchisement," which could easily beggar a man. Loyalty was a deadly serious matter to the ubiquitous Whig committeemen.[12]

By the end of 1774 affairs had reached the point where good Whigs defined Tories as persons whose bodies were in America, whose heads were in Great Britain, and whose necks they hoped to stretch between the two points. But English statesmen still saw hope for reconciliation, a phantom which they pursued almost until the achievement of American independence. "Every step taken by these infatuated people," ran one informed British view of 1775, "must defeat its own purpose." This largely ignored the fact that the "steps" Whigs took trod agonizingly heavily on Tory backs.[13]

While British policy makers temporized, Tories, with few exceptions, failed to organize. A few centers of loyalist strength—some Anglican ministers like Maryland's Jonathan Boucher (who preached with loaded pistols on his lectern after refusing to sign the association), or Samuel Peters and John Sayre of Connecticut—provided local Tories with the kind of stubborn leadership needed to counter Whig pressure. A very few colonials created Tory committees to beat the Whigs at their own game. In Maryland, Virginia, and North Carolina such Tory organizations flourished briefly, then withered when promised British assistance failed to materialize. Tories achieved some success by spreading whispers that all who signed the association would be hanged, and that the whole association scheme was a mere trick of Whig merchants to empty their overstocked wares upon the market at boycott-inflated prices, but such pinpricks failed to deflate the swelling Whig power.[14] Tory counterorganizations suffered from failing to keep their membership secret: Worcester's Whigs had merely to read handbills, which Tories generously printed to announce their meeting time, to ambush and arrest members of this incipient center of loyalism. Whig spies did not scruple to take Tory oaths in order to learn Tory secrets. As each Tory organization fell, as each Anglican minister bowed to pressure, recanted, or fled, Whiggery won the prestige that power affords; loyalism lost not merely present supporters but possible future recruits.[15]

Most loyalists remained quiescent, signed Whig oaths, and waited with some traces of smug assurance for the majesty of royal power to reassert itself. To many Tories, any Whig was an "idle projector," a "silly clown and illiterate mechanic." Tories were confident that the Whigs would overreach themselves, and then the "dirty, domineering Committees of Inspection" would be on the receiving end of royal justice. Feeling so, the Tories waited too long to help themselves. They permitted the numerically inferior Whigs to perfect their power and force Tories either to recant or to swell the stream of exiles heading toward the center of British strength at Boston.[16]

For a century and a half, accounts of loyalist sufferings at Whig hands have largely followed the pattern set by such Tory spokesmen as Jonathan Boucher, who blamed British official inaction for permitting Whig strength to develop unchecked, and who claimed that "no Tory has in a single instance misused or injured a Whig merely for being a Whig." But Tories shared in the responsibility for British inaction, and, where loyalists had the opportunity and the strength, they wielded whips, applied tar and feathers, and beat their victims with as much viciousness as any Whig displayed.[17]

More dismal still is the fact that this year of organized persecution was but the comparatively petty prelude of worse to come. From mid-1774 until mid-1775, Whigs proscribed Tories in the name of the association's boycott agreement. Then, in July, 1775, the issue of loyalty took on a wider definition and a mortal significance. As one Pennsylvanian, whose mild Toryism now changed into a firm Whiggism, expressed this change, "All nice distinctions . . . must now give way to resolute, active determination." News of the fighting at Lexington and Concord made the difference.[18]

Bloodshed invigorated Tory-hunting everywhere in the colonies. The Continental Association continued to serve as a standard Whig loyalty test, pledging subscribers to loyalty to the king but also to persistent opposition to royal policies. Even while insurgent Americans battled redcoats at Concord, besieged Gage in Boston, and invaded Canada, they maintained that their jousts with royal forces were true exercises of loyalty to the Crown! Theory and fact, obviously, needed a better wedding.

Whig leaders throughout the colonies were anxious for the Continental Congress to assume leadership in the task of suppressing Tories, and to centralize its administration in congressional hands. "Would it not be best," inquired a Maryland provincial assemblyman of the Congress, "to have one general [loyalty] test for all America?" Massachusetts, similarly, sought from Congress "a test by which all persons inimical to the rights and liberties of America shall be distinguished from their friends." Congress, however, refused to assume responsibility for producing this political litmus paper.[19] Still committed to conciliation rather than to independence, Congress vacillated on the Tory question, its membership contenting itself with recommendations to provincial assemblies and local committees to deal with local problems of disloyalty. Some Whig leaders like John Adams recognized that disloyalty was a transcolonial rather than a local problem, and that Congress was dodging its basic responsibility by decentralizing the loyalty program. Congress, Adams complained,

. . . left all the powers of government in the hands of [local] assemblies, conventions, and committees, which composed a scene of much confusion and injustice, the continuance of which was much dreaded by me, as tending to injure the morals of the people, and destroy their habits of order and attachment to regular government. However, I could do nothing but remonstrate.[20]

Thus, local Whig groups took the law of loyalty into their hands long before the Declaration of Independence, and enforced it by local standards and agencies. The local groups which took on the anti-Tory task were the same extralegal committees of safety (bearing a variety of titles but behaving everywhere with remarkable similarity) which were already enforcing the Continental Association. Once more Congress and committees exchanged functions and afforded each other vitality. The question of loyalty served to press the reluctant Congress closer to outright independence from Britain.[21]

Congress consistently recommended to local committee leaders that they deal with their Tories with some measure of restraint. But, in what one unhappy loyalist called the "infinite number of petty tyrannies," these sober injunctions rarely rated obedience. Lexington and Concord shifted Whig attitudes: what had once been radicalism was now moderation; what earlier had passed for caution was now suspect neo-Toryism. Local Whig leaders, responsible in reality to no higher authority for their actions in the cause of loyalty, made loyalty tests into weapons of savage coercion. Witness the events in New York City when, at news of Lexington, even soberly conservative citizens

Astonished by accounts of . . . hostility, in the moment of the expectations of terms of reconciliation, and now filled with distrust, . . . burst through all restraints . . . and . . . seized the city arms; . . . distributed them among the multitude, . . . increased the numbers and powers of the committee . . . to execute the Association of the Continental Congress. . . . Such a change of temper and conduct has entirely prostrated his Majesty's government in New York.[22]

The swift pace of events outdistanced the ability of many colonists to shift their attitudes toward loyalty. John Peters of Connecticut, for example, who had been a delegate to the First Continental Congress, pleaded with the Liberty Boys of his area to adopt a wait-and-see attitude. He was mobbed three times in one afternoon for refusing to re-swear the association. Peters, bitter and angry, did swear the oath and drilled the colonial militia, but in his heart he determined to support Britain rather than the Whigs. He secretly spied for General Gage and later openly espoused the royal cause. The loyalty test he had been forced to sign bore bitter fruit for the patriot cause.[23]

Loyalty tests sometimes worked out the opposite way as well. Whig committeemen of New York, including John Jay, James Duane, and Peter van Schaack, proclaimed a mass association subscription ceremony, and carefully took note of absentees. One such was a colonial judge, William Smith. When they accosted him for his delinquency,

Smith justified his nonjuring on the grounds that he proposed to pose as a Tory in order to serve the Whigs should overt war come. The committeemen approved Smith's deliberate perjury and Smith remained unmolested. But, ironically, Smith became a "sincere" Tory when the British Army took New York, while van Schaack, erstwhile arranger of Whig loyalty-testing ceremonies, reconverted to royal allegiance.[24]

South Carolina's loyalty-testing situation illustrates how clever Whigs used news of Lexington and Concord to justify harsh anti-Tory actions, and to nurture opposition to British authority in general rather than against a few particular British trade policies. The Carolina provincial assembly created a stern association test for the colony and Henry Laurens, president of the assembly, defended the measure. He asserted that he considered himself fully loyal to the king and denied Tory and conservative Whig assertions that the new test implied rebellion against the Crown. Laurens castigated some Carolinians who openly admitted swearing earlier Whiggish loyalty tests with mental reservations, and he insisted that no honest man could believe that perjury and liberty could coexist. The Carolina Association test passed, and gained an evil reputation among Tories and would-be neutrals as one of the most stringent in the turbulent colonies.[25]

Twelve times repeated, such experiences reflect the adroit achievement of Whig committeemen who created and enforced loyalty tests which in theory merely proclaimed a boycott of British goods, and claimed allegiance to the monarch whose officials, laws, and supporters they flouted and harassed. In thirteen seething colonies, Congress' surrender of loyalty-testing control to local authorities makes this story as various as the integrity and prejudices of the individuals concerned. The only common denominator was the association. As one student of loyalism in this period described it:

The association thus became the first decisive test of the politics of individuals. . . . It stamped the individual as a Whig or a Tory in the eyes of his neighbors, and treatment was meted out to him accordingly. It proved his political rectitude or depravity. Hesitation [to sign] involved suspicion; refusal, guilt.[26]

If, after Lexington, events had remained static, royal authority might have revived, loyalism could have organized, and the Continental Congress, timid about treason, would have achieved conciliation with Britain. But Congress had let independent local power run loose in the land in the name of loyalty, and created a Continental Army to besiege

British headquarters in Boston. Together, in an unplanned concert of words and deeds on the theme of loyalty, local committees and the Continental Army, dual illicit offspring of the extralegal Congress, by enforcing the association pushed their hesitant parent toward an outright assertion of independence. At the same time, local Whig authorities and the Whig army competed for control over loyalty-testing. At stake was the fate of thousands of colonists.

Under English law, every man in George Washington's Continental forces was a traitor. Congress might placate its conservative conscience by claiming persistent loyalty to George III, but Washington had the immediate responsibility for maintaining discipline in his corps of citizen-soldiers who were actively engaged in shooting at redcoats. His soldiers needed legal status from the legislators. Thus, a full year before it declared political independence from England, Congress created regulations for its army which made mutiny, sedition, and aiding the "enemy" offenses punishable by courts-martial. In effect, Congress had to place its need for the army's loyalty to itself above its official position of a primary loyalty to the king. Washington wasted no time enforcing his new authority. His officers created for the troops loyalty tests demanding fidelity to Congress' orders and officials. As early as July, 1775, one private soldier refused the oath and threatened to desert. A quick court-martial evoked the delinquent's promise to reform and his subscription to the oath, and Washington pardoned him.[27] But disloyalty in higher ranks soon appeared to plague army and Congress.

The treason of Benjamin Church threw all Whigs into confusion. A member of Boston's committee of correspondence, Massachusetts' provincial assembly, and the Continental Congress, Church was Washington's chief surgeon. He was also a spy for the British. Church's mistress betrayed him to Washington, who, because the brand-new Articles of War failed to cover treason (how could they, when Congress still claimed loyalty to England, automatically limiting treason to acts against that sovereignty?), turned the traitor over to Congress for disposition. Congress, embarrassed, refused to prosecute Church since that might amount to an open declaration of independence from Britain. Everyone was happier when Church escaped, took ship from America, and presumably drowned. But the episode impelled Congress to authorize Washington to impose the death penalty for traitors in the army.[28]

Church's defection pushed the reluctant Congress a big step toward outright independence. But far greater than the question of the loyalty of a few soldiers was the problem of thousands of uncertain Whigs and outspoken Tories who promised to become a reservoir of loyalty for the British to exploit. Since Congress persisted in avoiding this problem, Washington, by default, launched the Continental Army into the breach of loyalty-testing. It was the simple martial need for security which sent the Continental forces into action against "that infernal crew of Tories, who have laughed at the Congress, despised the friends of liberty, . . . and yet . . . walk the streets . . . with impunity." [29]

Worried Continental officers were not fighting phantoms. As events made the situation increasingly critical, many moderate colonists recoiled from earlier coöperation with Whigs and pronounced for Britain. In late 1775 and early 1776, Tory power seemed everywhere on the increase. Even a loyalist who was languishing in a Massachusetts prison for "refusing to be forced into rebellion" could muster enough spirit to pen these lines:

> I, poor d——l am here confined
> (A state which no way suits my mind)
> For being—you all know the story—
> A sad, incorrigible Tory,
> However, e'en so let it run,
> 'Tis a d——d long lane that has no turn,
> And when ye tide has all ebbed out
> The next thing 't does 'twill turn about
> And flow as high—nay sometimes more—
> As it was low water before.[30]

To prevent a reversal of the tide of loyalty, George Washington and the Continental Army entered the loyalty-testing business. Convinced of the dangers represented by untrustworthy Tory civilians in strategic areas, Washington wondered why "persons who are preying upon the vitals of their country [should] be suffered to stalk at large, whilst we know that they will do us every mischief in their power?" He considered Tories "abominable pests of society," and hoped they would all commit suicide. If Tories would not coöperate by self-extermination, Washington was prepared to help them along. "I think as you do," he wrote in December, 1775,

that it is high time a test act was prepared and every man called upon to declare himself; that we may distinguish friends from foes; nor have I any idea of a set of men being exempt from the common duties of society in any country, or community where they have been fostered in the sweet enjoyment of its liberties.[31]

But it became obvious that neither Congress nor the Whig state authorities were going to provide Washington with any other loyalty test than the inadequate association. The best Congress would do was to authorize Washington, *or* the states, *or* the local committees, to disarm Tories. Washington considered this permission enough. He launched loyalty-testing expeditions into the heavily Tory and strategically important Rhode Island and Long Island areas. By his orders, Continental troops worked closely with Whig committees, and turned over to the latter "all those who shall be detected in . . . infamous practices."

The Long Island raid offered an example of superb army-committee coöperation. Committeemen's black lists of suspect neighbors highlighted the targets for Washington's troops. As Continental raiders assembled suspected disloyalists, officers presented the prisoners with the choice of either swearing to two special loyalty oaths Washington had written for the occasion, or going to prison. One oath was a promise to surrender all arms; the other was a promise not to oppose "by thought, word or deed," any acts of the New York Provincial Convention or the Continental Congress. Previous subscription to Congress' association was no exemption from these novel tests.[32] Some Long Islanders, according to Whig committeemen, were too far sunk in Toryism to be regenerated by loyalty tests, and received no chance to swear but went straightway to jail. Such swift action and unnerving familiarity with individual politics produced heart-warming results, by Whig standards. Hundreds of Long Islanders swore the special army oaths, dozens divulged innocent or sinister arms caches, and other dozens, defiant nonjurors or those barred from taking the loyalty tests whatever their wishes, became committee prisoners. When the troops marched off, Long Islanders should have been safely loyal. But events soon proved that loyalty and loyalty tests did not necessarily coincide.[33]

Simultaneously, and similarly, Washington's second loyalty-testing expedition operated in Connecticut and Rhode Island under the command of immodest General Charles Lee. Lee's appearance in Providence was a nightmare to loyalists. To one Tory lady he was a "wicked madman," who carried from their homes helpless men whose only offense was their refusal to swear to the loyalty tests he imposed. But Lee's disloyalty-hunting received general Whig approbation. Rhode Island's delegates in Congress complained, however, that his loyalty tests infringed upon the sovereignty of the state's assembly, which alone had power over the citizenry of that area. Lee, his pride hurt, admitted error, but justified it on the grounds of Whig need "to administer a very strong oath to some of the leading Tories." Washington stilled the troubled waters by giving Lee's acts unstinting praise and expressing his "opinion that, if the same plan were pursued through every province it would have a very good effect." Lee emerged from this adventure with his reputation buoyed by Washington's praise (which may have inspired him to compete for Washington's place). Soon thereafter, Washington sent Lee off on another loyalty-testing expedition.[34]

Again the target was Long Island, where recent loyalty cleansings had failed to wipe Toryism from the peninsula. Lee arranged with the chief New York Whig committeeman, Isaac Sears, for close army-committee coöperation, and wrote new loyalty tests for Sears to apply in Long Island. Nonjurors were "irreclaimable enemies to their country," and were to go into "close custody in Connecticut." But Sears, despite his loose view of what a Tory was, found few Islanders willing to proclaim themselves as such by refusing the oaths. One of Sears's reports complained that he "tendered the oath to four of the greater tories, which they swallowed as hard as if it were a four pound shot they were trying to get down. On this day I have been able to catch but five tories, . . . who swallowed the oath." [35]

A few dozen more Whig loyalty tests found signatures and a baker's dozen nonjurors became Sears's prisoners. This little success blew up a storm of words so violent that Lee and Washington wondered if the results were worth the trouble. New York's provincial assembly censured Lee for "invading" New York's territory, arresting its citizens (most of whom, as it turned out, were not Tories at all), and requiring an unauthorized loyalty test. Only New York's officials were in the loyalty-testing business in that state, Lee was curtly informed, and his defense of immediate danger—"When the enemy is at our door, forms must be dispensed with"—lacked validity when the enemy failed to appear. Lee and Washington could agree that "not to crush . . . serpents before their rattles are grown, would be ruinous," but the two generals found themselves in a small minority when Congress stepped into this jurisdictional dispute.

New York's delegation to the Continental Congress—John Jay, John Alsop, James Duane, and Lewis Morris—introduced a resolution in March, 1776, that "no oath by way of test be imposed upon, exacted, or required of any of the inhabitants of these colonies, by military officers." The New Yorkers justified their proposal, not by rejecting loyalty tests as threats to liberty, but by asserting the natural monopoly of loyalty-testing which New York's assembly enjoyed in that colony.

No Continental Army officer had authority from Congress to impose loyalty tests upon civilians anywhere. "For God's sake," Jay pleaded with congressmen, "resist all such attempts in the future." When Congress approved the resolution, Lee's sensitive soul writhed. His bitter retort met placating words from his friends in Congress, who assured him that their criticism was against the precedent he might have set, not against him personally. Lee, convinced, let the matter drop.

Having knocked the Continental Army temporarily out of the loyalty-testing field, and itself remaining carefully outside that dangerous area, Congress inferentially signaled state assemblies and local committees to continue their antisubversive investigations. If the jurisdictional question was momentarily settled by default, the perennial problem of disloyalty continued its urgent pressure, impelling Whigs ever further toward a clean break from Britain.[36]

While Whigs everywhere waited tensely for expected British attacks, loyalty investigators of New York's alert provincial assembly unearthed a ring of traitors in high army and civil offices. Exiled royal governor Tryon had recruited David Matthews, mayor of New York City, and William Hickey of Washington's personal bodyguard (both of whom had sworn Congress' association and Lee's loyalty test), in a plot to capture Congress when the appearance of British forces should provide the opportunity. Hickey gained the dubious fame of being the first of Washington's soldiers to hang for treason, even before there was a nation to betray. But New York civil law recognized treason as a crime solely against the king. Congress was forced to take another step toward the chasm of independence. In June, 1776, it resolved that all Americans owed allegiance only to itself and to their colonies, and recommended that every member of the American union revise its treason statutes to conform to the realities of the time. Treason and disloyalty, as Elbridge Gerry exulted, were preparing a "fair way to a speedy Declaration of Independency." That immortal Declaration followed hard upon the Hickey plot; soon after, New York, now a state in a nation that had to prove its right to exist, redefined its treason statute, and sent Matthews to prison.[37]

Outright assertion of independence stiffened Tory spines and made loyalists of many nominal Whigs who had never dreamed that resistance to British laws would ever become rebellion against Great Britain. As one Whig jibe had it:

> The word, Rebellion, hath frozen them up,
> Like fish in a pond.

To Try Men's Souls

After July 4, 1776, individual acceptance or rejection of the Declaration became a common test of loyalty in all the self-proclaimed states. Whig committees, as in New York City, made house-to-house canvasses, requiring each inhabitant to signify if he was for or against separation. Those who refused, regardless of past loyalty tests they might have signed, and certainly regardless of past loyal conduct toward Whiggery, were automatically disloyal to America. What John Adams condemned as the absurdity of Americans prating words of loyalty to George III while they fought his troops, was finished. Now patriots and traitors were clearly in opposition, and treason was a crime deserving the most severe punishment. As one Continental Army officer expressed it:

I have often supposed a Declaration of Independence would be accompanied by a [congressional] declaration of high treason. . . . Can we subsist—did any State ever subsist, without exterminating traitors? . . . No one thing made the Declaration of Independence indispensably necessary more than cutting off traitors. It is amazingly wonderful, that having no capital punishment for our intestine enemies, we have not been utterly ruined before now. For God's sake, let us not run such risks a day longer. It appears to me, . . . that high treason ought to be the same in all the United States.[38]

But, after the Declaration of Independence as before, Congress kept out of the field of loyalty tests and treason laws. Its members had other things to worry about. Almost simultaneously with the Americans' proud assertion of independence, General Howe's redcoats flooded across Long Island, New York City, and New Jersey. Washington's battered Continental Army counted its losses in the last weeks of 1776, and raged over the baseness of civilian conduct. In the areas abandoned in the face of British might, thousands of civilians, firmly sworn to Whig allegiance, welcomed the royal forces with no apparent taint of conscience. Then, in a shattering stroke of martial audacity, Washington's Christmas attack on Trenton brought southwestern New Jersey back under American control—but under which Americans? Continental Army officers, Jersey officials, and Whig committeemen jostled each other in a jurisdictional rush to punish civilians who had proved faithless to the rebel cause during Howe's occupation. The absence of a congressional loyalty-testing policy brought Washington once more into a war of words with a state authority.

New Jersey had always seemed suspect to ardent Whigs. Sam Adams, for instance, felt that all residents there should "be engaged beyond the power of receding." General Nathaniel Greene demanded a "discretionary power to punish the disaffected." As Washington surveyed the newly won western Jersey scene, he knew that thousands of civilians within his lines had once sworn Whig loyalty tests and broken them when British officers offered royal pardons upon subscriptions to royal oaths. Washington, however, was willing to trust such flexible folk if they would once more assume the obligation of allegiance to the rebel cause.[39]

With John Adams' coöperation, Washington secured Congress' approval for the Continental Army to conduct a loyalty-testing program in New Jersey. On January 25, 1777, Washington was ready. His headquarters issued a proclamation throughout the American area (and agents carried it well into the British occupation zone as well) ordering all Jerseymen who, "influenced by inimical motives, intimidated by the threats of the enemy, or deluded by a [pardon and amnesty] Proclamation issued by Lord and General Howe," had foolishly cast off their allegiance to America, to come to his officials within thirty days and swear anew their loyalty to the United States. Nonjurors were to pay the penalty of exile into British lines. Any who refused the oath and did not leave American territory would be "deemed adherents to the King of Great Britain, and treated as common enemies of the American States." The situation seemed simple to Washington; loyal Americans swore loyalty to America. Disloyalists refused to swear.

Results at first seemed to justify Washington's confidence. Thousands of Jersey residents queued up before army oath commissioners and raised their hands in token of loyal submission. In return Washington promised them property and personal protection. There, to other Jerseymen, was the rub. For in the wake of Washington's troops a large number of former exiles from British occupation returned, demanding vengeance upon neighbors and relatives who had proved false to the rebel cause. Whig committeemen opened carefully compiled black lists of names of Tory traitors. Now, in the long-awaited moment of victorious revenge, they were blocked by the proclamation of the Continental general, guaranteeing protection to oath takers whose past perjuries made any oath a mockery. Their complaints reached Washington, who rejected them, declaring that it would be "bad policy" to punish past defectors and make Tory martyrs of them. "Lenity will operate with greater force," Washington felt, "than rigor." Americans would not indulge in personal persecutions "in imitation of the enemy." For the moment, his officers took precedence over state officials and local committeemen in loyalty-testing, and the swearing process proceeded peaceably.[40]

It did not, however, go smoothly. Administrative problems complicated seemingly clear lines of loyalty. Should those who chose exile take portable property with them? And what of those who, according to Whig committeemen, were using the thirty-day grace period to spy for the British? Did the existence of the month-long delay mean that men might wait a month before choosing to swear or not, or rather that all must swear immediately, with only sincerely uncertain folk privileged to delay? What form of oath (for Washington had prescribed none) should be used? And what of those civilians whose loyal conduct under British occupation had been exemplary, but who, for strange reasons, still refused the American loyalty test?

Washington answered the queries as best he could. Nonjurors might not take scarce horses or wagons with them, for the British would surely confiscate them. "No form of an oath is yet drawn up," he wrote, halfway through the thirty-day period of decision, "but you can easily strike off one that will answer the end designed." All civilians might have the full month to decide, without restraints upon their liberty, even from the vengeful Whig committeemen. And, in difficult cases, Washington cautioned subordinates to exercise the nicest discrimination, bordering, indeed, upon patent hypocrisy: "Nor do I think it a good policy," Washington wrote, "to insist rigidly upon those, whose general conduct has been friendly to us, to take the oaths—to release them from it by a general act would not be right—*but I would wish it to slip over as a matter unnoticed* [italics added]."

Such inconsistency served further to complicate loyalty-testing administration. Several dozen Elizabethtown men publicly announced that they were going to use the full thirty-day grace to clear up personal affairs, then refuse the American oath. Washington let himself become convinced that these determined nonjurors were British agents and ordered their immediate exile, in contradiction to his own earlier decision. His oath program, Washington felt, must not become "a Shelter for our Enemies to injure us under, with impunity." [41] In this he was sincere; Washington's deep conviction that loyalty oaths served rebel needs found expression in his report to Congress concerning his Jersey activities:

From the first institution of civil government, it has been the national policy of every precedent State to . . . engage its members to the discharge of their duty by the obligation of some oath. Its force and happy influence have been felt in too many instances to need any arguments to support the policy or prove its utility. . . . An oath is the only substitute that can be adopted to supply the defect of principle.

Clearly, Washington considered himself a trail blazer on a loyalty-testing path which he recommended that Congress and all the states follow. It hurt him to learn that his actions had not met universal Whig approval. Abraham Clark, signer of the Declaration of Independence and representative from New Jersey in Congress, alerted his colleagues to the dangers to state sovereignty inherent in Washington's loyalty-testing program. "It must render any man unpopular," Clark admitted, "to speak in favour of those who joined the enemy . . . but I think the General's proclamation a violation of our civil rights." He felt sure that Washington deserved Congress' censure. Clark's defense of civil over military power, of state over national acts, and his criticism of Washington, unleased a flood of calumny upon his unyielding head. Ardent patriots accused Clark of secret Toryism for criticizing anti-Tory actions. According to one indignant letter, Clark was aiding "those that are really disaffected, and such as want to lay by, and wait the Issue . . . endeavouring to play a d[ou]ble game, in which their present protections may . . . become a sure card."

Clark conceded that Washington did not wish to be a dictator. The loyalty-testing program at issue was the result, Clark felt, of evil influences in Washington's entourage, who had misled the overburdened general. But Congress had censured Lee for doing in New York precisely what Washington was imposing upon Jersey citizens. Congressional consistency and state dignity required similar censure for the latter offender. His resolution met the hard wall of Washington's congressional defenders; John Adams reported that the loyalty proclamation was "prudent and necessary." The state of New Jersey was not yet done, however, with the Continental Army commander.

Late in February, 1777, Governor Livingston of New Jersey asked Washington about the form of oath his military officers had required of Jersey civilians, in order to judge if the army test usurped a state loyalty oath that had graced the brand-new statute books of New Jersey since the past September. Washington was embarrassed. He could not supply the form of the army oath because he had set no form. And he had to admit that he had not even known the state oath law existed. For the latter, Washington was not to blame. The Jersey oath law applied only to state officials, not to common citizens, and it had not even had time to be printed before the British had taken over the state! Still, there it was on the books. Washington admitted partial error and happily let the matter drop. In any event, it was a teapot tempest, for by that time his commanders had completed their loyalty-testing program, the nonjurors to the army oath were already on their way to New York exile, and Washington had more to do than spill ink in argument with New Jersey. He had a bloody war on his hands with a British force readying to strike at Philadelphia.[42]

The lessons of the Jersey incident sank home. Never again during the Revolution did Washington, the Continental Army, or Congress presume to impose loyalty tests upon civilians, except for civil officials of Congress or the army. This does not mean that loyalty-testing ceased behind Whig lines. On the contrary, it increased, but was marked by decentralization and lack of standardization. Continental troops used state loyalty tests when such inquisitorial devices were necessary, and turned over to state authorities those who failed the tests by nonjuring or false swearing. Congress' timid refusal to support Washington's desire for a standard, trans-American loyalty-testing program resulted in six long years of unsystematized, local loyalty-testing. From early 1777 until the end of the Revolution, loyalty was a local matter.

In one area of loyalty-testing the Continental Army retained a relatively free hand. The self-conscious states insisted, indeed, that Washington bind his soldiers to patriotism by every available device, and loyalty tests seemed the obvious answer. So in October, 1776, Congress required that every soldier take an oath of allegiance to the United States and of obedience to Congress' commissioned officers. But as 1776 and 1777 passed their doleful events in review, Washington and Congress agreed that treason needed a tighter test to prevent its infection from further weakening the rebel forces. Washington pressured the harried congressmen to revise the soldier's oath to include abjuration of allegiance to Great Britain. Howe's successful Philadelphia campaign, in which hundreds of American military and civil officials, congressional and state, and thousands of ordinary civilians, proved false to earlier loyalty oaths to state and nation, underlined the urgency of Washington's pleas. A committee of Congress (which at different times included George Wythe, Robert Treat Paine, Charles Carroll, and James Wilson) consolidated earlier suggestions of means to "prevent persons disaffected to the interest of the United States from being employed in any of the important offices thereof." Early in February, 1778, Congress agreed to a new loyalty test for all federal civil and military officers to swear:

I ――― do acknowledge the United States of America to be free, independent and sovereign states, and declare that the people thereof owe no allegiance or obedience to George the 3d, King of Great Britain; and I renounce, refuse and abjure any allegiance or obedience to him; and I do swear (or affirm) that I will, to the utmost of my power, support, maintain, and defend the said United States against the said King George 3d and his heirs and successors, and his and their abettors, assistants and adherents, and I will serve the said United States in the office of ——— which I now hold, with fidelity, according to the best of my skill and understanding. So help me God.

Since Congress particularly feared treason in high military office (eleven of the twelve generals had formerly held royal commissions, and three were English-born Royal Army veterans), it required that nonjurors be cashiered, forfeit two months' pay, and face perpetual exclusion from government service. Optimistically, Congress required all officers to subscribe the new test within twenty days of its proclamation.[43] Washington had more pressing martial duties. Only after repeated importunities from Congress, and the threat of restricting postwar pensions to those who signed immediately, did Washington finally sign the new oath himself and arrange for his subordinate officers to affirm their loyalty. Washington assembled his generals and all signed except the unpredictable Charles Lee, who hesitated at renouncing the Prince of Wales. Lee finally signed. Benedict Arnold was absent, but signed later.

The spring months of 1778 witnessed successive swearing ceremonies as Washington's belated but urgent orders impelled subordinate officers to repeat the new formula of loyalty. In fact, the process went too quickly, and supplies of the oath forms ran out. Special messengers hurried new stocks to Washington's headquarters a half-dozen times and still could not keep up with the demand. Other administrative complications ensued because of deficient camp communications to men absent on leave, in scattered outposts, or in hospitals. Washington appointed special officers in his provost corps to travel from Canada to Georgia administering oaths, so that none of his officers should incur the financial penalties of innocent nonjuring. The momentous events then occurring made the loyalty-testing requirement a vexatious, time-consuming detail.[44]

It became more sinister when Washington learned that more than two dozen junior officers of one regiment were conspiring to refuse the oath, causing "some little boggle in this matter in other corps." Unsure whether treason or temperament was involved, unwilling to make a public display of his officers' disobedience and thus admit weakness in the already dispirited Continental ranks, Washington decided to do a little loyalty-investigating on his own. He assigned the Marquis de Lafayette to this delicate task. The French officer's report was a lengthy plea for Washington not to equate nonjuring with disloyalty. Lafayette learned that the recalcitrant officers felt that the new oath was a slur upon individual honor and collective dignity. Somewhat less idealistically, they feared that subscribing the congressional test would "freeze" them in their existing ranks and in perpetual subjection to Washington's leadership. But no taint of disloyalty, Lafayette insisted, was involved.

Convinced, Washington took time to counter each of the nonjuring officers' fears. He insisted that no diminution of dignity or binding agreement as to rank or command was concerned. Feeling that "every Oath should be a free act of the mind, founded on the conviction . . . of its propriety," Washington permitted nonjurors to use individual discretion "and [to] swear or not swear, as their conscience or feelings dictate." He also took advantage of the occasion to lecture his disobedient subordinates on the proper channels of military protest. His forbearance, and the nonjurors' isolation in this matter, succeeded. Every one of them signed the loyalty test.[45]

Washington continued enforcing the congressional loyalty oath for the duration of hostilities. Deserters from American ranks who, succumbing to Tory blandishments, violated their oaths, received harsh and immediate punishment. Fifty lashes in one instance, the death penalty in another, met enlisted offenders against the American loyalty tests. Commissioned officers who failed to sign the necessary oaths suffered courts-martial, loss of pay, reduction in ranks, and, in some instances, cashiering from the service. Manuals of military procedure continually cautioned army commanders to see to it that all new officers were properly sworn: "It is indispensable to their being admitted on duty." But the most diligent overseership failed to make the loyalty requirement operate smoothly. All through the war, and as late as October, 1782, Congress was forced to withhold pay from officers delinquent in oath-taking.

But in a sense far more basic than administrative inefficiency, the congressional loyalty test for civil and military officials failed. The major traitors of the time were fully sworn by this formula to loyalty to America. In a land rent by civil war, where linguistic and physical attributes failed to demarcate sides, such double-dealings were common. Congress' army test oath failed, therefore, to achieve its purposes. But Washington continued enforcing it as Congress required.[46]

The American states, jealous of their loyalty-testing prerogatives, refused the Continental Congress and the Army leadership in this field, but gave full attention to Washington's advice that "every State . . . fix upon some oath or affirmation of allegiance, to be tendered to all the inhabitants without exception, and to outlaw those that refuse it." The Declaration of Independence made the Continental Association boycott agreement obsolete as a loyalty test. British martial successes were, Washington felt, due in part to the lack of American loyalty tests, for many "well-wishers" to the American cause had succumbed to British power "for want of the necessary tie." Only those who swore loyalty to American independence, he agreed with Thomas Jefferson, should enjoy the "full rights" of citizenship, and "all who have not full rights are secret enemies." [47]

By 1778 every state boasted a treason law, varying widely from one another despite the common Tory and British enemy. As the preamble to Virginia's treason statute proclaimed, there were certainly "divers opinions" concerning "what cases shall be adjudged treason, and what not." Military support of the Crown was treason in Pennsylvania, while conspiracy to levy war against the state satisfied Massachusetts. New Hampshire rated as traitor anyone seducing citizens from their proper allegiance or asserting that the state's policies were deficient or that the obligations of earlier royal oaths were still in effect. The most common element was the offense of joining the enemy.

Since strictly defined acts of treason were difficult to prove and slow and costly to prosecute, all the states punished offenses less than treason, but injurious to the American cause. Bills of attainder and property confiscation laws served the American states by depriving Tory citizens of their assets while the disloyal owners were out of patriot reach behind British lines. Each state, had, by 1778, created a loyalty test for all its residents to swear. These loyalty tests were supposed to provide the first clear indication of which civilian was openly ready to place himself on record in favor of his state and nation, and which not. Nonjurors faced patterns of coercion different in each state, but basically similar in purposes and techniques. Those who refused state oath tests came under suspicion as potential disloyalists. If persistent in nonjuring, they faced imprisonment, fines, attainder proceedings, and possible exile into British lines after state authorities confiscated their property. Less officially, nonjurors faced the bitterness and almost unchecked vengeance of their neighbors.

New state authorities, from their inceptions, turned to the old association-enforcing Whig committees for sustenance and personnel. Committeemen screened potential voters and delegates to state constitutional conventions to insure that no known or suspected Tory exercised the privilege of loyal citizenship. The resulting state governments again used the extralegal Whig committees to cleanse slates of office-holders from any taint of disloyal candidates. These governments then created treason laws, attainder bills, confiscation acts, and loyalty tests. Lacking money, experience, and above all, time, the new American state governments turned once more to the Whig committees, regularized them by law into the state's administrative apparatus, and made them the local enforcers of state laws on loyalty. In every state, committeemen became loyalty enforcers, the founts of indictments for treason, attainder, and confiscation actions, and the appliers of state loyalty tests. In this manner the transference of power was made smoothly and quickly, permitting rebeldom simultaneously to create thirteen regular state governments in the midst of civil war, keep Tories in check, and resist British power.[48]

Giants of the Revolutionary generation, despite disappointment that the central government had not assumed the antidisloyalty task, were relieved that the job was now taken in hand by some authority. Revolutionary leaders fully agreed with General Greene's admonition that "patriotism is a glorious principle, but never refuse her the necessary aids." John Jay, soon to be New York State's chief loyalty tester, saw the Declaration of Independence as the Rubicon for all men, and welcomed the task of learning which bank of allegiance each man chose. John Adams and Washington agreed that loyalty tests were the cornerstone of discipline for troops and the source of patriotism for civilians, and Adams proved from classical history and Christian experience that loyalty oaths were wonder-workers in causes sacred and profane. Tom Paine, convinced that a "person . . . must be a Whig or a Tory in a lump," devoted successive issues of the *Crisis* papers to pleas for states to create, then firmly to enforce, stern loyalty tests by which patriots might know whom to trust and whom to punish *before* secret disloyalists injured the war effort. In the present crisis, Paine urged, patriots must measure the "public characters of all men," and "ought to know, square by square and house by house, who are in real allegiance with the United Independent States, and who are not. Let but the line be made clear and distinct, and all men will then know what they are to trust to." [49] But, unfortunately for the lofty purposes of Paine's plea and the needs of the American rebels for real internal security, no one was able to create the "clear and distinct" line of loyalty or to provide "the touchstone to try men by." Men used loyalty tests. They could not insure loyalty.

Insurrection Becomes Independence

The loyalty-testing processes of the American Revolution find their best illustration in the New York scene. In procedures regular and irregular, ranging from uncontrollable mobs to formal treason indictments, New York State was a model and a microcosm of rebel notions concerning the problem of internal security and the best methods of crushing disloyalty and insuring loyalty.

CHAPTER IV

Conceived in Liberty

In a vast inverted pyramid, New York State lay athwart the strategic center of insurgent America, its Hudson waterway connecting the inland Canadian border with the Atlantic far south in New York City. British command of that city and state could cut New England off from direct communication with the rest of the rebel states; Tory sentiment flourished there as nowhere else; loyalty there was a factor of unparalleled importance to both sides.

Whigs read maps as well as Britons. New York's provincial assembly, in the turbulent two years preceding the Declaration of Independence, encouraged Whig committees to enforce the Continental Association with liberal applications of terrorism and tar and feathers. But such sternness obviously failed to crush Tory conspiracies. Washington's troublesome adventures in military loyalty-testing early in 1775 centered on New York City. His efforts, however superficially successful, met the determined opposition of the provincial authorities to centralized policies within their jurisdiction.

July 4, 1776, separated preindependence tarring and feathering of Tories from the post-Declaration time of grimly professional loyalty-testing. Through 1776 and 1777, while British soldiers occupied New York City and inspired savage Indian raids on the state's exposed western and northern communities, New York created a state constitution and government. During that period, a congeries of extralegal committees, provincial authorities, and Continental forces suppressed Toryism as best they could. But a consistent thread is found in New York's search for a system of local loyalty-testing, as expressed in the resolution of the rebel state convention in late September, 1776, that "a committee be appointed for the express purpose of inquiring into and detecting all conspiracies which may be formed in this state against the

Liberties of America." Headed by John Jay, this commission entered enthusiastically upon its work, organized a secret service to spy upon suspect civilians behind rebel lines and within the British occupation zone, recruited its own thirty-man military company to enforce its decisions, and set up subcommittees in dozens of communities as watchdogs for the rebel cause. Existing Whig committees of preindependence days were absorbed into the commission's organization, thus retaining for the rebel cause the familiarity with local personalities and conditions which made Whig activities so effective.

The basic problem facing the New York loyalty probers was the proximity of the British stronghold in New York City. Refugees from British occupation and Tory repression there came before commission boards, pleading for sanctuary. Former Tories sought respectable Whig status and appealed for pardon for past errors and for exemptions from the penalties that normally accompanied such transgressions. Rebel patriots and spies submitted accusations of disloyalty which commission members had to sift. All this and more—travel passes, protection papers, mail censorship, trade permits—came before the commissioners, who had in almost every case to decide which appellant deserved punishment, succor, or privilege.

In conformity with the addiction of the times for loyalty tests, the New York commissioners created a measuring rod of fidelity to serve their needs as judges between the conflicting claims of individual civilians. All applicants for privileges, all accused of disloyalty, all former Tories or turncoating British soldiers, had as their first hurdle to swear a lengthy loyalty test which denied allegiance to Britain, promised loyalty and obedience to New York and to the Congress of rebel states, engaged the subscriber to expose and suppress all "Treasonable Plotts and Conspiracies," and ended with the declaration that his was an oath voluntarily sworn without mental reservation.

Throughout critical 1777, the rebel government of New York, beset with fear of British attack from east and north, relied heavily on state militia units and the Continental Army to court-martial disloyal civilians without even the cursory procedures the commission provided. Military hangmen made short work of presumed traitors, and cared not at all that these unfortunates bore certificates attesting to their earlier subscriptions to Whig loyalty tests. By midyear conditions were stable enough so that New York's Whigs began creating a permanent constitution, and offered an "act of grace" to convicted traitors who took the state test oath. A year later, the state created the second, permanent Commission for Detecting and Defeating Conspiracies with even broader powers, and with more intimate and regular channels interlocking it with other branches of the state's administration, especially with the property-confiscation apparatus. The two commissions together were the most important fact of life for thousands of New Yorkers from 1776 until hostilities ceased. Their personnel included some of the most influential men of the state—Philip Livingston, John Jay, Gouverneur Morris, John Beekman, Jeremiah Van Rensselaer, Leonard Gansevoort—at various times. But it was not prestige the commissioners enjoyed, but power.[1]

New York's legislature provided its commission with plenty of power. State laws echoed the commission-drawn loyalty test. It was the prerequisite for suffrage, office-holding, practicing law or other licensed professions, and residence and citizenship. Legislators authorized the commission to impose the test in all the varied cases involving "disloyalty," to punish nonjuring in cases short of treason, and to pardon transgressions by obtaining resubscriptions to the oath. By the end of 1777, the commission had woven a web of surveillance wherever rebel arms held sway. Possessed of their own militia force, commissioners issued warrants such as this for the arrest of accused individuals:

Whereas Peter M'Lean, . . . Shoemaker, stands charged with dangerous Designs and treasonable Conspiracies against the Rights of Liberties of . . . America, we so . . . require you to cause the said Peter M'Lean to be with all his Papers forthwith apprehended and secured.

The commissioners assumed power to correspond with governors of neighboring states and with the Continental Congress in order to arrange for safe detention centers for nonjuring Tories, and for Continental troops to assist the commissioners' forces in special instances. They exiled wives and children of Tories along with husbands and fathers, which evoked a blast from Governor Clinton putting a stop to the practice, except when the loyalty commissioners felt that the females and minors were really disloyal. The commissioners assumed the power, too, to begin confiscation proceedings, despite the existence of a sequestration board charged with that specific duty. But at the base of all the legitimate or assumed powers of the loyalty commission was the loyalty test, the oath of loyalty to state and nation.[2]

Under its wide powers to require every suspect New Yorker to subscribe the state's loyalty oath, the loyalty commission assembled long rosters of nonjurors. Commissioners equated nonjuring with disloyalty, asserting that an accused person's refusal to swear loyalty was the capstone of "sundry overt acts of disloyalty to this and the other United

States." Nonjurors were of many kinds. Some who at first refused later changed their minds and begged for a second opportunity, normally granted, to swear. Others held fast to their decisions, broke up their homes, and, in dreary convoys, waited for flag-of-truce arrangements to take them into British lines. More dangerous-seeming nonjurors were less lucky and went to prison. Benjamin Baker, for example, refused to swear the oath, "and declared that if he did he would perjure himself and that none but fools and rogues would take it." The commission jailed him without delay.

Wholesale nonjuring was a vexing problem, for no available prisons were large enough to accommodate entire villages. Argyle, New York, was visited by a British-Hessian-Tory patrol early in 1778, and its residents swore future neutrality in the war to avoid having their homes burned. When the British force left, the rebel loyalty commission returned to Argyle, and ordered its people to reswear the rebel oath. Initial confusion concerning which loyalty test took precedence ended in a decision to exempt Argyle from the general loyalty requirement, apply an American oath of neutrality to match the British oath, and hope that news of the privilege did not become too common. Quakers, too, were an annoyance. Refusing all oaths, yet living peaceably, they defied even the fearful power of the commissioners. New York finally decided to permit twelve non-Quakers to swear as proxy for each oathless Friendly neighbor as a public relations measure to counter Tory assertions of rebel harshness.[3]

By the strict letter of New York State law, the commission's power was far from unlimited. It could confine possible disloyalists at will, but in order formally to arrest them it had to secure indictments from civil grand juries. In some cases, grand jurymen, more familiar with the realities of loyalty in their neighborhoods than the loyalty commissioners, released accused persons for want of convincing evidence of disloyalty. But such cases were rare, and this apparent check on commission power was more theoretical than real. It took a brave grand juror publicly to taint himself by freeing persons accused of disloyalty, and an even braver attorney to risk his own freedom and career by defending a nonjuring, self-proclaimed "enemy to American liberty." Commissioners sometimes proved themselves humble enough to admit doubt concerning their abilities to judge men's inner motives, and petitioned the supreme court of the state for its opinion concerning the sincerity of a proffered loyalty oath. Such instances were also rare. The overwhelming majority of disloyalty accusations were commission business from start to finish.[4]

One case may serve best to illustrate loyalty-testing procedures in New York. Peter van Schaack of Kinderhook followed a Whiggish path in the early dissent against British policies, and served as a Whig committeeman until a local variant of the Continental Association faced him with the choice of swearing to take up arms against Britain or of abandoning his former comrades. He decided to refuse the association, and throughout 1775 and 1776 he lived quietly, except for the taunts and insults of Whig rowdies. Van Schaack simply wished to remain neutral, especially after the Declaration of Independence demanded separation from the mother country. But the state loyalty commission decided otherwise. Late in 1776 it proffered him the loyalty test. Schaack refused it. In December the commission ordered him to leave for a Boston exile within ten days.

Schaack enjoyed high social and political status. He went over the commission's head and appealed directly to the New York assembly, pleading to be left in neutral peace. In phrases powerfully buttressed by Montesquieu and Locke, he justified nonjuring. New York State, Schaack insisted, could not ethically require a loyalty oath to itself before the state was fully established. Nor should the loyalty commission exercise tyrannical powers in order to fight British despotism. How was any man to know precisely when the bond of allegiance to Britain was fully sundered? How was any state to demand this act of moral faith by force?

In Schaack's view, an honest man must exercise his "right to choose the State of which he will become a member." Should he decide to abandon Britain, he need not assume New York as his lawful sovereign. The "immutable laws of nature" of which the Declaration of Independence grandly spoke were Schaack's major defenses for his position. He insisted that if New York did not want him for mistaken reasons, then he had the full power to locate where he wished, and to take all his property with him. His obedience to Whig law entitled him to Whig protection. Schaack insisted that his nonjuring to Whig oaths was a matter of principle, but a matter on which no sacrifice would make him compromise.

Schaack's literary eloquence and powerful friends secured him a stay of sentence on his parole of neutrality. But his happiness was short-lived. In 1777 his wife's health deteriorated. Schaack's pleas for permission to take her to British-occupied New York City for medical care met the suspicious refusal of the loyalty commissioners, and Mrs. van Schaack died without recourse to the help she needed. Van Schaack's father died at almost the same time, and there began a sad progression of fatalities among his children. As if to cap his cup of sorrow, Schaack's eyesight began to fail.

In mid-1778 he appealed to Governor Clinton for a pass to go to England for ocular treatment, and was pleased to receive it. But, almost simultaneously, a summons from his old nemesis, the loyalty commissioners, brought him once more before that unfriendly body. Some of the commissioners had never forgiven Schaack for evading them the year before. Now armed with even greater powers, the commissioners again ordered Schaack to swear the state loyalty oath. He again refused. The commission, in conformity with New York State's 1778 "Banishing Act" sentenced Schaack to perpetual exile and confiscated his property. Sadly, Schaack succumbed to power beyond his ability to counter. To the commission's secretary, Leonard Gansevoort, Schaack's former law student, the bereaved man expressed his dismay at seeing Gansevoort's signature formalizing the decree of exile: "Leonard! you have signed my death warrant."

Schaack prepared to leave his home forever. He busied himself writing commentaries on the events that had made him a convicted and exiled traitor to his country because he had refused to swear loyalty to his state. He pointed to American protests against British parliamentary legislation a decade earlier, which had denied omnipotent power to any lawmaker. Could New York's current legislature, in loyalty oath and banishing laws, assume what its members had earlier denied? Public safety could not justify public tyranny. Making banishment contingent upon individual subscription to a loyalty test, Schaack insisted, was absurd. Swearing loyalty was a matter for conscientious consideration by every individual. Men who swore easily were the untrustworthy ones, not those who carefully considered the ethical, moral, and juridical aspects of what they swore. "If the propositions . . . in the oath are agreeable to their principles," he admonished, "it adds no obligation to allegiance which did not previously exist." No just man would swear an unjust oath. No man wishing to be neutral, as he was, could swear an oath of unconditional loyalty, for by that act neutral conduct was not merely unethical, but unlawful. But what was the consequence of such rectitude?

We are called before a board for punishing conspirators, when we are acknowledged to be no conspirators; before a board unknown to the constitution of this State, to be condemned without a trial, and to be punished without a crime. The utmost extent of all that is alleged, amounts to no more than a difference of opinion. . . . Measures calculated to make hypocrites, will naturally produce deception. Have you never been deceived by persons who have taken the oath of allegiance? Why then do you impose it?

But logic failed before the needs of loyalty. About to take ship for exile in England, Schaack sadly penned a parting note to his past friend, John Jay, the present loyalty tester. He repeated much of what he had already written, and pleaded with Jay to return to libertarian principles the Whigs seemed to have forgotten:

I think it is manifestly improper to tender it [the oath of allegiance] to persons of opposite principles, because it is a temptation to perjury, . . . because, if taken, it adds no obligation in point of morality, . . . because . . . it gives no security to the public; and I think this measure most cruel, because it is carried on at a time when no *state necessity* (which, though sometimes a reality is often a phantom, to which numbers of virtuous men have been made victims) can be made to justify it.

So Peter van Schaack, aged, weak in body but firm in spirit, left his home for a bitter exile he had neither desired in his conscience nor earned by his conduct. His name became a synonym for sedition among New York's rebel authorities, and it lingered into future generations, so that eighty years later in another American civil conflict, men said of his grandson that "the blood is tainted." [5] The records tell of others like Schaack, of many who swore loyalty unthinkingly and went to rebel or British prisons despite their oaths or because they violated them uncaringly, and of other men who survived the conflict unhurt despite multiple conflicting oaths. Records fail to tell, however, that the security of New York or the cause of American independence were rendered a whit stronger by all the oaths taken or refused.

Twelve other rebel states constructed loyalty-testing systems which differed from New York's only in details. In every state, once the British threat lessened, wartime loyalty tests proved useful for partisan politics and for achieving personal ends. There was, for example, the Maryland community where one Thomas Kerr had, long before the rebellion, incurred a full measure of local hatred. He swindled honest folk with defective plows, cheated his landlords on rents due them, and was too successful at cards. When war came, Kerr encouraged other men to join the rebel militia, but remained safely at home himself. A group of women in the village, bereft of their husbands because of Kerr's persuasiveness, finally could bear the sight of him no longer. They swore to a state security commissioner that Kerr was a Tory. At the hearing collusive witnesses stated that Kerr had cursed the commonwealth "and their God damned Laws . . . [and that] he would go . . . and take that [state] Oath and he would be no better Whig now than he would be then, that but for his wife and children he would have a Red Coat on directly."

Kerr, no angel and no patriot, was also no traitor, but he went to jail for misprision of treason, of which crime he was innocent. Not unsimilar charges of past Toryism, of perjury in swearing to loyalty tests, infested local politics in the United States during the Revolution and for some uncertain, varying period, depending upon the locality, after hostilities ceased. It was simpler at the height of the war. Then one of Washington's officers, who was coöperating with the New York loyalty commission, could order Continental troops to round up some "disaffected persons," with the injunction that

. . . if they will not come within the lines and swallow the oath of allegiance with a good stomach you must take the trouble to bring them in and use your utmost endeavours by usage becoming such villains to make them after a season valuable subjects.[6]

How valuable such subscribers became is doubtful. But thirteen state loyalty-testing apparatuses, plus the coöperating Continental Army, combed as much of America as they could and swore as many Americans as they could. The real purpose of all the loyalty laws and of the enforcing commissions was not to find any loyalty but to prevent disloyalty. Disloyalty to America multiplied where royal power was strong. This simple equation of fidelity and fear was quite clear to rebel civil and military commanders. Its opposite face, that loyalty to the king flourished where redcoats conquered, formed the basic strategical element for a succession of British commanders.

Far back in 1775 many Englishmen and Tories saw the problem of suppressing insurrection in quite simple terms. As the Marquess of Hastings, on duty with the British Army in Boston, wrote in easy confidence to a London friend, "You wished . . . that they [the Whigs] would oppose us in the field, and get heartily trimmed." Lexington and Concord provided "one part of your wish, and sooner or later [you] will undoubtedly have the other."[7] But British policy was ever two-edged, calling for martial force and simultaneously seeking reconciliation with the unruly colonists. Beset by these conflicting claims of duty, General Gage waited in Boston, while helpless Tories across America complained that Gage was far too lenient. "Had a few [Whigs] been killed at first," mourned one Tory sufferer from a Whig committee's attentions, "the rest would have been quiet." If Gage had but hoisted the royal standard, he predicted, "thousands would flock to it, that are as yet afraid to declare their sentiments." Britain *must* mark its friends in order to punish its enemies, insisted another Tory: "Why is not the King's standard erected if they mean to make any difference?" [8]

This was the basic British dilemma. Mere justice dictated that royal officers should succor Tories and convince uncommitted colonists to remain loyal. Imperial policy demanded that the king's officials should crush and punish Whigs and defeat rebel armed forces. But British military might was not unlimited. American territory was vast. The problem was to determine the best way to realize these ends at once.

Tory refugees from Whig wrath, safe in British-held Boston, convinced Gage and through him the British ministry that the American hinterland was basically loyal to the king. Only a few sinister leaders— Henry, the Adams duo, Hancock, the vexed Congregational clergy and Whig committeemen—were causing all the trouble. British generals should tap the El Dorado of loyalism by "invading" Whig territory, offering royal loyalty oaths to counter Whig associations, and inspiring counterrevolution to defeat the rebels. In return, British power must provide protection against Whig vengeance. It all seemed simple. Sworn loyalists would supplement thin British army lines and receive royal protection, and the Empire would gain the full fruits of loyalism. Nonjuring Whigs would receive their just deserts in British military and civil courts. The very idea was enough to make committee-ridden Tories rejoice in anticipation of revenge.

Although Gage had strong doubts concerning the reality of this roseate dream, he obediently set about carrying out his orders. Even while his troops drilled to crush Whig militiamen, his printers prepared impressively embossed copies of the first royal loyalty-testing proclamation of what was not yet, in early 1775, an American revolution. All colonists were to appear before their respective royal governors (many of whom were in unapproachable exile) and swear the royal oath of allegiance. Gage excluded only Sam Adams and John Hancock from the general amnesty which all swearers were to receive. It might work; a similar policy used in a very small area in East Florida in 1774 had succeeded. As Lord Dartmouth noted to Gage,

Such a plan, at the same time that it holds out a proper test of that disposition towards submission which you seem to think begins to show itself, will leave no excuse for those who shall refuse to make such submission, and will mark the necessity of . . . bringing to condign punishment those whose crimes have rendered them unfit subjects of the King's mercy.[9]

But Gage's proclamation was issued in a post-Lexington atmosphere redolent with bitter emotionalism. It found relatively few takers except in Boston where British power was strong and where most royal oath swearers were in any event already known as loyal Tories. Then, in stunning succession, came the Whig counterblockade of Boston, the capture of Ticonderoga and the invasion of stubbornly loyal Canada, and the gory, glorious fray at Bunker Hill. How fundamentally unsuccessful this first royal loyalty-testing experiment was may be measured by the fact that a moderate Virginian like George Washington ignored it and assumed command of the Continental forces besieging Gage in Boston. While all this was going on, Congress and conservative Whigs still claimed that they were loyal to George III. Nauseated by such patent hypocrisy, one bitter Tory penned a caustic essay, *The Strictures of a Loyal Yankee* (1775), which he discreetly circulated in manuscript among his most trusted New York friends, and in which he derided Whigs who "daily profess great loyalty to the King while our hearts are far from him; and in the same breath we drink damnation to him in our hearts—and with the same degree of insincerity we again profess our submission." [10]

King George had had enough. In August, 1775, he declared the American colonies in rebellion, ordered them blockaded, and commanded all loyal Americans to aid in suppressing the rebels. Gage dutifully published the royal edict and reissued his offer of pardon to all colonists willing to swear the royal loyalty test. For some Americans, the king's proclamation settled matters. They made their way, if they could, to British lines, swore the royal oath, and awaited events. Most colonists remained passive, however, unwilling and fearful to commit themselves in the unstable situation. And a few found British sternness the final justification for deciding on anti-British Whiggism. As one colonist expressed it, the royal loyalty order was "putting the halter around our necks, and we may as well die by the sword as be hanged like rebels." [11]

For most American Tories, Gage's loyalty-testing and military operations were dismal failures. They had asked for action, and he had replied with a loyalty-oath proclamation that merely inspired Whig committeemen to greater excesses. As the bitter poetry of John Trumbull expressed it:

> The annals of his first year:
> While wearying out the Tories' patience,

He spent his breath in proclamations;
While all his mighty noise and vapor
Was used in wrangling upon paper; . . .
While stroke alternate stunned the nation,
Protest, address, proclamation;
And speech met speech, fib clashed with fib,
And Gage still answered squib for squib.[12]

But such criticisms failed to swerve Britain from her course. Successive royal commanders sought an American land of unalloyed loyalism for eighty years of war. In the process British generals lost reputations and Britain lost America. Lacking unity in policy, and with inadequate armies to provide the promised protection in return for her proffered oaths, Britain gained not strength but weakness from her loyalty-testing program.

Sir William Howe followed Gage as British commander in America. Howe had royal permission to follow the lines Gage had set—martial suppression of rebellion and merciful amnesty to rebel oath takers. He also was to support incumbent royal governors, almost all of whom, in mid-1775, were in exile from their Whig-dominated colonies. One such official, Governor Dunmore of Virginia, dreamed of sparking Virginia's Tories into opposition to Whig control. But Dunmore mixed loyalty oaths with racial prejudices, and in the resulting witches' brew Howe's pardon program received a travesty of a trial.

After initial successes in securing Virginians' subscriptions to the royal oath, coincident with promises of British protection in return, Dunmore wrecked his auspicious beginning by freeing Negro slaves and indentured servants of rebel masters. To Virginians of whatever politics, this was outrageous interference with their "peculiar institution." Virginia's Whigs revived; Dunmore and his tattered remnants fled to the safety of British warships, whence he briefly sallied forth to burn Norfolk, thus further sullying Britain's already damaged reputation in the colony.

For the bulk of Virginia's Tories, Dunmore's flight blasted the tissue of British promises. They had exposed themselves to Whig wrath and had sworn loyalty to the king, who had promised them protection. Now there was no protection. Many Tories consequently abandoned their oaths to the king in favor of the Continental Association. Whig leaders wisely refrained from punishing any but the most prominent of the erstwhile loyalists, and were satisfied to move the latter to inland locations far from British influence. Dunmore's optimistic pledge to

98

Virginia Tories—"I promised you protection and that I will give you"
—became a butt of Whig satire throughout America.[13]

Despite this setback, Howe continued on the British loyalty-testing
course. He organized loyalist companies in Boston, and was overjoyed
to learn that Joseph Galloway of Pennsylvania and Governor Tryon
of New York boasted that thousands of known Tories waited only for
the British Army to appear in order to assert their loyalty.[14] The early
months of 1776 brought further uncertainty to Tory hopes. North
Carolina loyalists suffered the same fates as their Virginia neighbors.
This disappointment seemed as nothing compared to Howe's abandonment of Boston. When Howe sailed to Nova Scotia he carried with him
hundreds of American Tories, erstwhile citizens of all the American
colonies, who preferred exile in an unknown land to the prospect of
rebel wrath when Washington occupied Boston. Howe knew that his
retreat was mere preparation for an attack on New York. But Whigs
jubilated as Tory prestige sank all over America. Richard Henry Lee,
for instance, exulted about "our enemies' shameful flight from Boston," where, Lee asserted, "they left to the resentment of an injured
country, many Tories to whom they had promised protection." To
John Adams, Howe's flight was proof of rebel rectitude, and justification for outright independence from Britain. As Adams expressed it,
for Americans to continue in nominal allegiance to George III, "to
take [royal] oaths of allegiance . . . is such an absurdity, such irre-
ligion, that I am amazed it can be endured in any one spot in
America." The date of Adams' comment was April 15, 1776. The
"absurdity" had less than two months to endure.[15]

Then, as if to underline the ridiculousness of rebel pretensions to
independence in mid-1776, Lord Howe's redcoats relentlessly rolled
Washington back from Whig positions on Long Island, in New York
City, and in New Jersey. Everywhere in this area where Washington
had so recently and thoroughly applied rebel loyalty tests, royal forces
received ardent popular welcome.

Howe made New York City a center of royal power, a haven for
Toryism, and a strategic base for future attacks. All three purposes
found, in Howe's view, invaluable assistance in the royal oath and
pardon policy. His heralds and agents spread the proclamation in the
newly occupied territory and deep into Whig fastnesses. The first results were vastly encouraging to Howe and discouraging to rebel commanders. As John Adams recorded,

Many of the [Americans] . . . are natives of England . . . who have indentured over here. . . . They have no Tie to this country—They have no principles. They love Howe as well as Washington, and his Army better than ours.
These things give Howe great opportunity to corrupt and seduce them.

What was seduction to Adams was a proper patriotic passion to
Howe. His military subordinates made life inside the British lines
around New York City one long, repetitive, determined essay in creating loyalty, or at least conformity, by loyalty-testing. As one rebel
refugee from British occupation bitterly noted,

General Tryon with his Aid du Camps and 1500 of the Queen City Militia
. . . [went] to cram down the Oath of Allegiance in the rebellious counties. . . . After the business was done of making King's men of rebels, they
intended to have some hunting matches on Hempstead and Bushy Plains.

Such frivolity was all very well as a pastime, but Howe's orders made
British loyalty policies a very serious business. New Yorkers found that
royal military officers granted the scarce housing, food, and travel permits only to British oath takers. Merchants, preachers, teachers, arti-
sans, and professional men earned livings only by swearing loyalty to
the Crown. Property owners enjoyed protection from British soldiery
only if they displayed a certificate of having sworn. Necessities—firewood, food, shoes—and luxuries—mail, permits to buy or sell—were
only for those who swore loyalty. Nonjurors, if not dangerous, could
starve, so far as British policy was concerned. Some did. Oath takers
divided nonjurors' properties and privileges among themselves, and,
boasting British property protection certificates, made a good thing
out of British victory. Thousands of New Yorkers succumbed to such
personal pressures, repeated unceasingly for months and then years of
British occupation.

Since all who took the royal oath were, in theory, automatic recipients of the king's pardon for past rebellion, such swearers could again
vote and hold office. It is noteworthy that, in considering the resumption of civil government in New York in 1779, Lord Germain indicated
some doubt that royal oath takers had really achieved pure patriotism:
"It is . . . his Majesty's commandement," Germain ordered, "that you
do not appoint any person to . . . any . . . office, . . . of whose
Loyalty and attachment . . . there can be any ground to doubt." As a
practical matter, however, subscription to the royal loyalty oath was
the way for a repentant rebel to remove "any ground . . . [of] doubt"
from his record.[16]

British victories and statistically impressive successes in loyalty-testing brought defeatism and despondency to rebel hearts. The Continental Congress advised Philadelphians to accept the British pardons when redcoated forces defeated Washington near that city. Tory propagandists delighted to broadcast news of American defections. As one discouraged Continental officer wrote to his Connecticut father,

The British troops make headway wherever they attempt. . . . People join them almost in Captain's Companies to take the oath of allegiance. . . . Dear Father, no man, unless he be on the spot, can have a tolerable idea of it. . . . I am, Dear Sir, in great fear of our political salvation.[17]

Even Washington's bright courage momentarily dimmed before the success of Howe's pardon and loyalty-oath proclamations. He sadly read of the hundreds of prominent colonists in the New York–New Jersey–Pennsylvania triangle, who, after consistent Whig professions, had accepted Howe's terms. "Between you and me," Washington wrote his brother, "I think our affairs are in a very bad condition." More than Howe's troops occasioned his admission; Howe's loyalty-oath program was even more dangerous, for Americans "are making submissions as fast as they can." [18] George Washington's despondency was George III's happiness. By the end of 1778, Howe heard from London of the king's pleasure that

. . . so many of his faithful Subjects, of weight and credit, had come in, to avoid taking [rebel] Oaths which had been offered them, and that numbers of the People were inclined to accept the offers [of royal pardon]. . . . It has ever been the Opinion of His Majesty and His confidential Servants that such were the sentiments of a greater part of His Subjects . . . and that nothing but the Tyranny of their leaders prevented them from avowing it.

But London was a long way from America. General Howe learned that loyalty oaths were no guarantee of loyalty, and that his addiction to the royal pardon program absorbed more British military energies than its results warranted. Most subscribers to royal pardon applications added little to British power; more often such recreants, needing care, charity, and protection, were incubi to British officials.[19] And there were other reasons that belittled the seemingly impressive early effects of the royal loyalty program.

First, many Americans responded to the offer of royal pardon with an indignant rejection of the imputation that they had anything to seek pardon for. "I see the haughty Court of Great Britain . . . have sent an insulting Message offering pardon," noted Richard Henry Lee, and predicted, albeit erroneously, that Howe's proclamation "will be treated with the contempt it deserves." Similarly, a young New York City woman who refused the royal oath confided to her diary her indignation at the offer of British pardon:

Pardon! For What? A just indignation for rights trampled upon? It is said that many wealthy and influential persons have deserted the American cause. It is indeed a gloomy hour! But we *must* triumph. . . . It is God's decree that this people shall be free.[20]

Second, British loyalty-testing policies were marked from their inception by inconsistencies born of necessity on the one hand, and of unnecessary deviations from the king's orders caused by the vagaries of human nature on the other. Consider the problem of captured rebel war prisoners as an illustration of the first category. In British law, all armed traitors were susceptible of trial and capital punishment. But Britons were prisoners of rebels, too; rebel retaliation was probable should British treason trials become common. Britain was forced to treat captured rebels as war prisoners. But royal commanders needed recruits more than consistency in loyalty-testing. Captured Whigs might, if convinced of error or coerced by pressure, join royal regiments and man royal ships. "Able-bodied" Whigs were especially welcome, throughout the war, to become turncoats (royal warders were far less interested in the loyalty of ill, aged, or wounded Americans).

For many captured Americans, little pressure was needed. Facing indeterminate detention in foul prisons, hundreds lost enthusiasm for rebellion and changed sides by swearing the king's oath. Other American captives who claimed to have been forced into rebellion by coercive committees allegedly welcomed this opportunity to show their real convictions.[21] On the other hand, there were many captured rebels who displayed the best possible evidence of their loyalty to America; they refused to renounce their oaths to rebel authority and swear new loyalty tests to the king whom they had, in considered sincerity, cast off.

There was, for instance, the group of American prisoners who celebrated their second wretched Christmas in captivity on board a prison ship anchored off London by swearing to each other never to accept the king's oath and pardon. They solemnly cursed erstwhile comrades who had succumbed to the royal lure. Yet these brave men resolved not to condemn those who refused to join them in this defiant act, recognizing that no public gesture was real evidence of a man's inner convictions. Another English prison contained a captive American who, told he might receive a pardon upon recanting, retorted: "Pardon! D—— his Majesty and his pardon too. Who wants any of his pardons? What murder or treasons have we done pray?" The angered jailer threatened the stubborn prisoner with the noose and predicted that all rebels would hang when Britain conquered. "Overpower and subdue America—ah, that's the least of my concern," the captive responded. "You have not done it yet nor won't till the Devil's blind." [22]

Prisoners' resistance met British and Tory insistence. Recognizing that Americans were divided in civil war, British officials wisely permitted loyalist relatives and friends of captive rebels to do the king's work for them whenever possible. Loyalist Thomas Skinner's two sons joined the rebel army against his wishes, were captured, and heard from their father, whom Howe permitted to visit their New York prison, that he "would disinherit them, and never speak to them again, unless they would quit the [American] service, which they did." Less successful was the father of a captive rebel, who, armed with a copy of the royal oath proclamation, visited his son at the vile prison compound in New York's Old Sugar House. "Did you not see his excellency's proclamation," the irate Tory demanded, "wherein was set forth a free grace and pardon to all who would come in voluntarily? Why then did you not . . . quit the rebels?" The son, ill from battle wounds and prison conditions, could muster enough strength of will to chance alienating his beloved parent:

Father, you . . . must know that it was a very trying thing to me, to leave all my dear friends and turn myself out in the world naked, when I had not a friend or relative . . . but what were enemies to this once happy country. Believe me, dear father, I was not led astray by any man as you suppose. But on the contrary I weighed the matter carefully before I came into the [rebel] service, and the more I meditated the more I was led to believe that the cause in which my countrymen were engaged was a just one, and loudly called for the assistance of every well-wisher of his bleeding country.[23]

So the claims of patriotism often clashed with those of paternal affection, filial devotion, or even marital ties, and sometimes the victor was the royal loyalty policy. In other instances rebel allegiance kept its power over men in the face of brutal imprisonment and tearful pleas of loved ones. It was, according to a bitter woman whose father's Anglican ministership found expression in loyalty to the Crown, and whose husband's patriotism resulted in his Continental service as a rebel captain, a time when one saw on every hand "brother lifting up sword against brother, in unnatural warfare." Loyalty tests accentuated the civil nature of the war and made its expression more terrible than it would otherwise have been.[24] But humanitarian considerations were of little moment in the face of logistical needs for men.

Another cause of inconsistency in royal loyalty-testing, graver than personnel needs, was the pressure of vengeful Tories. From all over America during the long years of war, loyalists flocked to the only permanent haven of safety in New York City. They had suffered abuses to their bodies and losses to their purses because of their loyalty to the king. Most Tories felt that the only suitable reward for past Whiggism was not royal forgiveness on any terms, but a royal noose or Tory whipping squad. Loyalists had prepared treasured black lists of Whigs whom they destined for Tory vengeance. Royal officials joined Whig-hunting expeditions in newly occupied British areas, venting special spleen upon rebel committee personnel. William Franklin, for instance, "swares he will hang every one of those Committeemen and others that have sworn to the King . . . and then taken arms against the King afterwards," and New York's royal governor, Tryon, offered a reward of twenty-five silver dollars for every committeeman captured.[25] But vengeance upon former tormentors clashed with royal policy when hapless Whig committeemen received the king's pardon after swearing his oath. Almost always, vengeance took first place on the illogical agenda of human priority.

Whig propagandists quickly seized upon this handy cudgel. What value had Howe's promises of personal and property protection to royal oath takers when Howe's Tory officials persecuted whomever they wished? When British and Hessian troops, caring little for fine shades in colonial consciences, carelessly looted the property of consistent Tories and repentant Whigs alike, rebel criticisms of the value of the king's oath received the pragmatic affirmation of dreadful events. Soon after Howe invaded Long Island, for instance, a rebel officer reported that Howe's oath commissioners had issued hundreds of protection certificates to pardon seekers, but

. . . this did not exempt them from plunder when their new friends came across them. The country that we have reconnoitered since the enemy fell lower down is a scene of desolation. The poor people are pillaged of even their wearing apparel. Is this the promised *Peace, Liberty,* and *Safety?* [26]

British and Tory behavior to British oath takers made a travesty of British promises of protection. Howe's repetitive orders that such deviations from his program must cease were of little avail. Poor administration, inadequate channels of redress for the victims, and deliberate evasions of his orders diminished the value of swearing British oaths. Howe insisted that every American who swore loyalty to Britain should do so freely; British officials rounded up whole villages and, at bayonet points, under threat of immediate imprisonment or worse for nonjurors, with little care for nuances of individual interpretations of loyalty, staged mass swearing ceremonies. British threats to "destroy the whole country," if nonjuring persisted, could not be carried out, but the very threats belied Howe's mission as conciliator.[27] Howe meant well, but controlled his soldiers and the Tories less well. "And yet they speak of peace," taunted John Jay, "but hold daggers in their hands." To Tom Paine, the "only instance of . . . [British consistency] is that you have treated and plundered all alike." To a Whig South Carolinian, the "cruel edict" of the local British conqueror, that even women and children nonjurors must face exile into the wilderness, proved the unlikelihood of fair play from England. To rebels almost everywhere, except those directly under the guns of redcoats, there was no use for any American to swear loyalty to the king. It simply was not worth the effort.

Still, all might have been well for Howe's plans had his armies been able to hold the areas they conquered. Only New York City and its immediate environs remained permanently under royal control from 1776 until the end of the war. Here the British loyalty program worked at its best and most completely, despite inconsistencies. At least royal oath takers in New York were protected from rebel committeemen outside the British lines. But every other British occupation eventually failed; redcoated forces in Pennsylvania, Virginia, the Carolinas, and Rhode Island successively abandoned their positions. Each time the British retreated, albeit for the best of strategic reasons, they took with them many hundreds of despairing oath takers into exile, and left others behind to face the returning Whigs. In short, had Britain won more than mere battles, had royal arms *kept* the cities they had taken, then royal oaths might have meant more than they did to many colonists who cared little for rebellion but more for their own homes and skins.

Because Britain abandoned American cities and Tories, Americans learned to be cautious about taking British oaths. Rebel spokesmen exulted at this delightful turn of events. Paine pointedly reminded wavering Americans that Howe wanted soldiers rather than mere oath-taking, inactive sympathizers: "Your opinions are of no use to him unless you support him personally." American soldiers delighted to repeat this tale of Tory woe:

It seems a cowardly Tory of large landed estate in New York City had fled to the enemy in Philadelphia . . . and when he discovered their [imminent] departure . . . he applied . . . to know what he should do. The [British] officer told him he must . . . make the best shift he could. The Tory, still dissatisfied, told him all this was come on him for being loyal and faithful to the King and queried, what shall I do, I expected protection. The officer replied, go seek passage on board some vessel. The Tory with vehement anxiety queried, but what the Devil shall I do with my estate. The officer replied, Damn you, why did you not stay at home and fight to defend it . . . and so dismissed the applicant. . . . Then the disgruntled Tory returned home, mulled over his grievances, took the oath of allegiance to the state and to the United States, and enlisted in the Continental Army.[28]

In reciprocal, uncritical reaction, British officials grew increasingly careless of oath protection certificates in their disappointment at the scarcity of loyalist troops. Indeed, royal officials looked on uncaringly in some instances when illegal Whig vigilance committees beat turncoat rebels under the very guns of royal garrisons. "Happily," noted one high British officer, "not one honest man is injured upon the Occasion!" Britons, in short, became cynical about the worth of Americans' oaths, which were "making Loyalty a sure Game." Another British army officer, ready to retreat from Rhode Island, noted how the earlier enthusiasms of local Tories evaporated. He derided the British pardon policy and loyalty oaths, for he no longer believed in the promises of Americans. Howe's suggestion to Philadelphia Tories, as he prepared to evacuate that city, that they throw themselves upon Congress' mercy, abjure their British oaths, and reswear any rebel oath handy, increased cynicism concerning the worth of loyalty oaths in general and British oaths in particular among the men who should, theoretically, have held their value in the highest respect—the officers of the British Army. As General Burgoyne dolefully recorded after the Bennington reverse:

The knowledge that I acquired of the professors of "loyalty" was "fatal" and put an end to every expectation from enterprise. . . . Why did they not rise around Albany when they found Mr. Gates' army increasing by separate and distinct parties from remote distances? A critical insurrection from any one point would probably have assured the success of the campaign.[29]

Which came first—Tory disappointment at British defeats or British disillusionment at Tory promises—is of little moment. Perjury among a whole people, with mass and individual defections encouraged by British and rebel governments alike for their respective purposes, was the order of the day. From observations of imperfect human nature responding to elemental needs of survival by swearing to successive contradictory loyalty tests, came cynicism concerning human nature itself. On the Tory-British side, this pessimistic reaction is perhaps best expressed in the anonymous effort of a New Yorker who, in an epic *Toriade,* blasted the easy consciences of his countrymen:

> There's not a Rebel in this lengthy land
> Committee and subcommittee man, [but who]
> Are loyal all, and harmless as a hen
> I've done no harm, I've never took up gun, . . .
> Thus, thus, and thus, they carry one protest
> Believe me friend, they but rebelled in jest:
> For he, that was as black as a Jew's eye
> Faith, now comes out, as bright as old Tory. . . .
>
> Then issued forth a Proclamation free
> That all who would come in would pardon'd be
> This Proclamation, sixty days doth run
> Wishing that all, might to their King return,
> What more could King, or King's viceregents do
> For a deluded, wretched, rebel crew.
> Lo! Puritanic priests now preach and say
> Heed not, fight on my boys, till the Last-day,
> . . . And prevents good of Proclamation.
>
> Rhode Island now the British troops possess
> That rebel colony's metropolis
> Rebels think now 'tis the hour eleven
> Release the Tories they had taken
> Thinking before the Proclamation's end
> To seize thereon and make General Howe their friend
> Thro' all New England's long and wide extent
> The Whigs are all preparing to recant
> And strive to palliate former abuse,
> Most cordially the Tories now they use.

Continuing, the Tory poet described the stunning impact of the news of the British reverse at Trenton:

> The Whigs revive—They're valiant now and bold,
> The Puritanic priests 'bout ship again
> Pray that the British troops may all be slain
> Whigs now rest easy without absolution
> A Fig they say for Howe's kind Proclamation
> But lo, the amazing clemency of Howe
> Our gracious sovereign to resemble now
> Issues another Proclamation out
> Inviting every man to turn about

> To the King's name free pardon offers all
> E'en Congressman, patriot, and each general. . . .
>
> Many had taken the allegiate oath
> And to our Sovereign King plighted their troth
> Have since been taken on the Jersey shore
> Fighting the British troops, rebelling o'er
> Others upon Long Island's lengthy strand
> Supplying rebels with a liberal hand
> Tho' they have sworn allegiance to the King
> Yet miss no chance for a second rebelling.
>
> Amazing is the odds, 'twixt right and wrong
> When rebels are weak and loyal bold and strong.[30]

Almost as if hypnotized by the dream of inspiring counterrevolution among the Americans by loyalty oaths and pardons, British commanders and peace commissioners throughout the remainder of the war continued on the course Gage and Howe had begun long ago in 1775. As British statesmen became convinced that American resistance and French assistance made full victory impossible, they sought compromises based on retention of the rebel colonies in the Empire, on terms which would have satisfied the Whigs of 1775, but not the self-conscious Americans of 1778. All such British proposals maintained that the insurrectionists must seek the king's pardon and swear the king's oath as a condition of reconciliation. All failed.[31]

Approaching peace brought little balm to Tory hearts. Uncertainty for the future was well founded on the dangers of the present. American national and state anti-Tory laws had despoiled Tories of their property and posed the possibilities of imprisonment and capital punishment should they seek to regain it. Surely a grateful Britain would recall Tory sacrifices, and protect loyalist lives and properties by diplomatic weapons more successfully than she had on the battlefield.

British officers were sensitive to Tory needs. Lord Carlisle's 1778 instructions ordered him to see that under any truce he might make, "as far as circumstances will permit . . . no person shall be molested in any of the Provinces, for declaring his opinion upon any point of Government or for refusing to sign any Test or Association or to take any Oath." Circumstances, however, made a milder tone necessary four years later. Sir Guy Carleton's 1782 negotiations with Washington for an armistice contained the former's expression of "highest confidence that the Loyalists will be restored to their positions or a full compensation made them for whatever confiscations may have taken place." But Tories feared American tempers, and by the tens of thousands chose exile from their homeland rather than face whatever fate an independent United States might hold for them. "I shall probably sail for England," wrote one loyalist as the British evacuated New York in 1783, "unless there is a great change in the temper and conduct of the Americans who are at present very violent." He had large, and good, company. To Britain itself, and to British imperial possessions the world over, Tories took themselves to build new lives, and, incidentally, to strengthen the Empire's ties through their firm attachment to the king's cause.

Ironically, however, not all American Tories who wished to leave America with the last departing British troops could do so; there were not enough ships. British commanders ordered that only "truly loyal" Tories could get space. Who were the truly loyal? Those with British loyalty-oath certificates, they decided, who had been for at least twelve months sworn to royal fidelity. This was logistical necessity, not loyalty. And it served to break hearts and fortunes. In a mad scramble for shipping space, Tories accused each other of swearing falsely to royal oaths in the past in order to gain protection in the present. British officers had to initiate time-consuming loyalty probes to determine the validity of such charges, and the results were rarely conclusive.[32]

Losers in these loyalty contests, and more nominal Tories, found justification in imminent peace negotiations to succumb finally to the inevitable, and accept rebel victory and American loyalty oaths. American oath commissioners were busy men in 1782 and 1783, and their daily increasing tallies helped create what one honest turncoat called American "Vicars of Bray." This bitter rhymester described how elastic consciences had stretched the meaning of loyalty tests since 1774:

> . . . Britain was not quickly scared
> She told another story,
> When Independence was declar'd
> I figur'd as a Tory.
> Declared it was a Rebellion base
> To take up Arms—I cursed it
> For faith it seemed a settled case
> That we would soon be worsted.
>
> When penal laws were passed by vote
> I thought the test a grievance:
> Yet sooner than I'd loose a groat,

I swore the State allegiance,
The thin disguise could hardly pass
For I was much suspected,
I felt myself much like the Ass
In Lion's skin detected. . . .

But poor Burgoyne's announced my fate
The Whigs began to glory,
I now bewailed my wretched state
That e'er I was a Tory.
By night the British left the shore
Nor car'd for their friends a fig, Sir,
I turn'd the cat in pan once more
And so became a Whig, Sir.

I called the [British] army butchering dogs
A bloody tyrant King, Sir,
The Commons, Lords, a set of rogues
That all deserved to swing, Sir,
Since fate has made us great and free,
And Providence can't falter
So Congress till death my King shall be
Unless the times do alter.

For this law I will maintain
Until my dying day, Sir,
Let whatsoever King will reign
I'll still be Vicar of Bray, Sir.[33]

If defeated Tories could boast of duplicity, victorious rebels distrusted their promises of future loyalty to America. The *Providence Gazette,* for instance, insisted that words could not "convert lions into lambs, serpents into doves, or Tories into Sons of Liberty." Such American attitudes, combined with lack of British power to protect Tories, impelled loyalists to flee America with departing royal armies.

Once in safe havens of imperial power, these former Americans demanded royal recognition and recompense from the king for their sacrifices in his cause. For duplicity worked both ways. Despite the 1783 peace treaty between Britain and the United States, which ostensibly guaranteed protection for loyalists seeking their just debts and properties, American state governments disregarded these obligations. Vengeful rebels harassed returning Tories; state legislatures passed banishing acts and stay laws to prevent Tory resumption of property; some importunates died for insisting upon their rights as defined in the treaty. Congress could do nothing. Exiled Tories had to seek redress from the English government, therefore, for what American authorities refused to provide. Since many Tories felt betrayed by the 1783 treaty, and many politically important Englishmen agreed with them, the political pressure the Tories could exert on Parliament was substantial. In any event, most Britons agreed that American colonists who had endured great sufferings for their loyalty to England should find recognition and reimbursement.[34]

But how? Neither Briton nor Tory wanted royal rewards to go to any but the truly loyal. Who were they? Eight years of civil strife had taught men on both sides of the Atlantic that the "daily deliberate murders committed by pretended Whigs and reputed Tories (men who are actually neither one thing nor the other in principle) are too numerous and shocking to relate." It was scandalously common knowledge in England that British Generals Gage, Howe, Clinton, Burgoyne, and Cornwallis excused their successive defeats in America partially on the grounds of what Cornwallis called "the female fears" of most American Tories, whose professions of loyalty had been merely oral, and had failed to provide recruits for redcoated forces. If Britons despised such recreants, they owed much to other Tories who had steadfastly supported the king's cause, and consequently suffered death, poverty, and exile. England's problem, after 1783, was to find some way to identify its loyal American citizens. As American states, town meetings, and private associations, in rapid succession, displayed seemingly irreconcilable hatred toward their former neighbors, and forbade their return under threats of severest punishment, Parliament considered ways of meeting England's responsibilities.[35]

All through the war years, American Tories in English exile had conducted an organized campaign for restitution of damages suffered in the king's cause. The 1783 peace treaty proved the final argument in their favor. In that year Parliament created the first of successive commissions to "inquire into the Losses and Services" of all loyal claimants upon the royal bounty. On the face of it, the commissions' task should have been simple. But the problems were many. Divisions among the Tories themselves made establishment of criteria for loyalty a lengthy, imprecise, and eventually insoluble task. Certainly no one, British loyalty commissioner or Tory applicant, placed any faith in loyalty tests as evidence.

How could they? Claimants easily produced certificates of royal oath-taking. But adverse witnesses came forth to cast doubt upon these claimants' sincerity in swearing the royal oaths, accused applicants of having sworn American oaths as well, and demanded that the loyalty commissioners establish gradations of loyalty and give larger compensation to the "most" loyal. Such a hierarchy of allegiance proved impossible; as one weary royal loyalty commissioner recorded after five years of loyalty testing,

It is a distinction which has never been, nor can ever be rationally made, because it is impossible to ascertain the numerous and various degrees of loyalty produced by an infinite variety of acts, during a long continued rebellion. . . . Besides, were this possible, it would be fundamentally unjust, because the Loyalist whose person has been attainted . . . in consequence of *one* act of loyalty, has evidently suffered . . . as much "injury and damage" as he who suffered in consequence of ten thousand.[36]

All true loyalists were equally loyal, then, as claimants for British rewards. But more than a decade of calm, unhurried postwar investigations by able parliamentary commissions into the realities of loyalty-testing in the American Revolution proved that no loyalty test, British or American, was adequate to prove loyalty. In 1783, when the commission commenced work, it made possession of royal loyalty-oath certificates a prerequisite for all applications. Two years later the commissioners all but abandoned this requirement, having learned by that time that loyalty tests too often proved nothing. As one cynical Tory exile in Nova Scotia warned in 1781, "you are certainly mistaken [in equating loyalty oaths and loyalty]. . . . I should expect the premium mobile to be cowardice, and the hopes of worldly gain, and public applause." [37]

Royal loyalty commissioners could hardly make loyalty tests a valid guide to conduct for such people as Thomas Skelton, who had taken British oaths freely, but who had been a spy for the rebels. Nor did Isaac Titus fit into a neat category, for he had served the rebel militia as well as later supporting the king's colors, and yet, as an exile, petitioned for reimbursement for his losses. British officials received petitions from former servitors requesting character references detailing that the official had ordered the writer to take American oaths in order to gain the confidence of rebels and so conduct espionage. As one group of repentant South Carolina Tories wrote the commissioners, explaining their wartime subscription to American oaths,

Some of the Persons who were compelled to take the Oath to the State, . . . died Martyrs to their Loyalty in the Field of Battle. . . . The [South Carolina] Act of Attainder against them is likewise an unequivocal proof of their zealous Attachment to the British Government. . . . And therefore they trust that their taking of the Oath to the State, and temporary submission to the [rebel] Government . . . , being legally justified by cruel necessity to which they were reduced . . . cannot militate to their prejudice.

With loyalty tests clearly no valid guide to loyalty, the royal commissioners made each applicant's past acts rather than his loyalty oaths the key to the king's largess. Thousands of individual loyalty investigations, carried on in full consciousness of the altering contexts of time and place, in vivid awareness of the practical alternatives that faced so many of the applicants, proved to the royal loyalty commissioners that not one of the hundreds of loyalty-oath proclamations issued by British generals had served the king's cause. As the acidulous Thomas Jones commented,

The proclamations of Generals and Governors were become mere farces. The loyalists laughed at them, the rebels despised them, and by both they were held in contempt. They were great favourites with Governors, Generals, and Commissioners during the whole war. The American Rebellion was the first (I believe) in the universe attempted to be crushed, and reduced, by proclamations.[38]

Great Britain's postwar loyalty commissions had one advantage over their American equivalents; they were as centralized and unified as the wartime royal proclamations on loyalty had been. American postwar loyalty problems and policies, conversely, remained as disparate, contradictory, and local as they had been during the war years. State governments, almost totally free of treaty obligations or other national constraints under the Articles of Confederation, hounded Tories unmercifully. Some of them, especially where wartime tribulations had been mild, permitted discreet loyalists to return quietly to their homes and take up peaceful lives after swearing to the relevant state loyalty oath. Postwar American patriotism remained basically what it had been during the war years: a matter for time, place, and local predilection to determine, rather than for statutory loyalty tests to define. Wartime passions soon cooled, especially among upper-class Americans who looked with increasing dismay upon the "democratical" excesses of life under the Articles, and whose efforts were within a decade to result in a new American constitution.

John Jay, for instance, ardent New York State disloyalty hunter during the war, wished as early as mid-1783 that "all except the faithless and the cruel [Tories] may be forgiven." Jay criticized the postwar banishing act of his state, and, rather remarkably in view of his past words and deeds, came to regard the Revolution as "one in which men might conscientiously take opposite sides." Many American rebel leaders, with Alexander Hamilton as the outstanding example, made themselves champions of Tory claims for property restitution. As the first postwar decade passed, Americans let the loyalty-testing apparatus of the war years fall into abeyance. Ben Franklin's prediction of 1785— "The circumstances of the royalists are daily mending. . . . A stop is put to all prosecutions against them, and in time their offences will be forgotten"—soon came true. But Franklin rejected one Tory proposal that all loyalists become good Americans by swearing to American loyalty oaths on the grounds that "there could be no reliance on their oaths." In the United States as in England, men had learned to disbelieve the efficacy of enforced loyalty tests as valid guides to future good conduct.[39]

In successive Congresses convened under the Articles of Confederation, no loyalty test faced the legislators of the independent American republic. When a few score Americans met at Philadelphia in 1787 to recast the Articles into the mold which became the present Constitution, they heard proposals for a uniform loyalty test for American officials. Pennsylvania's brilliant James Wilson laid the ghost low:

Mr. Wilson [Madison recorded] said he was never fond of oaths, considering them as a left-handed security only. A good government did not need them, and a bad government could not or ought not to be supported. He said they might too much trammel the members of the existing government in case future alterations [in the Constitution] should be necessary.

The Constitution of 1787 finally contained a provision specifying a mere oath of office for the president, and a provision requiring an unspecified oath for federal and state officers. This satisfied both the pro-Constitutional group and anti-Federalists like William Maclay, senator from Pennsylvania to the first Congress under the new Constitution. Maclay successfully resisted a proposed loyalty-oath bill for federal officers. The bill in question, Maclay felt, justified his fears that Federalism was equatable with "a most . . . enormous Federal Judiciary, pompous titles, strong efforts after religious distinctions, coercive laws for taking oaths, etc." Against such "impolitic" and "high-handed measures," Maclay amassed successful resistance, and the resulting oath requirement was a simple statement of future fidelity for government officials.

So far was wartime anti-Toryism dissipated that Washington as president could uncaringly employ as federal officials such prominent former loyalists as Tench Coxe. Although anti-Federalists sought to make political capital of the presence of Tories in the Treasury Department, their efforts proved fruitless. Few Americans in 1790 could work up much excitement about the disloyalty of 1780. When, in 1792, James Madison surveyed the contemporary state of American political divisions, he casually dismissed past pro- or anti-Toryism as of no importance.[40] The loyalty tests of the American Revolution had largely run their course.

Not everyone realized this. Jonathan Boucher, whose Toryism had placed him in permanent postwar exile from America, suggested in 1797 that the Anglican Church in the United States needed reinforcements for its educational staff, and proposed that Americans admit enlarged numbers of Anglican personnel if the latter swore that in their teachings they would not "by words or action, do anything whereby to lessen their [students'] esteem of, and their obedience to, the present [United States] government." Boucher need not have worried, for few Americans were concerned with the possibility of Anglican ministers subverting the victorious American republic.

By the end of the Revolution most Americans would have agreed with the sentiment Franklin approved in 1776, concerning a French agent's willingness to swear to keep American plans secret even if he was tortured by the British:

He would have given me his oath for it, if I laid stress upon oaths; but I have never regarded them otherwise than as the last recourse of liars. Were it not for that, I would swear, . . . a full homage and inviolable fidelity to the august Congress of the most respectable Republic which has ever existed. But my attachment to you answers for my devotedness to that.[41]

So Franklin took the man's word of honor instead of requiring his oath of loyalty. It really made no difference in measuring this agent's loyalty. But it required long years, thousands of loyalty tests, and immeasurable heartbreak for Britons and Americans to learn this.

"The revolution which rendered the thirteen states independent ought to have made them happy," wrote a homesick, exiled Tory as the first postwar Christmas neared, ". . . but . . . the contrary remains a melancholy truth." [42] There were troubles enough in the barely united states of the infant American republic to justify his pessimism and to make the future of the republican experiment seem very dim. Long years of war and civil strife had left deep scars. Champions of revolutionary social ideals opposed more traditional programs.

Government weakness compounded with fiscal instability amidst the complexities of an imperfectly understood federal system. For most Americans, local loyalties took precedence over allegiance to the new nation. In what the historian John Fiske later termed "the critical period" of American history, the survival potential of the United States in its first postwar decade seemed low indeed.[43] Loyalty tests played a role in assisting and resisting the developing nationhood. State loyalty laws harassed returning Tories and embarrassed American diplomacy. And in several instances state loyalty laws operated upon Americans, to force them into conformity to the policies of state authorities.

The addiction of many Americans to paper-money panaceas designed to relieve them of debt and to realize democratic social aims, occasioned the crisis of Shays' Rebellion. Massachusetts crushed this movement with martial force, and followed this sternness with the mercy of pardoning the Shaysites upon their subscription to loyalty oaths to the state. Nearby Rhode Island reversed the social implications of the process, when, almost simultaneously, "radical" paper-money advocates gained control of the state's government and issued satisfying quantities of fiat currency. Subsequent "force acts" impelled reluctant creditors to accept the script until the Rhode Island courts declared the acts unconstitutional, in one of the first expressions of judicial review. Ignoring this judicial condemnation, the state legislature prescribed special loyalty tests for all residents to swear, attesting to the subscriber's willingness to accept the disputed paper as legal tender. Nonjuring automatically brought the penalty of disfranchisement. Violation of the oath, or perjury in swearing to its terms, incurred money fines and imprisonment. But the victory quickly backfired. The patent partisanship involved overturned the incumbent lawmakers. Their successors, by 1788, repealed the money issues and the loyalty tests which had protected them.[44]

A new federal constitution followed hard upon these troubles. Problems of paper money gave way to contending philosophies of government as the ideological tensions of the French Revolution threatened to disrupt the reformed republic. The mid-1790's saw the stronger national government sustain its revenue laws when it suppressed the resistance of western Pennsylvanians to the whisky excise. As Massachusetts had pardoned Shays' followers a decade earlier with a liberal application of loyalty tests, so the national authorities first overawed, then pardoned the whisky rebels by requiring them to swear allegiance to the United States.[45]

By 1798 two major political parties were in competition for control of national offices and the nation's destiny. The incumbent Federalists professed a monopoly of patriotism, and indulged in the seductive, simple, and sinister equation that any dissent from their doctrines was disloyalty to the nation. In the Alien and Sedition Acts the Federalists found expression for this conviction, and treated the country to an unprecedented and rarely repeated exhibition of political partisanship conjoined with official power. Their triumph was short-lived. As in Rhode Island, autocracy in the name of allegiance was the prelude to and major cause of political defeat.[46]

Jefferson's victory in 1800 lessened internal tensions, but the continuing pitfalls created by a world at war surrounded the determinedly neutral United States. In 1812 the American government abandoned neutrality in favor of war against England. Some Americans resented the choice of enemy to the point of advocating secession and treason. The ending of hostilities terminated New England's flirtation with disloyalty and, incidentally, placed a final quietus on the effectiveness of the Federalist party, which stood branded by its ten-year dalliance with treason.[47]

New, vaster problems followed the War of 1812. Territorial growth and material prosperity cost much in terms of increasing sectional antagonisms. By 1830, the price was more than one state—South Carolina—was willing to pay. Its decision pitted state against nation, and saw the revival of loyalty tests as political weapons.

CHAPTER V

State against Nation—1833

"The laws of South Carolina are more bloody than the iron code of Russia," commented a New England visitor in the South in January, 1833. To another contemporary commentator, the "extraordinary proceedings of South Carolina have . . . disturbed, and embarrassed . . . and agitated the public mind throughout the United States." Crisis was at hand, crisis adequate for Carolinians to make their state "more like a military camp than a peaceful State of the Union." [1] It was crisis born of a single, seemingly simple question. What were the powers of an American state in the Union?

Neither the federal Constitution nor the brief half century of national history afforded the clear answer that, in 1830, was necessary. Increasing sectional differences between North and South had become politically significant. In 1820 those differences strained the fabric of union, but political compromise had found a path to peace. Four years later a federal tariff law seemed to many Southerners proof that their section was doomed to perpetual subordination to Northern economic and social interests, which were antagonistic to Southern staple investments and to the South's social structure based on Negro slavery. Some Southern spokesmen, franker than most, bared the dusky motive inspiring Southern antitariff arguments. Robert J. Turnbull, for instance, warned that "the time approaches when Congress can take no vote that shall not be an expression on the subject of slavery." [2] In 1828, the ill-fated "tariff of abominations" became law, and the South found a leader to plead its cause.

John C. Calhoun offered a theory of the federal system which concluded that every state possessed the power to reject unjust federal law and, in ultimate instances, to reject the Union itself. Hearkening

back to the Kentucky and Virginia Resolutions which Jefferson and
Madison had penned to oppose the Alien and Sedition Acts, Calhoun
transformed those defenses of individual liberty into ramparts guard-
ing regional interests by state action, in order to safeguard, not liberty,
but slavery.[3] South Carolina took his theory and put it into practice.
In the process, the state's acts proved what Calhoun's theory denied:
that nullification and secession might protect Southern minorities
against Northern majorities, but that dissenting minorities within the
South could be oppressed quite as heavily by their fellow Southerners
as by any Northern acts. South Carolina's use of loyalty tests made a
mockery of Calhoun's theory.

By mid-1832 Calhoun's split with President Andrew Jackson was
reflected in the organization within South Carolina of two antagonistic
political groups. The States' Rights and Union party (Unionists) condemned nullification, in the words of Hugh S. Legaré, as a "revolutionary measure." Championing Calhoun's views, the States' Rights and
Free Trade party (Nullifiers) made opposition to the unsatisfactory
revision of the federal tariff law of July, 1832, their battle cry. State
elections of that year were fought on that issue. Nullifiers won control
of the legislature and Governor James Hamilton, Jr., ardent Nullifier,
called a popular convention for November to consider the tariff measure. Of 162 delegates, 136 were Nullifiers, who voided the vexatious
federal tariff law. Then they enacted a requirement, as part of the
nullification resolution, that all state officials (except legislators) swear
an oath "to obey and enforce the [nullification] ordinance and the acts
which should be passed to give it effect." [4]

Clearly, the Nullifiers were determined to suppress dissent by this
loyalty test while they themselves dissented from the federal legislation
in question. No Unionists would hold state office, Nullifier spokesmen
made clear, unless they were willing to place obedience to state actions
ahead of obligations to national allegiance. The test-oath issue, as one
participant in the heated events recalled, immediately became "the
principal question of importance." [5]

Partisanship evoked opposite definitions of patriotism. State Judge
Daniel Huger "spoke of the tyranny and oppression of . . . the shameful test oath," and wondered, "Can I be called a freeman, when I am
to be tried by a perjured judge and a packed jury?" Benjamin F.
Perry, editor of the Unionist *Greenville Mountaineer,* damned the
"inquisitorial oath," and aided Joel R. Poinsett and Christopher
Memminger in organizing state-wide Unionist correspondence and

militia societies. Unionist delegates to the convention joined in a "Remonstrance and Protest" which condemned the Nullifiers' program in general and their loyalty test in particular:

. . . the said [nullification] Ordinance has insidiously assailed one of the inalienable rights of man, by endeavouring to enslave all freedom of conscience, by that tyrannical engine of power,—a test oath.

it has disfranchised and proscribed nearly one-half of the freemen of South Carolina for an honest difference of opinion, by declaring that those whose consciences will not permit them to take the test oath shall be deprived of every office, civil and military. . . .

it has violated the independence guaranteed to the judiciary, by enacting that the judges shall take a revolting test oath, or be arbitrarily removed from office.[6]

Christmas, 1832, was not peaceful in South Carolina. Heated political arguments disrupted business and social meetings; some fearful Unionists sent their families and movable property out of the state, and removed themselves to safer areas. "It is said," wrote an informed Carolinian in Washington, "that the President is determined to execute the [federal] revenue laws . . . at the point of the Bayonet." [7] Two civil wars seemed imminent—one between the state and the national government, the second between two factions within the state.

Ethics were an early casualty. Poinsett, for instance, advocated that Unionists take the Nullifiers' test oath in order to retain their votes, positions, and influence and thus counter the Nullifiers' program from within. "To refuse to take the oath would be to give up the contest and leave . . . victory in the hands of our enemies," Poinsett pleaded. His plan was, admittedly, an approval of wholesale perjury.[8]

February 1, 1833, was the fateful deadline when the nullification ordinance, test oath included, was scheduled to take effect. Suspense mounted all through the preceding December and January, as the nation uneasily waited for events to determine whether peace or civil war would come. "I do not believe," optimistically wrote a prominent Virginian, "that the people of South Carolina are ripe for 'Secession' or are willing to resist, with arms, the General Government . . . unless after events should madden her into hostilities." But Governor Robert Y. Hayne, taking his oath as Hamilton's successor, placed his influence squarely with the Nullifiers: "I recognize no allegiance," Hayne warned, "as paramount to that which the citizens of South Carolina owe to the State." [9]

Ten days before the dreaded deadline, Nullifier leaders announced an indefinite postponement for initiating the disputed state law. A compromise tariff was in the making in Washington and, since other Southern states had evidenced no concrete support for South Carolina's stand, Nullifiers thought discretion the best course for the moment. They were displeased, however, that their victory over federal power which the new tariff bill represented should be mitigated by a simultaneous congressional enactment authorizing the president to enforce federal laws by federal troops if necessary.

Victims of their own rigid theory of state sovereignty, Nullifier leaders reassembled the state convention in mid-March, 1833, to consider the new federal laws. The convention "approved" the tariff law, and then "nullified" its accompanying Force Act. And, in the resolution voiding the Force Act, the convention included a new loyalty-test provision, requiring all Carolina officials to swear primary allegiance to the state or face immediate removal from office. The governor, good Nullifier, was to restaff such vacated posts, obviously, with good Nullifiers.[10] So the vexed test-oath issue, which could have died, revived instead.

Angered by this turn of events, fearful at the power of the partisan loyalty test to force Unionists from state office (which had already occurred in some instances), Unionists at the convention condemned the resurrected oath proposal. "What is this," Judge J. B. O'Neall demanded, "but depriving the people of their right to choose whom they will to serve them?" All loyalty tests, O'Neall insisted, "are the proper engines of the despot—they may be necessary to his safety. They cannot be necessary in free government."

Judge William Harper, framer of the original nullification ordinance, countered O'Neall's dramatic plea. The test oath, Harper insisted, was a device to sustain rather than to diminish civil liberties. It was designed to protect those worth protecting—which meant, he made clear, only those who were willing to swear to their primary loyalty to South Carolina. Against the Unionist objectors, Harper demanded, "what measures could . . . have been too strong?" Unionists were disloyal to their state. They should not hold office in that state's government. In time of crisis, mere "opinions" must give way to the need of the "sovereign" state government for loyal personnel.

Adherents of both sides repeated these themes, buttressing them from lofty excursions into the philosophy of allegiance and the history of America. The arguments changed few minds, but served more to make moderate men "sick at heart with the present controversy" and "disgusted with the suspicion and treachery" the loyalty issue was breeding.

The Unionists were in an unenviable position. Most of them detested the federal Force Act as much as any Carolinian could, yet felt that nullification and secession were improper remedies. By their stand, Unionists condemned themselves for advocating the primacy of "foreign" power in their state. But the real issue in early 1833 was the test oath. O'Neall made this clear: "I believe," he said in a bid for compromise, "that this Oath is the only cause that could continue . . . irritations." The bid failed. On March 18, 1833, the convention approved the oath ordinance and forwarded it to the legislature for statutory enactment. Loyalty tests were to remain an issue.[11]

Some Unionists despaired of peace, and abandoned South Carolina "because of the unceasing hostility of . . . [their] political opponents." Perry felt that remaining Unionists must brace themselves for more oppression, especially if the state legislature continued in its addiction to partisan loyalty tests. To placate the numerically superior Nullifiers, Perry and other Unionist leaders tried moderation. Unionists did not present candidates in the September elections in Charleston, which merely resulted in the election of an arch-Nullifier, H. L. Pinckney, to Congress.

Moderation failed on two counts. It did not swerve Nullifiers from their fondness for loyalty tests, nor did it diminish tension within the state. As the 1833 winter session of the South Carolina legislature approached, newspapers renewed discussion of the oath issue. Unionist writers warned their opponents to be satisfied with past victories at the risk of stretching Unionist patience beyond endurance. Backs stiffened as time ran out. James L. Petigru admitted that he could approach not one member of the opposition party for a rational discussion of the issue. The direst forebodings found justification when the legislature convened.[12]

Among the first acts of the December, 1833, meeting of the South Carolina legislature, overwhelmingly Nullifier-controlled, was one that abolished all existing commissions in the state militia. All who achieved election to vacant offices would have to swear, not only to the oath required in the state constitution, but also to this special test of loyalty: "I, A. B., do solemnly swear, or affirm, that I will be faithful and true allegiance bear to the State of South Carolina; and that I will support and maintain, to the utmost of my ability, the laws and constitution of this state and the United States; so help me God." Once more the

Unionist leaders sought to stave off crisis. They proposed an interpreta-
tive preamble to the militia oath bill: "That nothing herein contained
shall be construed so as to impair or in any manner affect the allegiance
now due by the constitution of the state and of the United States."
Nullifiers quickly defeated this proposal. They had adopted a clever
tactic in their strategic drive to insure internal conformity. Already in
control of the executive and legislative departments of the government,
they hoped by this oath test to capture the military branch as well.
Once in control, Nullifier politics and state policy would become in-
distinguishable.

Disgruntled Unionists maintained steady opposition to the military
bill and its oath measure. They aimed sharp forensic blows at its political motivation and practical consequences. What disturbed the Nullifiers most was the Unionist charge that the proposed oath was an
illegal addition to the oath already required of state officials by the
state constitution. Nullifiers, hurriedly responding to this argument,
proposed an amendment to the state constitution, replacing the existing oath requirement with still another oath, which all state officers
including militiamen would have to swear. This proposal was to go
before the people in the autumn, 1834, elections:

I do solemnly swear, or affirm, that I will be faithful and true allegiance bear
to the state of South Carolina so long as I may continue a citizen thereof; and
that I am duly qualified, according to the constitution of this state, to exercise the office to which I have been appointed; and that I will, to the best of
my abilities, discharge the duties thereof, and preserve, protect and defend
the constitution of this state and of the United States; so help me God.[13]

Over undiminished Unionist protests, the militia oath bill and the
constitutional amendment proposal passed both houses of the legislature by more than 3:1 ratios. Some moderate Nullifiers, wishing to
cease this badgering of the Unionists, found an effective party whip applied to evoke their votes.

Beaten in the legislature, Unionists continued their antioath struggle
before the bar of public opinion. The thirteen men who had voted
against the Nullifiers' oath proposals in the state senate, Unionists all,
issued a public protest against the oaths, and an explanation of their
opposition. Printed as a broadside, this document circulated widely
in the state, and made its way across the nation. The protesters centered their attack on the seeming innocence of the test. It was in that
innocence that the reptile lay, they claimed, for, unless the new oath
meant something it did not say, it was unnecessary. If, however, it

really meant that allegiance to the state took precedence over federal attachment, then the proposed oath was a violation of the national Constitution. And, in addition to being at least unnecessary and perhaps unconstitutional, it was surely impolitic "under existing circumstances, [and] . . . a direct imputation upon the patriotism of the protestants, and those whose principles they represent." To the thirteen state senators, the oath test was untimely; "in a time of excitement, when opposition to the General Government has almost annihilated the affections of our people for the Federal Union . . . —The undersigned *protest*— . . . that any act of legislation [should] even seem to encourage this alienation of feeling." [14]

A few Nullifiers publicly stated that the Unionists were wrong, that the very ambiguity of the oath formula was fortunate in that it would permit each subscriber to decide for himself just what it was that he was signing, and fix the focus of his allegiance as he wished. Unionists derided this reasoning as sophistry, and continued their criticism of every aspect of the new militia law and constitutional amendment. Greenville's Unionists swore to obey no officer who took the oath, and resolved early in January, 1834, that their district's militia officers refuse the new oath and retain their commissions despite the law. Perry tried to divert their passionate declamations toward a search for legal and more pacific means of defeating the obnoxious laws in future elections and in the courts. But the potential for social explosion remained; as Petigru wrote to a Unionist who had already fled from South Carolina, "The mountaineers, who are generally on our side, received the test oath and Military Bill with a yell of passion. Here in the city [Charleston] people are so worn out and tired that the blow excited very little feeling. But the mountaineers have taken the thing as violently as Nullification was taken."

Unionist leaders were able to head off a proposed party convention scheduled to meet before April 11, 1834 (election day for militia officers). Fearing that the inevitable expressions of resistance to the oath laws which would emerge from such a meeting might stiffen the Nullifiers' attitudes, Unionist policy makers used correspondence committees to disseminate opinions less publicly among their adherents. In the mounting excitement, as April drew near, Nullifier spokesmen repeated their assertion that the oaths were harmless, and that the tempest was merely the result of Unionist stirring in an otherwise placid political teapot. No other political issues were at hand to keep the Union party alive, Nullifiers charged, so the oath tests had become a convenient symbol. Perhaps so. Probably some among both parties were delighted to have the loyalty oaths about as tools with which to dredge up party support. But certainly this was not true of all the political leaders. Few men risk careers, lifetime friendships, and freedom for momentary political gain. Principles dominated the situation, and the line of demarcation between two differing views of the principle of allegiance ran squarely through the spotlighted oath tests.

As men waited for the fateful militia elections, South Carolina politics descended from the rarefied atmosphere of debate on the right of nullification, to the problem of insuring obedience to party policies within the state. In that descent a great state found itself on the brink of civil war. That armed conflict did not explode is a credit entry for moderate men on both sides of the political fence who sought peaceful modes of settlement. But it was a narrow escape from a perilous point to which the loyalty-test issue brought the state.[15]

On April 11, 1834, militiamen mustered to elect new officers. As planned, expected, and feared, several companies chose Unionists to command them. When these Unionist officers reported to senior officers for their commissions, they found the oath requirement waiting as a prerequisite, refused the oath, and received no commissions. One such incident, occurring in Charleston, provoked the first judicial test of the oath law.

Edward McCready had earlier been elected as lieutenant of the Charleston militia company. He was an avowed Unionist, a fact well known to Colonel Hunt, commanding officer of the regiment. Mc-Cready appeared before the colonel, exhibited his certificate of election, and asked for his commission and the oath. Colonel Hunt demanded that he swear to the special militia oath as well as to the one prescribed by the state constitution. McCready refused the additional test; Hunt withheld his commission; McCready sought out Judge Bay of the Charleston court for a writ of mandamus requiring Hunt to deliver the commission.

McCready's petition argued that the militia oath was invalid because it conflicted with the allegiance he owed to the dual sovereignties of federal and state governments. Bay denied this premise, reviewing colonial and Revolutionary War history to indicate that South Carolina had been independent since 1776, and that her citizens depended upon her for intimate, daily protection for which they must pay by offering primary allegiance. Certainly, the judge stated, the debated oath was of peculiar necessity for the state at this political moment when "the idea of consolidation had become so prevalent in many portions of the

United States," and in order to deny President Jackson's proclamation "that the primary allegiance of the citizens [of the states] was transferred to the United States" when the Union was formed. From history and from necessity Judge Bay upheld the oath requirement; McCready initiated an appeal to the state's higher courts. The first round went to the Nullifiers.

In a similar situation, James McDaniel, colonel-elect of the Twenty-seventh Regiment, found he could not obtain his commission without taking the test oath. McDaniel appealed to the court at Lancaster for a writ of mandamus to compel his commanding general to deliver the commission. Judge Richardson found the oath requirement unconstitutional, giving the second round to the Unionists. The general in question decided to appeal this decision. His brief before the higher court declared that the militia oath was well within ordinary legislative purview, and was substantiated by the action of a popular convention as well. He denied the ability of the court to criticize the expressed voice of the people as Judge Richardson had done.

Now two cases were pending before the South Carolina Court of Appeals; two judges contradicted each other in their views of the legitimacy of the militia oath and the powers of the legislature and the convention. Both cases merged into one hearing before the appeals tribunal; the best legal talent of both parties took their places on opposite sides of the crowded Columbia courtroom in May, 1834. And the people of the state and of the nation watched and waited for a final verdict.

Thomas S. Grimké began the argument against the validity of the oath test, and he made it quite clear that it was not alone for McCready that he spoke, "but that I come to speak in behalf of all who think with him." The attorney noted the intense public interest focused on the courtroom, recognized the emotionalism that had accompanied much of the preceding debate on the oath in the political arena, and rejoiced that "this subject is to be discussed calmly, fearlessly." Preamble finished, Grimké launched his attack. The strength of his offensive lay in his argument that the militia bill was an illegal superaddition to the constitutional oath of office. The militia oath and the constitutional oath were almost identical and therefore the former was superfluous. Grimké found an additional cause for denouncing the militia oath in the conflict he saw between it and the federal Constitution. The latter instrument of government was still supreme law, not to be abrogated by mere state legislation. And the federal Constitution specifically provided for divided allegiance, for two authorities over all the people, for a mixture of federal and state powers which the oath in question arrogated to the state alone.

His lengthy argument traveled over long reaches of historical time and came finally to the extralegal issues that the court was, in Grimké's opinion, testing even as it tested the statute in question. "I honestly believe it [the militia oath] to be a test oath," Grimké declared. Such an oath he defined as one that required the subscriber to declare an opinion with his signature or his refusal to sign. Opinion, to Grimké, was a matter for each man's conscience. As Grimké reviewed the history of man's intolerance toward man he described how similar tests had accompanied terrors of the past, when one group gained so much power in a political organism that dissenters faced total destruction merely for being dissenters. "We know," said Grimké, "that [the oath law has] . . . arisen out of these unhappy political contests, which led directly to the question of exclusive or divided allegiance." If this pernicious question continued to absorb the attention of South Carolina, if, as seemed to be threatening, outright violence marked the course of events, then Grimké feared that the downfall of the republic was near. For the test oath would give to those who wielded it an engine capable of forging "the indissoluble union of party and State—the perilous principle that the party *is* the State, and the natural fruits of such a maxim, that the friend of the ruling party is a patriot, its adversary the enemy of the country—that political heresy is treason, and the political schismatic, a traitor." Grimké, his plea finished, let Petigru take up the task.[16]

As the second assailant of the legitimacy of the militia oath, Petigru asserted that the loyalty test belied its seeming innocence by requiring subscribers to abjure allegiance to the United States. No honest man, Petigru insisted, could deny the plain meaning of the 1833 convention, when it so clearly differentiated between obedience and primary allegiance. The subsequent legislature which enacted the oath bill admittedly carried out the mandate of that convention. And, since it was superfluous to the existing state constitutional oath, and repugnant to the national Constitution, the militia oath itself was unconstitutional. The 1833 state convention had, in Petigru's opinion, exceeded its powers. The oath must fall.

William McWillie, the third antioath contender, and counsel for McCready, analyzed the entire debate as one centering on definitions of allegiance and the consequent political effects of the confusion of interpretations. McCready had refused the oath because he felt the test abjured duties he owed the United States. McWillie agreed with this contention. The federal government exists; it must have citizens. Both the national government of the United States and the state government of South Carolina were "sovereign" in specific ways. The problem before the court was one engendered by the indefinite interstices of state-federal relations. But, McWillie noted, the 1833 convention which had defined allegiance as totally due to the state had denied almost completely the existence of dual allegiance. Whether as a product of the convention or of a normal session of the legislature, the test oath was, to McWillie, incontrovertibly unconstitutional. That oath "disfranchises nearly one half of the free citizens of South Carolina, . . . [and] reduce[s] the whole Union party to the condition of hewers of wood and drawers of water." McWillie went further with this political condemnation of the oath, describing it as equivalent to a religious test, and asking: "What right has the legislature to swear me to any given set of political opinions, which it has not of religious?" Both matters were for individual consciences to decide. The roots of the test oath were firmly planted in the unsavory earth of partisan dispute; McWillie pleaded with the court not to uphold this oath since its legal parentage was dubious. "On doubtful grounds," he concluded, "you cannot, you will not permit the disfranchisement of so large a portion of your fellow-citizens. You will not permit the imposition of an odious test-oath—the worst and most universal enemy of human liberty. . . . If you sustain the oath, it must be on the most unquestioned constitutional grounds."

Thomas Williams' argument against the oath was more legalistic. He concentrated on identifying the disputed law as one that effectually modified the state constitution's oath-of-office provision without submitting the change to the people. Notice, he urged the court, that even the supporters of the bill had felt it necessary to suggest a similar amendment to the state constitution, confessing by that act their own uncertainty concerning the legality of the militia oath law. Such parliamentary trickery, Williams warned, might find favor with future legislatures to alter the structure of government as they pleased, to shift the balance of political power to conform to prevailing political winds, and thus make temporary legislation do the work of suppressing effective dissent until entrenched minorities might change the constitution of the state itself. Each administration might require an oath of officials and citizens in the state to protect it alone, and when that occurred, as it was, he alleged, occurring in the present case, democratic forms must die. No true citizen, he averred, could abjure his required allegiance to either state or nation. Allegiance must go to the power that provides protection. Both the federal Union and the state protected the citizens of South Carolina. No, the counsel warned, the test oath was nothing but a partisan demand upon the "people of South Carolina to swear to the truth of a particular political tenet." Despotism had arrived in South Carolina via the avenue of the oath.

Last of the string of antioath lawyers was Abraham Blanding, who recapitulated the arguments of his predecessors. His major contribution was an exhaustive survey of the nature of a federal system, which concluded that nullification as a process, and the test oath as a weapon, could destroy that system. They were both inconsistent with democracy and contradictory to a republican form of government. On the dual criteria of deviation from state constitutional procedure and violation of the nature of the federal Union, the test oath, in Blanding's view, was legally evil and morally untenable: "Ordinance [of nullification] and [oath] law must fall together." [17]

The assailants of the test-oath fortress rested; now the defenders of that bulwark of the Nullifiers rose to assume their task. For the state, Mr. Solicitor Player began a lengthy historical analysis of federal systems of the world, and the development of the concept of allegiance. In 1776 South Carolina became a sovereign state, and no superior authority existed. The protection the United States government afforded the citizens of the state did not divide that allegiance; the Holy Roman Empire and the Swiss cantons were historical proofs that protection by a central authority did not necessarily imply the ending of local allegiance. The disputed test oath added no duty to office-holding which was not already implicitly part of any incumbent or citizen. Loyalty and allegiance were requisite without the oath; why object to mere formalization *by* the oath?

More, Player claimed, the argument that the 1833 convention was deficient in authority was ridiculous. The "Convention was the people"; the legislature had heard its voice and responded with the test oath. Not only was its authority perfect in theory, but such a convention wedded fact and theory with the firm bonds of a ministry which no believer in democracy could deny. Therefore, Player concluded, the court had no right to hear the case at all, for no court suggested that its review function extended to an overseership of the fundamental political fabric which the people wove in convention. If the court did choose to render a decision in this case, then the court was arrogating to itself power supreme over all other elements of the body politic. No, a popular convention has "omnipotence over the subject matter; [a] despotic, absolute will, which . . . cannot err, because no inferior power can have official cognizance of its errors for correction." Player thus upheld the oath on the very ground upon which his attorney disputants had criticized it—as an uncheckable exercise of popular power. He then explained to the court why he had submitted his interpretation of its lack of jurisdiction: "I was impelled not more by a deliberate conviction that it was legally correct, than by an anxious hope that in this war of conflicting opinions, it might be the means of presenting, through this court, to an excited community, a nucleus around which the discordant elements might arrange themselves in harmony." [18]

To Robert Barnwall Rhett, the state's attorney general, who next assumed the task of defending the oath, sovereignty and allegiance were alike indivisible. All federal powers were in his opinion "trust powers," which the people of the states might revoke. The militia oath could not, therefore, contradict federal or state constitutions, for it merely restated the essential principle of the unalterable sovereignty of the state. The convention of 1833 empowered the legislature to act on a subject fully within its competence; the people of South Carolina had demanded such a pledge of fidelity to their interests. Could the court deny them? [19]

Completing the three-part defense of the oath, W. Peroneau Finley decried the opposition assertion that the oath law was equivalent to a religious test. No word on religion existed in the text of the oath, which Finley described as a mere oath of office and allegiance. It could not be a threat to thought or conscience. Nothing that the federal Constitution stated contradicted the South Carolina oath. Only President Jackson's "monstrous" public proclamations demanded total allegiance from all American citizens to the national government. But no oaths emanated from the ordinary American to the national government; it was the state, not the nation, which required the totality of loyalty. Nor did the test oath contradict or superadd to any part of the state constitution. The oath was a new thing, created in accordance with the traditional and legal rights of the people to meet a situation that seemed dangerous enough to warrant resistance to oppression from without and subversion from within. As an expression of the legislative will, the oath was valid, but it was even more so since it had received the sanction of a popular convention. Finley, too, questioned the right of the court to judge the case or to rule over the unrestrainable voice of the people emanating from a popular convention. The oath was part of the ordinance nullifying the Force Bill of the federal government, as necessary as guns for defense against that law. The sovereignty of each state, to Finley, was "as the very rock of our liberties." *His* allegiance was exclusively to his state. The militia oath could not be found exceptionable under such reasoning.[20]

In these arguments, the attorneys for both sides of the oath question had reviewed much more than the strictly legal questions involved in the dispute. They had paid a full share of attention to the political context that had surrounded the test-oath issue from its inception. Now that issue was ready for the decision of the court, and its three members, Judges O'Neall, David Johnson, and Harper, had in their hands a problem with which the most active minds of the state had been dealing for weary months. Judge O'Neall began the announcement of the court's decision by acknowledging the strained temper of the times, when "the waves of popular fury and party strife are continually breaking upon the very walls of the Temple of Justice." Recognizing that his decision might fan exacerbated political passions into flames, O'Neall declared the militia oath unconstitutional.

His opinion drew from Revolutionary history to substantiate his belief that allegiance in America was due the government of all the people. The national government was as legitimate, in O'Neall's view, as that of any state, for the people had created both. Constitutions of state and nation were equally sovereign, served as reciprocally necessary balances in American political life, divided functions and powers between the federal and state governments in order to preserve liberty. But the framers of the federal Constitution, with the approval of the states, had given primacy in certain arenas to federal powers over those of the states. This must be true in a functioning federal form of government, and O'Neall could not but doubt that it was this kind of judicious intermixture of powers that gave to the United States its peculiar popularity among the people of the world.

Sovereignty then, for O'Neall, was undivided, but adhered to both state and national governments. The citizen must pay due allegiance to both governments. South Carolina's own legislative history showed this had been true in the past; no laws before this test oath had presumed to demarcate allegiance as something appertaining exclusively to the state. Aliens had first to swear to uphold the Constitution of the United States and to abjure foreign allegiance before South Carolina admitted them to state citizenship. Certainly, O'Neall commented, some American territories knew no allegiance at all but for the national government. Allegiance and obedience were concomitant aspects of being an American, and an American of South Carolina citizenship could not

,divest himself by the state test oath of his dual obligations to two governments.

At the heart of O'Neall's criticism of the oath was his contention that the convention which had passed it had exceeded its powers. The origin of the disputed loyalty test was in a legislative resolution calling for a popular testimony on federal trade laws. The resulting convention had transgressed into unauthorized territory by presuming, without popular fiat, to define allegiance and require a test oath. It seemed obvious to O'Neall that the oath was in conflict with the duties of the citizen to the government of the United States. No state legislature could legitimately alter the political relationships of the citizen to the national government, nor was it within the province either of the state legislature or of a popular convention to attempt a statutory definition of those relationships. The test oath was void, as O'Neall saw it, because it either demanded something excessively greater than the existing state constitutional oath, or merely duplicated it. Either way, it had no reason for legitimate being. He received judicial support from his benchmate, Judge Johnson, who also alluded to the "bad passions" on this "question about which the parties have ceased to reason, and have settled down upon opposite conclusions, as aphorisms admitting of no discussion." His reasoning closely followed the path O'Neall had traced; two of the three-man court were in close agreement on the test oath.[21]

From similar patterns of reasoning, but from different assumptions, the last, and dissenting, member of the appeals court derived opposite conclusions. Judge Harper, stanch political Nullifier and jurist of great reputation, decided that the oath was a perfectly justifiable requirement and exercise of state power. To him South Carolina was a nation unto itself, bound by tenuous ties to a limited confederacy which was decreasingly beneficial to the interests of the state. Federal powers, such as those to make war or treaties, to coin money, and to punish treason, were not, to Harper, exercises of sovereignty. Rather they were expressions of the delegation of powers to the federal government by the states. Harper concluded his examination of the federal system with the pronouncement that total allegiance adhered to the state from each citizen, and that the oath in question could not violate any provision of the federal or the state constitution. And certainly, Harper believed, the convention that recommended the oath had full popular authority to do so; the courts of the state had, therefore, no jurisdiction in this matter at all. Politics, he insisted, had no place in a courtroom —but Harper directly succeeded this sound dictum with a full statement outlining the, to him, evil nature of tariffs, the damnable character of the Force Bill, and the state's absolute necessity to have officers faithful to it alone. The test oath did not, in his opinion, have anything at all to do with any officer's religious or political opinions, but concerned his acts alone, his conduct which might affect the safety of the state. The judge admitted that an officer with conscientious doubts about the sovereignty of South Carolina might take the oath, and that after swearing he might perform his duties properly without violating the test. Conflicts of allegiance would ensue, Harper believed, if ever nullification was to reoccur, or go the dreaded step further to secession. It was for that crisis of the future that Harper believed the majority of the people of the state had demanded and written the test oath of loyalty. Could any patriotic officer do less than sign it, or a perceptive judge not uphold it? [22]

The decision of the court against the militia test oath was immediately more political than judicial. Unionists hailed the event as a "glorious victory." Nullifiers saw it as a serious blow, a sharp rebuff from an unexpected quarter. Some states' rights spokesmen abandoned all patience with future procedural or legalistic maneuvers, and, urging that "Constitutions are but paper, and Oaths are but breath," concluded that "the only guarantee of liberty is arms." [23] But somewhat more sober counsel prevailed.

In the Nullifiers' armory of loyalty-test weapons, the proposed amendment to the state constitution, requiring a new loyalty oath of all state officers, was already half through the process toward popular ratification. The next step was a second two-thirds vote in its favor in each house of the state legislature.

While Nullifiers marshaled forces to accomplish this vital vote, they salved their dignity which the court had injured. Extremists among them advocated removing the two antioath judges from the bench, and nullification newspapers ranted against them. States' rights meetings echoed these condemnations, and demanded abolition of the Court of Appeals and enactment of a new state law of treason. Governor Hayne received pleas to withhold the disputed militia commissions, despite the court's condemnation of the militia-oath requirement. Unionists colored their prose with hues from the other end of the political spectrum. All waited for Hayne's action.

In mid-June Hayne made his decision public. He would abide by the court's decision, and issue commissions under the traditional oath contained in the state constitution. It seemed to Hayne that the Nullifiers would be foolish to flout the court by insisting on the condemned militia oath, when, in less than half a year, the constitutional amendment would be ratified and the new oath in full force. Hayne knew that his moderate course would alienate the more extreme members of his party, but, with Calhoun, William C. Preston, Hamilton, and George McDuffie, he agreed that it was best to tread softly in order to keep the oath question politically useful for the forthcoming October elections. At the same time Nullifier spokesmen hinted at severer measures—a new treason law, a remodeling of the Court of Appeals—which might come about if the Unionists blocked the constitutional amendment. Such shadowboxing had some effect. Petigru, for instance, wrote that although he would still oppose the oath amendment "as unwise and unjust," he would "acquiesce in it" if they would "do no more . . . than carry this amendment." [24]

Through the hot summer and the torpid autumn political argumentation centered on the oath issue. Tempers frayed, and such men as Huger were "against going to court about the test oath, but for fighting." Judge Richardson, Unionist, wanted his party to declare it would "never submit, and he says there will be a general emigration from the back country if the Constitution is altered." It proved easier, however, to maintain energy on the legalistic oath issue among the party leaders than among the general population of the state. By late September, with election day less than a month away, one important Unionist complained of the impossibility of arousing the "dormant sense of justice in our people." All the cards seemed stacked in the Nullifier deck, and those who would predict anticipated a victory for the oath at the polls, and the proscription of anti-Nullifiers in the state's services immediately thereafter. Union newspapers accused the enemy of bribery, corruption, and intrigue, but noticed with more surprise than malice the depths to which once honorable men were stooping in order to corral pro-oath votes. Not to be outdone, Nullifiers charged their opponents with plotting secret, armed revolution through the medium of correspondence committees. To swear or not to swear—this seemed to be the motif of the campaign, and few partisans chose to refer to national issues in preference to concentrating on the major state-wide point of interest—the test oath.

Tempers proved unequal to the task of maintaining complete calm; one incident in Charleston nearly precipitated a riot. Unionists were already tense over a "raid" the previous night which resulted in damage to the home of an adherent and some manhandling of resident Unionists by Nullifiers. Election night found a mob of several hundred

Nullifiers out to repeat the process at Union headquarters. From the besieged party rooms came a hail of duck shot; a half dozen on each side suffered minor wounds. The crowd dispersed to the Citadel, from which armory they demanded weapons with which to avenge the affront. Fortunately for the peace of the city and the state, perhaps of the nation, the commander of the armory refused their demands and the situation passed over.

Electoral victory went to the Nullifiers. They now had the two-thirds majority they needed to pass the oath amendment. The antioath party had made some gains, but not enough, because the Unionists were ineradicably stained with the brush of the obnoxious federal tariff. Nullifiers had a simple formula—patriotism—to sell. Unionists had the complex task of convincing the electorate that harm would come to the state if a new state loyalty oath faced South Carolina's officers.[25]

Now that the fateful election returns were in, there were several alternative courses of action left to the defeated Unionists. They could continue resistance at the hustings, for the people had still to vote on the amendment after the Nullifier-dominated legislature passed it. There was danger in this approach, for some of the Unionists, in Petigru's words, "were running wild." Petigru, pondering the situation, concluded that compromise was the best course. He believed that the legislature should resolve that the constitution, as amended by the oath, "leaves the question of dividing allegiance to the conscience and judgment of every man." The Unionist leader thought he could persuade most of his adherents to agree to this, although some were inflamed "more from passion than reason," and would view any Nullifier overtures as poisoned draughts. Late in November, Petigru presented his plans to a Unionist meeting. He was not, he assured his auditors, retreating in his abhorrence of the oath, which would remain unlawful to him "as long as it offended the conscience of my friends." No, Unionists would continue resistance. But how? Not again through the courts, for no judge would hear a case based on criticism of a part of the constitution. Not by arms, for the Unionists held themselves pledged to be a party of peace and conservatism. Only by continued political agitation, and by refusing the new oath when the time came for state officers to take it, could Unionists profitably function, and then claim that "a third of the State would be unrepresented" if Nullifiers enforced the oath. In this program, Petigru played for time.[26]

The state legislature met and hurriedly read the oath amendment, and with it bills to define treason and to reorganize the judicial system. This was the Nullifiers' arsenal, the expression of how far they were willing to go, as Petigru's speech a few days earlier had detailed the Unionists' maximum assertions. One group of Unionists refused to be quieted, and submitted a petition to the legislature which repeated their opposition to the oath amendment. The petitioners declared that among the most "sacred and inalienable benefits of citizenship" was that of electing officials to office. This right the proposed test-oath amendment would of necessity destroy, creating "political degradation," and if it did become an amendment to the constitution of the state all Unionists would fear "an almost inevitable tendency to increase domestic discord, and to provoke civil strife." Conciliation was needed if that strife was not to begin.

Both parties had set the stage for compromise. Nullifier David McCord approached Unionist Richardson and "told him if he would say on what terms or in what sense he would be willing to take the oath, they, that is David McCord and his friends, would meet them and try to bring about a pacification." Petigru had to exert himself to achieve Unionists' promises of coöperation, but he succeeded. Unionist terms were threefold: first, the state legislature must resolve that "the allegiance required by the proposed [oath] alteration of the Constitution is the allegiance which every citizen owes to the State consistently with the Constitution of the United States"; second and third, the Nullifiers must abandon the treason definition and judiciary reorganization laws. To smooth the way, former Governor Hamilton and Petigru planned to decrease resistance to compromise within their respective parties, for Petigru feared that "the rank and file [of the Nullifiers] was really in pursuit of a test oath." In private caucuses and public pronouncements, the leaders of both parties sought to quiet the disturbed political waters.

Hamilton used the Unionists' arguments in a report to the legislature, in a manner clearly to show the most extreme Nullifiers that the Unionists meant business. Clothing his words in a well-chosen defense of the oath amendment ("the oath implies no compulsory conformity of opinion," he maintained), Hamilton concluded with a plea for a rapid renewal of internal tranquillity on the vexed oath question. Feelings among his party members still ran high; some were against conciliation at all. Hamilton resorted to a party caucus of prominent Nullifier leaders to put across his views, and achieved substantial success.

He should have invited one more member to that meeting, for that same afternoon a Nullifier who was unconscious of the peace feelers tenuously connecting the two party leaders, embarrassed the negotiations by introducing into the legislative session a resolution proclaiming the inalienable right of South Carolina to define allegiance. It was put down with some strange bedfellows voting together. Other Nullifiers, better briefed, soothed the ruffled feelings of their innocent colleague by reading into the record that they gave "their cordial approbation to the sentiment . . . but for causes well understood by the house, and in a spirit of reciprocal reconciliation," they had to vote against such a proposal.[27]

The galleries, confused at the sudden switch, speculated in vain, as the whole minority Union party voted with Nullifiers for acceptance of the report of the Nullifier governor! Smiles illuminated legislative faces which had scowled at each other for months, and rousing bipartisan applause greeted one perfervid speech which pleaded for South Carolina's resumption of power "in the councils of the nation, based on a people united at home." Indeed, as one contemporary described the scene, it was "an overwhelming testimony of the total change of feeling which had been effected within the last twenty-four hours." Further to symbolize unity, the two parties joined to elect George McDuffie as governor. Compromise, a product of men ranging from Calhoun through minor party members, was in effect. Each man would decide for himself what he meant by his oath of office.

Not all South Carolinians were satisfied with the approval of mass perjury implicit in the settlement of the oath problem. Almost fifteen hundred signatures from Greenville and more than five hundred from Pendleton protested that the compromise sold Unionist interests for too small a price. Perry, from Greenville, joined his constituents in forcefully expressing his discontent. Even with the reservation of personal interpretation, Perry could not see how any Union man could take the oath. He termed the compromise "an abandonment of principle and a sacrifice of honor." No point of the compromise dealt with the major problem of defining loyalty and allegiance. Unionists had given up victory to the Nullifiers and lost honor for themselves in the surrender. What was gained was a legitimizing of successive perjuries about which everyone would know. Perry bemoaned the shifting bases of politics, and pledged himself never to "pollute my lips" with the oath. But a plaintive question which Poinsett asked was a more accurate gauge to party sentiment than Perry's caustic comments: "But what [else] could we do?" [28]

The test oath was dead as a political issue, but the controversial elements which had given vitality to the oath question did not die. Tariffs gave way to graver arguments concerning the nature of the Union, as the decade of the 1830's gave way to the ebullient 1840's and the fateful 1850's. Petigru had written, in the midst of Southern jubilation at the 1833 compromise tariff: "I am not sensible of any great happiness in thinking that instead of happening to me . . . [civil war] is reserved for my children, and a devilish day it will be." [29] He was right.

When the war of 1861–1865 came to the young American republic, some of the major figures of the thirty-year-past test-oath dispute in South Carolina were alive to see the results of their handiwork. Perry decided to follow his state when South Carolina voted for secession. He said then: "I have been trying for the last thirty years to save the State from the horrors of disunion. They are now all going to the devil and I will go with them." His Greenville district stood stanchly against secession until Perry helped change its mind. He claimed that South Carolina was unanimous for secession and that his district must not obtrude its feelings in the way of the will of the people. Greenville switched with him and supplied two volunteer companies to the Confederacy.[30] Christopher Memminger became a cabinet officer of the Confederate government. Perhaps Petigru was the chief Unionist who deserved the title as much during the Civil War as he did in the 1833 fight, for William T. Sherman wrote of the "noble service he rendered his country, by standing almost solitary in combatting the fearful heresy of 'Secession' which deluged our land in blood." [31]

However these veterans of the nullification and test-oath controversy of the 1830's looked upon civil war in 1860, there is no doubt that the earlier experience in local defiance of national law provided a fateful education for a fiery generation. Echoes of nullification theory of 1833 became secession fact in 1860. Patterns of loyalty-testing which South Carolina's Nullifiers found useful to defy Andrew Jackson were even more useful when Abraham Lincoln became the great ogre to the South.

CHAPTER VI

The House Divided

Civil War loyalty-testing divides naturally into three parts—Northern, Southern, and the ever-changing border region between the two. Americans of 1861–1865 lived under a complex of laws, edicts, and local understandings concerning their allegiance. Loyalty was a factor in the lives of millions, second only to the paramount fact of war itself.

It seemed for a time after the firing on Fort Sumter that the tale of unrestrained localism in loyalty-testing which had marked the American Revolution would be repeated north and south. In the North, however, Lincoln gradually raised relatively centralized Union loyalty tests to higher planes of political purposes. Confederate leaders never successfully emulated their sectional opponent. In the South, loyalty tests remained fixed in an internal security apparatus capable only of serving local police functions.

"Must I shoot a simple-minded soldier boy who deserts," demanded Abraham Lincoln when his internal security policies received criticism, "while I must not touch a hair of the head of a wily agitator who induces him to desert?" No, the harried president decided: "I think that in such a case, to silence the agitator, and save the boy, is not only constitutional, but, withal, a great mercy." [1] Here were the basic ingredients in the Northern antidisloyalty program of the Civil War—forceful prevention and punishment of subversion combined with the "great mercy" of which Lincoln spoke, the mercy of forgiveness rooted in his view of the presidential power.

When Lincoln took office the nation was already split on the rock of secession. After a short month of uneasy peace an unprecedented weight of wartime responsibilities fell upon his untried shoulders. Even as he called for troops to combat rebels in the field, prosecessionist mobs in Baltimore stoned volunteers rushing to protect the isolated capital, militiamen refused to swear to defend the Union, and federal army and navy officers resigned commissions rather than take up arms against insurgent states. Widespread pro-Southern sentiment in the North threatened to sever the vital northernmost tier of border states—Maryland, Kentucky, Missouri, and Arkansas—from the Union. Lincoln had to meet all these emergencies. An untried administration and a force of civil servants allegedly riddled with prorebel officeholders had to quell reported rebel plots, disarm disloyalty before it could become treason, and prevent disaffection from developing into sabotage.

If Lincoln did nothing about traitors, there were plenty of Northern patriots who were willing to take matters into their own hands. Excited vigilantes in divided border states, eager home guards, and suspicious police officers throughout the North imprisoned suspected secessionists. Tar and feather "parties" developed into tragic lynchings. Some Southern sympathizers found flight the better part of valor, but, from the viewpoint of ardent Northern Unionists, too many prorebels still infested the North.[2]

Northerners were quick to denounce each other for alleged pro-Confederate sympathies. Popular opinion, aided by Republican charges, tarred all Democrats with the sticky brush of treason because most Southerners were Democrats and that party had controlled the national government for twenty years preceding the secession movement. Political feuds, family quarrels, business competition; fear, distrust, hysteria; lawlessness in the name of loyalty combined to produce terror in many Northern and border communities. Perhaps it was true, as one proud vigilante of New York City boasted to Lincoln, that "the loyal people are good judges and know by instinct what giving aid and comfort to the rebels means." But Lincoln was less confident. He feared that the loyal peoples' "instinct," however energetic, was too local in application and too erratic in performance. Someone had to meet the disloyalty problem immediately, forcefully, and consistently. In Lincoln's view he, as wartime president, had the legitimate primary role and power in this matter.[3]

Soon after the war began Lincoln proclaimed martial law in especially sensitive Northern areas (the railroad line from Philadelphia to Washington, for instance), and suspended the privilege of the writ of habeas corpus in those places. Northern police and army officials, freed from traditional restraints of evidence requirements and due process guarantees, arrested hundreds of suspect civilians on the general charge of disloyalty. Some of them deserved imprisonment. Near Baltimore, federal troops arrested John Merryman, drillmaster of a company of prorebel sympathizers. His attorney tried to secure his release from military custody by a writ of habeas corpus. But the army officer in charge of the federal prison at Fort McHenry refused to honor the writ. His refusal provoked a blast from Roger B. Taney, Chief Justice of the United States, who, while on circuit, roundly condemned Lincoln's assumption of arbitrary powers.

Taney dealt with the Constitution in a vacuum of legalistic niceties. Lincoln, who also knew the Bill of Rights, believed that clear and immediate dangers justified its temporary and local suspension. "To state the question more directly," he later argued before Congress, "are all the laws, *but one,* to go unexecuted, and the government itself go to pieces, lest that one be violated?" Through four terrible years of civil war Lincoln kept a vision of a reunited nation clearly before him, and shaped Northern antidisloyalty policies to help achieve his dream. "The military arrests and detentions," he said in 1863, ". . . have been for *prevention,* and not for *punishment*—as injunctions, to stay injury, as proceedings to keep the peace—and hence, . . . they have not been accompanied with indictment, or trials by juries, nor in a single case by any punishment whatever, beyond what is purely incidental to the prevention." [4]

Behind the harshness, Lincoln's mercy palliated the worst features of the disloyalty prevention program. Neither time nor facilities permitted investigations of each charge of subversion or plea of innocence. It was utterly impossible for the Union to indict each suspect for treason. Lincoln could not undo wrongs which hapless civilians suffered at the hands of too-eager officials; he would not hazard the safety of the nation by freeing civilian prisoners who might then endanger the security of the Union. But Lincoln would trust the seemingly innocent man who, seeking freedom, would pay for it by swearing loyalty to the federal government. Lincoln's mercy was the mercy of trust in the honor of Americans, buttressed by his view of presidential power.

To translate attitude into policy, Lincoln placed William Seward, his Secretary of State, in charge of the antidisloyalty program in the North. Seward soon proved himself an energetic and resourceful amateur in police work, improvising men and measures to assist him in combating internal disaffection, weaving an antidisloyalty web which soon covered every corner of the North and extended into the nominally loyal border states.

Seward enlisted as counterespionage agents every Northern official who was willing to coöperate with him, and few dared incur suspicion of disloyalty or challenge patriotic feeling in their communities by refusing. In complete disregard of traditional political boundaries and of theories of the separation of powers, Seward enrolled municipal policemen, county sheriffs, city mayors, state governors, state and federal attorneys, federal marshals and postmasters, state militiamen and federal army officers as field agents, and empowered them to arrest any American citizen or alien resident who seemed disloyal. By means of the still-novel telegraph, Seward bound this motley crew to his Washington office. From his desk a stream of messages went to all corners of the nation, transmitting orders to arrest individuals, information on suspects, and allegations and accusations on mass subversion and individual sabotage. Under his orders federal army units and state militia troops assisted energetic amateur agents when local situations seemed too hot for routine handling. By midsummer, 1861, Seward could boast: "I can touch a bell . . . and order the arrest of a citizen of Ohio . . . and the imprisonment of a citizen of New York, and no power on earth, except that of the President of the United States, can release them." [5]

Seward's improvisations impressed many Northerners. A federal marshal in Connecticut overheard a civilian criticizing Lincoln at a public meeting, and threatened him with arrest. The speaker begged forgiveness for his impolitic remarks and promised better behavior. He also, once he and the marshal were alone, promised to inform on a group of prorebels in his community. The marshal took him before a justice of the peace who administered a loyalty oath to the deflated orator. According to the exultant marshal, this "gentleman has become *intensely loyal* since. Others who have heretofore expressed their views very freely in opposition to the Government, are as quiet as lambs. The loyal citizens here appear to be highly pleased with the result."

But Seward was unsatisfied with the operations of his hurriedly assembled corps of loyalty enforcers. He employed scores of private detectives as confidential agents in specific loyalty investigations, for infiltrating into suspicious and perhaps subversive organizations, and incidentally to check on the loyalty of other loyalty investigators. It was as one of Seward's operatives that Allan Pinkerton made his first reputation (and fortune) as a detective capable of handling delicate cases with political implications.

By midsummer, 1861, Seward was better satisfied with the quality of his antisubversion corps, for his agents were unearthing rich yields of potential traitors to the North. "The administration agents are becoming so vigilant," worried one Confederate secret agent in Maryland, "that . . . I fear to comment on political matters as my letters might be sent to Washington." The fearful man was not overpessimistic; a few days after he wrote this, a State Department detective at the head of a file of Union cavalry came at night to his home, and placed him in the notorious Old Capitol Prison in Washington. An alert postmaster enlisted in Seward's service had censored the incriminating letter, decided that the writer was disloyal, and reported to Seward.[6]

Government agents had broad definitions of disloyalty. In one three-week period in 1861, they arrested American civilians on these charges: of being a noisy secessionist and doing great mischief by his treasonable talk; of being an intimate friend and companion of one arrested for disloyalty; of giving consideration and power to the rebel cause by his open sympathy and support; of opposing the federal government; of having deep sympathy with the rebellion; of being a secessionist; of aiding the rebellion; of treason; of being a dangerous man; of having secession proclivities; of expressing gratification over rebel victory; of being a resident of Atlanta, Georgia; of attempting to run the blockade; of holding decided sympathies and sentiments for the rebels; of suspicion of being engaged in contraband trade; of taking and concealing a government balloon; of habitually leaving his home early in the evening on horseback and returning late at night, and of saying that the United States government was oppressive; of having used treasonable language and having hurrahed for Jeff Davis and having d——d old Lincoln; of having a misunderstanding with a government agent; of enticing soldiers away from camp; of inciting to desertion and of disorganizing commands; of being dangerous to the peace and welfare of Union-loving people; of dissuading enlistment in the service of the United States; of expressing the strongest secession sentiments; of suspicion of being on the way to join the rebel army; of raising a secession flag on his premises; of taking up arms against the government; of communicating information to the enemy; of visiting the insurrectionary states on commercial business; of purchasing arms for the use of the rebels; of betraying his brother-in-law, a federal army officer, to the enemy; of treasonable correspondence; of displaying Confederate buttons, emblems, and so forth; of selling Confederate songs;

of bridge-burning; of being a shrewd and dangerous spy; of attempting to enter insurrectionary states contrary to the president's proclamation; of refusing to take the oath of allegiance to the United States government (a civil servant); of gross violation of the criminal law; of furnishing a supply of stock to the rebel army.[7]

In the first hectic weeks of the spy-catching operation, prisoners arrested on such charges were lodged anywhere handy. But local jails soon overflowed with the addition of political prisoners to the war-swollen number of ordinary criminal types, and Seward received War Department permission to use military forts as detention centers. These stretched in a long arc of repression from Fort Warren in Boston to Fort Lafayette in New York and Fort McHenry in Baltimore. There were also specially improvised detention centers: the notorious converted residence in Washington called Old Capitol Prison, the rickety former warehouse on Gratiot Street in St. Louis, and a portion of the war-prisoner tent city in Chicago's Camp Chase. These "American Bastilles," as their unhappy inmates termed them, were guarded by Union troops, but it was State Department authority that placed men and women in the cells. Only that authority, or that of Lincoln which it represented, could release them.

But if it was terribly easy for an American to go to prison in 1861, for reasons no one bothered to tell him, it was almost as simple for him to get out. Granted that the alleged crime was not too serious, that evidence (if any existed) seemed inconclusive of more than suspicious behavior, then Lincoln's mercy—and loyalty test—took effect. "I have just left the President," noted Ward Hill Lamon, marshal of the District of Columbia, to a political prisoner who pleaded for swift release. At the White House Lamon had placed the prisoner's case before Lincoln and Seward. "They inform me," Lamon told the distraught inmate of Old Capitol, "that they must deal with you as they do with the others—And that you will be released upon your taking the oath of allegiance." [8]

Most prisoners were overjoyed to discover how easily they could go free, and cared little that they never learned why they had been arrested. Nor could officials, who often lost all records of individual cases, enlighten them. Most imprisoned men were willing to forego asking too many questions about civil rights. From political prisoners in a dozen jails came applications to take the oath. A salesman of mowing machines, arrested for having sketched Union fortifications in Kentucky, claiming that the sinister sketches were of mere agricultural implements, was willing to ignore the issue of justice and swear his loyalty to get out of Camp Chase. An eighty-year-old political prisoner invoked the Deity to support his guiltless life: "God knows my innocence of any sympathy with the rebellion. I have long been a Democrat thinking a man could be a Democrat and a Union man at the same time." This patriarch, sick, weak, brokenhearted over his son's prorebel sympathies which had by implication tarred the father with the same offense and landed the old man in prison, eagerly reached for the proffered Bible and took the required oath.[9]

Prisoners wrote to the most influential people they knew—politicians, ministers, army officers—for character references. "The statements are so satisfactory," Seward decided in the case of an Ohioan imprisoned for three months for allegedly selling horses to Confederate agents, "that I feel it my duty to discharge him on his taking the oath if he does so voluntarily and in seeming good faith in his motive." [10] A Delaware youth impetuously hid a runaway Union observation balloon which descended upon his farm. Imprisoned, he begged for release, noting his motherless childen at home and his repentance over his guileless act of folly. The oath freed him.[11] A Virginian who had voted for secession before the war, then found his home in federal lines, was the target of malicious accusations of disloyalty from his Unionist neighbors. The hapless man left a family ill with scarlet fever (three children died while he was in jail) and a wife frantic with worry. He took the oath in time to return home to bury his dead. "For God's sake," pleaded a sixteen-year-old New Yorker who was arrested in suspicious company, "release me from Fort McHenry. I will cheerfully take the oath of allegiance." A Bostonian: "I am not only willing but anxious to take the oath." A Pennsylvanian: "There has never been a time when my heart would not have responded to any oath that might have been required of me." A Maryland schoolteacher, who while drunk had shouted "Hurrah for Jeff Davis and damned be old Lincoln!" pleaded his pitiful salary and pledged future temperance. "When sober," Seward decided, "he is a quiet and peaceable citizen. He is too insignificant to do injury to any cause." Again, the oath freed the sufferer.

It freed men because Lincoln felt that if necessity impelled the Union to protect itself from internal harm by arresting suspect civilians, the cause of the Union gained nothing from keeping presumably harmless prisoners in jail. Of some Kentuckians who were arrested on their way to join the rebels, Lincoln said: "The exercise of clemency towards these misguided young men will do no harm to the cause of the United

States, but would have a good effect in the neighborhood in which the prisoners reside." Another Kentuckian (Lincoln knew life in Kentucky) gained freedom by oath "to show those rascals there that we believe ourselves strong enough to be generous." [12]

By August, 1861, federal prison officials offered all incoming political offenders the opportunity to swear future loyalty to the Union. If the prisoner was willing to swear the oath, then the rest was up to the jailer, who could study the case, decide the degree of disloyalty involved, and offer the oath on the spot. Often the Union officer would withhold decision so that the educational effects of a few weeks of incarceration might impress the prisoner, in the event that he had been guilty of indiscretion, if not disloyalty. If, on the other hand, a civilian prisoner had been captured in the act of treason or sabotage and seemed conclusively guilty, then prison officials offered him no oath test. Such a prisoner remained in jail, awaiting trial by military tribunal, utterly without recourse.

Antidisloyalty arrests naturally attracted attention. Newspapers, especially when plagued by a dearth of news from battle fronts, kept reporters busy fabricating tales of treason which ever-imaginative Union officials supplied from unsubstantiated accusations. Northern public opinion remained easily convinced that every community harbored nests of prorebel vipers. It required brave men to speak out for political prisoners; for associating with them, or defending them, might bring public condemnation of equal guilt. Thus, Northern attorneys who visited political prisoners to settle personal affairs (no lawyers were permitted to defend the inmates in a legal sense) were careful to deny personal sympathy with their incarcerated clients. Robert Gillen, an attorney of New York, discreetly told Seward that his request for a pass to see a prisoner at Fort Lafayette was dictated by "no sympathy with the traitors whatever and in my actions towards this man I shall act strictly in accordance with this principle." All visitors to political prisoners had to have passes from the prison commander, and each pass bore a loyalty oath which the visitor had to sign before he could talk with the prisoner. Some inmates ceased writing to friends and families, as did one who doubted that a brother in Maryland should search for evidence to free him, "as his own 'loyalty' may be suspected, if he makes any inquiries." [13]

Most civilian prisoners were nameless folk who somehow ran afoul of Seward's disloyalty prevention apparatus; their fates mattered little except to themselves and their families. But the dragnet scooped up more prominent persons. When powerful and vocal men found themselves suddenly prisoners in grim Northern jails, then Seward learned that his energetic agents could get him and the Lincoln administration into deep trouble.

Maryland had been a continuing headache to Lincoln from the first day of the war. The state commanded the avenues of communication between the capital and the North, and thousands of Marylanders were pro-Southern. Lincoln proclaimed martial law there, and federal officers struggled to keep bridge burners, smugglers, and spies under control. What really kept Seward's agents busy in Maryland was lesser subversive fry: wearers of secession emblems, youths seeking to slip across federal lines to join rebel forces, irresponsible rumormongers who magnified Confederate victories and Union reverses. In midsummer, 1861, however, Seward learned that a substantial number of the state's officials were allegedly conspiring to injure the Union cause.

Common gossip and uncommon loyalty investigations disclosed that many members of the Maryland state legislature were plotting to pass a secession ordinance when the state assembly convened in November. Since a strong force of General John A. Dix's Union troops was stationed in Maryland, such an ordinance would have been little more than gasconade. But it undoubtedly would have unnerved the North, still reeling from the effects of military defeat at Bull Run. The South would have gained a propaganda weapon, and a secession vote in Maryland might prove to Europeans, already doubtful that the Union could survive, that it was time to recognize the legal existence of the Confederacy.

Seward and Lincoln believed that prevention was worth much future cure, and agreed with War Secretary Simon Cameron that anyone "giving aid and comfort to the enemy . . . should be arrested even when there is want of positive proof of their guilt." [14] On the night of September 17, 1861, General Dix triggered into action the complex preparations he and Seward had made; artillerymen trained cannon down Baltimore's streets; infantry blockaded the major routes of travel in and through the state; cavalry galloped to scores of different strategic points, armed with lists of disloyal Marylanders which Seward's agents supplied. A substantial slice of Maryland's officialdom began the trek to federal prison.

Seward was surprised when these prisoners became an overnight *cause célèbre*. He was unprepared for the howl of outrage that the antiadministration press unleashed at this example of "Lincoln despotism over a sovereign state," and no less distressed by the extremist Republican press which demanded he shoot the prisoners forthwith, or at least keep them in jail for the duration. When Lord Lyons, the British ambassador, noted to Seward that these arbitrary arrests were increasing anti-Union feelings in Europe, and when Congress began an investigation of its own, Seward and Lincoln knew that they had to do something. To Congress, Lincoln answered that "the public safety" prevented him from divulging the reasons impelling the arrests. But he assured the legislators that "no arrest has been made, or will be made, not based on substantial and unmistakable complicity with those in armed rebellion against the . . . United States." He insisted that federal authorities had complete evidence in each case "which will, when made public, be satisfactory to every loyal citizen." [15] His words failed to satisfy congressmen or public. It was up to Seward, who decided that the best course was to get the imprisoned Marylanders released from jail as quickly as possible. The swiftest way to do that was for the prisoners to take the oath. Seward ordered prison commanders to offer the oath to each of the inmates. To Seward's chagrin, almost all refused to swear, content to rot in jail rather than compromise their principles.

This took courage. The prisoners were not young men. In individual cases health, reputations, and fortunes were already suffering from the effects of imprisonment. "I am 60 years old and disabled," William McNabb pleaded with Seward. "My continued confinement cannot possibly be necessary to the Government." McNabb, a Maryland legislator, was wrong. It was necessary as long as he refused the oath. Men like McNabb found themselves in the unhappy position which a fellow political prisoner set to the spirit of Hamlet's soliloquy:

> To swear or not to swear, that is the question.
> Whether 'tis nobler in a man to suffer
> Imprisonment, exile and poverty,
> Or take the oath amidst a sea of troubles,
> And by submission end them? To swear, to lie
> Once more, and, by a lie, to say we end
> Starvation, nakedness, and all the ills
> That Rebels are heir to—'tis a perjury
> Devoutly to be wished. To swear—to lie;
> To lie!—perchance a change; aye, there's the rub,
> For in that change the angry rebels may come,
> When from these lands the Federals are driven out,
> Must give us pause; there's the respect
> That makes a man of honor hesitate.

But who would bear at the dead hour of night
To be roused from his sleep,—dragged out of bed—
To be locked up in jail—to hold his tongue—
Before a mock tribunal to be tried,
And then condemned for deeds he knew not of,
When he himself these evils might avoid
By perjury? Who would detectives bear—
To look about before he opens his mouth,
But that the dread of bayonets and chains—
The provost-marshal, from whose iron grip
No victim e'er escapes, puzzles the will,
And makes us swallow every oath that comes,
Than fly to evils that we dread still more?

Thus, love of ease makes patriots of us all!
And thus our sympathies are sicklied o'er
With confiscation, banishment and death!
With this regard, we doff our principles,
And swallow Abe, the Nigger, and the Oath! [16]

A few of the prisoners decided to "swallow Abe" and the oath Abe demanded. But more stubborn men persisted in their defiant course. In long, bitter letters to friends, families, and newspapers, they criticized their jailers, denounced Seward, and anathematized Lincoln. These communications often found space in antiadministration newspapers, and proved so galling to Seward that he imposed censorship on all the imprisoned Marylanders' letters. He also ordered prison officials to conduct a discreet campaign of persuasion and argumentation to convince the prisoners to swear to the Lincoln oath, countered adverse newspaper accounts with "planted" material in such Unionist newspapers as the *Brooklyn Eagle* ("We never knew a man sent to prison," its editor wrote, "who did not consider his fare and treatment 'hard' "), and urged families and friends of the stubborn prisoners to pressure them to take the oath. Nothing seemed to do any good. Naturally, many Northerners considered any refusal to swear to the Union loyalty oath clear proof that the nonjurors were guilty of disloyalty. Such men, a federal district attorney concluded, "are not loyal in opinions or designs." A friend of one of the inmates puzzled over the latter's obstinate refusal to swear: "By refusing the oath does he not give cause to suspect that his heart is not in the right place?" [17]

Seward had no time to worry over implications. He wanted these men out of jail now that the critical Maryland elections were safely past. If they declined to conform to standard State Department loyalty procedures, Seward was willing to create extraordinary administrative channels for them. At the same time, he could give a public impression of exerting every effort to achieve justice. Seward established a series of special loyalty-investigating commissions, with instructions to interview each political prisoner, and to decide in every case whether the inmate was fit for release. It was thin disguise for an effort to pressure the prominent Maryland inmates out of jail.

The most prominent loyalty-investigating commission was composed of Judge Edwards Pierrepont of New York and Union army General John A. Dix; it toured federal prisons in Maryland, Delaware, and northern Virginia. Every prisoner found this notice on his cell door, the day before the commissioners arrived: "The undersigned, appointed by the Secretary of State to examine into the cases of the political prisoners, . . . desire these prisoners to be prepared tomorrow, to answer the question whether they would severally be willing to take the oath of allegiance to the . . . United States if they should be set at liberty." Most of the political prisoners welcomed the commissioners, pleased that at last the government was going to investigate their claims of innocence, until they realized that the notice concluded with the tricky phrase, ". . . further inquiry in each case to depend upon willingness to take the oath." There would be loyalty investigations only if the prisoner was willing to swear loyalty. Dix and the other loyalty commissioners hewed strictly to this policy. "Our citizens must be for the Union or against it," wrote Dix, "and if they refuse to give a pledge of fidelity to it, they can be regarded in no other light than as secret enemies." In a similar vein, he condemned those who refused the oath as self-confessedly guilty of disloyalty: "His refusal to accept it indicates the justice of his arrest." It seems hardly surprising that, as a loyalty investigator, Dix should have been somewhat less than fair to those prisoners who decided that they would not take the test of loyalty.[18]

Many of the die-hard nonjurors took to their pens in bitter attacks on the loyalty commissioners. "If my interview with the commission is considered an investigation," an angry inmate wrote to General Dix, "then all my anticipations for ever obtaining justice are at an end. I renew my claim to be discharged without conditions." And here was the heart of the matter, for what most of the nonjurors were objecting to in the oath requirement was that in taking it the prisoner assumed in the public eye an admission of guilt. After months in jail, still ignorant of precisely why they had been sent there in the first place, despite filth and poor food, rheumatism and distraught families, most of the Maryland men were ready to stay in prison rather than imply by taking the oath that their incarceration had been just. Most of the imprisoned Maryland officials demanded release with apologies from the government, rather than oaths from them to the government. It was a stalemate that the stubborn prisoners seemed unlikely to break.

The loyalty commissioners continued their work through the winter of 1861–62, netting a few in every prison who were willing to swear in order to gain their release, but on the whole failing in their real task—to get the political incubus of the imprisoned Marylanders off Seward's neck. Seth Hawley of Boston, loyalty commissioner at Fort Warren, was, according to one jubilant prisoner, "very much disgusted at the results of his mission, found but three or four that were willing to take the oath, and had to listen to a good deal of plain talk not at all complimentary to him or his master." The master, Seward, was still caught on a hook of his own making.[19] Seward, stubborn and proud, refused to recede. He gained Lincoln's public support. When an imprisoned Maryland official appealed directly to Lincoln for release without oath, Lincoln replied that the prisoner knew a way to get out of jail, the way of the oath. "If Mr. Davis is still so hostile to the Government," wrote Lincoln, "and so determined to aid its enemies in destroying it, he makes his own choice." [20]

The furor refused to die. Democrats the country over delighted in attacking Lincoln by calling Seward "tyrant" and "dictator." Political axes were sharp on both sides of the partisan fence. Many Republicans as well as Democrats, now that the federal Congress was in session, were anxious to clamp down on Lincoln's much-disliked Secretary of State. Congressmen of both parties were jealous of the tremendous power executive officers had assumed in the war crisis. Congress determined to investigate the executive loyalty-investigating system.

A committee of Congress, headed by Republican Senator Lyman Trumbull of Illinois, was charged with ascertaining the necessity for the habeas corpus suspension and the arbitrary arrests. In mid-December, 1861, the committeemen met with Seward to get his side of the story on record. Seward greeted the congressmen, welcoming all questions until the inquest became heated and bitter. Then he lost his temper. "Why the hell," he demanded of the legislators, "are you not fighting traitors at home instead of seeking their release here?" He didn't give a "damn," Seward shouted, whether those he arrested were innocent or guilty of treason; he was preventing them from damaging the Union, not punishing them for past injury to it. Would the senators suggest that his officers placidly await sabotage before they arrested subversives? [21]

Seward's answers may have been forceful, but this was no way to treat important congressmen. His operations had stepped on so many toes, hurt so many individuals, and undercut so many political props that even his own party was increasingly sure that he was, as loyalty controller at least, a liability. It was easy even for Lincoln's supporters to criticize Seward as internal security administrator. His administration of the program had been slipshod and erratic. Northern officials were under so little supervision in these matters that many became notoriously addicted to brutality and corruption. Seward never was able to centralize his sprawling, hurriedly assembled apparatus; he never really controlled it, and never defined the relationship of his motley conglomeration of officials to himself. Lincoln's administration was suffering from the improprieties of incautious counterspies.

Lincoln made it as painless as possible. The rigged Maryland election had resulted in a large Republican majority, hardly surprising because most influential Maryland Democrats were in jail, and Maryland voters had to take loyalty oaths at bayonet points before depositing their open ballots. Lincoln ordered the release of all political prisoners from Maryland on their simple parole not to do anything against the Union (a lesser commitment than an oath), if they would also promise to resign all state and federal offices they held when arrested. Seward simultaneously told reporters that tensions were easing in the North: "Summary and severe measures are no longer required and the Government may rely for the present upon the devotion and patriotism of the great mass of its citizens." He also alleged, truthfully enough, that diplomatic chores were absorbing an increasing part of his time.

It was transparently clear to cynical Washingtonians. "Seward gives it up as a bad job," they gossiped, when, early in February, 1862, it was officially announced [22] that the new secretary of war, Edwin M. Stanton, would assume charge of the antidisloyalty program as part of his duties. Stanton was an unknown quantity. He soon proved himself determined to coöperate with Congress as Seward had never done; he appeared before legislative investigating committees, including those inquiring into the arbitrary arrests of civilians and the conduct of military strategy, and the House committee investigating the disloyalty of civil and military officers. So far as civilian prisoners were concerned, Stanton followed Seward's last-announced policy of releasing as many as possible on oath.

By early 1862 the North was more secure internally. Whether this apparent safety was a result of nine months of energetic antidisloyalty action or of increasingly sophisticated martial dedication, or an indication that the danger of mass subversion had never actually existed, forms a still-debatable question.

For the remaining three years of the war, the civilian loyalty program was a War Department function, and became much more an arm of Lincoln's military strategy and political planning than it had ever been when Seward controlled it. Lincoln's concept of the loyalty oath as a measure for determining political acceptability broadened into a war and reconstruction weapon which moved south with advancing Union forces. When Stanton took charge of the antidisloyalty program early in 1862, loyalty tests went to war.

Northern congressmen found themselves following throughout the war a loyalty trail blazed by Lincoln's executive officers. Legislators criticized presidential suspension of habeas corpus privileges and denounced his policy of arbitrary arrests, but Congress finally ratified these policies.[23] Congress tried to lead the loyalty-testing processes, as it tried to make strategy and reconstruction policies instruments of congressional rather than executive control. It became one of the primary items in an intra-Republican struggle for control over the war. The problem of disloyal government officials formed the first phase of this Republican family feud.

Sensational stories of subversion among federal officials ran riot in the North in the tense months before hostilities commenced. From coast to coast, fearful popular opinion began to doubt that any public official was trustworthy. The editor of the *Chicago Tribune,* for instance, heard from a Washington correspondent that the commanding general of the United States Army, Winfield Scott, was a "hoary old double dyed traitor" who afforded secessionists "free hints of our plans." And the worried Governor of California warned the chief executive of Massachusetts: "Do not be surprised at any news of treason, however extraordinary, which you may hear." [24] In an upside-down world, when a nation disintegrated into warring sections, no man trusted his neighbor, and certainly not his public servants.

Lingering doubts troubled the North. Who could say that all pro-Southern officials had left government service, that traitors and rebel sympathizers were not still on the payroll of the nation, secretly plotting to end its life in a vast conspiracy of slaveholders? Republican politicians, flushed with electoral victory, eager to make names for themselves and their ambitious new party, hungry for all the spoils of office they could garner, uncritically added to dark tales of treason in the federal bureaucracy. Their condemnations of Democratic defections added to Northern uncertainty concerning the trustworthiness of the nation's official servants. Lincoln shared this uncertainty. But the hours in each day were too few for all that the harried president must do. Lincoln insisted to Congress that the loyalty of executive officers was an executive rather than a legislative concern, but let his cabinet officers deal individually with their own subordinates.

The only unanimous decision Lincoln's cabinet officers reached on the question of loyalty tests for government officials was that each employee should reswear his oath of allegiance. This obvious requirement of the first war month drove out of federal service some scores of officials who until then had sat on the fence of sectional allegiance. And some of them took the trains that were still running directly to the South (one of the anomalies of the confused early days of the war) to offer themselves to the rebel government. It surely could have been no intention of Lincoln's Cabinet to recruit for rebeldom! [25]

Soon, however, the trains stopped running. Severity replaced moderation for those federal officials who declined to take loyalty oaths. By July, 1861, and throughout the four years of war to come, the government officer who refused to swear loyalty faced imprisonment until he would swear. In one instance Seward ordered a secret agent of his department to "have an eye to E. B. Grayson. He has just resigned from the employ of Uncle Sam, refusing to take the oath. . . . He ought to be put in some safe place." Fort Lafayette was safe enough. In grim irony, the Confederate spies against whom the test oath was supposed to operate delighted in learning that they could normally secure federal employment without difficulty in the labor-hungry Northern capital, and they did not hesitate to swear all the Union loyalty oaths required. [26]

Each cabinet officer was free, in those loose times of administrative independence, to add whatever criteria of allegiance he chose to the standard oath requirement. Informality and lack of standardization did not, however, necessarily mean impartiality. Patronage considerations inextricably mixed with tests of loyalty; Republicans' loyalty oaths were generally worth more than those that Democrats swore, as prerequisites for federal positions. And, in a dozen Northern state governments, partisanship and patriotism mingled in similar unhealthy stews.

In none of the loyalty-security programs inaugurated by Lincoln's Cabinet was there any standardized opportunity for accused employees to seek redress. Suspect civil and military officers were not entirely without recourse, however, and in many instances the more energetic among them were able to convince supervisory officials of their innocence. Some accused officials took their cases directly to the President. Others wisely gained the support of influential politicians in their behalf, a factor which no cabinet officer could wisely ignore. Those employees who failed to convince their bureau heads that they were truly loyal faced the dismal road to one of the American Bastilles. Civil servants and military officers who lost positions and went to prison on disloyalty charges could not hope for redress in the courts. A few tried to sue for false arrest, but never carried their suits to a conclusion. They had no opportunity for review of their cases, nor to redress the wrongs which many of the imprisoned men claimed had been done them. The truth of their guilt or innocence remains uncertain even today.[27]

The executive employee loyalty program received very little publicity. Newspapermen found that with the exception of Postmaster General Montgomery Blair, cabinet officers refused to divulge details. Battles, in any event, usually made better headlines than bureaucrats. As a result the public was hardly conscious that the federal government was involved in combing its ranks for apparent security risks.

What did make headlines were the few cases of civil and military servants who became involved in genuine plots against the Union. Complaints that Washington remained a hotbed of secession sentiment and rebel espionage were rife all through the war. Northern public opinion continued to blame civil servants for providing the Confederates with intelligence which resulted in military defeats for Union forces. Charles Francis Adams, American ambassador to England, complained that "much of what is done at Washington is known to the Confederates by the treachery of subordinates yet retained by Government."[28] Congress, convening for its first wartime session in July, 1861, determined to find out why.

The first wartime Congress organized under the numerical domination of Republicans. Men representing many attitudes on important issues called themselves by that political title. Lincoln represented a moderate faction which saw the eventual political reconstruction of the nation as the primary war aim, and relegated the burning question of Negro emancipation to a place of secondary importance.

Other Republican congressmen—Sumner and Davis of Massachusetts, Lane of Kansas, Stevens of Pennsylvania, Wade of Ohio, and Trumbull of Illinois—proudly accepted the title of "radicals." Their radicalism consisted in large part of convictions that immediate Negro emancipation was a primary aim of the war and a prerequisite of reconstruction, of advocacy of the harshest punishments for rebels of the South and their sympathizers in the North, and of the assumption that congressional rather than presidential leadership should command the war effort. American history is in part a story of an institutional tug of war between Congress and president for primacy in national affairs. War and crisis normally have given the executive this coveted primacy; Lincoln and the legislatures of the Civil War could not escape history.

Republican congressmen, with their party in power for the first time, were eager to make names for themselves and anxious to realize their social and economic convictions. They were also hungry for the patronage that formed the needed sustenance of permanent political life, and so paid particular attention to the burgeoning federal military and civil services. A succession of intra-Republican struggles emerged from this complex background of individual ambitions, ideological convictions, and institutional traditions. Radical Republicans wanted Congress, under their control, to dominate the federal government and thus realize their economic policies and abolitionist beliefs. Lincoln firmly insisted that he, as president, had the sole constitutional right to direct the war, and exhibited himself as a moderate on the Negro and reconstruction issues.

Radical Republicans found a most useful argument when they claimed that rebel sympathizers remained in the military and civil services. It was easy for Northern congressmen to blame Union defeats in the field upon treason at home, convenient for radical Republicans to flay Democratic opponents as natural sympathizers with rebellion. It was strategically opportune for radicals to place their own, like-thinking men in positions in the federal bureaucracy, and such a patronage opportunity was heaven-sent.[29]

So radicals in the wartime Congresses unleashed oblique attacks upon Lincoln in the form of congressional investigating committees, whose members developed fine techniques for making political hay in the sunshine of newspaper headlines. Lincoln's determination to retain control of military strategy and higher military appointments eventually foiled the radicals' plans, but not before they injected an unhealthy political canker into federal administration. Congress launched this crusade in the name of loyalty.

A Republican representative from Wisconsin, Congressman John Fox Potter, became the torchbearer of radical plans. He was a colorful figure. A contemporary witness described him as "one of the very strongest men in the 39th Congress. . . . He has back-bone enough for half a dozen Congresses." Potter was an unqualified Unionist whose strictures against secessionists and their sympathizers achieved note even in the oratory-laden Washington atmosphere. In mid-July, 1861, Potter proposed that the House form an investigating committee to unearth federal employees who "are known to entertain sentiments of hostility to the Government . . . and who have refused to take the oath to support the Government." The House named him chairman, and newspapers almost immediately fastened the title "Potter's Committee" to this investigating group, for Potter soon obscured the other four committeemen from public consciousness. Potter let his constituents know of his new assignment, and learned that Wisconsin was "rejoiced to hear that the traitors who have been retained in our camp are now to be cleaned out." [30]

Potter launched his loyalty investigation by circularizing all federal department heads, asking them to list federal employees who had not sworn allegiance to the Union, or who were in any way possibly disloyal. As such lists returned to Potter's chambers from the executive offices, his staff arranged the names in several categories of possible danger to the nation. Potter completely ignored the fact that executive officers were already engaged in loyalty house cleanings in their own departments, and paid no attention to the detail that most of the names he listed represented men who were already, voluntarily or under protest, out of federal employment.

If Potter had stopped at this point his activities would have made no ripple at all on the surface of Civil War history. But he chose to go much further. He let it be known around Washington that he wanted information, and that he would protect all informants who provided his committee with leads to disloyal personnel. The swinging doors of Potter's committee room were soon opening to admit men and women who had accusations to make, but who wished to keep secret their identities as accusers of their fellows. Potter received an increasing load of mail; accusations, allegations, and affidavits followed one another in growing volume.

Some informants were too cautious even to write, much less to appear personally before the loyalty investigator. By mid-July Potter was arranging rendezvous with such hesitant souls, where they might safely unburden themselves of disclosures of past or future treason. He created confidential codes so that clerks could communicate with his staff in seeming innocence. His network grew with amazing rapidity. Only a month after he began work, Potter told the House of his "astonishment at the number of well-authenticated cases of disloyalty to the Government" which he had unearthed. When Potter encountered federal officials who refused to coöperate with his investigators, or to supply him with lists of suspect personnel, he "planted" or recruited informers in their departments. Such men, as Potter used them, were not merely to seek out alleged disloyalists, but were also to identify higher executive officials who were less than wholeheartedly willing to supply Potter with the information he demanded.

News of Potter's work spread rapidly through Washington. Once-voluble federal employees found discretion infinitely preferable to a place on Potter's dreaded roster of disloyalty, the existence of which became a hobgoblin haunting the dreams of clerks and secretaries. "You might as well ask a Patagonian for information as one of the clerks," noted a federal police officer, and the influential *Springfield Republican* commented on the sudden restraint that had fallen upon Washington's social world since Potter appeared as inquisitor: "Since it became publicly known that Potter's Committee was looking for them, traitors became more discreet in their manifestations." [31] By Christmas, 1861, Potter's fact-finding apparatus extended throughout Washington's federal bureaus and across the nation, traveled with diplomats to foreign shores, and extended to military and naval units in battle areas and training camps.

A daily drama of disloyalty was enacted in Potter's committee chambers. Most often the supporting players chose to remain anonymous, or performed under stage names like "Patriotic American," "Lincoln Man," or "Union Forever." Informants told tales of treason, described disloyalty, intimated infidelity. Here, often in emotional distress approaching hysteria, came the accused, who in some way learned of the charges against them, determined to deny, rebut, and to plead for lost position and reputation. Americans spoke of loyalty and disloyalty in terms of individual interpretation and action, condemned friends and families (sometimes their own friends and families) of aiding rebellion or of sympathizing with the enemy's cause.

A host of written accusations centered on federal personnel who refused the oath of loyalty, or who spoke disparagingly of its importance,

158

who satirized it in lampoons and demeaned it in cartoons. One anonymous informant accused eight treasury clerks of associating with subversive Democrats and declared that the unholy octet kept their jobs only through the direct intercession of secession supporters in the White House. Another writer cautioned Potter about a revenue officer then on patrol off New York, who allegedly cheered his wife's addiction to embroidering feminine underwear with Jefferson Davis' image, argued down his subordinates in wardroom debates over secession and abolition, and predicted military success for the South. Be warned, a third accuser admonished Potter, of a patent examiner whose pro-Southern sympathies endured from a Virginia boyhood, and whose daughter had danced with Confederate General Beauregard only three years before the war commenced.

Other patriotic informants warned Potter of federal civil and military personnel who spoke too much of sectional compromise, or too little of joy in Union victory; who criticized his committee or Frémont's abolitionist proclamations; whose wives, families, and associates were suspect; whose adult children chose to serve Secessia rather than the Union; whose past activity in Democratic party councils labeled them as presently untrustworthy; whose proslavery attitudes in the decades since 1820 did not change in 1861; who assertedly had secret caches of weapons in Washington homes awaiting the arrival of Confederate troops; who refused, or less than wholeheartedly performed, militia drill service when the first war actions imperiled the capital; who bought too few subscriptions to Republican party affairs; who substituted "Home of the Slave" for the correct line in the anthem, and loudly sang the burlesque after a night's carousing in the saloons of Washington; who saw no good in the seizure of Mason and Slidell or in confiscation or in the suspension of habeas corpus; who once knew the suspicious Vallandigham; who refused to reject Southern ancestry and accent as currently dishonorable; who bandaged rebel as well as federal wounded when the rout of Bull Run cast its human wreckage into the homes of government employees near Washington; who had helped to stock Southern arsenals with supplies before 1861, supplies which a later Confederacy was to seize; whose age, penury, or homosexuality made them susceptible to the notorious blandishments of allegedly omnipresent Confederate secret agents.

Accusations of disloyalty were directed at generals and admirals, cavalrymen and gardeners, file clerks and auditors, watchmen and pages, postal inspectors and surgeons, janitors and jailers. Potter's committee diligently listened, collected evidence in sworn testimony

and unsworn letter, assembled assertions of disloyalty into neat categories, stated its conclusions as to the guilt or innocence of the accused,
and forwarded the lot to executive officers. Here, as Potter defined his
task, his responsibility ended. From this point, as the loyalty investigator envisaged the proper method of unearthing subversion, the
course was clearly marked, with no complicating issues of jurisdiction
or justice. Potter's condemnation should have been enough signal for
executive superior officers to discharge the man concerned. Potter was
surprised and indignant to learn that it was not to be so simple.

Opposition to Potter's investigatory techniques arose first on the
House floor from a group of border-state Democrats. Did the House of
Representatives have the right, demanded Kentucky's Wickliffe, "to go
about the highways and byways, . . . and inquire of John Doe and
Richard Roe, 'Have you heard that such and such a man is not exactly
as he ought to be to hold office?' " Are not innocent men and women
being deprived of position, are not patriotic Americans being vilified
as traitors, is not the Union's cause suffering rather than benefiting
from Potter's investigations? Were not Potter's methods—the use of
secret testimony, the denial of the right of the accused to be heard in
rebuttal—usurpations of the executive function of overseeing its own
personnel? Were not the bulwarks of American liberty endangered in
Potter's committee rooms? Were not political partisanship and spoils
advantages for Republicans equated with loyalty to America?

It was, Potter replied, all beside the point. His defense rested upon
a lengthy description of secession, an emotional recital of the perils
which Union arms were facing because of Southerners and their sympathizers. His critics, Potter warned, were Democrats and lukewarm
Republicans, were they not? Had not the Democratic party planned
treason for twenty years in the very halls of Congress? Had not Democrats split the Union, were not Americans dying because traitors had
prostituted the Union to the harlot's goal of slave expansion? This
was no time for temporizing.

It was even more beside the point, Potter claimed, for Congressmen
to inject the question of civil liberties into the discussion. His committee was not a court but an investigating body created to gather data
and report its conclusions to the House. His methods could not involve
judicial safeguards and must maintain inviolate the anonymity of informants. Potter described the committee as a channel into which all
assertions of disloyalty might be launched and directed to the proper
executive authorities. The nation, Potter warned the House, needed
such a channel. He hinted that many high-level executive officers re-

maining on government payrolls were old-line Democrats, Brecken-
ridge and Buchanan men, who kept their offices in the absence of a
dedicated antislavery policy by Lincoln's administration. Could a lowly
clerk appear before them, inform on his fellows, and expect anything
but contumely? Fear of retribution would cancel patriotic willingness
to condemn others, Potter asserted; his committee provided a safe
arena of secrecy. There was evidence that even cabinet secretaries and
bureau heads defended disloyal cliques—could the House do less than
defend those who sought to expose these cliques?

No, Potter concluded, his critics were wrong through design or ignorance. War demanded sacrifice. Employees discharged because of evidence gathered by his committee suffered only a return to the general
level of citizens, and might evidence their patriotism by enlisting in
military service. But even if hurt occurred, even if reputations were
besmirched, his committee was necessary and its methods were justified.
Potter won the day.[32]

Newspaper accounts of the Wisconsin loyalty investigator's activities
carried Potter's name across the nation. Potter's Committee was a campaign weapon with which Republican orators and writers flayed the
Democratic foe in the 1862 congressional campaign. "The investigations of the . . . Potter Committee . . . are fully sustained," declared
one Republican election handbook. "Indeed," the partisan author lamented, "it can only be regretted that the investigations have not been
more searching and the removals more vigorous." [33]

But Potter met still other obstacles from another branch of government. He learned that his plan of action lost its smoothness when it
reached the rocky shoals of the executive offices. From "planted" or volunteer informants in every federal bureau, Potter heard that the
"Potter lists" were going astray, or rested ignored on administrators'
desks, or, worst of all, were opened to the accused to read, to contradict, and to rebut. Potter, furious, turned his attention to what he
considered these breaches of trust. He released stories to newspapers
condemning officials who assertedly protected disloyal inferior officers;
he castigated as un-American high administrative officers who rejected
his conclusions and maintained accused men in their jobs.[34]

Secretary of War Cameron, for instance, rejected all Potter's claims
concerning the disloyalty of military officers. Cameron insisted that
Potter had no jurisdiction under the Constitution or the House resolution which had formed the investigating committee, to oversee military
affairs. To add insult to what Potter felt was enough injury, Cameron

contemptuously returned Potter's lists, with clear indication, as Potter's informants furtively disclosed, that the War Secretary had paid little attention to them. Potter tried unsuccessfully to have the House censure Cameron for his independence, and inspired newspaper articles criticizing the unpopular cabinet officer. He was happier when Edwin M. Stanton replaced Cameron as Secretary of War in January, 1862. Stanton spent his first day in charge of the "great lunatic asylum" of the War Department conferring with Potter. Soon thereafter a widespread change in personnel was discernible among Stanton's employees. Potter had gained a victory.[35]

But he never could conquer crusty Navy Secretary Gideon Welles. In no uncertain terms Welles denounced Potter's extension of jurisdiction over allegedly disloyal naval officers. Potter had no business in that area of Navy Department policy, Welles declared, and nothing Potter could do shook him from that position. So far as civil servants of the Navy Department were concerned, Welles told Potter that he had cleaned house himself, and needed no help from Congress. As he had with Cameron, Potter tried to pressure the House into censuring Welles, but Potter's colleagues refused to coöperate.[36]

Potter was even more dismayed by Lincoln's frequent refusals to honor the investigator's accusations. Instead of cashiering a White House aide who found an unwanted place on Potter's list, Lincoln secured him an army commission (and the maligned man served the Union honorably for three years). When Isaac Miller, an aged Washington arsenal employee, pleaded with Lincoln for help because Potter's accusation of disloyalty against Miller threatened his job, Lincoln personally interceded. It took but a brief note from the President ("I have seen him, and believe him to be loyal") for Miller to retain his place. Instead of discharging Moses Kelley, an accused Interior Department clerk, Lincoln promoted him to be register of wills. Lincoln had his old and trusted friend, Ward Lamon, marshal of the District, investigate each of Congressman Potter's accusations which came to the attention of the White House. In each case Lamon handled, his conclusions contradicted those of the House investigating committee. Lamon's investigations inspired Interior Secretary Caleb Smith to reject a disloyalty accusation because "the testimony was so indefinite and from so irresponsible a source." And Lincoln and Lamon chortled together when a man whom Potter had accused of disloyalty wrote a blistering letter to Lamon concerning the legislator's ancestry. For this man, accused of disloyalty, had been for a half year past a federal soldier, a youthful veteran of a dozen bloody skirmishes.[37]

Potter met Lincoln's adroit resistance, too, when he combined investigatory activities with patronage-hunting. Time after time, Potter followed up a disloyalty accusation with a recommendation for a particular person to replace the accused. The Wisconsin investigator became wrathful when he learned that his recommendations met with ungratifying responses from Lincoln's chief officials. "Will you please inform me," he imperiously demanded of Lamon, "why Mr. Duffee is still retained [as a guard at the District jail]?" Potter added that Lamon's stubbornness in this matter was inexcusable; Potter's committee had accused Duffee of disloyalty; Potter had generously supplied Lamon with the name of a worthy successor to Duffee (that is, a Republican, loyal Wisconsin resident). Lamon was unimpressed. He had little to fear for he knew well how little his beloved chief valued Potter's work. So Lamon kept the accused guard on the disputed job, without, seemingly, endangering the Union cause.[38]

Whatever success Potter achieved as a loyalty investigator depended in large part upon his ability to guarantee anonymity to his informants. When executive officers opened the evidence to those accused, that cloak disappeared. Uninvited, sometimes refused admittance, but persisting in ratio to their determination to clear their names, government clerks gained hearings before Potter's Committee, seeking to prove their innocence. Their appearance was not important in itself, for no record exists of Potter's ever changing his mind and recommending dropping a name from his lists. What was important was that the accused knew they were accused, and of what, and probably by whom. That knowledge sounded the death knell for the Potter Loyalty Investigating Committee, a sentence which Potter implicitly acknowledged in the autumn of 1862 when he reported his conclusions to the House.

That report bravely repeated Potter's earlier defense of his committee and its methods, and condemned all who criticized him or who had not coöperated with him. It listed as positively disloyal or as untrustworthy security risks more than five hundred federal officials of all ranks and responsibilities. But the report also named Potter's sources of information. Newspaper accounts insured that everyone had a chance to read the sordid story of recrimination and innuendo which had been the heart of the investigating committee's work. This one report was the first and last for Potter's loyalty investigators. The House chose not to renew the committee's life for a second year, tacitly admitting Congress' temporary failure to crack Lincoln's control over the bureaucracy.

Potter and the other members of the committee returned to their regular congressional duties, and to face the 1862 electoral campaign for congressmen. Potter was defeated in his attempt at reëlection, in a Wisconsin campaign in which railroads figured more prominently than loyalty. Lincoln's political generosity extended even to this partisan gadfly who had tried so valiantly to disrupt the President's control over the civil administration of the government; he finally secured Potter a post as consular official abroad, where he could defend the Union from a safer distance.[39] Although Republican congressmen continued to criticize Lincoln's administration for coddling traitors long after Potter's political demise, they never again came as close to taking control of the executive departments as they had when the Wisconsin Republican was seeking traitors in the government offices.

Congress' momentary surrender of loyalty-investigating to the President produced a notable relaxation of tension among the war workers of Washington. Clerks talked more freely, now that the threat of Potter's informers was gone from the city. More importantly, by the end of 1862 the North was becoming adept at living at war. Hysteria partly gave way to system. The armed guards that had surrounded Lincoln in his first months as president disappeared, so that a surprised visiting Englishman wandered for hours about the White House without being challenged.[40]

At intervals during the war, Congress tried to regain the initiative in loyalty-testing. In July, 1862, radical Republican leadership passed an "ironclad" loyalty-oath law for all government officials, which required statements of past as well as future loyalty. Legislators belatedly wrote into law many of the loyalty-testing policies which cabinet officers had inaugurated earlier on their own responsibility—test oaths for pensioners, shipmasters, and passport applicants, for instance. Congress extended loyalty tests into areas where executive officers could not go; representatives and senators required the ironclad oath of past loyalty for themselves after a passionate yearlong debate, which resulted in the resignation of an indignant principled Democrat, Delaware's James F. Bayard, from the Senate. The national legislature also required that attorneys practicing in all federal courts take this oath; years later, this loyalty law brought the Supreme Court into the picture. Congress demanded, too, that anyone making any claim before a federal bureau or court be sworn to past and future loyalty.

Congress always ran late in the loyalty-testing race. At no time during the war years were legislators able to take the initiative from Lincoln, although he, in turn, was unable to prevent the partisan ravages which Congress' Committee on the Conduct of the War and the House loyalty-investigating committee wrought on the executive offices. Lincoln obeyed Congress. When it required the ironclad oath of civil and military officers, Lincoln ordered the oath applied. But Congress' loyalty tests never applied during the war to more than a few score thousands of Americans who in some way had direct connection with the federal payroll or privilege. Lincoln's loyalty policies affected millions.[41]

By early 1862, as Union troops began the first real penetrations of the South, Northern loyalty tests moved with them. The new War Secretary, Stanton, had to adapt what had begun as an emergency internal security measure under Seward, to the expanding needs of the Union. And Stanton also had to deal with the irritating heritage of Seward's political prisoners. He soon proved that he was going to follow the path Seward had marked. When a Seward-appointed loyalty enforcer bemoaned the change in bosses ("I know almost every disloyal man in my district. It will take a great deal of time for any new man to become as thoroughly conversant"), Stanton merely commissioned him into the army and kept him on the same job.

Under Stanton as under Seward the loyalty commissioners toured the American Bastilles offering loyalty tests to civilian prisoners who had, by someone's definition, been disloyal, or who might become so. Throughout the long years of war, it was common for Northern civilians to go to prison on unspecified charges and gain freedom on taking specified loyalty tests. But Stanton found that security, in any absolute sense, was unattainable.[42]

In August, 1862, Stanton empowered the army's judge advocate, L. C. Turner, to enforce the clumsy conscription system. Turner incautiously enlisted the same kind of motley administrative staff that had so plagued Seward. What was considered disloyal in one area went unpunished in another, and reports of excesses mounted. Stanton needed better weapons. In September he created a special, novel corps of civilian provost marshals, one for each Northern city and county. These new officers, civilians with military power, possessed general police authority backed by federal cavalry and infantry. Many civilian provosts launched spectacular raids into the haunts of suspected deserters and bounty jumpers. Stanton soon applied some brakes.

He created the office of provost marshal general, which Congress did not get around to authorizing for six months to come. To head the civilian-control part of this office, Stanton chose Simeon Draper, a New

York City attorney who had earlier broken a ring of "passport brokers" who forged loyalty-oath receipts for unsworn civilians. Stanton gave Draper a blank check to centralize the sprawling internal security system. Draper recruited a staff of lawyers as assistant provost marshal generals, and assigned one to each city and each congressional district. Each assistant took charge of all the manifold loyalty matters in his jurisdiction, and he alone reported directly to Draper. It worked. By early 1863 the internal security system of the North, while certainly not infallible, was for the first time in the war relatively efficient, consistent, and responsible. If it could not prevent or subdue such mass resistance as the New York City draft riots, it did keep lesser dissent in close check. The provost marshal system provided professionals, under national authority, for the internal security task at hand. It was the right combination.[43]

Civilian provost marshals were not, however, the solution to the problem which Stanton's army commanders faced in the growing portions of the South which were coming under Union command. As federal forces pierced the heart of Dixie, loyalty tests became war weapons.

CHAPTER VII

Yankee Provosts and Rebel Patriotism

Bungling amateurs in the difficult practice of war in 1861, Americans North and South had even less experience as occupation administrators. This lack particularly plagued the North, for Union forces faced the novel duties of conqueror almost from the outbreak of hostilities. These duties, in the opinion of General Sherman, were "the most difficult business of our army as it advances and occupies the Southern country." As was true of so much else in Civil War administration, occupation policies never achieved the twentieth-century desideratum of uniformity in practice. In dealing with Southern civilians "suspected to be hostile or 'secesh,' " Sherman recalled, Union commanding officers enjoyed relatively uninhibited roles. "It is almost impossible to lay down rules," Sherman confessed as late as 1864, "and I invariably leave the whole subject to the local commanders." [1]

Free to act as personal feelings and local needs dictated, federal army commanders exhibited widely varying conduct toward inhabitants of border and Southern areas. Ben Butler, who controlled captured New Orleans, won the enduring nickname of "Beast" from his unhappy subjects; McClellan seemed to the Virginians whose communities he occupied a milder and fairer conqueror. Almost from the first days of the war such disparities were evident. "The system," a Union general complained, "was no system at all." He was only partly correct.[2]

Certain factors common to all occupied areas imposed a semblance of similarity upon the conduct of Union officers. The Unionists were invaders in a hostile land. Military security against Confederate counterattack was every commanding officer's first and enduring responsibility. In many areas his troops had to wage continuing campaigns against irregular rebel raiders and guerrillas, prevent looting by Union troops as well as by nonpartisan robbers, and simultaneously counter sabotage and subversion. Ardent prorebels burned bridges, cut telegraph and railroad lines, and seduced Union soldiers to desert. Military courts prescribed firing squads, gallows, and prisons for obvious disloyalists, penalties sanctioned by the tenets of martial law and the necessity to survive. The conqueror necessarily became a policeman.

As policemen, but police almost without restraint from public opinion or civil law, different occupation commanders in Virginia, Louisiana, Tennessee, Kentucky, Missouri, and Arkansas came to similar conclusions concerning the best way to prevent subversion. In the first war year several Union generals—Pope, Halleck, Rosecrans, Butler, Frémont—proclaimed, without prearrangement, that all potentially disloyal civilians in their jurisdictions must leave their homes and depart into rebel lines. And, again without prearrangement, each of these disparate commanders resorted to loyalty tests to indicate who were loyal, and were therefore privileged to live in peace, and who were disloyal and must face prison or exile from homes and communities. As one Union officer reported to the army's judge advocate general, "It has been supposed that all citizens who refuse to take the oath should be arrested because their refusal is *prima facie* evidence of disloyalty and that they only wanted the opportunity to do the Government some injury." [3]

In the absence of law or direction on the subject, Union officers used any loyalty oath that seemed to fit the situation. Some officers found useful the successive loyalty tests that Congress prescribed for civil and military officers. State loyalty oaths provided another fruitful supply, for every Northern and border state adopted such tests during the war. Whatever the source or form, loyalty oaths were weapons ready to hand with which federal officers could combat unrest in newly-occupied areas.

There was more to war than battle. Even conquerors must eat, and mere humanity dictated that the conquered, too, must live. Once the first phases of securing their conquests from recapture and subversion were under way, Union commanders engaged in complex efforts to restore the shattered economic and political structures of their zones. Even the simplest step in this direction, however, involved federal officers in the process of discriminating among Southern civilians, affording privileges to some and withholding them from others. The policeman became a politician.

To prevent subversion and sabotage in newly occupied areas Union officers prohibited civilians from traveling. But to get food into towns from adjoining countrysides, farmers had to travel, and merchants had to buy and sell; cities required sanitation and utility services; doctors had to deliver babies; ministers had to marry and bury—life demanded its due even in war. Again without prearrangement, Union commanders everywhere resorted once more to loyalty tests to help decide upon whom the federal conqueror should bestow coveted permissions to travel, buy food and clothing, engage in business, plead cases of law, preach, teach, marry, or vote, and those who could not.

Such spontaneous use of loyalty oaths soon received formal encouragement from presidential proclamations and congressional enactments on subjects ranging from property confiscations and fugitive slave recapture and emancipation to political reconstruction. The vital border-state governments which Lincoln's quick and forceful acts had held in the Union responded with internal loyalty cleansings and with loyalty laws and tests which Union troops largely enforced. Federal treasury and postal agents, War Department counterspies, and State Department private detectives came to each occupied area as secondary waves of occupation. They brought with them federal laws on conscription, taxation, trade and mail systems, leasing plans for rebel property —and all these rules and laws restricted federal favors to loyal civilians. All encouraged federal officers to resort to loyalty-testing on an ever-increasing scale.

With the Union loyalty oath as lure, federal officers made the self-interest of individual Southerners work for Northern military security in occupied areas. "The reins are being tightened over us every day," mourned an unrepentant daughter of Dixie, as she observed her Nashville neighbors hastening to take advantage of proffered privileges by swearing the Union oath.[4]

Union generals, after the first hectic months of war, usually became too busy with larger matters personally to hold the loyalty reins, and delegated the time-consuming business of loyalty-testing. "I see from General Rosecrans' order," noted a Tennessee Unionist, "that it is left to the discretion of district commanders what assurance they demand of the citizens for their peaceful and orderly behavior."[5] District commanders, in turn, left this work largely in the hands of subordinates, and, almost everywhere the Union army went, the subordinate bore the title of provost marshal.

By War Secretary Stanton's orders, each federal army included a provost marshal unit, with subdivisions down to the company level. In addition, permanent units, under command of the provost marshal general of an army corps, were stationed in each major occupied city or town, and in nominally loyal border areas where Union military occupation was thinly disguised. It was the local provost who carried into action the policies which distant generals proclaimed. Each provost, despite a reporting system that theoretically permitted Washington headquarters to check on his activities, was a law unto himself. He was the most important man in the lives of the civilians in his jurisdiction, for he decided questions of life or death and poverty or prosperity for them, and usually there was no appeal.

Since so much depended upon the standards and quality of the individual provost, inconsistencies and inequities among men and areas were serious problems in the lives of the civilians of an occupied area. One provost required only male civilians to take loyalty oaths; the neighboring provost required adult women to swear; a third demanded the test of minor children as well. In one area refusal to take the oath was a crime drastic enough to warrant prison or exile for the nonjuror. Other nearby provosts cared little whether a man swore loyalty or not, so long as he conducted himself peaceably and obeyed regulations. It was up to the provost.

A provost's responsibilities required consummate tact, prudence, and judicious discretion. The provost was essentially a policeman for the army. Often he had to keep Unionists as well as prorebels in check, for the approach of federal armies freed antisecession Southerners from the grasp of Confederate policies no less repressive than the North's. Such Southerners often celebrated their freedom by beating, tarring and feathering, and imprisoning neighbors who had previously denounced Unionists to rebel authorities. Unionist vigilantes emerged from underground hideaways, armed with secret black lists of secessionists, upon whom they wreaked full measures of vengeance for past persecutions. It was what Champ Clark called the "evening-up time," which made so much of the border and the South into what Lincoln, who loved that land, sadly termed a "belt of desolation."

Personal hatreds motivated Unionists to condemn neighbors to provosts, and by far the commonest charge was disloyalty. Some provosts uncritically accepted these accusations at face value; Northern prisons became crowded with civilian inmates from occupation zones whom provosts arrested on the unsupported charges of self-described Unionists. Personal issues so bedeviled General Wright's command in Kentucky that he circularized his provosts, warning them that "old feuds and more recent dislikes have an influence in controlling the judgments of the most loyal." [6] Many provosts possessed neither the objectivity nor the time to pierce the passions surrounding accusations of disloyalty.

For this reason, too, Union army commanders and provosts turned to loyalty oaths to afford them a surer means than Unionists' accusations to achieve the primary task of pacification, and the secondary one of reconstruction. There are several case histories which illustrate the effectiveness of the test-oath tool, and show how well it was adapted to exploiting human needs and desires in the name of loyalty.

Fredericksburg, Virginia, approved secession in 1861, and its citizens permitted the few resident Unionists to leave peaceably when the war started. When federal forces approached in April, 1862, the decision of the Confederate commander not to defend the town spared battered Fredericksburg the horrors of siege. Fredericksburg's Mayor Slaughter soon realized that federal Provost Marshal General Marsena Patrick was a mild conqueror, who permitted all peaceable civilians to reside untroubled by Union troops, and welcomed all citizens of the town to resume normal occupations if they would give paroles (not oaths) pledging future neutrality. But the exiled Unionists returned to Fredericksburg with the federal army. They saw the people who had forced them to flee their homes enjoying the fruits of profitable trade with the specie-laden Union army, while they, good patriots, had lost everything. Their loud complaints to Stanton and to radical Republican congressmen brought quick results. Stanton censured Patrick for excessive leniency toward rebels.[7]

The clearest contemporary account of how effectively the loyalty oath served the Union as a pressure instrument is available in the diary of a town councilman of Plymouth, North Carolina, a small tobacco and fishing center. The currents of war largely bypassed its life until April, 1862, when three federal gunboats anchored off the single wharf the town boasted. Plymouth was occupied. In 1860, 10 of the 120 voters of Plymouth had voted against secession; the ten fled the town when the war started, leaving behind a clandestine group of convinced Unionists. These remained discreetly quiet until the small federal fleet appeared, whereupon they proceeded to harass the Confederate officials of Plymouth. The Union naval commander intervened and deployed marines to keep order. Plymouth rested in brief, uneasy peace.

The first night of Union occupation covert threats and counter-threats made their way to barricaded homes of prorebels and Unionists alike. The naval officer warned Plymouth's mayor that he would protect the Unionists if Confederate cavalry or vigilantes threatened them:

"If any of these men be injured by your authorities, then I will arrest two secessionists for every one of them."

Federal army units soon arrived and took up permanent occupation duty. With the troops came a provost marshal, who set up office in the mayor's chambers, and began the process that was to make Plymouth, where a mere 10 per cent had voted for the Union in 1860, 100 per cent Unionist in 1862—*if* Unionist and swearing to a Union loyalty oath meant the same thing. The provost welcomed Plymouth's Unionists as his assistants. Together they pored over the "Black Books" of prominent secessionists which the Unionists had secretly compiled. Troops under the provost's orders arrested some of the black-listed men and sent them north as political prisoners. But he left most of the townspeople alone, permitting fishermen, merchants, and farmers to go about their business without interruption. Plymouth's frustrated Unionists resorted to instigating disloyal remarks in order to gain revenge upon personal enemies. "How do you like the U.S. Flag over the Customs House?" a Unionist innocently asked a neighbor. "If I must speak of it, I don't like it," was enough of an answer to place the incautious speaker in prison.

A constant fear during the first months of Union occupation of Plymouth was that Confederate forces might retake the town. Then the secessionists would have revenge, and any resident who collaborated with the federal troops would face the consequences. But in June, 1862, a full regiment of Union cavalry took up station nearby. Plymouth's provost and Unionists breathed easier and increased the tempo of loyalty-testing. Most of the townspeople owned outlying farms, the fruits of which formed an essential supplement to fishing and other seasonal work. The provost ordered that anyone who wanted a pass to leave the town must take the Union oath. He insisted that he was coercing no one; any one who refused was free to remain at peace inside the town. But it hardly looked like peace. Unionists formed themselves into an armed home guard, and behaved so threateningly that many proud prorebels went to the hated Yankee provost to ask for protection against Unionist neighbors! Protection, the provost told them, was available for themselves, family, and property against Unionists, federal looters, or Confederate attackers, if they took the oath. A few did.

The provost soon after announced new municipal and county elections. Only loyal men, of course, could vote, and loyalty was equal to taking the oath. Unionist home guards, who knew everyone in the area, were poll watchers. On the day preceding the election, the provost proclaimed that only those who took the oath might obtain salt, or use fishing boats. More men succumbed, swore, and obtained coveted rights to buy, travel, and vote. Those who voted found only Unionists as candidates. It was a Unionist landslide.

Federal postal agents censored outgoing mail, incidentally preventing Plymouth's unsworn citizens from appealing to influential friends in the North for assistance. Federal treasury agents compiled rosters of property—real estate, slaves, tobacco stocks—belonging to disloyalists, and announced that owners who remained unsworn by a certain date faced confiscation of that property. The provost issued circulars describing fugitive Negroes he had in custody, noting that only loyal owners could reclaim them. When scarce grain seed, shoes, salt, and farming and fishing equipment arrived at Plymouth, the provost restricted selling and buying privileges to sworn men. Looters from two armies and from no army despoiled outlying farms left deserted or without protection because unsworn residents could not travel without a pass from the provost, and could get neither pass nor protection papers without an oath. Plymouth was impaled upon the point of the provost's pen as well as upon Union bayonets.

More and more citizens succumbed to this unrelenting pressure, but some unbending prorebels stood firm and resisted the temptations the oath symbolized. But their hearts hurt when they saw relatives and friends crowding the provost's office, begging for the magic oath that would end so many ills. Lifelong friendships broke on the oath issue. Shamefacedly, those who had taken the hated oath sought out their more principled neighbors to explain their conduct. Shame and revulsion mingled with forgiveness and tears, but the scars remained. A new stratification of Plymouth's society was building, based on a separation of the sworn from the unsworn, between those who enlisted in the Union army and the majority of the men, who remained civilians.

By December, 1862, only a dozen of the most convinced prorebels of Plymouth remained untainted by the Union oath of loyalty. They avoided the oath takers as the latter avoided them. Plymouth's Unionists pressured the provost to rid the town of this dangerous remnant of defiant men. One by one they disappeared into Northern prisons. Only one aged man, who had very influential connections among Northern politicians, received special dispensation to sign a limited parole not to aid the Confederacy. Armed with the parole, he bought seed and salt and made one last trip from Plymouth to his outlying farm. There, self-imprisoned by his refusal to swear, he remained for the rest of the war.[8]

Plymouth was a microcosm of Civil War loyalty-testing. New Orleans experienced the same sort of thing on a much grander scale, as did Tennessee when Andrew Johnson assumed the military governorship of that divided state. Missouri's succession of punitive army and state loyalty tests were vastly more pervasive and harsh than were similar tests in little Plymouth. But everywhere the same sorts of human reactions to administrative loyalty pressures, and the personal conflicts of patriotism and individual interpretations of loyalty, were the business of Americans. Everywhere, in the border and the occupied South, revengeful Unionists spurred the Union army to increasingly harsh measures. In New Orleans, for instance, a prorebel citizen described how that city's Unionists celebrated their rise to power:

All who have taken the Oath of Allegiance to the U.S. Government are very active in the discharge of their duties. They are even more active than the U.S. soldiers and press upon the citizens with a harder hand. . . . They are very vigilant in dispersing all assemblages of gentlemen upon the streets where the number exceeds the prescribed "crowd" of three. They make frequent complaints of persons for using seditious language. Those charged by them are generally found guilty and punished by fines or imprisonment. . . . One of these Home Guard policemen was asked "how many times he had taken the oath." The impertinent questioner was immediately arrested—the day following was brought into court—found guilty and fined.[9]

Everywhere the Union army went the ubiquitous provosts carried these pressures with them and made the taking of a loyalty oath a question of immense importance for hundreds of thousands of Americans. For, whatever the form of the oath, whoever the Union commander might be, the essentials remained relatively constant. A political lieutenant of General Butler best expressed this essential similarity:

General Butler knew that the hatred of the old Government could not be quelled simply by military occupation. He knew that loyalty to the Union was to be fostered by other means than the bayonet. . . . The policy of Major General Butler therefore, was to interest every man in business, so that he might come to have a pecuniary regard in the stability and success of the Government of the United States . . . and by taking the oath of allegiance required . . . and by depending on the protection of our flag, they must more and more become interested in our cause.[10]

The Union army provost was keeper of the keys and bearer of the oath. An example of the work of a busy provost is available from the headquarters records of the Union Army of the Frontier, stationed in Fayetteville, Arkansas. Its provost's orders were to suppress subversion and spur Unionism and loyalty in this deeply divided border state, and in order to carry out these basic instructions the provost daily decided technical questions of property and constitutional law, although he boasted no legal training. But as he said, the "summariness of martial law . . . enabled us to come to quick conclusions." Into his office came the full stream of the troubled life of the border. He was judge, jury, prosecutor, and sheriff in thousands of cases:

[He is] . . . empowered to arrest deserters, whether regulars, volunteers or militia, and all disloyal persons; to enquire into and report treasonable practices; to seize stolen or embezzled property belonging to the Government; to detect spies of the enemy, and put a stop to miscellaneous pillaging by lawless soldiers. A provost marshal in the enemy's country has . . . quite sufficient to harass him. Added to these labors, bonds are to be taken and safeguards given; a general pass system devised and occasionally reconstituted, oaths of allegiance administered and paroles subscribed; proofs of loyalty made and endorsed on vouchers, . . . in short, there is imposed upon him the general administration of the law during a suspension of civil process.[11]

When the Union army took Nashville, Tennessee, the provost there found himself the center of Unionist attraction. He heard men denounce others as secessionist leaders and rebel spies. He listened to the complaints of Unionists who claimed that prosecessionist neighbors were destroying their crops, running off their livestock, and shooting at their homes because of the Unionism of the complainants. Men and women offered themselves to him as informers, ready for a price to divulge real or fancied tales of secret societies of prorebel civilians. The provost often paid the price, and through his informers mounted several raids which in one instance netted the Union a prorebel guerrilla band, but in another produced nothing more than a bewildered meeting of religious cultists. The provost's office resounded to the pleas of Northern businessmen who wished to open trade in occupied Nashville; of Nashville merchants who desired to reopen shops under Union dispensation; of tearful women begging news of menfolk languishing in Northern prison camps. The Nashville provost coöperated closely with the political efforts of Military Governor Andrew Johnson to rebuild the state as a loyal part of the Union. Through the provost's office came orders that resulted in the creation of a home guard unit of civilian Unionists, well armed, dedicated to keeping former secessionists from voting, holding office, or practicing trades or professions.

In Nashville, as at Fayetteville, New Orleans, and Plymouth, words of loyalty and oaths of loyalty formed the bases from which provosts worked. Standards of loyalty differed from those held by provosts in other areas. But Union loyalty policies worked out to very similar conclusions in the lives of the people whom provosts ruled.[12]

All provosts administered systems of travel passes. In every occupied area the guns were hardly still before civilians came, begging permission to go about their business, to see their dead and wounded on the battlefield, or to find scattered families and property. An alert provost knew that this was the best time to close the loyalty trap. He had ready an adequate stock of pass forms, which provided space for the applicant's name, physical description, and destination, and for the provost's signature. But on the bottom or the reverse side of the pass the Union loyalty oath was also printed, and the civilian who received the pass had simultaneously to take the oath.

The provost at Clarksburg, West Virginia, devised a rough rule with which to measure the civilians who came to seek passes from him. First, he happily identified the "truly loyal" who "would walk boldly to the desk, and with free, open willingness subscribe to the required oath, seeming to regard the ceremony as a blessed privilege vouchsafed to them." The "truly rebel" class, on the opposite hand, seldom appeared before him voluntarily. But it was the undecided waverers who gave the provost the greatest trouble. He rarely knew who of this troubled group deserved the liberties that derived from taking the oath, and he often refused to proffer the oath even to some who asked for it if he could not judge "whether they held the obligation binding or not." Some Southerners came to him with glib phrases of assurance that they needed no oath test; with carefully folded copies of the *New York Tribune* peeking from their pockets to show how Unionist they were; with carefully displayed envelopes they had addressed (with no intention of mailing) to important Northern politicians as suggestions that they were above the need for oaths. Some brought bribes to exchange for oathless favors. And all, afraid to swear, admitted that their fear envisioned a returning rebel army venting its wrath upon all who had taken the Yankee test.

How could even the most Solomon-like provost make unalterable rules in the face of all these nuances of human conduct? Consider Tennessee in the early part of the war, where the rebel flag flew over the heaviest concentrations of Unionist sentiment, and the Northern forces occupied the most secessionist portion of the state. Here only the harshest security measures seemed useful at all, and neither side flinched from the most galling tests of loyalty and penalties for disloyalty. "Persons are being arrested all over for simple expressions of opinion," mournfully recorded a bereaved Tennessean, "and it is done without a murmur." [13]

If few were brave enough to murmur, many Southerners were strong enough in their sectional allegiance to withstand, at least for a time, the temptations of the Union oath. Thousands became political prisoners or displaced persons, exiled from homes and families, because they dared refuse. James Harrison of New Orleans, for instance, refused to take the oath because he felt it implied that he approved the war. Harrison was a Unionist of renown and had earlier risked his life to plead the cause of nationalism in the South. Yet he would not take a Union oath to prove that he was for the Union. He escaped provost's prison only because the judge advocate general of the army interceded for him. A Knoxville resident chose prison for refusing the oath, even though his young children were dying of whooping cough. He never saw two of them again. An aged man of Gallatin, Tennessee, faced the problem of welcoming his rebel son's widow to the family home. But the woman chose to continue a penniless exile, burdened with two children, rather than take the Union oath the provost stationed there demanded of her.[14]

Provosts dealt with a daily drama of principle, bravery, and even humor. In Nashville "a saucy, dashing young girl, of the Southern persuasion," faced General Rosecrans and his provost, who demanded she take the Union oath. She demurred, objecting that her mother had warned her that ladies did not swear. The officers insisted. "Well, General," she replied, "if I must swear, I will, but all the sins of the oath must rest on your shoulders. . . . 'G——d d——n every Yankee to H——l!" And she left the Union army headquarters unmolested, according to a Southern newspaper's account of her bravery.

A Louisiana lady appeared before the New Orleans provost with a request for the return of her fugitive Negro slaves. He asked her if she had taken the oath; her curt negative answer provoked reciprocal rudeness. The officer sought to shut her up with a terse "Hush!" She told him she would talk as much as she pleased and would never take the oath. Irritated, the officer made it clear that he did not "give a damn" whether she did or not. "You have *proved* yourself a gentleman, . . . sir, in swearing at an old lady," she retorted. According to her reminiscence, the officer was ashamed of his conduct—but she did not get her slaves.

Feminine forcefulness was sometimes more successful. Mrs. Roger Pryor went with her two young sons to the federal provost at Petersburg, Virginia, seeking a food-ration permit, and met the oath requirement head on. She had already decided that principles must give way before the physical needs of her children, and that she would swear falsely to the oath to get food, when the young officer pleased and startled her: "Neither will I require it of you, Madam," he said, as he gave her the coveted document. But a provost in Virginia, facing another woman who had come to him for permission to buy food, insisted upon the oath before he would give her the privilege. "I told him," she recorded, "it was impossible for me to do it, as it would be entirely false; & added that it could not be a matter of importance what women thought or wished." But her asperity failed to shake him. The proud woman, repelled by "that little creature's impertinence," exited, her pride intact but her larder still bare.[15]

Sarah Dawson's refugee family from Arkansas, en route to safer New Orleans, encountered the Union oath on board the steamboat bearing them to their goal. The family was already broken by the war; three beloved brothers were rebel officers, another was a Unionist politician on Butler's payroll in New Orleans. When a federal provost assembled the boat's haggard passengers and told them they might not land unless they took the Union oath, Sarah Dawson refused. The provost showed her lists of important Southerners who had already taken the oath, and insisted she join in the swearing. She bent her head, crying, and prayed for her rebel brothers and their cause. Her unhappy reverie ended when the provost called out "All right!" and pronounced her sworn. "Strange to say," she confided to her diary, "I experienced no change." She did not feel that she had taken the oath at all, nor did she consider it binding, but she did accept the travel pass which bore the notation that she was sworn to Union allegiance.

Union provosts generally made special efforts to get those Southerners to swear who had sons, husbands, and brothers in the rebel forces. Unionist neighbors eagerly pointed out who these were, and insisted that such folk, made guilty by the fact of kinship, be sworn to the Union test or take the consequences. An aged woman of Lebanon, Tennessee, found the oath requirement facing her when she asked for protection papers for her home. Her many grandsons were all rebels. She pleaded that she had no control over their actions. Her plea was effective, and she secured the needed protection without the oath. Nearby, in Maury City, a Tennessean faced General Negley to plead for a travel pass. The general asked the applicant for his loyalty oath. "Very well," the civilian answered, "just have it boxd up, and I'll take it out." The general patiently sought to make the civilian understand that the oath was one to support the government. "Why, General, I

already have seven children," came the response, "I can't think of supporting the whole Government, that's too much." Negley, impatient,
ordered the man to read the oath. "I can't read," he responded. Negley
lost patience. "Give him a pass anyhow, he has no sense." Perhaps not,
but the friends of the apparently stupid nonjuror chortled at the way
he had outwitted the impatient conqueror.[16]

As provosts increased pressures for oath-taking, some Southerners
resorted to evasions and deceits they would have found unthinkable
in other circumstances. A Virginia woman, wife of a political prisoner
and a distant relative of Lincoln, pleaded with the President to release
her husband. She claimed that the only charge against him was his
refusal to take the oath, that he was a consistent Unionist and had refused on grounds of principle only. Lincoln was ready to order his
release. Then, in a report of a loyalty investigation Stanton had ordered,
proof arrived that the man was really a secessionist of long standing,
and an undoubted rebel spy. A Nashville woman of high principle was
jubilant that other people had less lofty ethics than her own: "I bought
a quarter of beef, a great and unwonted luxury, from an old woman
from the country. Her husband would not take the oath, so she did it,
and brought in her marketing." [17]

Many Southern civilians found that the easiest way to get vital
protection papers from a Yankee provost was to let their womenfolk do
their arguing. It sometimes worked. Beautiful young women found
some Union officers susceptible to feminine charms and willing to
issue passes and protection papers without sullying the lips of a lovely
pleader with an obnoxious oath. But other provosts were made of
sterner stuff. A youthful New Yorker, provost near New Orleans in
1863, denounced the "mendacity of the applicants" for his favor:

The people send their women (young and pretty if they have them, otherwise
old and ugly) to put through their petty business which they are afraid to
manage themselves. . . . My office has lately been ornamented every day . . .
with the "gushing daughters of the sunny South." With Artemus Ward I can
only say "let em gush!!!"

The daughters of the "sunny South" proceeded to pillory this stern
young officer in correspondence between themselves. More fortunate
Southern ladies who lived in areas where Union officers of greater gal-
lantry respected the weaker sex, commiserated with their less fortunate
Louisiana sisters.[18]

The outstanding documented record of organized oath evasion is in
the diary of a Memphis attorney, John Hallum, who served in the

rebel army for a year before poor health secured him a medical discharge. He returned to Memphis just before Union troops took the city. The federal provost instituted oath requirements and proclaimed that he would send all civilians who refused the oath into rebel lines. Hallum wrestled with his sectional patriotism and love of family, realizing full well the effect his refusal of the oath would have upon his already damaged health and dwindling funds. But he determined to go into exile rather than swear falsely.

An unexpected windfall of gold dollars from an old debtor gave Hallum a way out of his difficulty. A few days after Hallum got the money, a civilian stranger approached him. This newcomer to Memphis had arrived with the new Union provost, and was known as a confidant of that officer. He offered Hallum a complete set of papers—passes, protection, permit to practice law—without the oath, for five hundred gold dollars. It meant that Hallum and his family need not move or lose their home. Hallum accepted. When he went to get the papers and pay the money, he found the provost's office physically divided into two sections. The front room, with the provost in attendance, performed regular business, requiring loyalty oaths of all applicants. The back room, overseen by Hallum's "fixer," was equally well organized, and accommodated men like Hallum who would buy their way out of the oath test.

Hallum paid his money and received the papers. Friends of Hallum, equally determined not to take the Union oath, made him their intermediary with the "back-room provost." Hallum collected $65,000 in six months and turned it over to the provost's discreet friend, who shared the booty with the provost. The rates for evading the oath varied from $10 to $1,500, depending in part upon the ability of the individual civilian to pay. Hallum found that the "fixer" was a scrupulously honest businessman, and enjoyed a harmonious relationship with him. Perhaps three hundred Memphis residents and their families found oathless safety through this illicit arrangement. Everyone kept the secret, since all concerned were risking prison in the transactions.[19]

A less well-kept secret involved an assistant provost in General Jerry Boyle's Kentucky command in 1861. Boyle had achieved a quick reputation as an enthusiastic oath giver. Civilians in his jurisdiction sometimes swore loyalty ten times in a single day in the course of normal working activities, or faced immediate arrest as political prisoners for refusing to swear. Boyle called a special election for Union-occupied Kentucky in November, 1861, and appointed a host of assistant provosts to oversee the polls. Each provost was ordered to insure that every voter was loyal; disloyal men could cast no ballot.

One of the assistant provosts, a Mr. Sharp, who liked the oath idea, fell into the profitable habit of sending federal troops out to round up as many civilians as they could. Then Sharp proffered the harried Kentuckians the Union oath, with a charge ranging from $1 to $25 each for the privilege of swearing, according to the amount of money the civilian had on him. Sharp cared nothing that many of those his dragnets caught had already sworn to the oath multiple times. But it disgruntled Kentucky's Unionists, whose patriotic idealism revolted at Sharp's mercenary tactics. Indeed, a future governor of the state withdrew his name from the Unionist ballot in disgust at Sharp's mercenary use of the oath test. Kentucky patriots protested to Congress about this practice. Nothing, apparently, was done, except that Lincoln ordered Boyle to confine arrests to those cases where good cause existed.

More publicized still were the oath evasions attendant upon Butler's occupation of New Orleans. This spectacular officer overturned the whole political and social life of that city and its environs with his oath requirements. He ordered that all who refused the oath register as "enemies to the United States" who must, by their self-confession of treason (refusal to swear), face exile into rebel lines. Thousands of Louisianans wished to stay outside Confederate territory, yet refused the Union oath. Their only hope was to get military passes for Union areas where Butler's rules did not hold sway. But passes meant oaths, unless one could buy a pass. Butler's immediate staff proved to be the answer. Apparently with their chief's knowledge, they initiated a thriving business in illicit passes and protection papers, reaping large sums from nonjurors who had the funds to escape the consequences of refusal to swear. What a rebel army newspaper called "the powerful aid of the almighty dollar" proved adequate to succor nonjurors.[20] Different in scale but similar in purpose were the "fines" which Union General Negley imposed upon civilians arrested by his provosts in mid-Tennessee. Negley's provost made a good thing of frequent roundups of civilians, who pleaded their innocence of crime and displayed certificates of loyalty oaths they had already taken. The provost disregarded these supposedly sacred protection certificates, and imposed fines ranging from $5 to $200 upon his hapless victims.

There were still other ways for determined Southerners to evade a provost's oath requirement. One Nashville widow, facing exile into Confederate lines because of her determined nonjuring, brooded over the problem of supporting her young children and herself among strangers. Then she realized that the provost who had sentenced her to exile was the husband of an old friend of happier prewar days. In bygone years the two women had corresponded regularly, and had written freely of common secession sympathies and antipathies to Northern abolitionists. The Nashville woman had saved all her friend's letters. Now she used them to blackmail her former friend's husband. "I notice," she wrote to the provost, "that your wife was once pro-Southern, but doubtless she has become converted. I think, unless the news gets out of this, that she may remain zealous in the Union cause." The barbed thrust found its mark; the news did not "get out." And the desperate Tennessee lady who had found it necessary to resort to blackmail in order to live unsworn to a cause in which she did not believe, at least found the satisfaction of success as tribute to her unsavory course. She lived out the war in her Nashville home.[21]

Bribery and blackmail were not the only means to evade loyalty tests. A nonjuring Mississippi family, for example, had to abandon their home by Union army orders. They left their considerable property in the name of a Unionist friend ("an old beau of Momma's") and were sure he would protect it for them. A Tennessee girl recalled a neighbor who had openly taken the oath in order to get protection, "which we are very glad to have him do, as he carries letters . . . gets passes for Ma, and has the wood hauled. . . . It is a mutual accommodation, and satisfies all parties." But this devoted daughter of the South could not resist venting her deep antipathy against a neighbor who had proved false to Dixie by admitting a genuine conversion to Unionism: "I give him some hard cuts, though, about people taking the oath." Nor could another likable young Southern woman refrain from exulting when an oath-bound neighbor lost property to federal army looters, despite the protection her oath entitled her to. "Yankee soldiers stole a good deal from Widow Hildebrands," the girl recorded, "but she had taken the oath, and I don't care much." War and loyalty-testing were coarsening the moral fiber of Americans.[22]

Although there were ways to get around Union loyalty tests, evasion sometimes proved to be a dangerous game. Incorruptible Union troops and Southern Unionists kept wary watch on too-lenient occupation officers. Union League organizations flourished in every occupied area, and their watchdog committees insured a requisite harshness in occupation policy.

Loyalty-conscious Unionists had resort to the solid phalanx of radical Republicans in Congress who assumed the mantle of keepers of the nation's loyalty conscience, and who were always receptive to allegations from any source which imputed the loyalty of a Union official. Wade heard that McClellan's provost and military governor at Norfolk, Virginia, were dangerously familiar with traitors, allegedly favoring rich secessionists over good Unionists, failing to require loyalty oaths as prerequisites for passes and protection papers, neglecting to insist upon loyalty tests as requirements for voting and holding local office. "In short," the complainant wrote Wade, "no convert can be made to the Union." This kind of accusation formed ammunition for the savage attacks that Republican political leaders maintained against McClellan in Congress and in the public press.[23]

A less spectacular case involved a Union provost, colonel of the Pennsylvania Volunteers, on occupation duty near Key West, Florida. His fellow officers reported him to the War Department because "he is charged with too much sympathy with the South and has favored the rebels at Key West so much that they have presented him with a sword." Stanton ordered his detectives to arrest the man, and began court-martial proceedings against him. A Missouri-based federal officer complained that civilians in his command secured passes from sinister "higher authorities." Women especially, he noted bitterly, obtained passes with little difficulty, and used their freedom to buy arms for Confederate guerrillas.

Negro troops in Union military service often were particularly vigilant about how their white officers behaved with Southerners. "A colored-man heart . . . is a fair synonym for a loyal heart," was the way one white commander of a colored regiment described how his troops felt about their former masters. And these troops "watched their [white] officers vigilantly, and even suspiciously, to detect any disposition towards compromise."

It was not easy for federal army officers to steer a middle course between tyranny and laxity in their rule over conquered civilians. It was even less easy when politics mixed with loyalty policies. McClellan was a favored whipping boy for radical Republican politicians, who chose to blame his military setbacks on sinister pro-Southerners whom, they alleged, he favored. McClellan, of course, was a Democrat, and was to be that party's presidential candidate in 1864, but as early as 1862 he had a reputation as a mild loyalty enforcer. What angered many of his more ardent junior officers was his predilection for accepting the oath of any Southerner who offered it. His troops joked about his failing. One of his provosts captured a rattlesnake, pondered its fate, and, in imitation of his chief's weakness, told his men to "swear it, and let it go."

Missouri's Union occupiers and Unionist state governments made their loyalty tests not merely a well-designed apparatus to prevent rebels from voting or holding office, but a partisan tool which several political factions among the Unionists learned how to use. The Blair family machine, for instance, found bitter opposition to their entrenched political power from radical Republican newcomers who ejected Blair supporters from the polls. The Union army became embroiled in the unsavory partisan stew when provost marshals lent their authority and troops to factions they favored. By the end of 1863 Missouri's constitution had received multiple amendments, which required citizens to swear that they had not committed any of eighty-six acts in order to vote or hold public office, or preach, teach, or conduct a business or profession. Similar situations in Tennessee, West Virginia, and Louisiana kept the loyalty pots boiling with the forced feed of political fuel long into the postwar period.[24]

Another division among Northerners stressed by the loyalty tests was the traditional rivalry between regular and temporary officers. Few regulars administered loyalty policies with any but routine energies. But the "political officers," whose rapid promotions embittered the hearts of professional soldiers, were much more apt to make loyalty crusades part of their well-publicized strategy and tactics in the South. Many regular officers on Buell's and Butler's staffs disapproved of their chiefs' propensities for widespread loyalty-testing. Many of the provosts who permitted Southerners to obtain travel permits and protection papers without oaths were regular officers.

When military policy conflicted with political policy, the loyalty program played another divisive role. In addition to the military officer in command of an area, Lincoln and Congress commissioned all kinds of improvised policy makers. In Tennessee, for example, the military commander found that a military governor and state-appointed commissions had functions parallel to, and powers that conflicted with, his own. All were interested in promoting as much loyalty as possible; all had different ideas on when and how to do it. In one instance, Buell, Union army commander, promised the residents of Belle Meade that they need fear no arrests as long as the many returned rebel soldiers among them remained peaceable. But the day after Buell's pronouncement, the military governor, Andrew Johnson, sent out troops *he* controlled who arrested scores of the people Buell had promised could remain in peace. Buell's officers wanted to invade Johnson's headquarters to teach him a lesson, but wiser counsel prevailed. Loyalty was a two-edged sword, and doubly dangerous because one of the sides was labeled "politics." [25]

Clever Southerners recognized that different Union officers held varying standards of loyalty, and played sharp games, often with great risks, in playing one off against another. A Mississippi woman, determined to get protection for her plantation, now inside federal lines near besieged Vicksburg, went to General McClernand, who demanded to know where her family was. She had to confess that her husband and two sons were in the rebel army. "Then, Madam," the general decided, "to get protection you must take the oath." She unhesitatingly replied: "I will starve first." To which the officer retorted: "Then, Madam, go home and starve; you cannot get protection." The resourceful woman shopped around among other Union officers. Her dignified demeanor and "the aweing glance of her fierce black eyes" finally evoked the coveted paper without the hated oath. Then Vicksburg fell to the Yankees, and all papers had to be renewed by new commanders. The woman held her course, refused the oath even when threatened with prison for refusing, and, aided by feminine friends who flattered a susceptible provost out of a protection paper, retained her home.

Southern women played an important part in this sectional game of outwitting the occupying federals. When the men of the family refused the oath, their women sometimes secretly took it in order to keep their too-proud-to-swear menfolk alive, for only those who had sworn were, in many localities, able to buy food. "We have long since ceased to expect to buy," mourned an unrepentant secessionist woman. The oath, for thousands of women less ardent in the cause of Dixie than herself, provided an easy way of loosening constricting prohibitions.[26]

Almost always a civilian in Union occupation areas could, if determined to remain unsworn, evade the consequences of nonjuring by obtaining the coöperation of a sworn neighbor or of a friendly army officer, or through political "pull" could receive special dispensation. Even in Tennessee, a notorious center of stern Unionist policy, adept Southerners imported reaping and mowing machines, scarce salt, flour, and other necessaries, through the kindness of oath-sworn friends. In some occupied communities, civilians actually drew straws to choose some among their number to take the Yankee oath, and thus become able to buy, sell, and travel in the interests of the whole group, the majority of which remained unsworn. Some unrepentant rebels found that the best way to rid themselves of a Unionist they disliked, or of a Northern officer they feared, was to accuse him of disloyalty to the Union and softness toward themselves! It was so easy—an anonymous note, a whisper to a provost of indiscreet associations, or of confessed leniency toward rebels, often sufficed. At a time when each man feared his neighbor, scruples against such vicious conduct went awry.

Even such clever duplicity faced unpredictable elements of chance when one provost succeeded another in a locality. The new officer normally renewed all passes and oath certificates, and in the process uncovered subterfuges and irregularities his predecessor had connived in or innocently permitted. Grant removed one provost, General Henry Price, from command in Kentucky on charges that he had been too soft toward the civilians in his jurisdiction. Price refused to take disgrace without resistance. He defended his past policy as one designed to improve the attitudes of the Kentuckians toward the federal government, and that had suppressed a ruinous guerrilla warfare which had decimated the counties he had commanded. His successor, according to Price, was resurrecting the phantom of rebellion by his harshness, his refusal to recognize Price's oath certificates, and his arbitrary arrests. "He has," Price charged, "sent under guard . . . quiet and peaceable citizens who have taken the oath of allegiance and actually banished them to Canada." Grant was too busy at Cold Harbor to investigate this situation. There were many such incidents when the predilections of one provost superseded those of another. For the Southerners concerned each change meant an anxious waiting period while a stranger decided their fates and the worthwhileness of their oaths. Each change in provost involved complex issues of the validity of protection papers, of travel permits, of food quotas, and of political privileges. It was a great gamble, and the stakes were always high for the men and women whom fate made pawns in the national game of loyalty.[27]

Because some Southerners resorted to deceit in loyalty matters, many Northerners concluded that all rebels' oaths were valueless. A New Yorker on provost duty in Louisiana, repelled by the hypocritical greed of many civilians whom he must convert to loyalty, described his nauseated reaction:

You can't imagine the pestiferous character of the rebels in this section . . . meanness, hypocrisy, and insolence; truckling to us as we advance; with bated breath and hang dog demeanor approaching an officer to beg a pitiful protection from the Government they despise and spit on. . . . No sooner has our rear guard passed them than they reassume the vocation of guerrillas.[28]

Federal troops hated being "taken in" by oath-sworn Southerners. The provost guard of Sherman's troops in Tennessee made friends with a young civilian couple whose farm, near the Union barracks, boasted the protection paper which meant that the owner had sworn the required test of loyalty. One spring day in 1863, the farmer invited the Yankee provosts on a turkey hunt. Instead of game birds, the host meant the Yankee guests to be the targets, for he had connived with Confederate guerrillas to ambush the trusting soldiers.

As things worked out the ambushing party was too weak. Union soldiers repelled the attack, and then considered what should be the fate of their untrustworthy, oath-taking friend. Some demanded that they lynch him on the spot, but enough decried this to send him to prison, while the disappointed lynchers derived some satisfaction from burning the informer's home to the ground. His wife, party to the deception, fled to the Southern lines. His father, innocent of complicity, suffered revocation of his protection and travel permits. Soon after, the imprisoned man escaped, just before the military court convened which would have tried him for violating his loyalty oath.

He was lucky to escape in time. Union military courts had little patience with oath violators. Many loyalty-oath forms bore the statement that automatic death sentences awaited those who violated its terms. Wherever federal forces found guerrillas, spies, or saboteurs who possessed Union oath certificates, the rattle of the firing squad, or the softer but no less deadly rasp of the gallows' rope, marked a final end to perjurers' careers. Few federal soldiers worried over the ethical problem of perjury. They were determined, however, that civilians whom they let live in the rear of Union armies because of loyalty-testing policies, should not strike them foul blows.[29]

In all these manifold applications of loyalty tests by Union armies, there had been almost no agreement on essentials of plan or purpose among Union officers. During the first three war years the utility of loyalty oaths made itself apparent to many officials. By late 1863 Lincoln was prepared to launch the most significant Union loyalty-testing program of all. From 1861 to 1863 Lincoln had experimented with plans for reuniting the occupied Southern areas with the political Union. In Arkansas, Florida, Louisiana, and Tennessee, his authority initiated various combinations of civil-military state governments. Lincoln learned from these improvisations. On December 8, 1863, he proclaimed a program for political reconstruction, the tentative system through which he felt that this war for the preservation of the Union could realize its objective.

At the heart of Lincoln's system was a loyalty test. It required repentant Southerners who wished to participate in new, loyal state governments, and desired to gain the material benefits accruing to Union oath takers, to swear future loyalty to the Union, and to accept the verdict of battle which was making certain the survival of that Union. Those who took the oath received Lincoln's pardon for rebelling. A pardoned man, as Lincoln defined the term, was exempt from all penalties for past subversion and treason. Why an oath of future loyalty? Congress had, in 1862, written its rigid "ironclad test oath" of past allegiance; radical Republican congressmen demanded to know why the president did not use their relatively harsher code of loyalty-testing in reconstruction. Lincoln's reason was simple: "On principle I dislike an oath which requires a man to swear he *has* done no wrong. It rejects the Christian principle of forgiveness on terms of repentance. I think it enough if a man does no wrong *hereafter*."

Lincoln, determined to exploit Unionist feeling in the still-defiant South, convinced that former rebels could become future loyal citizens by swearing an oath, sure that he, as wartime president, had full power and primary responsibility to do all that was necessary to reknit the Union, maintained his test oath over Congress' oath and reconstruction program. While Lincoln lived, his comparatively merciful reconstruction proposals, based on this simple test of future loyalty, were all that Southerners faced as a barrier to reëntrance into the nation's political life. The Confederate government did not appreciate his mercy.[30]

Rebel authorities, from the beginning of the war, recognized the threat to the Confederacy posed by Union loyalty programs. The Southern Congress, in 1862, professed to believe that Confederate war prisoners were coerced into taking the Union oath in order to gain release from Northern prison camps. General Robert E. Lee protested to McClellan that Union troops in Virginia imprisoned "peaceful citizens" for refusing the oath, and treated nonjurors so harshly that they finally succumbed to the loyalty test. McClellan denied the charge; Halleck insisted that no federal officer had ever "extorted" an oath of loyalty from a Southern soldier or civilian. Halleck went on to warn all Union officers against imposing an oath upon anyone.

This academic argument, carried on under flags of truce, avoided the real issue. Behind the Union offer of an oath lay the whole gamut of pressures and privileges that oath-taking brought, and the entire list of restrictions that nonjuring involved. "To call oaths given under such circumstances voluntary," wrote the editor of the Confederate army newspaper, *Daily Rebel,* "is downright foolishness." No, not foolishness. Circumlocution is a better word.

Confederate President Jefferson Davis fulminated against the "unheard-of conduct" of Union officers who exiled civilians for refusing to take the federal oath; rebel congressmen passed resolutions against Northern oath programs; rebel state governors promised Southerners that oaths taken to the Union "under duress" were not binding. But oaths were more than words, and it required more than words to counter their seductive attractiveness to civilians in occupied areas or Northern prisons. Oaths meant life, freedom, and property. And when Lincoln added the bonus of pardon and amnesty to the buying power of the oath he proclaimed in 1863, Union loyalty-testing accelerated, and achieved its final form as a propaganda weapon capable of sucking the will to resist from thousands of rebels.[31]

Southerners saw well enough that Lincoln possessed a deadly weapon in the loyalty test. "To conquer the South without fighting has been the great desideratum . . . from the beginning of the war," warned the *Richmond Examiner,* and the angry editorialist admitted that the Union oath program was effective among those Southerners whom he called "the weary, the cowardly, the base." These "shrewdly-conceived oaths" attracted what another ardent rebel writer termed "those perfidious and dishonorable classes who are ever ready, servilely, to bend their necks to the yoke of might, in order to grasp the thrift that fawning secures." Oath takers were "fitted for servitude, but unworthy of freedom." A Southern woman accurately described the Union loyalty tests as devices "to frighten our men into submission . . . and [into] the perjury of themselves; . . . devoid of all principles of manliness, courage, or bravery." And the sister of a Confederate general described how a former friend of theirs had *voluntarily* (unkindest cut of all) taken the Yankee oath in order to get a federal contract for pasturing horses. This "base character" boasted, perhaps in the excessive zeal of the new convert, that he hoped the war would last ten years, so that his suddenly swollen profits might continue. "I sincerely hope," the woman wrote, "he may never receive a dime for his sordid treachery. . . . He would sell his soul for money." [32] Lincoln cared less about the man's soul or his money than about the effect of such successive defections upon other civilians in the growing occupied areas of the South.

To make his program immediately effective, Lincoln ordered a corps of special oath commissioners, his private secretary among them, to rush the blank oath in new form to all occupied Southern cities and Northern prison camps. And his new loyalty test, with all it promised, was at once successful. By the end of 1863 Union military victories had split the South in twain. The end of the war, if distant, was already in sight. Fervid secessionists became increasingly discouraged as brave Southern resistance failed to achieve Northern recognition of the Confederacy's right to exist. Their discouragement accumulated until, capitulating, they admitted "an error of the head and not of the heart," and applied for Lincoln's oath.

The new oath was successful because it was an oath of future loyalty, rather than one testing the past, as Congress and some Union officers wanted. Lincoln saw that most Southerners supported the Confederacy, whether willingly or not. He deeply believed that America would benefit more from repentance than from repression, and insisted that only local men should govern neighbors. When, early in 1864, Tennesseans were able to choose between Lincoln's test of future loyalty and Johnson's harsher oath, which demanded an oath of past allegiance as a prerequisite for voting, a diarist noted that a "great many people are taking the [presidential] oath of amnesty but few are taking Johnson's oath." 33

Pro-Confederate civilians in Northern zones of occupation fought the Union oath with all the power they could. A few found ridicule effective. Belle Boyd, the famous rebel spy, made the most of a situation in Virginia where a dairymaid had to cross a Union check point on the way to milk her cows. Each day the girl had to get a new pass and swear a new oath. Belle pasted a sign between the horns of the lead cow: "These cows have permission to pass to and from the yard . . . for the purpose of being milked."

Other prorebels used more subtle social pressures to influence their friends and families against taking any Union oath. Ridicule, scorn, social ostracism—these were the common weapons that Southern civilians, especially women, launched against "galvanized" neighbors. Of a brother who succumbed to the lures of oath-taking, one Southern miss wrote: "I wish there was no blood in his veins that is in mine. I wish to Heaven he was no brother of mine." Although she publicly defended her brother's decision to change allegiance ("Let him be President Lincoln if he will and I would love him just the same"), privately she admitted her revulsion at his act.34

Perhaps the female of the Southern species should have received Lincoln's special attention. Young Kate Carney of Tennessee surely was worth a division of cavalry to the cause of Dixie, in influencing neighbors against the Yankee oath. She tells how

Mr. Duffer came in dressed as fine as any dandy. . . . He is in town for marrying to judge from his looks, and I must say I was not at all favorably impressed. It might have been the conversation he struck up about taking the oath. I said very little, but my remarks were pointed. He had too much Yankee about him for me.

But other Southern girls were less eager to sacrifice for Dixie. "Talk about dying for your country," said one, when a Union oath was required for wedding permits, "but what is that to being an old maid for it?" And what was dying, for other Southern misses, compared to missing a year of school, or failing to have a new frock or coach, or living without dances and parties if their families refused the Yankee oath? A Kate Carney fought the oath, and many Kate Carneys fought this way for the South. But other Southern women importuned their men to swear to *any* oath, in order that they and their families might enjoy necessities and luxuries. It was a story as complex and individual as humanity itself, a story that divided families and friends. Deep scars were represented in such comments as these, which one young Southern belle recorded: "Aunt Laura, formerly so bitter against the Yankees, is now urging us to go . . . and get letters protecting us." Or, of a former friend: "Miss W. Richardson . . . came back boasting that she had caught a Yankee beau. Imagine any girl falling so low."

The oath was heartbreak, envy, jubilation, hatred. "If I was a wife," decided Kate Carney, "I would say, go and die before taking that vile oath." Of families and former friends who, for selfish purposes, swore the Union oath or pressured their men to do so, she had only scorn. "Poor goose, I wish I had never been intimate with her, but I will never be so again," Kate bitterly noted of a girlhood chum who had made her father swear, so that the daughter might keep a carriage. Some Southern women were weaker than their fighting rebel men, or more property-conscious. In any event, the wife of Confederate General Alcorn, who remained at her Mississippi home when federal troops occupied the area, wrote her unrepentant husband that "I regret that many of our people have . . . [taken the oath], not many of the sterner sex, but several of the weaker." For thousands of Southern families, "it was a sad trial to hear of so many of our friends taking the oath. . . . I did think our friends were a little higher."

Higher than what? For the harassed Dawson family of Louisiana, abstract sectional ethics faded before pressing personal needs. An aged mother, ill and near death, was a reality apart from patriotism. So the family took Union oaths to get protection, buy food, and keep their home. Their unsworn neighbors cried "treason" against this devotedly rebel family. Pro-Confederate guerrillas threatened the Dawson men with hanging, the women with tar and feathers, and their home with the torch. The family finally fled to a haven made safe by a Unionist renegade relative in New Orleans, where federal troops could protect them against their former friends.[35]

In communities inside federal lines, where most of the population were pro-Confederate, taking the Union test of loyalty was a dangerous and brave act. Nimrod Porter, a farmer of Nashville, had sworn the Union oath, and was returning home from a trip which the oath made possible, when a rifle pointed at his heart impelled him to stop his buggy. The rifleman was a Confederate guerrilla who was "checking" on reputed Union oath takers. He charged Porter with the double offense of seeking to convince other Southern civilians to take the Union oath in order to save their property. Porter, an owner of three Negro slaves, was a man of mild political convictions. He also had a temper. He took his buggy whip to the guerrilla who decided to leave the scene at top speed and let local pro-Southerners attend to this stubborn man.

Another Southern farmer learned that living in a zone of Union occupation had all sorts of subtle dangers. This Virginian had refused the Union oath, but he heard gossip about himself which charged that he had secretly taken it in order to receive money for damages federal troops had done to his property. He was sure that his slaves or old personal enemies were behind these "slanders," and shrugged them off, but could not as easily ignore the probable effects of the charge that he had taken the oath: "I hope I shall not suffer seriously from their calumny," he noted, "but . . . outlive the prejudice it may engender." Depending upon where and when the situation permitted such open defiance of federal laws and oath, some Southerners freely told their neighbors that the Yankee oath equaled a death warrant for the signer.[36]

Threats of rebel military retaliation carried force. Hope beat brightly in prorebel breasts that Dixie's armies would rescue her oppressed supporters from Yankee occupation. And sometimes, often in the first years of the war, increasingly rarely as Northern power increased, it happened. When it did, those who had been oppressed under Union rule became oppressors.

Pensacola, Florida, March, 1863. Union army and naval forces were hurriedly evacuating their positions in the face of threatening rebel advances. Pensacolans who had, during the months of Union occupation, supported, fed, and housed these troops, keened over their fates now that the erstwhile protectors were fleeing. A Northern naval officer wrote his wife of the harried civilians who displayed the Union oath certificate and begged for a place on board the crowded transports, in order to evade the wrath they knew would come upon them once the Stars and Bars again floated over their homes. "They are a poor sickly mass of humanity," he wrote. "I pity them, poor things." The retreating Union fleet sailed away from Pensacola's docks, bearing perhaps two thousand of these refugees on board, displaced from families and homes because they had taken the Union oath, and because their commitment to the Northern cause made continued living in what was now Confederate territory too dangerous to chance. The Union loyalty-testing program experienced a real reversal, for protections had proved worthless. Unionists who had avowed their faith had climbed out on a loyalty limb which was now collapsing.[37]

Alexandria, Missouri, June 8, 1864. Striking out from New Orleans, Union forces under General Banks had reached Alexandria, where Banks proclaimed to all residents of the area that he was there to stay, and that if they wished to avoid prison or property confiscation, and receive protection, they must take the oath. Hundreds, impressed by the display of armed might, did so. Then came a forceful Confederate counterattack. Banks, no great gladiator, prepared to retreat, and ordered his troops to burn the town, making no exception for the property of oath takers. Tearful men and women watched their property consumed. But they could not stay, even though homeless, for the nonjurors of the region were figuratively and literally whetting knives in preparation for coming revenge. So Banks bore with him a corps of fearful people, wrenched by untimely oath from homes and habits.

Bolivar, Tennessee, June, 1863. After more than a year of Union occupation and loyalty-testing, federal forces hurriedly evacuated the area in the face of large-scale rebel advances. Most of the ardent Unionists of Bolivar went with the troops, abandoning their property. But some Unionists could or would not go, nor would many nonpolitical civilians who had taken the Union oath. Then the first of the Confederate forces appeared. Their arrival seemed to justify the most fearful imaginings of rebel retaliation, for the advance guard was a group of pro-Confederate guerrillas who had sprung up with the good news from the South. They rode the streets, shooting, threatening, cursing, but as an undesired tribute to their amateur marksmanship, doing no real harm. Within an hour, regular Confederate cavalry forces arrived in Bolivar and took charge.

Locked doors opened. Prorebel hearts exulted. First joy gave way to thoughts of revenge upon Unionist oath takers. Bolivar's citizens offered the Confederate commander lists of neighbors who had collaborated with the Yankees, which they had secretly compiled as they waited for the second coming of the rebels. Prorebel citizens supplied rebel officers with detailed accounts of the property which Yankee oath takers had confiscated, so that it might be reconfiscated. Confederate squads marched off to arrest Tennesseans who had taken the Union side.

Then—alarm! Union forces retook Bolivar. The process reversed. Unionists now demanded revenge, and denounced neighbors who had caused other Unionists to become political prisoners of the Confederacy. Union provosts issued new passes and protections based upon new loyalty oaths. The cycle was run.[38]

Hope for and fear of like event warmed and chilled many a rebel heart. Even gentle ladies of Dixie could write enthusiastically of the longed-for time or reckoning. "I am delighted to hear this morning that Little Rock is again in the Confederacy," exulted Miss Ida Fulton to an intimate lady friend. "Do write me all about the yankees leaving and how those of our people who took the [Union] oath of allegiance are treated by our authorities." They were treated roughly.[39]

Optimism or fear that rebel troops might return to Union-occupied sections formed a continuing though ever-decreasing obstacle to successful Northern loyalty-testing. When Union provosts near Nashville announced that every civilian must take the federal loyalty oath or face propertyless exile, a bitter woman prayed: "I hope that before they have a chance [to put the order into effect], our men will be back." The idea that rebels would return made many less ardent prorebel Southerners refuse the oath through fear of Confederate revenge and lack of confidence in Union victory. As Union forces in Mississippi readied for the amphibious attack on Vicksburg, a naval officer noted how few plantation owners came on board to get protection and take the oath. "They are fearful," the officer recorded, "that we will leave them to the mercies of our bitter and relentless foes." Civilians, unless they had strong ideological convictions indeed, did well to wait until the side they swore to was firmly in control of an area, before they signed a loyalty oath.[40]

They had reason for caution. St. Louis, among many other "occupied" cities, harbored a secret Southern vigilance committee whose members agreed to swear whatever Union oaths were required of them in order that they might remain in the town and "keep a sharp eye" on their neighbors' Confederate patriotism. These deliberate perjurers anonymously circularized Missourians with dire threats of vengeance ("Union military law cannot last forever, and then woe to the man who has robbed his neighbor!!") when rebel armies should return. This time they did not return.

John J. Tyler, of Loudoun County, Virginia, had the misfortune to live in an area that changed hands more than a dozen times in the first two war years. He went to successive Yankee and Confederate prisons, because he refused oaths to either side. His determined neutrality excited the anger or contempt of more convinced neighbors. Tyler was unusually fortunate, however, for he had influential friends in both sectional governments, who got him out of prisons without oaths. But there were few who had Tyler's kind of "connections."

Civilians without such influence chose to "bend to existing winds," as one federal provost marshal described it; they refused oaths and endured as best they could the penalties of nonjuring, rather than face the dreaded penalties for disloyalty to either side. How could prorebels seek Yankee protection when rebel hosts waited to reconquer all Southern land from the Yankees? "The Secesh about here are in fine spirits—spunky as ever, 'never say die,'" rpeorted a Confederate general's wife to her husband, "while those who from fear or other motives took the oath are as a general thing, morose and sullen." Woe was always coming for the derelict sons of the South who had taken the Yankee oath. "When the Confederates reach Nashville," the woman dreamed, "they will drive every man out of the country, who took so abominable an oath." Only—and this was the test stronger than loyalty—the Confederacy lost more battles than it won. Rebel troops returned to Union-occupied areas more and more rarely. Dixie and not the North became the battleground.[41]

Loyalty was a war weapon of the Civil War, and the fate of battles decided that Union loyalty tests were more numerous and more effective than their Confederate counterparts. As rebel fortunes waned through 1864 and 1865, and rebel hopes for a reconquest of Union-occupied Southern territory dimmed, Union loyalty-testing increased in tempo. Indeed, Union officers often faced the problem of decreasing the number of Southerners who desired to take the oath. "The trouble has been not to induce them to do it," one harassed provost marshal reported from Wilmington, "but to resist the pressure to take the oath, that there might be a little opportunity to discriminate and avoid being imposed upon." [42]

The effectiveness of Union loyalty-testing programs suffered from other causes than the rare recapture of territory by rebel troops. Civilians whose Unionism was adequate merely to taking the oath in order to get protection for their property, often suffered loss regardless of their oaths. "Mrs. Graves' [protection] papers," exulted an unrepentant nonjuror at an oath-sworn neighbor's discomfiture, "did not prove a perfect safeguard as the [Yankee] squad took all their good horses." Nor did their masters' protection papers often hold Negro slaves on Southern farms when the heady winds of freedom blew in with Union armies. Angry Southerners demanded the return of stolen horses and strayed Negroes, but few Union officers troubled to honor the demands of men whose only proof of patriotism was an oath certificate. Too many Northern officers doubted the genuineness of the oath, and were, in any event, too busy otherwise to worry about it.

But such callousness made many Southerners wonder if it was worth while to take the oath. Why bother, why expose oneself to retribution and ostracism, if Union troops did not fulfill the promise of protection the oaths implied? Southerners found that in many areas Union troops paid scant attention to protection papers issued by their officers. Sherman's forces glorified themselves as "the cotton-burners of the 16th Corps," and cared not at all that a Union loyalty oath supposedly exempted some Georgia cotton from the torch. Yankee soldiers joked about how they stole only those chickens and pigs that refused the Northern loyalty test. Some Union officers held all citizens of an area, sworn or not, financially responsible for the damage committed by Confederate cavalry depredations.

Many federal soldiers failed completely to see how swearing a Union oath made a Southerner less a rebel. In Missouri and Kansas, for instance, Union troops felt that every Southerner had participated in the bloody deeds of an earlier decade; in northern Virginia and South Carolina the blue-clad forces were convinced that the spirit of Calhoun still predominated. Unionists at Port Royal, Florida, suffered as much from riotous federal troops as they had from earlier rebel oppression. Union General Paine in Kentucky made his administration of civil affairs memorable by a two months' campaign of terror which imprisoned and impoverished thousands of civilians, oath takers and nonjurors alike. General Roberts in northern Virginia despaired of ending sabotage in his command until he resorted to depopulating whole counties. His orders exiled thousands of civilians who had taken the oath to prevent just such a fate. Rosecrans in Tennessee requisitioned Negro slaves to build Union fortifications, and made no distinction between loyal and nonjuring owners. When two Union commanders in an area refused to recognize each other's protection certificates, then civilians were reduced to despondency, never knowing if federal soldiers would honor the papers or not. The effect of such acts was to make more difficult the job of Northern provosts and oath commissioners: to tie Southerners' self-interest and national loyalty together by the oath. A few federal commanders realized this, and sought to curb the indiscriminate foraging that thinly disguised plain looting and robbery. But such orders were honored more in the breach than in the observance. The Civil War, for rebel and Yank alike, was often a looters' holiday, usually in the name of loyalty.[43]

Worst off of all Americans in this war of sections were those who lived in the no man's lands between rebel and Union armies. There were many such areas of indeterminate sovereignty, where unfortunate residents rarely knew for certain which side controlled their lives from one day to the next. Even less certain was the answer to the bitter question: To which side should the civilian adhere by his oath? Vigilantes of both sides, guerrillas, and plain nonpartisan looters and robbers pillaged happily in these troubled areas. Deserters from two armies, stragglers, the scum of war, made life uncertain and death common. A Tennessean recalls how

. . . our section was within the lines of first one side and then the other— now sprinkled with Federal soldiers, now with Confederates . . . and sometimes with irregular bands of gorillas [sic], bushwackers and tories, . . . all bent on rapine and plunder . . . the "Yankees" plundering and sometimes murdering rebel families and sympathizers, and the "rebs" treating in the same way . . . the families of Union men and sympathizers.[44]

Berkeley County, Virginia, was another such bedeviled area. Rebel forces raided it frequently but impermanently; Union troops compounded the evil by treating the county's residents as though all were prorebel, and as if not one had ever sworn loyalty to the Union, which many had. As Lincoln's close friend, Ward Hill Lamon, stated, such poor people were "unfortunate . . . in their place of birth or misguided in their place of habitation." [45]

Eventually the force of Union arms made the entire Southland a "misguided" place of residence. Northern victory made the success of Lincoln's loyalty program possible. The reverse, however, is not true. In bitterly divided Tennessee in mid-1864, Union General Payne launched a campaign against Confederate guerrillas, many of whom, when captured, proved to have Union oath certificates on their untrustworthy persons. Such men died. Payne made clear how he felt concerning the utility of loyalty tests as security measures. Peaceful civilians, he warned, "might think, feel [and] die secesh, but if they talked or acted treason, he would make them houseless, homeless, and lifeless." [46] If Payne was right in his policy, then an awesome amount of loyalty-swearing had gone for nothing.

CHAPTER VIII

Over These Prison Walls

"To become a prisoner of war," recalled a Virginian who survived the process, "was the one horror of a Confederate soldier." As this dispirited man entered a federal military prison late in 1861, he foresaw only three grim alternatives: ". . . to remain until we either died, were exchanged, or succeeded in subjugating the North." [1] Many died. Thousands were exchanged, in an erratic system that collapsed completely at frequent intervals. Hope for the third alternative, Southern victory, died a slow death on a hundred battlefields. Only a daring few escaped. For the great majority, however, there was only waiting, stretching into endless months and stagnant years. To Lincoln, the miseries of the prison camps accumulated into an intolerable moral pressure, which found release through the agency of loyalty tests.

During the first war months federal commanders freed captured rebels immediately after battle, on simple paroles of honor not to resume fighting against the Union until formal exchanges voided the paroles.[2] Such breezy informality did not long endure. It was patently absurd for federal officers to permit the outnumbered Confederacy so easily to regain the military services of these men. And it was as obviously inhumane for Lincoln to force captives to return to rebeldom via an exchange system, when so many did not wish to return.

Pleas for pardon rather than exchange increased in volume during the first war months. "Grant me the liberty," importuned a captive North Carolinian, "of taking the oath of allegiance to the USA and to remain in the [federal] lines . . . until my home is in the Union again." An imprisoned Kentuckian described himself as a "loyal man who deserted the Confederate Army after being impressed into it; I am willing to take the oath . . . and also to volunteer into the [U.S.] Army." Something, Lincoln felt, had to be done for such men.[3] Other federal officials agreed. Judge John Catron of Tennessee pleaded with War Secretary Stanton for the liberty of a twenty-year-old Kentucky relative, who had run away from home to join the rebels, "as did all the other young fellows in the neighborhood. As things stood it could not be otherwise at that time. . . . [His] family are Union people generally. . . . [He] will take the oath and give any [other] surety required. He gives up the rebellion."

Such a case exhibits how loyalty tests came to serve Lincoln both as a war weapon and as a preparatory phase for the reconstruction of the nation still to come. The South would lose a soldier if the imprisoned youth gained his freedom rather than exchange. Kentucky and the United States would possess a living example of Union moderation and power. The prisoner's family and friends in the ever-disturbed border area would be beneficially affected by his release, which, in Catron's words, would "quiet an unusual number of people. Can this be done—when, and how? The object is, mainly, to bring back this large connection of loyal people to a loyal sentiment and earnest support of the [federal] government, and this can only be accomplished by using moderate means." [4]

Other Unionist spokesmen urged that turncoat rebels would be proof that the vaunted unity of Dixie was a sham. A Union policy of freeing war prisoners willing to recant Confederate allegiance would encourage desertion among rebel troops, reveal the oppressive nature of the Southern government, and underscore the North's official contention that the rebellion was the work of a designing few rather than an expression of popular Southern will. Every captured rebel prisoner who took the oath lessened the number the North had to feed and guard. If the chameleons among the captives were willing to serve on the Western frontier, they freed federal soldiers for combat duty; if they chose federal military service they provided needed recruits for whom neither bounty payments nor cumbersome conscription machinery was required. Those who preferred to return to their homes within the Union lines, or to relocate in the North or in the unsettled West, added to the nation's agricultural and industrial productivity.

Emotional appeals reinforced the practical advantages of a freedom-through-loyalty-test policy. The President, congressmen, and generals received appeals from loyal partisans of captured rebels. Perhaps the most touching was this tragic story of a sorrowing Missourian. He told of his cousin, who

. . . was only fifteen years old when [he was] persuaded to join John Morgan's [Confederate] Regiment. His father and brother were very much opposed to his going but stronger influences took him away. The surgeon at the [prison] Hospital at Camp Douglas writes to the young man's parents that he . . . is fast declining and must shortly die. And his parents are anxious that he may be allowed to die at home. He is willing to take the oath of allegiance.[5]

With greater hope for the future, other Northerners told how their sons had been in school or in business in the South when war came, had joined rebel forces under duress and had been captured, and now wished to resume interrupted educations and careers. Prisoners added to these appeals, describing how they had perilously deserted rebel ranks at the first opportunity in order to achieve captive status under the Stars and Stripes. Such self-professed ardent Unionists, who claimed to have worn rebel gray only by force, now begged to be freed of the dread of exchange, which would return them to the rebeldom they had risked their lives and property to escape. Northern women entered the lists to champion individual captive rebels, and to plead that federal authorities permit their men to return to homes, hearths—and to "her." Children of prisoners penned scrawled, tear-stained appeals for "mercy and Daddy." [6] Indeed, the need for some federal policy toward repentant rebels was overwhelming. The much-used loyalty-oath test became the symbol and the tool of Lincoln's policy concerning the

. . . prisoners of war in our custody, . . . who wish not to be exchanged, but to take the oath and be discharged. . . . My impression [Lincoln stated] is that we will not ever force the exchange of any of this class; that, taking the oath and being discharged, none of them will again go to the rebellion; but, the rebellion again coming to them, a considerable percentage of them, probably not a majority, would rejoin it; that, by a cautious discrimination, the number so discharged would not be large enough to do any considerable mischief in any event, would relieve distress in at least some meritorious cases, and would give me some relief from an intolerable pressure.[7]

In early 1862 federal loyalty-testing of rebel war prisoners commenced. As in almost every matter of Civil War administration, Washington proposed and local commanders did pretty much as they pleased. Every federal general, provost marshal, and prison superintendent modified Lincoln's orders to suit real or fancied needs of the area involved. Some even ignored the President's wishes in this matter of loyalty tests for captured rebels.

Grant, for instance, permitted his subordinate commanders to offer loyalty tests on the still-smoking battlefield to all rebel troops, including deserters who surrendered at Vicksburg. Another point of view was exemplified by General Boyle, who refused to allow his command to have anything to do with loyalty oaths at the battle front and sent captives off to the rear immediately. Some federal provost marshals in Tennessee centralized oath administration in the capital city of the state; their colleagues in Missouri provided swearing facilities in every hamlet where captured or deserting rebels might appear. Superintendent Wood of the Old Capitol Prison in Washington faced each group of incoming war prisoners with an unnerving and unauthorized claim that any who refused the Union oath would hang. Other prison commanders were careful to make their tenders of the oaths a discreet, individual affair. Still others were so lackadaisical about the entire program that a rebel prisoner waited weeks after his initial incarceration before he had a chance to consider taking the oath. And some federal officers never afforded their rebel prisoners any opportunity to change allegiance.[8] The essential fact remained, however, that most captured Confederates had an opportunity to renounce the South, and thus gain freedom.

At dozens of prison camps in the North new captives received a printed from, often conjoined with a curt admonition from a guard to read it immediately. The form was entitled: "Voluntary Statement of Prisoners to the Provost Marshal General." Prisoners saw that it contained a score of questions concerning the captive's vital statistics and military history, and—here the bait hung enticingly—the inquiry "What terms do you ask to be released on?" That magic word—"release." If the prisoner seemed about to relegate the form to the trash heap, guards hastened to admonish him at least to keep it for a more thorough reading later. Should a rebel seem disposed to answer the questions immediately, pen and ink or pencil appeared for his use, and a federal officer was on hand to act as secretary if the prisoner was illiterate.

This form was the first intimation most prisoners had that there was a way out of the camps other than by escape, exchange, or death. It was the first, and very effective, step in the process by which federal officers hoped to carry out Lincoln's plan to convert rebels to Unionism by loyalty test and oath. Orders from the provost marshal general directed all prison superintendents to keep adequate supplies of the form on hand, "constantly make known to the prisoners that they can each day send this statement" to federal officers. In addition, there were to be copies in each prison tent, barracks, mess hall, and latrine, and near every bulletin board. Rebel captives blessed their bountiful keepers for providing such excellent writing paper for letters home, and many a prisoner enjoyed his first experience with toilet tissue through the largess of the loyalty program. Camp commanders stopped privileges for such disrespectful souls.

Other rebel prisoners were more impressed with the possibility for release which the form offered. Each man knew the temper of his comrades. Sometimes he felt it safe enough to talk openly of his interest in the federal questionnaire, and of his intention to fill out the form; groups combined their literary efforts, exchanging suggestions regarding questions of grammar and form most likely to please federal officials. More often, probably, a prisoner discreetly hid the blank form so that he might fill it out in safe privacy, free from the censure of more ardent Southern patriots than himself. He might then warily approach a guard, whisper his intention to complete the form, and arrange a clandestine meeting with camp officers.

Such a man was James A. Bosworth, a Texan, already a veteran of two years of combat on his eighteenth birthday, when he was captured in Arkansas. Bosworth, illiterate, met secretly with a federal officer to fill out the form. He described himself as a cattle tender, claimed that he had never before taken the oath of allegiance to the United States, and denied that he had plundered Unionist civilians or behaved cruelly to Union captives while in rebel service. Bosworth concluded his oath application in no uncertain terms: "I denounce the so-called Southern Confederacy and will bear allegiance to the United States." The officer who examined him decided that Bosworth was no rebel. "He claimed," the officer noted, "that he was sick most of the time during combat," and that "he does not know what he is" so far as ideological convictions were concerned. Bosworth, according to the officer's notes on the form, was not suitable material to carry out the President's ideas on reconstruction should he return to his home area. Better to refuse him the oath and let him suffer until exchanged.[9]

After a captive Confederate filled out the form, it went to the camp commander, who entered his recommendations and comments. Here many a prisoner's hopes for release died if the federal officer felt that the protestations of reawakened Union loyalty were insincere. If, however, the camp commander's subjective standards of loyalty were satisfied by the prisoner's statement, he forwarded it to the next link in the loyalty chain, the "oath commissioner."

Oath commissioners were civilian appointees of the War Department, who secured their posts through the governors of their states or from prominent Unionists. At each major prison camp, there were resident oath commissioners for all the states in the Union, including the states in rebellion (the latter staffed, of course, with refugee Unionists). These commissioners operated the "Prisoner Roll Office" of the camp, and made regular circuits to smaller prison compounds where there were no resident oath commissioners. They formed the basic loyalty review boards for war prisoners of the Civil War. In their hands they held the fates of thousands, daily deciding between imprisonment or freedom for captives who claimed conversion to Unionism. To the appropriate oath commissioner came the prisoners' completed statements; the next step was up to him.

What the next step was depended largely upon the predilections of the individual commissioner. If he was satisfied with the loyalty of the prisoner, he could immediately approve the application for release, administer the oath to the repentant rebel, and see him on his way outside the prison. But when the commissioner doubted the genuineness of the conversion, he initiated a loyalty probe. Most often, this inquiry centered on a demand that the prisoner supply detailed information concerning his past Unionism, including proofs that he had been an unwilling rebel, or had sincerely repented his insurrectionary life. Prisoners had to obtain unimpeachable references from loyal persons—an onerous task for those from the deep South who knew no refugee Unionists familiar with their histories. The commissioner judged this evidence, added his own conclusions concerning the personality of the prisoner, and decided to accept or reject the oath application.

A good oath commissioner was much more than a mere passive recipient of oath applications. When new prisoners arrived in camp, the commissioner surveyed them, and sought to pick out the influential men among them. If these men proved reluctant to apply for the oath, the commissioner essayed to convert them by persuasion. Naturally, a commissioner paid a good deal of attention to rebel officers, and counted it a good day when a Confederate colonel or captain converted to Union allegiance. Many a commissioner was a former politician of his state, and his intimate knowledge of who among the prisoners were important persons, worthy of proselytizing efforts, stood the Union cause in good stead.

Among the rare records of Civil War oath commissioners are those of two such officials whose activities were typical of many more. W. B. Campbell was the commissioner for Tennessee at the Camp Douglas, Illinois, war prison. He was an ardent patriot, a relative of the Unionist governor, and a friend of his divided state's fiery wartime commander, Andrew Johnson. Equipped with a stock of oath forms, a copy of Army General Orders, and a Bible, Campbell set up his office in a tent as close as possible to the prisoners' barracks. Only a palisaded wall separated him from the inmates. The camp superintendent secretly instructed sentries to permit individual prisoners to approach the wall day or night, in order to deposit their oath applications in a locked box provided for that purpose.

Campbell soon was busy enough to need assistance. He secured a clerk when G. H. Taylor, an ex-rebel Tennessean who had taken the Union oath after being captured, pleaded with Campbell to permit him to stay on in the hope of convincing others to take the same path to freedom. Taylor was a former frontier preacher, and his earthy sermons on the divine nature of allegiance, Union brand, was a potent asset in Campbell's work. Among the most powerful levers Campbell and Taylor had in stock to pressure wavering prisoners were letters from families of the inmates. Wives wrote to Campbell, telling how much their imprisoned men were needed to till the home fields and stave off starvation for their children. Frightened relatives told of injuries and indignities they were suffering at the hands of unprincipled guerrillas and bushwhackers, because "there is no man about the place." Campbell shrewdly showed these letters to the men concerned. Oath-taking increased.[10]

Bryan Tyson was the able oath commissioner for North Carolina at the federal military prison at Point Lookout, Maryland. Tyson was one of that heroic breed of Southern abolitionists who leavened the history of the prewar decades by their devotion to the cause of human freedom. When war came he felt it wise to leave North Carolina; he fled to Washington and became a clerk in a government department. But his ardent Unionism derived inadequate satisfaction from bureaucratic work. Tyson petitioned Stanton for more immediately useful wartime service. He enthusiastically entered upon the duties of oath commissioner, intermixing exhortations for loyalty with philippics against slavery.

Tyson did his best to publicize his position in rebel areas. He indulged in a voluminous correspondence with loyal leaders from his state, and placed advertisements in Northern newspapers, knowing that rebel troops eagerly scanned all the home town news at every opportunity. His propagandizing efforts soon received due reward. Captured Confederates at the prison where Tyson was stationed came to him with oath applications, and imprisoned Carolinians in federal prisoner-of-war camps in Washington, D.C., Elmira, New York, Chicago, and Ohio sent him pleas for his influence in their behalf. His reputation spread so far that one wavering Confederate whose brief rebel service ended in federal captivity wrote Tyson that

Shortly before leaving home my Father told me that if I was ever taken prisoner by writing to you I would be befriended by you. I am tired of the war and having previously consulted my Father on the subject I know of no greater favor you can do me than to use your endeavors to get me out of this prison. If you can accomplish this by vouching for my being a Union man I will readily take the oath.

By such means, combined with the power of his pen and his oratory, buttressed with judicious gifts of clothes, money, and tobacco to promising captives, Tyson effectively carried out his duties.[11]

Lincoln added to the roster of oath commissioners early in 1864, soon after he issued his December, 1863, proclamation of amnesty and reconstruction, which required past rebels to take a prescribed oath of future loyalty to the Union. In every rebel area, as federal troops eliminated Confederate opposition, Lincoln envisaged sworn Unionists resurrecting loyal state governments. A fine source of such state-making material was close at hand, among the oath takers of the prison camps. Lincoln sent his secretary, John Hay, on a tour of the major prisoner-of-war encampments, as the President's personal oath commissioner. Hay equipped himself with books of blank oaths in the new form, and launched a successful recruiting campaign among war prisoners who had escaped the attention of the regular commissioners.[12]

News of the federal loyalty-test policy spread amazingly swiftly. Former prisoners, free on oath, took with them to their homes the tidings of how they had gained release. But impatient federal officers and eager Unionists felt that the process of propagandizing rebels was still too slow, and desired to get the news of Lincoln's oath plan into the deep South. "Scarcely a day passes," a Union officer in Arkansas noted, "that a squad of rebels do not come in and ask the protection of the Government." He felt that many more would desert from Confederate service if they knew that they could receive federal protection and return to their homes if they took the oath. Fear of federal retribution kept lukewarm rebel soldiers from becoming overtly obedient Unionist citizens, this officer was convinced. He thought that Union commanders should spread the news that pardon awaited the oath taker.[13]

Colonel Russell A. Alger, of the Fifth Michigan Cavalry, agreed with these ideas. He told Lincoln and Stanton that "almost invariably, the first questions asked by [rebel] deserters coming within our lines are 'What are you going to do with us?' . . . [and] 'What privileges can we have, if we take the oath?' " But, Alger noted, Confederate officers had taken to quelling desertion by telling their troops that federal policy included imprisoning all deserters or impressing them into Union military service. Alger suggested that publicity provided the antidote:

The plan I would suggest for distributing [news of the oath program] is: let scouts carry it within the enemy's lines; let Cavalry expeditions be sent out, supplied with it; leave copies at every house possible, and scatter [them] wherever the enemy will be likely to find [them]. . . . Many will be found by rebel soldiers, and many more will be sent to them by mail from their friends.

With Lincoln's approval, Alger secured a stock of small-print amnesty and oath announcements and, with a regiment of cavalry, experimented with his idea on the Florida-Louisiana-Arkansas front. An anonymous Alabaman, who had fled North to evade Confederate military service, volunteered to return there, at the risk of his life, as a carrier of Lincoln's oath policy. "No doubt," he argued, "many [Alabamans] would like to . . . accept the terms offered under the amnesty oath." These primitive forms of psychological warfare were effective. Increasing numbers of rebel prisoners in federal camps, and of deserters from Confederate service, applied to take the Union oath as the war entered its third grim year.[14]

Confederate authorities did not, naturally, welcome the increasing desertions among their men which Lincoln's amnesty oath policy inspired. They prescribed death sentences for deserters whom rebel patrols caught absconding from the Southern cause. Confederate army newspapers pleaded with men in gray to reject the seductive lure of Lincoln's oath. "Our only hope," editorialized the *Daily Rebel,* organ of the Confederate Army of the West, "is to reject all thought of submission and trust in our strong right arms." [15] But such threats and appeals failed to stop the exodus from rebel ranks which eventually drained the heart from the Southern ability to resist.

Deserters from Dixie did not escape danger when they became Union prisoners, but often had to protect themselves from the ire of more ardently Confederate fellow inmates while they pondered the question of whether to apply for the Yankee oath. Then they had to wait for the slow loyalty-testing machinery to operate. It was never easy, in the goldfish-bowl life of a prison camp, for federal officers to keep secret the identity of prisoners who contemplated converting into Unionists.

The task was easiest when captive rebels decided to take the oath in groups. Such mass defectors protected each other throughout the process, and fended off the insults and injuries with which more patriotic Confederates greeted the announcement of their conversion. A disgusted Texan observed one such group taking the Union oath, condemned them as "all foreigners from Europe and British America," and helped toss rocks into their ranks as they marched out of the prison camp for frontier duty, newly clad in Union blue.[16]

Protecting oath takers was most difficult when incautious Union officials, perhaps ignorant of the dangers faced by turncoats, demanded public displays of returning loyalty from rebel prisoners. Superintendent Wood of Old Capitol Prison in Washington, and John Hay in Florida, resorted to such demands for overt oath-taking. Both found that they would have done better to exercise greater discretion.

In Southern eyes those captured rebels who swore to the Union oath were, as one imprisoned rebel patriot informed General Sherman, "base wretches, the curse of every country and of every cause, . . . miscreant and perjured villains." [17] To prevent defections and to punish those who had already committed themselves to Unionism, Southern war prisoners often took matters into their own restricted but still powerful hands. Within many federal prison camps ardent Confederates organized secret (and illegal) counterspy units and kangaroo courts to ferret out and punish those inmates who seemed impressed by the appeal of the oath. Warnings to such potential defectors, embellished with cabalistic signs and threats of violence, sufficed to dissuade many prisoners from taking the oath. And it was not too difficult to find out which prisoners were tending toward Unionism. Sometimes a bribable or sympathetic Union guard informed the vigilant rebels who had visited the oath commissioner. Sharp eyes among rebel prisoners pierced the blackness of night to discover a once trusted comrade furtively making his way toward a clandestine meeting with a federal officer to deliver an oath application. Such information then went to the secret committee of patriotic Confederates, and the stage was set for tragedy.

There was, for instance, Lieutenant J. W. Davis, of the proud Twentieth Virginia Cavalry. Davis and most of the officers of his regiment became captives at Fredericksburg, and were sent to Fort

The Loyal Nonconformist;

OR,

An Account what he dare swear, and what not.

I Fear an Oath, before I swear to take it;
   And well I may, for 'tis the *Oath of God*:
   I fear an Oath, when I have sworn, to break it;
   And well I may, for Vengeance hath a Rod.

And yet I may swear, and must too, 'tis due
   Both to my Heav'nly, and my Earthly King:
If I assent, it must be full and true;
   And if I promise, I must do the thing.

I am no *Quaker*, not at all to swear;
   Nor *Papist*, to swear East, and mean the West;
But am a *Protestant*, and shall declare
   What *I cannot*, and what *I can* protest.

I never will endeavour Alteration
   Of Monarchy, or of that Royal Name,
Which God hath chosen to command this Nation,
   But will maintain his Person, Crown & Fame:

What he commands, if *Conscience* say not nay,
   (For *Conscience* is a greater King than he)
For *Conscience-sake*, not *Fear*, I will obey;
   And if not *Active, Passive* I will be.

I'll pray that all his Subjects may agree,
   And never more be crumbled into parts;
I will endeavour that his Majestie
   M y not be King of *Clubs*, but King of *Hearts*.

The *Royal Oak* I swear I will defend;
   But   *Ivy* which doth hug it so,
I swear that is a Thief, and not a Friend,
   And about Steeples fitter for to grow.

The Civil-Government I will obey;
   But for Church-Policy I swear I doubt it;
And if my Bible want th'*Apocrypha*,
   I'l swear my Book may be compleat without it.

I dare not swear Church-Government is right
   As it should be; but this I dare to swear,
If they should put me to't, the Bishops might
   Do better, and be better than they are.

Nor will I swear for all that they are worth,
   That Bishopricks will stand, & Doomsday see;
And yet I'l swear the Gospel holdeth forth
   Christ with his Ministers till then will be.

That *Peter* was a Prelate they aver,
   But I'l not swear't when all is said and done:
But I dare swear, and hope I shall not err,
   He preach'd a hundred Sermons to their one.

Peter a Fisher was, and he caught Men:
   And they have Nets, & in them catch Men too;
Yet I'l not swear they are alike, for them
   He caught he say'd: these catch, & them undo.

I dare not swear that Courts Ecclesiastick
   Do in their Laws make just and gentle Votes;
But I'l be sworn that *Burton, Pryn* and *Bastwick*
   Were once Ear-witnesses of harsher Notes.

Archdeacons, Deans & Chapters are brave men,
   By Canon, not by Scripture: but to this,
If I be call'd, I'll swear, and swear agen,
   That no such *Chapter* in my Bible is.

I'll not condemn those *Presbyterians*, who
   Refused Bishopricks, and might have had'em:
But Mistris *Calamy* I'll swear doth do
   As well as if she were a *Spiritual Madam*.

For Holy Vestments I'll not take an Oath
   Which Linen most Canonical may be;
Some are for *Lawn*, some *Holland*, some *Scotscloth*;
   And *Hemp* for some is fitter than all three.

Paul had a Cloak, and Books, & Parchments too;
   But that he wore a *Surplice* I'll not swear,
Nor that his Parchments did his *Orders* shew,
   Or in his Books there was a *Common-Prayer*.

I owe assistance to the King by Oath;
   And if he please to put the Bishops down,
As who knows what may be, I should be loth
   To see *Tom Beckets* Mitre push the Crown.

And yet Church-Government I do allow,
   And am contented Bishops be the men;
And that I speak in earnest, here I vow
   Where we have one, I wish we might have ten.

In fine, the Civil Power I'le obey,
   And seek the Peace & Welfare of the Nation:
If this won't do, I know not what to say,
   But farewel *London*, farewel *Corporation*.

                               R. W.

Printed in the Year, 1 6 6 6.

The Alternatives of Williamsburg, 1775, showing
subscriptions to the Association Oath.

_I_ Nicholas Fish, Major in the Second New York Regiment
do acknowledge the UNITED STATES of AME-
RICA, to be Free, Independent and Sovereign States, and
declare that the people thereof owe no allegiance or obedience to George the Third, King of Great-Britain; and I renounce, refuse and abjure any allegiance or obedience to him;
and I do _Swear_ --- that I will to the utmost of
my power, support, maintain and defend the said United
States, against the said King George the Third, his heirs and
successors and his or their abettors, assistants and adherents,
and will serve the said United States in the office of
Major which I now hold, with fidelity,
according to the best of my skill and understanding.

Sworn before me Camp
Valley Forge May 14th 1778   _Nichs Fish, Major_

Enoch Poor B Genl

_I_ DO HEREBY CERTIFY, That
William R. Davie
hath taken and subscribed the Oath of Allegiance and Fidelity, as directed by an Act of
the General Assembly of the State of South-
Carolina, entitled, "An Act to oblige eve-
" ry free Male Inhabitant of this State, a-
" bove a certain Age, to give Assurance of
" Fidelity and Allegiance to the same, and
" for other Purposes therein mentioned."

July 28. 1778.   _W. Earl_

State and Continental Army Loyalty Oaths.

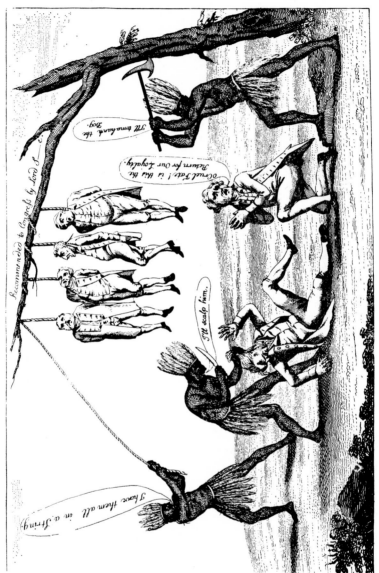

Is this a Peace, when Loyalists must bleed?   The SAVAGES let loose, OR   It is a Bloody Piece of work indeed.
The Cruel FATE of the LOYALISTS.

PROTEST.

The undersigned, members of the Senate of the State of South Carolina, impelled by the duty which they owe to their country and themselves claim the right respectfully, but earnestly, to set forth in the form of a Protest, the grounds of their opposition to the Bill passed, during the present session of the General Assembly of this State, entitled "A Bill to amend the fourth article of the Constitution of this State," wherein it is provided that all officers who shall be chosen or appointed to any office of profit or trust before entering on the execution of the duties thereof, shall take the following Oath; "I do solemnly swear (or affirm) that I will be faithful and true allegiance bear to the State of South Carolina, so long as I shall continue a citizen thereof, and that I am duly qualified according to the Constitution of this State, to exercise the office to which I have been appointed, and that I will, to the best of my abilities, discharge the duties thereof and that I will preserve, protect and defend the Constitution of this State and of the United States."

1st. By the Constitution of South Carolina, every person chosen or appointed to any office of profit or trust, is required before entering on the duties thereof to take an Oath or affirmation, that he is duly qualified according to the Constitution of said State to exercise the office to which he has been elected or appointed, and that he will to the best of his abilities, discharge the duties thereof, and that he will "preserve, protect and defend the Constitution of this State and of the United States"—If therefore by the proposed amendment in said Bill contained, that "he will be faithful and true allegiance bear to the State of South Carolina" nothing more is intended than to secure to the State, that duty and obedience which is consistent with our present Constitutions, then the undersigned protest against said amendment because its object is attained by the Oath or affirmation now prescribed by the Constitution—and the said amendment is therefore, unnecessary, unmeaning and inexpedient and calculated only to render the said oath or affirmation of uncertain and doubtful import.

2nd. If the proposed amendment be construed, to impose on officers hereafter to be chosen or appointed, an obligation, or allegiance inconsistent with the Federal Constitution or the Laws and treaties made in pursuance thereof—then the undersigned protest against said Bill—because, the same is in this respect, unconstitutional, null and void—Under the present oath, our citizens engage to "support, protect and defend the Constitution of this State and of the United States;" this obligation is precisely commensurate and co-extensive with all the duties to both governments, and the addition of any words attempting to explain it, must be attended with ruinous consequences.— For if they alter the obligation imposed by the present oath, it is a direct violation of the Constitution of the United States and not binding on our citizens; If they do not alter that obligation, it is useless, and calculated only to render doubtful what is now perfectly certain and intelligible; taking either view of the proposed amendment it is worse than useless.

3rd. Because, whether the obligation of the citizen or officer, to the State or Federal Government be paramount, identical or secondary, or whether as declared by the Convention of South Carolina in 1833. "Obedience only— and not allegiance is due by them to any power or authority to whom a control over them has been or may be delegated by the State," the undersigned solemnly protest that these questions can only be resolved, by the Constitution of the United States, which this assembly hath not authority to amend alter or abolish.

4th. That the duty and obligation of the citizen of this State being fixed and determined by the nature and fundamental principles of our Government—This assembly hath no authority to transfer their duty, obedience or allegiance, to any Prince, Potentate, State or authority whatsoever.

5th. That the passage of the Bill at the present period, and under existing circumstances, is a direct imputation upon the patriotism of the protestants, and those whose principles they represent; and they therefore solemnly protest against it as proscription for opinion's sake, and as tending to the expatriation of those who constitute a portion of the wealth and strength of the State.

6th. That in a time of excitement, when opposition to the General Government, has almost annihilated the affections of our people for the Federal Union, when wild and untenable theories, calculated to break down the true doctrine of State Rights and State Government, have been scattered with a profuse hand among them—The undersigned protest—that it does not comport with the interest and safety of the Republic or with the dignity and character of South Carolina that this assembly should by any act of legislation even seem to encourage this alienation of feeling, and thus lead to the dissolution of that Noble Fabric in which alone the liberty of the people and the rights of the states can be inviolably preserved.

Hereby protesting and affirming all and singular the matters and things, herein before contained and expressed, we have with our own proper hands; hereunto subscribed our names in the Senate Chamber, in the Town of Columbia this sixteenth day of December in the year of our Lord one thousand eight hundred and thirty three (1833.) and in the fifty eighth year of the Sovereignty and Independence of the United States of America.

RASHA CANNON, from Darlington.
JAS. CHESNUT, Senator from Kershaw.
JOHN DODD, from Spartanburg.
PAUL WESTON, from Christ Church.
ROBT. D. MONTGOMERY, Lancaster Dist.
JOSEPH KOGER Jr. Senator from St. Georges Dorchester.
BANISTER STONE, from Greenville District.
RICHARDSON, from Laurens District.
DAVID D. WILSON, from Williamsburgh District.
BENJAMIN GAUSE, Kingston Election District.
JOHN N. DAVIS, St. James Goose Creek.
RICHARD I. MANNING, Senator from Clarendon.
ALFRED HUGER, Senator from St. Thomas & St. Dennis.

Protest, 1833 (see pages 123–124).

PERMIT OF PROVOST MARSHAL.

By order of the Commanding General, *A H Marknell*
is allowed to pass from Louisville to *Owen Boro Ky* on the
Steam Railroad or otherwise. He having taken the oath to support the Constitution of the United States, and to be true and loyal to the United States and the Commonwealth of Kentucky—and that he will not divulge or reveal any thing he may see or hear within our lines, or give any aid or comfort to our enemies.

S Henry Denr
Provost Marshal.

LOUISVILLE, KY., *13 of Dec* , 1861.

Cause and Contrast, or the Beauties of the Passport-System.

CLERK.—"Well, sir, what can I do for you?"

PLUG.—"I wants to run the block——. When I'm at home, I travels on my muscle and runs wid de merchise."

CLERK.—"That's all right. Here is a passport."

WOUNDED SOLDIER.—"Will you oblige me with a passport to Manchester? I have been in the army since the commencement of the war—lost a leg at Gettysburg, and now desire to go to Manchester to see my family."

CLERK (abruptly).—"We are not granting passports to Manchester to-day."

FROM THE SOUTHERN ILLUSTRATED NEWS, SEPTEMBER 26, 1862

Civil War Passports

Gen. Dix's
PROCLAMATION

Know all men by these presents: that I, John L. Dix, (no relation to the rebel " Dixie") knowing that the feeling excited in the breasts of our brave Union army by the combination of colors known as red, white and red, are by no means agreeable, do hereby, by virtue of the authority vested in me, by His Majesty Abraham 1st, require and command all police officers of the city of Baltimore in the pay of His Majesty's government to suppress and cause to disappear all substances, whether in the heavens above, or in the earth beneath, or in the waters under the earth, bearing the said combination of rebel colors. All babies having red, white and red stockings on will be sent to Fort Lafayette. All houses built of red brick and white mortar, must be removed, or painted red, white and blue, in alternate stripes. All water-melons must be painted blue on the rind; and all mint candy, and barber's poles so colored are forbidden. All red and white cows are required to change their spots or take the oath of allegiance. Red and white variegated flowers must be altered to include blue. All white persons having red hair and moustaches or whiskers are hereby warned to have the one or the other dyed blue. No sun-rises or sun-sets which exhibit such combinations will be permitted, on pain of suppression. Persons are forbidden to drink red and white wines alternately. His Majesty is, however, graciously pleased to make an exception in favor of red noses, these last being greatly in vogue among Federal officers, and additional *lustre* having recently been shed upon such noses, by one of my former predecessors in this command.

Done at the Baltimore Bastile, this 4th day of September, the 1st year of Abraham's glorious and peaceful reign.

(Signed),   JOHN L. DIX, Maj. Gen.

SOUTHERN "VOLUNTEERS".

"Taking the Oath and Drawing Rations."
Statuette by John Rogers, 1865.

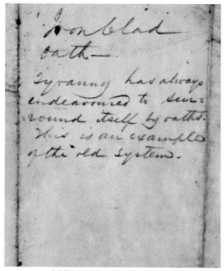

Comment on Ironclad Oath, *ca.* 1864, by anonymous War Department clerk, written on reverse of an oath form.

EXECUTIVE OFFICE,
Washington D.C.

July 17th 1865

R Ewell held as a Prisoner of War at Fort Warren having taken the oath of allegiance and given his bond in the sum of Ten Thousand Dollars for the faithful observance thereof is hereby permitted to return to his home in Virginia upon parole. To report once a week by letter to the Secretary of War at Washington City until further orders

Andrew Johnson
President U.S.

War Prisoner Parole, 1865.

Sir:

GENTLEMEN: With the view of being able to furnish Major-General SICKLES, Commanding this District, with the names of suitable persons, who may act as Registers of the Voters in the several Districts in the State, and also as Managers of Elections, under the Military Reconstruction Act and its Supplement, passed by the last Congress of the United States, I respectfully request you:

1. To furnish me with the names of four intelligent and trust-worthy citizens in each Battalion in your District, if that number can be found, and if not, any less number, who are competent to act as Registers.

2. The names of three persons, if they can be found, and if not, any less number, at each one of the Election precincts in your District, who will be competent to act as Managers of Elections.

These Registers and Managers will be required to take the following oath prescribed by the Act of July 2d, 1862:

"I, A. B., do solemnly swear (or affirm) that I have never voluntarily borne arms against the United States since I have been a citizen thereof; that I have voluntarily given no aid, countenance, counsel or encouragement to persons engaged in armed hostility thereto; that I have neither sought nor accepted nor attempted to exercise the functions of any office whatever, under any authority or pretended authority in hostility to the United States; that I have not yielded a voluntary support to any pretended government, authority, power or constitution within the United States, hostile or inimical thereto. And I do further swear (or affirm) that, to the best of my knowledge and ability, I will support and defend the Constitution of the United States, against all enemies, foreign and domestic; that I will bear true faith and allegiance to the same; that I take this obligation freely, without any mental reservation or purpose of evasion, and that I will well and faithfully discharge the duties of the office on which I am about to enter, so help me God."

You will also designate the precincts where there is no competent person able to take the above oath. It is very desirable that you should authoritatively ascertain, from each person named, whether he can do so. You will also give the Post Office address of each person named. The Registers, and perhaps the Managers of Elections, will be compensated for their services.

I cannot too earnestly impress upon you the vital importance of promptly acting upon the request contained in this communication, and of transmitting your answer at the earliest day practicable.

If an earnest and energetic effort is not made to procure the services of trust-worthy citizens to discharge these respective duties, they will be performed by strangers, who may not have a correct appreciation of the wants of the community.

James L. Orr

Governor of South Carolina.

Hon:

Richard Dozier,

Georgetown, S. C.

Reconstruction Loyalty Requirement, 1867.

The Only Spy Cure

Confidential

The SPY GLASS

A Bulletin of News and Better Methods issued by The American Protective League

| Vol. I | WASHINGTON, D. C., JUNE 28, 1918 | No. 2 |

How to Handle Espionage Cases

"The League Not Only Has Our Respect but also Our Admiration."

ADVERTISING is no part of the A. P. L. program. When, however, the chief of the Bureau of Investigation, Department of Justice, tells a thousand or more League men what he thinks of the organization and its record, *The Spy Glass* feels that the good word should be passed along for the encouragement and inspiration of all.

Chief A. Bruce Bielaski was tempted into breaking his habit of silence at the conference of the New York Division in Hudson theater, New York city, June 10. In a brief address he expressed his admiration for the League and the share it has taken in the enforcement of the war code of the United States. In part, he said:

"When Mr. Briggs came to Washington to urge the organization of the A. P. L., we did not know what its development would be. We did not know what our needs would be, but we knew that we had a growing problem and that we must have individual and organized service that we could not buy. When the United States declared war on Germany in April, 1917, its intelligence services were relatively small and some tremendous enlargement was absolutely essential. Yet the plan of forming a voluntary organization seemed doubtful.

What the League Means

"But the Attorney General, with confidence in the American people, believed that he could find in business men and other citizens of the country the help he needed. When he told the American Bar Association recently that the United States was the best policed nation in the world, he was thinking of the A. P. L. It has nearly 300,000 members, yet there has not been a single violation of duty, not a single flagrant performance of any kind by any Member.

"The A. P. L. has not only the respect but also the admiration of the Department of Justice. It is an inspiration to all the officials of the Department. And the Department of Justice has not been alone in profiting by the aid which you

---

> **WAR DEPARTMENT**
> **OFFICE OF THE CHIEF OF STAFF**
> **WASHINGTON**
>
> June 11, 1918
>
> Dear Captain Frey:
>
> I am just in receipt of a letter from Colonel D. E. Nolan, Chief of the Military Intelligence force abroad, to the effect that the photographs, drawings, and descriptions that you have been collecting for him contain much information of value, and in closing he states "The citizens of the United States who have donated the above mentioned articles, and the League which has collected them, have done something which definitely helps toward the success of the operations of our Army.
>
> Very sincerely yours,
>
> M. CHURCHILL,
> Lieutenant Colonel, General Staff,
> Chief, Military Intelligence Branch,
> Executive Division.
>
> By: A. B. COXE,
> Lieutenant Colonel, General Staff.

---

have given it. The War Department, the Department of State and every other Department which is functioning in this special field of investigation knows the A. P. L. and relies upon it.

"Many of us have had opportunities to go abroad and have had to give them up. The work here at home has, possibly, seemed more urgent. And that is the way I hope you will all feel about your work. You are doing it not because you cannot do something else, but because it is work which those going abroad could not do. To support the Government in the localities in which you live is to hold the Army safe and to carry out the purposes of the President. And we depend on the A. P. L. to do that very thing.

"It is my sincere hope that when this war has been won—as it will be—the American Protective League will continue to serve the nation."

THE first thing you need to know, in running down a reported violation of the Espionage and Sedition law—or of any one of several other laws in the war code of the United States—is whether the man involved is a citizen or an alien. It will throw much light on his character and conduct to know at the start whether he owes allegiance to this country, or belongs to a foreign nation which may be either friendly, strictly neutral, openly hostile or secretly antagonistic to America's purposes and ideals.

To know his citizenship or the country of his origin may give you an instant clue to the meaning of the action or speech alleged against him. This charge is to be proved or disproved. In the first event, at least, unmistakable legal evidence must be secured to make a case.

Five Important Classes

In the end you will probably find that he belongs to one of five groups:

I.—Native-born citizens disaffected by reason of their blood, sympathies or political opinions or bought by money or other considerations to do Germany's work.

II.—Naturalized citizens, born in enemy countries.

III.—Enemy aliens, subjects of enemy states.

IV.—Unfriendly aliens, born neutrals but sympathizing with or working for Teuton interests.

V.—Neutral or enemy aliens, inoffensive and desirous only of personal peace.

I.—If he is a native-born American it may be that his ancestry, sympathies or affiliations with pro-German groups or political movements have led him to take a position of disloyalty from which he is too obstinate to withdraw. The constitutional right to free speech, on which he has relied, has been much re-

American Protective League Badge Before and After
(see pages 287–288).

American Protective League

Organized with Approval and Operating under Direction of
United States Department of Justice Bureau of Investigation

19 .... N⁰ ....

TO WHOM IT MAY CONCERN

This is to certify that the bearer, whose signature appears on the margin hereof, is a regularly appointed member of the American Protective League, with the rank of........................

A. M. Briggs

CHIEF   DIVISION   GENERAL SUPERINTENDENT

American Protective League Membership Card.

Loyal Legion Lapel Insignia.

Loyal Legion of Loggers and Lumbermen

PLEDGE   № 64940

Aviation Section, Signal Corps, U. S. Army

To The Secretary of War:

I, the Undersigned, in consideration of my being made a Member of the Loyal Legion of Loggers and Lumbermen, do hereby solemnly pledge my efforts during this war to the United States of America, and will support and defend this Country against enemies, both foreign and domestic.

I further agree, by these presents, to faithfully do my duty toward this country by directing my best efforts in every way possible to the production of Logs or Lumber for the construction of Army Airplanes and Ships to be used against our common enemies. That I will stamp out any sedition or acts of hostility against the United States Government which may come within my knowledge, and will do every act and thing which will in general aid in carrying this war to a successful conclusion.

Dated this_____ day of_____ 1918.

- -

Loyal Legion of Loggers and Lumbermen

Date_____ **MEMBERS INFORMATION SHEET**   № 64940

District No._____

Name_____ Local No. _____

Address _____

Occupation _____

Age_____ Place of Birth_____

Naturalized_____ First papers_____ Final papers_____

Married_____ Children_____

Remarks _____

_____

_____

_____

_____

_____

Loyal Legion Enrollment Form.

Lafayette. Davis "acted queer," and became too intimate with Union guards to please his fellow officers. Then an alert prisoner saw him reading the oath-application form. A rebel prisoner who was a trusty-janitor at the oath commissioner's office accused Davis of applying to take the hated Yankee oath and become "galvanized" by swearing. Late one night his brother officers assembled a kangaroo court in a dark cell and confronted Davis with the accusations. Davis first denied the charge.

When Colonel Manning read a copy of . . . [Davis'] application [to take the oath] to him, he broke down, admitted the truth, and became very defiant. Colonel Manning suggested to the meeting that, as Lieutenant Davis had premeditatedly intended to dishonor his uniform of the Confederate States of America and insult by such act his brother officers, prisoners of war, that the bars and buttons be cut from his coat, and his coat turned inside out, and that he be ostracised by his fellow prisoners. This suggestion was quickly carried out.

Davis panicked, and threatened the rebel officers with revenge, and with punishment from his new Yankee friends. Tempers rose as language increased in violence. His former commander warned Davis to have the guards remove him from the prison immediately "as the prisoners were not in good temper to tolerate or overlook his insult to them by [his] taking the oath." Davis, "like a whipped cur," fled to the federal barracks, and was seen no more.

Other Confederate officers and enlisted men who followed Davis' path met with similar reactions from their former comrades in arms. "We jeered and hissed the party [of oath takers]," one indignant rebel recalled, "until we were hoarse, and nothing but [federal] bayonets prevented us from kicking them." Such men, to principled Southern soldiery, had "sold their birthrights for a mess of pottage"; turncoats were "disgracing themselves, dishonoring their uniforms, [and] leaving their comrades to suffer." This was written by a diarist who boasted that of his troop of six hundred "immortals," only eighteen had chosen the shame of swearing. "What nation," he exulted, "can present a better record than this? . . . What could be said that would be flattery of . . . the men who kept faith throughout the terrible ordeal?" But the diarist's esteem for the pure rebel patriotism of his regiment soon suffered a terrible blow. He and five trusted comrades, after months of toil, succeeded in tunneling under the camp walls. Briefly they exulted in the freedom they had gained without compromise of principles. Then one of their number betrayed them, and federal guards returned the bitter men to cells made drearier by the brief taste of liberty they had enjoyed. The informer, from fear and shame, and so "that he would not be put [back] in the same cell with us," took the Yankee oath, and gained solitary freedom. His wronged comrades at first plotted future revenge, then shrugged off the bad memory of a man "who was at heart a coward." Punishment for such a miscreant must come from above, they felt: "If he can hide his treachery from the world, he cannot hide it from his God. His sin will find him out." [18]

God had helpers. Perhaps the most effective antioath medicine was the knowledge that many Southern women looked with scorn upon men who changed allegiance. Picture beautiful young Kate Carney, for instance, visiting her brother, a war prisoner in a Yankee stockade near Murfreesboro, Tennessee. He told the strongly prorebel maiden that some of his cellmates were considering swearing to the Union oath. Kate half-shamefully, but proudly, admitted to her diary that "I forgot I was before so many men, especially when I began to see my old friends among them. I told them never to take the oath, and they answered, 'Don't worry, that had played out,' and a great many other things. They enraged the Yankees very much." Even when her beloved brother fell desperately ill in prison, this determined miss could still "hope that nothing will induce him to take the oath. . . . If he should take the oath I should trust no one." Kate rejoiced when word came to her that her imprisoned brother was determined to die before renouncing the Southern cause. She heard that one of the prisoners ("Just to think he was one of Morgan's men, too!") had taken the detested loyalty test. "Oh!" she wrote, "I hope the other poor fellows will not [do] such a thing. I feel so wretched when I have placed my confidence in any one, and it is betrayed, by [their] taking that awful oath."

Kate's standards concerning oath takers lowered but once, and then but a little, when a handsome young man was a guest at her home:

Mr. Watterson, a Confederate prisoner, who had taken the oath . . . ate dinner with us [Kate recorded]. He seems very polite and quite intelligent, and if he hadn't taken the oath I would think him quite nice. I must confess, to be crowded in that filthy jail, filled with vermin, with little air, with scarcely food to sustain life, and then [to be] threatened [that] if they did not take it [the oath] they would be forced back into their cells or else lose their lives, is some excuse.

It was fortunate for Lincoln's loyalty-oath policy that only a few Kate Carneys were able to get to rebel prisoners, and that women like Mrs. Rose Greenhow (who publicly harangued rebel captives against taking the Union oath) soon went to jail themselves. It was even more fortunate that a good many other daughters of Dixie were willing to plead with their imprisoned men to forget principles and swear to anything in order to get free of jail. And even the fiery Kate Carney found it possible to forgive a rebel soldier who took the Yankee oath when he heard that his wife was at the point of death.[19]

The Confederate soldier who took the Yankee oath and started on his way homeward (if his home was behind the ever-advancing Union lines) rarely knew what kind of reception he would receive there. A former rebel general, Alfred Beekley, took the Union oath and returned to his western Virginia farm. But border bitterness poisoned his neighbors against him. Former friends, distrusting him, pressured Union General John C. Frémont to remove the ex-rebel from their midst:

There is [War Secretary Stanton learned] a strong feeling of opposition among citizens of Western Virginia, to the return among them of men like this man Beekley, who left home to join in the rebellion. . . . Their presence is attended with mischievous consequences to the people of this neighborhood, and most of them engage, as soon as they return, in forming guerrilla parties to . . . injure . . . Union men, and murder them as well. I find this feeling more widespread and serious than I had been led to suppose it was.

As a favor to Beekley, Frémont rearrested him, and agreed to cancel the unhappy man's oath of allegiance! Beekley returned to a federal prison to await exchange, rather than remain a man without a country or a home.[20]

Other turncoat Confederates were but a little more fortunate. Some found that even Negro slaves in the border area scorned them, and considered their presence an insult to their masters who were still fighting for the sacred cause. But most oath takers found the way home eased by the mercy of kind persons, who provided nourishment and shelter for the weary travelers, already weakened by the rigors of prison. Not even the burning pro-Southernism of Susannah, a Negro house slave of Confederate General Harding, could criticize her mistress' act of mercy to one freed rebel:

Mistress [Susannah wrote to the general] loaned a horse to little Johnny Martin, your former race rider, who was here as a released prisoner. He said he wanted to go to his sister, having taken the [Union] oath of allegiance, and Mistress loaned him a horse to go on. He looks like a mere child, and home will suit him much better than soldiering.[21]

Once home, the former rebel soldiers faced the task of fitting themselves again into the traces of civilian life. In many communities the continued antipathy of neighbors toward those who had turned against the South made rehabilitation difficult. Nor was the process helped by a slipshod federal administration, which often failed to provide the oath taker with a certificate of his oath. Without this document, one pardoned rebel was rearrested as a spy at his Maryland home, and narrowly escaped a federal firing squad. Only less serious was the fact that ravenous Northern army commissaries and tax officials delighted in exercising their functions on anyone who could not prove himself a sworn Union supporter. But even when armed with the oath certificate, turncoat rebels in the divided border areas faced the wrath of pro-Southern guerrillas.[22]

Many a man who had taken the oath to secure Union military protection for his family and property found Northern troops reluctant to extend themselves in behalf of those they had so recently fought, and whose conversion they distrusted. Almost nobody, it appeared, honored the turncoat. And almost everybody was observing his words and deeds, waiting for a chance to report him to a provost marshal or oath commissioner as a perjured swearer.

But the lure of freedom was stronger than the dangers and stigmas attached to swearing. Rebel war prisoners applied in ever-increasing numbers during 1863 to take the Union oath. This at first made federal officials rejoice. "I am delighted," commented a Union officer to a successful oath commissioner, "to hear of the returning of loyalty among the Texans of which you speak. God grant that you may have an opportunity of releasing them from their bondage." He was less delighted when he received reports that the loyalty-test program was becoming a sort of automatic release mechanism for rebel war prisoners in many camps.[23] Lincoln had made it clear that only selected prisoners, those innocent of evil past intent and those who would be influential in furthering future sectional reunion, were to gain release by taking the oath. To return the loyalty-testing to its pristine purpose, the adjutant general, in August, 1863, proclaimed that

In general, the mere desire to be discharged upon taking the oath of allegiance will furnish no sufficient ground for such discharge; but in cases where it can be shown that the prisoner was impressed into rebel service, or can plead in palliation extreme youth, followed by open and declared repentance, with other reasons . . . may be specially reported. . . . The oath of allegiance, when administered, must be taken without qualification, and can in no case carry with it an exemption from any of the duties of a citizen.[24]

Oath commissioners obediently raised standards in loyalty clearances. In many cases they reversed decisions to free prisoners, some of whom had already taken the oath or were ready to do so. Protests from these men were loud and bitter. Some denounced the new policy as a federal fraud. "I had too much faith in the U.S. Government," one Texas Confederate lamented, "to think that she would hold out such inducements to men, get them to commit themselves, and then let them languish in prison for months afterwards." Others, feeling themselves similarly betrayed, detailed how their decision to apply for the oath had brought with it the obloquy of their fellow inmates. And still others, who described themselves as innocent Unionists whom rebel authorities had conscripted into military service, complained that Union guards "might as well hold one of their own men." A cousin of oath commissioner Bryan Tyson summed up the prisoners' feelings: "I have been in prison seven months. I am getting tired of the life. I don't like to make application [for the oath] and remain in prison. Can you do anything for me?" [25]

By early 1864 the federal loyalty-oath policy had again been reversed, and the loyalty-oath system was back to its unsystematic normal. Lincoln had issued his amnesty proclamation and he wanted as many repentant rebels as possible to take the oath he had prescribed. General Butler, in obedience to Lincoln's explicit instructions, saw to it that every military prisoner in Union hands received an oath-application questionnaire, and fresh stocks of oath blanks replenished dwindling supplies on the shelves of the oath commissioners.

Thus, in defiance of calumny in prison and ostracism at home, oath-taking among captured rebels continued to increase throughout the remainder of the war. "Fifteen of the privates . . . became weak-kneed," sadly noted one imprisoned Southern soldier, "took the oath, and went North, rejoicing in their infamy." He was happier when the imprisoned rebel son of a prominent Iowa politician refused the personal blandishments of the governor of that state to take the oath. But his spirit flagged again when a trusted captain of his regiment suddenly left the prison, a free man, an oath taker. A watchdog committee accurately accused another officer of the same offense. "He is notoriously worthless," the diarist sought to shrug off the defection, "bearing on his face the evidence of his character."

Ardent rebels did their best to stop the increase of Union-oath-taking among war prisoners. Watchdog committees increased their vigilance, and die-hards pledged themselves to perish in gallant assaults upon their Yankee guards rather than succumb to the lure of the oath. One literary weapon these men used to frighten new inmates away from the oath applications achieved wide currency:

> Whoeber takes de oath, they put him near the pribby
> Den work him like the debil, worse than in the Libby;
> Den they stop him up in blankets, throw snuff in his eyes
> And parole him on the island, and dey call him galvanized.[26]

Such pressures against the oath undoubtedly were momentarily effective. No one can know how many Southern men reached tentatively toward the Northern oath as toward a dream of home and family, but had quickly to retract their thoughts of swearing to the Union in the face of their comrades' bitter attitude toward oath takers. There must have been many such. Three rebel war prisoners on Governor's Island in New York harbor, for example, applied for the oath. They proved to the satisfaction of the resident oath commissioner, who carefully investigated their stories, that they were unwilling participants in the rebellion, helpless victims of wartime social pressures in Georgia. These three took the ultimate step in rejecting the Confederacy by conjoining their request for the Union oath with a declaration of intent to serve in the federal army after they secured release.

Then, late in October, 1862, only two days before federal officials were planning to give the trio the loyalty oath, the three switched again, claiming that they had volunteered for rebel military service in the first place and did not want to change sides. The Union officer in charge had no choice but to list them for exchange, but he noted in his report that the three "uncertain men" showed the physical effects of their comrades' solicitude for their patriotic welfare. "These three prisoners," the federal officer noted, "are considerably bruised and chastened. There is nothing I can do unless I transfer them to solitary cells." [27] And all the Union prisons taken together did not possess enough isolation wards adequately to protect all embryonic oath takers from the wrath of devoted rebel captives.

There were a few men, repentant enough, who could not stomach the thought of forswearing that for which they had fought, although by a certain stage in their prison experience they no longer considered the Confederacy as the recipient of their allegiance. A Philadelphia youth, wealthy, impetuous, had rushed to join the Southern army in 1861, had been captured, and, by mid-1863, was heartily sick of federal prison. His influential parents pulled powerful political strings to effect his release. But the young man, though "sick of his folly, and . . . not wish[ing] to be exchanged . . . with boyish pride and undiminished folly . . . objects to something in the oath, although adverse to all further connections with the rebels." He gained release from prison without the oath, when his family posted a bond of $10,000 for his good behavior, and sent him off to study law in Wisconsin.[28]

Perhaps the strangest war prisoners who refused the proffered Union oath were a dozen Negro servants of rebel officers who had been captured with their masters. Compassionate Confederates pleaded with their federal captors to release the slaves from prison, where they were suffering severely from the unaccustomed rigors of a Boston winter. The matter came before Stanton, who offered the Negroes their freedom from slavery and their liberty from prison if they would first swear to the Union loyalty oath. With quick unanimity the Negroes refused the oath, not because they objected to its terms, but because their families remained in South Carolina. They preferred to wait in the Northern prison until the slow mills of exchange returned them home, preferred even to return to slavery rather than attain free status, if freedom meant an unknowably long separation from wives and children. Such nobility of character achieved reward. Early in 1862 the twelve Negroes signed a special parole not to fight against the United States again, and a special flag-of-truce steamer returned them to the South.[29]

These exceptions from the incubus of the oath requirement were few in number. Captive rebels increasingly shrugged off the threats and the ridicule that more stubborn Confederate patriots heaped upon those who evidenced willingness to take the Yankee oath. More and more imprisoned Southerners applied for a loyalty test that might bring the longed-for liberty, and appealed to federal officials for the privilege of swearing to an oath that had already been a key to freedom for thousands. For one thing was becoming increasingly certain. The South was losing the war. As long weeks passed in 1864, only the most convinced Southern patriot could persuade himself that victory might yet come to Dixie.

Bitter winter became, for the imprisoned rebels, a more bitter spring; the early months of 1865 saw their beloved South sinking to final defeat. During the last weeks of the war men in prison camps met to argue the question of when it was timely for them, the defeated, to admit defeat. For many, surrender to the Yankee oath was unthinkable while a rebel army remained in the field, and while Lee commanded the destiny of the Confederate forces. "When General Lee has taken the oath of allegiance to Mr. Lincoln," wrote one rebel war prisoner to his old friend, Sherman, "then I will consider the propriety of my doing so." [30]

Then—Appomattox. "The end had come, and we were men without a country—soldiers without a flag. We were broken, indeed," mournfully recorded one captured Southerner. Prisoners at Northern camps applied in increasing numbers to take the oath, "to swallow the yaller dog," especially after Lee counseled all former rebels to reconcile themselves to the fortunes of war and accept defeat and Union.[31] At each camp, under orders from Washington, federal officers held daily roll calls of prisoners, to give the oath to all who wished it. No longer were applicants for the oath subject to loyalty investigations; the oath alone was now the key to freedom for all war prisoners who asked to take it. Every day more and more swore, and walked from the camps as free men. Lincoln's assassination briefly stopped the mass swearing ceremonies, and gave renewed heart to the intransigent minority among the captive rebels. "Many of us," recalled one of these stubborn men, "tried arguments, persuasion, and ridicule" to convince their less implacable comrades to reject the oath. But the process resumed, and most rebels, as a disgusted Southern patriot sneeringly noted, "were determined to take care of themselves."

Still, not all prisoners chose this easy way to homes and families. All during April and into May of 1865, while scattered Confederate forces still resisted surrender, a rugged minority of Confederates held their cause inviolable even while in prison. The oath "was the great topic of conversation [among the prisoners]," one of their number recorded, "and a good deal of bitter, angry feeling was engendered on both sides. . . . Shall I stand with arms folded and await my destiny?" Destiny overtook the man. Confederate President Jefferson Davis fell prisoner to the omnipotent Yankees, and all was at an end. There was nothing more for which to hold out—the Confederacy was dead. As the prison camps emptied, the dwindling few who remained as inmates capitulated. "I am heartily sick of prison life," complained one prisoner to his father in Virginia. "When they intend to release us I have not the slightest idea." [32] Administrative problems delayed hundreds in achieving freedom, and, naturally, Union soldiers took precedence in demobilization procedures.

Eventually the intricate business of getting the prisoners home was efficiently regularized. The Union Quartermaster Department furnished transportation and subsistence to all prisoners who took the oath, and for four months after the end of the war all a rebel needed to obtain space on a Union army train was an oath certificate. With an administrative bow to executive reconstruction plans, the army tried to have as many departing prisoners as possible take the amnesty oath Lincoln had prescribed. Whatever the machinery, the oath remained the way out of prison for the tens of thousands of ragged rebels who were the human sediment of scores of battles. Former rebels by the thousands took the Union oath, trooped outside the federal prison walls, heard the command "Break ranks!" and knew that they were free men, and would fight no more.[33]

The former war prisoners made their way toward uncertain futures, to a South devastated by four years of war, to homes often fire-blackened in the passage of arms just spent. Most of these men who had held out until the bitter end of hostilities felt no shame for the oaths they had taken to gain release. Yes, one grizzled veteran of the prison camps admitted when a newspaper correspondent asked him if he had taken the Yankee oath to get out of prison. "Yes, I took something. . . . I wanted to get home. General Lee had surrendered. I concluded that I wouldn't let their durned oath stop me, but I'd cuss along with the rest. So I took it and came home. Don't reckon that's much." Not even "fire-eating" Southern belles reproached a veteran Confederate who "went in at the first pop and been a-fightin' ever since," who took "their infernal oath—beg your pardon, ladies," and who resignedly concluded, "I don't reckon it'll make much difference." [34] No, it rarely made much difference, once the guns stilled and America turned to the task of reconstruction. In only a few localities did oath takers face the enmity of neighbors; only rarely were they known as "the meanest of the mean" for their words of allegiance to the enemy.

Perhaps the last carry-over from the wartime loyalty-testing system for war prisoners occurred in the camp at Elmira, New York, which had housed thousands of rebels. Through its gates had departed hundreds of inmates who had taken the Yankee oath. By June, 1865, the Elmira camp was almost empty, and government officials were hastening preparations to close it permanently.

One of the war prisoners, Joseph Allen, had sworn the Union oath in 1863, and after his release took a job as a clerk in the headquarters of the federal army guard detachment at Elmira. This able man soon gained the trust of his employers, handled large sums of federal money, and was in charge of seven junior clerks. Allen did a Herculean job of expediting the paper work involved in discharging war prisoners, and in readying Elmira for final closing. He did such a good job, in fact, that army officers in charge of the camp became accustomed to taking afternoons off, knowing that the efficient, trusted, former rebel was on hand to see that necessary tasks were done. Then, late in June, 1865, Allen disappeared. With him went more than twelve hundred dollars of federal army funds. In place of the money, Allen left a novel definition of loyalty—his certificate of the Union oath of allegiance.[35]

CHAPTER IX

South of the Border

To literary defenders of the lost cause, Northern loyalty-testing policies were another indication of the superiority of Confederate ethical standards and political practices.[1] But the facts of history require an opposite conclusion. Disloyalty was a plague to the South as to the North, and even more dangerous to the former. The Confederacy countered disloyalty as ruthlessly as, if less efficiently than, the Lincoln government.

Superficially, the South used much the same loyalty-testing methods and procedures as its Northern enemy. Certain factors, however, made loyalty-testing differ markedly between North and South. Southern localism affected internal security procedures in the Confederacy, as it did so much else. States' rights doctrines impelled local governments to demand and secure shares in antisubversion work from the Confederate sectional government. Loyalty-testing in the South was even less standardized, therefore, than in the North. More significant is the related difference of the South's failure to make loyalty tests useful for anything more than mere police work. The South lacked a Lincoln capable of bending loyalty tests into weapons of military significance and political influence.

Southern internal security systems long predated the Civil War, as local authorities and volunteer patrols controlled slave travel and suppressed abolitionism. During the excited secession winter of 1860–61, local, extralegal vigilance committees proliferated throughout the South, ready to meet the needs of independence and incipient civil war. When war came, patriotic emotionalism, fed on the heady fuel of propaganda, largely unrestrained by effective governmental authority on any level, unleashed excesses almost everywhere in the South.

Southern concepts of the code duello and individual justice cost heavily in terms of human suffering and in the inadequacy of Confederate loyalty-testing procedures.

The borderlands of the South offered the greatest scope for Confederate vigilante operations. Vicious vendettas raged in these "debatable lands" and broke more hearts than the clash of armies could shatter. The border nurtured the irregular. Jayhawkers, tories, bushwhackers, and guerrillas of whatever name, formed the human materials for the dreaded corps which Mosby and Quantrill assembled, and were the mainstay of the South's loyalty-testing apparatus on the border. Adept at evasion, expert at circumlocution, and deadly in action against weakly armed civilians or small Union detachments, vigilantes were inherently incapable of accepting centralized direction or control.

Nowhere in Dixie were the deeds of the irregulars bloodier than in the Southwest. A young woman, so ardent a Confederate that she chose Texas exile rather than swear loyalty to the Union in Louisiana, horrifiedly recalled how "we hear no news now but accounts of murders done and suffered. . . . Nothing seems more common and less condemned than assassination. . . . No one . . . seems surprised or shocked, but takes it as a matter of course that an obnoxious person should be put to death by some offended neighbor." [2]

This dreary picture was not, however, confined to the northern fringes of the Confederacy. When patriotism and passion combined, vigilantism flourished everywhere in the South. In the words of a stubborn old Unionist of North Carolina, "If a man said he was [for the] union, his life was threatened . . . [and] other men quelled this sentiment." [3]

During the state elections of 1860–1861, before hostilities began, the issue of secession was a basic loyalty test. A few candidates campaigned on frank antisecession platforms. Many others, however, found that their opponents were whispering insinuations of Unionism which sometimes ruined reputations for a lifetime. Charles Upton, a Virginian, refused to obey his seceded state's order canceling scheduled elections to the national Congress, opened a "side-poll" in Alexandria, and announced himself as a Unionist candidate. Vigilantes "visited," beat, and exiled Upton. Conversely, William Lander of North Carolina, no Unionist, lost a local election when an anonymous handbill accused him of past associations with abolitionists. Southern journalists suggested that such men as Upton and Lander should grace ropes' ends rather than legislative halls, and that any voter using a secret instead of an open ballot must be presumed to be a secret enemy. Local vigilantes responded admirably to the injunction of a Tennessee newspaper: "Mark every man that votes for the Union and have a cotton rope prepared for him."

Conformity, not security or loyalty, resulted. James Parton noted from Virginia in 1861 that "many of the . . . citizenry who were . . . strong Union submissionists are now as strongly for secession and a United Southern Confederacy." [4] The question remained—how united?

In August, 1861, the Confederate Congress required all "alien enemies" (men of Northern nativity) to tender their allegiance to the South or, within forty days, go into exile. Property confiscation acts followed. Thus, early in the war, Confederate policy paralleled its Northern counterpart; men must declare their loyalty by oath, or forfeit freedom and property. The banishing act immediately involved the Confederate army, which, through its provost marshals, controlled travel everywhere in the South, always with the participation of Confederate state and local authorities, home guards, and vigilante groups.

In order to leave the South, nonjuring alien enemies had to secure special passports from some authority. The forty-day limit inspired thousands of "alien enemies" to abandon their properties to eager speculators, and begin the weary trek northward. To add to their misery, some Southern provosts on the North-South border, knowing that Union authorities jailed all who had sworn loyalty to the Confederacy, required the distraught refugees to subscribe a rebel oath or stay in the South. Either way, the alternative was prison.

The whole process was attended with violence. Nonjuring aliens whose overt Unionism had been particularly obnoxious often found a Confederate noose rather than a pass the grim route out of Dixie. After a lynching in North Carolina, a spirited Southern lady exulted: "Never did any tree bear such quick fruit. In a day or two it was impossible to find a Lincolnite in all that region."

Southern opposition to the banishing policy was not, sad to relate, based on humanitarian grounds. Spy-conscious Confederates insisted that Northern secret agents formed the bulk of the refugees, accepted the easy equation that anyone unwilling to swear loyalty to the South was a spy, and denounced the seeming idiocy of permitting traitors to go North to report what they had seen.[5]

With the first agonized exodus of nonjuring refugees, the passport and loyalty-test system became a permanent part of Southern wartime life. Theoretically, passports were under the control of the Confederate military authorities, acting under the mantle of President Davis' suspensions of the habeas corpus writ privilege according to the stern tenets of martial law. Each rebel army command included a provost marshal detachment, with additional units permanently billeted at railroad termini, crossroads, and urban centers. Provosts received orders from the Police and Passport Division of the War Department, and from Provost Marshal General Alexander McKinstry, who was simultaneously head of the Secret Service and the Bureau of Intelligence of the Confederate land forces. Every provost was a loyalty tester, for all passes bore a loyalty oath. In addition to central government provosts, state civil and military authorities, local officials, home guards, and the ubiquitous vigilantes issued travel passes and loyalty tests of their own. Confederate provosts accepted this practice as a normal part of Southern living, which indeed it was. Multiplicity of authorities made uniformity impossible.

Pass and loyalty requirements generally faced every male traveler. Only in areas near Union lines, or where disloyalty was rampant, did white women need to carry the coveted forms. Every Negro, on the other hand, had to have a travel pass, but did not, in obedience to the color line, have to swear loyalty. By early 1862, anyone traveling in the South, even Confederate troops and civilian refugees from Yankee areas, were all too familiar with the passport-control system and with the provosts who administered it. A sympathetic English visitor noted that

Without the provost-marshal's or some "pass" no one can move about any road, river, or railroad—no, not even from county to county. The entrances to the steamboats, the toll-gates, and the doors of the [railroad] cars are blocked by armed sentinels, who will let no one enter or pass without the necessary voucher. They do their duty civilly enough, I must admit, but most rigorously, showing favor or excuse to no one, high or low.

Each pass bore the indicated destination of the traveler. Provosts on duty at the destination, aided by militiamen, recruits in training depots, home guards, and civilian vigilantes, made sure that the traveler went where his pass said he should go. Hotel- and tavernkeepers submitted guest registers to local provosts who canceled used passports against the names inscribed. Each month the provost submitted the canceled passes, and a report on passes still outstanding, to the Confederate provost marshal general, who combined them with similar reports from all the provosts of the army commands, and sent the accumulated tally to the Secretary of War. There were always some nota-

222

tions concerning those who refused to take a pass because of the oath requirement, usually reading "Imprisoned on suspicion of disloyalty."

This was a tight system, and its application by Confederate provosts even to women refugees from Yankee zones of occupation indicates how seriously the Southern officials treated it. Not even chivalric codes of conduct exempted Kate Cumming, for instance, when she fled to Chattanooga in 1862, and found that she could not register for a room in the hotel without a pass, but could not leave the hotel lobby in order to get one! She finally solved her dilemma by having a willing rebel soldier inform the local provost of her plight. The latter official gallantly came to the lobby, swore her to loyalty, and provided her with the necessary document.[6]

Since every Southerner, soldier or civilian, who for any reason had to travel faced a series of provosts, the efficacy of the control system depended entirely upon the industry and character of the individual provost. And since each provost was, like his Northern colleague, a work horse for his army, his office in any Southern town was likely to be a busy, crowded place. In Richmond, for instance, the provost was almost always surrounded by a crowd of people seeking some privilege or facing some penalty. The provost there, General John H. Winder, had to place armed guards at the entrance to control the crowd, and to permit a manageable few to enter at a time. Indeed, the fortunate recipients of passes and other favors had to leave by a discreet rear door, since the press of the crowd in front was too great to permit orderly departure by the normal exit.

A great contrast to such large-scale operations is provided by the provost at Ponchatoula, Louisiana, "a large, jolly man" who asked the few applicants for his favors almost no questions, and did not examine the baggage of blockade-running immigrants into the Confederacy. Most provosts were of the Richmond type: efficient, grim, humorless, staffed by men who used, and sometimes abused, their authority in the pursuit of loyalty.

The endless travel restrictions—swearing to loyalty, waiting in line, document inspections—exasperated many Southerners. It seemed debasing that their government should emulate the arbitrary security activities which Lincoln was using in the North (actually, the Southern travel-control system exceeded anything Lincoln undertook). Other Southerners resented what one described as the "right to travel as first class, but like a negro, show your pass." Even Southern congressmen were not exempt from the pass requirement despite fulminations in Congress and the press against "military tyranny." It irked Confederate

legislators to observe the provosts at work, enjoying "poking their bayonets at you" while examining a pass. Southern soldiers joined the
chorus of criticism. Combat veterans lost precious furlough time while
rear-area provost personnel examined their passes and required them to
swear loyalty to the Confederacy. As one angry soldier described it,

> There is not a more flagrant nuisance extant than the present passport system
> in the railroad trains in the interior of the country. In the vicinity of the
> camp it may be an absolute necessity, but at a distance from the army it is of
> no benefit whatever to anybody. It serves to keep a regiment, or more perhaps,
> of able-bodied soldiers and officers out of the field, and to keep a few quiet
> people at home, who are afraid to go out because of the difficulty involved in
> obtaining a permit from someone to travel. . . . What is the use of all this
> ridiculous ceremony? [7]

Perhaps the oath-taking part of the passport system was a mere
"ridiculous ceremony." Critics derided the fact that most provosts
accepted the required loyalty oaths of everyone who proffered them,
without bothering to ascertain the genuineness of these protestations
of fidelity. Other critics, conversely, condemned as violators of individual liberty and states' rights the more energetic provosts like
Winder in Richmond who did conduct loyalty investigations among
pass applicants. Samuel Day, for instance, a pro-Southern English journalist, applied for a pass to go to Union-occupied Norfolk from Richmond. Winder, after making Day swear loyalty as a prerequisite for
the pass, informed him that his oath included an implicit promise to
publish nothing concerning Confederate conditions. Day, angry, went
to the top. From Confederate War Secretary Benjamin he received
assurances that Winder had been overenergetic, and that the loyalty-
oath part of the pass was a mere form, a ceremony without significance.

Many Southerners agreed that the loyalty-test aspect of Confederate
travel passes was essentially meaningless. Few, however, would say so
as openly as Benjamin, for such admissions could invite consequences
too drastic to justify expressing the purest ethics. In rare cases such
frankness did intrude into the record.

A Southern-born British consular official, stationed in Richmond,
reported to London that in order to carry out his duties he had sworn
loyalty to the Confederacy. England, which never officially recognized
the Confederacy, was embarrassed, and the North, fearing that the
consul's oath presaged English recognition of the Confederacy, was
outraged. International tension lessened when the consul assured his
government that he had sworn the oath heedlessly, as thousands of

other Southland residents did every day. It meant no more than the height and weight statistics which also appeared on the pass he had sworn loyalty to obtain.

Critics attacked the pass system unceasingly, on the grounds that Southern states rather than the central government should issue passes and loyalty tests, that venal provosts corrupted the purposes of the system, and that spies swore any oath demanded in order to function. "Good and loyal citizens are arrested if they fail to carry passes," thundered obstreperous Governor Brown of Georgia, "while Federal spies procure or force passes, and travel our thoroughfares at their pleasure." [8]

Southerners who berated the Confederate central government for its rigorous pass system often added criticisms of the alleged laxness of that government in retaining spies and traitors on its payrolls. Like its Northern counterpart, the Southern central authority erected loyalty-testing systems more complete than their critics would acknowledge. The Confederate Constitution, for example, required all national and state legislators and executive and judicial officers to swear loyalty. Congressional law and army regulations required similar commitments from military officers and enlisted men, including aliens. Congress also required all voters in border-state elections to repeat words of loyalty as a prerequisite for casting ballots.[9] But south as north, the presence of loyalty tests failed to convince many people that loyalty was present.

Fear of Northern spies and Southern traitors in government positions remained a consistent and unnerving fact of Southern life. The specter of subversion haunted Secessia, a phantom that grew in proportion to the proximity of Union troops and the failing fortunes of Confederate forces. Blaming military reverses on traitors became almost a sectional game. Jefferson Davis, for instance, could write early in 1862 that "recent disasters have depressed the weak. . . . Traitors show the tendencies heretofore concealed." When defective boilers disabled a Confederate steamboat in Charleston's blockaded harbor, excited patriots immediately concluded that saboteurs were plying their devilish trade, which, as a diarist noted, "creates excitement, and suspicion of traitors among us." Mischievous youths who scrawled "God bless the Stars and Stripes" on Richmond's walls soon after Southern defeats in distant Tennessee, unwittingly initiated a week of hysterical spy-hunting in Virginia which resulted in the arrest of a few harmless old men whose open Unionism had heretofore gone respectfully unpunished. Loyalty tests failed, however, to unearth the sinister caucuses of covert

225

Unionists which rumor insisted were lodged in government offices.[10]

Richmond, capital and command center of the Confederacy, was the most hysterical and loyalty-conscious Southern city. Professional and amateur internal security agents kept constant watch on Judah Benjamin, holder of numerous cabinet portfolios. Even President Davis was a target for suspicion, and lesser officials walked a narrow path of conduct and associations.

Suffering from sectional schizophrenia as it did, the Confederacy never quite decided whether it welcomed Northern deserters or suspected them as spies, so it continued doing both. Even such a dedicated supporter of the rebel cause as Josiah Gorgas, the ingenious chief of the Confederacy's ordinance department, faced continuing accusations that the inadequacies of his organization were the deliberate result of his foreign (Pennsylvania) birth and secret Unionist sympathy. Many Southerners felt that all Northerners were automatically abolitionists. Many Northerners who chose to take up arms in defense of the South found it best to have made that choice as early in the war as possible. The eleventh-hour turncoat had no easy time. This was partly due to the resentment of Southerners when Yankees received positions which older sons of Dixie might have secured. "These gentry somehow succeed in getting appointments," fretted a Confederate civil servant, who had been in Richmond long enough almost to forget about his own Philadelphia origin.[11]

In the tense Confederate atmosphere, public suspicion found attractive targets in the civilian and enlisted personnel of the Army Signal Bureau. These telegraphers were the communications center for the Confederacy. Since Union commanders seemed to have no difficulty intercepting rebel telegrams, patriotic Southerners throughout the war uncritically condemned the telegraphers as deliberate disloyalists or dupes of Northern spies. The Signal Bureau, therefore, found itself successively investigated by committees of the Confederate Congress, the War Department, and several state governments, and by completely unofficial vigilantes. None unearthed anything more sinister than ineptitude. But no reports certifying to the absence of disloyalty seemed able to convince the Confederate public, or officialdom, for that matter, that no traitors fattened on the public payroll.[12]

As response to this conviction, the Confederate Congress, state legislatures, and lower units of civil government, as well as all levels of military authority, poured a plenitude of loyalty tests over the South. Congressional property confiscation procedures, for example, exhibit the interaction of national and local authorities. Sequestration commissioners, under War Department regulations, toured the South after 1863, as did colleagues whose duty was to reimburse loyal civilians for property which the Confederate army used. If, during either process, the commissioners detected an aroma of disloyalty among the claimants, they formed themselves into a loyalty review board on the spot, co-opted a board of loyal local citizens, and settled the matter then and there. It was a process without standards or appeal. Loyalty, south as well as north, was a great gamble.

A Virginia farmer, J. L. Mock of Mile Creek, learned how much of a gamble it was when he applied to a Confederate property commission for payment for his last two horses, which rebel troops had appropriated. The commissioners ordered him to swear loyalty to the South before they would hear his case. Mock, fearing that Union vigilantes in the area would "visit" him if he did, refused. The commissioners then ordered him to present himself in order to face disloyalty charges. Giving the whole matter up as hopeless, Mock abandoned farming, and headed for the hopefully oathless West.[13]

Another interaction between the Confederate loyalty commissioners and local authorities occurred frequently when the appearance of the former in a locality inspired the latter to a spree of loyalty-testing. Vigilantes announced "swearing days" coincident with the scheduled visit of the commissioners, and assembled the populations of whole villages to attest their fidelity by a variety of formulas. Almost all the oath tests did, however, contain the common elements of support of the Confederacy, renunciation of the Union, and commitments to "reveal . . . any knowledge . . . of any plot, conspiracy, or plan for an invasion to overthrow the . . . Confederate States." Often the Confederate commissioners arrived after the ceremony, to receive from laconic vigilantes the notation that some individuals, having refused to swear, were "Dead" or "Gone to the Yanks."

Most judges in the Confederate court system were relatively more conscious of procedures than the military commissioners or the vigilantes. In addition to requiring loyalty tests of plaintiffs and defendants, judges unauthorizedly applied the same tests to all court officers, and sometimes served as loyalty commissioners themselves. Confederate jurists found haled before them many suspected traitors against whom inadequate evidence existed for a treason indictment. (Indeed, not one treason trial ever reached the dockets of Southern civil courts. Military courts-martial took care of this matter.) Civil and military authorities competed for disloyalty jurisdiction as they did in the North. In one instance General Braxton Bragg arrested an Alabama civilian for allegedly spying for the North. Upon application, Judge James Scruggs granted a habeas corpus writ, required the harassed civilian to swear loyalty to the Confederacy, which he did, and released him, outraging rebel soldiers.

Judges like Humphreys of the Confederate District Court in Tennessee and Magrath of the South Carolina District Court gained spectacular reputations as administrators of loyalty tests. The latter's charges to juries were lengthy lectures on the duties of patriotic citizenship, the necessity to keep close watch on neighbors' words and deeds, and the sacredness of loyalty in general and of Southern loyalty tests in particular. Confederate judges, in addition, appointed property confiscation commissioners and reimbursement officials, and issued warrants for the apprehension of those accused of disloyalty by the property administrators. Still further, judges received affidavits from citizens accusing named individuals of general disloyalty or specific acts of treason or sabotage. Such affidavits resulted in loyalty investigations by any of a dozen authorities, ranging from Confederate army units and sequestration commissioners to state attorneys and vigilantes.[14]

Southern state governments were the main sources of loyalty tests during the experiment in rebellion. Texas' experience with loyalty tests began with secession, when Unionists, inspired by Governor Sam Houston's refusal to replace "United States" with "Confederate States" in his oath of office, tried to prevent other Texans from swearing the novel formula. Their efforts were successful until more numerous pro-rebel vigilantes disarmed them and offered the Unionists the alternatives of swearing the Confederate oath or gracing a Confederate noose. This ended the antioath movement, but did not end disloyalty in Texas.

More effective opponents of Confederate state loyalty tests were Southerners of unimpeachable rebel loyalty who put forth precedent concepts of individual liberty and state sovereignty. The first proposed state loyalty test that Georgians approved contained a clause requiring the state's officers to swear first to the Confederate, then to the state government. Secessionists debated the issue in lengthy committee and mass meetings, and decided that Georgia came first, where her revised state oath placed her.[15]

North Carolina offers the outstanding example of patriotic opposition to loyalty tests. As the state constitutional convention of 1861 considered a new state oath, that issue became a bottleneck on the busy agenda. "It is a question," wrote a delegate, "of great delicacy, requiring much pondering both as regards the law and its enforcement." It was a delicate question because antisecession sentiment had been strong in the state, although outmaneuvered and suppressed by secessionist sympathizers. Many of the delegates at the convention knew that their acts were unrepresentative of the wishes of thousands of their fellow citizens. Debate on the proposed test oath revealed that sensitive secessionist Carolinians had, as Northern critics jeeringly insisted, forced their state into rebellion.

William Pettigrew of Raleigh, sponsor of the oath bill, defended it in the convention, admitting that discord existed and that disloyalty must be crushed. His test oath merely required every North Carolina official and citizen to state whether or not he was loyal to the state and the section. If a citizen refused the oath, then he need only give security for future good behavior; failing that, he deserved the penalty of prison. "Where lies the hardship to this oath?" Pettigrew demanded. It did not impugn the patriot; rather it sought out the skulking traitor, who by self-admission of guilt in refusing to swear deserved contumely and penalty. And if some swore falsely and thus escaped detection? Pettigrew cared not for "these hardened in sin," and trusted that their own guilty consciences and the "Argus eyes" of rebel authorities would expose their perjuries. Wartime was emergency. "Tell me not," Pettigrew pleaded, "of the latitude which was proper in times of peace. . . . Our lives demand that we be a unit." Above all, Pettigrew pointed out that he had written to President Jefferson Davis about the oath law and Davis had supported it as a military necessity.

A few days later, however, Pettigrew reversed his stand. He had learned in the interim that most North Carolinians felt the oath proposal a partisan weapon aimed not at covert disloyalists, but at open Unionists who had never concealed their antipathy to secession. Such overt Unionists had never aroused much suspicion concerning their fidelity to the state. Since state loyalty, to Pettigrew, took precedence over allegiance to the new Confederacy, he was content to trust his state's Unionists to keep North Carolina's cause uppermost in their hearts without a new loyalty oath.[16]

Six war months later a new session of the convention continued consideration of the same loyalty-test proposal. Supporters showed that the test oath was substantially the same as the one the state had used during the Revolution almost a century earlier, and hoped that the halo of antique patriotism would cast its patina over this later crisis of arms. Representative Briggs, the bill's sponsor, described the oath as "an evidence of patriotism and no one but a traitor need have any hesitation about taking it." Opponents of the measure were no less forceful.

William Graham, stanch secessionist of Orange County, was the chief antioath spokesman. He derided the attempts to eulogize the loyalty test's antique character into an administrative asset. The oath had been adequate in 1776, when everyone knew who the disloyal Tories were, with or without an oath. Such a test law in 1861 would open the way for malignant personal and political passions, and twist the state's power to individual ends. Graham insisted that treason was a natural monopoly of concern for the Confederate central government. "Let us not," he begged his auditors, "render ourselves a subject of merriment, by taking better care of our [central] government than it takes care of itself."

Graham pictured the consequences of enacting the test into law. A horde of inquisitors would descend upon every North Carolina hamlet "with an oath in the left hand, and a sentence of banishment in the other." Each citizen would face a self-assumption of guilt until he took the oath. Would not patriotic North Carolinians sicken at being forced to take oaths under the compulsion of force? Could conscientious men assume that "it is right and proper to hunt through the consciences of all good men by an oath of discovery, in order to ferret out the bad?" No, it was best to unearth disloyal men by their actions, not by their words or lack of words.

With growing warmth Graham criticized the oath law. Suppose only fifty citizens of the state took the oath. They would then control every state office. What a perfect weapon for oligarchic control such a test was! North Carolina had already abjured the United States, and no reason existed to force an individual renunciation upon every Carolinian. Should North Carolina admit to the world that she was afraid of herself? Would she dare emulate the scorned actions of Northern tyrants by descending to the level of test oaths? "Who constituted us the searchers of hearts?" Graham demanded.

His eloquence received a rare reward. North Carolina at that time passed no loyalty test. The state's Quakers and Mennonites, dedicated by faith to refuse all oaths, momentarily breathed easier, although a few went into voluntary exile from the state in correct anticipation of worse to come.[17]

By mid-1862 the South was as honeycombed with oath tests as the North. All Confederate and state civil and military officers were sworn to their rebel fidelity by a congeries of statutory and extralegal loyalty tests. Government contractors, purchasing agents, and postal subcontractors, in addition, found some oath or other facing them, as did licensed professional practitioners, teachers, and craftsmen, and hundreds of ordinary civilians who sought travel passes. Despite all the tests of loyalty, however, fear of disloyalty mounted. Investigations into alleged disloyalty continued. Some were successful.

Rebel patriots rejoiced when one investigation disclosed a Confederate War Department clerk as a Union spy, who, after a brief court-martial, was hanged. More fortunate was Richard Thompson, a newspaperman on the respected *Charleston Mercury,* who was a Confederate home guard officer, sworn to rebel allegiance. Thompson also supplied the hated *New York Tribune* with anonymous articles and the Union army with equally anonymous information. A *Tribune* blunder disclosed his multiple role, and Thompson escaped barely in time. He joined the Union army.

Confederate conscription officers found their thankless task complicated by the test-oath requirement. Few potential deserters scrupled at swearing the oath. Men who refused it for conscientious, religious, or other personal reasons were often of unquestioned loyalty to the South, but they were barred from military or civilian service, and became burdensome political prisoners. Perjured swearers were more deadly to the South, conscription administrators made it clear, than nonjurors who suffered severely for their convictions. But manpower shortages took precedence over principles. Obvious perjurers were better, perhaps, than nothing. The best that vigilant Southern patriots could do was to accept such oaths, watch such men, and punish the least infractions of loyal conduct.[18]

In order to maintain strict surveillance over individuals and groups in Confederate ranks, Southern counterspies infiltrated doubtful units and sought to ascertain the true feelings of potentially disloyal men. In late 1861 the officers of a volunteer North Carolina regiment were anonymously accused of disloyalty. The state government sent a secret agent to join the regiment as an ordinary recruit. His report admitted that those accused had, in the heat of temper of the secession months, talked like Unionists. But he had unearthed no indication that the accused personnel were secretly organized into a "reconstruction society" or that they were anything but faithful to the South, as their loyalty oaths indicated. With this report the traduced regiment finally received the arms which cautious state officials had withheld on successive pretexts until they were sure that the weapons would go into the hands of patriots.

A similar situation existed in Arkansas in 1863, when Confederate cavalry, sorely needed at the front, had to expend time and strength in subduing bitter anticonscription sentiment among training regiment personnel. A subsequent loyalty investigation, again conducted by state officers, spotlighted one man as the apparent ringleader of the allegedly disloyal Arkansans. But the maligned individual was able to prove that he had been the subject of a malicious rumor deliberately instigated by local Unionists to get him arrested, because he was one of the most ardent and influential Confederate patriots in the area, with three hangings of pro-Lincoln neighbors to his credit. The disloyal person in this affair was a Confederate postal agent who combined spying for the North with his peripatetic duties for the South. He died before a rebel firing squad.

A loyalty investigation by Confederate central government authorities followed anonymous accusations that several justices of the peace in northern Virginia, perilously close to Union lines, were disloyal. The investigation disclosed the accuracy of the accusations, but arresting officers could do nothing about their quarry, for Union troops occupied the area just before the loyalty investigation ended.[19]

Few such accounts of specific loyalty probes survive. The few that do exist indicate that each disloyalty problem received special handling, for the South never achieved the relatively centralized antisubversion apparatus that Northern administrators created. Probably the most effective surveillance over Southern officials was unofficial, or, at best, was conducted by quasi-official vigilante and home guard personnel who made patriotic spy-catching one of their tasks. Local overseers of loyalty, men familiar with their neighbors and communities, suspicious and alert, were a constant feature of wartime Southern life.

The physical product of all the loyalty-testing, investigations, travel controls, and martial law were the human beings who, as in the North, refused loyalty oaths, or in some way seemed actually or potentially disloyal to the South. In emulation of the North, an imitation that Southerners rarely have admitted then or since, Southern internal security procedures produced a harvest of political prisoners whose general offense was disloyalty. Most of them, again as in the North, could regain freedom by swearing loyalty to their sectional jailer. Some never had the chance, and died from a vigilante's blow or in front of a military firing squad.

Early in the war a steady stream of suspects flowed into Southern prisons from the border states, arrested by the mélange of authorities involved in protecting the South against Southerners. A very few Confederate military commanders, like General McCulloch in Missouri, declared to unhappy civilians within their jurisdictions that "no oaths binding upon your consciences will be administered." Such moderation soon fell into abeyance. Confederate army provosts, civil judges, state civil and military officers, and the ubiquitous vigilantes made loyalty tests their primary security weapon. Initial Confederate successes in Tennessee, for instance, resulted in hauls of hundreds of suspect civilians who crowded prisons in the lower South. As one Confederate officer reported to War Secretary Benjamin, "To release them is ruinous; to convict them before a court at this time next to an impossibility; but if they are kept in prison for six months it will have a good effect." Benjamin agreed. The milder offenders, after benefiting from the salubrious climate of prison, were released if they took the Confederate oath. The ever-undermanned condition of rebel armies inspired provosts in charge of political prisoners to proselytize among able-bodied nonjurors. Freedom for them involved, in addition to swearing loyalty, enlistment in rebel forces. Persuasion often gave way to force.[20]

The resemblance of Confederate loyalty-testing goals and practices to their Northern counterparts was merely superficial. The variety of Southern agencies, uncoördinated, overlapping, undisciplined, had an Alice-in-Wonderland aspect that compounded the grim purposes of loyalty-testing with the grimmer excesses of unrestrained localism. Political prisoners bounced among the conflicting jurisdictions of competing Confederate authorities. The South never created a central agency akin to the North's Provost Marshal General Bureau to correlate and control its disparate agencies, and to supersede the vigilante in security work. The most common denominator in loyalty-testing in the South was the Confederate army military commission. But when such commissions, as part of their standard procedure, enforced state, local, and vigilante laws and policies as well as those of the Confederate government, when they advertised in newspapers for "all cases of seditious and traitorous persons against whom charges are preferred, without regard to time or place of committing the offense," and worked with no clear policy lines from the Confederate President or Congress, then uniformity became impossible.[21]

Closest to the relatively centralized Northern security system was the special Confederate army provost marshal unit in Richmond, under command of General Winder. He was a controversial figure throughout the war. A renegade Baltimorean, Winder staffed his corps with "plug-ugly" detectives, many of whom were also Northern turncoats. "How can they detect political offenders," demanded a critic of the provost's ungentle policies, "when they are too ignorant to comprehend what constitutes a political offense?" President Davis stubbornly refused to remove Winder long after the latter was an incubus to the central government (unlike Lincoln, who adroitly replaced Seward in a not dissimilar situation). Winder involved Davis in fruitless arguments with Southern state governors, and inspired widespread popular resentment among otherwise patriotic supporters of the rebellion. As one popular political satire had it, Winder's brutal methods offered Confederates

> The right to dream that all's impartial
> Which may be done by the Provost Marshal;
> To view the scum of all the nation
> Promoted to official station; . . .
> And give your safety the éclat
> Of bayonet courts and martial law.[22]

Winder's work, though most publicized, was relatively minor compared to the activities of the field commanders of Confederate armies. The latter were major suppliers of loyalty tests to civilians and contributors of political prisoners to Southern prisons. Throughout the war, Southern armies conducted loyalty probes in areas of doubtful security. Coöperating with state and local officers and the omnipresent vigilantes, army provosts rounded up civilians accused of disloyalty. Courts-martial settled many cases immediately. Lesser offenders, whose guilt was doubtful even by the elastic standards of a military tribunal, generally got off with a term in prison and eventual release upon swearing the Confederate oath. James Trakle, a fisherman of Mathias Point, Virginia, was accused by vigilantes of piloting federal spies across the Chesapeake. He was able to prove his innocence, but the local provost refused to release him. Trakle then came under Winder's harsh control, but secured release by swearing loyalty to the South after influential relatives appealed to President Davis in his behalf.

D. M. Hamilton's case had an opposite conclusion. He was a Mississippi steamboat pilot whom Confederate vigilantes accused of disloyalty. He insisted the charges were false, but, fearing Union vengeance upon his St. Louis family, refused the Confederate oath. Outraged Southern officers pressured him for two weeks, refusing him food for days at a time, until Hamilton acceded and swore the oath—and escaped to Union lines at the first opportunity.

Braxton Bragg was the most devoted user of loyalty tests among Confederate generals. In his Florida command early in the war Bragg demanded oath tests from all civil officials in the area. Bragg's provosts went a long step further and required all resident male civilians (white) to swear loyalty or become political prisoners. Nonjurors added their number to the swelling prison population of the South. Their crime consisted of having found something objectionable in this formula of fidelity:

I do most solemnly and sincerely swear before Almighty God, without mental reservation of any kind, that I will support and defend the Constitution of the Confederate States of America, and that I will . . . promise that I will endeavor to discover, and will report any and every unfaithful person of whom I may obtain reliable intelligence. So help me God.[23]

Outstanding among the records of political prisoners in the South is the testimony of the Reverend John Aughey of Tupelo, Mississippi. An open Unionist, Aughey refused the state test oath and went to prison, where a large company of inmates told him sad tales of sufferings incurred for nonjuring and for various acts equaling disloyalty. The grim Calvinist pondered and prayed, then disclosed that he saw no reason why political prisoners should not swear falsely to the rebel oath in order to save themselves and their families from death and destitution. He encouraged the young men to enter Confederate military units, swear loyalty as required, and desert at the first opportunity. "Naught but Punic faith," was the agreed response of his audience. As for himself, Aughey rejected perjured compromise, escaped, and added his account to the growing exilic literature that flooded the North. The problem of civilian prisoners was more serious for the South than for the North. Political offenders cost precious food and manpower. Refugees from the South appealed to Northern political leaders for exchanges of civilian prisoners. But Lincoln's efforts to arrange such exchanges were largely futile, and North and South kept their political prisoners until they could decide what to do with them.[24]

Meanwhile, Northern propagandists used tales of terror in the South (even as Southern propagandists used the Northern internal security system) to point to the self-contradictions of a section that claimed to fight for liberty while lowering itself to repression in the name of loyalty. Consider the dramatic story that Northern newspapers carried early in 1863, telling of an aged Tennessee Unionist who faced the Confederate provost in charge of Castle Thunder, Virginia, where the old man was imprisoned on a disloyalty charge. The provost admitted there was no real evidence and offered to release the man if he would take the Confederate oath. The septuagenarian proudly declined the proffered freedom, admitted that he had four sons in the Union army and that were he able he would be with them, but repeated earlier denials of treason to the South. Soon after, the old man died in prison, still unsworn to the South.

The case of John Minor Botts of northern Virginia, a prominent and open Unionist imprisoned in 1862, attracted national attention. Released on parole, Botts suffered successive reincarcerations as every kind of antidisloyalty entity in the Confederacy tried its unsuccessful hand at breaking his spirit and forcing him to take the rebel oath. Southern troops destroyed his farm and guerrillas looted what was left because, it was rumored, he had entertained Union General Meade. To many Americans North and South, this kind of persecution seemed mere harassment of a harmless old man.[25]

By early 1863 the problem of political prisoners had become more than merely embarrassing to the South. Thousands of men were occupied in rear-area internal security work, when their strength was urgently needed in combat zones. Annoying jurisdictional clashes between central and local authorities, and heated legalistic arguments among President Davis, the Confederate Congress, and state governors, consumed valuable time and exacerbated sensitive tempers.

Early in February, 1863, the Confederate Congress demanded that Davis supply it with lists of all civilians imprisoned under executive authority. Davis' reply revealed that some political offenders had been in various Southern prisons since January, 1861, months before the hostilities began. Most of them faced the general charge of "disloyalty"; almost all were residents of border areas. This report did no credit to Davis' government in the eyes of European powers, some of whose citizens were political prisoners of the South. Since the Confederacy even in 1863 was still hoping for European recognition and support in its war against the United States, it was especially awkward for Davis to have to list several British and French subjects among those incarcerated. Awkwardness went both ways, however, for neither European nation could effectively protest to the South since neither recognized its official existence. The upshot was that the Southern government quietly released all British political prisoners as soon as it could do so with dignity. It received European protests in a highhanded manner, however, which did nothing to ease strained relations.[26]

Another embarrassment the political-prisoner problem caused President Davis was its revelation of the snarled lines of authority in the Confederacy. Davis smarted at the criticisms that came his way from North as well as South, ridiculing a government that so vividly portrayed the problems of seeking to fight a war while simultaneously honoring theories of state sovereignty.

Davis tried to improve the situation. He ordered all Confederate army officers, prison commandants, state home guard commanders, and anyone else in the South who had anything to do with arrests for disloyalty, to submit monthly reports to the Confederate War Department, showing the vital statistics of each prisoner and the reasons for arrest. This reporting system was precisely what Lincoln and Seward had discarded as inadequate in February, 1862; the Confederacy was about to try it in March, 1863. The South had no better luck with it than Lincoln had had. Mere reporting, without supervision of disloyalty controls from the beginning, could not provide standardization of procedures and protection for civilians. And it failed to control the largest group of loyalty enforcers in the South—the vigilantes.

When these inadequacies became apparent, Davis tried to reach those who would or could not reach him with their reports. He appointed a corps of special commissioners to examine political arrests of civilians. These circuit riders, combining routine justice-of-the-peace duties with this new assignment, toured almost everywhere in the South, inquiring into internal security situations. They also had original jurisdiction in disloyalty matters, for the War Department empowered them to unearth disloyal combinations among citizens which existing subversion controls had failed to find.

How these special loyalty commissions operated is only dimly apparent, for few of their reports survived the war. One such document is the 1864 record of Special Commissioners Vowles and Sandes, circuit-riding in Alabama. In one day Vowles and Sandes heard nine cases of alleged disloyalty, brought before them by state and vigilante authorities. A man who admitted swearing Lincoln's amnesty oath received three months in jail and conscription into Confederate military service upon release. Another who was accused of aiding deserters from the rebel army enjoyed release upon taking the Confederate oath and paying a heavy fine in gold. A Tennessean who had insulted patriotic Knoxville women a year earlier by suggesting that the South might lose the war went to prison, to await his jailer's pleasure about releasing him on his oath of loyalty. Another Tennessean, who proved he was no Union spy, was released, but only on condition that he swear the rebel oath and report daily to the local provost. A British subject who had foolishly shown vigilantes his Union oath certificate, and a deserter from the Northern army, were released on their oaths, plus their immediate enlistment in the Confederate army. The commissioners rounded off their day by investigating the impeached loyalty of the local postmaster; they pronounced him innocent, but secretly advised vigilantes to keep him under close observation.

The work of such loyalty commissioners served more to obscure than to clarify the confused loyalty-testing picture. Since commissioners heard cases emanating from all the political jurisdictions of the South, as well as from extralegal vigilantes, they could not agree on standards or policy. The commissioners became an additional element in an already overcrowded administrative galaxy. Disloyalty was endemic in the South, but so was the antidisloyalty machinery the Confederacy erected to combat it. Localism became not a defense of democracy and civil liberty, but the chief abuser of that which it was supposed to protect.[27]

The Southern citizen, even if devoutly patriotic, could rarely be sure that his conduct satisfied the loyalty standards of all Southern agencies. In 1863, Tennessee's Episcopal Bishop Otey transmitted to England his written consent that a Pennsylvanian be ordained in a Northern bishopric. To Otey's hypersensitive neighbors, this equaled disloyalty. Otey successfully defended himself, but he was an uneasy man thereafter. Similarly, a young Louisiana girl, patriotic sister of a rebel civil officer, unthinkingly entertained weary Union troops at her home. Rebel vigilantes insisted that she had betrayed the South and her brother by waltzing with federal gallants. Embittered, she swore the Union oath and accepted protection from the Yankees in defiance of the suspicious neighbors who had so recently been her friends. But this unhappy young woman told her diary what her pride forbade her to say, that her rebel patriotism was unimpaired despite appearances. Appearances, however, were what counted.[28]

Defeatism was the commonest Southern synonym for disloyalty. To admit the possibility of Southern defeat or to advocate a reknit Union was to invite censure, prosecution, and persecution. But the degree of danger in pessimistic statements depended upon who and where the speaker or writer was. In the absence of effective censorship machinery a North Carolina rebel soldier could advise his brother by mail to "go to the other side, where you can get plenty and not stay in this one-horse, barefooted, naked and famine-stricken Southern Confederacy." It was not too unsafe for the *Augusta Chronicle and Sentinel*, secure in the favor of Georgia's Governor Brown, a stern believer in states' rights, to editorialize on the necessity of national reunification. But even moderate Southerners agreed that "this is a dangerous subject for discussion and one which may lead to dissension among ourselves and great peril to our cause. . . . May God preserve us from the necessity of a choice between reconstruction and subjugation." [29]

God and Confederate arms, two sacred institutions which fervid rebels delighted to make partners, did their best for four years to permit the South to escape this choice. As late as February, 1865, spokesmen of the Fourteenth Virginia Infantry sent a resolution to the faltering Confederate Congress: ". . . a Southern soldier or civilian who would lay down his arms and now submit is unworthy to breathe the air of freedom." The Fifty-seventh Virginia Regiment denounced those Confederates who were "recanting their allegiance" and insisted that "now is no time to dream of submission and reconstruction." To members of Humphrey's Mississippi Brigade, the "solemn obligation voluntarily incurred by us nearly four years ago, to serve the Confederate States faithfully against her enemies, . . . precludes us forever from the sacrilege of a re-construction." Forever is a long time. Even as the faithful few offered devotion to a cause already lost, Confederate authorities were relaxing antidisloyalty measures in helpless admission of impending defeat.[30]

As with civilian political prisoners, Confederate policies toward prisoners of war both aped and criticized Northern programs. Southern spokesmen condemned Union loyalty-oath lures which seduced thousands of captive Confederates from their allegiance, and insisted that only brute force elicited Union oaths from Southern soldiers. Such oaths, the Confederate government logically concluded, could not bind their subscribers. Less logically, Southern officials failed to admit that Confederate prisonkeepers indulged, when they could, in the same loyalty-testing policies as their Northern colleagues, although far less successfully.

Such sectional myopia was born of the urgent Confederate need to quell desertion from its armies. The death penalty awaited those who deserted or incited "mutiny, sedition, or desertion." A northern Virginia youth faced this sentence after a series of tragic misadventures. A rebel soldier, he fell captive at Antietam, and finally succumbed to his mother's entreaties to swear loyalty to the Union and gain release. Shame impelled him to run the Union lines and plead for reënlistment in his former Confederate regiment. Southern officers, after a court-martial, assured the youth that the Northern oath he had sworn was invalid, and reswore him to Confederate allegiance, and he fought once more against the Union he had sworn to defend.

A second case underlined the seriousness with which Confederate officials viewed their sectional allegiance. A rebel deserter had volunteered for Union military service and had been captured by Southern troops. Was he a traitor or a prisoner of war? Traitor, the Confederate court-martial and attorney general agreed; death was the sentence, for no Southerner had the right to modify the implications of the Southern oath he swore, although no Northern oath could burden his conscience.[31]

Such solemn pronouncements were made mockeries in every Confederate war prison, where rebel deserters and Union captives found that they could gain freedom if they abandoned former oaths in favor of novel tests of loyalty to the South. But rarely could the Confederacy offer Union soldiers the lure of returning to their homes, as the boundaries of Dixie contracted. Lacking this basic inducement, the Southern oath policy was much less effective than the Northern. Most often, Confederate camp commanders and provosts substituted force for persuasion.

Captured Union troops did not face the relatively sophisticated loyalty-testing machinery that the North applied to its captives. But imprisoned Northern soldiers, depending always upon their location and upon the personality of the camp commander, faced prison conditions so appalling that commanders exploited physical degradation to achieve loyalty conversions. At Andersonville, for instance, more than four thousand imprisoned federals swore loyalty to the South and joined Confederate military units, for "these men felt that the . . . United States had forgotten them . . . in not procuring . . . an exchange." [32]

Some Confederate prison officials were too impatient to wait for their charges to change their minds. The "Foreign Battalion" of the Southern army was theoretically formed by "aliens" who had voluntarily decided to fight for the South. It was actually composed mainly of former Union soldiers who had switched sides, by no means voluntarily in many instances. Some prisoners died rather than become turncoats. Others succumbed, swore, and donned rebel gray. Some newly captured Union troops were ordered by armed guards to raise their hands, and were told that they had just sworn loyalty to the Confederacy. Two Union officers, after being captured on a scouting party, were threatened with being shot as spies unless they abandoned the Union and accepted commissions in the Confederate army. Both refused, and escaped before the sentence of death was carried out.[33]

At Andersonville and Libby prisons the offer of release by loyalty oath was more standard and consistent than elsewhere in the South. The memoirs of Union prisoners who suffered the horrors of those places reveal how attractive that offer was. But relatively few succumbed. Unlike Southern captives in Northern camps, the captured Yankee could look ahead to eventual victory for his section and release. All the Southern oath could buy was a rebel uniform or an uneasy neutrality in an unfamiliar, losing land. War conditions rather than a purer Southern morality prevented the Confederacy from making the loyalty oath the effective war weapon Lincoln made of it.

Even in Libby's degradation, Northern prisoners could joke about the Confederate oath their jailers regularly offered them. In a rare moment of relaxation, captives put on a minstrel show wherein a black-faced interlocutor posed the question: "If Jefferson Davis released you on condition that you did not take up arms again during the war, would you accept?" His faithful respondent's earthy, negative reply evoked "three cheers, and three more, followed by a tiger that might have been heard at the [Confederate] 'Executive Mansion' on the hill." [34]

Since the South could not, by reason of its centrifugal internal organization and ever-deteriorating military situation, make loyalty tests positive tools for victory, it expended much official and individual energy in negatively combating Northern loyalty-testing policies. The effectiveness of Union loyalty tests was all too apparent. Increasing numbers of Southerners, caught by advancing Union forces, swore Northern oaths in order to keep property and positions. These defections evoked criticisms among more faithful, or safer, sons of Dixie. A soldier-journalist of the Confederate army unleashed a savage diatribe against such "Southern Yankees" who had exhibited "traits of character that we were not willing to believe existed in the South." One day, he confidently predicted, the Stars and Bars would triumph, and then those perjured villains would again seek to swear loyalty oaths to the South. Such "summer patriots" were unworthy of future trust, suffrage, or position under Confederate dispensation; "to reward men who are ready to be on either side, according to circumstances, is to offer a premium for disloyalty." No loyalty oaths were trustworthy, according to this cynical Southerner, for perjury was too common. "We want some more positive acts, better evidence than merely taking the oath of allegiance." [35] But his 1862 vision of inevitable rebel victory never came true; the South's dream of punishing Union oath takers died with the Confederacy.

So deep was the Confederacy's detestation of Southerners who broke Southern loyalty tests, that the South never overcame it sufficiently to make amnesty a war weapon as Lincoln had done. True, individual Confederate commanders pardoned deserters and forgave defectors. But Southern policy as a whole stubbornly refrained from a possible avenue of easing its increasingly desperate manpower shortage. Such shortsightedness derived from the very extent of Southern disloyalty, which convinced Confederate officials that all loyalty tests were useless as symbols of repentance. Kirby E. Smith, for example, commanding in Tennessee in 1861, proclaimed that all civilians should be left at peace if they swore loyalty to the Confederacy. But Smith could not suppress rebel vigilantes, and even his subordinates disobeyed him. Smith's provost reported that all local residents were pro-Union, Southern oath or no. "They will," he warned, "take the oath of allegiance with no intention to observe it." Cynicism and loyalty-testing are always poor companions.

They formed especially poor partners for the Confederacy, which officially accepted the premise that pardon for past treasons was unthinkable, that Southern loyalty oaths were perpetual, and that the sole effective loyalty guarantee the South had was its own military strength. "The time for such measures is past," decreed War Secretary Benjamin, when a subordinate reminded him that General Smith had promised Tennesseans protection if they swore the Southern oath. All past disloyalists, in the erratic course of Confederate loyalty-testing, faced prison rather than pardon.[36]

It was with this outraged dignity that Southerners viewed the conduct of Confederate military and civil officials, repeatedly sworn to loyalty to the South, who made the complete conversion from secessionist to Unionist and from rebel to reconstructionist. Then scorn became anger and cynicism gave way to fury.

In any pantheon of perjured traitors, E. W. Gantt of Arkansas rated a high position. In 1861 Gantt was a Confederate general who achieved a commendable record as a brave soldier until he was captured. While a prisoner of the North, Gantt recanted the heresy of secession. He returned to his home state in 1863, when Union forces were maintaining precarious control of its largest cities. Gantt became the spark of pro-Unionist feeling even in sections where the Confederate authority still held forceful sway. Among his favorite propaganda targets were the absolute military commissions which, created by Confederate General Hindman in that war-torn state, ordered more than four hundred

Arkansas civilians executed for disloyalty to the South. Gantt was anathema to all good rebels, a worthy successor, according to one Confederate journalist, to Judas Iscariot and Benedict Arnold. For he had not merely violated the oath he had sworn when he accepted Confederate command in 1861; he had done so blatantly and unashamedly, and was now expending all the zeal of the convert in effective anti-Southern activities. Their own loyalty tests were no joking matter to good rebels.[37]

Only on rare occasions did Southerners treat the Confederate loyalty oath with levity. Near Louisville, Kentucky, in June, 1864, a band of rebel guerrillas successfully attacked a federal troop train. The rebels, seizing the arms of the surrendered Union soldiers, loudly debated the fate of their prisoners. The nervous Northerners, fearing immediate execution, were overjoyed when their captors decided to leave the scene of their brief conquest and permit the Union troops to stay unharmed, if they first swore to the Confederate oath of loyalty. Shouting with unrestrained laughter, the Southern soldiers faced their captives, ordered them to raise their hands and swear eternal fidelity to the South. All did so. Then the warning whistle of another approaching Union troop train sounded. The Confederate irregulars hurriedly departed, leaving behind an embarrassed group of shaken Northern soldiers who admitted their part in the grim comedy because they knew that news of it would spread in any event. It did.

More spectacular were the adventures of Southern secret agents who planned a demoralizing coup into the North from Canada, which resulted in a single sally into the northern Vermont city of St. Albans. The raiders' target was the local bank, which they robbed, and then they forced the bank president and teller to swear to the Confederate oath. Then the group melted back into Canada, chortling over their successful robbery and about how disgusted their victims had appeared when discretion impelled them to pledge patriotism to the South.[38]

More general than humor was the widespread Southern anger at the news of Confederate officials who, in the face of Union occupation, failed to stand by the oaths they had sworn. To Confederate Judge Magrath, "oaths, which have been taken in the presence of God . . . have been mockingly, carelessly, cruelly broken and disregarded." In seeming inconsistency, Southern spokesmen criticized rebel officials who retained posts in the South without swearing to the required loyalty oaths. Judge R. A. Hill, for instance, realizing that his Mississippi jurisdiction was a veritable no man's land, permitted court officers to function without loyalty oaths. Michael Hahn, a Louisiana notary, never swore the statutory official oaths. Only the vagaries of human nature can explain how a people can simultaneously decry the efficacy of oaths to promote loyalty, reject the possibility of canceling the obligation theoretically imposed by such oaths, and criticize the laxity of officials who, agreeing, abandon oath requirements.[39]

Ranking higher in Southern detestation than the ordinary turncoat was the former rebel like Gantt, who, with the zeal of the convert to Unionism, sought to entice other Southerners to follow his path to perjury. There was, for instance, a widely (and illegally) disseminated pamphlet which described how the author had been bullied into rebel military service in 1861, and how he deserted to Union lines, swore Lincoln's oath, and luxuriated in the moral and material ease his swearing had won him. There were also the prolix products of Edwin H. Ewing's pen, which supported the Northern oath program in occupied Tennessee on the pragmatic basis of "Alas, . . . what choice have we?" but continued with vivid descriptions of the benefits oath takers derived. Such defections provoked the Confederate Congress to condemn the "imbecile and unprincipled usurper who now sits . . . in Washington City," and to deride the notion that the oath Lincoln offered would avail Northern strategy. Bombast like this merely served to indicate how worried the Southern leaders were over the threat presented by the Union oath.[40]

The fiercest blast at Northern oaths, and at Southerners who succumbed to them, came from the pen of Benjamin Palmer, a vigorous secessionist who served as Methodist chaplain to successive rebel army units stationed near his New Orleans home. One hot August Sunday in 1862 Palmer was preaching to a congregation of Southern soldiers when Yankee gunboats opened fire upon the assemblage from the nearby Mississippi River. Palmer, obdurate, refused to shorten his lengthy sermon even by one paragraph. Restive Confederate troops, preferring dugouts to Deuteronomy, fumed while Palmer resolutely finished his prayers, then all dived for protection.

True to his stubborn principles, Palmer chose exile rather than perjury when Butler's Union forces occupied New Orleans and demanded Northern oaths of all residents. When the Confederate Congress resolved that *all* citizens of Union-held Louisiana deserved the thanks of the Confederacy for widespread resistance and determined nonjuring to Union oaths, Palmer, a grim, unbending man, decided to "expose" Louisianans less loyal than himself. In his *Oath of Allegiance to the United States Discussed in its Moral and Political Bear-*

ings, published in 1863, he slashed in no uncertain terms at Southerners whose craven oath-taking was a "dishonor which must cleave to them forever." Palmer denied any logical or Scriptural basis permitting Southerners to take the Yankee test with mental reservations. His arguments helped to bolster the wavering morale of pessimistic Southerners. Many Confederates living in Union-occupied zones, fearful of the consequences of open anti-Union statements, anonymously sent illicit copies of Palmer's sermon to other Southerners who had already taken the Yankee oath. Some, seeing unhappy recipients of the sermon squirm in apparent tortured repentance, regretted their application of salt to already gaping wounds. "I had really forgotten that Mrs. Roselius had taken it," confessed a New Orleans woman who had seen to it that Mrs. Roselius received a copy of Palmer's sermon. "She cried as bitterly as the day she took the oath." [41]

Palmer's blast at Southern swearers to Yankee oaths unleashed a widespread debate among Confederates as to the merits of his arguments, further dividing Southerners from each other. The most forceful support of Palmer's position came from the Reverend W. H. Ruffner, Presbyterian minister at Lexington, Virginia. Ruffner agreed with Palmer on the "diabolical nature of the Union oath" and on a Southerner's inability to swear falsely to that oath while maintaining his ethical and religious integrity. But, from the deep recesses of Scripture and Calvinism, Ruffner found a Biblical escape valve which Palmer had failed to consider:

A loyal citizen of the Confederate States [Ruffner concluded] who has unhappily taken the oath of allegiance to the United States, is not bound to keep it; because, and only because, it binds him to sin, and was therefore null and void from the moment it was taken. His duty is not that of obedience to the sinful promise he has sworn to keep, but of deep repentance for having made it, and a public renunciation of the same.

Like Palmer, Ruffner pleaded with Southerners to refuse the Northern oath in order to save their souls and their Confederacy. If they must swear, Ruffner's casuistry found a perjured way out for them. But each Southern patriot had to realize that more than his own self and soul was at stake. Everyone who took the Union oath, Ruffner wrote, damaged the rebel cause and gained nothing in return. The North rejoiced at each oath sworn, and thus derived encouragement to continue the battle. Each subscriber to the Union oath gave the South an evil example that spread like fire through the dry tinder of weary discouragement, growing so rankly in this fourth year of war. And,

245

above all, rebel soldiers were discouraged by delinquencies on the home front.[42]

Strangely enough, or perhaps not so strangely, the rebel soldiers about whom everyone seemed so concerned were apparently much less extreme on this question than were most Southern civilians. Consider the articles that appeared on this question at the height of the Palmer furor. Signed "Confederate," and probably written by Henry Watterson, these articles pleaded with civilians to resist the Union oath as much as possible. But, because the oath was illegal, those who took it under compulsion were exempt from criticism. The only ones this soldier-writer really condemned were Southern civilians and officials who accepted the Yankee loyalty obligation without compulsion, and, worst of all, those who persuaded other Southerners to follow their "craven conduct" and sign the Union test. But how, asked the writer, was the Confederacy to know into which class an oath taker fell? It was best, therefore, to cast no stones; too much injustice had already been done by too-hasty rebel patriots; Southern reputations were going glimmering by the thousands as rumor, gossip, and misinformation accused loyal sons and daughters of Dixie of having taken the Union oath.

The writer offered specific examples. A Tennessee nonjuring exile from his home was *not,* the editorialist insisted, a secret Unionist as gossip implied, but rather a dutiful rebel soldier. Many of those whom Palmer had accused of swearing the Northern loyalty formula had taken not an oath, but a mere temporary parole, involving no shift of allegiance. And the soldier-journalist concluded:

I am satisfied that many men who took that oath are not guilty mentally, morally, or religiously, of any offence. They did it under duress. I have no excuse to offer for those men who, of their own free will and accord, aided the enemy. . . . They deserve the execrations of all true patriots.[43]

But even moderate rebel soldiers applauded events that showered seemingly just punishment upon those who had deserted Dixie for the pelf the Union oath offered. When the famed rebel guerrilla, Quantrill, despoiled Union-oath–protected Mississippi plantations in swift, savage raids, Confederate army spokesmen delighted in pointing out how proper such retribution was. Nor could these spokesmen hide their scorn for their former fellows in arms who had gone the whole way to Canossa, and, now sworn to Union allegiance, were wearing blue uniforms in place of gray. When the former rebel soldier-beau of a

246

Georgia girl appeared resplendent in a Union colonel's uniform, she noted with distaste: "I have no faith in Yankees of any sort, especially those miserable turncoats that are ready to sell themselves to either side. There isn't gold enough in existence to galvanize one of them into a respectable Confederate."

A "respectable" Confederate, then, was one who rejected the Union oath so long as Yankee pressures remained endurable. A rebel soldier-poet put this thought to rhyme, when the South heard of the severe Union loyalty program imposed by a federal general in eastern Arkansas:

> We have reliable information
> Concerning the Yankee occupation
> Of McMinnville. They are supremely sweet
> To every man and woman on the street
> They say their aim is not subjugation
> Grand larceny, or extirpation,
> All they ask of the people is that they
> Will let King Abraham have his way,
> To be sure, a most solemn affirmation
> Is required of a whole population,
> That they will not use a finger or arm
> In trying to do the yanks any harm.[44]

Confederates agreed that no true son or daughter of the South should take the Union oath unless forced into it. Would a patriotic Southerner so "forsake his God and country as to take an oath to Lincoln to support his despotism?" demanded aged William Pettrigrew. Speaking at Williamston, North Carolina, in midsummer, 1864, Pettigrew sadly admitted that rebel arms were losing the war and that Sherman's army was terribly close. But he demanded an end to pessimism: "You have everything at stake in this contest that man regards dear on earth." He pictured to his audience the consequences of Yankee occupation, and warned them that "buying" exemption from confiscation was a foolish dream: "Oath or no oath, submission or no submission, if they subjugate us, they intend to have everything in the land." Quantrill harangued a defeatist crowd in Richmond with the warning: "Woe unto all of you if the Federals come with an oath of loyalty in one hand and a torch in the other." This noted warrior exhorted the assembly to "meet the torch with the torch"; he knew that the South was already matching Northern oaths with rebel counterparts. Confederate authorities and vigilantes did their best to penalize

Southerners who, heedless of Pettigrew's and Quantrill's warnings and faithless to the South, swallowed the Yankee oath.[45]

Under Confederate national and state laws, all property of alien enemies was subject to confiscation. Confederate confiscation commissioners equated Southerners who took Union oaths with alien enemies, pragmatically writing them off as debits to the cause of Dixie once they subscribed the Northern loyalty test. It was easy for these Southern officials to learn who had weakened, and were overtly espousing the Northern side. Federal officials, anxious to impress the South with the numbers of defectors, and as anxious to impress their superiors with the zeal of their proselytizing efforts, published the names of Southerners who had sworn fealty to the Union in local and national newspapers. Southern officials made it a practice to scan these convenient rosters of Southern disloyalists and to confiscate the property of those who were listed. Even from behind Union lines, Confederate officials heard from organized vigilantes about the effectiveness of the Union oath program:

I have seated myself [wrote a North Carolina vigilante] to give you some information concerning the disloyalty of the people. . . . I don't yet know how many . . . have taken the oath of allegiance to the old United States . . . and organized a [Union] home guard. . . . I can't write my name to this for fear the home guard or the Yankees may get holt of it and betray me; you remember who conversed with you about the disloyalty of our people. . . . From a friend and well wisher of the CSA.[46]

So great was the fear that evil consequences would follow swearing the Union oath that some turncoat Southerners, after taking it, successfully pleaded with sympathetic Northern provosts to write a phrase like this after the oath certificate: "His avowals have been uniformly those of a consistent Southern man." A strange phrase to appear where it did! Other oath takers begged forgiveness from their friends and families, and wondered, pitifully enough, "how we are looked upon?" There were as many answers to that question as there were loyalty-testing authorities in the South.[47]

Ever-late in making effective use of Southern loyalty tests, the Confederacy waited until August, 1864, to welcome all "foreigners" who wished to seek domicile within the shrinking boundaries of Dixie, and to promise them full protection and subsistence upon their swearing the Southern oath. Lincoln had offered the same benefits to defecting

Southerners from the earliest weeks of the war, and had formalized them by his December, 1863, reconstruction and amnesty proclamation. But, early or late, the South could offer no reconstruction. Its protection offer, issued when the most unsophisticated observers could see the avalanching decline of rebel fortunes, was patently absurd.

Confederate spokesmen did, however, maintain their defensive barrage against the Northern oath until the very end. As late as March, 1865, a bare month before Appomattox, a rebel writer pointed to a recent Union oath order in occupied Memphis as proof of the fiendish nature of Northern arms. This order, in contradiction to Lincoln's announced pardon policy, imposed immediate exile upon every adult in the town not already sworn to some Yankee loyalty test. Confederate army newspapers copied the Union order, and in articles and handbills entitled "Yankee Despotism" spread it over the South, to "be attentively read by every man who in his own heart . . . contemplated submission to the foe and a return to the Federal Union." All that Lincoln had asked, the Southern editorialist noted, was that Southerners should perjure themselves by swearing the oath he had prescribed ("an oath of affection and loyalty to a government we detest and abhor"). But this new order proved that Lincoln's words did not control Lincoln's officers, that "our only hope is to reject all thought of submission and trust in our strong right arms." In March, 1865, rebel strength was ebbing rapidly.[48]

As the war neared its end, as the debacle of rebel arms neared, increasing numbers of Southerners gave up the loyalty ghost. They openly speculated among themselves about the property protection Lincoln's amnesty oath offered, looked with noticeably lessening scorn upon those Southerners who took Lincoln's oath and sought his pardon, and hurried to prove how antisecessionist they really had been all the time. For the basic limitation to the Confederate anti–Union-oath drive always remained—Southern armies retreated more than they advanced, Southerners faced trials of their allegiance because rebel armies failed to hold Southern territory. After 1863 it was impossible to block oath-taking by threats that rebel armies would repossess territory occupied by Union troops, for this occurred too rarely for the tactic to succeed. Nor could Confederate confiscation policies prove a consistently effective barrier once it was apparent that the South was losing the war. Men whose property the South sequestered for refusing the Confederate oath could anticipate regaining it when final Union victory came.

In the perverse complexity of Confederate confusion, Southerners who encouraged fellow rebels to perjure themselves when Yankee oaths were offered took an opposite stand when rebel oaths were involved. Southern officials who laughed at tales of evasions of Union oaths were dutifully grim when an oath marked "CSA" was violated or perjured. When Confederate Governor Henry Allen of Louisiana was asked in mid-1864 what he thought of the citizens of his diminished state who swore to federal oaths, he replied, "If you are true to such oaths you must be false to our country, and its cause." Union oaths were not binding because taken under duress, but, he warned, the stain remained. "Join the [Confederate] Army at once, and wash out the blot in the blood of your enemies," Allen advised, and insisted that this was the same advice he would give to a son of his own. Allen's advice went largely untaken, however, as did similar counsel of Virginia's Governor Letcher. Union troops remained in possession of most of both states.[49]

Southern loyalty tests differed in detail and effectiveness from their Northern counterparts. The real difference was not merely the failure of the South's internal security apparatus to accomplish what Northern administrators realized with the system Lincoln created. The South's loyalty-testing program failed because the Confederate military effort failed.

CHAPTER X

Postwar but Less than Peace

Confederate surrender meant that for the first time since 1783, Americans had to deal with countrymen defeated in civil war. During and after the American Revolution, state authorities handled the Tory problem. In 1865, eight decades of intervening history, combined with the fundamental alterations in governmental relationships created by the Civil War, made it inevitable that the victorious national government would dominate in reconstruction.

In the light of recent history the price the South paid for its abortive experiment in rebellion seems incredibly small. No mass executions, imprisonments, or confiscations followed Appomattox. The reconstruction decade has nevertheless become the bête noire of American history. In defiance of constitutional restraints, a congressional minority seized control of the national government and established military rule over the defeated Southern states, enforcing Negro suffrage and disfranchising tens of thousands of former rebels. Loyalty tests played a prominent part in this process.

Opposite loyalty-testing policies marked the major alternative paths to reconstruction when the Confederacy collapsed. The Lincoln plan of 1863, which Johnson continued without basic modification in its surface details, was essentially conservative. The oath of future loyalty it prescribed was the prerequisite for executive pardon for rebellion, and for suffrage and office-holding. Apart from emancipation, the presidential plan envisaged no alteration in Southern society, but accepted continued white political control in the South in the interest of rapid national reunification. In nine brief months of 1865, "loyal" state governments rose phoenixlike from the ashes of defeat, wrote new state constitutions admitting the end of slavery, staffed their offices with whites sworn by the simple presidential formula, and awaited the December meeting of Congress to admit their delegations and complete the reconstruction process. Such amazing speed was possible only because the loyalty test Southerners swore ignored the rebel past. In the words of a North Carolina jurist, presidential amnesty made possible "a great public good if the past can be forgiven and forgotten." [1]

Republican leaders, jealously devoted to theories of congressional rather than executive leadership, championing more than mere freedom for the South's Negroes, needing to broaden the sectional base of their party's none too stable structure, would neither forgive nor forget. In 1864 the Wade-Davis Bill set the guideposts for radical Republican concepts of reconstruction, under which Negroes and Unionist whites would assume political power in the South. Former Confederates would face the barrier of Congress' ironclad test oath of past loyalty, designed as an oath of federal office, here expanded into a wider arena. "This oath," commented an acute observer, "both in its letter and spirit is in utter antagonism to the policy of Mr. Johnson." Opposing loyalty-testing concepts created "an irreconcilable difference . . . [which] could have been healed only by the . . . Republicans consenting to abandon the whole question of reconstruction to the discretion of Mr. Johnson." The Republicans did not consent.[2]

In early 1865 there seemed to be other choices beyond Congress' or the President's plans. A few Northerners proposed keeping national loyalty-testing and internal security policies in permanent postwar operation, north and south. "National life," according to one such proposal, "should be perpetuated . . . by the ramification of test oaths into all departments of society—mechanical, mercantile, agricultural, and professional." Although this grandiose plan found no important political champion on the postwar national stage, local Republican leaders in the border states from Maryland to Arkansas did their best to make "treason, like consumption, hereditary." Wartime loyalty laws faded quickly from most of the North, however, finding their most durable refuge in the national capital.

Extreme, too, were the relatively small number of Southerners who would not accept defeat in any form and fled into exile, or chose the bitter path to suicide which unbending old Edmund Ruffin followed. A larger number acknowledged that their cause was lost, yet considered even Lincoln's plan too harsh. Spokesmen for this view naïvely expected reunification without any conditions. A few Northern Democrats, seeking to reknit the shattered sectional lines of their party, championed a reconstruction in which only the Southerners would do the reconstructing. The fact of four years of war made such assertions absurd and delusive.[3]

If some reconstruction process was necessary, many Americans in 1865 doubted the wisdom, the utility, and the morality of making loyalty tests the measure of loyalty or anything else. Moral considerations inspired a Missouri minister, who had seen Union, Confederate, and various partisan loyalty tests crisscross his divided state, to plead unsuccessfully that none sap the morality of the postwar generation:

It does not require the wisdom of Washington to discover that official and judicial corruption as well as the loss of private, social, and public virtue, is in a great measure, the baneful result of the reckless and utter disregard of the "religious sanctions" of the thousand and one "test oaths" and "oaths of allegiance" administered during and since the war.[4]

Cynicism rather than moral considerations marked Northerners who decried loyalty tests on the grounds that they were less evil than useless. "Of all the serious jokes of this war," commented *Harper's Weekly*, "that oath of allegiance seems to be the chief." Thousands of Northern veterans agreed with the reaction of a Union provost, whose comment —"What terms can bind men who have already broken faith?"—reflected the wholesale deceits, evasions, and perjuries that Southerners practiced during the war. Hosea Biglow, a popular comic character, set the theme to dialect rhyme: "Ez fer dependin' on their oaths an' thet, 'Twun't bind 'em more'n the ribbin' roun' my het." A Northern Methodist leader felt that "it is worse than folly to talk of accepting their professions of loyalty and anti-slavery. Who believes in Southern professions?" Cynicism penetrated even into Lincoln's Cabinet, where Treasury Secretary Chase protested Union loyalty-testing policies, and War Secretary Stanton approvingly read this 1863 report from William Whiting, War Department solicitor:

Taking oaths of loyalty is not giving proof of loyalty. The obligation of an oath may or may not be binding on those who assume them. . . . [The] taking of an oath is one circumstance entitled to consideration in weighing proofs of loyalty submitted by an applicant [for presidential pardon]. . . . His previous conduct must be examined; the motives, the real intent of the applicant should be searched out; . . . if his intent is not proved to be loyalty, all oaths, professions, and appearances of loyalty are deemed as false pretences.[5]

To Try Men's Souls

Whiting's proposal for individual investigation of every Southerner's intent in swearing future loyalty to the North was far beyond the administrative capacity of the period. It was even further from the purposes of Lincoln's pragmatic plan of reconstruction, which accepted human nature for what it was. The loyalty test Lincoln prescribed was concerned neither with absolute purity nor with cynical negativism. He designed it to do precisely what this letter, written by a wounded rebel soldier awaiting discharge from a Northern prison hospital in May, 1865, proves that it accomplished:

I think it is the duty now of all good men to take the oath of allegiance to the U.S. . . . for the following reasons: in the 1st place we have no government to be loyal to, 2nd, not even a state government, 3rd, 'tis our duty to try to do the best we can for ourselves. No one I presume will be allowed to vote unless they take the oath and we should try to send good men to the legislature and convention . . . and as Senators to go to Washington. If every Southern State will send two good Senators we will with the aid of the Democratic Party (which is bound to be very strong) of the North be able to check the Republican Party in their wild schemes. Now this isn't half I might say of the benefits which may be derived from taking the oath but it is enough to satisfy any reasonable mind.[6]

Lincoln, seeking such "reasonable minds" among Southerners almost from the first days of the war, consistently followed the loyalty-testing path that he defended before Congress in 1863. "There must be a test," he insisted, ". . . so as to build only from the sound; and that test is a sufficiently liberal one which accepts as sound whoever will make a sworn recantation of his former unsoundness." Lincoln's Northern and border-state supporters denounced the cynics who rejected all Southerners' oaths as useless, as did this excited Missouri Unionist:

Contemplate for a moment the statement . . . that no rebel can possibly reform. That when he takes the most solemn oaths he cannot be believed! That all such declarations are hypocritical. . . . If it has been discovered that four or five million of the people of the United States have become so corrupt that when they offer to renew their allegiance they cannot be trusted . . . [w]hat assurances have we that the residue of our population may not . . . fall into the same category?

In 1865 the practical choices for Southerners lay not in any of the extreme suggestions but within the roads to political regeneration marked by Lincoln's or Congress' plan, by the presidential oath of future loyalty or the legislative test of past loyalty. Granted, one pamphleteer argued, that loyalty tests were no "infallible mode" of mark-

254

ing loyalty. But who, he queried rhetorically, "can at the present propound a better test?" The best minds of the nineteenth century, "with our present imperfect means of penetrating men's real purposes," offered no practical alternative. Loyalty oaths, he concluded, "must be used in the reconstruction if we are to commence . . . separating the true from the false, the loyal from the disloyal." [7]

Lincoln's death was a godsend to the radical Republicans. They celebrated Johnson's succession, confident that this stern former military governor of wartime Tennessee would share their attitudes and plans. In his first weeks as president Johnson sounded gratifyingly like a radical. But by May, 1865, he had seemingly committed himself to Lincoln's reconstruction plan. He could not as easily assume his predecessor's political abilities. Doctrinaire where Lincoln had retained a skillfully flexible pragmatism, Johnson faced a postwar situation in which the most sensitive leadership was necessary.

When Congress convened for its first regular postwar session in December, 1865, Johnson hoped to present it with a completed reconstruction. Every former rebel state would have an elected delegation on hand, pardoned by the President's proclamation and oath. Congress would satisfy itself of the validity of their credentials in a purely ministerial sense, and admit them, and the nation would be reunited politically as well as militarily.

This pretty dream failed for reasons centering on radical Republican manipulation and exploitation of the loyalty issue. In a series of colossal blunders, Johnson and the Southerners involved in his reconstruction process failed to recognize that in this postwar scene the kind of exclusive wartime leadership Lincoln had achieved was no longer possible, especially in the absence of Lincoln's mastery over men. Worse, once having committed those blunders, Johnson and his supporters stubbornly maintained their courses. Republican leaders proved themselves more adept than their opponent in the White House in sensing the mood of the North, and manipulating popular attitudes toward loyalty tests in favor of their partisan plans.

Johnson made his first error in connection with the reopening of federal civil services in the conquered South. These included postal, revenue, and judicial offices. All federal personnel were required by Congress' 1862 ironclad test-oath law to swear to their past loyalty. It was a real problem to find enough qualified white men residing in the areas where they were to function and able to swear that they had never aided the rebellion. Johnson mistook this problem for an opportunity. He intermixed the federal services in the South with the state reconstruction governments he was creating, by appointing men to those offices upon nomination of the Southern provisional governors. Presidential authority permitted these nominees to assume federal positions after illicitly modifying Congress' oath or substituting for it the executive test of future loyalty. Almost all these men were therefore illegally in office. Almost all were former rebels. That they were uniformly honest, capable, and loyal in the sense of accepting the verdict of defeat seems more than likely from the evidence. But that it would have been much wiser for Johnson to have chosen Southern Unionists rather than former rebels, qualified Negroes, and federal army veterans, seems equally certain.

Related and more important was the second presidential error. In all the former rebel states Johnson appointed provisional governors and staffs to initiate reconstruction. All were former rebels; almost all were former slaveholders and former and present Democrats. They were also technically federal civil servants, paid from War Department funds, susceptible to the ironclad oath test which few if any could take. Like the revived federal bureaucracy in the South, the state authorities formed by presidential initiative in 1865 were illegitimate when measured by the ironclad scale.

The third and most egregious error, because most capable of popular diffusion and exaggeration, resulted from the same causes as the first two. In 1864 Congress had extended the ironclad-test-oath requirement to its own members. Political wisdom prescribed that all congressmen-elect from the South be able to surmount that political hurdle by their readiness to swear to their past loyalty. In a touching tribute to the leaders of their lost cause, Southern electorates chose a group of civil and military leaders of the Confederacy to represent them in the national Congress. This delightful sentimentality played directly into radical hands.

From Republican supporters in the South, from touring journalists eager to discover evidences of lack of repentance among Southerners, from Union army officers in Dixie who found the elevation of former enemies too strong a political medicine to swallow, Republican leaders amassed plentiful evidences of executive indiscretions. Radical spokesmen stressed the theme of the inutility of an oath of future loyalty "to transmute ruffians and bullies into civilized Christians and gentlemen all at once." Republican strategists convened in secret caucuses to prepare for the climax of 1865, when the revived Southern states sent delegates to the United States Congress.

To his credit, Johnson learned from his errors. In October, 1865, he ordered a stop to the practice of appointing Southerners to federal offices if they would not swear to their past loyalty as required. All through the summer and fall of that year he pressured Southern nominating conventions to choose men for office only if they could meet the ironclad test oath's requirements. A few successes rewarded him. Some Southerners withdrew their names from election slates. But the great majority of candidates ignored Johnson's pleas. The result was enough to make a Union army staff officer on Arkansas occupation duty abandon earlier support of presidential reconstruction plans and adopt radical tenets of Republicanism. He wrote Thaddeus Stevens:

My God—Can any sane man look at the men who fill the so-called State Legislatures and then say that the [Southern] States are loyal? Who are the men they send to Congress and then ask that you give them seats? Majors, Colonels, and Generals of the rebel army from whose foul hands we have just wrested the sword of rebellion. To admit such men into the councils of the nation would disgrace every soldier who fought in the late war and I for one would curse the day I ever drew my sword in defence of such a Union.

But the loyalty-test issue could serve radical Republicans only up to the point of Congress' convening. Among the Southern delegates-elect were a few men from the border states who could legitimately swear to any test of past loyalty, and others who announced they would swear any oath required. Congress had to keep every one of the Southern delegations out if its Republican directors were to prove their contentions of legislative precedence in reconstruction matters.[8]

During the war Republican congressmen had perfected techniques of excluding unwanted members on disloyalty charges, and of countering executive acts through legislative investigating committees. When Congress met on December 4, 1865, Republican preparedness paid off. No Southern delegation had the opportunity to swear to any oath of office. Congress organized its Joint Committee on Reconstruction to inquire into each delegate's substantive qualifications, and to offer the loyalty test only to those applicants who had not merely been loyal in the past, but were politically in harmony with radical plans for the future. The Southern state governments of 1865 were left in a constitutional limbo, eventually to wither into nothingness despite Johnson's continued support. The new year of 1866 initiated a second phase of the struggle for control over reconstruction and for domination over the national government.

Congress' action in barring all Southern delegations unleashed a widespread debate concerning the constitutional power of the legislature to do what it had already done. Angry Southern spokesmen condemned the Republican tactic, and asserted that the South was the surprised victim of a revolutionary Republican plot. Victim, undoubtedly; surprised, not at all. Even in August, 1865, some Southerners were acute enough to see the handwriting on the political wall. Louisiana's J. C. Alcorn, for instance, after a discouraging conference with Johnson, wrote his wife: "I doubt very much whether any of the Southern States will be admitted to representation in the ensuing Congress." The radical-oriented *Cleveland Leader* echoed widespread Northern editorial comment when, a full month before Congress met, it candidly admitted: "We will not . . . be surprised, that when the roll of the House is called . . . it will contain the name of no rebel or representative of rebels." Johnson's warnings to the South to elect men capable of swearing their past loyalty had been heard, if disobeyed. "They become candidates knowing this fact," one of his correspondents dolefully assured him in November. From speeches, sermons, and broadsides, Southerners had a half year of warning not to play into Republican hands. Consecutive columns of advice from A. H. H. Stuart of Virginia and W. A. Graham of North Carolina to hearken to Johnson's advice were reprinted in dozens of Southern newspapers. The South may have been outraged, but it was not taken unawares.[9]

Throughout 1866 the nation's attention centered on Washington. Successive attempts at a reconciliation between Johnson and the radical leadership failed, and Northern Democrats frankly adopted him as their party's champion. Johnson helplessly vetoed Republican measures, and Congress' reconstruction committee systematically kept the Southern delegations at arm's length. Simultaneously, Johnson unsuccessfully sought to have Congress repeal the ironclad test oath, or at least to modify its absolute prohibition of employment in federal service of anyone with any taint of past disloyalty, voluntary or not, in his record. By mid-1866 Democrats were committed against continuation of the test oath, and Republicans were equally committed to its unmodified perpetuation.

Except, that is, when it was politically inconvenient. By this time Republicans had promised the excluded South that ratification of the Fourteenth Amendment was necessary for admission. Tennessee, strongly Unionist, ratified, and her Senator David T. Patterson presented his credentials for a seat in the upper house. A Republican purist pointed out that Patterson, although unquestionably ever loyal to the Union, had during the war, at the behest of Tennessee's Unionists, held an insignificant Confederate office in order to protect his loyal neighbors. Patterson admitted the charge, but insisted that he felt completely able to swear to his real past loyalty to the Union. Weeks of intra-Republican debate followed, concerning how thin the plating on the ironclad oath might be worn in favor of expediency. Ethics gave way; Patterson, admittedly perjuring himself, swore that he had never aided or held office under the rebel authority, and he became a United States senator. But only such narrow-minded literalists as Democrats generally, and the Republican editor of the theological periodical *The Right Way,* were unkind enough to highlight Republican inconsistency:

[Patterson] . . . unquestionably committed an act of perjury and the United States Senate tolerated the act in their presence. He took a solemn oath before Almighty God which he knew and they knew to be false; . . . a form of words understood to have no force, as a pleasant piece of irony, as a good jest, and all this with the mockery of a solemn appeal to the "God of Truth!" The whole country should awake to this new danger and should cry out in alarmed and indignant protest.[10]

The unpleasant Patterson business buried, Republicans closed ranks in defense of the ironclad oath. In the November, 1866, congressional elections, Republicans made the oath issue part of the first "bloody-shirt" campaign, equating votes for Democrats with a cataclysmic repeal of the test-oath law. Rewarded by a majority in both houses of Congress, Republicans began, early in 1867, to create the reconstruction program they had demanded three years earlier in the Wade-Davis Bill. Then a discordant note from an almost forgotten quarter interrupted their jubilations. The Supreme Court had something to say about loyalty tests.

Courts, constitutions, and bills of rights, whether federal or state, Northern or Southern, had utterly failed to protect American civil liberties during the war years. There were few protests from the bench as legislators and executive officials exercised unrestraind authority. Taney's vigorous denunciation of martial law in 1861 went unheeded. The 1863 decision of Minnesota's supreme court, voiding that state's loyalty-test law which made mere silence on the part of one challenged for disloyalty proof of the accusation, went unpublicized even in Minnesota. More in harmony with the times was the California decision, the same year, upholding the similar loyalty law there as a necessary and desirable war weapon. In areas closer to the fighting fronts than Minnesota and California, no one challenged loyalty tests in court actions until after the war ended.[11]

Missouri was the first postwar arena. By 1865 the state's rigged constitution was a frank political weapon of the Missouri radical Republican organization. An oath test, part of that constitution, required every official, licensed professional or tradesman, and voter to swear innocence of eighty-six past acts, each equaling disloyalty. The Missouri Supreme Court sustained the validity of the state test law as a valid exercise of state authority beyond the power of courts to negate.

West Virginia, born of violence and division, had made the federal ironclad test oath its model for the same purposes as those behind Missouri's test law. Republican rulers of the infant state were outraged when West Virginia's appeal court declared the state test oath unconstitutional as a violation of civil liberties guaranteed by the national and state constitutions. In quick reaction to such judicial temerity, the West Virginia legislature repassed the condemned statute, and the cowed judges acquiesced in admitted helplessness. The box score for 1865 clearly supported the continuation of loyalty laws.

But federal lower courts in the South changed the picture. Federal judges had found great difficulty in resuming operations in former rebel areas because few attorneys were able or willing to swear the ironclad oath, which Congress early in 1865 had extended to court personnel. In three instances, attorneys applying to practice in federal lower courts insisted that the presidential pardon they possessed exempted them from Congress' past-loyalty requirement. They claimed in addition that the oath was attaintive in purpose and ex post facto in effect. Three federal judges agreed, and held the ironclad test oath in their jurisdictions inapplicable and unconstitutional.[12]

Similar issues pended before the United States Supreme Court. Hoping to escape the necessity for commitment on these delicate questions, the judges delayed the cases involving them as long as they could, but by the end of 1866 delay was no longer possible. One case involved a civilian arrested, tried, and condemned for disloyalty during the war by an army court in an area where civil courts were functioning. A second case concerned a Roman Catholic priest-teacher of Missouri who refused to swear the state test oath and who suffered arrest, fines, and imprisonment as a result, although no one suggested that he had ever been disloyal. The best legal talent Democrats could muster took his case through Missouri's courts, which upheld the oath as a valid exercise of state police power, and thence to the national Supreme Court. The third case involved a former rebel general and congressman, A. H. Garland of Arkansas, who petitioned to return to his prewar practice before the Supreme Court without having to swear the ironclad oath. Garland held that his presidential pardon took precedence over the ironclad oath and that the congressional test law was invalid in any event. Taken together, the three cases involved every aspect of the critical political struggle then gathering momentum between Johnson and the radical Republicans dominating Congress.

In three momentous decisions (of which two, in the Garland and Cummings cases, were five to four), the Supreme Court held that civilians in peaceful areas were not amenable to the jurisdiction of martial law, and that the federal ironclad oath for attorneys and the Missouri state oath for teachers were unconstitutional because they violated the constitutional prohibitions against bills of attainder and ex post facto laws. Equally vigorously, the minority of judges in each case upheld the respective government's contentions and oath regulations as proper exercises of popular sovereignty with which no court in a democratic society could tamper, and which no presidential pardon could supersede. Internal security, the dissenters insisted, took precedence over civil liberty even if loyalty tests admittedly injured men of unimpeachable loyalty.

What seemed like a clear victory for the Lincoln-Johnson view of the primacy of the presidential pardoning power and the undesirability of tests of past loyalty proved ephemeral. Republican congressional attacks on the Supreme Court, involving threats to impeach the majority jurists and even to abolish the court itself, succeeded in frightening the court out of the civil liberties arena. Congress proceeded with its plans for reconstructing the South. As finally perfected, those plans would impose martial law over civilians in the entire South and would apply the ironclad test oath to millions of Southerners. The court had spoken for the first time in its history in defense of civil liberty. Its words could not check a determined Congress.[13]

Events proved that the power to determine the qualifications of congressmen, combined with subjective interpretations of loyalty-test requirements, gave a determined majority in Congress control over the court and the executive, and, finally, over the states themselves. Civil war made loyalty a Republican property. Opponents of loyalty tests were, in the Republican lexicon, disloyal. The political utility of this equation became obvious as early as 1864, when, after spirited Democratic opposition, Republicans applied the ironclad-test-oath law to congressmen. They received an unexpected political bonus when Delaware's Democratic Senator James Bayard resigned rather than sign the oath. No one offered evidence of Bayard's disloyalty. Republicans, however, successfully associated Bayard's principled stubbornness with implicit disloyalty. Indeed, one patriot lodged a disloyalty complaint against Bayard with Northern army provosts, who set out to arrest the Delawarean, but Lincoln interceded to halt arrest proceedings.[14]

The Bayard episode clearly suggested that the test oath for congressmen was an invaluable Republican adjunct if, and it was a large qualification, all Democrats possessed Bayard's high morality, and were willing to exclude themselves from Congress by nonjuring. There were, unfortunately, Democrats of easier conscience. Maryland's Senator Reverdy Johnson, for example, openly advocated subscription to any loyalty test in order to sustain Democratic opposition to all Republican programs.

If Democrats interpreted the test-oath guardian subjectively, then Republicans would offer it as subjectively. In 1865 they stood the Southern congressmen-elect off at arm's length, refusing to let the eager applicants for admission into Congress decide on individual ability to swear past loyalty. The test oath was the Republcian key to Congress, and the Joint Reconstruction Committee turned it at its partisan pleasure. Republican congressional leaders permitted Tennessee's Patterson to take the oath in 1866, patently perjuring himself, because Tennessee had to have a senator if Republicans were to realize their objectives.

Early the following year radical strategists, who consistently denied Johnson his frequent requests for modification of the past-loyalty parts of the test-oath law so far as federal employees were concerned, showed that they could manipulate the oath requirement in their favor whether they modified it or kept it sacrosanct as a congressional test. Maryland Senator-elect Phillip Thomas was ready to swear the oath when Republican charges of past disloyalty automatically referred his case to their elections committee. As a loyal Northern state, Maryland was not under reconstruction rule. The Thomas situation was too bare an evidence of congressional power for Republicans to relish, especially since the Marylander's chief offense had been to subsidize his adolescent son's wartime flight to join the Confederacy. Thomas insisted that he was ready to swear the oath, then face a perjury proceeding. Senators debated his case for a full year. Finally the Republican majority overbore other, less flexible Republicans, and decided that Thomas was loyal enough to swear loyalty.[15]

In the heyday of their congressional control, Republicans impeached the President (in part for his violations of the test-oath law in 1865–1866), overawed the courts, and ruled the former rebel states in the hope of realizing the social, economic, and political goals of their party. The test oath kept Southern delegates out of Congress until Southern states accepted increasing Republican conditions. Congressional committees functioned as loyalty review boards in dozens of disputed-elections cases arising from the corrupt turbulence of local Southern politics. Democrats delighted as aspiring contenders for Republican seats in Congress from the South accused each other of disloyalty and consequent inability to swear the oath. In some instances Democrats joined in the game. They accused Republican congressmen-elect from the South of disloyalty in order to delay their admission and to highlight the patent inconsistency of Republican professions and practices.

As long as Johnson held office, Republicans blamed all reconstruction problems on him, a process that Robert Ingersoll shrewdly saw must stop when Grant became president:

We can't run the machine [any longer] merely by making faces at Andy Johnson. . . . The people said why in hell . . . don't we have peace in the South—Andy Johnson—Why are not some of the traitors hung?—Andy Johnson— . . . What the devil makes the roads so muddy—measles so bad—whooping cough so prevalent—Why G——d d——n it, Andy Johnson. We can sing this song only until tomorrow.[16]

Tomorrow came, and under a Republican president reconstruction was no less troublesome than under Johnson. Radical state machines in the South, although supported by federal troops and reinforced by cadres of scallawags and carpetbaggers, had as much trouble staffing government offices with men able to swear past loyalty as ever Johnson had known.

Republican strategy based itself on the Fourteenth Amendment, which empowered Congress rather than the President to pardon specified classes of past rebels. Southern radicals, however, persisted in electing men to Congress who were disqualified not only by the Fourteenth Amendment's disfranchising clauses but by the far wider bar of the ironclad-oath requirement. Radical leaders needed these men in Congress. The resulting conundrum inspired doubtful virtue from ethical inconsistency. In mid-1868, radical congressional leaders secured Democratic support and overcame inconveniently consistent Republican opposition in order to modify the sacrosanct ironclad-oath requirement for national legislators. Congressmen-elect whom Congress pardoned under the Fourteenth Amendment could henceforth swear merely to their future rather than to their past loyalty to the Union.

Unfortunately for Republican happiness, most Southerners, even good Republican supporters, were disfranchised by the ironclad oath's blanket provisions rather than by the Fourteenth Amendment's highly selective disabilities. Three years of continual problems after 1868 convinced Republican congressional leaders that adjustment to this unpleasant fact of life was necessary. In February, 1871, Congress again modified the ironclad-oath requirement, permitting all former rebels to use the 1868 formula of future loyalty. This was a bit too blatantly cynical even for Grant to stomach. He vetoed the 1871 bill, stating that he would have signed a repeal of the whole ironclad-oath law without protest, but that the measure at hand discriminated against loyal Northerners, merely relieving "from taking a prescribed oath, all of those persons whom it was intended to exclude from such offices, and to require it from all others." Fuming at Grant's obtuseness, Republicans and Democrats passed it over his veto.[17]

After 1871 the ironclad oath as a partisan exclusion tool was a dead letter. Only Northerners whom no one accused of past disloyalty swore to it; Southerners swore a future-loyalty oath which Lincoln and Johnson would have approved, but which radical Republicans had condemned all during the war and for five years after hostilities ended. The test oath remained a mere anachronism suitable for Republican "bloody-shirt" ammunition in every election campaign, but bearing no relationship to wartime loyalty facts or postwar legislative needs. Democrats made the repeal of all surviving loyalty tests an article of party faith to prove to the South that the Democratic party deserved Southern support. Republicans, gradually losing and acknowledging the loss of the Southern states from their roster of reliable political adjuncts, defended loyalty-testing remnants with renewed vigor.

One such persistent remnant was a past-loyalty oath test, dating from 1862, which faced all federal jurors. In April, 1871, Democrats succeeded in repealing it as the price of coöperation with Republican efforts to modify the ironclad oath. Three years later, completely inexplicably, the defunct jurors' oath law reappeared in a revised codification of federal statutes. Five years of confusion resulted. Federal courts in the South were hamstrung by a series of contests alleging incapacity and perjury of jurors, resulting from indecision concerning the vitality of the resurrected oath law. Not until 1878 did the Supreme Court decide that the legal ghoul was alive.

Radical reconstruction ended, but the remnants of loyalty tests survived. Democrats, led by New York's Congressman Samuel "Sunset" Cox, made a crusade of repealing them, and although lawmaking processes sometimes completely halted in filibusters and parliamentary chicanery, the tactics finally succeeded. In May, 1884, President Arthur signed the law repealing the ironclad and jurors' test-oath statutes. In their demise the nation took a long step forward on the road to reunion. In their lifetimes the loyalty-testing laws reflected little credit upon their defenders or their attackers, nor, history indicates, did they have very much to do with loyalty.[18]

At the height of the postwar loyalty-test controversy, Congress, in 1871, created the Southern Claims Commission to compensate loyal citizens of the South for private property used by Union armed forces during the war. Remarkably, the legislators specified no loyalty test to determine the fitness of applicants for compensation. The able, cautious commissioners had a free hand in the loyalty-testing arena within the confines of Congress' generalized dictate that "the party claiming to be loyal must prove his loyalty."

Five years and thousands of loyalty investigations later, the commission reported to Congress that "we have not had occasion to lay down any general tests of loyalty." Painstaking, lengthy, objective inquiries into the realities of life in the locality of each applicant replaced loyalty tests in the commission's procedures. "The cases vary so greatly," the commissioners advised Congress, "that it is difficult to lay down any general and absolute rules." In a remarkable appreciation of the complexities of human relationships involved in the turmoil of civil war, the commission offered this summary of its criteria of operation:

We find, by experience, that to form a correct opinion as to whether a claimant was or was not loyal during the war, . . . [w]e must . . . look to his surroundings, to the vicinity where he lived, the pressures that bore upon him, the opportunity he had to show his loyalty by aiding the Union cause; his acts and omissions to act; whether he was threatened, molested, or injured, in person, family, or property; whether he rendered any aid to the Confederate cause; . . . in short, to all the circumstances of the case.[19]

The American Revolution and the American Civil War both impelled the creation of postwar commissions to reward wartime loyalty.

In 1783 as in 1871, administrative commissions assumed this task for their respective governments, and history records the similarity of their conclusions and procedures. The obvious qualification exists that such deliberate, calm, scholarly inquiries as the royal commission to compensate loyalists and the Southern Claims Commission conducted were impossible as procedural techniques during the crisis of war.

This qualification does not, however, alter the conclusion that the loyalty tests of the Civil War and Reconstruction failed to perform their nominal function—that of identifying and measuring loyalty. They became partisan weapons of great power and of such widespread application that a member of Lincoln's Cabinet, Edward Bates, defined loyalty as "adhesion to *my* clique." They became, too, so patently useless as indexes to actual allegiance that eight years after Lee surrendered Congressman Garrett Davis of Kentucky proposed that the United states offer "a reward for the discovery of an invention which would provide a proper way of determining loyalty." And, perhaps worst of all, Civil War loyalty tests debased the notion of patriotism and the very concept of loyalty, so that the popular humorist Petroleum V. Nasby could treat loyalty oaths in this manner:

Twict durin' the fratrisidle struggle which drencht this happy land in goar, I wuz drafted into a service I detested . . . and the eggins—the ridin' upon rails—the takin' uv the oath—but why should I harrow up the public buzzum? I stood it all till one night I wuz pulled out uv bed . . . and by a crowd uv laffin' soljers compelled to take the oath and drink a pint uv raw, undilootid water! That feather broke the back uv the camel. The oath gave me inflamashen uv the brane and the water inflamashen uv the stumick, and for six long weeks I lay, a wreck uv my former self.[20]

The Civil War had seen a much greater extension of the national government's power in pursuit of loyalty than had been true during the American Revolution. Loyalty tests were gradually percolating upward in administrative inspiration from the localism of the Revolutionary committees to the relative centralism of the Civil War. In the next crisis of American loyalty—World War I—this trend toward national control of loyalty-testing continued at an accelerated pace.

CHAPTER XI

Amateur Spycatchers of World War I*

"I agree that the nation has a duty to protect itself," Upton Sinclair wrote President Wilson late in 1917. Less agreeably, the novelist complained that Wilson's subordinates "in . . . drawing the line [between liberty and security] have come much too close to the methods of Autocracy." Almost all commentators, no matter how critically they have viewed home-front repressions of the World War I period, have suggested no more than an accidental coincidence between popular excesses and national policy. Instances of brutal vigilantism derived, in such analyses, not from the intent of legislators but from the intensity of public zeal. The editorialist Francis Hackett, for example, concluded that "with impetuous patriots demanding a new pass-word of allegiance every minute, the wonder is not at how many outrages there are, but how few." Historian William A. Dunning expressed much the same view when he compared the civil liberties story of World War I with that of the Civil War. Dunning praised Wilson for the relative restraint of his internal security procedures and for the procedural regularity of his methods, as compared to Lincoln. In World War I, Dunning insisted, the United States government had no connection with mob outrages or deliberate antiradicalism.[1]

Some evidence supports these contentions. Loyalty-oath tests were conspicuously absent from national security programs in World War I, reflecting Newton D. Baker's disinterest in such indexes to loyalty: "It may be," Baker replied to a suggestion for a national loyalty test, "that the formulation and repetition of some particular pledge [of loyalty] will be of fundamental help, but I am not quite sure." There, for Wil-

* The contents of this chapter were given in part as a paper at the 1956 meeting of the American Historical Association, St. Louis.

son's administration, the matter dropped, although similar suggestions received the warmest reception in state governments across the nation.[2]

Like Lincoln, Wilson insisted on executive leadership of the war effort against the demands of Congress for control. Oregon's Senator Chamberlain, for example, would have made the entire nation a war zone under martial law. Wilson's objections resulted in the relatively milder Espionage Act of June, 1917, which provided for twenty-year jail terms and fines up to $10,000 for anyone interfering with troop enlistments or industrial production. But the Espionage Act, Wilson learned, failed to touch individual oral or written antiwar sentiments. Ardent patriots concluded that the continued presence of critical street-corner speakers proved that the Wilson administration coddled pacifists, and insisted that the mobs that lynched and beat such orators would continue their vigilantism unless the government took a sterner course. Under these pressures Wilson approved a draft sedition bill prepared by Justice Department officials, which Congress enacted into law in May, 1918. Taken together, the Espionage Act and its 1918 amendment, known popularly as the Sedition Act, provided more latitude to federal suppression of dissent than America had known in its history. As the Detroit federal attorney exulted, until these were on the statute books "we were unable in many instances to prosecute pro-Germans. Since then we have given them the cold steel." Upon these statutory lances more than 6,000 Americans impaled themselves for a multitude of offenses which wartime attitudes made synonymous with disloyalty.[3] Censorship, conscription, mass imprisonment of enemy aliens, and the complex of commodity-rationing followed the same pattern of executive inspiration, legislative acquiescence, and, again, enforcement by a burgeoning federal bureaucracy.

Wilson, like Lincoln, faced the problem of possible disloyalists among the personnel of that bureaucracy. Unlike his predecessor in the White House, Wilson followed an administratively consistent course in harmony with Congress in this matter, while keeping executive leadership unimpaired. Four days after the war declaration, Congress voted Wilson authority to set loyalty standards for all civil servants. In a confidential order anticipating Congress' permission, Wilson had instructed the Civil Service Commission to

. . . remove any employee when . . . the retention of such employee would be inimical to the public welfare by reasons of his conduct, sympathies, or utterances, or because of other reasons growing out of the war. Such removal may be made without other formality than that the reasons shall be made a matter of confidential record, subject, however, to inspection by the Civil Service Commission.

The Civil Service Commission assumed the power to refuse all applications for employment "if there was a reasonable belief that . . . [this] appointment was inimical to the public interest owing to . . . lack of loyalty." Its agents conducted 135 loyalty investigations in 1917, and 2,537 more in 1918. In the latter year 660 applicants were debarred from federal employment for questionable loyalty, a tiny percentage of the total of federal workers. But there were many agencies not under commission control, and thousands of loyalty investigations were conducted by other internal security agencies. Despairing of slow civil service recruiting practices, federal departments employed tens of thousands of workers outside civil service procedures, with the result that the established loyalty regulations were only partially effective in their coverage.[4]

What was done, however, received remarkably little publicity. Throughout the war, Wilson's critics insisted that the executive offices were a refuge for pro-German pacifists and, later, for pro-Bolshevik radicals. George Creel of the Committee on Public Information was a popular target for antiadministration congressional sniping. "Jumping on George" was a favorite sport of Republican legislators, according to the historian of Creel's department, and charges of disloyalty formed the bases for similar attacks on many of Wilson's appointees, including the President's private secretary. Self-appointed saviors of the nation's patriotism like Theodore Roosevelt and Cleveland Moffett of the American Defense Society never stopped their attacks on the loyalty of the wartime civil officials. Wilson ignored them as best he could, fending off an incipient congressional investigation of the loyalty of government employees, and the whole matter remained an inconspicuous item in the exciting events of wartime America.[5]

Less inconspicuous was the matter of the loyalty of military and naval personnel. Popular fears insisted that Americans of German ancestry were untrustworthy and that German spies infested the armed forces. The Army War College suggested that every soldier face a loyalty probe before embarking for France, but War Secretary Baker vetoed this "time-wasting and conspicuous formula" and replaced it with an order empowering all company commanders to arrest any officer or soldier for suspected disloyalty. When suspicion was too slight to justify arrest, Military Intelligence placed the suspected man under surveillance. Theoretically, men of German ancestry were not suspected merely on the basis of their Teutonic cognomens. "It is unlikely," Baker stated, "that, in the choice of spies . . . the German secret service would choose men of German names, since these would naturally be open to suspicion." But the Senate made a field day of Colonel Carl Reichman's confirmation in rank, and incidentally ruined the career of a professional soldier of outstanding record.

Only a few soldiers and sailors faced courts-martial for disloyal utterances. Like the matter of the loyalty of civil servants, the processes established to determine the fidelity of military and naval personnel received almost no publicity. Indeed, the fact that every single commission granted to an officer in World War I was prefaced by an inquiry into that individual's loyalty, remained entirely outside the public consciousness. Few of the subjects of loyalty probes were ever aware that they had been investigated. The same was true of the thousands of Red Cross workers, religious and entertainment personnel, and other volunteer civilians who went overseas.

World War I loyalty-testing processes for military personnel, though benefiting from the discreet lack of publicity which embraced them, caused suffering among the small number of individuals who failed to meet whatever loyalty standards superior officers held. Unless an accused officer secured a court-martial review of his case, he had no effective appeal. An anonymous accusation of disloyalty removed a captain's name from the roll of medical officers due to sail to France. He had abandoned a rich private practice to join a special neurosurgical unit of the army. Denied the opportunity to do his specialized work, he served out the war as a home-front personnel assignment officer, angrily demanding, but never securing, an investigation into the disloyalty charges against him. Although popular imaginings inspired wild tales of hundreds of soldiers and sailors shot for disloyalty, lengthy terms in federal prisons—some of twenty-five or thirty years— were the most severe penalties imposed by courts-martial. Disloyalty in the armed forces and civil services was never a great problem in World War I. Only wartime hysteria and political partisanship made it appear so.[6]

Thus, on the surface, the Wilson administration seems worthy of exemption from connection with the monstrous interferences with American's civil liberties which popular hatred of *Kultur* engendered. The plethora of superpatriotic private organizations were critics rather than colleagues of the wartime President. State councils of defense and committees of public safety which used emergency powers to crush unpopular groups like the Non-Partisan League and the IWW, and to harass in the meanest fashion hyphenated Americans for no cause other than their nativity, operated as they did through no desire of President, Cabinet, or Congress.

But below the surface America's home-front history in World War I requires a different verdict for the Wilson administration, which created two loyalty-testing organizations which operated secretly and extralegally. These two unique creations—the American Protective League and the Loyal Legion of Loggers and Lumbermen—wove an antidisloyalty web across America and brought terror to the lives of thousands of innocent, loyal persons.

In the tense weeks preceding American entrance into World War I, worried federal and state officials shared a widespread, uncritical fear of the seemingly omnipotent German spy machine. The Kaiser's secret agents would surely recruit among the German- and Austro-Hungarian–Americans, and infest the United States with wholesale Black Tom tragedies. The nation was fearfully unprepared. Since 1916, Wilson's commitment to neutrality had kept American counterspy services at a minimum. A cabinet survey in February, 1917, revealed depressing weakness. Army Intelligence consisted of two officers; so far as counterespionage was concerned, Naval Intelligence did not exist at all. Investigative staffs of the Justice, Post Office, and Treasury departments were already overburdened with peacetime civil duties. In the face of such weakness, cabinet officers quietly prepared for the feared consequences of a war declaration. War Secretary Baker posted thin lines of regulars at strategic termini and near immigrant population and industrial centers. Attorney General Thomas W. Gregory ordered federal attorneys across the nation to maintain "constant vigilance" and requested municipal police chiefs to keep known pacifists and German sympathizers under observation. April brought war—and nothing happened.

The war initiated a tremendous physical expansion in all government agencies, including those charged with internal security. From two officers in early 1917, Military Intelligence expanded to more than 300 uniformed officers and 1,000 civilian employees by the time the Armistice was signed, and other agencies increased by even greater ratios.[7] In the first months of the war, however, before expansion could get well under way, Gregory asked every loyal American to act as "a volunteer detective." District attorneys, he ordered, were to welcome complaints "of even the most informal and confidential nature," so that "citizens should feel free to bring their suspicions and information to the . . . Department of Justice." Obediently, federal attorneys placed newspaper advertisements to run for the duration, in the spirit of this Boston item: "Your patriotic duty: To report disloyal acts, seditious utterances, and any information relative to attempts to hinder the United States . . . to the U.S. Department of Justice."

Results were staggering. In May, 1917, Gregory reported receipt of a thousand accusations of disloyalty a day; a year later, the flood had increased to fifteen hundred. Most of them, Gregory admitted, were from what he called "hysterical women and . . . men, some doubtless actuated by malice and ill-will, and the vast majority utterly worthless." Gregory's assistant, John Lord O'Brian, confessed his astonishment at this response and at the willingness of Americans to "become arms of the Secret Service and to devote their entire time to the patriotic purpose of pursuing spies." The Attorney General also insisted that all this accusatory information would remain confidential and in the custody of his department. It did not.[8]

The same impulsion toward patriotic oversight of others' activities which choked Gregory's mail had already, before the United States entered the war, created the American Protective League, a private volunteer organization with the unique sanction of the Department of Justice.

Late in 1916, Albert M. Briggs, owner of a Chicago advertising agency, learned that the federal attorney there had to chase criminals in streetcars while lawbreakers enjoyed fleeter automobiles. Briggs arranged with wealthy friends to make automobiles available to Justice Department agents on voluntary loan. Soon after the new year of 1917, Briggs proposed to Attorney General Gregory and the Bureau of Investigation head, A. Bruce Bielaski, that he form a nationwide extension of the Chicago group—a volunteer, amateur adjunct to the Justice Department. Gregory, knowing the paucity of federal strength, fearing a rash of sabotage, agreed after securing presidential and cabinet approval.

Briggs and two wealthy, patriotic, able men, Victor Elting and Charles D. Frey, abandoned private activities, moved to Washington, and, in March, quietly opened American Protective League headquarters. From private funds, replenished by contributions solicited from trusted friends, they circularized hundreds of acquaintances and references across the nation, inviting them to prepare for patriotic service to the Justice Department. Gregory, meanwhile, ordered federal attorneys everywhere to coöperate with local league units as they formed and to recruit new ones.

In an America still at uneasy peace, not even the magic APL letterhead—"Organized with the Approval and Operating under the Direction of the United States Department of Justice, Bureau of Investigation"—evoked many recruits. The league leaders grew discouraged. Bielaski, assigned as league overseer, rallied them:

The future [he wrote Briggs] undoubtedly holds a large amount of work . . . and we are relying upon the League to help do it when the occasion comes. I appreciate the fact that in some cities there is now very little for your organization to do, but it will be a source of comfort and assistance to us, if it will . . . maintain its organization in order that we [can] make use of it when the time comes.[9]

The time came. When the United States went to war, popular interest in league work spread rapidly and the APL national headquarters blossomed into a busy center of a nationwide network of amateur counterspies. Every league member boasted a code number, identification card, badge, and confidential manual, and swore an oath of loyalty and secrecy. Members who were classed as "inactive" followed their normal routine and merely reported on the words and deeds of their friends and associates. Active leaguers, in addition, handled case investigations assigned to them. Every agent paid his own expenses; none was salaried.

APL organizing activities proceeded with great speed and amazing secrecy, in view of the method of recruiting and the numbers of individuals involved, during the first war months. Not until September, 1917, did minuscule newspaper notices acknowledge publicly the existence of the league; Justice Department requests to publishers for coöperation in retaining APL anonymity achieved results. In midsummer, 1917, the league numbered 90,000 members organized in 600 locals. By war's end 350,000 APL agents staffed 1,400 local units across the country. By January, 1918, every federal attorney had an APL local at his disposal. From a free taxi service in Chicago, the APL developed swiftly into a nationwide apparatus. As it developed in size, it also perfected its internal organization.[10]

Heading the APL were its three founders. Briggs's contributions were largely the initiation of the small-scale Chicago idea and its extension to Washington. His bumptious energy found no comfortable niche as the league expanded, but he remained active in its leadership. Elting, the suave, intensely patriotic, sophisticated friend of high administration officials, was the "front-office man." Quiet, efficient, tireless Frey dealt with the daily routine of the league headquarters. This tripartite national directorate met daily with Bielaski and John Lord O'Brian at the nearby Justice Department building to receive orders and submit reports.

League headquarters supplied all locals with circular instructions, manuals of operation, assignments to investigations, and the weekly APL publication, the *Spy Glass*. This journal provided "pep talks," general instructions, and suggestions concerning methods of operation. One issue, for example, dealt with loyalty investigations. The *Spy Glass* editorialist suggested that APL agents pose as automobile salesmen, credit investigators, or newspapermen in order to get information. Agents must establish the loyalty of witnesses as well as of the subject of the inquiry, the *Spy Glass* warned, and all seeming trivia must be noted and included in the resulting dossier, which should then go to the local Justice Department office.

APL national headquarters appointed a director for each state as administrative intermediary between Washington and the state's locals. By September, 1917, existing state directors agreed that standards for admission to the APL were too low. "Stringent rules should be made at once," they petitioned Washington headquarters. "They [APL agents] have access to all Department of Justice work." Soon after, each loyalty tester of the APL underwent loyalty clearances before assuming his duties. APL agents from a different area investigated the potential investigator. Such cross-checking produced little internal friction, for each APL local lived in administrative isolation from its fellows. Communication, at least according to the neat chart of organization gracing the wall of Washington headquarters, existed only through state directors.

In his role of inspector of APL internal matters, the state director was supposed to be the basic disciplinarian of the league. He could, theoretically, suspend locals from affiliation and individuals from membership. But the league's very intimacy with Justice Department work, the financial autonomy of its members, and the volunteer nature of the whole apparatus made such penalties illusory. Neither state nor national APL directors possessed effective coercive power over APL locals or members. In practice, state and national league officials became office managers rather than supervisors.[11]

Success or failure for the APL as a whole, then, depended largely upon the quality of the chief of an APL local and its membership. Many chiefs nominated themselves, as did a *New York Tribune* employee resident in Connecticut and a North Carolina textile-mill owner who knew "that labor troubles have their inception in the activities of agents of the Kaiser." With great acuity the league directors searched among the upper social, economic, and political crust of each community for local chiefs and members. Bankers, businessmen, mayors, police chiefs, postmasters, ministers, attorneys, newspaper editors, officers of religious, charitable, fraternal, and patriotic societies, factory owners and foremen, YMCA workers and chamber of commerce leaders, insurance company executives, and teachers were favored sources of league personnel. Such men possessed means and leisure to devote to APL work, and opened their professional, business, and official records for APL use. Many were also members of draft boards, war-bond sale committees, food- and fuel-rationing units, and state defense councils, affording the league illicit access to information denied even to commissioned government investigators.

Consider the position of the head of the Metropolitan Trust Company of New York, who in August, 1917, was invited to form an APL local in his company. He asked President Wilson to certify to the respectability of the league, which Wilson did. Soon hundreds of Metropolitan agents, visiting thousands of homes and businesses in their daily rounds, were simultaneously conducting league inquiries. A Texas insurance company was similarly welcomed into league work; Gregory rejoiced at "the facilities naturally afforded by your corps of inspectors located throughout Texas, and in certain adjoining states." [12]

The resulting social, economic, and, often, political homogeneity of APL membership, combined with the essential uncontrollability of league locals, resulted in tragic miscarriages of the lofty initial purpose of the amateur sypcatchers. For the American Protective League came into being to help federal agents catch German spies, and there were no spies for them to pursue. By the end of 1917 this was perfectly clear in Washington. Gregory decided, fatefully, to keep the APL in existence, but to direct its vast, growing staff and energies toward necessary if more humdrum wartime tasks. He ordered the APL to coöperate with the multitude of special federal and state war agencies dealing in matters as varied as food-rationing and vice control, and offered APL services to the army, the navy, and the Civil Service Commission to investigate the loyalty of the personnel in those departments. Gregory monopolized the more professionally taxing work of collecting evidence for regular Justice Department agents for prosecutions under the Espionage and Sedition acts.

Lacking demanding tasks, APL members in many communities,

especially in smaller centers isolated from direct Department of Justice or league supervision, assumed the role of guardians of their neighbors' consciences. Enjoying the magic of their connection with the government and the power of their impressive badges, lacking official accountability, mixing their private attitudes with league work, APL men fell prey to their prejudices and subjective standards of patriotism. League members, for example, simply refused to obey repeated orders to keep hands off Espionage and Sedition acts investigations. Gregory circularized the APL and the Justice Department in May, 1918, with this injunction:

[The acts] . . . should not be permitted to become a medium whereby efforts are made to suppress honest, legitimate criticism . . . or discussion . . . nor . . . for personal feuds or persecution. . . . Protection of loyal persons from unjust suspicion and prosecution is quite as important as the suppression of actual disloyalty. . . . [C]are should be exercised to avoid unjustified arrests and prosecutions.

More informally, Gregory wrote to an old friend, who combined teaching duties at the University of Texas with the chieftainship of an APL unit. The leaguer had complained to Gregory that regular Justice Department agents had monopolized all investigations involving possible German espionage, and demanded a continuing share in this work. According to the Attorney General of the United States,

There is quite a good deal of hysteria in the country about German spies. If you will kindly box up and send me from one to a dozen I will pay you very handsomely for your trouble. We are looking for them constantly, but it is a little difficult to shoot them until they have been found. . . . Keep your shirt on.[13]

Some APL units heeded Gregory's orders and performed a multitude of useful subsidiary services for the war effort. They patrolled industrial plants, bridges, and tunnels, and checked claims for draft exemptions and the veracity of ration books. APL men assisted war-bond salesmen and army provosts suppressing vice and liquor centers near military camps. And the third of a million APL agents became the primary loyalty investigators for the civil and military services, and for the dozens of private welfare groups connected with the war effort.

When the war started no adequate mechanism existed for security clearances. The APL, with Gregory's permission, assumed this task. APL instruction manuals and special issues of the *Spy Glass* offered neophyte APL investigators advice on how to make character investigations. One such article suggested that the final success or failure of

American arms would depend upon the quality of officer leadership. Every applicant for a military commission, every civil servant with more than clerical responsibilities, all welfare group officials who were to do overseas work, rated loyalty investigations. The APL newspaper warned leaguers that a loyalty inquiry implied no guilt, and that unjustified innuendoes of disloyalty might ruin a career and a life. A confidential APL manual warned that "no two cases are exactly alike for the reason that no two men are exactly alike." The pamphlet advised all APL loyalty testers to examine a substantial cross section of the subject's ancestors in enemy countries, his social, political, and church affiliations, his attitude toward the *Lusitania* sinking and the rape of Belgium, what he had said about war bonds, draft dodgers, and the Espionage Act. Had he purchased enough bonds, dug victory gardens, and appeared at patriotic rallies? Did neighbors recall untoward statements he might have made, did he own stock in enemy-held corporations, was his labor union respectable? But caution was the watchword in loyalty-hunting, and the manual pleaded for objectivity and fullness in reporting. Officials would normally put full cre dence in the decision of the loyalty investigator; APL reports received almost complete acceptance in Washington. Thus the APL agent became the judge, the jury, and sometimes the executioner in the lives of many who knew nothing of his existence.[14]

Some APL locals did a professionally respectable job in loyalty investigations. The New York City office, which handled 5,046 loyalty clearances during the first seven months of the war, figured that each case required four interviews, two hundred miles of traveling, and three weeks' time. Other league locals, especially those in small towns, were far less thorough, and immeasurably less prompt. Irate complaints from the army, the navy, the Civil Service Commission, the YMCA, the Red Cross, the Jewish Welfare Board, the Knights of Columbus, and the Over There Theatre League, all of whose personnel required loyalty clearances, reached high levels. Army commanders complained because needed replacement officers did not reach France. The Red Cross suffered a vacuum in its Paris office because of dilatory APL work. The civil service lost scarce personnel to private industry on account of bungled APL investigations.

The result was that Gregory and Military Intelligence rechecked APL loyalty reports. They learned that most league personnel were neither thorough, objective, nor reliable. APL amateurs were often too credulous in accepting unsupported allegations of disloyalty. Others equated labor-union connections, minority ethnic descent, or racial factors with lack of allegiance. In one instance leaguers made the Democratic affiliation of an applicant for an army commission reason enough for an adverse conclusion concerning loyalty. This applicant learned through his own resources of the APL verdict, went directly to the Secretary of War, and was cleared by a second inquiry conducted by the professionals of Military Intelligence.

Most APL loyalty investigation troubles, however, were caused more by sloppiness than by sinister motives. Sometimes successive APL agents from different locals conducted repetitive investigations of the same individual and reached different conclusions concerning his loyalty. In a few burlesque instances, APL men, unknown to each other, accused one another of German-inspired espionage as they maintained unsynchronized surveillance over an applicant for a naval commission. Worse, some leaguers also put Department of Justice agents and Military Intelligence men in embarrassing positions by getting them arrested for spying.

Such inefficiency almost ruptured the close relations the APL had enjoyed with Military Intelligence since mid-1917, when the league formed a local in the army agency, and some APL men took direct commissions in Military Intelligence. But in December, 1917, the Military Intelligence head, Colonel Van Dieman, raised an official storm concerning poor APL work. The protest went to the White House and thence to Gregory. He, in turn, berated the league's directorate, which sent this telegram to all APL locals:

Bureau of Investigation . . . requests APL to make no more investigations of commissioned officers in any Department. . . . The request is made because the investigation of an officer is a delicate matter and any suspicion directed against him at any time in his career, unless cleared up, will impair his usefulness forever afterward.

Thus chastened, the league thenceforth restricted itself to transmitting unevaluated information to the appropriate federal agencies, without attempting to weigh its significance or make conclusions concerning its validity. By war's end, the APL had made more than three million loyalty investigations. What proportion of these reached negative conclusions concerning loyalty, and how many Americans lost an opportunity to serve their country and unknowingly had their patriotism impeached, are questions that existing league records fail to answer.[15]

In loyalty investigations, as in all APL work, amateurishness limited the effectiveness of the sprawling, growing organization. Early in May,

1918, for instance, an APL agent carelessly left a packet of completed loyalty reports on a Washington streetcar. The lost dossiers were returned within a day to league headquarters, but not before their contents became grist for the capital's rumor mills. When unwitting subjects of the league's investigations—army officers, Metropolitan Opera performers, and some Smith College faculty—learned that they had been included in APL investigatory operations, they raised a storm that reached the White House, and reverberated through the executive departments. Elting received the penultimate blast from Gregory. The APL director, momentarily despondent, confessed to a trusted subordinate that "the perfect deluge of people . . . who think they are born sleuths . . . as a matter of fact . . . are all about 100% rotten." [16] Rotten or not, the APL continued.

APL violations of secrecy regulations were often less accidental than the streetcar loss episode, and formed a constant problem for the Justice Department and the league's directors. Some publicity-hungry leaguers "tipped off" journalists concerning APL operations and Justice Department work. Clumsy sleuthing by league agents warned subjects of investigation and blocked official prosecutions under wartime statutes. "Damned fool," was Elting's comment about a Long Beach, California, APL chief who publicly boasted of past achievements and future plans. Removing the secrecy veil was not always the APL's fault. Red Cross officials proved especially troublesome, divulging to individuals barred from overseas employment because of APL loyalty reports the reasons for the adverse decision, the names of witnesses, and the league personnel involved. League headquarters was the complainant in this instance.[17]

Despite its secrecy fetish in the Red Cross episode, money troubles impelled the league to lift its confidential cloak. As an unpaid, semi-official, volunteer federation, each league local subsisted itself. The APL as a whole lived off members' contributions and the subsidies of patriotic patrons (often in the form of free office space, printing, stenographic help, and use of private corporations' vehicles, expense accounts, and telephone and telegraph budgets). By the end of 1917 the league was selling subscriptions to the *Spy Glass* to select private persons, state defense committees, and other private patriotic groups not blessed by Justice Department sanction. Expenses continued to outstrip income, however. By the summer of 1918 Elting had worked out a plan for a nationwide fund-raising campaign attended by all the advertising techniques wartime America had developed. The American Bankers' Association agreed to administer the campaign, and when

Gregory, Bielaski, and O'Brian approved it, the money troubles of the league's directors seemed about to end. But Wilson intervened early in September; as Gregory sadly reported to Elting,

I asked him [Wilson] what he thought of my approval of the plan for financing the APL. He expressed his appreciation of the work done by that body, but he said he felt there should be no further official indorsements of plans to raise money. Of course, the Government has no right to interfere with the [private] raising of money for any legitimate purpose.[18]

Inconsistency born of its nature plagued the APL in more ways than the matter of secrecy or operating funds. Officially, the league held that the "enrollment of women . . . is contrary to the national policy of the organization." Such nice Victorianism meant less to many APL locals, however, who employed women as agents in some instances. Leaguers who were drafted or enlisted into military service frequently took their APL badges and concerns with them, and sent reports on fellow soldiers' loyalty to national headquarters, APL locals, Military Intelligence, state defense councils, and even newspapers. General C. G. Morton, Twenty-ninth Division commander at Camp McClellan, Alabama, found such a situation in his staff, where a captain, a former leaguer, was investigating and completely unnerving all the officer personnel. High-level reverberations again reached Elting. "To avoid future embarrassment," he ruled, all leaguers had to resign from the APL upon joining the colors. On the other hand, APL men as such received commissions in the Provost Marshal Corps and in Military Intelligence, and retained their dual status throughout the war.[19]

At the opposite extreme were some league agents who became convinced that their APL cards exempted them from the draft. Ironically, other leaguers investigated the delinquents. The results suggested that because many APL men performed simultaneous draft-board duties, colleagues' requests for deferment because of APL affiliation were easily granted. The league's national directors circularized all locals, instructing the members to comply with conscription regulations. Whether or not they did so is unknown. It is certain that government records of prosecutions for selective service violations include no mention of action against APL delinquents.

League violations of federal and state laws included the activities of APL members in Kansas who mixed sleuthing with illicit importations of bootleg whisky and of prostitutes for use at army training cantonments into the legally dry and supposedly moral state. Treasury agents who uncovered the plot delighted in bringing the evidence to Gregory, who again called Elting in for an unpleasant conference. And APL men everywhere exceeded their powers by arresting citizens on the strength of the league's affiliation with the Justice Department. Thousands of such incidents went unreported until long after the war; thousands of frightened Americans never questioned the impressive APL badge. A few, however, did protest. "Under no circumstances," Elting warned, "should any of our members approach a man and try to arrest him or even threaten such a thing." Suits for false arrest might follow, he predicted. But, as in draft exemptions and prohibition evasions, no prosecutions of APL agents for false arrests ensued.[20]

Tragedy, however, did ensue. In New York City APL agents illicitly arrested a civilian, coincidentally an honorably discharged veteran of overseas service, for disloyalty, and took him to league headquarters. He managed to communicate with his attorney, who, after accusing the league agents of physical brutality toward his client, added this postscript to a complaint addressed to Gregory:

I know that we live in extraordinary times, calling for unusual methods, but I do not believe it is the policy of our Government to put weapons of oppression into the hands of private organizations. . . . There are many professional patriots at large, who can not distinguish between serving the country and having the country serve them.

When queried from Washington, New York APL authorities insisted that they knew nothing of the incident. Their victim, after ten days of extralegal imprisonment, managed to convince his captors of his innocence and was released. No one suffered except himself.

A similar instance concerned William Bayard Hale, suspected of pro-German espionage, and simultaneously investigated by the APL, the Treasury Department, Military Intelligence, and the New York State Council of Defense. Hale alleged that government agents had beaten him. Inquiries revealed that all the investigators were accusing each other of the offense, with most suspicion falling on the APL. But the incident faded out in acrimonious interbureau memoranda. Physical brutality was never official policy, but the ubiquitous APL was never more than a semiofficial agency under few restrictions, which its members did not feel inclined to follow. "The government is not responsible for mobs that hang innocent men, that paint houses yellow, and run up and down the country trying to crush honest discussion," George Creel argued. True, but the government sanctioned the existence of a nationwide organization that in many instances led the mobs, wielded the paintbrushes, knotted the nooses, and interfered with "honest discussion." The federal government found that it could not successfully curb the APL's vigorous expressions of patriotism.[21]

APL excesses were most sinister when they combined with the social, racial, and class prejudices of league members, who often used their unrestricted powers for partisan and personal goals. League personnel were overwhelmingly recruited from among older, financially upper-class, and politically conservative persons. The flurry of anti-German sentiment in the early war months became increasingly an antiradical, anti-Bolshevik, antiliberal, and anti-Socialist attitude which APL members shared. Unfortunately, leaguers often intermixed these terms. Since they could also mix their loyalty-testing duties with multitudes of other private and wartime functions, and enjoyed access to treasures of confidential private and government documents, the tendency toward excess which the league often exhibited reached into the most sensitive arenas of the nation.

West Coast APL groups collected evidence for state and federal procedural indictments against the Industrial Workers of the World, but also instigated mob attacks on "wobblies." Midwest league locals saw the German menace in terms of the hated Non-Partisan League, and tried to wreck its personnel and program. Eastern leaguers found Socialist party and labor-union activities targets for vigilant attention, and placed heavy hands on immigrant groups. Negroes were peculiarly attractive objects of league activities in the South.

Few victims of APL excesses had the courage or knew enough to complain about their sufferings. The Civil Liberties Bureau raised a courageous, if weak, voice in protest. Bernard Baruch privately "expressed himself as thoroughly disgusted with such star chamber methods, which he went so far as to say reminded him of the days of the Bastille and of the Spanish Inquisition," but he never officially made his feelings part of the record. More effective was the protest of the leaders of the Milwaukee locals, International Association of Machinists. These skilled aristocrats of organized labor were much in demand for wartime industrial production. APL agents, closely identified with the prosperous industrialists of the city, hounded the union, disrupted its meetings, and destroyed its papers. They also threatened uncoöperative machinists with induction if they demanded increases in wages or betterment of working conditions; the presence of league personnel on Milwaukee's draft boards made this no empty boast.

Union officers finally complained through Samuel Gompers to Gregory. The Attorney General learned that

On account of the [APL] activities . . . our men are in constant turmoil, making it hard for our [union] representatives to control our men. . . . Our members are loyal and do their work faithfully. . . . We are called upon almost daily to help maintain industrial peace, but our influence is going to be seriously hampered if men, operating under the guise of Government officials, are going to be permitted to use such tactics as they do in Milwaukee.

Similar situations existed in the booming Buffalo, New York, and Chicago areas. In each instance the Justice Department tried to stop the egregious practices, but in none were they altogether successful, and in all much damage to individuals and to the war effort resulted before the government intervened.[22]

Wilson's administration was much more receptive to complaints concerning the APL from respected labor unions than from the Socialist party, but one episode was too blatant to overlook. In Cleveland, the APL local teamed with the "Red Squad" of the city police and in mid-1918 launched a series of spectacular raids on Socialist meetings. In one of these a Negro speaker was kicked and beaten by APL men and then arrested by the police. With totally unnecessary violence, other Americans were illicitly confined by APL members for as long as a week and then released without explanation. "If true," O'Brian warned Elting, "every one of these items would constitute an unlawful and unconstitutional infringement with the rights of free speech and assemblage." Regular Justice Department agents investigated the charges and confirmed them, but no punishment was meted out to the impulsive APL men.[23]

Evidences of class consciousness in APL membership, proofs that league locals indulged in excesses, and truths concerning the bigotry, intolerance, and partisanship of individual leaguers do not, however, make the United States government a willing participant in these irregularities. The Socialist newspaper, the *New York Call,* for example, stated that the Justice Department deliberately commissioned the APL less because of concern for German espionage than for antiradical purposes. Disrupting Socialist meetings was more to league taste, the writer insisted, and individual APL men "shadowed labor and Socialist organizers and workers, and promoted and aided in the prosecution that led to the imprisonment of IWW leaders, Eugene V. Debs, and other Socialists and radicals." A Communist spokesman condemned

. . . the licensing by the Department of Justice of anti-labor strike-breaking groups of employers—such as the NSL [National Security League], the ADS [American Defense Society], the Knights of Liberty, [and] the APL—whose express purpose was the crushing of labor organizations and all class activities of the workers, and who inaugurated in this country a reign of terror similar to that of the Black Hundreds in Russia.

These accusations were in part true. The accuracy of the Communist claim that in many American communities vigilantism flourished under the protection of local law emerges only too clearly from the record of the home front. It is a commonplace that the charge of the same critics, denouncing the "so-called Public Safety Commissions and similar organizations [that] were constituted by authority of the Government" as "made up of representatives of the Chamber of Commerce and Employers' Associations which usurped the powers of Legislatures and municipal administrations," had some validity.

But the APL, alone of all the numerous patriotic groups of the war, enjoyed the distinction of being auxiliary to a federal government department. And the league was not created to be antilabor or antiradical. The Justice Department gave it sanction to meet a German spy threat that never materialized. It grew beyond the administrative control of its founders and official guardians. League members as individuals and in groups acted in seeming substantiation of the Communist and Socialist charges, but never because of the wishes of the federal government or of the league directors. The league's amateur counterspies, with no spies to catch, and without effective administrative controls from above, fell prey to the lowest aspects of human nature, and badly mixed patriotism and prejudice. But only in not punishing such offenses adequately, and in keeping the league in existence after its basic inutility was apparent, was the federal government at fault. It was fault enough.[24]

If, on the one hand, the APL Arizona local inspired and conducted the monstrous Bisbee deportations as an anti-IWW move, the work of the New York City and Washington, D.C., locals in boring into two vexatious, patriotic, conservative groups must also be considered. These two organizations were the National Security League and the American Defense Society. Both had their origins in the prewar preparedness crusade; both turned their militantly patriotic, influential membership to Americanization and loyalty programs when the war started. The rash of state and federal internal security laws received their cordial support.

Neither the NSL nor the ADS, despite repeated pleas, was able to secure the kind of official sponsorship which the APL enjoyed, though many of their members also belonged to the APL. By autumn, 1917, the unwillingly unofficial patriots were firm critics of Wilson's prewar progressivism, wartime leadership, and postwar plans. S. Stanwood Mencken, Security League president, and Theodore Roosevelt consistently suggested that Wilson was both pro-German and radical and that the federal government's "soft" policy toward Bolsheviks betrayed the presence of sinister influences in the White House. Creel thought that the problem represented by these organized gadflies "is being solved very rapidly by my constant refusal to recognize either of them in any way." But he was wrong. Herbert Croly, editor of the *New Republic,* was closer to reality when he complained to Wilson that

. . . the American Defense Society and the American [*sic*] Security League . . . who are setting themselves up . . . as the only true arbiters of loyalty and . . . are gaining a great deal of prestige from the fact, are the very people who will subsequently make the task of realizing the constructive purposes which lie behind American fighting excessively and unnecessarily difficult.

This potential threat to Wilson's plans for a postwar League of Nations inspired the President to order Gregory to investigate both critical groups. The Attorney General turned the task over to Elting. Carefully selecting only the most trusted APL men from among big-city locals which were most firmly under Justice Department control, Elting set to work. Some startling information soon came to light.

APL agents, after boring into the superpatriotic groups from within, reported that the NSL had become a property of the most conservative wing of the Eastern and Midwestern Republican party machines. In the 1918 congressional election, for instance, the NSL set up "loyalty courts," imperiously summoned congressmen before them, and adjudged as disloyal all who voted for the federal income tax amendment, for anti-injunction laws, and against stern internal security legislation. The NSL circulated millions of copies of its "loyalty test" across the nation, and the resulting Democratic defeat may find partial explanation in its work. Wilson's supporters angrily determined to hang the NSL's dirty linen in public view. With Elting's sanction, the APL "leaked" some of its acquired evidence to friendly newspapers.

As for the American Defense Society, APL investigations revealed that it, too, was acting in a spirit of partisan Republicanism. The society's favorite target, after the Justice Department refused to make the ADS an official government adjunct, was Gregory, whom it accused of harboring pro-Germans in his department. Defense Society members in hundreds of instances implied that they were quasi-official federal agents and were exercising vigilante functions in the cause of loyalty.

After the 1918 congressional elections, lame-duck Democrats started a congressional investigation of both groups. Wilson willingly departed from traditional executive reluctance to keep executive files from legislative use and provided congressional probers with APL files on the two troublesome groups. The resulting committee report (March, 1919) castigated the NSL for its misuse of the cause of patriotism in interfering with elections and for ruining individuals' reputations for partisan purposes.[25]

This was the single best piece of investigation the APL conducted so far as professional standards of police work and league obedience to orders were concerned. It was, however, noteworthy because it was exceptional. APL work generally was of far lower quality. Only in the largest cities, where the Justice Department maintained firm reins on APL operations, did the amateur agents of the league perform consistently valuable services even in the secondary tasks to which they were assigned. Everywhere, personal feuds, political enmities, financial opportunism, racial, religious, and class prejudices—all the ills of power almost unrestrained by effective authority—resulted in innumerable acts of terror, unmeasurable injuries to individual self-respect and dignity, incalculable and unnecessary fear.

APL deficiencies offered opportunity for the realization of personal ambitions among Wilson's cabinet officers. Treasury Secretary William G. MacAdoo early in the war exhibited himself as the most influential enemy of the league, but not because of antipathy to APL violations of constitutional safeguards or of protest against the extraordinary connection of the government with this private organization. Personal ambition inspired MacAdoo's unrelenting attacks.

Next to the Justice Department, the prewar Treasury agency mustered the largest force of federal investigators. A traditional rivalry existed between the two staffs which continued during the war. One Treasury agent, for instance, told a postwar congressional committee that

It is possible, even in time of actual war, for extraordinary detective work to be done without overthrowing constitutional safeguards. . . . [A]gents of the Treasury Department have . . . scorn and contempt for the crude and lawless methods of the Bureau of Investigation of the Department of Justice. . . . I think it would be truthful . . . to compliment the Secret Service of the Treasury Department by way of contrasting it with the Bureau of Investigation.[26]

Less frankly, MacAdoo clothed his ambitious purposes in a consistent demand for centralization of all federal investigative operations in the Treasury Department. He correctly charged that the multiplicity of existing security agencies resulted in conflicting jurisdictions, uncorrelated standards, and inefficiency. In one instance, MacAdoo divulged to the Cabinet that Military Intelligence agents had lodged an unfavorable report on Gregory's wife's loyalty; in another, MacAdoo hinted that what Senator Chandler P. Anderson had recorded as "an anonymous letter campaign" impugning the loyalty of a member of the Council of National Defense was inspired by the uncontrollable APL. In a long series of cabinet memoranda, MacAdoo conducted a powerful offensive against the APL as the spectacular symbol of all he wished to terminate. He met an equally determined opponent in Attorney General Gregory. A feud broke out between the two men, born partly of personal antipathy and nourished on MacAdoo's ambitions to increase his own power and influence. He also happened to be correct in his arguments.

Gregory hit back forcefully. He told the Cabinet that the Justice Department maintained effective liaison with all other federal investigative corps and state defense councils. "This Department," Gregory insisted to Wilson, "invariably confers with . . . and never has the slightest difficulty in cooperating with . . . [other] department[s]." Wilson, anxious to keep peace in his official family, was willing to let the matter drop. Realizing this, MacAdoo briefly retreated, attributed Gregory's heated indignation to excessive sensitivity, and magnanimously expressed regret at the "petty jealousies" which were disrupting cabinet accord on internal security policy. But MacAdoo secretly turned his Treasury sleuths loose on an investigation of the APL.[27]

This was the spring of 1917. The war and the APL were new phenomena. Treasury agents easily collected evidence of the league's sloppiness, but not enough to support MacAdoo's more serious accusations of APL responsibility for interbureau confusion. In early June, MacAdoo found a focus for a new charge against the APL in the league badge, which, he claimed, too closely resembled the Treasury agents' emblem. MacAdoo exploited the issue for far more than it was worth. To Wilson, he expressed regrets at increasing the President's burdens, but added, "I regard this organization as having very harmful possibilities." MacAdoo likened the APL to the American Revolutionary committees "through which many injustices and abuses resulted." But from Gregory, MacAdoo carefully concealed his general antipathy to the league's mushrooming strength in a specialized attack on the league badge. The Treasury head wrote Gregory of his astonishment that "you personally have sanctioned the formation and activities of this private association [the APL] operating under the name of 'Secret Service.' " This phrase, according to MacAdoo, was a monopoly of the Treasury Department's agents.

Specifics finished, MacAdoo made his general attack on the APL. Its excesses, he charged, resulted from the lack of government control over recruitment and internal discipline. Confidential information in irresponsible APL hands "is detrimental to the public interest and the public service." Of course, he piously continued, were the "confusing appellation" altered, he would have no complaint. "I am . . . not advised," MacAdoo patronizingly wrote, "as to whether or not there is authority of law for such sanction . . . [of a private organization] by the Department of Justice," but he strongly hinted that there was not. When any citizen could, merely by paying the dollar initiation fee, boast of "Secret Service" affiliation, "you can readily see," MacAdoo concluded, "that thoroughly irresponsible and untrustworthy people may be taken in." 28

Gregory, bitterly angry with MacAdoo, after two weeks of conferences with the league's directors, answered the Treasury Secretary's charges. He told MacAdoo what the Treasury head already knew, that the whole Cabinet had approved the formation of the APL. Gregory revealed that the wartime expansion of the regular Justice Department staff was only 25 per cent, and attributed this modest increase to the work the APL performed for the government. Less accurately, Gregory claimed that every APL local and agent was under close Bureau of Investigation supervision, and that "the work of the League has been of the very highest character, inspired by the most patriotic motives, and tremendously helpful to the National Government."

As to the badge, Gregory indicated that he realized MacAdoo's complaint concerning this emblem was a mere ruse. The APL would alter all future badges (existing emblems proved beyond the power of Gregory to recall, so tenuous was Justice Department control over the APL) to read "Auxiliary to the U.S. Dep't of Justice" rather than "Secret Service." And in a last cutting phrase in a very caustic thirteen-page memorandum, Gregory informed MacAdoo that "following your example, I am sending a copy of this letter to the President."

Wilson disappointed both Gregory and MacAdoo. The President told the Attorney General that the White House had received complaints concerning the APL from many others besides the Treasury Secretary. It seemed to Wilson that "it would be dangerous to have such an organization operating in the United States," and he asked Gregory "if there is any way in which we could stop it."

In impassioned defense of his administrative offspring, Gregory convinced Wilson that the APL was necessary, presumably for the internal security of the United States. The evidence indicates, however, that at this point continued APL existence was more essential for Gregory's cabinet prestige than for counterespionage. The teapot tempest over the league badge ended by Wilson's passing the matter off as a jest. The intelligence services remained uncoördinated, APL agents received modified badges, and an opportunity to terminate the league passed untaken. Gregory later regretted that he had permitted the APL to survive. And MacAdoo, resilient, tireless, and ambitious, continued sniping throughout the war at the booming APL and the concomitant Justice Department expansion in functions and prestige.[29]

In mid-1918, a year after the badge dispute, APL members provided their detractors with the best possible argument for ending the league's life. That year had been marked by unofficial, dreadful violence on the home front, ostensibly in the cause of furthering patriotism. Lynchings, beatings, and unjust prosecutions under state and federal espionage and syndicalism laws, were, according to many complainants, the work of APL men in combination with their manifold connections in public and private channels. By June, 1918, Wilson, Gregory, Creel, and other high officials were conducting energetic public relations campaigns deploring the "mob spirit" in war. Intemperate patriotism, according to the President, was providing actual German agents with propaganda that American democracy was a sham. Gregory circularized the Council of National Defense and state councils, as well as all APL locals, in this spirit:

The suppression of sedition . . . rests entirely with the Department of Justice. It is a technical and difficult task which outside agencies are likely to confuse and obstruct. . . . [U]ndertake no work for the detection and repression of sedition except such as is expressly requested or authorized by . . . the U.S. Department of Justice and done on its behalf.[30]

It was far easier to make requests than to achieve obedience. Almost simultaneously with Gregory's appeal, APL ebullience exploded.

Soon after the war began, when Gregory realized that the APL had no German spies to catch, he had offered league services to dozens of wartime home-front agencies. By the end of 1917 the commonest duty of most APL locals was assisting in the conscription process. At the request of the provost marshal general, at least one APL member sat on "each local and district exemption board [in the country] to accomplish the location and apprehension of delinquent registrants."

In a series of nationwide dragnets, the Justice Department launched a vast "slacker roundup" in mid-1918, and the APL plunged into this assignment with the greatest enthusiasm. In dozens of cities, government agents and their volunteer auxiliaries raided theaters, hotels, restaurants, train and bus termini, factories, offices, and private homes. They herded thousands of men—young and old, hale and infirm, civilian and uniformed—into overcrowded detention centers as preliminary to checking their draft cards. And, in many places, it was a rugged preliminary. Home guardsmen used bayonet points freely, municipal police bludgeoned reluctant civilians, and—for Gregory the worst of all —APL agents, freely flashing their badges and eagerly describing to interested journalists the league's connection with the Justice Department, illicitly arrested citizens and enthusiastically joined in the general physical excesses of the "slacker raids." A storm blew up in Washington. Congressional investigations pinpointed APL transgressions and guilt in hundreds of instances. It all fell into Gregory's lap, where MacAdoo, never relaxing his private vendetta against Gregory and the APL, tried to keep it as long as possible.

Gregory had a distressing interview with Wilson, followed by a series of similar conferences with the APL directors. The Attorney General learned that the most outrageous league units in the slacker raids had been those he had earlier felt were the most controllable and the best in the APL: the big-city New York and Chicago locals. His own inquiry completed, Gregory made a fateful public pronouncement. The APL, he stated, had been led into breaches of propriety "by an excess of zeal for the public good." But this "does not excuse their action[s]," Gregory inexorably continued. No league member was competent to pose as a regular agent of the Justice Department, as many had during the slacker raids. The APL was a mere unofficial auxiliary and nothing more.[31]

This was the first time in the war that the true nature of the APL was specified in such detail to the public. APL reaction to Gregory's statement revealed that league personnel everywhere had consistently claimed far more than their real status allowed. Posing as Justice Department colleagues rather than auxiliaries, APL men had secured information, contributions, and coöperation. With Gregory's words, fears of multiple libel and damage suits haunted APL agents, patriotic landlords withdrew rent-free quarters, and glib informants became suddenly dumb. Other federal departments—Post Office, Military Intelligence, Council of National Defense—temporarily withdrew all work and coöperation from league units. APL members began mass resignations. It seemed that the slacker raids were the death knell for the league.

APL national directors, the head of the New York City league local, Gregory, O'Brian, and Bielaski spent two September weeks in lengthy conferences and long-distance telephone exchanges. More discreet interviews occurred among Wilson, Gregory, and MacAdoo, who considered the effect of disavowing the APL on the incipient congressional elections. On September 21, Gregory called a press conference. He repeated his condemnation of APL excesses in the slacker raids, but after praising past APL contributions to home-front security, he called upon the league to continue its work under Justice Department auspices. His carefully chosen words restored the league's legitimacy. Contributions and coöperation resumed and resignations slowed. Popular attention shifted to the momentous battle news from France. The crisis passed.[32]

Gregory's decision seemed to please no one. Many leaguers felt unfairly treated, and believed, as did E. H. Rushmore, chief of the New York City local, that "the unhappy denouement of the slacker raid . . . is connected with [Democratic] politics." Many APL members expressed their discontent by exerting their energies and using their intricate web of influence to defeat Democratic candidates in the 1918 congressional elections. As one ardent Wilsonian sadly wrote Gregory after the Republican victory in that critical contest,

Are you aware that the . . . members of this League are for the most part Republicans, and have used this League to further the ends of the Republican party—as the last election plainly shows[?] This Protective League under the name of patriotism has blackened the name of Democratic government in every possible manner. . . . You say that the . . . [APL] conducted 3,000,000 [loyalty] investigations—but at what a cost to Democracy—the election of a Republican Congress. Oh, it was a subtle game, and they won it. They had no hesitation in swearing falsely of the disloyalty of decent Democrats. They have made the name of Democracy a reproach.

Gregory wearily penned "No answer" on the top of this emotional message. The elections were irrevocably past, the war was now won, and the degree of APL influence in providing a Republican majority for the Congress that would have to deal with the momentous questions of peace, the League of Nations, and the postwar internal policies of the nation, was now a historical rather than an administrative problem.[33]

Why had Gregory persistently continued league life when, soon after hostilities commenced, it became increasingly obvious that the threat of German espionage which the APL was supposed to counter failed to materialize? Part of the answer must lie in the personal antipathies and administrative jealousies existing between MacAdoo and Gregory. There are other reasons, some more creditable to Gregory. All APL locals were understandably reluctant to forward proofs of their excesses to Washington. The Arizona APL, for example, buried accounts of its participation in the Bisbee tragedy. Kansas leaguers suppressed reports of members' profiteering and blackmailing outrages made possible by APL access to confidential government and private records. Buffalo, New York, league personnel obscured their dual status as agents of antiunion industrialists. Lacking proof of APL guilt, Gregory hesitated to condemn the league on the basis of unsupported complaints.

In many ways, the league's largest locals performed valuable services. New York City's local, the nation's largest, dealt with 29,680 draft evasion cases, aided in liquor and vice suppression near training camps, completed 15,000 loyalty investigations for the War Department alone, and dealt with a motley array of other matters for more than three dozen federal and state wartime agencies. And, except for the disaster of the slacker raids, this local operated under relatively consistent Justice Department control. Even the tiniest locals, like the one in Glen Falls, New York, were able to collect pictures of the French-German border area for military use, and to aid in war bond sales.

And, last, as the war months progressed, Gregory belatedly realized that the third of a million administratively undisciplinable leaguers, recruited from among the most influential men in their communities across the nation, having the most damaging information at hand concerning millions of their largely unsuspecting countrymen, could not cavalierly be dismissed. Political repercussions might be disastrous. Personal tragedies would too clearly result if APL files were not first safely secured. The war had made the amateur spycatchers too powerful for their nominal master—the federal government—to control; APL internal organization was anarchic by nature.[34] Only the return of peace and the removal of the urgent spur of wartime patriotism offered Gregory the opportunity to disband the league. When peace came, the question was, would he do so?

On the day before the Armistice, League Director Briggs tried to evoke an answer to this question. In a New Orleans speech, he reviewed the positive contributions of the league and insisted that it should become a permanent postwar fixture "in helping the returning soldiers to re-establish themselves." Briggs incautiously added a suggestion that the United States cancel all Allied war debts. His addendum was Mac-Adoo's opportunity. The Treasury Secretary complained to Gregory of the embarrassment Briggs's speech was causing Wilson, for Allied governments mistook the league for an official American spokesman. Gregory in turn censured Briggs, but requested that the league continue existing assignments for the moment.

Elting then sought to force a decision. A postwar APL must exist, he publicly argued, to carry on naturalization investigations, and to uncover "organizations advocating the overthrow of or change in our government by unlawful means. . . ." Privately, Elting circularized the league members to stay on their jobs until Gregory's decision became known.[35] His request brought a variety of responses. Many league chiefs echoed the plaintive statement of the Westchester County, New York leader, who described how financial contributors were, "with the enthusiasm of the war gone," canceling their fiscal offerings. A few leaguers felt as did the chief of the Los Angeles local:

We believe that an attempt to perpetuate the organization in peace times would be impotent. . . . The character of its membership inevitably would change from the best elements of the communities to men of quite another type, and eventually . . . the League would [be]come . . . an organization devoted to . . . the interests of some class of the population against another class, or, worse still, be prostituted to political ends. We feel that it would be far better for the League to take a clean death and decent burial.

Perhaps the strongest impulsion for a postwar league was what the pro-APL *New York Times* called "the machinations of intestine foes . . . [and] the secret backers of our Bolsheviki in their several variants." This was Elting's repeated argument in his appeals to Gregory for a continuation of league life.[36] December, 1918, was far gone before Gregory announced his decision.

On December 26, Elting made public the death notice for the league. Gregory let him do so in order to "save face" for the league's directors, who graciously if belatedly admitted that "with peace there is no place for organized citizen espionage." February 1, 1919, was set as the terminal date for all league activities, and Gregory pleaded urgently that every league local immediately send all its files to the Justice

Department and that all leaguers turn in their badges and identity cards.

The APL demobilized as sloppily as its members had conducted most of its administrative actions. Some units sent in all files as ordered. Many others "edited" their records, carefully excising derogatory material. A few chiefs let leaguers keep dossiers on which they had worked as souvenirs; others donated locals' files to their respective states' historical depositories. Almost all APL members kept their impressive badges for their own purposes.[37]

In the APL's last weeks of life, its national headquarters busied itself with pleasant formalities. Congress voted its thanks to the league which Gregory echoed in commendations for the *Spy Glass* and in his official reports. The league's directors commissioned Emerson Hough, author of popular juvenile novels, to write a history of the APL, and graciously provided him with carefully edited league case files as his total source materials. Then, on February 1, 1919, the tripartite national directorate sponsored a final banquet at the Hotel Astor in New York City. Hundreds of guests listened to enthusiastic praise of the league they had created and staffed. An orchestra played the national anthem, and the American Protective League went out of existence—almost.[38]

For almost a year after the league's official termination, some locals played the role of old soldiers, and refused to die. Almost every week of 1919 brought the Justice Department unsettling news that league locals were continuing wartime investigations but with postwar, anti-radical motives now frankly acknowledged. An APL "watchdog" unit that had functioned since 1917 within the American Bar Association "to keep the Bar pure" maintained its activities. Individual leaguers who took APL badges into private detective work, often in industrial police specialties, proved a vexing problem. The nominally defunct APL provided energetic Red-hunters for New York State's Lusk Committee's notorious raids on radical centers, and former leaguers and league files provided personnel and evidence for the federal government's "deportations delirium." APL veterans graced the staffs of Military Intelligence, the Justice Department, congressional investigating committees, and several states' legislative loyalty probers. League experience often proved a useful entree for federal and state patronage positions. And some former APL men took their wartime techniques into the postwar Ku Klux Klan.

If remnants of the league twitched with stubborn postwar life, the idea that had inspired the APL—of coöperative, amateur, government-affiliated internal security—remained a vital, troublesome force throughout the ensuing decade, and penetrated deeply into the social fabric of America. Ohio's Governor Cox (Democratic presidential candidate in 1920) thought it perfectly proper to ask the Justice Department for APL wartime loyalty reports on Ohio schoolteachers. His inquiry reached A. Mitchell Palmer, Gregory's successor as Wilson's Attorney General, before Palmer launched his "Red raids" and while the new head of the Justice Department was deeply troubled by demands similar to Cox's. Palmer conferred with O'Brian who reminded the new Attorney General that "our files contain not only authentic information but an infinitely greater amount of misinformation, some of it based on malevolent motives." This was "particularly true," O'Brian noted, "of information gathered by the A.P.L." O'Brian suggested that Palmer make a public statement that the Justice Department "would never depart from its traditional policy of refusing to exploit confidential information." The APL experience had convinced O'Brian how miscellaneous was the information amateur counterspies dredged up, and how varied were its uses.[39]

So Governor Cox did not receive his requested information, and, for a time, Palmer hewed to the sound line O'Brian had set. When private patriotic groups, including the powerful American Defense Society, applied in increasing numbers for formal Justice Department affiliation, Palmer steadfastly refused. "Espionage conducted by private individuals or organizations," Palmer piously observed, "is entirely at variance with our theories of government." Amateur internal security operations would destroy public confidence in constituted authorities, upset community life, and imperil standards of objectivity and justice. Palmer's refusal to offer the seal of his department to any private group failed, however, to retard the growth of unofficial but nonetheless influential self-constituted patriotic arbiters the least bit. The APL experience provided precedent for many postwar patriots. It was also, for many former leaguers, what one APL veteran called "an inspiration and a joy." This man, who had worked in the business-like atmosphere of the New York City league local, believed that "there is not a man but is a better American for what the League alone made it possible to do." In his view, "our work will stand . . . in pure clean-cut unselfish patriotism beyond anything this side of our boys in the trenches." [40]

League files do not, unfortunately, substantiate this emotional valedictory. Most APL locals, lacking any wartime assignments at all, wrote unit histories such as this one from the chief of the Alma, Kansas, league cell:

I did not think my work of any great importance. . . . The principal part was to assist people to 'BE GOOD.' I reported about 25 cases of unpatriotic citizens to the Department of Justice, and . . . took their affidavits that they would be more careful in their remarks and swearing anew their allegiance to this country. . . . We had a German Banker who was a German Sympathizer and . . . was not 100% American. We had him on the carpet and told him it was time . . . to commence buying Liberty Bonds. . . . On our last drive I went with a committee of Six to him and told him he was Chairman for the United War Work. . . . He got busy. . . . Above all things the Protective League has had a great Moral Effect on the community by the people knowing that Uncle Sam was among them at all times and they not knowing who was keeping tabs on them. That alone had a wonderful effect on the German Lutherans. I assisted in a very quiet way in closing the German Lutheran Schools of this County.[41]

This self-portrait of a typical league local is a more revealing index to APL work than the big-city units could afford, or the glowing tributes of the league's government sponsors could depict. As Bielaski told a postwar congressional committee, the APL received Justice Department sanction early in 1917 because "we prepared for eventualities that did not materialize." [42] Lacking German spies to catch, the sprawling league mechanism assumed or was assigned a complex of investigative tasks all of which could have been better handled by regular authorities. APL work involved an inordinate amount of bungling, inefficiency, and duplication. Illegal acts by extralegal leaguers accentuated APL irresponsibility and added to the vigilantism of the war years and the postwar period. APL locals too often became preserves of private interests which defined loyalty in subjective terms. APL work involved heartbreak for uncountable numbers of Americans whose only fault was not fitting some leaguer's definition of patriotic conduct. In some communities, the APL became synonymous with local government, enjoying awful access to private and official records, and controlling both mobs and police authorities.

To the postwar United States, the APL bequeathed a corps of men imbued with its methodology and with a tested devotion to combating the real or fancied dangers America faced. APL experience encouraged authorities to trespass beyond their limited powers. The wartime forces that sustained the APL contributed to the postwar intolerance that marred the history of the 1920's. America's first total war left a permanent peacetime heritage. "It is unfortunate," Lewis Mumford wrote in 1919, "that no administrative authority has power to deal with the viscous states of mind which were . . . manufactured for purely bellicose purposes."

296

Fear of German spies created the APL. Although government officials like Gregory and Creel knew by mid-1917 that internal security had been achieved and that disloyalty was no grave problem, they kept the fear of German espionage alive. The APL fits neatly into Walter Lippmann's category of an institutional effort wherein the "effort itself has become the aim." [43] Loyalty-testing became the APL's chief effort and the league was the major loyalty-testing agency of World War I, but many leaguers ignored and distorted the purposes of that testing. At its best, the APL was merely a useful adjunct to responsible authorities. But at its worst, and the worst aspects of the APL have been too long obscured in panegyrics, the league was a force for outrageous vigilantism blessed with the seal and sanction of the federal government. It died unsung, except in its own annals.

Another loyalty-testing agency of World War I enjoyed an official connection with federal authorities. It was relatively restricted in geographical area and purpose. Its story centers in the timberland of the far Northwest. The Loyal Legion of Loggers and Lumbermen, administratively joined to the APL on the loyalty-testing level, also has a tale to be told.

CHAPTER XII

Timber and Treason

Air power captured the American imagination long before the United States entered World War I. With the war declaration, patriotic speakers and writers easily convinced uncritical Americans that their factories would build clouds of aircraft to beat down the Hun. The airplane—that fascinating American invention; industrial production—that supreme American achievement, would quickly defeat the Central Powers and exempt American soldiers from the degradations of trench warfare. But despite huge money appropriations, rich natural resources, and immense industrial preparation, no useful numbers of aerial warcraft appeared. Injured patriotism demanded reasons for the delay. Army Chief of Staff Peyton C. March recalled how "everyone who could claim the right was investigating the Air Service, and everyone else was demanding an investigation."

By the end of 1917 an array of inquisitors was loose in the aircraft industry, seeking villains but accepting scapegoats. President Wilson appointed the sculptor Gutzon Borglum as his investigator, and the latter made nationwide headlines with accusations of German espionage, Socialist sabotage, and capitalist profiteering in airplane production centers. Congressional investigating committees, groups from several state legislatures, and representatives of half a dozen private patriotic organizations were simultaneously repeating Borglum's work, and many of his accusations as well.

War Secretary Baker created the most constructive investigating group when he appointed Charles Evans Hughes to head an inquiry of warplane production. Hughes's prestige momentarily quieted popular clamor. His report, in substantial measure the result of APL investigations into disloyalty and corruption charges, indicated that carelessness rather than sabotage, inexperience more than treason, had restricted warplane production.[1]

If disloyalty was not the cause of snarled assembly lines, it seemed the reason limiting supplies of the special woods needed for airframe construction. In the tall timberlands of the Northwest where grew in abundance the stately Sitka spruce, the Port Orford cedar, and the Douglas fir, the labor problems that had long bedeviled the area were as rugged as the mountains on which the trees proliferated. For a turbulent decade before the war, near chaos marked worker-management relations. Industrial sabotage, strikes, and violence were common as the IWW and the more conservative American Federation of Labor made substantial organizing inroads into the ranks of timber-workers. Employers, refusing to recognize either organization, responded with black lists, injunctions from coöperative judges, and importations of industrial detectives and immigrant workers. Excesses bred reprisals in an unrelenting "bread-and-butter" conflict.

American entrance into the war failed to calm the intransigent enmities of the timber area despite patriotic appeals by federal and state governments. In midsummer, 1917, the AFL and the IWW again called strikes, demanding an eight-hour day and condemning the atrocious living conditions of the lumberjacks. Production soon fell far short of swollen wartime needs. Employers' trade associations insisted that sinister pro-Germanism inspired the strikes. In the already explosive West Coast atmosphere, such charges set off destructive reactions. Citizens' groups and patriotic societies joined mobs of soldiers and sailors in attacks on IWW speakers and assembly halls; state conspiracy indictments and federal Espionage Act prosecutions hamstrung "wobbly" leadership; terror followed accusations of treason in the timberlands.

Washington's Governor Lister and War Secretary Baker unsuccessfully pleaded with the Lumbermen's Protective Association to grant the eight-hour day. The President's Mediation Commission's findings, supported by the report of a secret agent of the War Department, convinced federal authorities that employers' intransigence, employees' substandard working and living conditions, and the instability of the supply of migratory workers, combined to create an almost complete lack of communication between workers and management. These factors also gave strength to radical IWW appeals. Most immediately important, they resulted in an inadequate wood supply.[2]

Early in September the strikes officially ended, but their heritage still hampered timber-cutting and promised future interruptions of wood production. In mid-October, at Felix Frankfurter's suggestion, the War Department and the Council of National Defense sent an army officer, Colonel Brice P. Disque, on an investigating tour of the lumber area. Disque, forty years old in 1917, had nineteen years of army service behind him, as well as a brief wardenship of Michigan Penitentiary. Although he knew nothing of logging, he had the ability to listen and the imagination to consider novelties. As an officer of the Army Signal Corps, then in charge of military aviation, Disque knew the need for planes. And as an individual, he detested the IWW.

On his Western tour, Disque heard some employers suggest that the only solution to timberland labor troubles was for military forces to clear out all union organizers at bayonet points; more moderate operators welcomed federal mediation. At one lumber camp he exercised his winning personality and the appeal of his uniform to convince local workers and managers to meet in conference, with himself as mediator. An idea was born of Disque's ingenuity.

Early in November Disque received Baker's permission for a novel experiment in American administrative history. He was given command of the new Spruce Production Division of the Signal Corps. Within this military unit he was to create a labor union composed of civilians, organized and directed by officers of the national army, coöperating with federal, state, and municipal military and civil authorities, and designed to stop labor unrest, to stabilize the lumber industry, to increase timber production, and to serve as the primary loyalty-testing agency for the geographically isolated lumber camps.[3]

On November 30, 1917, Disque organized the Loyal Legion of Loggers and Lumbermen at Portland, Oregon. He and an imaginative subordinate, Lieutenant M. E. Crumpacker, had ventured west armed with substantial resources. They had, first, a specialized army division which even in late November numbered 7,000 men, and by March, 1918, had grown to twice that size. Through the coöperation of the provost marshal general's office, Disque was able to scour draft-board and training-depot personnel records to locate men with lumbering experience, reroute them to his command, and station them in convenient Northwest camps. They were his ultimate weapon against recalcitrant workers as well as against uncoöperative employers. These troops, under military discipline, could break strikes, supplement civilian lumberjacks when production required, or do whatever else Disque ordered.

Second, Disque carried credentials from J. A. B. Scherer, coördinator and chief field agent of the national and state councils of defense, to Dr. Henry Suzzallo, chairman of the Washington State Council. Under these instructions, Suzzallo offered Disque his closest coöperation, as well as the considerable wartime powers of that state body. Disque also secured Department of Justice coöperation, access to its files on the IWW, and an order to the Northwest APL locals to provide the army officer with whatever services and personnel he requested.

Patriotism formed the most public part of Disque's armory. He and Crumpacker designed membership insignia for the LLLL before there were any members. A lapel button an inch in diameter depicted the letters "LLLL" over a stylized American warplane dutifully convoying a speeding troop transport ship. Beneath them, in turn, a crossed woodsman's ax and saw and the legend, "Authorized by the Secretary of War," flanked by silhouetted fir trees, completed the emblem.

But even this impressive battery of assets did not guarantee Disque easy success. He had to convince workers and management, both bitter and stubborn after a decade of industrial strife, to accept overseership, arbitration, and production quotas. Union leaders of the IWW and the AFL had little cause to trust government intervention; employers' spokesmen expressed distrust of what they called Wilson's prolabor administration and policies. Disque relied on more than lapel buttons to turn the trick.[4]

Disque sent a group of subordinate army officers to tour Northwest lumber camps and speak to lumberjacks, managers, and owners. Their major theme was the promise of material benefits for all and government objectivity at all times if the lumber camp in question affiliated with the LLLL. Union men, once convinced of Disque's sincerity concerning the government's willingness to recognize both the AFL and the IWW as bargaining agents, proved vastly more sympathetic than the mill and camp operators. Disque took it upon himself to meet with prominent lumbermen in secret rendezvous arranged by the Washington, Oregon, and California state councils of defense. Here he frankly asserted the anti-IWW purpose of the Loyal Legion and asked for the coöperation of timber operators, many of whom were also state council members. As one of the latter recorded,

According to [Dr. Henry] Suzzallo [chairman of the Washington State Council and president of the University of Washington] the IWW leaders are as "smart as rats." The [state] Council, however . . . [is] a good mouser. . . . Officials of the Washington Council assured me that when they could get federal support for some important local movement their authority and influence was increased at least 100%.

Disque offered such "federal support" for "important local movements." State defense councilmen in turn promised him their coöperation, and the timber operators, impressed, stated their willingness to go along with the Loyal Legion on a cautious wait-and-see basis. They had not long to wait.[5]

In the first week of December, Disque heard of a work stoppage at a small lumber mill near Portland. He convinced the owner and the striking workers to accept his arbitration, and heard a long catalogue of substandard working and living conditions from the latter. From his army unit Disque ordered troops and materiel to the mill site. Soldiers unloaded quartermaster's stores of bunks, rations, and cleaning equipment, applied unaesthetic but sanitary olive-drab paint to barracks, rubbed GI soap and insecticides on floors that had rarely endured cleaning, and supplied army recipes for the lumberjacks' meals. A company of the timber-wise troops remained at the camp when the main body withdrew. And there also remained the first Loyal Legion local. There soon were many others.

By the end of 1917 this scene was repeated throughout the three timber states of the Northwest. Three hundred LLLL locals, listing 35,000 members, graced Disque's rosters at the new year. It was an amazing achievement in rapid organization, made possible by Disque's capable leadership, the power and resources of the government behind him, and the spur of patriotism he applied. By war's end his administrative creation had swelled to 1,100 locals in seven states, numbering 125,000 members. Its purpose was always, first, to spur timber production. Its methods were based, in deference to the LLLL's goal, on patriotism and pressure. And its secondary function from the beginning was to suppress labor unrest and disloyalty, terms that often became synonyms in the Loyal Legion lexicon.

The Loyal Legion remained from beginning to end a paramilitary labor union organized and directed by army officers, under Disque's tight control. Unlike the American Protective League, the only comparable World War I loyalty-testing organization, the LLLL was regional rather than national, under military rather than civilian direction, public rather than secret, with strict internal discipline replacing APL local autonomy, and with loyalty-testing a secondary rather than a primary organizational function. In the APL, every one of the third of a million leaguers dealt with internal security. Almost all Loyal Legionnaires, on the other hand, were simple lumberjacks; only a small proportion of the LLLL personnel were involved in loyalty-testing. But that small number were the heart of the legion's effectiveness. They were the secretaries of the LLLL locals.

But, in the LLLL as in the APL, loyalty-testing achieved similar results. In their pursuit of loyalty both organizations commonly transgressed traditional boundaries of the federal system, mingling national, state, and municipal powers, personnel, and information sources in a manner unknown in America since the Civil War. And subjective regional, class, and private preconceptions became inextricably confused with the loyalty-testing purposes of the APL and the LLLL.[6]

As an able industrial diplomat and labor relations director, Disque cleverly maintained the patriotic and material lures the LLLL offered as the legion's most effective recruiting devices for ordinary lumberjacks. Each applicant for membership read and signed this oath in a solemn, flag-bedecked ceremony:

I, the undersigned, . . . do hereby solemnly pledge my efforts during the war to the United States of America, and will support and defend this Country against enemies, both foreign and domestic. I further agree . . . to faithfully do my duty toward this country by directing my best efforts in every way possible to the production of Logs or Lumber for the construction of Army Airplanes and Ships to be used against our common enemies. That I will stamp out any sedition or acts of hostility against the United States Government which may come within my knowledge, and [I] will do every act and thing which will in general aid in carrying this war to a successful conclusion.

An attached information sheet gave the applicant's vital statistics, including naturalization history, vocational record, union activities, and, under "Remarks," space for the legion secretary to add data concerning the patriotic reliability of the putative legionnaire. Once admitted to membership, the new LLLL man received an identification card and the increasingly coveted lapel pin. Then the benefits of participation in the Loyal Legion were his. All were designed to keep him on the job.

A professional editor, now an army officer, commenced publication of the *Four L Bulletin,* a monthly journal that throughout the war stressed the tremendous need for lumber. Its contributors offered eulogistic comparisons of the devoted lumberjack and the front-line soldier; its editorials demanded unrelenting vigilance against the pro-German industrial saboteur. The Committee on Public Information supplied LLLL locals with a flood of loyalty literature. Isolated lumber camps suddenly found themselves included on the itineraries of Liberty Bond sales groups, and, more enjoyably certainly, of entertainment companies that brought popular theatrical personalities like Mary Pickford to the rugged mountain timber sites. At Disque's suggestion, President Wilson cut a phonograph record appealing for higher lumber quotas, which, according to the tactful LLLL head, was extremely effective "in appealing to . . . [lumbermen's] patriotism and sense of duty" (no rank-and-file reaction exists to support Disque's statement). Patriotic posters from a score of wartime agencies accentuated the patriotic theme, as did lectures on American history offered by legion secretaries and itinerant army officers. Military bands toured LLLL-affiliated camps. Disque played this patriotic chorus like a skilled musician. He was willing to try all techniques, ascertain their effectiveness, and drop those that seemed unproductive.

Each legion local had a sanitary committee, under direction from Disque's Portland headquarters. From the recommendations of such committees came the first code of industrial conditions which the timberlands had ever known. The code provided minimal standards to replace the execrable food and housing conditions lumberjacks had long deplored. It required resident medical officers, adequate safety precautions, qualified cooks, and facilities for the families of married workers. Except for the eight-hour day, which management stubbornly refused to concede, the LLLL seemed on the way to providing precisely the improvements that the AFL and the IWW had been demanding for a decade. Such improvements were, of course, paid for from public taxes. There were no contributions from legion members, or subventions from lumber operators whose properties were vastly improved in value by LLLL activities.

Disque soon found himself running a complex, growing organization involving labor-management relations, maternity services, cookbooks, and counterespionage. His staff of army officers divided the West Coast into seven administrative districts. In each district the army officer in charge sought to establish an LLLL local at every lumber mill, camp, and kiln, as well as to supervise existing units. If he met situations beyond his power to handle, he could call upon Disque, who never relaxed unitary control of the legion, for aid.[7]

Resistance to LLLL policies came from both sides of the labor-management fence. Timber operators detested Disque's willingness to admit AFL and, worse, IWW members into Loyal Legion locals, and to provide the working and living conditions those groups had long demanded. It seemed to the *American Lumberman,* trade journal of the employers, that the LLLL experiment proved the anticapitalism of the Wilson administration:

When we consider the situation without prejudice or passion [the editor of that publication asserted] it is really pitiable to see the Government grovelling in the dust, and showing a willingness to practically paralyze a great industry simply to placate these agitators who are playing into the hands of our enemies.

Senators McCumber of North Dakota and Chamberlain of Oregon echoed the lumber operators' complaints in Congress. McCumber, an outspoken foe of organized labor, condemned the fact that "on the West Coast the Government itself stepped in, forced [lumber]yards either to close business or to recognize labor unions with all their disastrous rules." [8]

Disque alternately pleaded with and threatened stubborn employers. Patriotic appeals for coöperation formed his first-line weapon which usually brought to terms all but the most stubborn timber operators. When such arguments failed, Disque switched to another persuasive tack. His Loyal Legion, Disque asserted to a closed meeting of employers, was technically a part of the military forces. When LLLL recruits swore the legion oath, they placed themselves under military discipline. Anyone interfering with LLLL activities from within or without could face military courts-martial. Nonlegionnaires who blocked timber production could, he asserted, come under Espionage Act prosecution.

Disque admitted that he accorded the IWW bargaining status. But so did other federal, state, and municipal wartime agencies. Wobblies cut wood as well as the next man. His legion would enroll them, give them the conditions that the IWW had demanded for so long, and keep a sharp eye on all former and present wobblies. The Four L's had internal safeguards against IWW sabotage about which Disque refused to talk, but which he asserted were operating efficiently. When lumberjacks joined the LLLL, Disque argued,

We promised . . . in consideration of their signing the [loyalty] pledge, and showing their Loyalty to the Government, . . . that the Government intended to take an active interest in their welfare, and to consider them as much a part of the military forces . . . as though they were in uniform, and actually enlisted in the service. . . . The members are now demanding protection from the common enemy, the IWW. . . . To rid the [LLLL] Locals of the pro-German IWW disguising as a loyal man is the protection they demand.[9]

Patriotic coercion proved futile in one major disagreement between labor and management. The eight-hour-day issue continued to bedevil the lumber industry, and both the AFL and the IWW persisted in demanding the shorter workday. Employers resisted as insistently. The President's Mediation Commission's recommendation favoring the eight-hour day received union approval and employers' vehement rejection. Timber production remained erratic and inadequate. Disque, realizing that this single issue could nullify all past LLLL achievements and prevent future gains, plunged into the murky waters of the eight-hour dispute and exhibited himself as a skillful, knowledgeable manipulator of governmental processes.

Early in 1918, at Disque's suggestion, Senator Chamberlain sponsored a bill authorizing government seizure of timberland and lumber processing plants and products for LLLL use. The senator argued that anyone who resisted Loyal Legion membership was disloyal and his property rightly should revert to patriotic ownership. His bill stayed discreetly in committee, but its patent threat remained. Disque simultaneously reinforced the effects of Chamberlain's proposal with intimations that recusants would lose equipment priorities, find their non-LLLL personnel conscripted, and face public stigmatization as pro-Germans. Employers who joined the legion and accepted its code of standards, including the eight-hour day, gained a patriotic aura, a stable labor force under semimilitary discipline, assured profits, and an end to strikes and industrial sabotage.

After playing his multifaceted instrument of coercion and persuasion as urgently as he could, Disque hurried to report to War Secretary Baker in Washington. There, Felix Frankfurter, counsel for Wilson's Mediation Commission, agreed with Disque's contention that all federal contracts could include an eight-hour-day stipulation. And Disque was delighted to find that his coöperating colleagues on the West Coast were supplying him with precisely the kind of ammunition he needed to secure top-level support for the LLLL. Baker received such timely messages as this telegraphic plea from the head of the Washington State Defense Council:

Inefficiency in production of spruce continues despite remarkable efforts made by . . . Disque. . . . Absolutely essential for Government to give Disque extra-ordinary powers and to clean up labor inefficiency . . . caused by a discontent which can be materially eradicated only by establishment of eight hour day . . . by executive order.

Armed now with the threat of presidential action, Disque returned to Portland and again convened a meeting of timber operators. His strategy proved largely successful. Over considerable opposition the lumbermen agreed to the shorter workday without reduced wages, on condition that no decrease in production result. A few truly dedicated men closed their operations for the duration of the war rather than give in to what they felt were unnecessary sacrifices to union demands. But for the first time in the timberlands of the West, labor conditions began to approximate those of other industries, and credit for achieving this progressive reform belongs to the Loyal Legion's remarkable chieftain.[10]

Against lumberjacks who refused to join the LLLL in the first months after its formation, Disque followed a policy as cautious as the one he used with employers. He promised AFL and IWW leaders that the LLLL welcomed their members into the legion. As a result of Disque's adroit mastership of the 4-L administration, this promise found a place in the Loyal Legion constitution. Similarly, that document forbade LLLL interference with proselytizing by labor unions among unorganized legion members. A legionnaire had every theoretical right to join the AFL and even the IWW if he wished to. On the other hand, Disque also promised that timberworkers who did not want LLLL affiliation would face no discrimination in those camps flying the legion banner. He desired no "closed LLLL shop." Nor did the Loyal Legion organizer see anything wrong in a lumber camp's simultaneous employment of unorganized workers, AFL and IWW members, LLLL cardholders who might at the same time be members of the labor unions, and detachments of the uniformed soldiers of the Spruce Production Division. He insisted that the legion was an autonomous unit of the War Department, designed to express the government's paternalistic concern for workers' welfare, organized to act as an objective mediator in labor-management disputes, structured on democratic lines of ascending authority based upon the wishes of its members. Its purpose was to increase timber production and nothing else. Its total administrative machinery was, Disque insisted, open and unobjectionable.[11]

These soft promises of early 1918 became translated into strikingly different LLLL practices once settlement of the eight-hour-day dispute overcame the primary obstacle to legion expansion.

The basic LLLL unit was the local, composed of the workers and the owners of the affiliated lumberyard, kiln, camp, or mill. Each legion local was in charge of a secretary, who was appointed by the army officer in charge of the administrative district. The legion secretary was the heart of the loyalty-testing process of the 4-L's. He functioned on a public and a secret level. His public duties included maintaining the local's records, enforcing the code of industrial conditions, and arranging for his local to receive its full share of patriotic speakers and literature. His secret duty was to combat disloyalty, sabotage, and enemy propaganda.

Disque chose his men carefully. Some secretaries were soldiers in mufti, assigned from Military Intelligence or volunteers from the Spruce Production Division. The Lumbermen's Association supplied a small number of private detectives for Disque's use. But by far the largest portion came from the coöperative American Protective League units of the Northwest states, whose members volunteered in large numbers for LLLL assignments. Regardless of his administrative origin, every legion secretary found that once he accepted his assignment, General Disque (his promotion came early in 1918) was a stern, demanding taskmaster. No amount of martial oversight, however, sufficed to keep all legion secretaries to a standard loyalty-testing line.

In an organization that grew as rapidly as the LLLL, it was inevitable that some subordinates would not be men of the highest caliber. Legion secretaries took existing social, economic, and racial attitudes with them into 4-L service. Many secretaries shared dislikes concerning Orientals, Mexicans, IWW and AFL members, and what one Loyal Legionnaire called "rotten radical foreigners." Since the LLLL possessed close lines of coöperation with army draft boards, state defense councils, federal Justice Department attorneys (through the APL), and municipal police authorities, individual prejudices easily translated into official prosecutions. Even within the LLLL itself, secretaries manipulated job assignments, pay scales, and choice housing billets to fit subjective standards which most often found equation in individual concepts of "loyalty." [12]

Some zealous secretaries, for example, refused to accept into legion membership any applicant who retained IWW or AFL affiliation, despite the LLLL constitutional provision forbidding such discrimination. Samuel Gompers' complaints caused Disque to order a stop to this practice. Simultaneous secret orders, however, enjoined secretaries to keep separate rosters of wobbly and AFL members in the Loyal Legion, and to maintain special oversight of these stubborn men.

Similarly, legion secretaries illicitly interfered with AFL recruiting efforts among LLLL members, again in violation of the 4-L constitution. In geographically isolated lumber camps, the powerful leverage that secretaries could apply often succeeded in blocking AFL organizers. Irate AFL officials (the IWW was *persona non grata* by this time) unsuccessfully complained, but found it difficult to prove anything. One alert AFL man took a different tack. He wrote an innocent letter to the War Department asking if the LLLL really was part of the army, and if all civilian legionnaires were paramilitary, as Disque had consistently alleged. His letter accidentally reached the desk of a busy officer who was completely ignorant of the legion. The officer's reply, that the LLLL had no War Department sanction, occasioned a crisis in the Northwest. Disque was able to repair the damage only by securing a public telegram from the War Secretary restoring legion legitimacy.[13]

In a series of confidential circulars, Disque sought to standardize his secretaries' security functions. He warned his subordinates that uneducated, credulous lumberjacks could seemingly sound disloyal through ignorance more than design. "If a member talks disloyally," he ordered, ". . . do all you can to convert him and make him a better citizen." But if persuasion failed, Disque authorized sterner measures. The legion secretary concerned was to discharge such a member dishonorably from the LLLL and from his job, and notify Disque's headquarters of the incident. Disque then sent the delinquent's name to the coöperating federal, state, and municipal security agencies for further action.

The foregoing instructions applied to the most innocent cases that legion secretaries unearthed. More sinister lumberjacks received harsher treatment. Some timberworkers, including AFL personnel resentful of legion successes and policies, alleged that every signature to the LLLL loyalty oath robbed the subscriber of his civil rights and civilian status. In another confidential circular to legion secretaries, Disque enjoined them to resist

. . . the malign whisperings of enemies in your camps. . . . [Instruct legionnaires to pay] no heed to the nonsense that you are signing away your constitutional rights by taking the Legion's pledge of loyalty. Such stories are enemy stories, the work of Spies and Traitors. Your pledge to the Government . . . is only a visible and tangible evidence of loyalty. . . . It is your individual duty to combat such sinister propaganda. . . . The Head Quarters of this Division looks to you to prevent all acts of sabotage and sedition. . . . This duty the Government expects of you, to prevent all "aid or comfort" to the enemy in any way.[14]

Unfortunately, however, Disque's headquarters never clearly defined precisely what disloyalty, sedition, or sabotage involved. When legion secretaries found untrustworthy LLLL members, their instructions were to conduct a loyalty investigation of the suspect. Legion records indicate that many such inquiries resulted in conclusions that the subject was "Bolshevik," "pro-German," or a "disloyal wobbly saboteur." Those records also reveal that even when men were found innocent of "disloyalty," they lost their jobs, were black-listed throughout the timberlands, and, if of conscriptable age, often found themselves suddenly in uniform. A few such men were, ironically, assigned to Disque's division, but were now under unquestionably military discipline.

When legion loyalty probes returned a guilty verdict, Disque turned the evidence over to Military Intelligence, the Bureau of Investigation, a state defense council, or local city police for prosecution under pertinent wartime statutes. The result was, therefore, that the minuscule LLLL loyalty-testing contingent, superficially numbering merely the several hundred local secretaries, actually possessed tremendous personnel and institutional resources through the legion's manifold connections. The Loyal Legionnaire accused of disloyalty found himself the center of a complex web of investigative agencies. Most of them, like the APL and Military Intelligence, operated secretly. All tested loyalty.[15]

Within LLLL locals, secretaries perfected their own security machinery. They recruited "stool pigeons" from among complaisant lumberjacks, and provided them with favored job assignments, promotions, and outright bribes for information concerning other legionnaires' loyalty. Such intimate sources of information permitted the secretaries to anticipate grievances and head off decreases in timber production, as well as to oversee disloyalty.

By the end of January, 1918, Disque felt his legion structure strong enough for him publicly to strike against lumberjacks who refused to join the LLLL. Since the legion commander had consistently insisted that his organization was democratic in form, it seemed best to open this drive from below, rather than from his headquarters. It worked out this way. The Port Ludlow local secretary received his orders from Disque, and found a willing informant to pen an open letter for all LLLL men to read. His essay castigated lumberjacks "in our midst . . . who scorned to pledge themselves in backing our President." These pro-German "lepers among clean men" still cut wood and reaped the benefits of legion activities, yet refused to accept membership in its ranks. "Shall we nourish snakes to our breast," he demanded, "who may, at any moment, turn and strike?" No, the theoretically spontaneously motivated woodcutter concluded. "Let us . . . make it so unpleasant for these disloyal few that they will seek employment elsewhere."

This officially inspired ground swell of opinion produced the desired results. At Port Ludlow and elsewhere, LLLL members refused to work with nonjurors. This gave Disque a free hand. At legion conventions in Spokane and Portland, he informed the assembled army officers and legion secretaries that

The Loyal Legion has not forced any one to join it. . . . You will find men among your own crews who are not willing to join at once. . . . Give them every chance in the world to see that they are on the wrong track. Then if they refuse to join tell them to get out; we have no place for a man not willing to sign a pledge of loyalty today.

Soon thereafter, Disque also reversed his earlier stand concerning the freedom of the AFL to recruit in the LLLL camps. In short, by mid-1918 he was committed to closed LLLL shops, and his legion apparatus was under instructions (issued through the façade of the rigged conventions) to equate nonjuring with disloyalty.[16]

The Loyal Legion experiment was many things to many people. To one literate lumberjack, the LLLL's success in achieving the eight-hour day and settling industrial acrimony proved that most timberworkers were not wobblies, and that those who were red-card holders were not automatically disloyal. The President's Mediation Commission, "with great common sense," had left labor relations in the Northwest to Disque to deal with. His Loyal Legion had achieved what no earlier efforts had come close to doing: providing peaceful communication between workers and management.

Similar praise came from the editor of the *New Republic,* who insisted that Disque benefited the country by coöperating with loyal IWW members, enrolling them in the Loyal Legion, and filling the vacuum created by employers' earlier refusals to bargain collectively with the AFL. Disque gave the disgruntled timberworkers what they had been branded as disloyal for demanding. Instead of commandeering private property, the LLLL had saved it. Rather than subsidizing "disloyal" wobblies, as resentful employers insisted, the legion punished such erring lumberjacks. There had been much "irrelevant eloquence" in Congress concerning the legion, the editor asserted. What the legislators needed was a trip to the tall timber country to see for themselves the beneficial results of Disque's industrial diplomacy.[17]

Congress sent one man, instead. He was J. A. B. Scherer, coördinator of the national and state councils of defense, who had been influential in providing support for the LLLL since its inception. Scherer, head of what today is the California Institute of Technology, knew West Coast labor conditions well, if not objectively. After a tour of legion installations in June, 1918, he reported that

The most interesting change in Washington [State] . . . is concerned with the IWW. The pernicious activities of the organization have almost entirely disappeared. . . . When Capt. [*sic*] Disque was leaving for the lumber camps last fall, I gave him a letter . . . which has brought about cooperation between the federal authorities and the State Council of Defense. By means of this cooperation the Loyalty League [LLLL] has almost completely eradicated the disloyalty which affected the lumber output of the far northwest so disastrously. . . . Disque deserves great credit for the manner in which he has dealt with his men. . . . Members of this League make it very uncomfortable for newcomers lacking in patriotism.[18]

Yes, Disque had a good press, and enthusiastic supporters. Even publications normally critical of any action of Wilson's administration applauded this experiment in military labor unionism, as did the editor of the *Outlook*. Disque's "superb result" was harmony in labor-management relations. The legion's publication preached healthy American patriotism to a hundred thousand lumberjacks; its commander suppressed the "very dangerous spirit of antagonism between employer and employee in our lumber camps." Disque, according to this account, "is certainly doing a fine bit of industrial diplomacy." Even the president of the Washington State Federation of Labor (AFL), W. M. Short, admitted that the LLLL performed valuable services as a wartime agency.[19]

Loyal Legion accomplishments and failures may best be measured against its objectives. Its basic aim was to increase the production of timber suitable for warplane construction. The gross production figures are impressive. From roughly 5½ million board feet per month in November, 1917, to almost 23 million by the Armistice is a large increase. Not all the wood was of aircraft quality, however, although it was all used in less demanding construction.

To accomplish the major legion aim, Disque created immensely improved labor conditions, wage scales, and channels of communication between workers and employers. In the process he succeeded in stealing IWW thunder by anticipating wobblies' demands. He also, less in keeping with the stated policy of the President, bitterly antagonized the more traditional unionists of the AFL, who, by the war's end, were almost as completely excluded from legion camps as were the wobblies.

A secondary objective of the legion was to inculcate patriotism among its rank and file as well as among its employer members. As Disque described this motive to Wilson, the legion appealed

. . . to each man's sense of duty as a citizen . . . to bend his best efforts at this time to further the Government's war program. . . . In return for this manifestation of loyalty on the part of employers and employees, it is our policy to show, in some tangible way, the Government's appreciation.[20]

For employers the "tangible appreciation" was patriotic satisfaction, combined with substantial improvements in their property paid for from public funds. For timberworkers, the patriotic impulse was reinforced by vast improvements in working conditions, and a sense of participation in the nation's martial effort so great that even hard-bitten, nonjuring wobblies discreetly acquired legion lapel buttons to wear when away from the camps. For thousands of uneducated lumberjacks, the legion was their first school, and the initial identification of their vocation with the larger social aspects of the West and its communities.

Less success, however, attended the third purpose of the LLLL—to suppress disloyalty. In December, 1918, Disque's alter ego, Captain Crumpacker, told a 4-L convention that "sedition and sabotage were generally stamped out throughout the Northwest. . . . Strikes and sabotage and violence have been put aside." His statement assumed that sabotage and violence existed before the legion stepped in, and that they were motivated by pro-German purposes for anti-American ends. With millions of other Americans, Crumpacker and Disque equated IWW membership with disloyalty, and these two army officers bent the energies of the legion to the tasks of suppressing wobbly strength and punishing all disloyalty. The entire legion apparatus, however, including its manifold administrative connections with other internal security agencies, laid claim to detecting precisely one case of disloyalty adequate for indictment under the federal Espionage Act. This instance involved three legionnaires, former wobblies, who while on leave from their LLLL camp tried to convince a crew of fire fighters to strike while a forest fire was raging in the Olympic National Forest. Beyond this victory, the legion records are silent on the matter of suppressing disloyalty.[21]

Fragmentary records indicate, however, that lesser instances of nonconformity received unofficial legion attention, still in the name of antidisloyalty. Lumberjacks who refused to join the legion were beaten, black-listed, and conscripted. Legion secretaries boasted that their surveillance system was so effective that it prevented German agents and, later in the war, Bolshevik radicals from realizing their nefarious purposes. But LLLL records do not bear this out, nor do the files of the other internal security agencies that worked in close harmony with the legion.

That sabotage existed in the timber country no serious student of the subject denies. But industrial sabotage—the blind reaction of helpless men retaliating upon society by the most direct means at hand—is a felony. Only the perfervid fears of overimaginative souls could translate this municipal crime into treason. Industrial sabotage did motivate the inhibiting of war production, and Disque realized this. His achievement was to insist upon and obtain better living and working conditions for the long-suffering timberworkers of the Northwest. But not even the strict administrative supervision Disque maintained over the legion succeeded in restraining his less discriminating subordinates. Although he denied responsibility when legion secretaries inspired soldiers of the Spruce Production Division to break up IWW and AFL meetings, he was noticeably lax in punishing such transgressions, or in preventing repetitions of similar acts.

The Loyal Legion suffered, as did all wartime America, from its unclear concept of what loyalty and disloyalty meant. Certainly the legion increased timber supplies and bettered industrial conditions. But it did not create loyalty nor did its diligent loyalty-testing disclose the organized, mass disloyalists who were believed to infest the timberlands of the Northwest. They did not exist. The most incisive study of the labor picture in that area, by C. R. Howd, explains why:

It is a superficial and an essentially false analysis of the causes of the labor disturbances before and during 1917 to attribute them to union or radical propaganda or to the wickedness or ignorance of individual employers or employers' associations. The roots lie much deeper, in the very texture of the industry itself.[22]

Of the two administrative experiments sponsored by the federal government in World War I—the American Protective League and the Loyal Legion of Loggers and Lumbermen—only the latter survived as an organization into the postwar world. But peacetime life soon dissipated the patriotic motive of the LLLL. With army affiliation removed, the Loyal Legion became a barely disguised company union. Its supporters and detractors waged a continuing war of words regarding the legion's wartime utility and postwar desirability.

In fine irony, the basic purpose for which the Loyal Legion had been created—adequate wood supplies for warplane production—was nullified by events beyond the power of the legion's leaders to control. None of the fine woods 4-L lumberjacks cut ever flew over France as components of American-built aircraft. The wartime American aircraft industry was a failure.[23] It was a failure because too much had been demanded from it in too short a time. Inexperienced manufacturers and designers compounded errors which impatient military commanders condemned, but the latter's frequent changes of production specifications played an important part in confusing factory schedules. American strategy, too, was at fault. Planners pointed the peak industrial effort to 1919; the German surrender in 1918 came too early. But it was disorganization rather than disloyalty, error rather than espionage, and a heritage of exacerbated labor relations rather than sinister subversion, which kept American-built warplanes from the skies of France.

CHAPTER XIII

Path to the Patriotic Present

"I am not thinking about indemnities or just reprisals [from Germany] or anything of the sort," confessed Secretary of State Robert Lansing, three days after the Armistice. "I am anxious over the question of how we can check Bolshevism and the dangers which threaten the very structure of society." Few Americans then shared Lansing's urgent anxiety over the menace of Marxism. The United States hastily demobilized its armed forces. The War and Justice departments abandoned their wartime administrative progeny, the LLLL and the APL. When A. Mitchell Palmer replaced Gregory as Attorney General early in 1919, he at first continued his predecessor's policy of refusing to regrant official status to any of the private patriotic groups which clamored for the honor, or to release wartime APL loyalty dossiers for postwar use.

A good many Americans, if uncaring about Russian Bolshevism, were deeply concerned over domestic radicalism, and uncritically conjoined the two. With the German enemy prostrate, these worried patriots demanded that the Attorney General initiate Espionage Act prosecutions against "Bolsheviki activities in this country." The Justice Department refused. The Espionage Act was a war statute, Gregory decided, directed against organized interference with military operations. "I deem it of the utmost importance that this Department does not allow itself to be led into prosecuting . . . agitation against which Congress has not legislated." If Congress wanted "Bolsheviki agitation" suppressed, "Congress should so provide." Even under Gregory's relatively moderate administration and in the first few restrained months of Palmer's incumbency, however, the Justice Department kept "in close touch with all this [radical] agitation." But such surveillance was

316

quietly conducted and its results were kept secret in Bureau of Investigation files.

Initial postwar caution concerning communism reflected sad wartime experiences with uncontrollable popular hysteria over the Hun. Years later, John Lord O'Brian recalled "the constant popular demand that restraints be imposed upon . . . persons suspected of disloyalty but against whom there was little, if any, substantial proof," and how during the war Americans carelessly accepted continual interferences with traditional civil liberties in the headlong pursuit of loyalty. Throughout 1918, a galaxy of officials headed by President Wilson pleaded for curbs on vigilantism and for restraints in official antidisloyalty procedures. With peace at hand, with urgent diplomatic issues to master, with complex reconversion problems requiring solution, few executive officials wished for a new disloyalty program or felt that the need for one existed.[1]

Congress was a different matter. Legislators, in traditional resentment at wartime expansion of executive powers, saw peace as an opportunity for a return to the limelight. Wartime loyalty-testing had already completed the fateful symbiosis between radicalism and disloyalty, both subjectively defined. It was an easy step for congressmen to extend the wartime equation into the postwar period.

Senator Lee Overman of North Carolina became the patriotic pacesetter. He was in charge of a judiciary subcommittee inquiring into wartime propaganda efforts by German-American brewers. With the Senate's approval, Overman shifted his group's attention to "pacifists, socialists, radicals, Bolsheviks, free-love college professors, and their ilk." Against the spectacular background of the Seattle general strike, obliging witnesses pictured an America honeycombed with Marxist subversion, especially in labor unions and educational systems. The most voluble witness was Archibald E. Stevenson, former Justice Department agent in charge of antiradical surveillance. Stevenson offered long lists of names of alleged revolutionary radicals and organizations he claimed desired to overthrow American government. Similarly obliging was A. Bruce Bielaski, head of the Bureau of Investigation, who more restrainedly but no less uncritically added to his former subordinate's spectacular story. In the process, supposedly sacrosanct APL files found their way into the Senate committee's possession, thence into the eager public press. Hundreds of indignant Americans thus learned that they had been investigated, judged, and damned without their knowledge, for their opinions rather than their

317

acts. Attorney General Palmer, it appeared, had changed his mind concerning his earlier decision to keep APL files inviolate.[2]

The Overman Committee's deliberations spotlighted New York City as the center of American Bolshevism. New York State's legislature, dominated by upstate, Protestant, agricultural spokesmen, launched an inquiry into the loyalty of the urban, alien, hyphenated population of the metropolis. Stevenson shifted his activities from Washington to become counsel for the New York Lusk Committee. He did not shift his preconceptions.

The spectacular Lusk raids resulted. In incongruous partnership reminiscent of the war period, the committee's staff assembled city police, private detectives, remnants of APL locals, and members of veterans' organizations. The motley raiders rent asunder such open centers of dissenting opinion as the Rand School, IWW headquarters, and the minuscule group of left-wing Socialists. Attentive journalists made the Lusk-Stevenson partnership nationwide copy. They could not, unfortunately, transmute the documents the committeemen seized into evidence warranting indictments in the courts.

What the Overman and Lusk activities did do was to awaken a national uneasiness over the unexpected complexities of postwar readjustment. The weak, factionalized, tiny group of American devotees of Marx became, in the minds of an uncritical national audience, an immediate menace to all virtuous domestic traditions. Bombing outrages in 1918 and 1919, never solved, were unquestioningly ascribed to radicals. Radical propaganda found, in the conclusions of state legislatures across the nation, its major source of dissemination in un-American schoolteachers, labor leaders, and social reformers. Unsettling strikes in the coal and steel industries and, even more frightening, among Boston's police force, seemed proof to worried Americans that ubiquitous agitators were overturning the nation.

The result was a rash of state laws prohibiting the display of red flags, requiring new loyalty oaths of teachers, and providing for the punishment of peacetime sedition. American liberalism, which had anticipated revival in 1919, found its hopes dashed not only in Wilson's failure to align the United States in the League of Nations, but in domestic American intolerance. There could be only a dismally affirmative reply to Thorstein Veblen's query of late 1919: "Is the smoke barrage of 'Bolshevism' now to be used to hide the actual suppression of honest differences of opinion . . . ?"[3]

The House of Representatives answered Veblen's question by refusing to seat Victor L. Berger, a regularly elected Wisconsin Socialist who was awaiting trial under a federal Espionage Act indictment. In emulation of their legislative ancestors of Reconstruction, the incumbent congressmen found that Berger was too disloyal to swear the oath of office. Berger went back to Wisconsin and achieved an impressive reëlection to Congress, whereupon he was again refused admission. Yet, although Berger was subsequently found guilty of violating the Espionage Act, his exclusion from the House was a legislative act which can find justification only if congressmen possess substantive rather than ministerial powers concerning the qualifications of applicants for admission.

As Lusk followed Overman, so New York's legislature followed Congress. Early in 1920 the New York Assembly refused to seat five Socialist assemblymen duly elected from New York City constituencies. The arguments of the Berger case found repetition in this smaller arena. But historical and constitutional denials of the right of the legislators to exclude new members on the grounds of opinion found few auditors. That opposition existed at all is tribute to the courage of a relatively small group of attorneys, publicists, educators, and legislators. One congressman even had the temerity, as the press termed it, to vote against excluding Victor Berger.[4]

Attorney General Palmer bid fair to overshadow antiradical legislative action. In June, 1919, after a murderous bomb exploded in front of his Washington home, Palmer reversed his earlier moderate course. He established a new division in the Department of Justice to investigate American radicalism more systematically than had been true under Gregory. J. Edgar Hoover, named to head this novel unit, adapted his Library of Congress experience to collecting systematized files of radical organizations, publications, personnel, and, soon, the fingerprints of the latter. W. J. Flynn, new head of the Bureau of Investigation, issued this August, 1919, instruction to all his agents:

The bureau requires a vigorous and comprehensive investigation of anarchistic and similar classes, Bolshevism, and kindred agitations advocating change in the present form of government by force or violence. . . . In making daily or partial reports all information of every nature, whether hearsay or otherwise, shall be included.

Under the Alien Law of 1918 the federal government could deport undesirable aliens by decision of the Department of Labor. Palmer launched the series of spectacular "Red Raids" which resulted in the often brutal imprisonment of more than four thousand suspected alien radicals in the winter of 1919–20. Through an administrative sleight of hand, Palmer took the control of deportation proceedings from Assistant Secretary of Labor Louis F. Post who, along with Labor Secretary William Wilson, had resolutely refused to make membership in radical organizations synonymous with offenses punishable by deportation.

The Palmer raids coincided in time with the Lusk Committee's exploits, the exclusion of Berger and the New York Socialists, and serious labor unrest climaxing in the Centralia tragedy. Palmer's deportation proceedings succeeded in sending out of the country a wretched few hundred aliens, who never had the opportunity to plead their innocence and whose guilt the government never proved.[5]

Through it all, President Wilson rested in the bed of pain to which his struggle for ratification of the League of Nations had brought him. Now bitter, and uncaring for his prewar progressivism, he left American liberalism leaderless and all but helpless in the face of the determined onslaughts of Palmer, Postmaster General Burleson, and their emulators in a dozen states. Wilson stubbornly refused to consider a general amnesty or individual pardons for the thousands of Americans in prison for violations of the Espionage Act or for conscientious objection which transgressed what the conscription processes permitted. The White House remained silent through the Berger exclusion, the egregious excesses of the Department of Justice, and the 1919 impositions of censorship by the Post Office.

Liberalism and consistent conservatism found as little encouragement from the United States Supreme Court. If Justice Holmes's "clear-and-present-danger" doctrine of the Schenck case required some immediacy of crisis to justify legislative antidisloyalty action, it left the determination of immediacy to the legislators and administrators concerned. Holmes's magisterial opinion in the Abrams case, a classic plea for "free trade in ideas," was a dissent from a majority decision which upheld the inclusion of opinion as justifiable grounds for federal prosecution.

American participation in World War I and American home-front loyalty-testing had paved the way for the postwar surge of patriotic excesses. "No feature of the great war was so radical a departure from [American] precedents," Palmer wrote late in 1919, ". . . as the invasion of private rights and private property." There were more histori-

320

cal precedents than Palmer realized, and his contribution to extending the wartime "invasion of private rights" to the postwar scene was a major one.[6]

While the alleged focus of this furor over patriotism—the American Communists—floundered from one divisive schism to another, federal and state prosecutions under espionage laws and syndicalist and conspiracy statutes struck at the IWW, the Non-Partisan League, labor unions generally, and radicals specifically. "There was scarcely a ripple on the surface of American life," the secretary of the Civil Liberties Bureau (later the American Civil Liberties Union) sadly recalled, "when two hundred forty nine men and women . . . were torn up from their roots and shipped . . . to Russia."

If there was no crisis in America's conscience over widespread infringements of civil rights in the name of loyalty, there were individuals who refused to be swayed by the turgid climate of opinion. Assistant Secretary of the Navy Franklin Roosevelt, for example, refused to fire civilian employees of the Navy Department on grounds of Socialist party membership even at the height of the public furor over the Socialist New York assemblymen. But, as vice-presidential Democratic candidate two years later, Roosevelt eulogized the slain American Legionnaires of Centralia as "martyred members" who "gave their lives in the sacred cause of Americanism." More consistent champions of liberalism opposed loyalty-testing excesses, while believers in conservatism vigorously and with far greater success supported further extensions of loyalty tests into American life.[7]

Opposition to loyalty-testing was inconsistent, but it was not totally insensitive. Palmer's 1919 alien deportation raids, and his efforts all through that year to needle Congress (in the process portraying himself to the public as the guardian of America) into passing peacetime sedition and censorship statutes, were the height of the postwar anti-radical crusade. Palmer found himself under congressional investigation, during which a committee of prominent attorneys castigated the loyalty-testing techniques of the Bureau of Investigation. In answer to the question, "Are civil liberties worth saving?" another phalanx of noteworthy lawyers lambasted Palmer in print. "I thought perhaps I saw the tide make its first turning back," exulted William Hard in the *New Republic,* when former government internal security agents revealed to Congress how they planted incriminating evidence among labor unionists, performed as *agents provocateurs,* and lobbied among congressmen for harsher statutory restrictions upon radicals. The result was that no peacetime sedition or censorship statutes emerged from Washington.

Congressmen immersed themselves in the 1920 election contest. Democratic defeat on the League of Nations issue saddened American liberals of the Wilson wing. But Harding's victory meant, in seeming inconsistency with common accounts of that election, a great decrease in federal loyalty-testing activity. On the day before Wilson left the White House he approved Congress' resolution repealing most of the wartime internal security laws, but refused still to pardon imprisoned victims of those laws. Harding found no difficulty in releasing Debs and other federal wartime prisoners. Albert de Silver, brilliant young official of the American Civil Liberties Union, found reason to write, in May, 1921, that

They are getting some sense down in Washington, too. The new administration . . . is an administration of practical politicians, and while the Republican boys can certainly not lay any claim to any taint of intellectuality, . . . they have . . . more practical horse sense than the Democrats ever had. The new Attorney General [Daugherty] is a nice fat man with a big cigar in his face and instead of getting excited as Palmer used to do he grins when somebody talks about revolution and says, well, he thinks it probably best "not to agitate the agitator" too much.

Only the most "hard-boiled of the heresy chasers," de Silver noted, still sought congressional sedition laws. An "era of good feeling" in Washington prevailed as the Harding administration sought its peculiar brand of "normalcy." [8]

Attorney General Harry Daugherty's Bureau of Investigation failed to live up to de Silver's initial estimate. Federal agents investigated radical organizations, but the failure of Congress to provide peacetime sedition statutes forced Daugherty to turn over to the several states the evidence that his officials collected. Bureau of Investigation personnel helped states to prosecute alleged revolutionaries in an intimate partnership which crisscrossed traditional boundaries of the federal system as easily as those once sacrosanct divisions had been transgressed during the Civil War and World War I. Such mutuality paid off in dozens of successful state prosecutions under equally numerous state antiradical loyalty laws, ranging from the Sacco-Vanzetti case to that of the social worker Anita Whitney. Congressmen learned in 1924 that secret agents of the Justice Department were shadowing them, censoring legislators' mail, and "pumping" senators' servants. Such common wartime techniques earned oratorical censure from the floor of Congress but failed to stop the condemned practices.[9]

Another loyalty-testing practice born of World War I experience brought the Justice Department into intimate partnership with private organizations engaged in suppressing radicalism. With the Armistice, a host of supporters of Americanism launched into unceasing activity. These groups were as varied in purpose, techniques, and membership as the Ku Klux Klan, the American Legion, and the Daughters of the American Revolution. In numerous states their representatives secured passage and enforcement of loyalty-oath laws, flag-salute requirements, and criminal syndicalist and sedition statutes. On the federal level, under the Daugherty administration of the Justice Department, they established a novel kind of extralegal, working relationship.

Congress, in investigating Palmer's 1920 raids and Daugherty's leadership of the Justice Department in 1924, learned that favored private patriotic groups enjoyed access to "secret" Bureau of Investigation loyalty dossiers, including those of the wartime APL. The National Civic Federation, for example, found constant "leaks" available to its ambitious director, Ralph M. Easley, from friends in bureau offices. In reciprocal gratitude, these private organizations acted as probureau pressure groups, defended the bureau before Congress, and demanded ever-increasing appropriations for its antiradical work. Members of the patriotic societies appeared regularly to offer testimony to congressional committees and state legislatures concerning the allegedly ubiquitous liberal-radical minions of the Communist menace. Patriotic groups received Justice Department assistance in assembling black lists of subversive individuals and organizations which achieved headlines even when they failed to elicit national sedition legislation. Former APL men were influential in the entire process. The educative effects of the war were bearing fruit throughout the twenties.[10]

Still, such egregious deviations from American tradition did incur opposition. The most extreme antiradical proponents of loyalty-testing after World War I never achieved what Harding's commissioner of education desired:

There is altogether too much preaching of these damnable doctrines of Bolshevism, Anarchy, Communism, and Socialism, in this country today. If I had it in my power I would not only imprison, but would expatriate all advocates of these dangerous un-American doctrines. I would even execute every one of them—and do it joyfully.

Under Daugherty's successor, Harlan F. Stone, the Attorney General's office held the Bureau of Investigation to tighter control than it had known under Palmer's last year and the Harding administration. The United States Supreme Court began a cautious bridging between the Bill of Rights and the Fourteenth Amendment. In 1925 the court erected the first span of that bridge, when, in the Gitlow case, it held invalid, so far as the complainant was concerned, a New York State antianarchy law that was doing general antiradical service.

But the court's flirtation with federal judicial protection of civil rights against state actions was erratic, inconclusive, and contradictory. Jurists were slowly building a barrier to intemperate state loyalty-testing, but learned in the process that loyalty tests were a complex problem in a political democracy which was simultaneously a federal system. In the twilight zones of federalism, state police powers, individual civil rights, and the goal of national unity were confused in a mosaic of contradictory constitutional and judicial trends.

In the post–World War I decades, the states tested loyalty without federal competition. The situation had seemingly returned to the pattern set during and after the American Revolution. Localism had then preëmpted control of loyalty-testing from the central government. During the Civil War Lincoln had made national loyalty-testing programs far outdistance those of Northern states. When Congress assumed leadership in Reconstruction, the inspiration for loyalty legislation still remained national. In World War I Wilson revived the theory and practice of executive leadership in this field. But wartime recourse to the APL experiment reintroduced localism into loyalty-testing. The postwar resurgence of states' rights sentiment joined easily with antiradical patriotism. As the decade of the twenties ended, loyalty-testing was a local matter in America, except as the Supreme Court unevenly restricted state powers in this touchy arena.[11]

When depression blighted America, widespread unrest made legislators newly conscious of the Communist menace. America's distress, worried patriots argued, was Russia's opportunity to subvert this land to Marxism. The result was a growing number of increasingly stringent state loyalty-test laws for teachers and a widespread campaign in segments of the press for extensions of such tests to other areas of society. In Congress the 1930 Fish Committee and the 1934 McCormack-Dickstein investigations into un-American activities provided evidence for patriotic societies to use in pursuit of more loyalty tests. John Dos Passos feared that America's concern with outward symbols of patriotism so confused the real issues of the day that a new "Red hysteria" worse than that of 1919 was in the making, a hysteria that would make "even the coolest neutrality . . . look like Red radicalism." [12]

Depression dimmed the faith of hundreds of thousands of Americans in the virtues of political democracy and economic capitalism, and some flirted more or less seriously with totalitarian doctrines both left and right. Part of this loss of faith, however, resulted from the antics of the devotees of loyalty-testing on all levels of government, from cynicism engendered by the corruption of the business community, and from sheer hopelessness. When the Supreme Court refused citizenship to a middle-aged woman because as a pacifist she would not first swear to defend the United States, American liberals saw more nonsense than patriotic rectitude in the decision. And, in most cases, these flirtations with communism and neofascism proved to be temporary.

Most Americans, by far, remained moderate. In every congressional session after 1930, legislators' proposals for renewed federal loyalty-testing laws died because of liberal opposition and more pressing domestic and international problems. On the state level, however, the flood of loyalty tests continued unabated. They continued to express themselves in loyalty-oath requirements for increasing categories of public servants (especially teachers), voters, and recipients of state largess.

The new crop of loyalty laws coincided with the rise of fascism and Naziism, and many of the state tests included abjuration of these totalitarian doctrines as well as of communism. But almost everywhere in America, state and congressional legislative loyalty investigators concerned themselves far more with the latter ideology than with the former. Harold Ickes pointed this out when an editorial in the *Houston Chronicle* condemned a Texas speech he had made late in 1935 as Communist propaganda, implicit in his support of the New Deal. Ickes wrote to Jesse Jones, owner of the newspaper. The editorial was inconsequential "even if I thought it was goofy," Ickes stated. If the editor had really read the speech, he would have found an equal detestation of Marx as well as of Mussolini.

Ickes accurately described a condition of his time. American public opinion, as measured by legislative attention, newspaper space, and the novel techniques of the pollsters, found leftist radicalism more sinister than its rightist counterpart, equated all labor unrest with Marxist intrigue, and feared internal revolution more than external aggression. In sensitive reaction to these nuances of American life,

Congressman Martin Dies, Democrat of Texas, began to investigate disloyalty.[13]

Aided by a largely sympathetic press coverage and exploiting newspaper, radio, and newsreel media to the fullest, Dies launched a loyalty crusade which lasted until 1944. From 1938 to the end of 1941 he conducted a series of spectacular inquiries into American fascism and communism. His committee's investigators developed fine techniques of exploitation of witnesses and of subjective arrangement of evidence. Bathed in the welcome effulgence of publicity, Dies made the committee a "one-man show," largely negating the constructive accomplishments of its first year.

The most objective student of Dies's work, Father A. R. Ogden, concludes sadly that the Texan's ambitions came to cloud his judgment. In his myopic search for sensationalism, Dies injured innocent, loyal Americans, confused large segments of the public during a period of growing crisis, and produced no results worthy of the effort, expense, and strains involved. Dies, an anti-Roosevelt leader, made his loyalty-investigating committee serve political rather than patriotic ends.

From 1930 through an entire decade, one or more congressional investigating groups successively promised Americans the complete exposure of subversive activities in the country. They all failed to keep that promise. In part, that failure is attributable to the committeemen's subjective warping of their mission to the search for politically lucrative ends. But another, even more basic reason exists for the failure of legislative inquiries into disloyalty.

That reason emerges from a 1940 FBI inquiry into the inability of the federal government successfully to prosecute any of the accused subversives which its own personnel and Congress' investigators had found. The FBI's solicitor concluded that bureau agents and legislative loyalty probers tended to accept at face value the denials of subversive activity which American Nazis and fascists provided. Such trust permitted known agents of the German government to escape from the United States with the greatest ease, after they were under federal grand jury indictment. According to the FBI self-examination,

It would be possible to show a great many of the same errors and inconsistencies, probably attributable to the same lack of background and expert training in this specialized field [of internal security] in other portions of the FBI['s work] and equally in the work of the McCormack and the Dies Committees.[14]

Naziism rather than Marxism threatened America as 1940 neared, as it threatened the peace, territorial integrity, and human dignity of all nations and of all people. Involved fully in their popular-front concern against the Hitler menace to Russia, American Communists generally (the periods of the Russo-Finnish War and of the brief Moscow-Axis accord excepted) abandoned their disruptive tactics and pleaded for internal American harmony rather than discord. German agents in the United States, meanwhile, conducted a consistent campaign of ethnic division, racial and religious bigotry, and more traditional forms of espionage. The concern of most American loyalty investigators with communism proved an invaluable assistance to Hitler's spies and their organized American champions of a prostituted conservatism.

America must consider itself incredibly fortunate that the decade of consistent Nazi espionage in this country failed almost completely to achieve its purposes. In contempt of democracy's ability to withstand the siren song of totalitarian ideology, Germany recruited inept agents for American work and clumsily duplicated its American apparatus among competing and overlapping jurisdictions. Nazi agents and their American supporters found, after Pearl Harbor, that the United States was capable of an unprecedented, unified war effort. They found, too, that Americans now knew how to combat actual disloyalty as never before in their history.[15]

When war broke out in Europe in 1939, American neutrality assumed the same kind of primary importance it had achieved after 1914. Memories of World War I experiences in loyalty-testing also remained in official consciousness. Six days after the Polish blitzkrieg began, President Roosevelt placed the FBI in sole charge of all internal security and antisubversion matters:

The Attorney General has been requested by me to instruct the Federal Bureau of Investigation . . . to take charge of investigative work in matters relating to espionage, sabotage, and violations of the neutrality regulations. This task must be conducted in a comprehensive and effective manner *on a national basis,* and all information must be carefully sifted out and correlated in order to avoid confusion and irresponsibility.

The President requested all law enforcement agencies in the United States, federal, state, and local, to turn over to the FBI all disloyalty and espionage investigation and information.[16] To put Roosevelt's request into action, Attorney General Robert Jackson called a conference of state governors, police officials, and attorneys to meet in August,

1940, with their opposite numbers in the federal departments and with Justice Department personnel. John Lord O'Brian and other prominent bureaucratic veterans of World War I loyalty-testing addressed the gathering, stressing the need for centralized handling of any future disloyalty problem. J. Edgar Hoover, already on the road to a unique form of public adulation, pleaded against "amateur handling of such vital matters." Roosevelt substantiated their warnings against the "untrained policeman" and the "fussy and malicious busybody." The "cruel stupidities of the vigilante," he asserted, offered only opportunities for the fifth column. And Jackson capped the proceedings with a well-balanced survey of past American internal security problems, concluding that

The detection of spies is no job for merely well-meaning citizens, however patriotic. The foreign agent and the skilled spy are trained to their jobs and can be dealt with only by one who is trained to his job. Amateur efforts or mob efforts almost invariably seize upon people who are merely queer or who hold opinions of an unpopular tinge, or who talk too much or otherwise give offense.

This concerted appeal to patriotic efficiency succeeded. An almost completely unpublicized gentlemen's agreement emerged from the conference, granting primacy in loyalty-testing to the national executive branch, unanimously promising local restraint of incipient extralegal internal security action. It promised, too, that existing state sedition laws would go unenforced during the war crisis to give precedence to the brand-new federal Smith Act, which emerged from Congress simultaneously with the conference.[17]

It was barely in time. Two months earlier, Governor Lloyd Stark of Missouri had called for a "sixth column" to combat American fascism; for local organizations "composed of all loyal citizens, patriotic men and women," to "listen quietly" for un-American words and to observe unpatriotic conduct. But after the Washington conference in August, Stark abandoned his patriotic crusade.

With the Japanese attack on Pearl Harbor, worried liberals girded themselves to face a renewal of World War I patterns of popular obloquy and local persecution. But neither occurred. The American Civil Liberties Union, surprised, conducted a national survey in early 1942 of attacks on constitutional rights. Its correspondents reported that "there was not a case of mob violence or vigilantism . . . ; spy-hunting . . . was left to the proper authorities rather than to loyalty leagues and neighbors."

There were exceptions. The major blot on the loyalty record of World War II was the Japanese relocation program. Born of a union of traditional antipathy to Orientals and wartime hysteria, this monstrous miscarriage of justice disclosed neither sabotoge nor espionage. But even this sorry event was handled by officials rather than by vigilantes. Loyalty-testing in World War II remained from 1941 through 1945 where the 1940 conference had placed it: in the hands of executive departments of the national government.

The result was that relative consistency, restraint, and regularity marked the war years, as compared with all of America's previous wars. National, executive monopoly of loyalty-testing produced a remarkably superior pattern of patriotism and a surer retention of internal security than any earlier generation of Americans had known. From once turbulent Butte, Montana, scene of endemic unrest a wartime generation earlier, a surprised and pleased commentator offered this valedictory to the unexpectedly serene wartime conditions: "It's a strange contrast to 1917–18," he wrote. "Perhaps we have come of age." [18]

Perhaps. In World War II as in 1917, federal officials refused even to consider using loyalty oaths as valid tests of loyalty. In the American Revolution and in the Civil War, tens of thousands of Americans had become enmeshed in loyalty-testing webs. In World War I more than 2,500 federal indictments under security statutes were issued. Only 26 emerged from World War II. Attorney General Gregory waited until December, 1918, to monopolize to his office all Espionage Act prosecutions. In 1942 Attorney General Francis Biddle ordered a similar monopoly of centralized federal prosecutions only two weeks after Pearl Harbor. The Supreme Court, for the first time in its history, ventured to defend civil rights during hostilities when in 1944 it restricted the applicability of the 1917 Espionage Act to the existing war by holding that "an American citizen has the right to discuss [wartime leadership] . . . either by temperate reasoning or by immoderate and vicious invective without running afoul of the Espionage Act." In this most popular of American wars, infringements on civil liberties and mass applications of loyalty tests were far less necessary than ever before.

But not everyone thought so. In mid-1939, more than two years before the United States entered World War II, the FBI acknowledged receiving scores of "tips" daily from nervous patriots who saw espionage in their neighbors' conduct. The Dies Committee in Congress and the New York State Rapp-Coudert investigations encouraged popular fears of mass subversion, insisted that Communists and (always to a lesser degree) fascists honeycombed America's official offices and schools, and published lengthy lists of alleged subversive individuals and organizations. Dies gladly clashed with President Roosevelt when the Texan accused more than 500 government employees of being on the mailing list of a Communist front organization. The result was a draw, and the battle, fought in the pages of the public press, continued.[19]

It continued, before Pearl Harbor, more on issues arising from the New Deal than from the threat of the New Order. Federal relief agencies, according to Dies and other congressional critics of Roosevelt's policies, were a thriving center of subversion. Dies's free-swinging accusations in large part resulted in the fateful inclusion, in the 1939 Hatch Act and in emergency relief appropriation laws from 1939 through 1941, of stipulations forbidding federal employment or relief to any member of a political party or organization "which advocates the overthrow of our constitutional form of government." The Hatch Act provided that the Civil Service Commission investigate the loyalty of federal employees. The loyalty provisions of the relief laws required loyalty oaths from recipients of federal largess. The Works Progress Administration was the favored prewar target for Dies and his colleagues. Of almost 2,000,000 WPA workers in mid-1940, 429 refused to sign the loyalty oath and were dropped. But only Dies suggested that every one of the nonjurors was thereby disloyal. And no evidence ever was offered to substantiate his charges that a menacing proportion of the remainder had submitted perjured affidavits of loyalty.[20]

After Pearl Harbor the Civil Service Commission enlarged its loyalty investigation staff and proceeded, without the benefit of precise definitions of loyalty or disloyalty from Congress, to execute Congress' loyalty order. From the first, the commission's staff proved inadequately trained and excessively prone to subjective concepts of loyalty. Civil service investigators inquired if federal employees were atheists, supported the Dies Committee, favored Franco, and listened to Archibald MacLeish's poetry. Often in collaboration with FBI personnel, the investigators assembled their reports and sent their conclusions to the employee's regional headquarters, and, if the decision of that body was appealed, to the commission's Loyalty Board (established in 1941) for final review.

Such procedures, when combined with the evident prejudices of many loyalty investigators, evoked widespread protest from liberal spokesmen, chiefly that old nemesis of Dies, Interior Secretary Ickes. The crusty "curmudgeon" enlisted President Roosevelt and Attorney General Biddle in his determined opposition to Dies's continuing press and radio charges that the war administration was infested with Communists. Dies supplied the Attorney General with the names of more than 2,000 federal employees supposedly tainted by membership in subversive organizations. After lengthy inquiry by a special interdepartmental committee Biddle created, precisely two on Dies's roster were disciplined, not discharged, for misjudgment in work rather than misprision of treason.[21]

World War II loyalty-testing of federal employees never reached the status of an "American Gestapo," as the most excited of American liberal journals claimed. Roosevelt's leadership of the war effort followed the Lincoln-Wilson pattern, and this included loyalty procedures. Cabinet officers and heads of war emergency administrative boards successfully defended accused employees before Congress and in public print. Roosevelt seconded the demand of the United Federal Workers of America for greater procedural protection in loyalty probes, and in 1943 the Civil Service Commission clamped down on the subjective pattern of its investigators' inquiries and set firmer standards of definition. "Remember that you are investigating . . . loyalty," the new instructions stated. "You are not investigating whether . . . views are unorthodox or do not conform to those of the majority of the people."

Similar commendable restraint marked a vast loyalty-testing program which received almost no publicity and produced remarkably little friction. The Special Agent Corps of the provost marshal general's office assumed the tremendous job of clearing the millions of civilian workers needed in war plants and at military bases. Applicants for military commissions also had to pass the loyalty procedures of this organization. These were tasks that the amateur spycatchers of the APL had performed in World War I. In this second global conflict, Americans profited from their experiences in the first, and made the responsibility a national, professional monopoly.

Events indicate that the loyalty testers did a good job. No cases of sabotage marred the production story. On the other hand, known Communists, their sympathizers, and less clearly associated critics of capitalism were cleared for war work and army commissions. The needs of personnel for production and fighting took precedence over the antipathy of many of the loyalty-clearance staff to radicals and liberals. None of the postwar disclosures of Communist penetration into American government and industry have suggested that any actual Russian agents benefited from this sophisticated policy.[22]

Thwarted in direct attacks on Roosevelt, and by the President's determined retention of control over the civil service, Dies and his like-thinking congressional colleagues shifted to more oblique actions. Rummaging through his Un-American Activities Committee's files, Dies selected the most promising alleged subversive federal employees, and succeeded in maneuvering Congress into resolving not to pay salaries to the individuals he named. This resolution was made the tail to a vital appropriations bill.

Many of the victims of Congress' strategy felt unable to resist, and accomplished Dies's purposes by resigning. But a few more determined proscribed employees brought suit for salary payments, and the Attorney General refused to oppose such suits. Three years later the Supreme Court upheld the employees' contention that the legislative salary bar was an unconstitutional bill of attainder. And, noteworthily, all these civil servants had initially passed the loyalty clearances that Dies had championed. All were outstanding liberals politically and intellectuals professionally. None, except in Dies's perfervid imaginings, were disloyal.[23] A total of 1,000 federal employees out of the almost 8,000,000 hired during the war were discharged or refused employment on disloyalty findings (three were on Dies's lists). A third of these were laborers, many of whom were Italian-Americans with romantic attitudes toward Mussolini. Of the remainder, potential rather than proved disloyalty was the basis for adverse administrative decisions.

That the war-swollen federal bureaucracy harbored disloyal Americans is beyond doubt. Roberto Vallecilla sent data on warplane production to German agents, and W. K. Matheson acknowledged accepting bribes from Japanese spies. But in both cases loyalty tests failed to reveal the disloyalty of these men. The FBI deliberately let them remain in their unimportant posts until detailed, lengthy, professional counterespionage work uncovered their derelictions. And neither civil service, provost marshal, nor FBI loyalty probes served to expose the spying of covert Russian agents like David Greenglass, who passed all loyalty tests and worked in the supersecret Manhattan Project creating the atomic bomb.[24]

World War II loyalty-testing, the Japanese relocation program always excepted, achieved advances in procedural regularity and maintenance of civil liberties beyond anything earlier wartime generations had known. Critics of administration programs remained free to voice and write their strictures. Even during the stresses of this greatest of world conflicts, busy American officials found time to correct the most glaring abuses. Loyalty-testing improved in intelligence of conception and standards of operation all through the war years, except when the interferences of legislative self-seekers conflicted with executive control of this task.

Ironically, the Communist menace which had needlessly worried American patriots since 1919 became a real threat in 1945. Russia's resistance to Hitler's legions energized world Marxism to new endeavors. Marxist imperialism made the postwar American Communist party, which had long since been a complaisant tool of Russian foreign policy, a legitimate concern of all Americans. After 1945, that concern expressed itself in a renewed recourse to loyalty-testing. The patriotic past joined the vital, unstable center of the twentieth century.

After each of America's great wars, congressmen have sought to recapture the wartime leadership, functions, and powers which the incumbent presidents of our wars have gathered. The Reconstruction period after the Civil War and the upsurge in legislative action after World War I offered a pattern for what might occur when Germany and Japan finally surrendered. As World War II closed, all loyalty-testing procedures fell into decay. Early in 1945 a new House un-American activities committee humbly sought advice from the Brookings Institution concerning proper procedural and substantive standards for loyalty-testing. The Institution's able report stressed the need for restraint on the part of legislators and for coöperation between Congress and President if internal security was to be obtained without infringing upon civil liberties.[25]

Humility, restraint, and coöperation were early casualties of postwar politics and international tensions. Expansive communism inspired unprecedented, expensive American leadership of the free world. Many troubled Americans searched for a cause of Russian gains and American inadequacies in the cold war, and found a ready reason in domestic disloyalty. Nationalist failure in China, debatable diplomacy at Yalta, and Communist acquisition of atomic "secrets" seemed to outweigh the accomplishments of American diplomacy and arms in Greece, in the Berlin airlift, and in Korea. Resulting national frustration inspired an unprecedented search for disloyalty in America. In the dozen years after 1945 that search permeated all levels of government and society, strained party lines, made reputations, and broke hearts. Post–World War II loyalty tests seemed a novel problem of the present.

When President Truman issued his 1947 executive order initiating the loyalty-security program for federal employees, he struck a new note in the expanded concept of executive powers. In all previous peacetime loyalty-testing experience, Congress rather than President had taken the lead.

Controversy greeted the order. Some critics condemned it as totally unnecessary, others as needful but excessively rigorous, and still others as too mild. Truman may well have headed off more stringent congressional action in this arena, but Ickes insisted that the order resulted from cabinet hysteria engendered by Attorney General Tom C. Clark's pressures upon the President. The listing of alleged subversive organizations, association with which equated "disloyalty" for a federal official, by the Attorney General has been one of the most fertile sources of disagreement. Never before in American history, even during war crises, had the government officially established public black lists for security purposes.[26]

The vast literature supporting and condemning the executive loyalty order has searched deeply into complex and contradictory aspects of contemporary American life. American liberals had long crusaded for the kind of executive initiative that Truman exhibited, but exempted the field of civil rights from governmental interference even in the cause of security. Conservatives, who decried extensions of federal functions, demanded that the security program increase in rigor, scope, and effectiveness. Disagreement centers upon the means the program used rather than the ends it sought. The nation's servants, it seemed, could not have their positions and at the same time enjoy traditional privileges of citizenship.

The procedural structure erected by the 1947 program did not protect the civil rights of accused civil servants. Inadequately trained loyalty investigators confused anti-Communist liberal and radical affiliations with Marxist sympathies, made egregious errors of fact and interpretation, and causelessly impaired the careers of the officials whom they investigated. Partisan criticism, meanwhile, condemned the program as insufficient to unearth subversives.

Mounting criticism concerned with the inadequacies of the program and with the inequities arising from its operation impelled Truman to move two ways at once. He approved the suggestion of Hiram Bingham, chairman of the Loyalty Review Board, that the existing Korean conflict justified dismissing government employees for "reasonable doubt" of their loyalty rather than for suspicion of disloyalty. Truman proclaimed this harsher formula in April, 1951.[27]

Two months earlier, Truman had created the Commission on Internal Security and Individual Rights, headed by Fleet Admiral Chester Nimitz. It was to seek to combine the dual goals specified in its title. Almost from its inception, the Nimitz Commission was the object of suspicion and abuse from the same spokesmen who were accusing Truman and past Democratic administrations of coddling Communists on the federal payroll. According to columnist George Sokolsky, Nimitz "was an innocent dupe behind which the treasonous [Truman] Administration hoped to sulk." All members of the Nimitz Commission voluntarily subjected themselves to loyalty investigations. Opponents of its work, who at first hinted at subversion within the commission, then sought and found other avenues of attack.

It is perfectly clear [Nimitz learned in March, 1951] that there are certain Senators on both sides of the aisle who . . . resent the fact that the President raised our Commission just as both the House and the Senate have re-activated their own inquiries into the field involving subversives.

Democratic Senator Pat McCarran of Nevada killed the Nimitz group before it could fairly begin work. McCarran, chairman of the Senate Judiciary Committee, applied the "conflict-of-interest" law, designed to prevent former federal employees from profiting from their past official duties, to the Nimitz Commission members. Truman's appeal to the Nevadan that the special investigatory group be exempted from the law met firm and vindictive refusal. Thus, the Nimitz Commission, which had begun to approach the loyalty-testing problem in a scholarly, careful manner, became the victim of intraparty politics and of presidential-congressional institutional competition. It was the most hopeful experiment in the complex, exacerbating, unending loyalty-security picture. It died young.[28]

The loyalty-testing problem remained to face Republican President Dwight Eisenhower. Soon after he assumed office, Eisenhower modified the loyalty-testing program. His 1953 directive decentralized the security apparatus to the agency level and altered the criteria for dismissal to include categories of security risks—homosexuals, alcoholics, persons undergoing psychiatric treatment—without reference to subversion. But security risk and disloyalty had already become a fixed duo in the public mind. The Eisenhower modification did not basically alter the loyalty-testing structure.

Other executive orders and legislative requirements have extended loyalty-security processes to passport applicants, port employees, industrial workers, American officials in the United Nations, recipients of government research grants, and scientists engaged in official research and development programs. The military services and the Atomic Energy Commission conduct their own clearance procedures. The American national government, in short, has been involved in an unending, dozen-year-long search for subversives. How effective this drive has been no one has yet satisfactorily proved.[29]

Congressmen of both parties have doubted that it was successful. As an institution, Congress plunged into the postwar disloyalty problem in an effort to restore some measure of legislative initiative. Hearkening to the pull of history, to the American Revolutionary tale of legislative supremacy, to the Civil War Potter Committee, the Committee on the Conduct of the War and its postwar offspring, the Committee on Reconstruction, to the Chamberlain and Overman committees during and after World War I, and to the spectacular precedent Martin Dies had set before and during World War II, legislators sought to repeat their patterns.

The most successful congressional bid for legislative dominance in American history was the Joint Committee on Reconstruction. Its Republican majority overruled a Republican president, dominated Congress, intimidated the Supreme Court, and very nearly overturned the delicate balance of the federal system. Party lines had never bound Congress' disloyalty-hunting committees in any period of American history. Republican Potter in 1861 took issue with Republican President Lincoln, Democratic Senator Chamberlain with Democratic President Wilson, as did Dies with Franklin Roosevelt and McCarran with Truman. World Wars I and II and the intervening depression expanded all executive functions tremendously, even as they inspired a vast increase in all governmental operations. After 1945, congressmen leaped to the breach of legislative initiative in loyalty-testing. As before, their weapon was the congressional investigating committee. In numerous instances in the post–World War II period, congressional investigating committees involved in the loyalty-testing controversy came close to repeating the Reconstruction precedent.

The fateful year was 1950, when Congress passed the Internal Security Act over Truman's veto, and Republican Senator Joseph McCarthy realized the potentialities of the Communist threat. After that year Congress' already ardent demands for primacy in loyalty-testing reached a climax in McCarthy's demands for legislative leadership, not merely of the loyalty program, but of all federal executive functions as well. In unceasing, spectacular, unnerving crescendo, McCarthy made disloyalty a weapon of statecraft. After achieving considerable success during Eisenhower's first years in the White House, Senator McCarthy indulged in his direct challenge to the army and to the presidency which culminated in the dramatic television trial of 1954. Since then congressional competition with the executive in loyalty-testing has diminished, but has not disappeared. It may always revive.

Legislative loyalty-testing evoked outrageous generalizations concerning American democratic procedures. Partisan politics erred in offering "twenty years of treason" as a vote-getting formula. Congressional investigators sinned in sponsoring the "Fifth Amendment Communist" formula, in publicizing proofs of past error into probabilities of present and future treason, and in exploiting legislative powers for personal and partisan ends. "The legislature," James Madison had warned, "is everywhere extending the sphere of its activity and drawing all power into its impetuous vortex." To keep this "enterprising ambition" in check, Madison felt that "the people ought to indulge all their jealousy and exhaust all their precautions." The cold war, the Communist threat, and the need for internal security have offered Congress its greatest opportunity for self-assertion since Reconstruction. Loyalty-testing in legislative hands throughout American history is a dismal picture of localism, subjectivity, and partisanship. Modern techniques of mass communication merely add to its exploitative potentialities, but not, unfortunately, to its efficiency or objectivity.

Executive, national management of loyalty-testing emerges from history as the proper pattern. It is far from perfect. The army's 1955 pamphlet, "How To Spot a Communist," was almost burlesque in its naïveté, and its oversimplifications were so patent that journalistic ridicule impelled its recall. Other executive loyalty-testing inadequacies and excesses are less easily corrected. But in the hands of a president who can strike the delicate balance between exercising the vast crisis powers of his office and maintaining harmony with Congress, executive control of loyalty-testing is far more correctable than congressional control.[30]

It is noteworthy that in World Wars I and II the federal government's loyalty-testing programs largely ignored loyalty oaths. True, for limited purposes, as in selecting interned German aliens for release in 1918 or "relocated" Americans of Japanese descent for release in 1944, federal executive officials did prescribe oath tests. Beyond these carry-overs from the past, such obsolete indexes to patriotism remained dormant.[31]

Since Hiroshima, however, state and local governments across America have "discovered" loyalty-oath tests. By 1956 no less than forty-two states, and more than two thousand county and municipal subdivisions and state and local administrative commissions required loyalty oaths from teachers, voters, lawyers, union officials, residents in public housing, recipients of public welfare, and, in Indiana, wrestlers.

State legislative loyalty-investigating committees emulated their congressional prototypes. California's State Senator Jack Tenney made a political football of the careers of dozens of persons; the Broyles Commission in Illinois repeated the tale. Test-oath requirements ruptured great universities, chiefly the University of California, in a tragic and unnecessary indulgence in partisanship and prejudice. Out of Americans' proper concern over communism, local activity in loyalty-testing created disunity and tragedy, but found no subversives.[32]

The American federal system is dynamic. In changing allocations of powers and functions between national and state authorities rests the ability of America to learn from the past in order not merely to cope with the present but also to prepare for the future. The Constitution is written, but not static.

Since 1945 a novel states' rights movement has professed to protect the future by flaying the past. Its proponents have added an amendment to the Constitution limiting the number of terms a president may serve, and in the proposed Bricker amendment would restrict executive freedom in diplomacy. Self-proclaimed contemporary conservatives have switched sides on the historical train that throughout the American experience has linked conservatism with efficient, growing national power in functional areas. Localism in loyalty-testing partakes of this Calhoun-like fear of the growth of national authority. In uncaring self-contradiction, champions of states' rights in 1957, who decry national civil rights protection, adulate the FBI, which is the outstanding example of federal government police power.

Federalism—the distribution of policy-making power between nation and states—is an innately complex system of government. Within its context nation and states have both vastly increased in functional responsibilities in the past century and a half. But as both have grown, the pressures of historical necessity have shifted the exercise of certain functions increasingly to the national level. The framers of our Constitution prepared for this elasticity by limiting local power in diplomacy, coinage, and military affairs.[33]

Modern needs would properly add loyalty-testing as an arena wherein local control must abdicate in favor of national monopoly. Localism in loyalty-testing permitted seventeenth-century excesses from such diverse sources as New England's Puritans, Nathaniel Bacon, and Jacob Leisler. During the American Revolution the Continental cause suffered from internal inconsistencies, excesses, and vagaries inspired by lack of unified control of loyalty-testing. The nineteenth century saw reaffirmations of this pattern. South Carolina's abortive nullification experiment of 1833 involved local loyalty tests which split that state's unity in defiance of the needs of the hour, and prepared for the tragic rupture of the Civil War three decades later.

In that Civil War, local loyalty-testing reached its peak. Terror compounded tragedy as multitudinous patriots made loyalty their property, and enforced it by local standards. Only Lincoln's concepts of the purposes of the war and of the peace lifted Civil War loyalty-testing above the fully ignoble and useless. And in the Reconstruction that followed, local loyalty tests dominated partisan politics in a dozen states, denying suffrage and office to thousands in the interests of party and self.

World War I found a nation better able to deal with the needs of total conflict. National loyalty-testing control remained imperfect, however, largely because federal officials incautiously opened the internal security arena to the pressures of local purposes in the APL and the LLLL. World War II saw the most heartening indication in our history of the application of the lessons of the past to current needs. The 1940 federal-state agreement assigning loyalty-testing control to the national government wrote the brightest home-front story of any American war. Vigilantism remained subdued so far as loyalty was concerned. Internal security was achieved to an almost incredible degree. And security is the purpose of valid loyalty tests.

In this connection, the post–World War II resurgence of localism in loyalty-testing is an aberration in history. Of local loyalty laws, Professor Robert E. Cushman wrote in 1951:

These range from the registration of Communists to their expulsion from . . . city limits. A number of the measures have been held unconstitutional; many of them are grotesque in their stupid brutality. In suggesting that these state and local measures violate the principles of a sound federalism, I am not again stating a technical constitutional objection. . . . What I do maintain is that the very delicate balance which a democratic nation must seek to maintain

339

between the demands of internal security and civil liberty calls for the wisest statesmanship of which we are capable on the national level. The difficult problems involved ought not to be bungled by state legislatures, city councils, or town police.

Cushman called the roll of current state and local action in loyalty-testing. Maryland's Ober Act deprived "subversives" of political rights and imposed $20,000 fines and prison sentences to twenty years. Tennessee proclaimed the death penalty for treason. Birmingham, Alabama, exiled Communists from its boundaries under penalty of prison for remaining. Cumberland, Maryland, organized citizens' "watchdog committees" to expose Reds. The Mayor of McKeesport, Pennsylvania, stated that "we are going to treat Communism in McKeesport just as Americans would be treated in Moscow if they violated the Russian laws." And, almost everywhere, state and local legislative committees and police officials utilized and expanded the Attorney General's list of subversive organizations at their pleasure.[34]

In 1956 local loyalty-testing received its most severe check. The Supreme Court of the United States, in the Nelson case, spoke out in favor of national control of loyalty-testing. It was not an easy decision for the court to reach. For twenty years the justices have championed an affirmative view of the powers of national and state governments to express legislative needs largely without judicial interference. But the jurists have tended to exempt one arena of American life from the suzerainty of legislative police power—civil liberties. At the same time, the court's inquiries into the federal system have resulted in its consistent grant to Congress of plenary powers in legitimate areas of national authority.

In the Nelson case the Supreme Court decided that the antisedition statute of the state of Pennsylvania intruded into an area that Congress had already preëmpted. The 1940 Smith Act, the 1950 Internal Security Act, and the 1954 Communist Control Act clearly established Congress' desire for leadership in loyalty-testing. State loyalty laws like the Pennsylvania statute in question, according to Chief Justice Warren, varied from "studiously drawn" to "vague [statutes] . . . almost wholly without . . . safeguards." For the majority of the court, Warren denied the viability of concurrent state jurisdiction in antisubversion lawmaking. *Pennsylvania* v. *Nelson* was a valid reading of American history. Unfortunately, the majority opinion confined itself exclusively to an examination of the problem of federalism, rather than of the limitations on civil rights implicit in the state statute under review.[35]

If the Supreme Court's judgment is obeyed, the problem remains to achieve an acceptable loyalty-testing program on the federal, executive level. The answer is not in Thurman Arnold's satirical advice on "How Not To Get Investigated" which, to point out the excesses involved in the existing loyalty-security program, proposed that federal personnel insulate themselves from all ideas, attitudes, and associations. He properly concluded that such protection against disloyalty accusations would breed employees who would sagely see, hear, and speak no evil of American society, but who would also think not at all.[36] This is too high a price for any security system. It is outrageously expensive for a system that has failed, in the opinion of many critics, to achieve either protection for the government or safeguards for traduced employees.

The postwar security program has operated from its inception in the spirit of all loyalty testers of the past. It has not sought loyalty, but rather has tried to punish past disloyalty and to prevent future disloyalty. As William Penn stated of the motives for loyalty tests in his troubled time, "When men grew corrupt, they distrusted each other; and had recourse to extraordinary ways to awe one another into Truth." And when an English jury refused to convict the Quaker for disloyal nonjuring, the presiding judge made this classic, irate appeal to the ultimate justification of *raison d'état:* "Till now I never understood the reason of the policy and prudence of the Spaniards in suffering the Inquisition among them. And certainly it will never be well with us till something like the Spanish Inquisition be in England." [37]

Presidents Truman and Eisenhower have both sought to temper security goals with justice for the accused. Both have failed. Procedural standards have been inadequate, and Congress seems determined to avoid the Supreme Court's intent as stated in the 1957 Jencks case, which required that the FBI open its files to persons prosecuted on the basis of evidence contained in those files. But not even the June, 1957, recommendations of the Commission on Government Security could remove existing inadequacies from the security structure. The Attorney General's listings of subversive organizations has been broadened in size and use by federal and state legislators, school boards, and private industry. This extrapolation has inspired serious infringements upon traditional American concepts of an unfettered society.

Advocates of reforms for the existing system would correct these procedural excesses. Demarcating between official positions of a "sensitive" nature, which require rigorous loyalty clearances, and routine posts in agencies far removed from strategic data, is a popular and logical step. Federal subsidy for counsel to protect accused employees is justifiable and far from prohibitively expensive. Application of the "conflict-of-interest" principle to former FBI agents, to prevent exploitation of official information for private gain, is an approach to this problem worthy of study. Refining the application of the Attorney General's lists to include consideration of the degree of the accused employee's participation and of the carry-over of the black-listed organization's ideals into his work, is a necessary procedural reform.

Out of such revisions might emerge better procedural safeguards, leading to improved substantive protection. It is difficult to see how their application would inhibit the primary purpose of the security program, that of protecting the government from employing untrustworthy persons. Assignment of FBI agents to assist accused personnel to prove loyalty is as much the government's responsibility, if justice is its goal, as the traditional police functions of amassing indexes to disloyalty. Providing government-financed counsel for the accused with power to subpoena witnesses and documents will protect the innocent and neither assist the guilty nor hinder the government.[38]

Beyond these desirable reforms of the existing system, an increasing condemnation of the need for a security system at all has emerged from the decade-long experiment in loyalty-testing. In March, 1957, for example, the American Jewish Congress noted that the executive loyalty program had outlived the "emergency" for which President Truman created it. If abandonment of the total present program is impossible, this body urged incorporation of the procedural and substantive modifications already noted.[39]

It is doubtful that political considerations would permit ending of the security program even if the desirability of termination was to be agreed upon in the White House. Intraparty stresses caused by disputes over the leadership of the loyalty-clearance system are far from healed. Public sensitivity to the question of Communists in government is merely lessened rather than dormant.

A total reliance upon existing federal security laws to punish actual past disloyalty by traditional judicial prosecutions is an attractive alternative to the present system. The past ten years' history indicates that such a reliance would have imperiled American security not at all. The questionable statistical accomplishments of the legislative inquiries or the executive system in ousting "security risks" from official employment fail to show how clearly those discharged persons were a present danger to the nation.

Even more questionable is the thesis that a loyalty-security system is necessary at all. That the present apparatus has been conceived in haste and nourished in a substandard partisan environment is patent. There can be no doubt that it has been a major factor in the unsavory tendencies toward a fearful conformity which have marked the domestic American scene since the victorious close of World War II. Social tensions, translated into political pressures, brought loyalty-testing perilously close to disrupting much in the American system of government which the loyalty-security system was designed to protect.[40]

But the executive departments must protect themselves against future espionage and infiltration as well as against past acts. Indeed, fear of the past and the future, rather than judicious consideration of the present, has been the major obstacle to effective executive loyalty-testing. At no time have any of the federal agencies supplied the primary need of a valid loyalty program—a definition, a standard, a viable agreement on what loyalty is. Lacking this prerequisite, subjectivity, partisanship, sheer stupidity, and vindictiveness in the operation of the executive system have justified the criticisms made of it.[41]

Defining loyalty is a philosophical problem. The difficulties involved in its realization are endless. Men in the present and past have ignored this need. They relied on loyalty oaths and other tests which prescribed absolutes of past conduct for suspected disloyalists. Mere emulation of the past in an uncritical search for security in the future is to turn a deaf ear to history and to the present needs of political democracy involved in unprecedented crisis. If executive officials have advanced beyond Lincoln's use of loyalty-oath tests, they have not yet reached Lincoln's calm appraisal of human nature and democracy's resiliency: "On principle, I dislike an oath which requires a man to swear he has not done wrong. It rejects the Christian principle of forgiveness on terms of repentance. I think it enough if a man does no wrong hereafter." [42]

History records two examples relevant to the present difficulty. After the Revolution the Royal Commission, appointed to reimburse American loyalists, and the post–Civil War Southern Claims Commission, created to adjudge Southerners who claimed consistent wartime Unionism, had to deal with many of the kinds of problems facing loyalty-testing today. True, money rather than security was at stake in both instances. But both commissions had to establish criteria for loyalty and make decisions concerning human conduct in crisis situations.

These precedents suggest that the 1953 Eisenhower decentralization order requires reversal. They suggest, too, that loyalty clearances and criteria may best be made by a permanent commission possessing plenary powers, rather than by existing agencies. A loyalty-security commission, like dozens of other existing regulatory agencies, would have its own expert staff, and should have a nonpartisan directing group composed of men of national prominence exempt from political pressures and responsible for creating standards adequate to the task. Its procedures would include all the reforms advocated for the existing system.

The 1951 Nimitz Commission came close to these criteria. Its files indicate the cautious, scholarly, and objective manner in which it approached its assigned task. "Without sound 'principles of evaluation' there is no 'Rule of Law,' " stated a preliminary memorandum. "Frequently exoneration of an employee on a Loyalty charge means merely 'human nature' tendency to find the 'evidence' of Disloyalty too meagre but [the] safety of the Agency is assured through using the Security Program for dismissing the suspect employee."

The precedent of the Nimitz Commission, killed in its infancy, deserves revival. In such an approach, government employees would enjoy as much protection as organized labor, industrialists, manufacturers, aircraft operators, and bankers have before pertinent government bodies regulating their fields. Congress' legitimate concerns, if exercised with necessary restraint, would center on ascertaining the degree to which such an agency, rather than the entire federal bureaucracy, achieved its responsibilities, and on preventing it from exceeding its prescribed duties. And the courts, troubled by the dual need for the government to achieve internal security and for the judiciary to protect civil liberties, would have a consistent body of administrative practice for review.[43]

Three decades ago, William Butler Yeats offered this doleful prophecy of mid-century life:

> Things fall apart; the centre cannot hold;
> Mere anarchy is loosed upon the world,
> The blood-dimmed tide is loosed, and everywhere
> The ceremony of innocence is drowned.
> The best lack all conviction, while the worst
> Are full of passionate intensity.

Herman Melville was more hopeful almost a century ago when, as civil war and mass disloyalty rent the land, he offered this poetical plea for moderation and humility:

Yea and Nay—
Each hath his say;
But God he keeps the middle way.
None was by
When He spread the sky;
Wisdom is vain, and prophesy.[44]

Between Melville's humanistic skepticism and Yeats's dreary pessimism rests the measure of the current generation, seeking absolutes of loyalty and of much else. Absolute security, as Justice Holmes said in another connection, is achieved only in the graveyard. Never in America's history have loyalty tests provided security. That security has emerged from within, from strengths garnered by lives and sacrifices freely offered. Until the past history of the inutility of loyalty tests to provide loyalty is recognized, American unity and Americans' rights will suffer.

NOTES

Abbreviations

AHA	American Historical Association
AHR	*American Historical Review*
CSA	Confederate States of America
HL	Huntington Library
LC	Library of Congress
MHS	Massachusetts Historical Society
NA	National Archives
NYHS	New-York Historical Society
NYPL	New York Public Library
SCHGM	*South Carolina Historical and Genealogical Magazine*
UNC	University of North Carolina
TQHGM	*Tyler's Quarterly Historical and Genealogical Magazine*
VMHB	*Virginia Magazine of History and Biography*
WMQ	*William and Mary Quarterly*

[1] Herman Melville, *Battle-Pieces and Aspects of the War* (New York: 1866), p. 260.

[2] Quoted in Lindsay Rogers, "Civilian Control of Military Policy," *Foreign Affairs*, XVIII (Jan., 1941), p. 291.

[3] Thorstein Veblen, *An Inquiry into the Nature of Peace* (New York: 1917), p. 31.

[4] Milton Greenberg, "The Loyalty Oath in the American Experience" (unpublished Ph.D. thesis, University of Wisconsin, 1955), offers a most useful guide to loyalty-oath usage.

[5] Art. 3, sec. 11.

[6] Telegram, Baker to R. J. Briggs, Feb. 11, 1918, Newton D. Baker Papers, LC.

NOTES TO CHAPTER I

Old Loyalties in the New World

(Pages 1–22)

[1] Quoted in R. Lewis and A. Maude, *The English Middle Classes* (New York: 1950), p. 40.

[2] 31 Henry VIII, c. 8.

[3] Quoted in St. George K. Hyland, *A Century of Persecution under Tudor and Stuart Sovereigns* (London: 1920), p. 61.

[4] Thomas Wilson, "The State of England, Anno Domini 1600," Royal Historical Society *Publications*, 3d series, LXII [Camden Miscellany, XVI, Part I] (1932), 41–42.

[5] *True Law of Free Monarchies*, in C. H. McIlwain, ed., *The Political Works of James I* (Cambridge: 1918), p. 53.

[6] For the quotation, see James's *An Apologie for the Oath of Allegiance*, in *ibid.*, pp. 85–86. Thomas G. Law, *A Historical Sketch of the Conflict between Jesuits and Seculars in the Reign of Queen Elizabeth* (London: 1889), and C. J. Ryan, "The Jacobean Oath of Allegiance and English Lay Catholics," *Catholic Historical Review*, XXVIII (July, 1942), 159 ff., contain full accounts of the divisive effects of the Tudor loyalty-testing policies.

[7] Most useful were S. M. Koenigsberg and M. Stavis, "Test Oaths: Henry VIII to the American Bar Association," *Lawyers Guild Review*, XI (Summer, 1951), 111–126; F. Pollock, *Essays in Jurisprudence and Ethics* (London: 1882), chap. 7; Arthur J. Klein, *Intolerance in the Reign of Elizabeth, Queen of England* (Boston: 1917).

[8] Quoted in Alexander Brown, *The First Republic of Virginia* (Boston: 1898), pp. 10–11. English background is in E. P. Cheyney, "Some English Conditions Surrounding the Settlement of Virginia," *AHR*, XII (April, 1907), 507–528, and W.

Notes

Notestein, *The English People on the Eve of Colonization, 1603–1630* (New York: 1954).

[9] Brown, *op. cit.*, pp. 12–13; Susan M. Kingsbury, ed., *The Records of the Virginia Company of London* (Washington: 1906–1935) , III, 4–6.

[10] W. W. Hening, ed., *The Statutes-at-Large of Virginia* (New York: 1823) , I, 97–98.

[11] Peter Force, comp., *Tracts and Other Papers Relating . . . to the Colonies in North America* (Washington: 1836–1846) , III, 20–21, 30.

[12] Quoted in M. N. Stanard, "The Real Beginnings of American Democracy," *VMHB*, XXX (April, 1922), 163.

[13] Kingsbury, *op. cit.*, I, 400; IV, 117–118, 420.

[14] Hening, *op. cit.*, I, 166.

[15] "Memorial in Regard to Passengers Out of England, 1637," *VMHB*, IX (Jan., 1902), 271; J. C. Hotten, *The Original Lists of the Persons of Quality, Who Went from Great Britain to the American Plantation, 1600–1700* (London: 1874), pp. 35–60.

[16] "Instructions to Sir Francis Wyatt," *VMHB*, XI (July, 1903), 54.

[17] "Petition of Captain Richard Morrison to the Privy Council," *VMHB*, XI (Jan., 1904), 284–285; "Virginia Under Governor Harvey," *ibid.*, III (July, 1895), 21; "Virginia in 1629 and 1630," *ibid.*, VII (April, 1900) 373–374; "Virginia in 1639–40," *ibid.*, XIII (April, 1906), 378–379; "Virginia in 1641–49," *ibid.*, XVII (Jan., 1909), 14–33.

[18] "Notes of Proceedings of the Privy Council on Virginia Affairs," *VMHB*, VIII (April, 1901), 404–405; P. A. Bruce, *Institutional History of Virginia in the Seventeenth Century* (New York: 1910), I, 151–157.

[19] Hening, *op. cit.*, I, 277; "Virginia in 1635," *VMHB*, VIII (Jan.-April, 1901), 302–306; "Acts, Orders and Resolutions of the Virginia Assembly, 1643–1646," *ibid.*, XXIII (July, 1915), 237.

[20] "Proceedings in York County Court, 1661," *WMQ*, XI (July, 1902) , 28.

[21] William MacDonald, ed., *Select Charters and Other Documents Illustrative of American History* (New York: 1899) , p. 31.

[22] R. P. Stearns, "New England Way in Holland," *New England Quarterly*, VI (Dec., 1933) , 747 ff.

[23] W. Bradford, *Of Plimouth Plantation* (Commonwealth ed.; Boston: 1898), pp. 1–111.

[24] R. C. Winthrop, *Life and Letters of John Winthrop* (Boston: 1864–1867), I, 298.

[25] MacDonald, *op. cit.*, pp. 41–42.

[26] K. B. Murdock, ed., *Selections from Cotton Mather* (New York: 1926), p. 90.

[27] The decision to eject noncomformable settlers is in H. E. Egerton, *A Short History of British Colonial Policy* (3d ed.; London: 1910), p. 45. The oath text is in N. B. Shurtleff, ed., *Records of the Governor and Company of the Massachusetts Bay in New England* (Boston: 1853–1854), I, 354. More extensive commentary is available in Charles Evans, *Oaths of Allegiance in Colonial New England* (Worcester: 1922) , and L. C. Wroth, *A Historical Study of the Oath of a Free Man* (New York: 1939) .

[28] Thomas Hutchinson, *Papers* (Albany: 1865) , II, 132.

[29] Lechford's *Plain Dealing* is quoted from MHS *Collections*, 3d series, III (1833), 83.

[30] Hutchinson, *op. cit.*, I, 216–217; R. B. Morris, "Massachusetts and Common Law," *AHR*, XXXI (April, 1926), 443 ff.

[31] G. L. Kittredge, "Dr. Robert Child the Remonstrant," Colonial Society of Massachusetts *Publications*, XXI (March, 1919), 1–146.

[32] A. P. Newton, *The Colonizing Activities of the English Puritans* (New Haven: 1914), pp. 82–88, 183; W. L. Sachse, "Migration of New Englanders to England," *AHR*, LIII (Jan., 1948), 251 ff.

[33] J. K. Hosmer, ed., *The Journal of John Winthrop* (New York: 1908), I, 128; II, 299–301; Edward Randolph, *Letters and Official Papers, 1676–1703* (Boston: 1898–1909), I, 18; W. Winslow, "The Colonial Customs Service in New England and Its Relationship to the American Revolution," MHS *Proceedings*, XLVI (June, 1913), 441.

[34] B. C. Steiner, *Beginnings of Maryland, 1631–1639* (Baltimore: 1903), p. 15.

[35] J. T. Scharf, *History of Maryland* (Baltimore: 1879), I, 40; Hening, *op. cit.*, I, 552.

[36] Scharf, *op. cit.*, I, 66–68; C. M. Andrews, *British Committees, Commissions, and Councils of Trade and Plantations, 1622–1675* (Baltimore: 1908), p. 11.

[37] A. B. Hart, ed., *American History Told by Contemporaries* (New York: 1897–1929), I, 247–250.

[38] J. L. Bozman, *The History of Maryland* (Baltimore: 1837), II, 595–600; C. M. Andrews, *The Colonial Period of American History* (New Haven: 1937), II, 330–331.

NOTES TO CHAPTER II

Torchbearers of Colonial Loyalty-Testing

(Pages 23–60)

[1] Quoted in Joseph Frank, *The Levellers* (Cambridge: 1955), p. 122.

[2] P. H. Hardacre, *The Royalists during the Puritan Revolution* (The Hague: 1956); C. F. Mullett, "Protestant Dissent as a Crime," *Review of Religion*, XIII (May, 1949), 339 ff.; Mullett, "Toleration and Persecution in England, 1660–1689," *Church History*, XIX (March, 1949), 3 ff.

[3] J. L. Bozman, *The History of Maryland* (Baltimore: 1837), II, 311–312, 335; G. B. Stratemeier, *Thomas Cornwaleys: Commissioner and Counsellor of Maryland* (Washington: 1922), chap. 11.

[4] B. C. Steiner, *Maryland during the English Civil Wars* (Baltimore: 1907), p. 111; C. M. Andrews, *The Colonial Period of American History* (New Haven: 1937), II, 330–331.

[5] Bozman, *op. cit.*, II, 696; A. P. Dennis, "Lord Baltimore's Struggle with the Jesuits, 1634–1639," AHA *Annual Report* (1900), Part I, 124.

[6] "Langford's Refutation (1656)," *Maryland Historical Magazine*, IV (March, 1909), 43–63. See also Bozman, *op. cit.*, II, 403.

[7] Quoted in J. T. Scharf, *History of Maryland* (Baltimore: 1879), I, 202.

[8] Nathaniel C. Hale, *Virginia Venturer: A Historical Biography of William Claiborne, 1600–1677* (Richmond: 1951), chaps. 12–13.

Notes

⁹ *Archives of Maryland* (Baltimore: 1883——), V, 142; J. H. Latané, *Early Relations between Maryland and Virginia* (Baltimore: 1895), pp. 173–186.

¹⁰ Andrews, *op. cit.*, II, 319–330.

¹¹ *Archives of Maryland*, V, 134–152.

¹² *Ibid.*, IV, 58, 153–160, 162–163.

¹³ *Ibid.*, IV, 101, 124, 159, 225–226.

¹⁴ B. C. Steiner, "The Protestant Revolution in Maryland," AHA *Annual Report* (1897), 281 ff.; Francis E. Sparks, *Causes of the Maryland Revolution of 1689* (Baltimore: 1896), *passim*.

¹⁵ Scharf, *op. cit.*, I, 383; William S. Perry, ed., *Historical Collections Relating to the American Colonial Church* (Hartford: 1870–1878), IV, 171.

¹⁶ W. W. Hening, ed., *The Statutes-at-Large of Virginia* (New York: 1823), I, 360–361; "Virginia in 1650–1652," *VMHB*, XVII (July, 1909), 282–283.

¹⁷ "Papers from the Records of Surry County," *WMQ*, III (Oct., 1894), 122; Hening, *op. cit.*, I, 360–367.

¹⁸ Perry, *op. cit.*, I, 244; "Captain William Carver," *WMQ*, III (Jan., 1895), 163–165; Lyon G. Tyler, "Major Edmund Chisman, Jr.," *WMQ*, I (Oct. 1892), 91–92; "The Church in Lower Norfolk County," *Lower Norfolk County Virginia Antiquary*, IV (1902), 34, all contain details. T. J. Wertenbaker, *Virginia under the Stuarts, 1607–1688* (Princeton: 1914), chap. 4, offers background, and "Bacon's Rebellion [Eggleston MSS]," *WMQ*, IX (July, 1900), 6–10, presents contemporary comment.

¹⁹ Wertenbaker, *op. cit.*, p. 40; the convenient compilation of contemporary sources in C. M. Andrews, *Narratives of the Insurrections, 1675–1690* (Reprint ed.; New York: 1952), pp. 108–140, is supplemented by P. A. Bruce, *Institutional History of Virginia in the Seventeenth Century* (New York: 1910), I, 175–198. Unreliable for this study was T. J. Wertenbaker, *Torchbearer of the Revolution* (Princeton: 1940). For the latest scholarship on these events, and an interpretation that agrees more closely with mine, see Wilcomb E. Washburn, *The Governor and the Rebel: A History of Bacon's Rebellion in Virginia* (Chapel Hill: 1957).

²⁰ "The Aspinwall Papers," MHS *Collections*, 4th series, IX (1871), 177–181.

²¹ Hening, *op cit.*, II, 543; Andrews, *Narratives of the Insurrections*, pp. 20–23; Wertenbaker, *Virginia under the Stuarts*, pp. 159–162; P. Force, comp., *Tracts and Other Papers Relating . . . to the Colonies in North America* (Washington: 1836–1846), I, 393.

²² Hening, *op. cit.*, II, 343–349; Andrews, *Narratives of the Insurrections*, pp. 29–30, 119.

²³ Andrews, *Narratives of the Insurrections*, pp. 34, 120–121; Wertenbaker, *Virginia under the Stuarts*, p. 172.

²⁴ "The Aspinwall Papers," p. 183; "Papers from the Records of Surry County," p. 122; Wertenbaker, *Virginia under the Stuarts*, pp. 183–184; Andrews, *Narratives of the Insurrections*, pp. 34, 122, 135–138.

²⁵ *History of Bacon's and Ingram's Rebellion in Virginia* (Cambridge: 1867), pp. 19–21.

²⁶ "Virginia in 1677–1678," *VMHB*, XXIII (April, 1915), 146–152; Andrews, *Narratives of the Insurrections*, pp. 38–39, 139; Wertenbaker, *Virginia under the Stuarts*, p. 186.

²⁷ "Virginia Colonial Records," *VMHB*, XIV (Jan., 1907), 287–288; "Instructions to Lord Culpeper," *VMHB*, XXVII (July-Oct., 1919), 330; Thomas Grantham, *An*

Historical Account of Some Memorable Actions Particularly in Virginia (London: 1716), p. 23; "Papers from the Records of Surry County," pp. 125–126.

²⁸ R. M. McElroy, "The Great Virginia Rebellion of 1676," N.Y. Society of Colonial Wars *Publications*, no. 19 (Nov., 1912), 1–23.

²⁹ N. B. Shurtleff, ed., *Records of the Governor and Company of the Massachusetts Bay in New England* (Boston: 1853–1854), IV, part 1, pp. 79–80.

³⁰ Thomas Hutchinson, *Papers* (Albany: 1865), II, 50–51.

³¹ "Maverick's Account of New England," MHS *Proceedings*, XXI (Oct., 1884), 241; "Clarendon Papers," NYHS *Collections* (1869), 17.

³² Hutchinson, *op. cit.*, I, 233; Samuel Pepys, *Diary* (Baybrooke ed.; London: 1854), III, 314.

³³ Hutchinson, *op. cit.*, II, 146–147; Percy L. Kaye, *English Colonial Administration under Lord Clarendon, 1660–1667* (Baltimore: 1905), chap. 4.

³⁴ Edward Randolph, *Letters and Official Papers, 1676–1703* (Boston: 1898–1909), II, 307.

³⁵ R. P. Bieber, "The Plantation Councils of 1670–1674," *English Historical Review*, XL (Jan., 1925), 104–106; John Evelyn, *Diary* (London: 1906), II, 327–328.

³⁶ B. L. Borough, "Edward Randolph, Royal Agent of the Restoration" (unpublished Ph.D. thesis, Stanford University, 1949).

³⁷ Perry, *op. cit.*, II, 5–7; "Winthrop Papers," MHS *Collections*, 5th series, I (1871), 502–504; Hutchinson, *op. cit.*, II, 216–218, 239; Randolph, *op. cit.*, II, 207–218, 257–276, 289.

³⁸ Borough, *op. cit.*, pp. 11–57; Randolph, *op. cit.*, II, 305–320; III, 1–36.

³⁹ M. G. Hall, "Randolph, Dudley, and the Massachusetts Moderates in 1683," *New England Quarterly*, XXIX (Dec., 1956), 513–516; Randolph, *op. cit.*, I, 107–110; III, 36–51, 60–64, 77–108, 142–144, 193, 233–234; IV, 22–23, 52–57; Hutchinson, *op. cit.*, II, 256–257; Perry Miller, *The New England Mind: from Colony to Province* (Cambridge: 1953), pp. 128–142.

⁴⁰ Hutchinson, *op. cit.*, II, 311–312; "Dudley Records," MHS *Proceedings*, 2d series, XIII (Nov., 1899), 224–236, 258–263; Randolph, *op. cit.*, IV, 117; VI, 186; V. F. Barnes, *The Dominion of New England* (New Haven: 1923).

⁴¹ C. F. Mullett, "Religion, Politics, and Oaths in the Glorious Revolution," *Review of Politics*, X (Oct., 1948), 462 ff.; Mullett, "A Case of Allegiance: William Sherlock and the Revolution of 1688," *Huntington Library Quarterly*, X (Nov., 1946), 83 ff. Older and useful is T. Lathbury, *A History of the Nonjurors* (London: 1845).

⁴² G. H. Guttridge, *The Colonial Policy of William III in America and the West Indies* (Cambridge: 1922), chap. 2.

⁴³ J. R. Reich, *Leisler's Rebellion: A Study of Democracy in New York, 1664–1720* (Chicago: 1953), is the major guide for this section, but Reich paid little attention to loyalty tests. L. H. Leder, "Jacob Leisler and the New York Rebellion of 1689–1691" (unpublished M.A. thesis, New York University, 1952), was very useful, as was his "Records of the Trial of Jacob Leisler and His Associates," NYHS *Quarterly*, XXXVI (Oct., 1952), 431–437.

⁴⁴ E. B. O'Callaghan, ed., *Documentary History of the State of New York* (Albany: 1849–1851), II, 3–4; "Documents Relating to the Administration of Jacob Leisler," NYHS *Collections*, I (1868), 245 ff.

⁴⁵ "Documents Relating to the Administration of Jacob Leisler," pp. 259–265.

⁴⁶ *Ibid.*, pp. 268–288; O'Callaghan, *op. cit.*, II, 10–13.

Notes

[47] O'Callaghan, *op. cit.*, II, 4; "Documents Relating to the Administration of Jacob Leisler," 270–289.

[48] Andrews, *Narratives of the Insurrections*, p. 329; O'Callaghan, *op. cit.*, II, 16–23.

[49] *Documents Relative to the Colonial History of the State of New York* (Albany: 1853–1857), III, 614–616.

[50] O'Callaghan, *op. cit.*, II, 88–100.

[51] *Ibid.*, II, 36–37, 76–77, 113–114.

[52] *Ibid.*, II, 76–77, 262–264, 288–290; Reich, *op. cit.*, pp. 99–107.

[53] Quoted in Borough, *op. cit.*, p. 189; see "Documents Relating to the Administration of Jacob Leisler," pp. 300–310; and A. Reppy, "The Spectre of Attainder in New York," *St. John's Law Review*, XXIII (Nov., 1948), 1 ff., for details.

[54] W. Gandy, ed., *The Association Oath Rolls of the British Plantations* (London: 1922), pp. 30–32.

[55] L. W. Labaree, *Royal Instructions to British Colonial Governors, 1670–1776* (New York: 1935), I, 33–34, 302–436; II, 520; J. Martel, "The Second Expulsion of the Acadians," *Dalhousie Review*, XIII (Oct., 1933), 362; O. W. Winzerling, "The Removal of the Acadians from New France to Louisiana, 1763–1785" (unpublished Ph.D. thesis, University of California, Los Angeles, 1949).

[56] W. J. Hinke, ed., "Journey of Francis Louis Michel," *VMHB*, XXIV (April, 1916), 125–128.

[57] Everett Kimball, *The Public Life of Joseph Dudley: A Study of the Colonial Policy of the Stuarts in New England, 1660–1715* (New York: 1911), pp. 65 ff.

[58] E. F. Slafter, *John Checkley; or the Evolution of Religious Tolerance in Massachusetts Bay, 1710–1744* (Boston: 1897), pp. 32–40; Cotton Mather, *The Religion of an Oath* (Boston: 1719), *passim*.

[59] A. E. McKinley, *The Suffrage Franchise in the Thirteen English Colonies in America* (Philadelphia: 1905); E. B. Greene, *The Provincial Governor in the English Colonies of North America* (New York: 1898), pp. 54–55.

NOTES TO CHAPTER III

Insurrection Becomes Independence

(Pages 61–87)

[1] "A Tory Returns to Buckingham," *WMQ*, 2d series, XV (Oct., 1935), 411–412.

[2] "Belknap Papers," MHS *Collections*, 6th series, IV (1891), Part I, pp. 120–121.

[3] Hutchinson to Dartmouth, Dec. 14, 1773, in J. K. Hosmer, ed., *The Life of Thomas Hutchinson* (Boston: 1896), p. 301. See E. D. Collins, "Committees of Correspondence in the American Revolution," AHA *Annual Report*, Part I (1901), 245–271.

[4] "Letters of John Andrews," MHS *Proceedings*, VIII (July, 1865), 330–332, 338–411; Great Britain, Audit Office Transcripts, XIV, 469–470, NYPL.

[5] C. E. Carter, ed., *Correspondence of Thomas Gage* (New Haven: 1931–1933), I, 359; R. B. Morris, "Legalism versus Revolutionary Doctrine," *New England Quarterly*, IV (April, 1931), 213; A. M. Schlesinger, "Political Mobs and the American Revolution," American Philosophical Society *Proceedings*, XCIX (Aug., 1955), 244–250.

[6] The quotation is in W. MacDonald, ed., *Select Charters and Other Documents*

Illustrative of American History (New York: 1899), p. 366. Theodore Fisch, "The Revolutionary Committee System in Massachusetts, Virginia, and New York, 1772–1775" (unpublished M.A. thesis, University of Illinois, 1945), chaps. 1–4, offers excellent detail, and W. Millis, *Arms and Men: A Study in American Military History* (New York: 1956), pp. 22–25, is provocative.

[7] M. B. MacMillan, *The War Governors in the American Revolution* (New York: 1943), pp. 23–35, has Dunmore's complaint and other data. See, too, M. W. Willard, ed., *Letters of the American Revolution, 1774–1776* (Boston: 1925), pp. 67–68; W. V. Wells, *Life and Public Services of Samuel Adams* (Boston: 1865), II, 4–5; Peter Force, ed., *American Archives* (Washington: 1837–1853), 4th series, I, 1061–1063.

[8] The first quotation is in E. H. Tatum, Jr., ed., *The American Journal of Ambrose Serle* (San Marino: 1940), pp. 89–90. See, too, P. Davidson, *Propaganda and the American Revolution* (Chapel Hill: 1941), chaps. 1–6; R. W. Gibbes, ed., *Documentary History of the American Revolution* (New York: 1853–1857), I, 111–134, 179–184; "Colden Papers, 1765–1775," NYHS *Collections*, LVI (1923), 265.

[9] M. C. Tyler, *The Literary History of the American Revolution, 1763–1783* (New York: 1897), pp. 54–55.

[10] L. Sabine, *Biographical Sketches of Loyalists of the American Revolution* (Boston: 1864), I, 184.

[11] D. E. Johnson, "Worcester in the War for Independence" (unpublished Ph.D. thesis, Clark University, 1953), chap. 4.

[12] J. Gay, *The Farmington Papers* (Hartford: 1929), p. 89; "The Loyalty of Barnstable in the Revolution," Colonial Society of Massachusetts *Publications,* XXV (1923), 330–345; William Eddis, *Letters from America* (London: 1792), p. 217; J. Stuart to W. Drayton, July 18, 1775, Emmet Collection #6579, NYPL; Force, *op. cit.,* 4th series, II, 337–338.

[13] Dunmore to Dartmouth, Dec. 24, 1774, in D. P. Coke, *Notes on the Royal Commission on the Losses and Services of the American Loyalists, 1783–1785* (Oxford: 1915), p. xiv.

[14] J. Sullivan to D. Fowle, March 10, 1775, John Sullivan Papers, NYHS. See, too, Willard, *op. cit.,* pp. 12–14; H. A. Cushing, ed., *The Writings of Samuel Adams* (New York: 1907), III, 145.

[15] "Indictment of Tory Associators," RG 93, NA; Sabine, *op. cit.,* II, 242–246; C. H. Van Tyne, *Loyalists of the American Revolution* (New York: 1902), pp. 72–74; Audit Office Transcripts, XLV, 469–470, NYPL; W. H. Siebert, "Loyalist Troops of New England," *New England Quarterly,* IV (Jan., 1931), 108–147.

[16] R. Mansfield to S. Peters, Jan. 12, 1776, Richard Peters Papers, I, 21, NYHS; J. Boucher, *Reminiscences of an American Loyalist* (Boston: 1925), pp. 105–113.

[17] Boucher, *op. cit.,* p. 139; Otis G. Hammond, *Tories of New Hampshire in the War of the Revolution* (Concord: 1917), pp. 26–27; Andrew M. Davis, *The Confiscation of John Chandler's Estate* (Boston: 1903), pp. 12–16.

[18] Griffith J. McRee, ed., *Life and Correspondence of James Iredell* (New York: 1857–1858), I, 259–260.

[19] Force, *op. cit.,* 4th series, III, 819; IV, 1285.

[20] C. F. Adams, ed., *Works of John Adams* (Boston: 1850–1856), III, 33.

[21] For example, see William Duane, ed., *Extract from the Diary of Christopher Marshall Kept in Philadelphia and Lancaster during the American Revolution* (Albany: 1877), pp. 45–46.

[22] "Colden Papers, 1765–1775," pp. 288–289. See also W. C. Ford, ed., *Journals of*

the Continental Congress (Washington: 1904–1937), IV, 205; E. C. Burnett, ed., *Letters of Members of the Continental Congress* (Washington: 1921–1936), I, 338; Force, *op. cit.*, 4th series, IV, 665, 765; H. Onderdonk, Jr., *Documents and Letters Intended to Illustrate the Revolutionary Incidents of Queens County* (New York: 1846), pp. 29, 44.

[23] "Narrative," John Peters Papers, NYHS.

[24] Thomas Jones, *History of New York during the Revolutionary War* (New York: 1879), I, 41–45.

[25] "Miscellaneous Papers of the General Committee, Secret Committee, and Provincial Congress," *SCHGM*, VIII (July, 1907), 141–150.

[26] A. C. Flick, *Loyalism in New York during the American Revolution* (New York: 1901), pp. 47–48.

[27] J. C. Fitzpatrick, ed., *The Writings of George Washington* (Washington: 1931–1944), III, 367.

[28] Force, *op. cit.*, 4th series, III, 1158; A. French, *General Gage's Informers* (Ann Arbor: 1932), pp. 197–201.

[29] J. Sullivan to Washington, Oct. 29, 1775, in J. Sparks, ed., *Correspondence of the American Revolution* (Boston: 1853), I, 71–72.

[30] W. O. Raymond, "Benjamin Marston of Marblehead," New Brunswick Historical Society *Collections*, III (1907), 85; Force, *op. cit.*, 5th series, II, 821.

[31] Washington to W. Ramsay, Dec. [?], 1775, in Fitzpatrick, *op. cit.*, IV, 201. See also C. P. Nettels, *Washington and American Independence* (Boston: 1951), p. 191.

[32] Washington to Livingston, Jan. 6, 1776, in Continental Army Orderly Book, HL; see also Burnett, *op. cit.*, I, 293, and Ford, *op. cit.*, III, 280.

[33] Frank Moore, comp., *Diary of the American Revolution* (New York: 1858–1860), I, 198; Audit Office Transcripts, XLIV, 641–643, NYPL; Appraisement of Sundry Arms Taken from Non-Associators, NYHS; Proceedings of the Committee of Safety of Brookhaven, 1776, HL; Burnett, *op. cit.*, I, 300.

[34] Force, *op. cit.*, 4th series, IV, 806; N. Greene to Gov. Ward, Dec. 31, 1775, Nathaniel Greene Papers, HL; Ann Hulton, *Letters of a Loyalist Lady* (Cambridge: 1927), p. 85; W. C. Ford, ed., *The Writings of George Washington* (New York: 1889–1893), III, 310.

[35] Sears to Lee, March 5, 1776, in Onderdonk, *op. cit.*, pp. 52–53.

[36] Burnett, *op. cit.*, I, 389–390, 405–409; Force, *op. cit.*, 5th series, V, 342; Flick, *op. cit.*, pp. 90–91; Ford, *Journals of the Continental Congress*, III, 280.

[37] Ford, *Journals of the Continental Congress*, II, 229; V, 475–476; C. P. Nettels, "A Link in the Chain of Events Leading to American Independence," *WMQ*, 3d series, III (Jan., 1946), 36–47; Fitzpatrick, *op. cit.*, V, 182; Burnett, *op. cit.*, I, 506.

[38] Burnett, *op. cit.*, II, 319–320; Hearing of Pownalboro Committee of Safety, Samuel Peters Papers, I, #26, NYHS; Audit Office Transcripts, XXXIX, 95–97; Sabine, *op. cit.*, I, 213; II, 148.

[39] J. D. Sergeant to Adams, Sept. 11, 1776, Samuel Adams Papers, NYPL; Greene to President of Congress, Dec. 21, 1776, Nathaniel Greene Papers.

[40] Ford, *Writings of George Washington*, V, 235; Tatum, *op. cit.*, p. 180; Fitzpatrick, *op. cit.*, VII, 61–62; C. L. Lundin, *Cockpit of the Revolution* (Princeton: 1940), pp. 120–121, 160–164.

[41] Fitzpatrick, *op. cit.*, VII, 120, 142–143; Washington to S. Parson, Feb. 8, 1777, and to W. Maxwell, Feb. 9, 1777, Washington Papers, LC.

[42] Burnett, *op. cit.*, II, 243, 293; Fitzpatrick, *op. cit.*, VII, 61; Ford, *Writings of George Washington*, V, 222–223.

[43] T. Bland to Washington, Nov. [?], 1777, Washington Papers; Ford, *Journals of the Continental Congress*, VI, 893–894; X, 68, 114–118; Force, *op. cit.*, 5th series, II, 1408; III, 814; N. P. Waldenmaier, *Some of the Earliest Oaths of Allegiance to the United States of America* (Lancaster: 1944), pp. 2–9.

[44] Burnett, *op. cit.*, III, 71, 190–191; Ford, *Journals of the Continental Congress*, XII, 1281; S. Moyland to Washington, May 30, 1777, and W. Maxwell to same, June 14, 1777, Washington Papers; Fitzpatrick, *op. cit.*, X, 331, 429; "Revolutionary Army Orders," *VMHB*, XIII (April, 1906), 343–348.

[45] Fitzpatrick, *op. cit.*, XI, 373, 410–412.

[46] Ebenezer Thayer's Orderly Book, HL; Orderly Book #69, RG 93, NA; Fitzpatrick, *op. cit.*, XXI, 23; XXIV, 215.

[47] Ford, *Writings of George Washington*, V, 222–223; undated fragment, Thomas Jefferson Papers, #1003, LC.

[48] J. W. Thompson, "Anti-Loyalist Legislation during the American Revolution," *Illinois Law Review*, III (June, Oct., 1908), 81–90, 147–171; B. Chapin, "The Law of Treason during the American Revolution, 1765–1783" (unpublished Ph.D. thesis, Cornell University, 1951); Van Tyne, *op. cit.*, chap. 6.

[49] W. M. Van der Weyde, ed., *Life and Works of Thomas Paine* (New Rochelle: 1925), II, 314–317; Fitzpatrick, *op. cit.*, VII, 105–106; B. Knollenberg, ed., "The Revolutionary Correspondence of Nathaniel Greene and John Adams," *Rhode Island History*, I (April, 1942), 50.

NOTES TO CHAPTER IV

Conceived in Liberty

(Pages 88–117)

[1] Dorothy C. Barck, ed., "Minutes of the Committee and First Commission for Detecting and Defeating Conspiracies in the State of New York," NYHS *Collections*, I (1924), 1–26; II (1925), 427–428; *Minutes of the Commission for Detecting and Defeating Conspiracies in the State of New York* (Albany: 1909), I, 67; A. C. Flick, *Loyalism in New York during the American Revolution* (New York: 1901), pp. 119–124; P. Force, ed., *American Archives* (Washington: 1837–1853), 2d series, II, 714.

[2] Emmet Collection, #6938, NYPL, has the committee warrant. Other data are in Henry P. Johnston, ed., *The Correspondence and Public Papers of John Jay* (New York: 1890–1893), I, 90–91; George Clinton, *Public Papers* (New York: 1899–1914), II, 581.

[3] B. F. Stevens, ed., *Facsimiles of Manuscripts in European Archives Relating to America, 1773–1783* (London: 1889–1895), XII, 1228; Force, *op. cit.*, 5th series, III, 1204; Barck, *op. cit.*, I, 261–262; II, 425; *Minutes of the Commission . . .*, I, 117–128, 172–193; II, 478, 747.

[4] *Minutes of the Commission . . .*, I, 44; R. D. Younger, "Grand Juries and the American Revolution," *VMHB*, LXIII (July, 1955), 167 ff.

[5] H. C. Van Schaack, *Life of Peter van Schaack* (New York: 1842), pp. 59–76, 109–

Notes

123, 474-475; "H" to A. O. Hall, Sept. 6, 1861, RG 59, NA; L. Sabine, *Biographical Sketches of Loyalists of the American Revolution* (Boston: 1864), II, 380.

⁶ J. Stark to W. Ballard, July 4, 1778, Washington Papers, LC; C. H. Van Tyne, *Loyalists of the American Revolution* (New York: 1902), pp. 192-198. On Kerr, see his trial record, in Personal Papers, Miscellaneous, LC.

⁷ To Earl of Huntington, June 9, 1775, Hastings Papers, HL.

⁸ A. D. Spalding to J. Peters, *ca.* May, 1775, John Peters Papers, NYHS; M. W. Willard, ed., *Letters of the American Revolution, 1774-1776* (Boston: 1925), pp. 45-46.

⁹ For Dartmouth's letter see C. E. Carter, ed., *Correspondence of Thomas Gage* (New Haven: 1931-1933), II, 192-193. See also T. S. Anderson, *Command of the Howe Brothers during the American Revolution* (New York: 1936), pp. 27-42.

¹⁰ John Peters Papers.

¹¹ E. C. Burnett, ed., *Letters of Members of the Continental Congress* (Washington: 1921-1936), I, 114; Force, *op. cit.,* 4th series, III, 240-241.

¹² M. C. Tyler, *The Literary History of the American Revolution, 1763-1783* (New York: 1897), p. 438.

¹³ Dunmore to N. M. Carey, Oct. 24, 1775, Benedict Collection, HL. See also Anderson, *op. cit.,* chap. 1; I. S. Harrell, *Loyalism in Virginia* (Durham: 1926), pp. 39-44; J. Sparks, ed., *Correspondence of the American Revolution* (Boston: 1853), I, 88-89.

¹⁴ G. W. Kyte, "Some Plans for a Loyalist Stronghold in the Middle Colonies," *Pennsylvania History,* XVI (July, 1949), 177 ff.

¹⁵ "Papers of William Heath," MHS *Collections,* 7th series, IV (1904), 10; J. C. Ballagh, ed., *The Letters of Richard Henry Lee* (New York: 1911-1914), I, 173.

¹⁶ Adams' statement is in B. Knollenberg, ed., "The Revolutionary Correspondence of Nathaniel Greene and John Adams," *Rhode Island History,* I (July, 1942), 73. The Tryon incident is in Louisa S. Wells, *Journal of a Voyage from Charlestown, South Carolina to London* (New York: 1906), p. 43. Germain's order is in Thomas Jones, *History of New York during the Revolutionary War* (New York: 1879), II, 401. For general data see T. J. Wertenbaker, *Father Knickerbocker Rebels* (New York: 1948), chaps. 4-5.

¹⁷ Nov. 25, 1776, Ebenezer Huntington Papers, HL.

¹⁸ Force, *op. cit.,* 5th series, III, 1275, has Washington's letter. Howe's oath offer is discussed in Greene to Washington, Nov. 5, 1776, Nathaniel Greene Papers, HL.

¹⁹ Stevens, *op. cit.,* XII, 1185.

²⁰ Lee to T. Adams, June 29, 1778, Thomas Adams Papers, Virginia Historical Society; Grace Barclay, *Diary; or, Personal Recollections of the American Revolution* (New York: 1866), pp. 57-58.

²¹ O. Anderson, "The Treatment of Prisoners of War in Britain during the American War of Independence," Institute of Historical Research *Bulletin,* XXVIII (May, 1955), 63-83.

²² R. Livesey, ed., *The Prisoners of 1776: Compiled from the Journal of Charles Herbert* (Boston: 1854), p. 208; "Diary of Jonathan Carpenter," Vermont Historical Society *Proceedings* (1872), viii-ix.

²³ Elias Cornelius, *Journal of a Revolutionary Surgeon* (Washington: 1903), pp. 9-10; Great Britain, Audit Office Transcripts, XXXIX, 43, NYPL.

²⁴ Barclay, *op. cit.,* pp. 20-21; Barck, *op. cit.,* I, 216.

²⁵ Audit Office Transcripts, XIV, 309-310; Sabine, *op. cit.,* II, 365-366.

²⁶ T. Tilghman to W. Duer, Nov. 8, 1776, Tench Tilghman Papers, NYHS.

²⁷ J. Bailey to Washington, Aug. 19, 1782, Washington Papers; Barck, *op. cit.*, I, 119–138, 213, 263, 283; David Fanning, *Narrative* (New York: 1865) , p. 65.

²⁸ The anecdote is in S. Huntington to J. Huntington, June 5, 1778, Ebenezer Huntington Papers, HL. Other data are in Johnston, *op. cit.*, I, 105–111; W. M. Van der Weyde, ed., *Life and Works of Thomas Paine* (New Rochelle: 1925), II, 269–270.

²⁹ Burgoyne's comment is in Clinton, *op. cit.*, I, 160–161. See also E. H. Tatum, Jr., ed., *The American Journal of Ambrose Serle* (San Marino: 1940), pp. 154–172; Jones, *op. cit.*, I, 239–240; Frederick Mackenzie, *Diary* (Cambridge: 1930), II, 326, 581–582.

³⁰ John Peters Papers.

³¹ Stevens, *op. cit.*, XIV, 1190. Conciliation efforts are ably surveyed in Alan S. Brown, "William Eden and the American Revolution" (unpublished Ph.D. thesis, University of Michigan, 1953), pp. 109–151.

³² Secret Instructions to Lord Carlisle, April 12, 1778, U.S. Revolution Miscellany, LC; Royal Army Embarkation Orders, April 5-Aug. 7, 1783, LC; G. Carleton to Washington, Aug. 9, 1782, Mordecai Gist Papers, Maryland Historical Society. See also W. O. Raymond, ed., *Winslow Papers, A.D. 1776–1826* (New Brunswick: 1901) , p. 80.

³³ Winthrop Sargent, *Loyalist Poetry of the Revolution* (Philadelphia: 1857), pp. 94–98.

³⁴ The *Gazette* is quoted in Van Tyne, *op. cit.*, p. 219, and see James H. Stark, *The Loyalists of Massachusetts and the Other Side of the American Revolution* (Boston: 1910) , pp. 94–95.

³⁵ R. T. Halsey, *Impolitical Prints* (New York: 1939), p. 24, details Edmund Burke on loyalists. B. F. Stevens, ed., *The Campaign in Virginia, 1781, . . . The Clinton-Cornwallis Controversy* (London: 1888), II, 44, 199–264; O. Zeichner, "The Loyalist Problem in New York after the Revolution," *New York History*, XXI (July, 1940), 284–302, offer contrasting data. The statement on political murder is in O. H. Williams to brother, June 19, 1781, Williams Papers, Maryland Historical Society.

³⁶ J. Eardley-Wilmot, *An Historical View of the Commission for Enquiring into the Losses, Services, and Claims of the American Loyalists* (London: 1815), pp. 161–163.

³⁷ "Metonius, Jr.," to S. Peters, May 5, 1781, Samuel Peters Papers, NYHS. See also *Proceedings of the Commission on Loyalist Claims,* Ontario Bureau of Archives (Ontario: 1905), I, 11–21.

³⁸ E. Alfred Jones, ed., *The Journal of Alexander Chesney* (Columbus: 1921) , pp. 145–149. Thomas Jones's comment is in his *History*, II, 27. On British and American policies to encourage their respective agents to swear to the enemy's loyalty tests, see Audit Office Transcripts, I, 222–232; XXIX, 267; [?] to Washington, Nov. 28, 1783, and Washington to E. Hunter, Dec. 1, 1783, McDougall Collection, NYPL.

³⁹ On Jay, see Van Schaack, *op. cit.*, p. 395. A. H. Smyth, ed., *The Writings of Benjamin Franklin* (New York: 1905–1907), IX, 313, 348–350, offers his reflections. Recent studies are R. L. Brunhouse, *The Counter-Revolution in Pennsylvania, 1776–1790* (Philadelphia: 1942) , and Allan Nevins, *American States during and after the Revolution* (New York: 1924) .

⁴⁰ M. Farrand, ed., *Records of the Federal Convention of 1787* (New Haven: 1911),

Notes

II, 67; William Maclay, *Journal* (New York: 1927), p. 6; G. Hunt, ed., *Writings of James Madison* (New York: 1900–1910), VI, 106; for charges of employing former Tories, see Sabine, *op. cit.*, I, 341; *Albany Register*, May 30, 1800; and *United States v. Haswell* (1799).

⁴¹ See J. Boucher, *View of the Causes of the American Revolution* (London: 1797), pp. 195–196. Franklin's statement is in Force, *op. cit.*, 4th series, VI, 781–782 n.

⁴² S. Peters to S. Huntington, Dec. 6, 1784, Samuel Peters Papers, II, 24.

⁴³ Merrill Jensen, *The New Nation* (New York: 1950), offers sharp contrast to John Fiske, *The Critical Period of American History* (Boston: 1888).

⁴⁴ For Shays' Rebellion, see R. B. Morris, "Insurrection in Massachusetts," in Daniel Aaron, ed., *America in Crisis* (New York: 1952); William Bentley, *Diary* (Salem: 1905), I, 55; J. G. Holland, *History of Western Massachusetts* (Springfield: 1855), I, chaps. 16–18. On Rhode Island, see F. G. Bates, *Rhode Island and the Formation of the Union* (New York: 1898), pp. 107–145, and T. Durfee, "Gleanings from the Judicial History of Rhode Island," *Rhode Island Historical Tracts Number 18* (Providence: 1833), pp. 52–58.

⁴⁵ L. D. Baldwin, *Whiskey Rebels: The Story of a Frontier Uprising* (Pittsburgh: 1939), pp. 209–217, 243.

⁴⁶ James M. Smith, *Freedom's Fetters: The Alien and Sedition Laws and American Civil Liberties* (Ithaca: 1956), *passim*.

⁴⁷ F. M. Anderson, "Opposition to the War of 1812," Mississippi Valley Historical Association *Proceedings*, VI (1912–1913), 176 ff.

NOTES TO CHAPTER V

State against Nation—1833

(Pages 118–138)

¹ Quotations are in B. C. Steiner, ed., "The South Atlantic States in 1833, as Seen by a New Englander," *Maryland Historical Magazine*, XIII (Sept., 1918), 275; Letter of W. Hendricks, March 2, 1833, Portfolio 195, #2, Rare Book Room, LC.

² D. F. Houston, *A Critical Study of Nullification in South Carolina* (New York: 1896), pp. 49–51. Full bibliography is in C. S. Sydnor, *The Development of Southern Sectionalism, 1819–1848* (Baton Rouge: 1948).

³ On Calhoun, see C. M. Wiltse, *John C. Calhoun, Sectionalist, 1840–1850* (Indianapolis: 1951). C. S. Boucher, *The Nullification Controversy in South Carolina* (Chicago: 1916), pp. 2–20, offers perceptive background.

⁴ Boucher, *op. cit.*, p. 219; Houston, *op. cit.*, pp. 109–111; H. D. Capers, *Life and Times of Christopher G. Memminger* (Richmond: 1893), pp. 36–75; J. P. Carson, *Life, Letters, and Speeches of James Louis Petigru* (Washington: 1920), pp. 90–103.

⁵ Address on anniversary of the 1833 test oath, George McC. Wetherspoon Papers, DU.

⁶ Carson, *op. cit.*, pp. 108–109; L. A. Kibler, *Benjamin F. Perry, South Carolina Unionist* (Durham: 1946), pp. 145–147; Boucher, *op. cit.*, p. 282; B. F. Perry Diary, UNC.

⁷ Armstrong to C. J. Faulkner, Dec. 8, 1832, C. J. Faulkner Papers, DU; J. H. Easterby, *A History of the College of Charleston* (Charleston: 1935), pp. 86–88; E. P. Guion to D. Cameron, Nov. 27, 1832, Duncan Cameron Papers, UNC.

[8] S. G. Stoney, ed., "The Poinsett-Campbell Correspondence," *SCHGM*, XLII (April, 1941), 38–39; C. J. Stillé, *The Life and Public Services of Joel R. Poinsett* (Philadelphia: 1888), pp. 77–78, contain the correspondence.

[9] Hayne's inaugural is in Carson, *op. cit.*, p. 107. For the Virginian's letter, see "Nullification and War," *TQHGM*, I (April, 1920), 278.

[10] *Speeches Delivered in the Convention of the State of South Carolina, held in Columbia in March, 1833* (Charleston: 1833), pp. 20–34; Houston, *op. cit.*, p. 122. A. Brown to H. Brown, March 4, 1833, Hamilton Brown Papers, UNC, surveys moderate views.

[11] Kibler, *op. cit.*, pp. 153–155. *Niles' Register*, March 9, 23, April 6, 1833, reports speeches, as does *Speeches Delivered in the Convention . . . of South Carolina . . .*, pp. 34–78, including oath text.

[12] *Niles' Register*, April 6, 13, June 29, 1833; Kibler, *op. cit.*, pp. 159–160.

[13] Boucher, *op. cit.*, pp. 316–319; *Niles' Register*, July 13, Sept. 7, 14, 1833.

[14] Dec. 16, 1833, in Broadside Collection, Rare Book Room, LC.

[15] Carson, *op. cit.*, p. 130. All court proceedings are in South Carolina Court of Appeals, *The Book of Allegiance* (Columbia: 1834), of which pages 113–123 contain Petigru's speech.

[16] *The Book of Allegiance*, pp. 14–67.

[17] *Ibid.*, pp. 113–133, 188.

[18] *Ibid.*, pp. 202–209.

[19] *Ibid.*, pp. 93–113, and H. H. Perritt, "Robert Barnwell Rhett: Prophet of Resistance, 1828–1834," *Southern Speech Journal*, XXI (Winter, 1955), 103–119.

[20] *The Book of Allegiance*, p. 92.

[21] *Ibid.*, pp. 189–209, 228.

[22] *Ibid.*, pp. 226–248.

[23] W. Lenoir to L. Williams, Feb. 4, 1834, Lenoir Family Papers, UNC.

[24] *Niles' Register*, July 5, 1834; Carson, *op. cit.*, p. 153.

[25] Hugh S. Legaré, *Writings* (Charleston: 1846), I, 126; Boucher, *op. cit.*, p. 352 n. 1; Carson, *op. cit.*, pp. 155–163.

[26] Carson, *op. cit.*, pp. 166–171.

[27] *Ibid.*, pp. 168–170; *Niles' Register*, Nov. 22, Dec. 27, 1834; Diary of Philip Phillips, Phillips-Meyers Papers, UNC, contain these details.

[28] Kibler, *op. cit.*, p. 170; Stoney, *op. cit.*, p. 50. The argument against taking a false oath is in William Lenoir's essay, "Call to the Surviving Patriots of 1776," Lenoir Family Papers.

[29] Carson, *op. cit.*, p. 122.

[30] Kibler, *op. cit.*, pp. 348–351.

[31] Carson, *op. cit.*, p. 420.

NOTES TO CHAPTER VI

The House Divided

(Pages 139–166)

[1] R. P. Basler, ed., *Collected Works of Abraham Lincoln* (New Brunswick: 1953–1955), VI, 266–267.

[2] John B. Jones, *A Rebel War Clerk's Diary* (New York: 1935), I, 13–14.

Notes

[3] The quotation is in J. Center to E. M. Stanton, Sept. 30, 1862, Turner-Baker Papers #2554, NA. For Lincoln's view of executive power, see J. G. Randall, *Constitutional Problems under Lincoln* (rev. ed.; Urbana: 1951), chaps. 2, 3.

[4] Randall, *op. cit.*, chaps. 6, 7. Quotations are in Basler, *op. cit.*, IV, 430; VI, 303. See also J. T. Dorris, *Pardon and Amnesty under Lincoln and Johnson* (Chapel Hill: 1953), pp. 9–28; H. M. Hyman, *Era of the Oath: Northern Loyalty Tests during the Civil War and Reconstruction* (Philadelphia: 1954), pp. 1–20; Gerald I. Jordan, "The Suspension of Habeas Corpus as a War-Time Political Control Technique" (unpublished Ph.D. thesis, University of California, Los Angeles, 1941).

[5] A. Sanborn, ed., *Reminiscences of Richard Lathers* (New York: 1907), p. 229. For judicial reaction, see *Ex parte Benedict*, 3 Fed. Cas. Nos. 159, 162 (1862); Jordan, *op. cit.*, chaps. 1–4.

[6] Files of G. Pendleton and S. L. Veech, RG 59, NA; H. M. Hyman, "Oroville's Reputation Redeemed," *Pacific Historical Review*, XXV (May, 1956), 173–178.

[7] *War of the Rebellion: . . . Official Records of the Union and Confederate Armies,* War Department (Washington: 1880–1901), 2d series, II, 290–294, 349.

[8] Lamon to C. J. Faulkner, Oct. 24, 1861, W. H. Lamon Papers, HL.

[9] File of W. J. Allen, Turner-Baker Papers; W. Hamilton to L. C. Baker, Sept. 10, 1861, F. H. Pierpont Papers, DU.

[10] Seward to R. Anderson, Sept. 24, 1861, RG 59, NA.

[11] File of J. S. Bacon, RG 77, NA.

[12] Files of C. Follins, D. Lucchesi, W. Frank, M. Ives, G. Harbin, M. Haldenback, and W. Tolle, RG 59, NA.

[13] File of C. Gayerré, Turner-Baker Papers #1689, for Gillen's statement, and Eldridge Collection, HL, for visitor's pass. Lawrence Sangston, *The Bastilles of the North* (Baltimore: 1863), p. 93, offers more data.

[14] *Official Records of the Union and Confederate Armies,* 2d series, I, 586.

[15] Basler, *op. cit.*, IV, 523; J. M. Brewer, *Prison Life!* (n.p.: n.d.); W. D. Hoyt, "Thomas John Claggett," *Maryland Historical Magazine*, XLVII (June, 1952), 128 ff.

[16] File of W. McNabb, RG 59, NA. The Hamlet parody is in J. J. Williamson, *Prison Life in the Old Capitol* (West Orange: 1911), p. 62 n.

[17] File of A. DeCosta, RG 59, NA.

[18] File of A. Lynch, *ibid.*, has Dix's statements and commission orders. See also Samuel P. Day, *Down South; or an Englishman's Experiences at the Seat of the American War* (London: 1862), II, 242.

[19] E. S. Kilborn *et al.* to Seth Hawley, Nov. 15, 1861, in C. MacGill Papers, DU, and Horace S. Fulkerson, *A Civilian's Recollections of the War between the States* (Baton Rouge: 1939), pp. 399–405.

[20] Basler, *op. cit.*, IV, 522–523; V, 86–87; Sangston, *op. cit.*, pp. 85–88; and Dennis A. Mahoney, *The Prisoner of State* (New York: 1863), pp. 399–403, offer participants' details.

[21] *Congressional Globe,* 37th Cong., 2d sess., p. 2114.

[22] Feb. 15, 1862, William Owner Diary, LC; Basler, *op. cit.*, V, 86–87.

[23] Congressional attacks on Lincoln for arbitrary arrests are surveyed in an article by Charles Warren, *New York Times*, May 12, 1918.

[24] H. Smith to Charles Ray, Oct. 1, 1861, C. Ray Papers, HL.

[25] Hyman, *Era of the Oath*, chap. 1.

[26] File of E. B. Grayson, RG 59, NA. See also n. 42 below.

[27] Hyman, *Era of the Oath*, pp. 1–20.

[28] Adams' quote is in the file of D. Holland, RG 59, NA.

[29] T. H. Williams, *Lincoln and the Radicals* (Madison: 1941), should be compared to David Donald's provocative essay in *Lincoln Reconsidered* (New York: 1956), pp. 103–127.

[30] Howard Glyndon (pseud.), *Notable Men in the House of Representatives* (New York: 1862), p. 15; H. I. Paine to Potter, Aug. 29, 1861, John Fox Potter Papers, State Historical Society of Wisconsin. The committee report is in *Loyalty of Clerks and Other Persons Employed by the Government*, U.S. 37th Cong., 2d sess., H. Rept. 16 (Washington: 1862).

[31] See *Loyalty of Clerks . . .* , *passim*, and the Potter Papers. Quotations are in C. H. Winder to brother, Sept. 24, 1861, RG 59, NA, and *Springfield Republican*, Nov. 22, 1861.

[32] *Loyalty of Clerks . . .* , *passim*, and Hyman, *Era of the Oath*, pp. 1–5.

[33] W. A. Cook, *The Administration of Abraham Lincoln Sustained by the Sages and Heroes of the Revolution* (Washington: 1864), pp. 21–22.

[34] Anonymous to Potter, Dec. 11, 1861, Potter Papers, and William Owner Diary, I, 37.

[35] A. H. Meneely, *The War Department, 1861* (New York: 1928), pp. 202–204; F. A. Flower, *Edwin McMasters Stanton* (New York: 1905), p. 119.

[36] Critical references to Welles are in the Potter Papers, too numerous to cite.

[37] S. Cameron to Potter, Sept. 20, 1861, and A. Reed to Lincoln, Oct. 16, 1861, in *ibid*. J. P. Usher to J. M. Edmunds, April 2, 1863, W. H. Lamon Papers; Basler, *op. cit.*, IV, 530–531, 556; V, 25.

[38] Potter to Lamon, Sept. 6, 1862, Lamon Papers; for a Lincoln anecdote on patronage, see E. Dicey, *Six Months in the Federal States* (London: 1863), I, 226.

[39] *Loyalty of Clerks . . .* , pp. 34–60; Basler, *op. cit.*, VI, 70.

[40] G. G. Lawrence, *Three Months in America in the Summer of 1863* (London: 1864), p. 29.

[41] Hyman, *Era of the Oath*, chaps. 1–3.

[42] On multiple perjuries ordered by Union and Confederate authorities for espionage purposes, see T. N. Conrad, *A Confederate Spy* (New York: 1892), p. 29, and see J. Bradley, *The Confederate Mail Carrier* (Mexico, Mo.: 1894), pp. 20–21; H. T. Kane, *Spies for the Blue and Gray* (New York: 1954), *passim*.

[43] *Official Records of the Union and Confederate Armies*, 2d series, II, 291–292, 333–335; VI, 998; Jordan, *op. cit.*, chap. 4–6. The civilian provost marshals were incorporated into the military structure when the provost marshal general's office was legitimized by Congress in March, 1863.

NOTES TO CHAPTER VII

Yankee Provosts and Rebel Patriotism

(Pages 167–198)

[1] R. S. Thorndike, ed., *The Sherman Letters* (New York: 1894), p. 230; see also A. H. Carpenter, "Military Government of Southern Territory, 1861–1865," AHA *Annual Report* (1900), Part I, pp. 467 ff. Sections of this chapter have appeared in

Notes

my "Deceit in Dixie: Southerners' Evasions of Union Loyalty Tests," *Civil War History*, III (March, 1957), 65–82.

[2] *War of the Rebellion: . . . Official Records of the Union and Confederate Armies*, War Department (Washington: 1880–1901), 2d series, I, 97.

[3] *Ibid.*, IV, 466–468.

[4] Cornelia McDonald, *A Diary* (Nashville: 1934), p. 133.

[5] P. S. White to W. B. Campbell, Aug. 23, 1863, David Campbell Papers, DU. On Lincoln's inability to correct this, see R. P. Basler, ed., *Collected Works of Abraham Lincoln* (New Brunswick: 1953–1955), V, 344.

[6] *Official Records of the Union and Confederate Armies*, 2d series, V, 300.

[7] Mayor Slaughter's Memoranda, in Slaughter Collection, HL, and M. D. Conway, "Fredericksburg First and Last," *Magazine of American History*, XVII (June, 1887), 449–469; Marsena Patrick Diary, LC.

[8] H. G. Spruill, Memoranda, in Pettigrew Family Papers, UNC; R. C. Hawkins, "Early Coast Operations in North Carolina," in R. U. Johnson and C. C. Buell, eds., *Battles and Leaders of the Civil War* (repr. ed.; New York: 1956), I, 633–659. Plymouth later changed hands several times.

[9] Journal of a Louisiana Rebel, July 28, 1862, NYHS.

[10] Col. Warmouth's plea to a military commission on question of oath violation, 1864, H. C. Warmouth Papers, UNC.

[11] A. W. Bishop, *Loyalty on the Frontier* (St. Louis: 1863), pp. 105–106.

[12] *Ibid.*, pp. 108–110; Thomas W. Humes, *The Loyal Mountaineers of Tennessee* (Knoxville: 1888), pp. 230–231, 273.

[13] Journal of David M. Turnure, Aug. 19, 1862, NYHS; T. F. Lang, *Loyal West Virginia from 1861 to 1865* (Baltimore: 1895), pp. 60–61.

[14] C. Woolley to Holt, Feb. 23, 1863, Joseph Holt Papers, LC; W. Lenoir to R. Lenoir, Nov. 13, 1863, Lenoir Family Papers, UNC; S. E. Belcher to W. B. Campbell, Aug. 3, 1863, David Campbell Papers, DU.

[15] John B. Jones, *A Rebel War Clerk's Diary* (New York: 1935), I, 313; Mrs. R. A. Pryor, *Reminiscences of War and Peace* (New York: 1905), pp. 376–377; McDonald, *op. cit.*, p. 157; K. M. Rowland and M. L. Croxall, eds., *Journal of Julia Le Grand* (Richmond; 1911), pp. 215–217.

[16] Sarah M. Dawson, *A Confederate Girl's Diary* (Boston: 1913), pp. 382–384; *Daily Rebel*, Oct. 7, 1862; N. Green to W. B. Campbell, Aug. 22, 1863, Campbell Papers.

[17] Basler, *op. cit.*, VI, 441–442; McDonald, *op. cit.*, p. 133.

[18] R. F. Wilkinson to his father, June 19, 1864, R. F. Wilkinson Letters, NYHS; M. E. Garrett to her mother, Oct. 26, 1863, Lenoir Family Papers.

[19] John Hallum, *The Diary of an Old Lawyer* (Nashville: 1895), pp. 280–287; testimony supported in Smith-Brady Commission Report, NYPL.

[20] Basler, *op. cit.*, V, 370; *Daily Rebel*, Nov. 5, 1862; *Digest of Cases of Contested Elections, 1865–1871*, U.S. 41st Cong., 2d sess., H. Misc. Doc. 152 (Washington: 1871), pp. 358–443.

[21] Mrs. A. W. Brown to Col. J. G. Parkhurst, Jan. 27, 1861, Parkhurst Papers, DU.

[22] K. P. Hale Recollections, UNC; Kate S. Carney Diary, May 7, 1862, UNC.

[23] Wiley Britton, *Memoirs of the Rebellion on the Border, 1863* (Chicago: 1882), p. 407; C. R. Aulit to Wade, June 24, 1862, B. Wade Papers, LC; J. C. Andrews, *The North Reports the Civil War* (Pittsburgh: 1955), pp. 286–287.

[24] T. Eidner to E. M. Stanton, April 1, 1863, Turner-Baker Papers #2045, NA, describes the Key West episode, and Britton, *op. cit.*, p. 366, deals with Missouri.

Thomas W. Higginson, *Army Life in a Black Regiment* (Boston: 1900), pp. 149–150, pictures Negro troops' attitude, and for McClellan and state loyalty tests, see H. M. Hyman, *Era of the Oath: Northern Loyalty Tests during the Civil War and Reconstruction* (Philadelphia: 1954), pp. 35–47.

[25] On the Buell-Johnson fiasco, see Mrs. Harding to her husband, July 24, 1862, Harding-Jackson Papers, UNC.

[26] Horace S. Fulkerson, *A Civilian's Recollections of the War between the States* (Baton Rouge: 1939), pp. 171–175.

[27] On duplicity, see Mrs. Harding to her husband, June 8, 1862, Harding-Jackson Papers. For Price, see his letter to Grant, Aug. 15, 1864, Eldridge Collection, HL, and Hyman, "Deceit in Dixie."

[28] R. F. Wilkinson to his father, Oct. 26, 1863, Wilkinson Letters.

[29] O. O. Winther, ed., *With Sherman to the Sea; the Civil War Letters, Diaries, and Reminiscences of Theodore F. Upson* (Baton Rouge: 1943), pp. 48–54; Report of Divisional Provost Marshals, Dec. 7, 1863, RG 107, NA.

[30] Lincoln to Stanton, Feb. 5, 1864, in Basler, *op. cit.,* VIII, 108–109, 153–154, 169–170. Radical reaction is in Hyman, *Era of the Oath,* pp. 48–49.

[31] *Official Records of the Union and Confederate Armies,* 2d series, IV, 251, 310–311, 393, 561; Jefferson Davis, *The Rise and Fall of the Confederate Government* (New York: 1881), II, 593; *Daily Rebel,* Sept. 26, 1862. Pertinent is J. Yates to Lincoln, Feb. 1, 1864, R. T. Lincoln Papers, LC.

[32] The *Examiner* editorial is in Frederick S. Daniel, *The Richmond Examiner during the War* (New York: 1868), p. 115. Alexander Harris, *A Review of the Political Conflict in America* (New York: 1876), pp. 354–355, Mrs. S. A. B. Putnam, *Richmond during the War* (New York: 1867), pp. 155–156, and M. Southal to Gen. Harding, Aug. 11, 1863, Harding-Jackson Papers, have the quotations in the order used.

[33] Overton Bernard Diary, Dec. 16, 1863, and Nimrod Porter Diary, Feb. 22, 1864, both in UNC.

[34] L. A. Sigaud, *Belle Boyd, Confederate Spy* (Richmond: 1944), pp. 40–41; Dawson, *op. cit.,* pp. 316–317; Kate S. Carney Diary, May 29, 1862, UNC. A satire on Lincoln's oath offer was presented by touring companies and was well received by Confederate troops; see J. H. Hewitt, *King Linkum the First: A Musical Burletta,* ed. R. B. Harwell, Emory University Publications, Sources, and Reprints, Series I (Atlanta: 1947).

[35] Kate S. Carney Diary, June 15, July 2, 1862; Dawson, *op. cit.,* pp. 70–75, 343–344; Mrs. J. L. Alcorn to husband, Aug. 29, 1863, James A. Alcorn Papers, UNC; E. F. Andrews, *The War-Time Journal of a Georgia Girl, 1864–1865* (New York: 1908), pp. 255–256.

[36] Nimrod Porter Diary, July 18, 1863; O. M. Sanford, "A Virginian's Diary in Civil War Days," *Americana,* XVIII (Oct., 1924), 367.

[37] F. Smith to wife, March 26, 1863, F. E. Smith Papers, DU.

[38] Unidentified newspaper clippings in William Owner Diary, LC, covers Alexandria, and for Bolivar, J. H. Bills Diary, April 18, June 9, 15, 1863, UNC.

[39] Ida Fulton to Miss Wright, Aug. 11, 1864, T. Hunter-Holmes Papers, DU.

[40] Kate S. Carney Diary, June 18, 21, 1862; C. S. Foltz, *Surgeon of the Seas* (Indianapolis: 1931), p. 277.

[41] On the St. Louis secret society, see Missouri Report, 1864, Turner-Baker Papers, and Tyler's plight is in his letter to Lamon, July 16, 1863, and in Lamon's to Chase,

Notes

Jan. 25, 1863, W. H. Lamon Papers, HL. The Southern woman's reaction is in M. Southall to Gen. Harding, July 30, 1864, Harding-Jackson Papers.

[42] Basler, *op. cit.*, VIII, 104; *Official Records of the Union and Confederate Armies*, 1st series, XLVII, part 3, p. 92; *General Orders, 1863*, U.S. Army, Adjutant General (Washington: 1864), #107; *General Orders, 1865*, U.S. Army, Adjutant General (Washington: 1866), #242.

[43] J. Q. Anderson, ed., *Brokenburn: The Journal of Kate Stone, 1861–1868* (Baton Rouge: 1955), pp. 181–182; Wiley Britton, *The Civil War on the Border* (New York: 1891), I, 145–147; Britton, *Memoirs of the Rebellion . . .* , pp. 118–131; E. M. Coulter, *The Civil War and Readjustment in Kentucky* (Chapel Hill: 1926), pp. 221–227; F. Smith to wife, March 10, 1862, F. E. Smith Papers; R. M. Ewing to Gen. Harding, Aug. 17, 1862, Harding-Jackson Papers; H. B. Short to W. Pettigrew, May 19, 1863, Pettigrew Family Papers, UNC.

[44] J. A. Pitts, *Personal and Professional Reminiscences of an Old Lawyer* (Kingsport: 1930), pp. 107–108.

[45] Lamon to Chase, Jan. 25, 1864, W. H. Lamon Papers.

[46] *Daily Rebel*, July 12, 1864.

NOTES TO CHAPTER VIII

Over These Prison Walls

(Pages 199–218)

[1] J. C. Williams, Civil War Record, Virginia State Library.

[2] *General Orders, 1861*, U.S. Army, Adjutant General (Washington: 1862), #44.

[3] J. M. Perkins to Seward, Jan. 22, 1862, and C. W. Coleman to same, May 1, 1862, RG 59, NA.

[4] Catron to E. M. Stanton, May 26, 1862, W. H. Lamon Papers, HL.

[5] John Hay to Lamon, Dec. 27, 1864, Lamon Papers.

[6] Anne Donnetty to Lamon, Jan. 1, 1865, Lamon Papers; file of A. Archimaud, Turner-Baker Papers, NA; H. M. Hyman, "New Yorkers and the Civil War Draft," *New York History*, XXXVI (April, 1955), 170.

[7] J. G. Nicolay and J. Hay, eds., *Complete Works of Abraham Lincoln* (Gettsyburg ed.; New York: 1905), X, 44.

[8] Gen. M. L. Smith to Grant, July 15, 1863, in J. Devereux Papers, UNC; Grant's Special Order #82 (undated), Confederate States of America Archives, DU.

[9] All data from file of J. Bosworth, RG 109, NA; H. M. Hyman, "Civil War Turncoats," *Military Affairs*, XXII (Fall, 1958), 134–138.

[10] G. H. Taylor to W. B. Campbell, Feb. 24, 1866, David Campbell Papers, DU, supplies detailed reminiscences of the commission system.

[11] Quotation in H. C. Smith to Tyson, April 4, 1865, Bryan Tyson Papers, DU. See also B. H. Pierce to Gov. Pierpont, May 9, 1862, F. H. Pierpont Papers, DU.

[12] T. Dennett, ed., *Lincoln and the Civil War in the Diaries and Letters of John Hay* (New York: 1939), pp. 160–161.

[13] W. Britton, *Memoirs of the Rebellion on the Border, 1863* (Chicago: 1882), pp. 126, 183–184.

[14] R. P. Basler, ed., *Collected Works of Abraham Lincoln* (New Brunswick: 1953–1955), VII, 176–177; [?] to Holt, Dec. 24, 1864, Joseph Holt Papers, LC.

[15] *Daily Rebel,* March 15, 1864.

[16] J. Cobb to A. Burt, Oct. [?], 1864, Armistead Burt Papers, DU.

[17] D. F. Boyd to Sherman, April 7, 1864, D. F. Boyd Papers, UNC.

[18] J. O. Murray, *The Immortal Six Hundred* (Winchester: 1905), pp. 178–180; H. C. Dickinson, *Diary, Morris Island, 1864–1865* (Denver: n.d.), pp. 90, 150–152, 167–171.

[19] Kate S. Carney Diary, May 7, 23, 29, June 14–17, 30, July 6, 1862, UNC; I. Ross, *Rebel Rose: Life of Rose O'Neal Greenhow* (New York: 1954), pp. 124–125.

[20] File of A. Beekley, RG 59, NA.

[21] Susannah to Gen. Harding, Aug. 25, 1862, Harding-Jackson Papers, UNC.

[22] File of H. Young, RG 59, NA.

[23] J. Gray to Col. Warmouth, April 11, 1864, H. C. Warmouth Papers, UNC.

[24] *General Orders, 1863,* U.S. Army, Adjutant General (Washington: 1864), #286.

[25] J. M. McAlpine to Holt, Sept. 12, 1864, Joseph Holt Papers; G. W. Tyson to B. Tyson, Dec. 14, 1864, B. Tyson Papers.

[26] Poem is in Dickinson, *op. cit.,* pp. 127–128. Lincoln's orders to Butler are in Basler, *op. cit.,* VIII, 103.

[27] H. Storms, late Commissary General, to R. Murrat, Dec. 9, 1862, RG 59, NA.

[28] S. Treat to Holt, Aug. 29, 1863, Joseph Holt Papers.

[29] Files of W. Robinson and R. Brooks, RG 59, NA.

[30] D. F. Boyd to Sherman, April 7, 1864, D. F. Boyd Papers.

[31] Murray, *op. cit.,* pp. 189–190.

[32] W. P. Smith to father, June 6, 1865, F. E. Smith Papers, DU; Dickinson, *op. cit.,* pp. 180–188.

[33] J. O. Casler, *Four Years in the Stonewall Brigade* (2d ed.; Girard: 1956), pp. 284–285.

[34] E. F. Andrews, *The War-Time Journal of a Georgia Girl, 1864–1865* (New York: 1908), pp. 29–30; *Nation,* Sept. 21, 1865.

[35] Clay W. Holmes, *The Elmira Prison Camp* (New York: 1912), pp. 278–279.

NOTES TO CHAPTER IX

South of the Border

(Pages 219–250)

[1] See Lyon G. Tyler, *A Confederate Catechism* (Richmond: 1930), p. 31; Jefferson Davis, *The Rise and Fall of the Confederate Government* (New York: 1881), II, 285–288, 458, 468–469. Basic monographs on Confederate internal security problems are G. L. Tatum, *Disloyalty in the Confederacy* (Chapel Hill: 1934), and E. Lonn, *Foreigners in the Confederacy* (Chapel Hill: 1940).

[2] The quotation is in J. Q. Anderson, ed., *Brokenburn: The Journal of Kate Stone, 1861–1868* (Baton Rouge: 1955), pp. 226–227. E. C. Barksdale, "Semi-Regular and Irregular Warfare in the Civil War" (unpublished Ph.D. thesis, University of Texas, 1941), covers vigilantes, and see John H. Aughey, *Tupelo* (Lincoln: 1888), pp. 46–50, and John K. Bettersworth, *Confederate Mississippi* (Baton Rouge: 1943), pp. 252–266.

[3] A. K. Pearce to B. Tyson, Nov. 25, 1865, B. Tyson Papers, DU.

[4] See Parton's letter to Col. J. Morton, March 13, 1861, Morton-Halsey Papers,

Notes

University of Virginia. John Taffe, *An Address to the Churches of Christ in Kentucky* (Cincinnati: 1866), pp. 58–59, has the Tennessee newspaper statement. On Lander, see Hillsboro, N.C., *Recorder*, Oct. 29, 1861. For Upton, *Digest of Cases of Constested Elections, 1834–1865*, U.S., 38th Cong., 2d sess., H. Misc. Doc. 57 (Washington: 1865), pp. 368–380.

⁵ The quotation is in a letter from "Caroline" to her mother, Nov. 12, 1861, W. Pettigrew Papers, UNC. Lonn, *op. cit.*, pp. 385–386, covers the Banishing Act. The file of J. W. Packard, RG 59, NA, deals with Confederate provosts' functions. Lincoln's reaction is in E. Dicey, *Six Months in the Federal States* (London: 1863), I, 225. For Southern dissatisfaction, see John B. Jones, *A Rebel War Clerk's Diary* (New York: 1935), I, 81.

⁶ W. C. Corsan, *Two Months in the Confederate States* (London: 1863), pp. 148–149, has the quotation. Kate Cumming, *Gleanings from the Southland* (Birmingham: 1895), p. 82, relates her experience. Walter Lord, ed., *The Fremantle Diary* (Boston: 1954), p. 107; *War of the Rebellion: . . . Official Records of the Union and Confederate Armies*, War Department (Washington: 1880–1901), 2d series, II, 1361–1557; Confederate Provost Marshal Records, RG 109, NA, and the A. H. Brown Record Book, UNC, offer manifold details.

⁷ Jones, *op. cit.*, I, 113; Corsan, *op. cit.*, p. 72; *Daily Rebel*, April 2, 1863, the last of which contains the soldier's complaint.

⁸ Louise B. Hill, *Joseph E. Brown and the Confederacy* (Chapel Hill: 1939), p. 219, has Brown's statement. On the consular official, see M. L. Bonham, *The British Consuls in the Confederacy* (New York: 1911), pp. 74–76. See also Samuel P. Day, *Down South; or an Englishman's Experiences at the Seat of the American War* (London: 1862), II, 222; C. C. Hopley, *Life in the South* (London: 1863), I, 293; Texas state passport in A. D. Bache Papers, HL.

⁹ CSA Constitution, Art. 6, sec. 4; *Military Laws*, CSA, Department of Henrico (Richmond: 1863), pp. 15, 38–39; *Daily Rebel*, March 23, 1864.

¹⁰ Davis to J. E. Johnston, Feb. 28, 1862, J. E. Johnston Papers, HL; A. R. Childs, ed., *The Private Journal of Henry William Ravenel, 1859–1887* (Columbia: 1947), pp. 93–94.

¹¹ Jones, *op. cit.*, I, 65–67, 89, 270; F. E. Vandiver, ed., *Civil War Diary of Josiah Gorgas* (University, Ala.: 1947), p. 63; W. H. Russell, *My Diary North and South*, ed. F. Pratt (New York: 1954), p. 109; Frederick S. Daniel, *The Richmond Examiner during the War* (New York: 1868), pp. 69–70.

¹² J. C. Andrews, *The North Reports the Civil War* (Pittsburgh: 1955), pp. 18–21; Jones, *op. cit.*, I, 70–71, 102–104, 374; *Calendar of the Ryder Collection of Confederate Archives at Tufts College*, WPA, Historical Records Survey (Boston: 1940), pp. 69–70; petition re Confederate telegraphers, Sept. 20, 1862, Kie Oldham Papers, Arkansas Historical Society.

¹³ *Circulars, 1864*, CSA, War Department (n.p.: n.d.), #161, Dec. 10, 1863; J. L. Mock to J. Bell, Feb. 28, 1864, W. H. Lamon Papers, HL.

¹⁴ Proceedings of Sequestration Commissioner R. B. Reynolds, *ca.* May, 1862, RG 109, NA. William M. Robinson, Jr., *Justice in Grey* (Cambridge: 1941), is fullest on Confederate courts: see also *Daily Rebel*, Jan. 27, 1863; T. W. Humes, *The Loyal Mountaineers of Tennessee* (Knoxville: 1888), pp. 125–153; C. W. Hall (pseud.), *Threescore Years and Ten* (Cincinnati: 1884), pp. 152–154, 199; proceedings in First Brigade court-martial in R. Boykin Papers, UNC; affidavits against disloyal persons, Oct.-Nov. 1861, Pettigrew Family Papers, UNC.

[15] E. W. Winkler, ed., *Journal of the Secession Convention of Texas, 1861* (Austin: 1912), p. 257; J. Farber, *Texas, C.S.A.* (New York: 1947), pp. 315, 433; letters seized from R. I. Freeman of Macon (in his file), RG 59, NA; Thomas C. Bryan, *Confederate Georgia* (Athens: 1953), chap. 9.

[16] Speech, June, 1861, in W. Pettigrew Papers, UNC.

[17] W. A. Graham, *Speech in the Convention of North Carolina, December 7, 1861, on the Ordinance Concerning Test Oaths and Sedition* (Raleigh: 1862), *passim.;* Graham to Andrew Johnson, July 25, 1865, W. A. Graham Papers, UNC.

[18] Sallie A. B. Putnam, *Richmond during the War* (New York: 1867), p. 211; Thompson to Lamon, undated, W. H. Lamon Papers; Albert D. Richardson, *The Secret Service: the Field, the Dungeon, and the Escape* (Hartford: 1865), pp. 404, 428–429; R. H. Jackson to T. Hunter, Feb. 16, 1863, T. Hunter-Holmes Papers, DU; W. D. Pender to J. F. Hoke, May 11, 1861, Chief Justice Hoke Papers, UNC; A. L. Hull, *Annals of Athens, Georgia, 1801–1901* (Athens: 1906), pp. 274–275.

[19] H. G. Spruill to W. Pettigrew, Dec. 9, 1861, Pettigrew Family Papers; report to Gov. H. Flanagan, Jan. 17, 1863, Kie Oldham Papers; *Calendar of the Ryder Collection of Confederate Archives . . . ,* p. 63.

[20] Day, *op. cit.,* II, 173–174; E. M. Coulter, *The Civil War and Readjustment in Kentucky* (Chapel Hill: 1926), p. 172. Tatum, *op. cit.,* pp. 37, 148–150.

[21] *Official Records of the Union and Confederate Armies,* 2d series, II, 1361–1557; IV, 857; R. B. Patrick, ed., *Opinions of the Confederate Attorneys General, 1861–1865* (Buffalo: 1950), pp. 114–115.

[22] An East Tennessean, *Secession or Prose in Rhyme* (Philadelphia: 1864), pp. 15–16. Comments on Winder are in Jones, *op. cit.,* I, 71, 96.

[23] Report on his trial in J. Trakle Papers, DU. On Hamilton, see Loyalty Book #2, RG 174, NA. Bragg's activities are best described in a report on his Pensacola policies in the Maryland Historical Society, with other data in *Official Records of the Union and Confederate Armies,* 2d series, II, 1550–1557.

[24] Aughey, *op. cit.,* pp. 108–290; D. Cadwell to Wade, June 23, 1862, Benjamin Wade Papers, LC; R. P. Basler, ed., *Collected Works of Abraham Lincoln* (New Brunswick: 1953–1955), IV, 469.

[25] Richardson, *op. cit.,* p. 385; C. C. Webster, "John Minor Botts, Anti-Secessionist," Richmond College *Historical Papers,* I (June, 1915), 29–30.

[26] *Report,* CSA Army, Department of Henrico (n.p.: n.d.), pp. 1–8; Lord Lyons to E. Molyneux, March 14, 1862, Lord Lyons Papers, DU; Bonham, *op. cit.,* pp. 81–106.

[27] *General Orders, 1863,* CSA Army, Adjutant and Inspector General, (Richmond: 1863), pp. 31–32, 82, 210, describes the reporting system. J. L. M. Curry Papers, Book B, pp. 107–109, LC, and reports on prisoners brought before commissioners, RG 109, NA, deal with the special loyalty commissioners Davis appointed.

[28] J. H. Otey Papers, UNC; Sarah M. Dawson, *A Confederate Girl's Diary* (Boston: 1913), pp. 65–66.

[29] The soldier's statement is in B. I. Wiley, *The Plain People of the Confederacy* (Baton Rouge: 1943), p. 86; the Georgia newspaper and quotation are in Childs, *op. cit.,* pp. 200–201.

[30] *Resolutions,* CSA Congress, House (n.p.: n.d.); Jones, *op. cit.,* II, 390.

[31] Davis, *op. cit.,* II, 585; *Daily Rebel,* Sept. 8, 1864; *Regulations for the Army of the Confederate States,* CSA War Department (Richmond: 1864), p. 408; Patrick, *op. cit.,* pp. 238–242; *Official Records of the Union and Confederate Armies,* 2d series, VII, 478–479.

Notes

[32] L. Ballarsh to Wade, Jan. 25, 1865, B. Wade Papers.

[33] C. D. Scott to Holt, Jan. 4, 1865, Joseph Holt Papers, LC; D. M. N. Palmer, *Four Weeks in the Rebel Army* (New London: 1865), p. 18; Richardson, *op. cit.*, p. 390.

[34] A. N. Hayes, "Wartime Recollections," *Magazine of History*, XXI (Aug.-Sept., 1915), 91.

[35] *Daily Rebel*, Sept. 20, Oct. 18, 1862.

[36] Humes, *op. cit.*, pp. 140–141; Jones, *op. cit.*, II, 279.

[37] E. W. Gantt, *Address in Favor of Re-Union in 1863* (New York: 1863); Tatum, *op. cit.*, pp. 43–44.

[38] *Daily Rebel*, June 28, 1864; J. D. Horan, *Confederate Agent* (New York: 1954), pp. 248–253.

[39] A. G. Magrath, *Opinion in the Sequestration Cases and Report of Cases in the District Court, South Carolina* (n.p.: 1861), p. 4; Lonn, *op. cit.*, p. 329; Bettersworth, *op. cit.*, p. 216.

[40] E. H. Ewing, *Letters Accepting the President's Amnesty* (Nashville: 1864), pp. 1–6; A Texan, *To the Men of the South* (Philadelphia: 1863), p. 4; *Journal of the Congress of the Confederate States of America, 1861–1865*, U.S. 58th Cong., 2d sess., S. Doc. 234 (Washington: 1905), VI, 536–537.

[41] B. M. Palmer, *The Oath of Allegiance to the United States Discussed in Its Moral and Political Bearings* (Richmond: 1863); K. M. Rowland and M. L. Croxall, eds., *Journal of Julia Le Grand* (Richmond: 1911), pp. 73, 150–151, 201–203, 279–282.

[42] W. H. Ruffner, *The Oath: A Sermon on the Nature and Obligations of the Oath of Allegiance* (Lexington: 1864).

[43] *Daily Rebel*, March 28, April 2, 1863.

[44] *Ibid.*, July 22, 1863; March 27, April 1, Sept. 3, 1864; E. F. Andrews, *The War-Time Journal of a Georgia Girl, 1864–1865* (New York: 1908), p. 75.

[45] On Quantrill, see Barksdale, *op. cit.*, pp. 262–263. Pettigrew's speech is in the Pettigrew Family Papers, UNC.

[46] "CSA" to Pettigrew, May 24, 1862, Pettigrew Family Papers.

[47] On the pass modification, see C. S. Foster to Lamon, May 14, 1861, W. H. Lamon Papers. The inquiry on Southern reaction is in J. C. Johnston to Gen. Spruill, Feb. 2, 1863, Pettigrew Family Papers.

[48] *General Orders from January 1862 to December 1864*, CSA War Department (Columbia: 1864), Nos. 62, 65; *Daily Rebel*, March 15, 1865.

[49] *Official Records of the Union and Confederate Armies*, 2d series, IV, 561; J. Letcher, *Message of the Governor of Virginia* (Richmond: 1862), p. 3; Allen is quoted in the Lynchburg, Virginia, *Weekly Register*, Aug. 27, 1864.

NOTES TO CHAPTER X

Postwar but Less than Peace

(Pages 251–266)

[1] K. E. St. Clair, "The Administration of Justice in North Carolina during Reconstruction, 1865–1876" (unpublished Ph.D. thesis, Ohio State University, 1939), quoted p. 146, and see pp. 1–192.

[2] G. L. Prentiss, "The Political Crisis," *American Presbyterian and Theological Review*, n.s., IV (Oct., 1866), 625–630.

[3] W. A. Cook, *The Administration of Abraham Lincoln Sustained by the Sages and Heroes of the Revolution* (Washington: 1864), p. 23; for Southern attitudes, see T. N. Page, "The Southern People during Reconstruction," *Atlantic Monthly*, LXXXVIII (Sept., 1901), 293.

[4] W. M. Leftwich, *Martyrdom in Missouri* (St. Louis: 1870), II, 44–46.

[5] *Harper's Weekly*, Nov. 9, 1861, p. 706; *War of the Rebellion: . . . Official Records of the Union and Confederate Armies*, U.S. War Department (Washington: 1880–1901), 2d series, IV, 553–554. Biglow is in *The Right Way*, May 12, 1866. H. D. Farish, *The Circuit Rider Dismounts* (Richmond: 1938), pp. 41–42, has the Methodist quote. On Chase, see H. M. Hyman, *Era of the Oath: Northern Loyalty Tests during the Civil War and Reconstruction* (Philadelphia: 1954), p. 35. Whiting's report to Stanton, Feb. 25, 1863, is in RG 107, #W2735–138, NA.

[6] A. C. Jones to aunt, May 13, 1865, A. C. Jones Papers, UNC.

[7] R. P. Basler, ed., *Collected Works of Abraham Lincoln* (New Brunswick: 1953–1955), VIII, 50–56. On the Missouri Unionist, see S. T. Grover (pseud.), *Remarks on the Existing Rebellion* (St. Louis: 1865), pp. 13–14. The defense of Lincoln's oath is in H. C. Deming, *Speech on the President's Plan of State Renovation* (Washington: 1864), p. 8; that plan is best analyzed in J. G. Randall and R. N. Current, *Lincoln the President* (New York: 1955), IV, chaps. 1–2, 15.

[8] J. S. Brisbin to Stevens, Dec. 29, 1865, Thaddeus Stevens Papers, LC.

[9] Alcorn to Mrs. Alcorn, Aug. 26, 1865, J. A. Alcorn Papers, UNC; *Cleveland Leader*, Oct. 31, 1865. J. C. Bradley to A. Johnson, Nov. 15, 1865, Andrew Johnson Papers, LC, is from the President's correspondent. Southerners' knowledge of the test-oath requirement is in C. L. Mosby, *Congressional Test Oath Examined* (Lynchburg: 1865), and C. Gayarré, *Lecture on Oaths, Amnesties, and Rebellions* (New Orleans: 1866); *Raleigh Daily Sentinel*, Nov. 18, 1865; A. H. H. Stuart broadside in W. A. Graham Papers, UNC.

[10] *Report of Committee on the Credentials of David T. Patterson*, U.S. 39th Cong., 1st sess., S. Rept. 139 (Washington: 1866). Quoted editorial comment is in *The Right Way*, Aug. 4, 1866, and *Cleveland Leader*, July 31, 1866.

[11] W. N. Trenerry, "The Minnesota Rebellion Act of 1862," *Minnesota History*, XXXV (March, 1956), 1–10; *Cohen v. Wright*, 22 California 293 (1863).

[12] *Missouri v. Garesché*, 36 Missouri 256 (1865); *Ex parte Faulkner*, 1 West Virginia 269 (1866); *In re Shorter*, Fed. Cas. No. 12811 (1865); *Ex parte Law*, Fed. Cas. No. 8126 (1866); *In re Baxter*, Fed. Cas. No. 1118 (1866).

[13] *Ex parte Milligan*, 4 Wall. 2 (1866); *Cummings v. Missouri*, 4 Wall. 277 (1867); *Ex parte Garland*, 4 Wall. 333 (1867); W. A. Russ, Jr., "The Lawyers' Test Oath during Reconstruction," *Mississippi Law Journal*, X (Dec., 1937), 156 ff.; O. K. Fraenkel, "Law and Loyalty," *Iowa Law Review*, XXXVII (Winter, 1952), 153–174; Z. Chafee, Jr., *The Blessings of Liberty* (Philadelphia: 1956), pp. 164–167; Hyman, *op. cit.*, pp. 107–120.

[14] See Bayard's *Speech against the Validity of the Test Oath* (Philadelphia: 1864), and in Turner-Baker Papers #506, RG 94, NA, are the data on the arrest attempt. Public equation of antioath attitudes with disloyalty is evident in Judge David McDonald, "Diaries," *Indiana Magazine of History*, XXVIII (Dec., 1932), 296.

[15] *Congressional Globe*, 40th Cong., 2d sess., 1263–1271; Hyman, *op. cit.*, pp. 127–128.

Notes

[16] Hyman, *op. cit.*, pp. 128–142. E. I. Wakefield, ed., *Letters of Robert G. Ingersoll* (New York: 1951), pp. 156–157.

[17] *Message of the President of the United States*, U.S. 41st Cong., 1st sess., S. Exec. Doc. 42 (Washington: 1871).

[18] Hyman, *op. cit.*, pp. 145–146.

[19] *Summary Reports in All Cases Reported to Congress as Disallowed under the Act of March 3, 1871*, U.S. Commissioner of Claims (Washington: 1876), pp. 5, 60; Frank W. Klingberg, *The Southern Claims Commission* (Berkeley and Los Angeles: 1955), exhaustively treats this subject.

[20] See H. K. Beale, ed., "The Diary of Edward Bates, 1859–1866," AHA *Annual Report* (1930), Part IV, p. 431. Davis' comment is in *Congressional Globe*, 41st Cong., 3d sess., 1871. Nasby's statement is in D. R. Locke, *The Moral History of America's Life Struggle* (Boston: 1874), pp. 8–9.

NOTES TO CHAPTER XI

Amateur Spycatchers of World War I

(Pages 267–297)

[1] Sinclair to Wilson, Oct. 22, 1917, Woodrow Wilson Papers, LC; F. Hackett, "With Malice Towards None," *New Republic*, Nov. 17, 1917, p. 1; W. A. Dunning, "Disloyalty in Two Wars," *AHR*, XXIV (July, 1919), 625–630, and C. L. Rossiter, *Constitutional Dictatorship* (Princeton: 1948), pp. 250–253, compare Lincoln and Wilson.

[2] Baker to R. J. Biggs, Feb. 8, 1918, Newton D. Baker Papers, LC. On state loyalty laws see Z. Chafee, Jr., *Freedom of Speech* (New York: 1920), pp. 110–112, 399–405; E. F. Dowell, *History of Criminal Syndicalism Legislation in the United States* (Baltimore: 1939), and W. D. Carey, "State Councils of Defense," *State Government*, XIV (April, 1941), 106.

[3] *Annual Report, 1918*, U.S. Attorney General (Washington: 1919), pp. 14–30, has background of security laws. Superpatriots' pressures on Wilson are in C. Moffett to Wilson, Aug. 16, 1917, Wilson Papers; R. S. Baker, ed., *Woodrow Wilson, Life and Letters* (New York: 1939), VIII, 100–101; F. L. Paxson, *American Democracy and the World War* (Boston: 1936–1948), II, 291. The Detroit attorney's statement is in his letter to Gregory, Aug. 8, 1918, RG 60, NA.

[4] Civil Service Commission data are in *Annual Report, 1918*, U.S. Civil Service Commission (Washington: 1918); press release, Sept. 5, 1950; letter, World War I commissioner H. B. Mitchell to H. M. Hyman, June 17, 1955. Wilson's orders are in File 2, Box 116, Wilson Papers. Commission orders are in *List and Index of Presidential Executive Orders, Unnumbered Series, 1789–1941*, WPA Historical Records Survey (Newark: 1943), p. 218.

[5] On Creel, see J. R. Mock and C. Larsen, *Words That Won the War* (Princeton: 1939), pp. 60–61; E. W. Young, *The Wilson Administration and the Great War* (Boston: 1922), pp. 119–121. On Wilson's resistance to Congress, based on his fear of a repetition of the Civil War experience, see Baker, *op. cit.*, VII, 185–186, 251–252, and Robert Lansing to Tumulty, June 28, 1918, Robert Lansing Papers, LC.

[6] For the War College, see Baker to Gen. Sibert, June 8, 1917, N. D. Baker Papers,

LC, and F. Palmer, *Newton D. Baker* (New York: 1931), I, 357–360, for policy. On Reichman, see T. Bliss to Baker, Aug. 18, 1917, Wilson Papers, and Baker to Wilson, same date, Baker Papers. On Landon, see "Dick" to Borah, July 9, 1918, William E. Borah Papers, LC. A. A. Schiller, *Military Law and Defense Legislation* (St. Paul: 1941), pp. 526, 601–602, surveys loyalty aspects of the Articles of War, and see *Digest of Opinions*, U.S. Army, Judge Advocate General (Washington: 1942), pp. 201–352.

[7] Fear of German-Americans is in George Creel, *How We Advertised America* (New York: 1920), p. 167, and of spies, in *Literary Digest*, Oct. 6, 1917, p. 9. On internal security strength, see P. C. March, *The Nation at War* (New York: 1932), pp. 226–230; data given by John Lord O'Brian in interview with H. M. Hyman, June 9, 1955; Palmer, *op. cit.*, I, 100–102. Gregory's acts are in his Circulars, Nos. 657, 661, 667, and 838, RG 60, NA.

[8] *New York Times*, May 13, June 12, 1918, has Gregory's plea and the Boston advertisement. The "spy mania" is described in J. L. O'Brian, "Uncle Sam's Spy Policies," *Forum*, LXI (April, 1919), 409; Gregory to J. W. Byrns, May 9, 1917, RG 60, NA; same to R. E. Vinson, May 8, 1918, T. W. Gregory Papers, LC.

[9] Early APL history is derived from an interview with John Lord O'Brian, June 9, 1955, and a letter from A. Bruce Bielaski to H. M. Hyman, Aug. 11, 1955. Accounts in E. Hough, *The Web: The Authorized History of the American Protective League* (Chicago: 1919), and F. Strother, *Fighting Germany's Spies* (New York: 1918), are unreliable. Gregory's order to all agents, March 22, 1917, RG 60, NA, requires cooperation with the APL; some to A. M. Briggs, May 3, 1917, *ibid.*, has the quotation. On cabinet approval, see Gregory to MacAdoo, June 12, 1917, National Headquarters File, APL Papers, RG 65, NA.

[10] See *New York Daily News*, Sept. 8, 1917, for publicity. Other data in National Headquarters File, APL Papers.

[11] Directors described in interview with O'Brian, June 9, 1955. *The Spy Glass*, Aug. 24, 1918, covered loyalty investigations. C. C. Arthur to Gregory, telegram, Sept. 17, 1917, has state directors' plea. Other data in National Headquarters File, APL Papers.

[12] T. W. Dynan to Tumulty, Aug. 9, 1917, Wilson Papers, covers the Metropolitan Trust Company. Gregory to A. R. Roberts, May 20, 1918, RG 60, NA, deals with the Texas company. League recruitment policies are covered in Preliminary Report of NYC APL Headquarters, APL Papers. *Circular Letters and Telegrams*, U.S. Provost Marshal General (mimeographed), #395, LC, deals with draft board–APL identity.

[13] Justice Department Circular #838, RG 60, NA, has Gregory's injunction on the Espionage and Sedition Acts. On the University of Texas, see same to T. U. Taylor, April 15, 1918, Gregory Papers.

[14] *The Spy Glass*, July 25, 1918; APL, *In re Military Intelligence Investigations* (n.p.: n.d.), and A. Eisemann, *APL Investigations for the United States Department of Justice* (New York: 1918), offer these data.

[15] The telegram, Dec. 8, 1917, and other data are in National Headquarters File, APL Papers. E. H. Rushmore to Directors, Nov. 20, 1918, New York File, *ibid.*, has that city's details. For Red Cross and similar groups' matters, see directors' circular, June 3, 1918, in California File, *ibid.* On interbureau confusion, see memorandum of Nov. 10, 1917, conference, Box 5, *ibid.* See also J. R. Mott to Wilson, Aug. 24, 1918, Baker Papers, and Baker, *op. cit.*, VIII, 360–361.

[16] See exchange of communication, Baker and Gregory, April 1-May 8, 1918, Baker

Papers; Elting to E. H. Rushmore, May 26, 1918, Box 5, APL Papers, for the closing quotation.

[17] Chief, APL Long Beach local to Elting, Aug. 23, 1918, California File, APL Papers. On the Red Cross, see New York APL to Headquarters, April 3, 1918, *ibid.*

[18] File #186751, RG 60, NA.

[19] J. R. Mock, *Censorship, 1917* (Princeton: 1941), pp. 208–209; see Elting to Mrs. N. Baker, March 26, 1918, Box 8, APL Papers, on employing women. On APL employment in armed forces, see Gen. C. G. Morton to Adjutant General, Washington, Sept. 9, 1917, RG 60, NA, and Elting to M. Barclay, Oct. 25, 1918, Box 6, APL Papers.

[20] Power to arrest is covered in Elting to W. Cherry, Jan. 9, 1918, Headquarters File, APL Papers. APL excesses are surveyed in Frey to C. A. Case, June 13, 1918, Kansas File, *ibid.*, and summarized in Gregory to Elting, Feb. 8, 1918, #186751–41, RG 60, NA. Elting's circular, Feb. 31, 1918, Box 9, APL Papers, warns all APL personnel of past errors.

[21] Hyacinth Ringrose to Gregory, Sept. 6, 1918, #186751, RG 60, NA. On Hale, see Baker, *op. cit.*, VII, 335, and the correspondence in Boxes 128 and 129, Wilson Papers. The Creel quotation is in his "Public Opinion in War Time," *Annals of the American Academy of Political and Social Science*, LXXVIII (July, 1918), 192.

[22] L. Milner, *Education of an American Liberal* (New York: 1954), surveys Civil Liberties Union activities. Chandler P. Anderson Diary, LC, entry for Feb. 17, 1918, has Baruch's statement. International Association of Machinists to Gregory, Aug. 31, 1918, File #186751, RG 60, NA, deals with that situation. On antiliberal sentiment, see H. E. Stearns, *Liberalism in America* (New York: 1919), pp. 92–154. APL class consciousness permeates all APL Papers; references are too numerous to cite.

[23] O'Brian to Elting, Sept. 10, 1918, File #186751, RG 60, NA.

[24] *New York Call*, June 2, 1919. *Report of Joint Committee to Investigate Seditious Activities*, New York Legislature (New York: 1920), I, 812, quotes the Communist accusation.

[25] On the Bisbee episode, see Arizona File, APL Papers. *Investigation of the National Security League*, U.S. 65th Cong., 3d sess., H. Rept. 1173 (Washington: 1919), documents NSL activities. Baker, *op. cit.*, VII, 480–486, and Creel to Wilson, Oct. 1, 1918, George Creel Papers, deal with the American Defense Society. George Croly to Wilson, Oct. 19, 1917, Wilson Papers, has the quotation used. On NSL and ADS accusations against Wilson, see C. Moffett to Gregory, April 17, 1918, RG 60, NA, and *New York Tribune*, July 15, 1918. N. Hapgood, *Professional Patriots* (New York: 1927), surveys the organized patriotic societies.

[26] Quoted in *Hearings before a Subcommittee of the Committee on the Judiciary, on a "Report upon the Illegal Practices of the Department of Justice," Made by a Committee of Lawyers*, U.S. Senate, 66th Cong., 3d sess. (Washington: 1921), p. 209.

[27] Correspondence dated April 26, 1918, Baker Papers, and entry of May 14, 1918, Chandler P. Anderson Diary, have charges against Gregory's wife and the Council of National Defense member. MacAdoo's preparations secured Lansing's support; see memoranda April 4–19, 1917, Lansing Papers. Other data in Gregory to Wilson, April 17, 1917, Gregory Papers; same to same, memorandum, same date, Wilson Papers; MacAdoo to Wilson, July 8, 1917, Wilson Papers; and C. F. Warren to Gregory, July 16, 1917, RG 60, NA.

[28] MacAdoo to Wilson and Gregory, June 2, 1917, Wilson Papers; H. Cummings and C. McFarland, *Federal Justice* (New York: 1937), p. 422.

[29] Gregory to MacAdoo, June 12, 1917, RG 60, NA. Same to Wilson, June 14, 1917, Wilson Papers, has quotations from Wilson, and Wilson to Gregory, July 12, 1917, in Baker, *op. cit.,* VII, 159, has Wilson's decision.

[30] Bulletin #99 and supplement, June 11, July 19, 1918, RG 60, NA; *New York Times,* July 23, 1918.

[31] *New York Times,* Sept. 12, 13, 1918; *Nation,* Sept. 14, 1918, p. 282; O'Brian to A. M. Dockery, April 15, 1918, File #186751–52, RG 60, NA, deal with the APL–draft raid connection.

[32] Memoranda of meetings and telephone conversations, Sept. 21, 1918, RG 60, NA, have all data.

[33] E. H. Rushmore to directors, Sept. 24, 1918, Headquarters File, APL Papers, has the party politics charge. S. Mahon to Gregory, Nov. 22, 1918, File #190470, RG 60, NA, deals with the Republican party accusation.

[34] Final report, New York City local, Oct. 28, 1918, APL Papers; *Glen Falls Times and Messenger,* March 27, 1918; interview with John Lord O'Brian, June 9, 1955.

[35] *New Orleans Times Picayune,* Nov. 10, 1918; MacAdoo to Gregory, Nov. 19, 1918, and Gregory to Briggs, Nov. 21, 1918, RG 60, NA. Elting's nudge is in *Philadelphia Inquirer,* Dec. 9, 1918. Military Intelligence tried to keep its APL unit going; see Capt. J. T. Evans to H. A. McLaughlin, Nov. 26, 1918, New York File, APL Papers. Other data are in *New York Times,* Nov. 22, 1918, and in unidentified newspaper clips on APL future in American Civil Liberties Union Archives, NYPL.

[36] A. F. Quincy to Elting, Dec. 19, 1918, New York File, APL Papers, deals with money problems. Objection to continuation is in O. P. Adams to directors, Dec. 5, 1918, California File, *ibid.* Editorials favoring a postwar APL are in *New York Times,* Nov. 23, 1918, and Lexington, Kentucky, *Herald,* same date.

[37] Gregory's decision in *New York Times,* Dec. 27, 1918. Demobilization data are in Headquarters File, APL Papers, and in W. G. Leland and N. D. Mereness, *Introduction to the American Official Sources for the Economic and Social History of the World War* (New Haven: 1926), pp. 455–474.

[38] Tributes to the APL are in *The Spy Glass,* Dec. 28, 1918, and Jan. 25, 1919; the banquet is in *New York Times,* Jan. 26, 1919. See also *Annual Report, 1918,* U.S. Attorney General (Washington: 1919), p. 15, and Gregory to Elting, Feb. 1, 1919, RG 60, NA.

[39] O'Brian to Palmer, April 30, 1919, RG 60, NA, discusses Cox's request. On the Bar Association, see F. L. Polk to Gregory, Jan. 17, 1919, *ibid.;* E. E. Swift to same, Nov. 18, 1918, *ibid.,* deals with APL patronage and private detective activities. *Report of Joint Committee to Investigate Seditious Activities,* I, 21, and *Hearings before the Committee on Rules; Investigation of the Administration of Louis F. Post,* U.S. 66th Cong., 2d sess., on H. Res. 522 (Washington: 1920), pp. 87–96, deal with committee use of APL veterans. On the Klan, see *Invitation to Membership to World War Patriots* (Atlanta: n.d.).

[40] Circular #952, March 31, 1919, and Palmer to Mrs. W. Brown, April 5, 1919, RG 60, NA, cover his policy. R. W. Floyd to E. H. Rushmore, Oct. 2, 1918, New York City File, APL Papers, has the quoted tribute.

[41] Report, Alma, Kansas local, Dec. 14, 1918, APL Papers.

[42] *Brewing and Liquor Interests and German and Bolshevik Propaganda,* 66th Cong., 1st sess., S. Doc. 62 (Washington: 1919), II, 2251–2252, has Bielaski's testimony.

[43] L. Mumford, "Patriotism and Its Consequences," *Dial,* April 19, 1919, pp. 406–407; W. Lippmann, *Liberty and the News* (New York: 1920), pp. 55–57.

Notes

NOTES TO CHAPTER XII

Timber and Treason

(Pages 298–315)

¹ P. C. March, *The Nation at War* (New York: 1932), pp. 199–200. A. Sinsheimer, "Hughes Aircraft Report: A Vindication," *Automotive Industries,* XXXIX (Oct., 1918), 741–750, has the text of the report and background.

² C. R. Howd, *Industrial Conditions in the West Coast Lumber Industry,* U.S. Bureau of Labor Statistics, Bulletin #349, Miscellaneous Series (Washington: 1924), p. iii; J. S. Gambs, *The Decline of the I.W.W.* (New York: 1932), p. 239; *Report, Unrest in the Lumber Industry of the Pacific Northwest,* U.S. President's Mediation Commission (Washington: 1918), pp. 13–15. On the army agent, see File #190657, RG 60 NA.

³ Frankfurter to Baker, Sept. 4, 1917, Newton D. Baker Papers, LC. Details on Disque are in A. M. Bing, *War-Time Strikes and Their Adjustment* (New York: 1921), pp. 270–272, and E. B. Mittleman, "The Loyal Legion of Loggers and Lumbermen," *Journal of Political Economy,* XXXI (June, 1923), 323–330. Biographical details on Disque are in *Report of Subcommittee on Aviation, Select House Committee on Expenditures in the War Department,* Part I, 66th Cong., 2d sess. (Washington: 1920), p. 29. Baker saw Disque's plan as "the velvet touch of the glove that covered War's steel hand." F. Palmer, *Newton D. Baker* (New York: 1931), II, 181–182.

⁴ *History of the Spruce Production Division,* U.S. Army, Signal Corps (Washington: 1921), pp. 1–16; C. Todes, *Labor and Lumber* (New York: 1931), p. 41. On other data, see report, June 4, 1918, in J. A. B. Scherer Papers, in possession of Mr. R. Schwarzman, Los Angeles, which are far more revealing than Scherer's *The Nation at War* (New York: 1918).

⁵ *History of the Spruce Production Division,* p. 19, and Bing, *op. cit.,* pp. 271–272, detail the recruiting and unit-management reactions.

⁶ Growth statistics are in *History of the Spruce Production Division,* p. 20. Data on the legion's *modus operandi* are in File #190657, RG 60, NA.

⁷ B. P. Disque, "How We Found a Cure for Strikes," *System, The Magazine of Business,* XXXVI (Sept., 1919), 381–382; S. H. Clay, "The Man Who Heads the Spruce Drive," *Review of Reviews,* LVII (June, 1918), 633–635, offer data on these activities. Disque to Wilson, Dec. 19, 1917, Woodrow Wilson Papers, LC, deals with the phonograph record. The loyalty-oath and membership data are in File #190657, RG 60, NA.

⁸ Quotations are in Bing, *op. cit.,* pp. 252–253. See also W. A. Wolff, "The Northwest Front," *Collier's,* April 20, 1918, pp. 10–11, 32.

⁹ Disque's speech reported in File #190657, RG 60, NA, also containing Gregory's decision that the LLLL was not part of the armed services (March 16, 1918). On federal coöperation with the IWW, see *Nation,* Dec. 14, 1917, p. 717, and Bing, *op. cit.,* pp. 261–262.

¹⁰ On Chamberlain, see *New Republic,* April 6, 1918, pp. 284–285. *History of the Spruce Production Division,* chap. 3, describes Disque's strategy. The quoted paragraph and the Mediation Commission are in Frankfurter to Baker, Jan. 16, 1918, and H. Suzzallo to Baker, Jan. 17, 1918, Newton D. Baker Papers, LC.

[11] "Objects of the LLLL," Bulletin #3, undated, which appeared soon after a meeting between Disque and AFL leaders in Portland, Jan. 30, 1918; bulletin and report on the meeting in Oregon File, APL Papers, RG 65, NA.

[12] Bulletin #3, LLLL.

[13] Bing, *op. cit.,* pp. 270–272.

[14] LLLL Confidential Bulletin #1, Dec. 29, 1917, RG 60, NA.

[15] LLLL Confidential Bulletin #2, Dec. 29, 1917, *ibid.,* deals with interagency coöperation and covers existing disloyalty cases.

[16] LLLL Bulletin #6, Jan. 28, 1918, signed by Member #23972, *ibid.,* has the complaint against nonjurors. In this instance, the Port Ludlow secretary was an APL agent; see his report in Washington File, APL Papers. On Disque's speeches and LLLL action, see Howd, *op. cit.,* p. 79.

[17] M. Denman, "Majority of Lumberjacks Are Not I.W.W.," *New Republic,* March 30, 1918, p. 265, and an editorial, "Colonel Disque and the I.W.W.," *ibid.,* April 6, 1918, pp. 284–285.

[18] Report of visit to Washington and Montana, June 4, 1918, J. A. B. Scherer Papers.

[19] "The Loyal Legion of Loggers and Lumbermen," *Outlook,* July 31, 1918, p. 510; for the comment of the AFL official, see *Portland Oregonian,* Dec. 21, 1918.

[20] Production figures are in E. C. Hole, "The Real Status of the Loyal Legion," *American Lumberman,* March 15, 1919, p. 41. Disque's letter to Wilson, Dec. 19, 1917, is in the Wilson Papers.

[21] Howd, *op. cit.,* pp. 75–76, 84–85, and H. Weintraub, "The I.W.W. in California, 1905–1931" (unpublished M.A. thesis, University of California, Los Angeles, 1947), chap. 7, deal with the disloyalty aspect.

[22] Howd, *op. cit.,* p. iii, has the quoted paragraph. See also Mittleman, *op. cit.,* p. 329, and the report on the LLLL in File #190657, RG 60, NA.

[23] R. S. Gill, "The Four L's in Lumber," *Survey,* May 1, 1920, pp. 165–170; R. Winstead, "Enter a Logger: An I.W.W. Reply to the Four L's," *ibid.,* July 3, 1920, pp. 474–477, and R. P. Boas, "The Loyal Legion of Loggers and Lumbermen," *Atlantic Monthly,* CXXVII (Feb., 1921), 221–226, best survey this problem.

NOTES TO CHAPTER XIII

Path to the Patriotic Present

(Pages 316–345)

[1] Lansing to R. S. Hungerford, Nov. 14, 1918, Robert Lansing Papers, LC. Gregory's decision concerning Bolsheviks is in memorandum, Nov. 20, 1918, RG 60, NA. Palmer's approval is subscribed beneath Gregory's signature. For O'Brian, see his "Civil Liberty in War Time," New York Bar Association *Reports,* LII (1919), 310, and his *The Government and Civil Liberties: World War I and After* (Lexington, Va.: 1952), pp. 149–152.

[2] *Brewing and Liquor Interests and German and Bolshevik Propaganda,* 66th Cong., 1st sess., S. Doc. 62 (Washington: 1919), is the Overman Committee report. On Stevenson, see "The New Sherlock Holmes," *Nation,* Feb. 1, 1919, p. 155.

[3] L. H. Chamberlain, *Loyalty and Legislative Action* (Ithaca: 1951), pp. 1–52, offers exacting scholarship on the Lusk Committee. Z. Chafee, Jr., *Freedom of*

Notes

Speech (New York: 1920), pp. 358–364, surveys state sedition statutes. The best general treatment is R. K. Murray, *The Red Scare: A Study in National Hysteria, 1919–1920* (Minneapolis: 1955). Veblen's query is in *Dial*, Nov. 30, 1919, p. 497.

⁴ *Case of Victor L. Berger of Wisconsin*, 66th Cong., 1st sess., H. Rept. 413 (Washington: 1920); *Brief of the Special Committee To Defend the Socialist Members of the N.Y. Legislature, January 20, 1920*, Association of the Bar of the City of New York (New York: 1920), and Chafee, *op. cit.*, pp. 314–364, cover these materials.

⁵ Flynn's order is quoted in *Report upon the Illegal Practices of the U.S. Department of Justice*, National Popular Government League (Washington: 1920), p. 37. See also A. M. Palmer, "The Case against the Reds," *Forum*, LXIII (Feb., 1920), 173–185; L. F. Post, *The Deportations Delirium of Nineteen-Twenty* (Chicago: 1923); *Hearings before the House Committee on Rules; Investigation of the Administration of Louis F. Post*, 66th Cong., 2d sess. (Washington: 1920). The American Civil Liberties Union Archives, NYPL, are rich in contemporary accounts. For changing Bureau of Investigation personnel and practices, see M. Lowenthal, *The Federal Bureau of Investigation* (New York: 1950), pp. 36–268.

⁶ A. M. Palmer, "Why We Seized German Property," *Forum*, LXII (Dec., 1919), 584, has the quotation. For Wilson, see A. B. Kuttner, "A Study of American Intolerance," *Dial*, March 28, 1918, pp. 284–285, and H. E. Stearns, *Liberalism in America* (New York: 1919), pp. 99–101.

⁷ On Communist weakness, see T. Draper, *The Roots of American Communism* (New York: 1957). W. J. Ghent, *The Reds Bring Reaction* (Princeton: 1923), pp. 3–7, distinguishes between anticommunism and reaction. L. P. Todd, *Wartime Relations of the Federal Government and the Public Schools* (New York: 1945), pp. 217–220, shows the inability of teachers and intellectuals to cope with the attacks. On Roosevelt, see A. M. Schlesinger, Jr., *Crisis of the Old Order, 1919–1933* (Boston: 1957), pp. 360, 365.

⁸ K. H. Claghorn, "Aliens and Sedition in the New Year," *Survey*, Jan. 17, 1920, pp. 422–423, shows the connection between "foreigner" and ' disloyalty." "Are American Liberties Worth Saving?" *Nation*, April 17, 1920, pp. 506–508, offers lawyers' comments on Palmer. W. Hard, "Perhaps the Turn of the Tide," *New Republic*, Feb. 11, 1920, pp. 313–316, covers the investigation of Palmer and the Justice Department. On amnesty, see L. Robins, *War Shadows* (New York: 1922). The de Silver statement is in W. Nelles, *A Liberal in Wartime: The Education of Albert de Silver* (New York: 1940), pp. 204–206.

⁹ Lowenthal, *op. cit.*, pp. 269–293, and Z. Chafee, Jr., "Freedom of Speech and States' Rights," *New Republic*, Jan. 26, 1921, deserve close attention.

¹⁰ N. Hapgood, *Professional Patriots* (New York: 1927), pp. 86–188, is the best account. On Easley, see W. Irwin, "This Gentleman Worries Too Much," *Hearst's International*, XLVI (Sept., 1924), 81 ff.; S. Howard, "Our Professional Patriots," *New Republic*, Aug. 20, Sept. 3, 10, 17, 24, Oct. 15, 1924; R. W. Dunn, "Meet Mr. Easley—Plutocrat Patriot," *Locomotive Engineers Journal*, LX (July, 1926), 497–499. E. P. Herring, *Group Representation before Congress* (Baltimore: 1929), pp. 223–224, and E. L. Hunter, *A Sociological Analysis of Certain Types of Patriotism* (New York: 1932), pp. 11–142, deal with pressure-group activities.

¹¹ Chafee, "Freedom of Speech and States' Rights," underlines contradictions of state-federal interaction. On the cases, see G. Foster, Jr., "The 1931 Personal Liberties Cases," *New York University Law Quarterly Review*, IX (Sept., 1931), 64–81.

H. K. Beale, *Are American Teachers Free?* (New York: 1936), p. 702, has the commissioner's quotation.

[12] E. Wilson, "Foster and Fish," *New Republic*, Dec. 24, 1930, p. 162; John Dos Passos, "Back to Red Hysteria," *ibid.*, July 2, 1930, pp. 168–169; J. A. Wechsler, *The Age of Suspicion* (New York: 1953), pp. 13–134.

[13] On the Schwimmer case, see D. D. Bromley, "The Pacifist Bogey," *Harper's Magazine*, CLXI (Oct., 1930), 554. A. R. Ogden, *The Dies Committee* (Washington: 1945); R. K. Carr, *The House Committee on Un-American Activities, 1945–1950* (Ithaca: 1952), pp. 1–18, cover the committees. R. G. Swing, "Patriotism Dons the Black Shirt," *Nation*, April 10, 1935, pp. 409–411, critically views attempts at new federal security laws. K. M. Gould, "Legislating Loyalty," *American Scholar*, IV (Summer, 1935), 345 ff., surveys state loyalty testing laws. Ickes' address at the University of Alabama, May 27, 1935, and his letter to Jones, Dec. 18, 1935, are in the Harold Ickes Papers, LC.

[14] Ogden, *op. cit., passim.* The FBI report is in the "Memorandum of Past Investigations of Nazi Activities in the U.S., Prepared by the Solicitor General of the FBI, January, 1940," Ickes Papers.

[15] Hans L. Trefousse, "Failure of German Intelligence in the United States, 1935–1945," *Mississippi Valley Historical Review*, XLII (June, 1955), 84 ff.

[16] S. I. Rosenman, ed., *The Public Papers and Addresses of Franklin D. Roosevelt* (New York: 1938–1950), IX, 478–479.

[17] *Proceedings*, Federal-State Conference on Law Enforcement Problems of National Defense (Washington: 1940), *passim.* Francis Biddle, in a letter to me of July 26, 1955, kindly supplied details. The Smith Act was almost dormant during the war years, but its assertion of national leadership in security matters is patent.

[18] Stark's pleas is in *New York Times*, June 4, 1940. Milner, *op. cit.*, pp. 296–298, and "Civil Liberties and the War," *New Republic*, June 22, 1942, pp. 848–849, deal with the ACLU survey. M. Grodzins, *Americans Betrayed: Politics and the Japanese Evacuation* (Chicago: 1949), and D. S. Thomas and R. S. Nishimoto, *The Spoilage* (Berkeley and Los Angeles: 1946), detail loyalty policies among the evacuees.

[19] "Free Speech in War Time," *Commonweal*, March 27, 1942, pp. 547–548, compares World Wars I and II. C. L. Rossiter, *Constitutional Dictatorship* (Princeton: 1948), pp. 266–267, treats executive leadership, and is the source of the quotation. Chamberlain, *op. cit.*, pp. 68–152, covers the Rapp-Coudert Committee. For the 1939–1941 period, see W. Gellermann, *Martin Dies* (New York: 1944); Ogden, *op. cit.*, chap. 13; and R. F. Brandt, "The Dies Committee: An Appraisal," *Atlantic Monthly*, CLXV (Feb., 1940), 232–237.

[20] G. M. Kammerer, *The Impact of War upon Federal Personnel Administration, 1939–1945* (Lexington: 1951), pp. 117–120, covers prewar requirements. On the WPA, see the *New York Times*, Aug. 4, 1940.

[21] On procedures, see Kammerer, *op. cit.*, pp. 117–134. Ickes' role is in his voluminous correspondence, Ickes Papers, too numerous to cite.

[22] Kammerer, *op. cit.*, p. 125, has the commission's statement. On the provost marshal general's Special Agent Corps, see Senator Clinton Anderson to Chester Nimitz, Feb. 7, 1951, in Nimitz Commission Records, RG 220, NA, and *Office of the Provost Marshal General: World War II: A Brief History*, U.S. Provost Marshal General's Bureau (typescript; Washington: 1946).

[23] *United States* v. *Lovett*, 328 U.S. 303 (1945); F. L. Schuman, "Bill of Attainder

Notes

in the 78th Congress," *American Political Science Review*, XXXVII (Oct., 1943), 819 ff.; G. J. Norville, "Bill of Attainder—A Rediscovered Weapon against Discriminatory Legislation," *Oregon Law Review*, XXVI (Feb. 1947), 78 ff.

[24] H. F. Pringle, "Snooping on the Potomac," *Saturday Evening Post*, Jan. 15, 1944, pp. 19 ff.; Kammerer, *op. cit.*, pp. 117–134.

[25] *Suggested Standards for Determining Un-American Activities*, Brookings Institution (Washington: 1945).

[26] H. Ickes, "Hysteria in the Justice Department," *New Republic*, July 4, 1949; L. A. Nikoloric, "The Government Loyalty Program," *American Scholar*, XIX (Summer, 1950), 285–293, and E. Bontecou, *The Federal Loyalty-Security Program* (Ithaca: 1953), pp. 1–34, offer the best accounts.

[27] Bingham to Chester Nimitz, Feb. 16, 1951, Nimitz Commission Records, details his role. The new formula had already received judicial approval in *Friedman* v. *Schwellenbach*, 159 F.2d 22 (1946), C.C.A.D.C.

[28] Sokolsky is quoted in W. Shelton, "Last Chance for Sanity," *Nation*, Feb. 24, 1951, pp. 169–170. Truman's order creating the commission, and the events terminating it, are in *New York Times*, Jan. 24, Oct. 28, 1951. The quotation is in a letter, J. A. Danaher to Nimitz, March 2, 1951, Nimitz Commission Records.

[29] E. Bontecou, "President Eisenhower's 'Security' Program," *Bulletin of the Atomic Scientists*, IX (June, 1953), 215 ff. Most useful on indicated matters are A. Yarmolinsky, *Case Studies in Personnel Security* (Washington: 1955); *Industrial Personnel Security Review Program, 1st Annual Report*, U.S. Secretary of Defense (Washington: 1956), and S. Weinstein, *Personnel Security Programs of the Federal Government* (mimeographed; n.p.: 1954).

[30] *Federalist*, no. 48, has Madison's statement. C. Rossiter, *The American Presidency* (New York: 1956), is complete on this theme. On the army pamphlet, see *New York Times*, July 14, 19, 1955. Of the vast literature on congressional investigating, most useful are A. Barth, *Government by Investigation* (New York: 1955); Telford Taylor, *Grand Inquest: The Story of Congressional Investigations* (New York: 1955), and M. Straight, *Trial by Television* (Boston: 1954). E. N. Griswold, *The 5th Amendment Today* (Cambridge: 1955), covers that important theme.

[31] C. Wittke, *German-Americans and the World War* (Columbus: 1936), chap. 5; Grodzins, *op. cit.;* and Thomas and Nishimoto, *op. cit.*, survey loyalty tests in World Wars I and II.

[32] "Local Governments and Loyalty Problems," *American City*, LXVI (Dec., 1951), 169; E. L. Barrett, Jr., *The Tenney Committee* (Ithaca: 1951); W. Gellhorn, ed., *The States and Subversion* (Ithaca: 1952); and V. Countryman, *Un-American Activities in the State of Washington* (Ithaca: 1951), fully cover local loyalty-testing.

[33] E. S. Corwin, *Total War and the Constitution* (New York: 1947), p. 70.

[34] R. E. Cushman, "American Civil Liberties in Mid-Twentieth Century," *Annals of the American Academy of Political and Social Science*, CCLXXV (May, 1951), 1–8.

[35] *Pennsylvania* v. *Nelson*, 350 U.S. 497 (1956).

[36] T. Arnold, "How *Not* To Get Investigated," *Harper's Magazine*, CXCVII (Nov., 1948), 61–63.

[37] See Penn's view in his *A Treatise on Oaths* (London: 1675), p. 10 of which has the statement quoted. The English judge is quoted in W. O. Douglas, *The Bill of Rights—at Home and Abroad* (Philadelphia: 1953), p. 3.

[38] M. L. Ernst, "Some Affirmative Suggestions for a Loyalty Program," *American Scholar*, XIX (Autumn, 1950), 452–460; *Report on the Federal Loyalty-Security*

Program, Special Committee of the Association of the Bar of the City of New York (New York: 1956), and R. E. Cushman, *Civil Liberties in the United States* (Ithaca: 1956), chap. 7, constructively criticize the executive program. See E. V. Rostow, "Needed: A Rational Security Program," *Harper's Magazine,* CCXV (July, 1957), 33 ff., and *New York Times,* June 23, 1957, on the Supreme Court cases of that year.

[39] *New York Times,* March 24, 1957.

[40] *Considerations Regarding the Loyalty Oath as a Manifestation of Current Social Tension and Anxiety,* Group for the Advancement of Psychiatry, Symposium no. 1 (Oct., 1954).

[41] J. H. Schaar, *Loyalty in America* (Berkeley and Los Angeles: 1957), pp. 171 ff.

[42] R. P. Basler, ed., *Collected Works of Abraham Lincoln* (New Brunswick: 1953–1955), VIII, 169.

[43] Memorandum of suggestions for Sen. Danaher, March 5, 1951, Nimitz Commission Records, contains the Nimitz Commission statement. Bontecou, *The Federal Loyalty-Security Program,* chap. 6, discusses the courts' problems with current security cases. M. Grodzins, *The Loyal and the Disloyal* (Chicago: 1956), ably sets current concerns over security into meaningful terms.

[44] Melville's "Conflict of Convictions (1860–1861)," is in his *Battle-Pieces and Aspects of the War* (New York: 1866), p. 18. Yeats's "The Second Coming," *ca.* 1921, is in his *Collected Poems* (definitive ed.; New York: 1956), pp. 184–185.

BIBLIOGRAPHY

BOOKS

Aaron, Daniel, ed. *America in Crisis*. New York: Knopf, 1952.

Adams, C. F., ed. *Works of John Adams*. Boston: Little, Brown, 1850–1856. 10 vols.

Anderson, John Q., ed. *Brokenburn: The Journal of Kate Stone, 1861–1868*. Baton Rouge: Louisiana State University Press, 1955.

Anderson, Troyer S. *Command of the Howe Brothers during the American Revolution*. New York: Oxford University Press, 1936.

Andrews, Charles M. *British Committees, Commissions, and Councils of Trade and Plantations, 1622–1675*. Baltimore: Johns Hopkins University Press, 1908.

――――. *The Colonial Period of American History*. New Haven: Yale University Press, 1937. 4 vols.

――――. *Narratives of the Insurrections, 1675–1690*. Reprint ed. New York: Barnes and Noble, 1952.

Andrews, E. F. *The War-Time Journal of a Georgia Girl, 1864–1865*. New York: Appleton, 1908.

Andrews, J. Cutler. *The North Reports the Civil War*. Pittsburgh: University of Pittsburgh Press, 1955.

Archives of Maryland. Baltimore: Maryland Historical Society, 1883――. 67 vols.

Aughey, John H. *Tupelo*. Lincoln, Neb.: State Journal, 1888.

Baker, Ray S., ed. *Woodrow Wilson, Life and Letters*. New York: Doubleday, Page, 1939. 8 vols.

Baldwin, L. D. *Whiskey Rebels: The Story of a Frontier Uprising*. Pittsburgh: University of Pittsburgh Press, 1939.

Ballagh, J. C., ed. *The Letters of Richard Henry Lee*. New York: Macmillan, 1911–1914. 2 vols.

Barclay, Grace. *Diary; or, Personal Recollections of the American Revolution*. New York: Randolph, 1866.

Barnes, Viola F. *The Dominion of New England*. New Haven: Yale University Press, 1923.

Barrett, E. L., Jr. *The Tenney Committee*. Ithaca: Cornell University Press, 1951.

Barth, A. *Government by Investigation*. New York: Viking, 1955.

Basler, R. P., ed. *Collected Works of Abraham Lincoln*. New Brunswick: Rutgers University Press, 1953–1955. 9 vols.

Bates, F. G. *Rhode Island and the Formation of the Union*. New York: Columbia University Press, 1898.

Beale, H. K. *Are American Teachers Free?* New York: Scribner's, 1936.

Bentley, William. *Diary*. Salem: Essex Institute, 1905. 4 vols.

Bettersworth, J. K. *Confederate Mississippi*. Baton Rouge: Louisiana State University Press, 1943.

Bing, Alexander M. *War-Time Strikes and Their Adjustment*. New York: Dutton, 1921.

Bibliography

Bishop, A. W. *Loyalty on the Frontier*. St. Louis: Studley, 1863.

Bonham, M. L. *The British Consuls in the Confederacy*. New York: Columbia University Press, 1911.

Bontecou, E. *The Federal Loyalty-Security Program*. Ithaca: Cornell University Press, 1953.

Boucher, Chauncey S. *The Nullification Controversy in South Carolina*. Chicago: University of Chicago Press, 1916.

Boucher, Jonathan. *Reminiscences of an American Loyalist*. Boston: Houghton, Mifflin, 1925.

——. *View of the Causes of the American Revolution*. London: Robinson, 1797.

Bozman, John L. *The History of Maryland*. Baltimore: Lucas and Deaver, 1837. 2 vols.

Bradford, William. *Of Plimoth Plantation*. Commonwealth ed. Boston: State Printers, 1898.

Bradley, James. *The Confederate Mail Carrier*. Mexico, Mo.: 1894.

Britton, Wiley. *The Civil War on the Border*. New York: Putnam, 1891. 2 vols.

——. *Memoirs of the Rebellion on the Border, 1863*. Chicago: Cushing, Thomas, 1882.

Brown, Alexander. *The First Republic of Virginia*. Boston: Houghton, Mifflin, 1898.

Bruce, Philip A. *Institutional History of Virginia in the Seventeenth Century*. New York: Putnam, 1910. 2 vols.

Brunhouse, R. L. *The Counter-Revolution in Pennsylvania, 1776–1790*. Philadelphia: Pennsylvania Historical Commission, 1942.

Bryan, Thomas C. *Confederate Georgia*. Athens: University of Georgia Press, 1953.

Burnett, Edmund C., ed. *Letters of Members of the Continental Congress*. Washington: Carnegie Institution, 1921–1936. 8 vols.

Capers, Henry D. *Life and Times of Christopher G. Memminger*. Richmond: Waddey, 1893.

Carr, R. K. *The House Committee on Un-American Activities, 1945–1950*. Ithaca: Cornell University Press, 1952.

Carson, James P. *Life, Letters, and Speeches of James Louis Petigru*. Washington: Lowdermilk, 1920.

Carter, C. E., ed. *Correspondence of Thomas Gage*. New Haven: Yale University Press, 1931–1933. 2 vols.

Casler, J. O. *Four Years in the Stonewall Brigade*. 2d ed. Girard: Appeal Co., 1956.

Chafee, Z., Jr. *The Blessings of Liberty*. Philadelphia: Lippincott, 1956.

——. *Freedom of Speech*. New York: Harcourt, Brace, 1920.

Chamberlain, L. H. *Loyalty and Legislative Action*. Ithaca: Cornell University Press, 1951.

Childs, A. R., ed. *The Private Journal of Henry William Ravenel, 1859–1887*. Columbia: University of South Carolina Press, 1947.

Clinton, George. *Public Papers*. New York: State Printer, 1899–1914. 10 vols.

Coke, D. P. *Notes on the Royal Commission on the Losses and Services of the American Loyalists, 1783–1785*. Oxford: Hart, 1915.

Conrad, Thomas N. *A Confederate Spy*. New York: Ogilvie, 1892.

Cornelius, Elias. *Journal of a Revolutionary Surgeon*. Washington: Tompkins and Sherman, 1903.

Corsan, W. C. *Two Months in the Confederate States*. London: Bentley, 1863.

Corwin, Edward S. *Total War and the Constitution*. New York: Knopf, 1947.

Coulter, E. M. *The Civil War and Readjustment in Kentucky*. Chapel Hill: University of North Carolina Press, 1926.

Countryman, V. *Un-American Activities in the State of Washington*. Ithaca: Cornell University Press, 1951.

Creel, George. *How We Advertised America*. New York: Harper, 1920.

Cumming, Kate. *Gleanings from the Southland*. Birmingham: Roberts, 1895.

Cummings, Homer, and Carl McFarland. *Federal Justice*. New York: Macmillan, 1937.

Cushing, Harry A., ed. *The Writings of Samuel Adams*. New York: Putnam, 1907. 4 vols.

Cushman, R. E. *Civil Liberties in the United States*. Ithaca: Cornell University Press, 1956.

Daniel, Frederick S. *The Richmond Examiner during the War*. New York: privately printed, 1868.

Davidson, Philip. *Propaganda and the American Revolution*. Chapel Hill: University of North Carolina Press, 1941.

Davis, Andrew M. *The Confiscation of John Chandler's Estate*. Boston: Houghton, Mifflin, 1903.

Davis, Jefferson. *The Rise and Fall of the Confederate Government*. New York: D. Appleton, 1881. 2 vols.

Dawson, Sarah M. *A Confederate Girl's Diary*. Boston: Houghton, Mifflin, 1913.

Day, Samuel P. *Down South; or an Englishman's Experiences at the Seat of the American War*. London: Hurst and Blackett, 1862. 2 vols.

Dennett, T., ed. *Lincoln and the Civil War in the Diaries and Letters of John Hay*. New York: Dodd, Mead, 1939.

Dicey, Edward. *Six Months in the Federal States*. London: Macmillan, 1863. 2 vols.

Dickinson, Henry C. *Diary, Morris Island, 1864–1865*. Denver: Williamson-Haffner, n.d.

Donald, David. *Lincoln Reconsidered*. New York: Knopf, 1956.

Dorris, J. T. *Pardon and Amnesty under Lincoln and Johnson*. Chapel Hill: University of North Carolina Press, 1953.

Dowell, E. F. *History of Criminal Syndicalism Legislation in the United States*. Baltimore: Johns Hopkins University Press, 1939.

Draper, T. *The Roots of American Communism*. New York: Viking, 1957.

Duane, William, ed. *Extract from the Diary of Christopher Marshall Kept in Philadelphia and Lancaster during the American Revolution*. Albany: Munsell, 1877.

Eardley-Wilmot, John. *An Historical View of the Commission for Enquiring into the Losses, Services, and Claims of the American Loyalists*. London: Nichols and Bentley, 1815.

Easterby, John H. *A History of the College of Charleston*. Charleston: privately printed, 1935.

Eddis, William. *Letters from America*. London: privately printed, 1792.

Egerton, Hugh E. *A Short History of British Colonial Policy*. 3d ed. London: Methuen, 1910.

Evans, Charles. *Oaths of Allegiance in Colonial New England*. Worcester: American Antiquarian Society, 1922.

Evelyn, John. *Diary*. London: Macmillan, 1906. 3 vols.

Fanning, David. *Narrative*. New York: Sabin, 1865.

Bibliography

Farber, James. *Texas, C.S.A.* New York: Jackson, 1947.

Farish, Hunter D. *The Circuit Rider Dismounts.* Richmond: Vietz, 1938.

Farrand, Max, ed. *Records of the Federal Convention of 1787.* New Haven: Yale University Press, 1911. 3 vols.

Fiske, J. *The Critical Period of American History.* Boston: Houghton, Mifflin, 1888.

Fitzpatrick, John C., ed. *The Writings of George Washington.* Washington: Government Printing Office, 1931–1944. 39 vols.

Flick, Alexander C. *Loyalism in New York during the American Revolution.* New York: Columbia University Press, 1901.

Flower, F. A. *Edwin McMasters Stanton.* New York: Wilson, 1905.

Foltz, Charles S. *Surgeon of the Seas.* Indianapolis: Bobbs-Merrill, 1931.

Force, Peter, ed. *American Archives.* Washington: 1837–1853. 9 vols.

———, comp. *Tracts and Other Papers Relating . . . to the Colonies in North America.* Washington: Force, 1836–1846. 4 vols.

Ford, W. C., ed. *Journals of the Continental Congress.* Washington: Government Printing Office, 1904–1937. 34 vols.

———. *The Writings of George Washington.* New York: Putnam, 1889–1893. 14 vols.

Frank, Joseph. *The Levellers.* Cambridge: Harvard University Press, 1955.

French, A. *General Gage's Informers.* Ann Arbor: University of Michigan Press, 1932.

Fulkerson, Horace S. *A Civilian's Recollections of the War between the States.* Baton Rouge: Claitor, 1939.

Gambs, John S. *The Decline of the I.W.W.* New York: Columbia University Press, 1932.

Gandy, Wallace, ed. *The Association Oath Rolls of the British Plantations.* London: privately printed, 1922.

Gay, Julius. *The Farmington Papers.* Hartford: 1929.

Gellermann, William. *Martin Dies.* New York: Day, 1944.

Gellhorn, W., ed. *The States and Subversion.* Ithaca: Cornell University Press, 1952.

Ghent, W. J. *The Reds Bring Reaction.* Princeton: Princeton University Press, 1923.

Gibbes, Robert W., ed. *Documentary History of the American Revolution.* New York: Appleton, 1853–1857. 3 vols.

Glyndon, Howard (pseud.). *Notable Men in the House of Representatives.* New York: Baker and Godwin, 1862.

Grantham, Thomas. *An Historical Account of Some Memorable Actions Particularly in Virginia.* London: Roberts, 1716.

Greene, Evarts B. *The Provincial Governor in the English Colonies of North America.* New York: Longmans, Green, 1898.

Griswold, E. N. *The 5th Amendment Today.* Cambridge: Harvard University Press, 1955.

Grodzins, M. *Americans Betrayed.* Chicago: University of Chicago Press, 1949.

———. *The Loyal and the Disloyal.* Chicago: University of Chicago Press, 1956.

Guttridge, George H. *The Colonial Policy of William III in America and the West Indies.* Cambridge: Cambridge University Press, 1922.

Hale, Nathaniel C. *Virginia Venturer: A Historical Biography of William Claiborne, 1600–1677.* Richmond: Dietz, 1951.

Hall, C. W. (pseud.). *Threescore Years and Ten.* Cincinnati, 1884.

Hallum, John. *The Diary of an Old Lawyer.* Nashville: Southwestern, 1895.

Halsey, R. T. *Impolitical Prints.* New York: New York Public Library, 1939.

Hammond, Otis G. *Tories of New Hampshire in the War of the Revolution.* Concord: New Hampshire Historical Society, 1917.

Hapgood, Norman. *Professional Patriots.* New York: Boni, 1927.

Hardacre, P. H. *The Royalists during the Puritan Revolution.* The Hague: Nijhoff, 1956.

Harrell, I. S. *Loyalism in Virginia.* Durham: Duke University Press, 1926.

Harris, Alexander. *A Review of the Political Conflict in America.* New York: Pollock, 1876.

Hart, Alfred B. *American History Told by Contemporaries.* New York: Macmillan, 1897–1929. 5 vols.

Hening, W. W., ed. *The Statutes-at-Large of Virginia.* New York: 1823. 12 vols.

Herring, E. P. *Group Representation before Congress.* Baltimore: Johns Hopkins University Press, 1929.

Higginson, T. W. *Army Life in a Black Regiment.* Boston: Houghton, Mifflin, 1900.

Hill, Louise B. *Joseph E. Brown and the Confederacy.* Chapel Hill: University of North Carolina Press, 1939.

History of Bacon's and Ingram's Rebellion in Virginia. Cambridge: Wilson, 1867.

Holland, J. G. *History of Western Massachusetts.* Springfield: Bowles, 1855. 2 vols.

Holmes, Clay W. *The Elmira Prison Camp.* New York: Putnam, 1912.

Hopley, Catherine C. *Life in the South.* London: Chapman and Hall, 1863. 2 vols.

Horan, James D. *Confederate Agent.* New York: Crown, 1954.

Hosmer, James K., ed. *The Journal of John Winthrop.* New York: Scribner's, 1908. 2 vols.

——. *The Life of Thomas Hutchinson.* Boston: Houghton, Mifflin, 1896.

Hotten, J. C. *The Original Lists of Persons of Quality, Who Went from Great Britain to the American Plantations, 1600–1700.* London: Chatto and Windus, 1874.

Hough, Emerson. *The Web: The Authorized History of the American Protective League.* Chicago: Reilley and Lee, 1919.

Houston, David F. *A Critical Study of Nullification in South Carolina.* New York: Longmans, Green, 1896.

Howd, Cloice R. *Industrial Relations in the West Coast Lumber Industry.* U.S. Bureau of Labor Statistics, Bulletin #349, Miscellaneous Series. Washington: Government Printing Office, 1924.

Hull, Augustus L. *Annals of Athens, Georgia, 1801–1901.* Athens: Banner, 1906.

Hulton, Ann. *Letters of a Loyalist Lady.* Cambridge: Harvard University Press, 1927.

Humes, Thomas W. *The Loyal Mountaineers of Tennessee.* Knoxville: Ogden, 1888.

Hunt, G., ed. *Writings of James Madison.* New York: Putnam, 1900–1910. 9 vols.

Hunter, Earle L. *A Sociological Analysis of Certain Types of Patriotism.* New York: Maisel, 1932.

Hutchinson, Thomas. *Papers.* Albany: Prince Society, 1865. 2 vols.

Hyland, St. George K. *A Century of Persecution under Tudor and Stuart Sovereigns, from Contemporary Records.* London: Paul, Trubner, 1920.

Hyman, H. M. *Era of the Oath: Northern Loyalty Tests during the Civil War and Reconstruction.* Philadelphia: University of Pennsylvania Press, 1954.

Jensen, Merrill. *The New Nation.* New York: Knopf, 1950.

Johnson, R. U., and C. C. Buell, eds. *Battles and Leaders of the Civil War.* Repr. ed. New York: Thomas Yoseloff, 1956. 4 vols.

Bibliography

Johnston, Henry P., ed. *The Correspondence and Public Papers of John Jay*. New York: Putnam, 1890–1893. 4 vols.

Jones, E. Alfred, ed. *The Journal of Alexander Chesney*. Columbus: Ohio State University Press, 1921.

Jones, John B. *A Rebel War Clerk's Diary*. New York: Old Hickory Bookshop, 1935. 2 vols.

Jones, Thomas. *History of New York during the Revolutionary War*. New York: New-York Historical Society, 1879. 2 vols.

Kammerer, G. M. *The Impact of War upon Federal Personnel Administration, 1939–1945*. Lexington: University of Kentucky Press, 1951.

Kane, Harnett T. *Spies for the Blue and Gray*. New York: Hanover, 1954.

Kaye, Percy L. *English Colonial Administration under Lord Clarendon, 1660–1667*. Baltimore: Johns Hopkins University Press, 1905.

Kibler, L. A. *Benjamin F. Perry, South Carolina Unionist*. Durham: Duke University Press, 1946.

Kimball, Everett. *The Public Life of Joseph Dudley*. New York: Longmans, Green, 1911.

Kingsbury, Susan M., ed. *The Records of the Virginia Company of London*. Washington: Government Printing Office, 1906–1935. 4 vols.

Klein, Arthur J. *Intolerance in the Reign of Elizabeth, Queen of England*. Boston: Houghton, Mifflin, 1917.

Klingberg, Frank W. *The Southern Claims Commission*. Berkeley and Los Angeles: University of California Press, 1955.

Labaree, Leonard W. *Royal Instructions to British Colonial Governors, 1670–1776*. New York: Appleton-Century, 1935. 2 vols.

Lang, Theodore F. *Loyal West Virginia from 1861 to 1865*. Baltimore: Deutsch, 1895.

Latané, John H. *Early Relations between Maryland and Virginia*. Baltimore: Johns Hopkins University Press, 1895.

Lathbury, Thomas. *A History of the Nonjurors*. London: Pickering, 1845.

Law, Thomas G. *A Historical Sketch of the Conflict between Jesuits and Seculars in the Reign of Queen Elizabeth*. London: Nutt, 1889.

Lawrence, G. G. *Three Months in America in the Summer of 1863*. London: Whittaker, 1864.

Leftwich, W. M. *Martyrdom in Missouri*. St. Louis: Southwest, 1870. 2 vols.

Legaré, Hugh S. *Writings*. Charleston: Burges and James, 1846. 2 vols.

Leland, W. G., and N. D. Mereness. *Introduction to the American Official Sources for the Economic and Social History of the World War*. New Haven: Yale University Press, 1926.

Lewis, R., and A. Maude. *The English Middle Classes*. New York: Knopf, 1950.

Lippmann, Walter. *Liberty and the News*. New York: Harcourt, Brace, 1920.

Livesey, R., ed. *The Prisoners of 1776*. Boston: Rand, 1854.

Locke, D. R. *The Moral History of America's Life Struggle*. Boston: Richardson, 1874.

Lonn, Ella. *Foreigners in the Confederacy*. Chapel Hill: University of North Carolina Press, 1940.

Lord, Walter, ed. *The Fremantle Diary*. Boston: Little, Brown, 1954.

Lowenthal, M. *The Federal Bureau of Investigation*. New York: Sloane, 1950.

Lundin, C. L. *Cockpit of the Revolution: The War for Independence in New Jersey.* Princeton: Princeton University Press, 1940.

McDonald, Cornelia. *A Diary.* Nashville: Cullom and Ghertner, 1934.

MacDonald, William, ed. *Select Charters and Other Documents Illustrative of American History.* New York: Macmillan, 1899.

McIlwain, C. H., ed. *The Political Works of James I.* Cambridge: Harvard University Press, 1918.

Mackenzie, Frederick. *Diary.* Cambridge: Harvard University Press, 1930. 2 vols.

McKinley, Albert E. *The Suffrage Franchise in the Thirteen English Colonies in America.* Philadelphia: University of Pennsylvania Press, 1905.

Maclay, William. *Journal.* New York: Boni, 1927.

MacMillan, Margaret B. *The War Governors in the American Revolution.* New York: Columbia University Press, 1943.

McRee, Griffith J., ed. *Life and Correspondence of James Iredell.* New York: Appleton, 1857–1858. 2 vols.

Mahoney, Dennis A. *The Prisoner of State.* New York: Carleton, 1863.

March, Peyton C. *The Nation at War.* New York: Doubleday, Doran, 1932.

Melville, Herman. *Battle-Pieces and Aspects of the War.* New York: Harper, 1866.

Meneely, A. Howard. *The War Department, 1861.* New York: Columbia University Press, 1928.

Miller, Perry. *The New England Mind: from Colony to Province.* Cambridge: Harvard University Press, 1953.

Millis, Walter. *Arms and Men: A Study in American Military History.* New York: Putnam, 1956.

Milner, Lucille. *Education of an American Liberal.* New York: Horizon, 1954.

Mock, James R. *Censorship, 1917.* Princeton: Princeton University Press, 1941.

———, and C. Larson. *Words That Won the War.* Princeton: Princeton University Press, 1939.

Moore, Frank, comp. *Diary of the American Revolution.* New York: Scribner, 1858–1860. 2 vols.

Murdock, K. B., ed. *Selections from Cotton Mather.* New York: Harcourt, Brace, 1926.

Murray, John O. *The Immortal Six Hundred.* Winchester, Va.: Eddy, 1905.

Murray, Robert K. *The Red Scare: A Study in National Hysteria, 1919–1920.* Minneapolis: University of Minnesota Press, 1955.

Nelles, Walter. *A Liberal in Wartime: The Education of Albert de Silver.* New York: Norton, 1940.

Nettels, C. P. *Washington and American Independence.* Boston: Little, Brown, 1951.

Nevins, Allan. *American States during and after the Revolution.* New York: Macmillan, 1924.

Newton, Arthur P. *The Colonizing Activities of the English Puritans.* New Haven: Yale University Press, 1914.

Nicolay, J. G., and J. Hay, eds. *Complete Works of Abraham Lincoln.* Gettysburg ed. New York: Tandy, 1905. 12 vols.

Notestein, W. *The English People on the Eve of Colonization, 1603–1630.* New York: Harper, 1954.

O'Brian, John L. *The Government and Civil Liberties: World War I and After.* Lexington: University of Virginia Press, 1952.

Bibliography

O'Callaghan, E. B., ed. *Documentary History of the State of New York*. Albany: Weed, Parsons, 1849–1851. 4 vols.

Ogden, A. R. *The Dies Committee*. Washington: Catholic University of America Press, 1945.

Onderdonk, Henry, Jr. *Documents and Letters Intended to Illustrate the Revolutionary Incidents of Queens County*. New York: Leavitt, Trow, 1846.

Palmer, Don M. N. *Four Weeks in the Rebel Army*. New London: Ruddock, 1865.

Palmer, Frederick. *Newton D. Baker*. New York: Dodd, Mead, 1931. 2 vols.

Patrick, Rembert B., ed. *Opinions of the Confederate Attorneys General, 1861–1865*. Buffalo: Dennis, 1950.

Paxson, Frederick L. *American Democracy and the World War*. Boston: Houghton, Mifflin, 1936–1948. 3 vols.

Pepys, Samuel. *Diary*. Baybrooke ed. London: Colburn, 1854. 4 vols.

Perry, William S., ed. *Historical Collections Relating to the American Colonial Church*. Hartford: privately printed, 1870–1878. 5 vols.

Pitts, J. A. *Personal and Professional Reminiscences of an Old Lawyer*. Kingsport, Tenn.: Southern, 1930.

Pollock, Frederick. *Essays in Jurisprudence and Ethics*. London: Macmillan, 1882.

Post, Louis F. *The Deportations Delirium of Nineteen-Twenty*. Chicago: Kerr, 1923.

Pryor, Mrs. Roger A. *Reminiscences of Peace and War*. New York: Macmillan, 1905.

Putnam, Mrs. Sallie A. B. *Richmond during the War*. New York: Carleton, 1867.

Randall, J. G. *Constitutional Problems under Lincoln*. Rev. ed. Urbana: University of Illinois Press, 1951.

———, and R. N. Current. *Lincoln the President*. Vol. IV. New York: Dodd, Mead, 1955.

Randolph, Edward. *Letters and Official Papers, 1676–1703*. Boston: Prince Society, 1898–1909. 7 vols.

Raymond, William O., ed. *Winslow Papers, A.D. 1776–1826*. St. John: New Brunswick Historical Society, 1901.

Reich, Jerome R. *Leisler's Rebellion, A Study of Democracy in New York, 1664–1720*. Chicago: University of Chicago Press, 1953.

Richardson, Albert D. *The Secret Service: the Field, the Dungeon, and the Escape*. Hartford: American, 1865.

Robinson, William M., Jr. *Justice in Grey*. Cambridge: Harvard University Press, 1941.

Rosenman, S. I., ed. *The Public Papers and Addresses of Franklin D. Roosevelt*. New York: Random House, 1938–1950. 13 vols.

Ross, Ishbel. *Rebel Rose: Life of Rose O'Neal Greenhow*. New York: Harper, 1954.

Rossiter, C. L. *The American Presidency*. New York: Harcourt, Brace, 1956.

———. *Constitutional Dictatorship*. Princeton: Princeton University Press, 1948.

Rowland, K. M., and Croxall, M. L., eds. *Journal of Julia Le Grand*. Richmond: Waddey, 1911.

Russell, William H. *My Diary North and South*. Ed. Fletcher Pratt. New York: Harper, 1954.

Sabine, Lorenzo. *Biographical Sketches of Loyalists of the American Revolution*. Boston: Little, Brown, 1864. 2 vols.

Sanborn, Alvan, ed. *Reminiscences of Richard Lathers*. New York: Grafton, 1907.

Sangston, Lawrence. *The Bastilles of the North*. Baltimore: Kelly, 1863.

Sargent, Winthrop. *Loyalist Poetry of the Revolution*. Philadelphia: Collins, 1857.

Schaar, J. H. *Loyalty in America.* Berkeley and Los Angeles: University of California Press, 1957.

Scharf, J. T. *History of Maryland.* Baltimore: Piet, 1879. 3 vols.

Scherer, J. A. B. *The Nation at War.* New York: Doran, 1918.

Schiller, A. A. *Military Law and Defense Legislation.* St. Paul: West, 1941.

Schlesinger, A. M., Jr. *Crisis of the Old Order, 1919–1933.* Boston: Houghton, Mifflin, 1957.

Shurtleff, N. B., ed. *Records of the Governor and Company of the Massachusetts Bay in New England.* Boston: White, 1853–1854. 6 vols.

Sigaud, Louis A. *Belle Boyd, Confederate Spy.* Richmond: Dietz, 1944.

Slafter, Edmund F. *John Checkley; or the Evolution of Religious Tolerance in Massachusetts Bay, 1710–1744.* Boston: Prince Society, 1897. 2 vols.

Smith, James M. *Freedom's Fetters: The Alien and Sedition Laws and American Civil Liberties.* Ithaca: Cornell University Press, 1956.

Smyth, Albert H., ed. *The Writings of Benjamin Franklin.* New York: Macmillan, 1905–1907. 10 vols.

Sparks, Francis E. *Causes of the Maryland Revolution of 1689.* Baltimore: Johns Hopkins University Press, 1896.

Sparks, Jared, ed. *Correspondence of the American Revolution; Being Letters of Eminent Men to George Washington.* Boston: Little, Brown, 1853. 4 vols.

Speeches Delivered in the Convention of the State of South Carolina, held in Columbia in March, 1833. Charleston: Van Brunt, 1833.

Stark, James H. *The Loyalists of Massachusetts.* Boston: Stark, 1910.

Stearns, Harold E. *Liberalism in America.* New York: Boni and Liveright, 1919.

Steiner, Bernard C. *Beginnings of Maryland, 1631–1639.* Baltimore: Johns Hopkins University Press, 1903.

———. *Maryland during the English Civil Wars.* Baltimore: Johns Hopkins University Press, 1907.

Stevens, Benjamin F., ed. *The Campaign in Virginia, 1781, . . . The Clinton-Cornwallis Controversy.* London: 1888. 2 vols.

———. *Facsimiles of Manuscripts in European Archives Relating to America, 1773–1783.* London: Malby, 1889–1895. 24 vols.

Straight, M. *Trial by Television.* Boston: Beacon, 1954.

Stratemeier, G. B. *Thomas Cornwaleys: Commissioner and Counsellor of Maryland.* Washington: Catholic University of America Press, 1922.

Strother, French. *Fighting Germany's Spies.* New York: Doubleday, Page, 1918.

Sydnor, C. S. *The Development of Southern Sectionalism, 1819–1848.* Baton Rouge: Louisiana State University Press, 1948.

Tatum, Edward H., Jr., ed. *The American Journal of Ambrose Serle.* San Marino, Calif.: Huntington Library, 1940.

Tatum, Georgia L. *Disloyalty in the Confederacy.* Chapel Hill: University of North Carolina Press, 1934.

Taylor, Telford. *Grand Inquest: The Story of Congressional Investigations.* New York: Simon and Schuster, 1955.

Thomas, D. S., and R. S. Nishimoto. *The Spoilage.* Berkeley and Los Angeles: University of California Press, 1946.

Thorndike, Rachel S., ed. *The Sherman Letters.* New York: Scribner, 1894.

Todd, Lewis P. *Wartime Relations of the Federal Government and the Public Schools.* New York: Columbia University Press, 1945.

Bibliography

Todes, C. *Labor and Lumber*. New York: International, 1931.

Tyler, Moses C. *The Literary History of the American Revolution, 1763–1783*. New York: Putnam, 1897.

Van der Weyde, William M., ed. *Life and Works of Thomas Paine*. New Rochelle: Paine National Historical Association, 1925. 10 vols.

Vandiver, F. E., ed. *Civil War Diary of Josiah Gorgas*. University: University of Alabama Press, 1947.

Van Schaack, H. C. *Life of Peter van Schaack*. New York: Appleton, 1842.

Van Tyne, C. H. *Loyalists of the American Revolution*. New York: Macmillan, 1902.

Veblen, Thorstein. *An Inquiry into the Nature of Peace*. New York: Macmillan, 1917.

Wakefield, Eva I., ed. *Letters of Robert G. Ingersoll*. New York: Philosophical Library, 1951.

Waldenmaier, N. P., *Some of the Earliest Oaths of Allegiance to the United States of America*. Lancaster: privately printed, 1944.

Washburn, Wilcomb E. *The Governor and the Rebel: A History of Bacon's Rebellion in Virginia*. Chapel Hill: University of North Carolina Press, 1957.

Wechsler, James A. *The Age of Suspicion*. New York: Random House, 1953.

Wells, Louisa S. *Journal of a Voyage from Charlestown, South Carolina to London*. New York: New-York Historical Society, 1906.

Wells, William V. *Life and Public Services of Samuel Adams*. Boston: Little, Brown, 1865. 3 vols.

Wertenbaker, Thomas J. *Father Knickerbocker Rebels*. New York: Scribner, 1948.

———. *Torchbearer of the Revolution*. Princeton: Princeton University Press, 1940.

———. *Virginia under the Stuarts, 1607–1688*. Princeton: Princeton University Press, 1914.

Wiley, B. I. *The Plain People of the Confederacy*. Baton Rouge: Louisiana State University Press, 1943.

Willard, M. W., ed. *Letters of the American Revolution, 1774–1776*. Boston: Houghton, Mifflin, 1925.

Williams, T. H. *Lincoln and the Radicals*. Madison: University of Wisconsin Press, 1941.

Williamson, James J. *Prison Life in the Old Capitol*. West Orange, N.J.: privately printed, 1911.

Wiltse, C. M. *John C. Calhoun, Sectionalist, 1840–1850*. Indianapolis: Bobbs-Merrill, 1951.

Winkler, E. W., ed. *Journal of the Secession Convention of Texas, 1861*. Austin: Austin Printing Co., 1912.

Winther, O. O., ed. *With Sherman to the Sea; the Civil War Letters, Diaries, and Reminiscences of Theodore F. Upson*. Baton Rouge: Louisiana State University Press, 1943.

Winthrop, R. C. *Life and Letters of John Winthrop*. Boston: Ticknor and Fields, 1864–1867. 2 vols.

Wittke, C. *German-Americans and the World War*. Columbus: Ohio State University Press, 1936.

WPA, Historical Records Survey. *Calendar of the Ryder Collection of Confederate Archives at Tufts College*. Boston: Historical Survey, 1940.

———. *Lists and Index of Presidential Executive Orders, Unnumbered Series, 1789–1941*. Newark: Historical Records Survey, 1943.

Wroth, Lawrence C. *A Historical Study of the Oath of a Free Man.* New York: Wooly Whale, 1939.

Yeats, W. B. *Collected Poems.* Definitive ed. New York: Macmillan, 1956.

Young, Ernest W. *The Wilson Administration and the Great War.* Boston: Badger, 1922.

PAMPHLETS

APL. *In re Military Intelligence Investigations.* N.p.: n.d.

Association of the Bar of the City of New York. *Brief of the Special Committee To Defend the Socialist Members of the N.Y. Legislature, January 20, 1920.* New York: 1920.

Bayard, James. *Speech against the Validity of the Test-Oath.* Philadelphia: 1864.

Black List. Philadelphia: 1802.

Brewer, J. M. *Prison Life!* N.p.: n.d.

Brookings Institution. *Suggested Standards for Determining Un-American Activities.* Washington: 1945.

Cook, W. A. *The Administration of Abraham Lincoln Sustained by the Sages and Heroes of the Revolution.* Washington: 1864.

Deming, H. C. *Speech on the President's Plan of State Renovation.* Washington: 1864.

Douglas, W. O. *The Bill of Rights—at Home and Abroad.* Address before the 10th Anniversary Dinner, Friends Committee on National Legislation. Philadelphia: 1953.

Durfee, T. "Gleanings from the Judicial History of Rhode Island," *Rhode Island Historical Tracts Number 18.* Providence: 1883.

An East Tennessean. *Secession or Prose in Rhyme.* Philadelphia: 1864.

Eisemann, A. *APL Investigations for the United States Department of Justice.* New York: 1918.

Ewing, Edwin H. *Letters Accepting the President's Amnesty.* Nashville: 1864.

Federal-State Conference on Law Enforcement Problems of National Defense. *Proceedings.* Washington: 1940.

Gantt, E. W. *Address in Favor of Re-Union in 1863.* New York: 1863.

Gayarré, C. *Lecture on Oaths, Amnesties and Rebellions.* New Orleans: 1866.

Graham, William A. *Speech in the Convention of North Carolina, December 7, 1861, on the Ordinance Concerning Test Oaths and Sedition.* Raleigh: 1862.

Group for the Advancement of Psychiatry. *Considerations Regarding the Loyalty Oath as a Manifestation of Current Social Tension and Anxiety.* Symposium no. 1. N.p.: Oct., 1954.

Grover, S. T. (pseud.). *Remarks on the Existing Rebellion.* St. Louis; 1865.

Hewitt, J. H. *King Linkum the First: A Musical Burletta.* Ed. R. B. Harwell. Emory University Publications, Sources, and Reprints, Series I. Atlanta: 1947.

Ku Klux Klan. *Invitation to Membership to World War Patriots.* Atlanta: n.d.

Letcher, J. *Message of the Governor of Virginia.* Richmond: 1862.

Magrath, A. G., *Opinion in the Sequestration Cases and Report of Cases in the District Court, South Carolina.* N.p.: 1861.

Mather, Cotton. *The Religion of an Oath.* Boston: 1719.

Mosby, C. L. *Congressional Test Act Examined.* Lynchburg: 1865.

Bibliography

National Popular Government League. *Report upon the Illegal Practices of the U.S. Department of Justice.* Washington: 1920.

Palmer, B. M. *The Oath of Allegiance to the United States Discussed in its Moral and Political Bearings.* Richmond: 1863.

Penn, W. *A Treatise on Oaths.* London: 1675.

Robins, L. *War Shadows.* New York: 1922.

Ruffner, W. H. *The Oath: A Sermon on the Nature and Obligations of the Oath of Allegiance.* Lexington: 1864.

South Carolina, Court of Appeals. *The Book of Allegiance.* Columbia: 1834.

Special Committee of the Association of the Bar of the City of New York. *Report on the Federal Loyalty-Security Program.* New York: 1956.

Stillé, Charles J. *The Life and Public Services of Joel R. Poinsett.* Philadelphia: 1888.

Taffe, John. *An Address to the Churches of Christ in Kentucky.* Cincinnati: 1866.

A Texan. *To the Men of the South.* Philadelphia: 1863.

Tyler, Lyon G. *A Confederate Catechism.* Richmond: 1930.

Weinstein, S. *Personnel Security Programs of the Federal Government.* N.p.: 1954.

Yarmolinsky, A. *Case Studies in Personnel Security.* Washington: 1955.

PERIODICAL LITERATURE

"Acts, Orders and Resolutions of the General Assembly of Virginia, 1643–1646," *VMHB,* XXIII (July, 1915), 225–255.

Anderson, F. M. "Opposition to the War of 1812," Mississippi Valley Historical Association *Proceedings,* VI (1912–1913), 176–188.

Anderson, O. "The Treatment of Prisoners of War in Britain during the American War of Independence," Institute of Historical Research *Bulletin,* XXVIII (May, 1955), 63–83.

"Are American Liberties Worth Saving?" *Nation,* April 17, 1920, pp. 506–508.

Arnold, Thurman. "How *Not* To Get Investigated: Ten Commandments for Government Employees," *Harper's Magazine,* CXCVII (Nov., 1948), 61–63.

"The Aspinwall Papers," Part I, MHS *Collections,* 4th series, IX (1871), 1–488.

"Bacon's Rebellion [Eggleston MSS]," *WMQ,* IX (July, 1900), 1–10.

Barck, Dorothy C., ed. "Minutes of the Committee and First Commission for Detecting Conspiracies in the State of New York," NYHS *Collections* (1924–1925). 2 vols.

Beale, H. K., ed. "The Diary of Edward Bates, 1859–1866," AHA *Annual Report* (1930), Part IV.

"Belknap Papers," MHS *Collections,* 6th series, IV (1891), Part I.

Bieber, Ralph P. "The Plantation Councils of 1670–1674," *English Historical Review,* XL (Jan., 1925), 93–106.

Boas, R. P. "The Loyal Legion of Loggers and Lumbermen," *Atlantic Monthly,* CXXVII (Feb., 1921), 221–226.

Bontecou, E. "President Eisenhower's 'Security' Program," *Bulletin of the Atomic Scientists,* IX (July, 1953), 215–218.

Brandt, R. F. "The Dies Committee: An Appraisal," *Atlantic Monthly,* CLXV (Feb., 1940), 232–238.

Bromley, D. D. "The Pacifist Bogey," *Harper's Magazine,* CLXI (Oct., 1930), 553–565.

"Captain William Carver," *WMQ,* III (Jan., 1895), 163–165.

Carey, W. D. "State Councils of Defense," *State Government,* XIV (April-June, 1941), 105–106, 133–136.

Carpenter, A. H. "Military Government of Southern Territory, 1861–1865," AHA *Annual Report* (1900), Part I, 467–498.

Chafee, Z., Jr. "Freedom of Speech and States' Rights," *New Republic,* Jan. 26, 1921, pp. 259–262.

Cheyney, E. P. "Some English Conditions Surrounding the Settlement of Virginia," *AHR,* XII (April, 1907), 507–528.

"The Church in Lower Norfolk County," *Lower Norfolk County Virginia Antiquary,* IV (1902), 32–34.

Claghorn, K. H. "Aliens and Sedition in the New Year," *Survey,* Jan. 17, 1920, pp. 422–423.

"Clarendon Papers," NYHS *Collections,* II (1869), 1–162.

Clay, S. H., "The Man Who Heads the Spruce Drive," *Review of Reviews,* LVII (June, 1918), 633–637.

"Colden Papers, 1765–1775," NYHS *Collections,* LVI (1923).

Collins, E. D. "Committees of Correspondence in the American Revolution," AHA *Annual Report* (1901), Part I, 245–271.

"Colonel Disque and the I.W.W.," *New Republic,* April 6, 1918, pp. 284–285.

Conway, M. D. "Fredericksburg First and Last," *Magazine of American History,* XVII (June, 1887), 449–469.

Creel, G. "Public Opinion in War Time," *Annals of the American Academy of Political and Social Science,* LXXVIII (July, 1918), 185–194.

Cushman, R. E. "American Civil Liberties in Mid-Twentieth Century," *Annals of the American Academy of Political and Social Science,* CCLXXV (May, 1951), 1–8.

Denman, M. "Majority of Lumberjacks Are Not I.W.W.," *New Republic,* March 30, 1918, p. 265.

Dennis, A. P. "Lord Baltimore's Struggle with the Jesuits, 1634–1639," AHA *Annual Report* (1900), Part I, 107–125.

"Diary of Jonathan Carpenter," Vermont Historical Society *Proceedings* (1872), vii–x.

Disque, B. P. "How We Found a Cure for Strikes," *System, The Magazine of Business,* XXXVI (Sept., 1919), 379–384.

"Documents Relating to the Administration of Jacob Leisler," NYHS *Collections,* I (1868), 239–426.

Dos Passos, John. "Back to Red Hysteria," *New Republic,* July 2, 1930, pp. 168–169.

"Dudley Records," MHS *Proceedings,* 2d series, XIII (Nov., 1899), 222–287.

Dunn, R. W. "Meet Mr. Easley—Plutocrat Patriot," *Locomotive Engineers Journal,* LX (July, 1926), 497–500.

Dunning, W. A. "Disloyalty in Two Wars," *AHR,* XXIV (July, 1919), 625–630.

Ernst, M. L. "Some Affirmative Suggestions for a Loyalty Program," *American Scholar,* XIX (Autumn, 1950), 452–460.

Foster, G., Jr. "The 1931 Personal Liberties Cases," *New York University Law Quarterly Review,* IX (Sept., 1931), 64–81.

Fraenkel, O. K. "Law and Loyalty," *Iowa Law Review,* XXXVII (Winter, 1951), 153–174.

"Free Speech in War Time," *Commonweal,* March 27, 1942, pp. 547–548.

Gill, R. S. "The Four L's in Lumber," *Survey,* May 1, 1920, pp. 165–170.

Gould, K. M. "Legislating Loyalty," *American Scholar,* IV (Summer, 1934), 345–356.

Hackett, F. "With Malice Towards None," *New Republic,* Nov. 17, 1917, pp. 1–3.

Bibliography

Hall, M. G. "Randolph, Dudley, and the Massachusetts Moderates in 1683," *New England Quarterly*, XXIX (Dec., 1956), 513–516.

Hard, W. "Perhaps the Turn of the Tide," *New Republic*, Feb. 11, 1920, pp. 313–316.

Hayes, A. N. "Wartime Recollections," *Magazine of History*, XXI (Aug.-Sept., Nov.-Dec., 1915), 89–97, 217–225.

Hinke, William J., ed. "Journey of Francis Louis Michel," *VMHB*, XXIV (April, 1916), 113–141.

Hole, E. C. "The Real Status of the Loyal Legion," *American Lumberman*, March 15, 1919, p. 41.

Howard, S. "Our Professional Patriots," *New Republic*, July 24, Aug. 20, Sept. 3, 10, 17, 24, Oct. 15, 1924.

Hoyt, W. D. "Thomas John Claggett," *Maryland Historical Magazine*, XLVII (June, 1952), 128–134.

Hyman, H. M. "Civil War Turncoats: A Commentary on a Military View of Lincoln's War Prisoner Utilization Program," *Military Affairs*, XXII (Fall, 1958), 134–138.

———. "Deceit in Dixie: Southerners' Evasions of Union Loyalty Tests," *Civil War History*, III (March, 1957), 65–82.

———. "New Yorkers and the Civil War Draft," *New York History*, XXXVI (April, 1955), 164–171.

———. "Oroville's Reputation Redeemed," *Pacific Historical Review*, XXV (May, 1956), 173–178.

Ickes, H. "Hysteria in the Justice Department," *New Republic*, July 4, 1949, p. 14.

"Instructions to Lord Culpeper," *VMHB*, XXVII (July-Oct., 1919), 326–335.

"Instructions to Sir Francis Wyatt," *VMHB*, XI (July, 1903), 54–57.

Irwin, W. "This Gentleman Worries Too Much," *Hearst's International*, XLVI (Sept., 1924), 81–82.

Kittredge, G. L. "Dr. Robert Child the Remonstrant," Colonial Society of Massachusetts *Publications*, XXI (March, 1919), 1–146.

Knollenberg, B., ed. "The Revolutionary Correspondence of Nathaniel Greene and John Adams," *Rhode Island History*, I (April, July, 1942), 45–55, 73–83.

Koenigsberg, S. M., and M. Stavis. "Test Oaths: Henry VIII to the American Bar Association," *Lawyers Guild Review*, XI (Summer, 1951), 111–126.

Kuttner, A. B. "A Study of American Intolerance," *Dial*, March 28, 1918, pp. 282–285.

Kyte, G. W. "Some Plans for a Loyalist Stronghold in the Middle Colonies," *Pennsylvania History*, XVI (July, 1949), 177–190.

"Langford's Refutation," *Maryland Historical Magazine*, IV (March, 1909), 42–64.

Lechford, Thomas. "Plain Dealing: or News from New-England," MHS *Collections*, 3d series, III (1833), 55–128.

Leder, H., ed. "Records of the Trial of Jacob Leisler and His Associates," NYHS *Quarterly*, XXXVI (Oct., 1952), 431–457.

"Letters of John Andrews," MHS *Proceedings*, VIII (July, 1865), 316–412.

"Local Governments and Loyalty Problems," *American City*, LXVI (Dec., 1951), 169.

"The Loyal Legion of Loggers and Lumbermen," *Outlook*, July 31, 1918, p. 510.

"The Loyalty of Barnstable in the Revolution," Colonial Society of Massachusetts *Publications*, XXV (1923), 265–348.

McDonald, David. "Diaries," *Indiana Magazine of History,* XXVIII (Dec., 1932), 282–306.

McElroy, R. M. "The Great Virginia Rebellion of 1676," N.Y. Society of Colonial Wars *Publications,* no. 19 (Nov., 1912), 1–23.

Martel, J. "The Second Expulsion of the Acadians," *Dalhousie Review,* XIII (Oct., 1933), 359–371.

"Maverick's Account of New England," MHS *Proceedings,* XXI (Oct., 1884), 231–249.

"Memorial in Regard to Passengers Out of England, 1637," *VMHB,* IX (Jan., 1902), 271–272.

"Miscellaneous Papers of the General Committee, Secret Committee, and Provincial Congress," *SCHGM,* VIII (July, Oct., 1907), 133–150, 189–194.

Mittleman, E. B. "The Loyal Legion of Loggers and Lumbermen," *Journal of Political Economy,* XXXI (June, 1923), 313–341.

Morris, R. B. "Legalism versus Revolutionary Doctrine," *New England Quarterly,* IV (April, 1931), 195–215.

———. "Massachusetts and Common Law," *AHR,* XXXI (April, 1926), 443–458.

Mullett, C. F. "A Case of Allegiance: William Sherlock and the Revolution of 1688," *Huntington Library Quarterly,* X (Nov., 1946), 83–103.

———. "Protestant Dissent as a Crime," *Review of Religion,* XIII (May, 1949), 339–343.

———. "Religion, Politics, and Oaths in the Glorious Revolution," *Review of Politics,* X (Oct., 1948), 462–474.

———. "Toleration and persecution in England, 1660–1689," *Church History,* XIX (March, 1949), 3–28.

Mumford, L. "Patriotism and Its Consequences," *Dial,* April 19, 1919, pp. 406–407.

Nettels, C. P. "A Link in the Chain of Events Leading to American Independence," *WMQ,* 3d series, III (Jan., 1946), 36–47.

"The New Sherlock Holmes," *Nation,* Feb. 1, 1919, p. 155.

Nikoloric, L. A. "The Government Loyalty Program," *American Scholar,* XIX (Summer, 1950), 285–298.

Norville, G. J. "Bill of Attainder—A Rediscovered Weapon against Discriminatory Legislation," *Oregon Law Review,* XXVI (Feb., 1947), 78–113.

"Notes of Proceedings of the Privy Council on Virginia Affairs," *VMHB,* VIII (April, 1901), 404–405.

"Nullification and War," *TQHGM,* I (April, 1920), 276–281.

O'Brian, J. L. "Civil Liberty in War Time," New York Bar Association *Reports,* LII (1919), 275–313.

———. "Uncle Sam's Spy Policies," *Forum,* LXI (April, 1919), 407–416.

Page, T. N. "The Southern People during Reconstruction," *Atlantic Monthly,* LXXXVIII (Sept., 1901), 289–304.

Palmer, A. M. "The Case against the Reds," *Forum,* LXIII (Feb., 1920), 173–185.

———. "Why We Seized German Property," *Forum,* LXII (Dec., 1919), 584–593.

"Papers from the Records of Surry County," *WMQ,* III (Oct., 1894), 121–126.

"Papers of William Heath," MHS *Collections,* 7th series, IV (1904).

Perritt, H. H. "Robert Barnwell Rhett: Prophet of Resistance, 1828–1834," *Southern Speech Journal,* XXI (Winter, 1955), 103–119.

"Petition of Captain Richard Morrison to the Privy Council," *VMHB,* XI (Jan., 1904), 284–285.

Bibliography

Prentiss, G. L. "The Political Crisis," *American Presbyterian and Theological Review*, n.s., IV (Oct., 1866), 625–630.

Pringle, H. F. "Snooping on the Potomac," *Saturday Evening Post*, Jan. 15, 1944, pp. 19–21.

"Proceedings in York County Court, 1661," *WMQ*, XI (July, 1902), 28–38.

Raymond, W. O. "Benjamin Marston of Marblehead," New Brunswick Historical Society *Collections*, III (1907), 79–110.

Reppy, A. "The Spectre of Attainder in New York," *St. John's Law Review*, XXIII (Nov., 1948), 1–67; (April, 1949), 243–290.

"Revolutionary Army Orders," *VMHB*, XIII (April, 1906), 337–350.

Rogers, Lindsay. "Civilian Control of Military Policy," *Foreign Affairs*, XVIII (Jan., 1941), 280–291.

Rostow, E. V. "Needed: A Rational Security Program," *Harper's Magazine*, CCXV (July, 1957), 33–40.

Russ, W. A., Jr. "The Lawyers' Test Oath during Reconstruction," *Mississippi Law Journal*, X (Dec., 1937), 154–167.

Ryan, C. J. "The Jacobean Oath of Allegiance and English Lay Catholics," *Catholic Historical Review*, XXVIII (July, 1942), 159–184.

Sachse, W. L. "Migration of New Englanders to England," *AHR*, LIII (Jan., 1948), 251–278.

Sanford, Orlin M. "A Virginian's Diary in Civil War Days," *Americana*, XVIII (Oct., 1924), 353–368.

Schlesinger, A. M. "Political Mobs and the American Revolution," American Philosophical Society *Proceedings*, XCIX (Aug., 1955), 244–250.

Schuman, F. L. "Bill of Attainder in the 78th Congress," *American Political Science Review*, XXXVII (Oct., 1943), 819–828.

Shelton, W. "Last Chance for Sanity," *Nation*, Feb. 24, 1951, pp. 169–170.

Siebert, W. H. "Loyalist Troops of New England," *New England Quarterly*, IV (Jan., 1931), 108–147.

Sinsheimer, A. "Hughes Aircraft Report: A Vindication," *Automotive Industries*, XXXIX (Oct., 1918), 741–750.

Stanard, M. N. "The Real Beginnings of American Democracy," *VMHB*, XXX (April, 1922), 157–168.

Stearns, R. P. "New England Way in Holland," *New England Quarterly*, VI (Dec., 1933), 747–792.

Steiner, B. C. "The Protestant Revolution in Maryland," AHA *Annual Report* (1897), 281–353.

———, ed. "The South Atlantic States in 1833, as Seen by a New Englander, . . . Henry Bernard," *Maryland Historical Magazine*, XIII (Sept., 1918), 267–294.

Stoney, S. G., ed. "The Poinsett-Campbell Correspondence," *SCHGM*, XLII (April, 1941), 31–52.

Swing, R. G. "Patriotism Dons the Black Shirt," *Nation*, April 10, 1935, pp. 409–411.

Thompson, J. W. "Anti-Loyalist Legislation during the American Revolution," *Illinois Law Review*, III (June, Oct., 1908), 81–90, 147–171.

"A Tory Returns to Buckingham," WMQ, 2d series, XV (Oct., 1934), 411–412.

Trefousse, H. L. "Failure of German Intelligence in the United States, 1935–1945," Mississippi Valley Historical Review, XLII (June, 1955), 84–100.

Trenerry, W. N. "The Minnesota Rebellion Act of 1862," *Minnesota History*, XXXV (March, 1956), 1–10.

Tyler, L. G. "Major Edmund Chisman, Jr.," *WMQ,* I (Oct., 1892), 89–98.

"Virginia in 1629 and 1630," *VMHB,* VII (April, 1900), 368–386.

"Virginia in 1635," *VMHB,* VIII (Jan.-April, 1901), 299–306, 398–407.

"Virginia in 1639–40," *VMHB,* XIII (April, 1906), 375–388.

"Virginia in 1641–49," *VMHB,* XVII (Jan., 1909), 14–33.

"Virginia in 1650–1652," *VMHB,* XVII (July, 1909), 278–291.

"Virginia in 1677–1678," *VMHB,* XXIII (April, 1915), 146–155.

"Virginia under Governor Harvey," *VMHB,* III (July, 1895), 21–34.

Webster, C. C. "John Minor Botts, Anti-Secessionist," Richmond College *Historical Papers,* I (June, 1915), 9–37.

Wilson, E. "Foster and Fish," *New Republic,* Dec. 24, 1930, pp. 158–162.

Wilson, Thomas. "The State of England, Anno Domini 1600," Royal Historical Society *Publications,* 3d series, LXII [Camden Miscellany, XVI, Part I] (1932).

Winslow, W. "The Colonial Customs Service in New England and Its Relationship to the American Revolution," MHS *Proceedings,* XLVI (June, 1913), 441–474.

Winstead, R. "Enter a Logger: An I.W.W. Reply to the Four L's," *Survey,* July 3, 1920, pp. 474–478.

"Winthrop Papers," MHS *Collections,* 5th series, I (1871).

Wolff, W. A. "The Northwest Front," *Collier's,* April 20, 1918, pp. 10–11, 32.

Younger, R. D. "Grand Juries and the American Revolution," *VMHB,* LXIII (July, 1955), 167–184.

Zeichner, O. "The Loyalist Problem in New York after the Revolution," *New York History,* XXI (July, 1940), 284–302.

THESES

Barksdale, E. C. "Semi-Regular and Irregular Warfare in the Civil War." Unpublished Ph.D. thesis. University of Texas, 1941.

Borough, B. L. "Edward Randolph, Royal Agent of the Restoration." Unpublished Ph.D. thesis. Stanford University, 1949.

Brown, Alan S. "William Eden and the American Revolution." Unpublished Ph.D. thesis. University of Michigan, 1953.

Chapin, B. "The Law of Treason during the American Revolution, 1765–1783." Unpublished Ph.D. thesis. Cornell University, 1951.

Fisch, T. "The Revolutionary Committee System in Massachusetts, Virginia, and New York, 1772–1775." Unpublished M.A. thesis. University of Illinois, 1945.

Greenberg, M. "The Loyalty Oath in the American Experience." Unpublished Ph.D. thesis. University of Wisconsin, 1955.

Johnson, D. E. "Worcester in the War for Independence." Unpublished Ph.D. thesis. Clark University, 1953.

Jordan, G. I. "The Suspension of Habeas Corpus as a War-Time Political Control Technique." Unpublished Ph.D. thesis. University of California, Los Angeles, 1941.

Leder, L. H. "Jacob Leisler and the New York Rebellion of 1689–1691." Unpublished M.A. thesis. New York University, 1952.

Bibliography

St. Clair, K. E. "The Administration of Justice in North Carolina during Reconstruction, 1865–1876." Unpublished Ph.D. thesis. Ohio State University, 1939.

Weintraub, H. "The I.W.W. in California, 1905–1931." Unpublished M. A. thesis. University of California, Los Angeles, 1947.

Winzerling, O. W. "The Removal of the Acadians from New France to Louisiana, 1763–1785." Unpublished Ph.D. thesis. University of California, Los Angeles, 1949.

OFFICIAL PUBLICATIONS

CSA. Army. Adjutant and Inspector General's Office. *General Orders, 1863.* Richmond: 1863.

———. ———. *General Orders from January 1862 to December 1864.* Columbia: 1864.

———. Department of Henrico. *Report.* N.p.: n.d.

———. ———. *Military Laws.* Richmond: 1863.

CSA. Congress. House. *Resolutions.* N.p.: n.d.

CSA. War Department. *Circulars, 1864.* N.p.: n.d.

———. *Regulations for the Army of the Confederate States.* Richmond: 1864.

New York State. *Documents Relative to the Colonial History of the State of New York.* Albany: Weed, Parsons, 1853–1857. 15 vols.

———. *Minutes of the Commission for Detecting and Defeating Conspiracies in the State of New York.* Albany: 1909. 3 vols.

———. Legislature. *Report of Joint Committee to Investigate Seditious Activities.* New York: 1920. 4 vols.

Ontario Bureau of Archives. *Proceedings of the Commission on Loyalist Claims.* Ontario: 1905. 2 vols.

U.S. Army. Adjutant General's Office. *General Orders, 1861.* Washington: 1862.

———. ———. *General Orders, 1863.* Washington: 1864.

———. ———. *General Orders, 1865.* Washington: 1866.

———. Judge Advocate General. *Digest of Opinions.* Washington: Government Printing Office, 1942.

———. Signal Corps. *History of the Spruce Production Division.* Washington: Government Printing Office, 1921.

U.S. Attorney General. *Annual Report, 1918.* Washington: Government Printing Office, 1919.

U.S. Civil Service Commission. *Annual Report, 1918.* Washington: 1918.

U.S. Commissioner of Claims. *Summary Reports in All Cases Reported to Congress as Disallowed under the Act of March 3, 1871.* Washington: Government Printing Office, 1876.

U.S. Congress. House. *Loyalty of Clerks and Other Persons Employed by the Government.* 37th Cong., 2d sess., H. Rept. 16. Washington: 1862.

———. ———. *Digest of Cases of Contested Elections, 1834–1865.* 38th Cong., 2d sess., H. Misc. Doc. 57. Washington: 1865.

———. ———. *Digest of Cases of Contested Elections, 1865-1871.* 41st Cong., 2d sess., H. Misc. Doc. 152. Washington: 1871.

———. ———. *Investigation of the National Security League.* 65th Cong., 3d sess., H. Rept. 1173. Washington: 1919.

———. ———. *Case of Victor L. Berger of Wisconsin.* 66th Cong., 1st sess., H. Rept. 413. Washington: 1920.

———. ———. *Hearings before the Committee on Rules; Investigation of the Administration of Louis F. Post.* 66th Cong., 2d sess. Washington: 1920.

———. ———. *Report on Subcommittee on Aviation, Select House Committee on Expenditures in the War Department,* Part I. 66th Cong., 2d sess. Washington: 1920.

———. Senate. *Report of Committee on the Credentials of David T. Patterson.* 39th Cong., 1st sess., S. Rept. 139. Washington: 1866.

———. ———. *Message of the President of the United States.* 41st Cong., 1st sess., S. Exec. Doc. 42. Washington: 1871.

———. ———. *Journal of the Congress of the Confederate States of America, 1861–1865.* 58th Cong., 2d sess., S. Doc. 234. Washington: 1905. 6 vols.

———. ———. *Brewing and Liquor Interests and German and Bolshevik Propaganda.* 66th Cong., 1st sess., S. Doc. 62. Washington: Government Printing Office, 1919. 3 vols.

———. ———. *Hearings before a Subcommittee of the Committee on the Judiciary, on a "Report upon the Illegal Practices of the Department of Justice," Made by a Committee of Lawyers.* 63d Cong., 3d sess. Washington: 1921.

U.S. President's Mediation Commission. *Report, Unrest in the Lumber Industry of the Pacific Northwest.* Washington: 1918.

U.S. Provost Marshal General. *Circulars and Telegrams.* Mimeographed. Washington: *ca.* 1917–1919. 32 vols.

U.S. Provost Marshal General's Bureau. *Office of the Provost Marshal General: World War II: A Brief History.* Typescript. Washington: Army Service Forces, 1946.

U.S. Secretary of Defense. *Industrial Personnel Security Review Program, 1st Annual Report.* Washington: Government Printing Office, 1956.

U.S. War Department. *War of the Rebellion: . . . Official Records of the Union and Confederate Armies.* Washington: Government Printing Office, 1880–1901. 128 vols.

JUDICIAL CASES

Cohen v. *Wright,* 22 California 293 (1863).

Cummings v. *Missouri,* 4 Wallace 277 (1867).

Ex parte Benedict, 3 Fed. Cas. Nos. 159, 162 (1862).

Ex parte Faulkner, 1 West Virginia 269 (1866).

Ex parte Garland, 4 Wallace 333 (1867).

Ex parte Law, Fed. Cas. No. 8126 (1866).

Ex parte Milligan, 4 Wallace 2 (1866).

Friedman v. *Schwellenbach,* 159 F.2d 22 (1946), C.C.A.D.C.

In re Baxter, Fed. Cas. No. 1118 (1866).

In re Shorter, Fed. Cas. No. 12811 (1865).

Missouri v. *Garesché,* 36 Missouri 256 (1865).

Pennsylvania v. *Nelson,* 350 U.S. 497 (1956).

United States v. *Lovett,* 328 U.S. 303 (1945).

NEWSPAPERS

Daily Rebel (Chattanooga), 1862–1864.

Cleveland Leader, 1865–1866.

Bibliography

Glen Falls Times and Messenger (New York), March 27, 1918.
Hillsboro Recorder (North Carolina), Oct. 29, 1861.
Lexington Herald (Kentucky), 1918.
Lynchburg Weekly Register (Virginia), Aug. 27, 1864.
New Orleans Times-Picayune, 1918.
New York Call, 1919.
New York Daily News, 1917.
New York Times, 1865–1869, 1917–1920, 1942–1958.
New York Tribune, 1918.
Niles' Register, 1833–1835.
Philadelphia Inquirer, 1918.
Portland Oregonian, 1918.
Raleigh Daily Sentinel (North Carolina), 1865.
The Right Way, 1865–1866.
Springfield Republican (Massachusetts), 1861.
The Spy Glass, 1917–1918.

MANUSCRIPTS

Arkansas Historical Society
  Kie Oldham Papers
Duke University
  Armistead Burt Papers
  David Campbell Papers
  Confederate States of America Archives
  C. J. Faulkner Papers
  T. Hunter-Holmes Papers
  Lord Lyons Papers
  C. MacGill Papers
  Parkhurst Papers
  F. H. Pierpont Papers
  F. E. Smith Papers
  J. Trakle Papers
  Bryan Tyson Papers
  George McC. Wetherspoon Papers
Huntington Library
  A. D. Bache Papers
  Benedict Collection
  Eldridge Collection
  Nathaniel Greene Papers
  Hastings Papers
  Ebenezer Hungtngton Papers
  J. E. Johnston Papers
  W. H. Lamon Papers
  Orderly Book, Continental Army
  Orderly Book, Ebenezer Thayer
  Proceedings of the Committee of Safety of Brookhaven, [L.I.,] 1776
  C. Ray Papers
  Slaughter Collection

Library of Congress (Manuscripts Division unless noted otherwise)
  Chandler P. Anderson Diary
  Newton D. Baker Papers
  William E. Borah Papers
  British Army Embarkation Orders, 1783
  Broadside Collection, Rare Book Room
  George Creel Papers
  J. L. M. Curry Papers
  Thomas W. Gregory Papers
  Joseph Holt Papers
  Charles Evans Hughes Papers
  Harold Ickes Papers
  Thomas Jefferson Papers
  Andrew Johnson Papers
  Thomas Kerr Papers
  Robert Lansing Papers
  Robert T. Lincoln Papers
  E. McPherson Scrapbooks, Rare Book Room
  William Owner Diary
  Marsena Patrick Diary
  Thaddeus Stevens Papers
  U.S. Revolution Miscellany
  Benjamin Wade Papers
  George Washington Papers
  Woodrow Wilson Papers
Maryland Historical Society
  Mordecai Gist Papers
  O. H. Williams Papers
National Archives, collections identified by Record Group (RG) number.
  RG 59. State Department Records
  RG 60. Attorney General Records
  RG 65. American Protective League Records, Justice Department
  RG 77. Records of the Office of the Chief of Engineers
  RG 93. Revolutionary War Records
  RG 94. Turner-Baker Papers
  RG 107. Secretary of War Records
  RG 109. Confederate Army Records
  RG 174. Department of Labor Records
  RG 220. Nimitz Commission Records
New-York Historical Society
  Appraisement of Sundry Arms Taken from Non-Associators
  Journal of a Louisan Rebel
  Journal of David M. Turnure
  John, Richard, and Samuel Peters Papers
  John Sullivan Papers
  Tench Tilghman Papers
  R. F. Wilkinson Letters
New York Public Library
  Samuel Adams Papers

Bibliography

American Civil Liberties Union Archives
Emmet Collection
Great Britain, Audit Office Transcripts
McDougall Collection
Smith-Brady Commission Report
State Historical Society of Wisconsin
John Fox Potter Papers
University of North Carolina, Southern Historical Collection
James A. Alcorn Papers
Rev. Overton Bernard Diary
J. H. Bills Diary
D. F. Boyd Papers
R. Boykin Papers
A. H. Brown Record Book
Hamilton Brown Papers
Duncan Cameron Papers
Kate S. Carney Diary
J. Devereux Papers
H. W. Dickins-Randolph Papers
W. A. Graham Papers
K. P. Hale Recollections
Harding-Jackson Papers
Chief Justice Hoke Papers
A. C. Jones Papers
Lenoir Family Papers
J. H. Otey Papers
Benjamin F. Perry Diary
Pettigrew Family Papers
W. Pettigrew Papers
Phillips-Meyers Papers
Nimrod Porter Diary
H. C. Warmouth Papers
University of Virginia
Morton-Halsey Papers
Virginia Historical Society
Thoms Adams Papers
L. S. Joynes Papers
Virginia State Library
Civil War Record of J. C. Williams
The J. A. B. Scherer Papers were used with the kind permission of Mr. Richard Schwarzman of Los Angeles, California.

INDEX

Index

Index

Carleton, Sir Guy, 108
Carlisle, Earl of, 108
Carroll, Charles, 82
Catron, John, 200
Chamberlain, George E., 305, 306
Charles I, 7, 13, 17–18
Charles II, 29, 31, 40, 41, 45
Chase, Salmon P., 253
Checkley, John, 58–59
Cheesman, John, 32, 38
Cheyney, Thomas, 11
Child, John, 17
Child, Robert, 16–17
Church, Benjamin, 73–74
Civil Liberties Bureau, 280, 321, 322
Civil Service Commission, 268–269, 330, 331
Civil War loyalty tests, 139–266
Claiborne, William, 19–20, 23, 25, 26
Clark, Abraham, 81
Clark, Tom C., 334
Clinton, George, 90, 93
Colonial period loyalty tests, 1–60
Commission on Government Security, 341
Commission on Internal Security and Individual Rights, 335
Communism, 331–345
Confederate army loyalty-testing policies, 221–225, 226–228, 231–239, 242–243, 246–249
Congress, 153–163, 183, 256, 257–262, 268, 317, 329–332, 333, 336–337. *See also* Loyalty tests; Potter Committee
Congress, Confederate, 221, 223, 226, 249–250
Continental army, 73–84, 89. *See also* Loyalty tests, American Revolution
Continental Association, 64–71
Continental Congress, 64, 72, 75, 76–77, 78, 82–83, 84
Coode, John, 29
Copley, Leonard, 30
Cotton, John, 15
Council for New England, 11
Council of National Defense, 289, 291, 300
Cox, James D., 295
Cox, Samuel Sullivan, 264
Creel, George, 269, 281, 289, 297
Croly, Herbert, 285
Cromwell, Oliver, 26, 30, 40
Crumpacker, M. E., 300, 313. *See also* Loyal Legion of Loggers and Lumbermen

Cummings v. *Missouri,* 260–261. *See also* Test oath cases
Cushman, Robert E., 339

Daugherty, Harry, 322
Davis, Garrett, 266
Davis, J. W., 209
Davis, Jefferson, 189, 216, 222, 225, 226, 229, 234, 236–237
Day, Samuel, 224
Declaration of Independence, 77–78
Dies, Martin, 326, 330, 332
Dies Committee, 329, 332
Disque, Brice P., 300–314. *See also* Loyal Legion of Loggers and Lumbermen; Loyalty tests, World War I
Dix, John A., 147, 150
Dominion of New England, 46
Dongan, Thomas, 49
Dos Passos, John, 324–325
Draper, Simeon, 165
Drummond, William, 32, 38
Duane, James, 66, 71, 76
Dudley, Joseph, 46, 58
Dunmore, Earl of, 65–66, 98
Dunning, William A., 267

Easley, Ralph M., 323
Edward VI, 2
Eisenhower, Dwight D., 335–337
Elizabeth I, 3
Elting, Victor, 272, 273–274, 279–281, 285, 293. *See also* American Protective League
Erasmus, Desiderius, 2
Espionage Act, 268, 319
Ewing, Edwin H., 244

Finley, W. Peroneau, 130–131
Fish Committee, 324
Flynn, W. T., 319
Fourteenth Amendment, 258, 263, 264
Frankfurter, Felix, 300, 306
Franklin, Benjamin, 114, 115
Franklin, William, 104
Frémont, John C., 211
Frey, Charles D., 272, 273–274. *See also* American Protective League

Gage, Thomas, 63–64, 66, 71, 95–97, 108. *See also* British army; Loyalty tests, American Revolution
Galloway, Joseph, 66, 99
Gansevoort, Leonard, 90, 93
Gantt, E. W., 242–243, 244

Index

Index